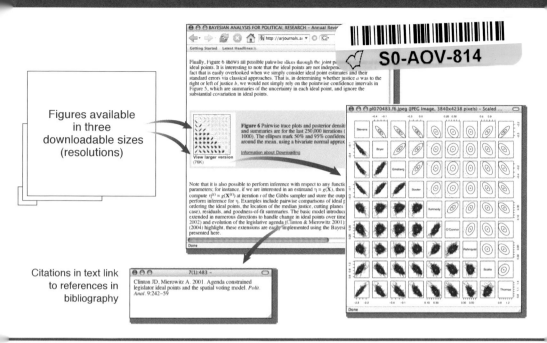

Figures available in three downloadable sizes (resolutions)

Citations in text link to references in bibliography

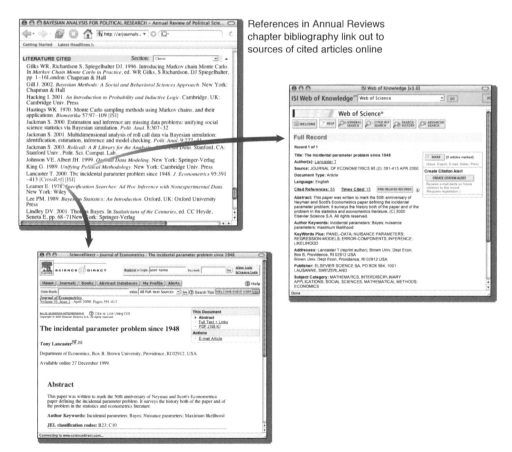

References in Annual Reviews chapter bibliography link out to sources of cited articles online

ANNUAL REVIEW OF
POLITICAL SCIENCE

ANNUAL REVIEW OF POLITICAL SCIENCE

VOLUME 8, 2005

NELSON W. POLSBY, *Editor*
University of California, Berkeley

www.annualreviews.org   science@annualreviews.org   650-493-4400

ANNUAL REVIEWS
4139 El Camino Way • P.O. Box 10139 • Palo Alto, California 94303-0139

ANNUAL REVIEWS
Palo Alto, California, USA

International Standard Serial Number: 1094-2939
International Standard Book Number: 0-8243-3308-X

TYPESET BY TECHBOOKS, FAIRFAX, VA
PRINTED AND BOUND BY MALLOY INCORPORATED, ANN ARBOR, MI

PREFACE

Some years ago, an eminent physician of my acquaintance asked me an arresting question. He had just been offered a big government job, as Assistant Secretary for Health in the Carter Administration. As a person who had spent a good bit of his career studying health policy, the idea intrigued him. So he set about to conduct what lawyers call a "due diligence" inquiry into the possibility. What, he wanted to know, did Assistant Secretaries actually do? In particular, what did Assistant Secretaries in the Health field do? Could I put together a reading list for him, something that would bring him up to speed on this obviously significant topic near the very center of the American government?

The short answer was, No I could not. To the best of my knowledge no such literature existed. That would still be my answer today, three decades later. Indeed, there is barely such a literature bearing on the conduct of any of the senior cabinet offices. A reading list might be cobbled out of book-length reconstructions of the formation of specific public policies on various matters dealt with by cabinet-level government departments, an executive branch equivalent to the bill-becomes-a-law literature about the legislative process, serious journalists' books like *The Power Game* by Hedrick Smith[1] or *The System* by Haynes Johnson and David Broder.[2]

But there is still, even to this day, nothing that political scientists would recognize as "systematic" explorations of the political world inhabited by members of a President's cabinet. I award honorable mention to two books: Victor Navasky's *Kennedy Justice*,[3] an account of how Robert Kennedy ran the Attorney General's shop in the administration of his brother, and Robert Reich's *Locked in the Cabinet*, an amusing memoir by Bill Clinton's friend and fellow Rhodes Scholar recounting some of his adventures as Secretary of Labor.[4]

We can already surmise how atypical these accounts must be. A central problem facing any cabinet-level official is bound to be maintaining rapport with the President. What are the lessons a typical cabinet official might draw from a description of the life of a cabinet official who is the brother of the President? Bob Reich's memoir is better on that score; he did posterity the courtesy of falling out of step with the Clinton economic strategy and therefore had some presidential access problems more typical of what ordinary cabinet officials must put up with.

Of course we don't really know how typical. Likewise relations with relevant interest groups, Congress, public opinion, and agency professionals, all potentially problematic relationships for a cabinet official. How do the officials who manage these relations well—or badly—do it? Where, as my friend put the matter, is the literature?

An *Annual Review* ought in ideal circumstances to be able to generate an answer or two, provided only that there actually are books and articles out there for an alert scholar to pull together. I am hoping that out of the woodwork will come some scholar who can take up this particular challenge and show me that I just didn't look hard enough, or looked in the wrong places.

From time to time I hope to use this space to indicate gaps like this one in our scholarly knowledge, and to solicit the help of the profession in plugging them up. Although editors must reconcile themselves mostly to a passive role in the creation of scholarly knowledge, not always. Every once in a while it feels good to leaven our expressions of satisfaction with the contributions we commission—such as the worthy articles in this volume—with a mild challenge.

Nelson W. Polsby
Editor

[1]Smith H. 1988. *The Power Game: How Washington Works*. New York: Random House
[2]Johnson H, Broder DS. 1996. *The System: The American Way of Politics at the Breaking Point*. Boston: Little Brown
[3]Navasky VS. 1971. *Kennedy Justice*. New York: Atheneum
[4]Reich RB. 1997. *Locked in the Cabinet*. New York: Knopf

Ⓡ *Annual Review of Political Science*
Volume 8, 2005

CONTENTS

PROSPECT THEORY AND POLITICAL SCIENCE, *Jonathan Mercer*   1

THE RELATIONSHIP BETWEEN THEORY AND POLICY IN
   INTERNATIONAL RELATIONS, *Stephen M. Walt*   23

DOES DELIBERATIVE DEMOCRACY WORK?, *David M. Ryfe*   49

CONSTITUTIONAL REFORM IN BRITAIN: THE QUIET REVOLUTION,
   Vernon Bogdanor   73

IMMIGRATION AND POLITICS, *Wayne A. Cornelius and Marc R. Rosenblum*   99

MAKING SENSE OF RELIGION IN POLITICAL LIFE, *Kenneth D. Wald,*
   Adam L. Silverman, and Kevin S. Fridy   121

STRATEGIC SURPRISE AND THE SEPTEMBER 11 ATTACKS, *Daniel Byman*   145

UNPACKING "TRANSNATIONAL CITIZENSHIP," *Jonathan Fox*   171

THE POLITICAL EVOLUTION OF PRINCIPAL-AGENT MODELS,
   Gary J. Miller   203

CITIZENSHIP AND CIVIC ENGAGEMENT, *Elizabeth Theiss-Morse and*
   John R. Hibbing   227

THE DEVELOPMENT OF INTEREST GROUP POLITICS IN AMERICA:
   BEYOND THE CONCEITS OF MODERN TIMES, *Daniel J. Tichenor and*
   Richard A. Harris   251

TRANSFORMATIONS IN WORLD POLITICS: THE INTELLECTUAL
   CONTRIBUTIONS OF ERNST B. HAAS, *John Gerard Ruggie,*
   Peter J. Katzenstein, Robert O. Keohane, and Philippe C. Schmitter   271

THE GLOBALIZATION OF PUBLIC OPINION RESEARCH, *Anthony Heath,*
   Stephen Fisher, and Shawna Smith   297

RISK, SECURITY, AND DISASTER MANAGEMENT, *Louise K. Comfort*   335

THEORIZING THE EUROPEAN UNION: INTERNATIONAL ORGANIZATION,
   DOMESTIC POLITY, OR EXPERIMENT IN NEW GOVERNANCE?,
   Mark A. Pollack   357

THE GLOBALIZATION RORSCHACH TEST: INTERNATIONAL ECONOMIC
   INTEGRATION, INEQUALITY, AND THE ROLE OF GOVERNMENT,
   Nancy Brune and Geoffrey Garrett   399

CONSTRUCTING JUDICIAL REVIEW, *Mark A. Graber*   425

INDEXES
Subject Index   453
Cumulative Index of Contributing Authors, Volumes 1–8   477
Cumulative Index of Chapter Titles, Volumes 1–8   479

ERRATA
An online log of corrections *Annual Review of Political Science*
chapters may be found at http://polisci.annualreviews.org/

RELATED ARTICLES

From the *Annual Review of Anthropology*, Volume 34 (2005)

    Caste and Politics: Identity Over System, Dipankar Gupta

    Intellectuals and Nationalism: Anthropological Engagements,
      Dominic Boyer and Claudio Lomnitz

From the *Annual Review of Psychology*, Volume 56 (2005)

    The Social Psychology of Stigma, Brenda N. Major and Laurie T. O'Brien

    Presidential Leadership, George R. Goethals

From the *Annual Review of Sociology*, Volume 30 (2004)

    Reflections on a Half-Century of Organizational Sociology, W. Richard Scott

    Values: Reviving a Dormant Concept, Steven Hitlin and Jane Allyn Piliavin

    Social Cohesion, Noah E. Friedkin

    The "New" Science of Networks, Duncan J. Watts

    The Use of Newspaper Data in the Study of Collective Action,
      Jennifer Earl, Andrew Martin, John D. McCarthy, and Sarah A. Soule

    Advocacy Organizations in the U.S. Political Process, Kenneth T. Andrews
      and Bob Edwards

    Protest and Political Opportunities, David S. Meyer

    Gender and Work in Germany: Before and After Reunification,
      Rachel A. Rosenfeld, Heike Trappe, and Janet C. Gornick

    *America's Changing Color Lines: Immigration, Race/Ethnicity,
      and Multiracial Identification*, Jennifer Lee and Frank D. Bean

    Sociology of Terrorism, Austin T. Turk

    Comparative-Historical Methodology, James Mahoney

Annu. Rev. Polit. Sci. 2005. 8:1–21
doi: 10.1146/annurev.polisci.8.082103.104911

PROSPECT THEORY AND POLITICAL SCIENCE

Jonathan Mercer

Department of Political Science, University of Washington, Seattle,
Washington 98195-3530; email: mercer@u.washington.edu

Key Words   decision making, framing, loss aversion

■ **Abstract**   Prospect theory is the most influential behavioral theory of choice in
the social sciences. Its creators won a Nobel Prize in economics, and it is largely
responsible for the booming field of behavioral economics. Although international
relations theorists who study security have used prospect theory extensively, Americanists, comparativists, and political economists have shown little interest in it. The
dominant explanation for political scientists' tepid response focuses on the theoretical
problems with extending a theory devised in the lab to explain political decisions in
the field. This essay focuses on these problems and reviews suggested solutions. It suggests that prospect theory's failure to ignite the imagination of more political scientists
probably results from their aversion to behavioral assumptions and not from problems
unique to prospect theory.

INTRODUCTION

A decade of laboratory experiments revealed that people systematically violate
the axioms of subjective expected utility theory (Kahneman et al. 1982). These
findings led two psychologists, Daniel Kahneman and Amos Tversky, to create
prospect theory—a descriptive theory of decision making under risk. They argued
that how we interpret our choices, as gains or as losses, influences how much risk
we will take. How we frame information should not influence our judgment, but it
does. As politicians know well, people feel differently about a policy guaranteed to
ensure a 90% employment rate than they feel about a policy guaranteed to provide
a 10% unemployment rate. Kahneman & Tversky (1979) found that framing a
policy as a loss (10% unemployment) will put someone in a domain of loss, and
framing it as a gain (90% employment) will put someone in a domain of gain. If
we frame an outcome as a loss, we will assume more risk to avoid that outcome
than if we framed the identical outcome as a gain. The observation that a frame
influences risk acceptance was surprising for at least two reasons. First, we should
pay attention to our absolute gains and losses or our total welfare, not changes
in our welfare relative to some arbitrary reference point. Second, whether we are
in a domain of gain or loss should not affect our attitude toward risk. Yet, we
tend to take risky bets when we are in a domain of loss. Kahneman & Tversky

created an elegant and generalizable theory that has become the leading alternative to subjective expected utility arguments.

If the findings from the lab extend to the field, then the political implications are profound. We should expect policy makers in a domain of loss to take risks they would be unlikely to take if they were in a domain of gain. They might escalate a military intervention that is going poorly, gamble on a risky rescue mission, choose war over peace, or embrace radical economic reform because they are in a domain of loss. More generally, risk aversion might account for the relative stability of the international system, explain how one might solve collective action problems, and help identify the best way to influence an adversary. Kahneman & Tversky's research has had an enormous influence on decision theory (Read 2002) and in economics. As acknowledged by the Nobel Prize committee when it awarded Kahneman (Tversky died in 1996) the 2002 Nobel in economics, their research is largely responsible for the creation of behavioral economics. Of the 2000 most recent citations to Kahneman & Tversky's 1979 article, about half are in economics, business, management, or finance journals; more than a third are in psychology; and the rest are distributed among various fields, such as law, mathematics, health, sociology, statistics, and engineering. Political scientists are responsible for about a twentieth of the citations. Between 1985 and 2003, Kahneman & Tversky's article was cited eight times in the *American Political Science Review*.[1] What explains prospect theory's limited influence in political science?

Prospect theory is influential in political science only among international relations (IR) theorists who study international security (for reviews, see Levy 1992, 1997, 2000; McDermott 2001, 2004). Prospect theory has received little attention in the fields of American politics and comparative politics, with a few exceptions (e.g., Hansen 1985, Pierson 1994, Weyland 2002). Most surprising, political economists have shown no interest in prospect theory. Psychological (or behavioral) economics has become a "hot" topic for graduate students in economics, as centers devoted to it have opened at universities in the United States, Europe, Israel, and Japan (Altman 2002, Hilsenrath 2002). Kahneman's Nobel Prize in economics confirmed Richard Thaler's observation that psychological economics "is no longer considered radical" (Uchitelle 2001)—at least not in economics. Some political scientists still view approaches that rely on psychological assumptions rather than rationalist assumptions as "radical" (Treisman 2004, p. 348). Although political economists were among the first political scientists to use prospect theory (Mastanduno 1993, Pauly 1993, Spar 1993), they are now among the least likely to use it (Elms 2004).

Prospect theory's influence in IR/security, but neglect in the rest of political science, is puzzling. Part of the explanation is institutional. Jervis (1988) was one of the first political scientists to use prospect theory concepts, and his students at Columbia University knew a good idea when they saw one (Cha 2002, Davis

---

[1]Citation data extracted from the Social Sciences Index Database of the Institute for Scientific Information.

2000, Farnham 1997, McDermott 1998). The other part of the explanation, and the focus of this review, is theoretical and methodological, and ultimately sociological. Simply put, studying choices between gambles in the lab is different from studying complex political decisions in the field, where precise measurement of domain, risk, and the influence of other factors is impossible. Kahneman (2000) believes prospect theory concepts, such as loss aversion, may illuminate strategic choices in the field, but he dismisses IR theorists' attempts to test prospect theory against expected utility theory. Although Kahneman is equally dismissive of expected utility theory (which he views as descriptively invalid), and despite prospect theory's influence in economics and related disciplines (Kahneman & Tversky 2000, Sunstein 2000), prospect theory has nonetheless failed to ignite the imagination of Americanists, comparativists, and political economists.

To address political scientists' tepid response to the most influential behavioral theory of choice in the social sciences, this review focuses not on the details of prospect theory (best presented by McDermott 1998, pp. 15–44), which tend to slip away in most empirical applications of the theory, but on the two aspects of it that political scientists generally regard as the most problematic. First, prospect theory provides no insight on how actors locate themselves in a domain of gain or loss. An actor's domain drives the rest of the theory, so determining whether an actor is in a domain of gain or loss is crucial. Second, assessing risk acceptance or risk aversion is easy in the lab but hard in the field. For political scientists, the most powerful aspect of prospect theory is its observation that people hate to lose even more than they love to win and that this will systematically bias their attitudes toward risk. If we cannot determine how an actor frames likely prospects, or if we cannot know what constitutes a risky choice, then the puzzle becomes understanding prospect theory's influence in IR, not its absence in the rest of political science.

ASSESSING DOMAIN

When we must choose between prospects, we typically frame our choices as gains or losses relative to some reference point. Rather than insert the frame by assumption, Kahneman & Tversky manipulated the experimental environment to put subjects in a domain of either gain or loss. By presenting subjects with information framed as gains or losses—an employment versus an unemployment frame when discussing economic policy, or a survival versus a mortality frame when discussing health policy—Kahneman & Tversky found that people would reverse their preferences depending on their domain. How we are presented with information should not influence our assessment of that information. Rather than focus on net gains and losses, we repackage information as representing a gain or a loss from some reference point. Most people accept the frames they are given, making them pliable to manipulation.

Psychologists create experiments that permit them to isolate variables of interest. Kahneman & Tversky (1979) created experiments in which it "is reasonable to assume either that the original formulation of the prospects leaves no room for further editing, or that the edited prospects can be specified without ambiguity" (pp. 29–30). Outside of the lab, we create our own frames, and this complicates using prospect theory to explain political decisions. Political scientists using or reviewing prospect theory always point out the lack of a theory of frames. As Levy (1997) noted, prospect theory "is a reference-dependent theory without a theory of the reference point" (p. 100). Whether an actor is risk acceptant or not depends on whether the actor is in a domain of loss, which is why the absence of a theory of frames is potentially such a problem.

Political scientists using prospect theory all wrestle with the problem of determining an actor's or a group's frame. The obstacles are formidable and the temptation to reason backwards, from choice to domain to frame, is strong. We create both our frames and our choices, and disentangling them is hard. Should we focus on individuals (Davis 2000, Farnham 1997, McDermott 1998) or on groups (Berejekian 1997, Taliaferro 2004)? Is cognition (McDermott 1998) or emotion (Farnham 1997) the key to explaining frames? If slight changes in design can affect framing effects in the lab (Boettcher 2004), then predicting frames in uncontrolled field settings is daunting. The observation that rational choice models suffer similar defects—rationalists do not have a theory of preference, and one can often reverse a rational model's predictions by changing slightly its parameters (Neral & Ochs 1992, Jung et al. 1994)—may comfort political psychologists but hardly solves the problems. As Jervis (2004) suggests, "Ingenuity and careful research can reduce, but not completely eliminate, these difficulties" (p. 172). Political psychologists rely on one or more of five complementary techniques for determining an actor's domain: status quo as reference point, aspiration as reference point, heuristics, analogies, and emotion.

Status Quo as Reference Point

Actors commonly use the status quo as a reference point for determining their domain. When we are satisfied with the status quo, we tend to be in a domain of gain; when we are dissatisfied, we tend to be in a domain of loss. Because satisfaction is subjective and because no general theory of satisfaction exists (Kahneman et al. 1999), analysts must study the details of a decision maker's situation, goals, and motivation. In many cases, assessing an actor's domain is simple: Is the status quo acceptable or not? When actors find their political position deteriorating, they are likely to view themselves in a domain of loss. Examples include Kaiser Wilhelm in the first Moroccan crisis (Davis 2000, Taliaferro 2004), the Japanese leadership before the attack on Pearl Harbor (Levi & Whyte 1997), President Carter during the Iranian hostage crisis (McDermott 1998), Prime Minister Eden in the Suez crisis (McDermott 1998, Richardson 1993), President Truman during the Korean War (Taliaferro 2004), and President Kennedy in the Cuban missile crisis (Haas 2001, Whyte & Levi 1994). In each case, foreign policy setbacks led policy makers to desire a return to a pre-crisis status quo.

Political scientists also use economic incentives, domestic politics, and a government's institutional structure to help identify what actors are likely to view as an appropriate reference point. For example, Mastanduno (1993) uses domestic structures, such as congressional pressure or the pressure of business groups, to explain the executive branch's tendency to frame trade policy in terms of loss avoidance. Mastanduno argues that this frame explains U.S. bargaining strategy in trade policy with Japan. Berejekian (1997) uses the changing market opportunities for European companies that benefit from the release of chlorofluorocarbons (CFCs) to predict how they will frame negotiations over limiting CFCs, which in turn explains the preferences and bargaining strategies of the European Community leading up to the 1987 Montreal Protocol. Cha (2002) suggests that a combination of international factors (such as the collapse of the Soviet Union) and domestic factors (such as the death of Kim Il Sung and a rapidly deteriorating domestic economy) led the North Korean leadership to view the status quo as unacceptable. Weyland (2002) uses economic crises to account for domain. Situational factors, such as an economic collapse, throw leaders and citizens into a domain of loss where the pre-crisis status quo becomes the standard reference point. Similarly, Fanis (2004) establishes actors' domain by examining economic data such as growth rates and government policies. After the Chileans elected Salvador Allende as president, he pursued economic policies that hurt the interests of leading economic sectors in Chile and these groups framed this period as a loss.

However, dissatisfaction with the status quo may also result from an actor being in the domain of gain. One can imagine that President George W. Bush, riding high in the polls after an apparently decisive military victory in Afghanistan, allowed himself the luxury of viewing the Iraqi status quo as unacceptable because he was in a domain of gain. Like a gambler in the black, Bush made bets with "house" money (Thaler & Johnson 1990) that he felt he could afford only because he was in a domain of gain. The apparent U.S. victory in Afghanistan put Secretary of Defense Donald Rumsfeld in a buoyant mood, and the President sought to use the momentum to push hard on Iraq (Woodward 2004, pp. 37, 39). Woodward reports that the Vice President's Chief of Staff "felt that keeping the focus on Afghanistan initially was wise, and now with Afghanistan going well, he believed if the war on terrorism was properly and broadly defined that Iraq had to be dealt with" (Woodward 2004, p. 50). The point is not that President Bush was either risk acceptant or risk averse, but that his dissatisfaction with the status quo may have been a consequence of his being in a domain of gain. Had the war in Afghanistan initially gone poorly, President Bush might have viewed the status quo in Iraq as acceptable. Because prospect theorists expect risk aversion in the domain of gain, they have been slow to consider the possibility that dissatisfaction with the status quo may be a consequence of success rather than failure.

Aspirations

An actor's reference point may not be the status quo but rather a point to which the actor aspires. How to distinguish dissatisfaction with an existing status quo from an aspiration for a new status quo is not always clear. In some cases, the distinction may be unnecessary. Because knowing what is going on inside North Korea is difficult, Cha (2002) settles for making a strong case that the North Korean leadership must be in a domain of loss. If their reference point is the status quo, then "the widening economic gap between North and South" puts Kim Jong Il in a domain of loss (Cha 2002, p. 59). If the reference point is an aspiration for the North's domination of a North-South Union, then Kim Jong Il is even deeper in a domain of loss. Knowing exactly how Kim Jong Il frames prospects might be helpful, but knowing that he is probably in a domain of loss, and thus likely to be risk acceptant, may tell policy makers all they need to know.

Taliaferro (2004) suggests that a careful analysis of an actor's perceptions is more useful than objective measures of determining an actor's domain (such as polling data or economic indices). Taliaferro draws on "realist" assumptions that states care more about relative than absolute gains to argue that a focus on relative power will reveal the reference point a political leader is likely to select. If a state's position relative to other states is ascendant, then the status quo becomes the reference point; if the state is in a position of relative decline, then some future aspiration becomes the reference point. An investigator can discover this reference point by examining private deliberations that provide a "baseline of expectations in planning documents, white papers on national security goals and strategies, public pronouncements, instructions to subordinates, and diplomatic communications" (Taliaferro 2004, p. 47). A nontautological assessment of an actor's aspiration level is easier said than done.

Were the Germans before the 1905 Moroccan crisis in a domain of loss primarily because of the 1904 entente between France and England (Taliaferro 2004), or because the Germans felt slighted that the French would attempt to steal Morocco in violation of its treaty commitments and without compensating Germany (Davis 2000)? Davis suggests that the Germans pursued a policy that risked war over territory of marginal value because they focused on changes from the status quo rather than on the overall position of Germany. The only thing necessary for eventual German hegemony in Europe was patience. If the Germans viewed French moves in Morocco as a challenge to German prestige, then they should have been satisfied early in the crisis with the forced ouster of French Prime Minister Delcassé in April 1906 and a return to the pre-crisis status quo. However, if their true aspiration was the destruction of the Anglo-French Entente, then even Delcassé's humiliating ouster would not satisfy. Taliaferro suggests that the Germans were in a domain of loss even after their initial humiliation of France; thus, they continued a risky policy that ended in failure. Because policy is often incoherent and evolves with the situation, it is usually possible to find evidence for a variety of different reference points. The detailed reconstruction of German decision making is necessary to understanding how people make decisions, but it demonstrates as well how difficult it is to establish a specific reference point.

For example, although I have posited that President George W. Bush was in a domain of gain before the U.S. invasion of Iraq in March 2003, maybe he was in a domain of loss even after the initial American success in Afghanistan. Not unlike the German leadership after its initial humiliation of the French, the White House kept its eye on the prize, which was overthrowing Saddam Hussein. Apparently, the President was keen on war with Iraq immediately after the 9/11 terrorist attacks (Clarke 2004, Woodward 2004) and perhaps even before them (Suskind 2004). President Bush viewed anything less than crushing Saddam Hussein's Iraq as a loss. Given this aspiration, the President was willing to engage in a risky war because he was in a domain of loss. Although the validity of prospect theory depends on a correct assessment of an actor's motivation, there is nothing within prospect theory to help with that assessment.

Elms (2004) provides a potential solution to the problem of the slippery aspiration point. Rather than rely on subjective assessments of actors, she argues that in trade disputes, "most losses and gains are measured in sales or market penetration in the target market, making domain easier to determine" (Elms 2004, p. 249). Interest groups representing firms aspire to improve their access to foreign markets, which means these groups will always frame disputes as losses to American firms. Spar (1993) focuses, in part, on the Japanese aspiration to develop an indigenous fighter jet. The Japanese aspired to greater military and technological autonomy, whereas the United States was content with the status quo. Spar explores how U.S. leaders were able to shift everyone's frame to focus not on possible gains but on possible losses to reach a compromise solution. Spar's explanation is messy, complicated, and in the details probably correct: "In reviewing the overall story of the FSX, it is clear that no single decision-making theory is sufficient to explain either the process or the outcome" (p. 87). Neither Elms nor Spar (nor Berejekian, Cha, Fanis, Mastanduno, or Weyland) conclusively demonstrates the ability to identify an actor's reference point, but their reliance on economic indices is an appropriate and potentially powerful solution to the problem and supports Elms's suggestion that political economy and prospect theory are well suited for each other.

Heuristics

Political psychologists also use heuristics to explain how people interpret their environment and locate themselves in a domain of either gain or loss (McDermott 1998, Stein 1993, Taliaferro 2004). Because we are cognitively incapable of adhering to normative models of decision, we solve complex inference problems by relying on a variety of heuristics—cognitive shortcuts that systematically bias our judgments. Tversky & Kahneman (1974) identify three heuristics as especially important. The first is the "representativeness" heuristic. We decide the probability that object or event A belongs to class B or originates from process B by determining how similar A looks to B. The more A resembles B, the higher the probability that A is a member of B or was produced by B. The problem is that we should also pay attention to other factors, such as the prior probability or base rate frequency of an outcome. Subjects typically ignore base rates and focus exclusively on similarity. The second is the "adjustment and anchoring" heuristic.

Once people have an initial assessment of a problem—even if the assessment is arbitrary—they will use it to anchor subsequent judgments and thus inadequately revise their beliefs to accommodate new information. The third is the "availability" heuristic, which is our tendency to assess probability based on how easily an object or class comes to mind. The more visible or salient an event, the easier it is to recall, which leads us to overestimate its frequency.

Psychologists in the lab easily trigger heuristics that lead to systematic bias, which in turn can explain why someone will put himself into a domain of gain or loss (Tversky & Kahneman 1974). This research cannot specify when one heuristic will trump another. One psychologist complained that current research on heuristics and biases tells us that judgments of probability are "sometimes influenced by what is similar (representativeness), comes easily to mind (availability), and comes first (anchoring). The problem with these heuristics is that they at once explain too little and too much" (Gigerenzer 1996, p. 592). Because a heuristic exists to explain any error, using them ex post is easy but not always helpful. For example, one can use "representativeness" to explain neglect of base rate probabilities and "adjustment and anchoring" to explain excessive attention to base rate probability. One can explain why an actor prefers one analogy over another by emphasizing "availability"; the salience or vividness with which the analogy comes to mind explains why it is available, and we know what is salient by identifying the choice of analogy. The limitations are obvious and are similar to the stimulus-and-response work of behaviorism: We can identify a stimulus only after identifying a response, which makes the stimulus a property of the actor and not the environment (Chomsky 1959). Although the "heuristics and biases" research program helps us understand how people reason, rather than how they ought to reason, the literature remains somewhat of a grab-bag, which may explain why psychologists test for domain's effects rather than for what affects domain. The psychologists' strategy of examining only the consequences of an actor's domain is unavailable to political scientists who study decision making in the field.

Taliaferro suggests that we use heuristics to determine how long and in what circumstances an actor will adhere to a particular aspiration. An aspiration may become a perceptual anchor that proves resistant to new evidence, and an aversion to loss coupled with the "endowment effect" (which holds that people value what they possess more than what they covet) means that actors will not update their goals and preferences; thus, they will stick doggedly to regaining past losses rather than revise their expectations downward (Taliaferro 2004, p. 45). It is difficult to assess the observation that the longer we adhere to an aspiration the less likely we are to change it. When an aspiration level changes, a heuristic will be available to explain the change. For example, after the Americans fought their way back to the 38th parallel in the Korean War, they bumped their aspirations from the prewar status quo to the goal of liberating all of Korea from communism. Taliaferro acknowledges that prospect theory would not anticipate Truman's gamble to continue the war even after returning to the prewar status quo. Taliaferro attributes this anomalous behavior to a desire to recover sunk costs. Given this new aspiration, the Truman administration was still in a domain of loss, which would then explain the U.S. push to the Yalu. The Chinese counter-offensive pushed Truman deeper into a domain of loss, but rather than escalate, the Americans revised their expectations downward (because they had not held them for long) and settled for the status-quo ante at the 38th parallel. The detailed reconstruction of the Truman administration's beliefs and expectations during the war is illuminating. The explanation is plausible, and it demonstrates that our preferences change with the circumstances. Nevertheless, the explanation can be no better than the theory on which it rests, and a theory of framing that rests on heuristics and biases provides no guidance about when people will be influenced by which heuristic.

Analogies

The analogies we use may reveal how we frame our choices. McDermott (1998) suggests that "historical analogies can provide powerful references for the development of frames" (p. 52). For example, President Carter's advisers could frame the Iranian hostage problem in several ways. Secretary of State Cyrus Vance repeatedly invoked World War II hostage crises that ended with the safe release of the American hostages without recourse to U.S. military action. In contrast, National Security Adviser Zbigniew Brzezinski viewed the crisis as the administration's own Bay of Pigs and used the Israelis' successful raid at Entebbe to support military action (McDermott 1998, p. 51). Richardson (1993) uses the availability heuristic to explain why, during the Suez crisis, the British viewed Egyptian President Gamal Abdel Nasser as another Hitler and drew quickly on the Munich analogy, whereas the Americans worried about Europeans entrapping them in another war. Mastanduno (1993) demonstrates the influence of the Smoot-Hawley Tariff analogy in trade policy to explain some otherwise puzzling behavior of the first Bush administration, and Pauly (1993) draws on the analogy of interwar monetary anarchy to capture the views of U.S. trade officials in the 1970s. Each author uses analogies either as evidence of an actor's domain or as an explanation for that domain.

One can never be certain that analogies do what one thinks they do. In a given instance, do analogies influence beliefs or do beliefs influence the choice of analogy? Which analogies are likely to be most salient and why? Careful users of analogies address these problems, but even they cannot solve them perfectly (Houghton 2001, Khong 1992). Despite these limitations, analogies can tell us a lot about an actor's domain. Prospect theory demands identifying an actor's domain but not the source of that domain. Whether domain explains analogies or analogies explain domain, we can use analogies to capture how an actor frames her environment. However, if policy preference explains the use of analogy, then the analogies become a consequence, not a cause (Levy 2000). For example, if Vance's and Brzezinski's competing policy preferences explain their use of analogies, then their analogies were part of a rhetorical strategy to advance a policy rather than a source of the policy preference (Riker 1996).

Emotion

Although Kahneman & Tversky emphasized cognition, emotion is central to prospect theory. Actors do not consult utility; they experience it (Kahneman 1994, Kahneman & Tversky 1984). As one decision theorist noted, "The effects of changes from reference points are *feelings*, or changes in hedonic states" (Read 2002, p. 471). "Experienced utility" captures the finding that we care more about recent changes in our welfare than we do about our total value position. We are not indifferent to our net assets, but what influences us most is the direction of change, whether it is a gain or a loss relative to some reference point. Emotion's influence on decision making is thus fundamental to prospect theory and to political science more generally (Bueno de Mesquita & McDermott 2004, McDermott 2005). My subjective feelings of gain or loss influence my choices. Although greed is important and provides the inspiration in most rationalist treatments of self-interest (Hirschman 1977), other emotions, such as fear, anger, regret (Jervis 1992, McDermott 2004), panic, desperation (Welch 1993a), pride (Gries 2004), desire for justice (Rabin 2002, Welch 1993b), or trust (Mercer 2005) may be equally important.

Emotion is not merely a consequence of a frame but can be a source of framing. Farnham (1997) demonstrates that our feelings can cause us to reframe our choices which, in turn, can cause us to reverse our preferences. For example, President Franklin D. Roosevelt viewed war in Europe as undesirable but as having no direct impact on the United States, and thus he opposed U.S. intervention. As the 1938 Munich crisis unfolded, Roosevelt's view remained constant. He expected war and he expected the Allies to win. The crisis provided no new information about German intentions, the dangers for Europe, or the risks for the United States. In the midst of the crisis, Roosevelt realized that war was no longer highly probable but certain and he began to feel emotionally engaged in the crisis: "as the president became increasingly affected by the emotional impact of the news from Europe, he began to experience the prospect of war as a loss" (Farnham 1992, p. 229). Bombarded by frantic and emotionally charged messages about impending war in Europe, Roosevelt reframed the war as a loss to the United States. Farnham confirms the general psychological insight that often preferences are not prior to a choice but are constructed during a choice (Shafir & LeBoeuf 2002). We figure out our preferences as we go along, which means they are neither stable nor hierarchical. It is not abstract ideas, dry information, or heuristics that explain President Roosevelt's domain, but feelings, mood, and the affect-laden reports of imminent war.

Welch (1993b) finds additional evidence that feelings influence how we frame our prospects. Although Welch is not a prospect theorist—in this work injustice, not loss aversion, drives risky behavior[2]—he notes that his approach provides clues for how actors will frame their choices. Welch argues that feelings of injustice, defined as a perceived discrepancy between entitlements and benefits, explains

---

[2] A new book (Welch 2005) uses insights from prospect theory but arrived too late for review.

why policy makers take big risks for marginal gains. A perception of injustice "engages powerful passions that have the effect of increasing the stridency of demands, amplifying intransigence, reducing sensitivity to threats and value trade-offs, increasing the willingness to run risks, and increasing the likelihood of violent behavior" (Welch 1993b, p. 20). For example, the French never adjusted to the loss of Alsace to the Germans, but the Germans never adjusted to the gain because they did not feel entitled to it. Losing Alsace did not trigger a feeling of injustice in the Germans; it did not put them in a domain of loss. Research in behavioral economics (Rabin 2002), behavioral game theory (Colman 2003), and organizational theory (Tyler & Dawes 1993) supports the view that people are routinely influenced in nontrivial ways by the justice motive. In some cases, Welch's justice motive provides an alternative explanation to prospect theory while also helping prospect theorists locate a national leader's reference point.

Emotion might also figure in the debate over how broadly to define an actor's domain of loss or gain. Whereas cognition is like a magnet (dedicated, focused, and limited), emotion is like heat (diffuse, spread across issues, enduring). The more important emotion is to determining an actor's frame, the more we should expect failure in one policy area to influence an actor's attitude toward risk in an unrelated policy area. Because we adjust to gains quickly—a process Jervis (1992) calls "renormalization"—but adjust to losses slowly, success should not have the same cross-situational effects as does failure. Frijda (1988) suggests that people respond asymmetrically to pleasure and pain, quickly becoming accustomed to pleasure but not to pain. As a result of this hedonic asymmetry, negative emotions are probably of greater consequence than positive emotions. If so, losses in one policy area outweigh equivalent gains in another and put the actor in a domain of loss.

Each of these five approaches provides creative and imperfect ways to identify how actors are likely to frame an issue. Enough people have worked on the problem of assessing how actors frame choices outside the lab to permit the conclusion that a theory of frames is beyond our grasp. Instead, political scientists have developed different approaches with various strengths and weaknesses that allow us to determine an actor's domain with various degrees of confidence. Anyone uncomfortable with these hedges should switch to mathematics, stay in the lab, or simply assume an actor's domain and be done with it.

EMPIRICAL APPLICATIONS OF LOSS AVERSION

No one likes to lose, and in this sense we are all loss averse. But for prospect theorists, loss aversion means that we will assume more risk to avoid a prospect framed as a loss than we will to obtain the identical prospect framed as a gain. Loss aversion, and its attendant biases—such as a preference for the status quo or a tendency to endow something we possess with greater value merely because we own it—has far-reaching implications. It suggests that fear of loss and not hope of gain causes most wars, that threats against a state in the domain of loss may backfire, that we should anticipate lower than optimal levels of trade (because people overvalue goods in their possession), and that radical economic plans aim to avoid losses rather than to secure equivalent gains. Although political scientists typically use prospect theory to explain conflict, several studies suggest that actors in a domain of loss will cooperate to avoid further losses.

For example, Mastanduno (1993) uses loss aversion to explain why the United States and Japan adopted a risky cooperative economic strategy, Spar (1993) notes the "dramatic appeal of loss aversion" to explain U.S.-Japanese cooperation over the development of a fighter aircraft, Welch (1993a) argues Israel cooperated with the United States to avoid damaging relations with Washington, and Fanis (2004) uses loss aversion to explain how economic actors in Chile overcame a collective action problem to form a coalition. Looming losses concentrate the mind and encourage actors to accept policies that they might otherwise reject. Although it is tempting to view either a rational or psychological explanation as best within a given case, Spar's (1993) study led her to conclude that "a model that combines bureaucratic politics and an orthodox utility maximization perspective offers a compelling account of how the process unfolded at several critical junctures" (p. 91). Sometimes policy makers adhere to normative models of choice, sometimes they do not, and only by considering the process of decision making is it possible to reach a sensible conclusion about either path.

Weyland extends loss aversion to comparative politics. He challenges the view that dictatorships engage in radical economic reform more easily than democracies by emphasizing the importance of loss aversion for both leaders and citizens in Latin American democracies. Two conditions are necessary for radical economic reform to occur. First, the public must be risk acceptant, which means they must be in a domain of loss. Second, new leaders must emerge who are free from past failed policies and who view themselves in a domain of loss. These leaders will reject the established political constraints and embrace radical economic reform. Weyland uses structure to explain frame, and frame to explain economic choices: "By demonstrating how these situational conditions affect individual choices, my prospect-theory interpretation provides a firm microfoundation for widely used crisis arguments" (Weyland 2002, p. 7). Weyland makes a compelling case in his study of Argentina, Brazil, Peru, and Venezuela that changes in frame—not changes in assets—best explain the initiation and consequences of radical economic reform. Nonetheless, identifying loss aversion is difficult. It is not always obvious whether Weyland's actors are any more risk acceptant than a skydiver who relies on an emergency parachute after the primary one fails.

Identifying Loss Aversion

Demonstrating loss aversion's effects is difficult for at least three reasons: They may be artifacts of the lab and thus vanish in the field; measuring loss aversion outside the lab is hard; and loss aversion in the domain of loss can be rational.

LOSS-AVERSION EFFECT OR ARTIFACT?   Some observers express skepticism that experiments in the lab reveal how people behave outside the lab. For example, Kahler (1998) suggests that the "transfer of experimental laboratory data, no matter how robust, to real-world choice situations is a flawed strategy: even the most ingenious experiments cannot capture the subjective perceptions of risk that are present in markets or international bargaining" (p. 928). Although applying hypotheses contradicted in the lab to explain behavior in the field might be a flawed strategy, it is hard to see how the reverse would be true. It is not obvious why we should have more confidence in theories that at the behavioral level are "demonstratively wrong" (Jones 2001, p. x) than in those that are demonstratively right. Vernon Smith, who received the 2002 Nobel Prize in economics for his pioneering work in experimental economics, views experimental and behavioral economics (and specifically prospect theory) as complementary (Smith 2003; see also Camerer 2000). Other economists use the ingenious experiments of behavioral decision theorists to explain and predict how people respond to market risks (Shiller 2000, Shleifer 2000). Researchers find that "experts" are as likely as "novices" to allow the framing of a problem to influence their decisions, and when subjects are given greater incentives to reason accurately they make the same mistakes as before but with greater enthusiasm (Le Boeuf & Shafir 2003). Thinking hard does not help one escape from framing effects any more than it allows one to escape from an optical illusion. Ultimately, of course, whether experiments tell us how people behave in real settings is an empirical question, which is why political scientists who use prospect theory are committed to detailed empirical case studies.

HOW CAN LOSS AVERSION BE MEASURED IN THE FIELD?   Measuring loss aversion is harder in the field than in the lab. As Levy (1992) points out, in the field it is often difficult to know "which prospect or strategy involves the greatest risks or how the actor evaluates the relative risks" (p. 301). McDermott (1998) addresses the problem by using an economic definition of risk: The greater the outcome variance in a choice, the riskier the choice (pp. 38–39). The more extreme the possible outcomes, the riskier the choice; the more moderate the outcomes, the less risky the choice. Rather than view risk as a product of an individual's personality, McDermott interprets risk as a feature of the situation as understood by the actor. Although we should keep in mind Kowert & Hermann's (1997) finding that people vary in their propensity for risk, our theories of personality are not well developed, which makes it difficult to know who by disposition is risk acceptant or risk averse.

McDermott's approach to defining risk helps one escape from the tautology of using domain to determine risk, but, as she notes, it does not solve the problem. Reaching a consensus on what constitutes a risky choice can be difficult. Was President Bush being risk averse or risk acceptant when he launched a preventive war against Iraq in March 2003? That the war caused more problems than it solved is irrelevant to assessing the riskiness of the policy. If President Bush believed that Iraq would either use weapons of mass destruction against the United States or provide them to terrorists, then inaction could be portrayed as having the greatest variance in outcome. Even access to primary sources might not resolve the debate over the riskiness of an actor's policy. For example, was President Eisenhower pursuing a risk-averse strategy in the 1956 Suez crisis (McDermott 1998) or merely a rational strategy (Richardson 1993)? This problem, like many, is as serious as one wishes to make it. Observers, like actors, will sometimes differ in their assessment of risk, and this makes prospect theory difficult to test.

LOSS-AVERSION EFFECT OR RATIONAL DECISION?   Loss aversion can be rational. A wild gamble to avoid a loss can be rational if one has nothing left to lose, or if one holds certain beliefs and desires that make that gamble rational. Goemans illustrates the first type of rational gamble: when one has nothing left to lose (see also Downs & Rocke 1995, pp. 56–75). Goemans (2000) suggests that states persist in losing war efforts in an attempt to escape domestic political punishment for failure. Semirepressive, moderately exclusionary regimes will gamble that through luck or a new strategy they can win a war. For example, the German leadership in 1917 felt their prospects for victory in World War I were grim and for this reason they embraced unrestricted submarine warfare. "The German leadership was now willing to try a very risky strategy because they estimated that was the only way to achieve the terms of settlement necessary to stave off punishment..." (Goemans 2000, p. 97). Although the risky bet on naval warfare did not maximize the expected utility of the German people, German leaders knew that any defeat would (at a minimum) end their careers and usher in a new social order. (Of course, if leaders know that they cannot survive even small losses, then these leaders should not start wars that they know they might lose.) Goemans's careful analysis demonstrates that actors in semirepressive and moderately exclusionary regimes can be both rational and risk acceptant in the domain of loss.

Distinguishing rational from irrational gambles demands testing alternative explanations against empirical cases. Policy makers confronting important decisions should approximate rational decision making. Often they do not. For example, in a study with a contemporary echo, Richardson (1993) examined British decision making during the Suez crisis to test prospect theory and rational choice models of decision making (pp. 176, 183–185, 187):

> [T]he process bore little or no relation to rational norms. There was no systematic evaluation of options or calculation of their costs and consequences. Having resolved to fight, British leaders, for their part, simply discounted all risks attendant on that decision. . ... They made no effort to marshal international support for their action. . ... No serious effort was made to establish the financial costs of anticipated military operations. . ... Moreover, the initial estimates that were made were extraordinarily optimistic. . ... Although Treasury officials warned of the dangers of "going it alone," the chancellor and the Egypt Committee remained undeterred. . ... [T]here appears to have been very little planning for future developments once Nasser was toppled; only a casual assumption that he would be replaced by a more compliant leader.

British decision makers were obsessed with overthrowing Nasser. Their exaggerated fear puzzled the Americans. President Eisenhower commented, "I just can't believe it. I can't believe that they would be so stupid as to invite on themselves all the Arab hostility to Israel" (Richardson 1993, p. 175). Richardson found no evidence that British decision makers were seeking gains: "The focus was entirely on the avoidance of the threat posed to British prestige and the British economy" (Richardson 1993, p. 187). The American policy makers, in contrast, used a rational decision-making process. Richardson embraces this evidence as supporting rational models; she does not attempt to either explain it away or adjust her argument to fit the data. The striking similarity between American decision-making processes before the preventive war against Iraq and British decision making in the Suez crisis challenges rational models, although whether it supports or undermines prospect theory depends on whether the Bush administration was in a domain of gain or loss.

A second type of rational gamble depends on an actor's beliefs and desires. For example, Taliaferro (2004) argues that the fear of loss, in terms of both material assets and diminished reputation for resolve, leads to a foolish acceptance of risk. Loss aversion might explain why countries initiate wars or risky military actions and, having begun them, why they persist even when the chance of victory seems remote. The Russians in Afghanistan, the Americans in Korea and Vietnam, the French in Algeria, and the Israelis in Lebanon all threw good money after bad in the hope of avoiding loss. Few things can be harder than admitting that one is responsible for an unnecessary war and, as Taliaferro demonstrates, the desire to gamble to make good on lives lost and money spent is enormous.

An irrational loss aversion may explain these bad bets, but alternative explanations exist. Actors can embrace risky strategies not because of the framing of prospects but because they believe in the "domino" theory, in which small losses quickly become big losses (Gaddis 1982). Alternatively, actors may accept risk to avoid getting a reputation for irresolution, not because they are averse to loss, but because the costs of acquiring such a reputation outweigh the benefits of ending a war (Schelling 1966). Although the domino theory has never made much sense (Jervis & Snyder 1991) and rational actors should probably not worry about their reputations for resolve (Mercer 1996, Press 2005), it would be rational for someone in the grip of these beliefs to be loss averse. It would not be rational, as Taliaferro notes, for one to worry more about losing a reputation than gaining a reputation. Prospect theory can explain this asymmetrical concern for reputation, which seems to be the rule rather than the exception.

Identifying a case of loss aversion and its effects can be as difficult as identifying an actor's domain, although it is probably no more difficult than identifying an actor's preferences. Loss aversion has the virtue of experimental support. Prospect theory emerged because normative models of risky choice repeatedly and systematically failed to explain or predict behavior. These impressive deviations demanded a new theory, and prospect theory is the best alternative we have for this type of problem. Rational theories can help decision makers by explaining how rational actors should behave if everyone adheres to normative decision theory. Behavioral theories help by explaining how people tend to reason.

Policy Implications of Loss Aversion

The policy implications of loss aversion come in two stripes: Beware loss aversion in your own policies, and anticipate loss aversion in the policies of others. The first is harder to implement than the second. It is not always clear what we can do to avoid psychological biases. Behavioral finance has become popular in part because it not only tells us what we do wrong—we tend to sell winning stocks too soon and hold on to losing stocks too long (Odean 1998)—but also tells us what we can do differently (buy index funds!). Awareness of biases is not always sufficient to change behavior. However, knowing how other people reason may help in designing policy toward others.

In strategic settings, where my best move depends on your move, knowing what you are likely to do is more helpful than knowing what you should do. For example, although defection is the rational choice in the game of Prisoner's Dilemma, 30 years of experimentation on this and strategically equivalent games (such as commons dilemmas) has invariably found what one researcher calls "rampant cooperation" (Colman 2003, p. 147). In a variety of games of strategic choice—such as Matching, Centipede, and Ultimatum games—the rational choice is typically the worst choice because people do not do what they are "supposed" to do (Colman 2003). If people think differently than they are supposed to, then knowing how they are supposed to think is not helpful and can be a source of mistakes (Mercer 2005). Better understanding when people will, for example, behave in a risk-averse or risk-acceptant way should help us in our strategic interactions.

For example, loss aversion may be key to understanding when a threat or a promise works best. Davis (2000) draws on prospect theory to provide an elegant answer to an important puzzle: When will threats deter but not cause unwanted escalation, and when will promises deter but not cause increased demands? Threats increase the risks and costs to a challenger, and promises decrease the risks and costs to a challenger. Davis combines earlier, empirically driven work on deterrence failure (e.g., Lebow & Stein 1987) with prospect theory to argue that threats should be most effective against actors who seek gains and least effective against actors who seek to avoid losses. Promises should be most effective against actors who seek to avoid losses and least effective against actors who seek gains. Davis wrings from prospect theory not only when which type of influence attempt is best, but also what type of threat or promise is likely to be most effective. For example, a promise that reduces or eliminates a target's losses should be more effective than one that augments some other value (Davis 2000, p. 37). Davis provides no insight, independent of detailed historical analysis, on how we can determine an actor's motivation. Instead, he notes that prospect theory leads us to expect fear of loss, more than hope for gain, as a dominant motive for aggression. If this expectation is correct—and his empirical chapters suggest that it is—then deterrence theorists' emphasis on threats is likely to cause conflict, not deter it.

Whereas Davis focuses on the use of threats and promises, Schaub (2004) uses loss aversion to explain Schelling's (1966) intuition that causing action (compellence) is harder than causing inaction (deterrence). Giving up something we possess makes us feel differently than not getting something we want. How an adversary frames prospects influences the value of these choices. An actor that frames discontinuing action as a loss may assume more risk to continue that action than would an actor who has the capability of action but has not yet begun it. For example, it will be harder to compel a state to surrender a chemical weapon once it has been developed than it will be to deter a state from developing such a weapon. Because of the framing effects of loss aversion, compellence is harder than deterrence.

One policy implication for political economists concerns the importance of "transaction costs" (such as the costs of preventing cheating or of acquiring information) to explain suboptimal levels of trade. If people endow their possessions with greater than market value because they own them, then suboptimal levels of trade should result. The observation challenges the Coase Theorem—that the price difference between buyers and sellers should be negligible—and thus challenges a central notion of economic rationality. Psychologists found evidence supporting the argument that the endowment effect ought to make firms "reluctant to divest themselves of divisions, plants, and product lines even though they would never consider buying the same assets" (Kahneman et al. 1990, p. 227). As Jervis suggested, the endowment effect is not only a source for stability (because people value what they have more than what they covet) but also has important implications for bargaining (Jervis 1992; see also Taliaferro 2004, p. 31). Because actors overvalue what they own, they may reject bargains or trades that a neutral observer would recommend. If loss aversion and the endowment effect are characteristics of preferences, then an exclusive focus on the structural impediments to trade misses an important part of the explanation.

CONCLUSION

The intuitive idea that we hate to lose more than we love to win, and so will take more risk to avoid a loss than we will to secure an equivalent gain, is the basis for prospect theory. Prospect theory is not a fad, a curiosity, or a way to capture idiosyncratic behavior. It is the most influential behavioral theory of choice in the social sciences. Political scientists who use prospect theory are methodologically sophisticated (e.g., McDermott 2002) and are aware of its problems and limitations. Despite their best efforts, they have failed to create either a theory of frames or a way to measure risk that guarantees a consensus.

These limitations probably do not explain the failure of prospect theory to spread widely in political science. The substantial theoretical problems with prospect theory are not obviously greater than the problems with rationalist models, and prospect theory, like most behavioral theories, can be as elegant, parsimonious, and formal as rationalist alternatives (Kanner 2004, Rabin 2002). Although economists' use of prospect theory does not validate the theory, its influence in economics belies the notion that it cannot handle complex environments and high stakes. Because most political scientists rarely use psychological theories, it seems likely that the resistance is to the discipline of psychology rather than to problems unique to prospect theory.

Although advocates of influential ideas sometimes attribute their influence to the quality of their ideas (Katzenstein et al. 1998), Jervis (1998) notes that an idea's influence is sometimes independent of its explanatory power. Such is probably the case with prospect theory. The resistance to prospect theory in political science mirrors what Rabin (1998) referred to as economists' "aggressive uncuriosity" (p. 41) toward behavioral assumptions, which he correctly anticipated would fade as economists became familiar with psychology. If behavioral economists continue to prosper, a new generation of political economists is sure to follow. None of this is meant to diminish the problems with extending prospect theory to explain how political actors make decisions under risk. These problems should not be dismissed, but neither should they be exaggerated, and always they should be viewed in a comparative light.

ACKNOWLEDGMENTS

I thank Robert Jervis, Elizabeth Kier, and Rose McDermott for excellent comments and critiques.

The *Annual Review of Political Science* is online at
http://polisci.annualreviews.org

LITERATURE CITED

Altman D. 2002. A Nobel Prize bridges economics and psychology. *New York Times,* Oct. 10:C1

Berejekian J. 1997. The gains debate: framing state choice. *Am. Polit. Sci. Rev.* 91:789–805

Boettcher WA. 2004. The prospects for prospect theory: an empirical evaluation of international relations applications of framing and loss aversion. *Polit. Psychol.* 25:331–62

Bueno de Mesquita B, McDermott R. 2004. Crossing no man's land: cooperation from the trenches. *Polit. Psychol.* 25:271–87

Camerer CF. 2000. Prospect theory in the wild: evidence from the field. See Kahneman & Tversky 2000, pp. 288–300

Cha VD. 2002. Hawk engagement and preventive defense on the Korean peninsula. *Int. Sec.* 27:40–78

Chomsky N. 1959. Review of B.F. Skinner, *Verbal Behavior. Language* 35:26–58

Clarke RA. 2004. *Against All Enemies: Inside America's War on Terror.* New York: Free

Colman AM. 2003. Cooperation, psychological game theory, and limitations of rationality in social interaction. *Behav. Brain Sci.* 26:139–53

Davis JW. 2000. *Threats and Promises: The Pursuit of International Influence.* Baltimore, MD: Johns Hopkins Univ. Press

Downs GW, Rocke DM. 1995. *Optimal Imperfection? Domestic Uncertainty and Institutions in International Relations.* Princeton, NJ: Princeton Univ. Press

Elms DK. 2004. Large costs, small benefits: explaining trade dispute outcomes. *Polit. Psychol.* 25:241–70

Fanis M. 2004. Collective action meets prospect theory: an application to coalition building in Chile, 1973–75. *Polit. Psychol.* 25:363–88

Farnham B. 1992. Roosevelt and the Munich crisis: insights from prospect theory. *Polit. Psychol.* 13:205–35

Farnham B. 1997. *Roosevelt and the Munich Crisis: A Study of Political Decision-Making.* Princeton, NJ: Princeton Univ. Press

Frijda NH. 1988. The laws of emotion. *Am. Psychol.* 43:349–58

Gaddis JL. 1982. *Strategies of Containment: A Critical Appraisal of Postwar American National Security Policy.* New York: Oxford Univ. Press

Gigerenzer G. 1996. On narrow norms and vague heuristics: a reply to Kahneman and Tversky 1996. *Psychol. Rev.* 103:592–96

Goemans HE. 2000. *War and Punishment: The Causes of War Termination and the First World War.* Princeton, NJ: Princeton Univ. Press

Gries PH. 2004. *China's New Nationalism: Pride, Politics, and Diplomacy.* Berkeley: Univ. Calif. Press

Haas ML. 2001. Prospect theory and the Cuban missile crisis. *Int. Stud. Q.* 45:241–71

Hansen JM. 1985. The political economy of group membership. *Am. Polit. Sci. Rev.* 79:79–96

Hilsenrath JE. 2002. Nobel winners for economics are new breed. *Wall Street J.*, Oct. 10:B1

Hirschman AO. 1977. *The Passions and the Interests: Political Arguments for Capitalism Before Its Triumph.* Princeton, NJ: Princeton Univ. Press

Houghton DP. 2001. *U.S. Foreign Policy and the Iran Hostage Crisis.* New York: Cambridge Univ. Press

Jervis R. 1988. War and misperception. *J. Interdiscipl. Hist.* 18:675–700

Jervis R. 1992. Political implications of loss aversion. *Polit. Psychol.* 13:187–204

Jervis R. 1998. Realism in the study of world politics. *Int. Organ.* 52:971–91

Jervis R. 2004. The implications of prospect theory for human nature and values. *Polit. Psychol.* 25:163–76

Jervis R, Snyder JL, eds. 1991. *Dominoes and Bandwagons: Strategic Beliefs and Great Power Competition in the Eurasian Rimland.* New York: Oxford Univ. Press

Jones BD. 2001. *Politics and the Architecture of Choice: Bounded Rationality and Governance.* Chicago: Univ. Chicago Press

Jung YJ, Kagel JH, Levin D. 1994. On the existence of predatory pricing: an experimental study of reputation and entry deterrence in the chain-store game. *RAND J. Econ.* 25:72–93

Kahler M. 1998. Rationality in international relations. *Int. Organ.* 52:919–41

Kahneman D. 1994. New challenges to the rationality assumption. *J. Inst. Theor. Econ.* 150:18–36. Reprinted in Kahneman & Tversky 2000, pp. 758–74

Kahneman D. 2000. Preface. See Kahneman & Tversky 2000, pp. ix–xvii

Kahneman D, Diener E, Schwarz N, eds. 1999. *Well-being: The Foundations of Hedonic Psychology.* New York: Russell Sage Found.

Kahneman D, Knetsch JL, Thaler RH. 1990. Experimental tests of the endowment effect and the Coase Theorem. *J. Polit. Econ.* 98:1325–48. Reprinted in Sunstein 2000, pp. 211–31

Kahneman D, Slovic P, Tversky A, eds. 1982. *Judgment under Uncertainty: Heuristics and Biases.* New York: Cambridge Univ. Press

Kahneman D, Tversky A. 1979. Prospect theory: an analysis of decision under risk. *Econometrica* 47:263–91. Reprinted in Kahneman & Tversky 2000, pp. 17–43

Kahneman D, Tversky A. 1984. Choices, values, and frames. *Am. Psychol.* 39:341–50. Reprinted in Kahneman & Tversky 2000, pp. 1–16

Kahneman D, Tversky A, eds. 2000. *Choices, Values, and Frames.* New York: Cambridge Univ. Press

Kanner MD. 2004. Framing and the role of the second actor: an application of prospect theory to bargaining. *Polit. Psychol.* 25:213–39

Katzenstein PJ, Keohane RO, Krasner SD.

1998. *International Organization* and the study of world politics. *Int. Organ.* 52:645–85

Khong YF. 1992. *Analogies at War: Korea, Munich, Dien Bien Phu, and the Vietnam Decisions of 1965*. Princeton, NJ: Princeton Univ. Press

Kowert PA, Hermann MG. 1997. Who takes risks? Daring and caution in foreign policy making. *J. Confl. Resolut.* 41:611–37

LeBoeuf RA, Shafir E. 2003. Deep thoughts and shallow frames: on the susceptibility to framing effects. *J. Behav. Decis. Making* 16:77–92

Lebow RN, Stein JG. 1987. Beyond deterrence. *J. Soc. Issues* 43(4):5–72

Levi AS, Whyte G. 1997. A cross-cultural exploration of the reference dependence of crucial group decisions under risk: Japan's 1941 decision for war. *J. Confl. Resolut.* 41:792–813

Levy JS. 1992. Prospect theory and international relations: theoretical applications and analytical problems. *Polit. Psychol.* 13:283–310

Levy JS. 1997. Prospect theory, rational choice, and international relations. *Int. Stud. Q.* 41:87–112

Levy JS. 2000. Loss aversion, framing effects, and international conflict: perspectives from prospect theory. In *Handbook of War Studies II*, ed. MI Midlarsky, 193–221. Ann Arbor: Univ. Mich. Press

Mastanduno M. 1993. Framing the Japan problem: the Bush administration and the Structural Impediments Initiative. See Stein & Pauly 1993, pp. 35–64

McDermott R. 1998. *Risk-Taking in International Politics: Prospect Theory in American Foreign Policy*. Ann Arbor: Univ. Mich. Press

McDermott R. 2001. The psychological ideas of Amos Tversky and their relevance for political science. *J. Theor. Polit.* 13:5–33

McDermott R. 2002. Experimental methods in political science. *Annu. Rev. Polit. Sci.* 5:31–61

McDermott R. 2004. Prospect theory in polit-

ical science: gains and losses from the first decade. *Polit. Psychol.* 25:289–312

McDermott R. 2005. The feeling of rationality: the meaning of neuroscientific advances for political science. *Perspect. Polit.* In press

Mercer J. 1996. *Reputation and International Politics*. Ithaca, NY: Cornell Univ. Press

Mercer J. 2005. Rationality and psychology in international politics. *Int. Organ.* 59(1):In press

Neral J, Ochs J. 1992. The sequential equilibrium theory of reputation building: a further test. *Econometrica* 60:1151–69

Odean T. 1998. Are investors reluctant to realize their losses? *J. Financ.* 53:1775–98. Reprinted in Kahneman & Tversky 2000, pp. 371–92

Pauly LW. 1993. The political foundations of multilateral economic surveillance. See Stein & Pauly 1993, pp. 93–127

Pierson P. 1994. *Dismantling the Welfare State? Reagan, Thatcher, and the Politics of Retrenchment*. New York: Cambridge Univ. Press

Press DG. 2005. *Calculating Credibility*. Ithaca, NY: Cornell Univ. Press. In press

Rabin M. 1998. Psychology and economics. *J. Econ. Lit.* 36:11–46

Rabin M. 2002. A perspective on psychology and economics. *Eur. Econ. Rev.* 46:657–85

Read D. 2002. Book review: *Choices, Values and Frames*. *J. Behav. Decis. Making* 15:467–73

Richardson L. 1993. Avoiding and incurring losses: decision-making in the Suez crisis. See Stein & Pauly 1993, pp. 170–201

Riker WH. 1996. *The Strategy of Rhetoric: Campaigning for the American Constitution*, ed. RL Calvert, J Mueller, RK Wilson. New Haven, CT: Yale Univ. Press

Schaub G. 2004. Deterrence, compellence, and prospect theory. *Polit. Psychol.* 25:389–411

Schelling TC. 1966. *Arms and Influence*. New Haven, CT: Yale Univ. Press

Shafir E, LeBoeuf RA. 2002. Rationality. *Annu. Rev. Psychol.* 53:491–517

Shiller RJ. 2000. *Irrational Exuberance*. Princeton, NJ: Princeton Univ. Press

Shleifer A. 2000. *Inefficient Markets: An Intro-duction to Behavioral Finance.* New York: Oxford Univ. Press

Smith VL. 2003. Constructivist and ecological rationality in economics. *Am. Econ. Rev.* 93:465–508

Spar D. 1993. Co-developing the FSX fighter: the domestic calculus of international cooperation. See Stein & Pauly 1993, pp. 65–92

Stein JG. 1993. International co-operation and loss avoidance: framing the problem. See Stein & Pauly 1993, pp. 2–34

Stein JG, Pauly LW, eds. 1993. *Choosing to Co-operate: How States Avoid Loss.* Baltimore, MD: Johns Hopkins Univ. Press

Sunstein CR, ed. 2000. *Behavioral Law and Economics.* New York: Cambridge Univ. Press

Suskind R. 2004. *The Price of Loyalty: George W. Bush, the White House, and the Education of Paul O'Neill.* New York: Simon & Schuster

Taliaferro JW. 2004. *Balancing Risks: Great Power Intervention in the Periphery.* Ithaca, NY: Cornell Univ. Press

Thaler RH, Johnson EJ. 1990. Gambling with the house money and trying to break even: the effects of prior outcomes on risky choice. *Manage. Sci.* 36:643–60

Treisman D. 2004. Rational appeasement. *Int. Organ.* 58:345–73

Tversky A, Kahneman D. 1974. Judgment under uncertainty: heuristics and biases. *Science* 185:1124–31. Reprinted in Kahneman et al. 1982, pp. 3–20

Tyler TR, Dawes RM. 1993. Fairness in groups: comparing the self-interest and social identity perspectives. In *Psychological Perspectives on Justice: Theory and Applications,* ed. BA Mellers, J Baron, pp. 87–108. New York: Cambridge Univ. Press

Uchitelle L. 2001. Economist is honored for use of psychology. *New York Times,* April 28:B14

Welch DA. 1993a. The politics and psychology of restraint: Israeli decision-making in the Gulf War. See Stein & Pauly 1993, pp. 128–69

Welch DA. 1993b. *Justice and the Genesis of War.* New York: Cambridge Univ. Press

Welch DA. 2005. *Painful Choices: A Theory of Foreign Policy Change.* Princeton, NJ: Princeton Univ. Press. In press

Weyland KG. 2002. *The Politics of Market Reform in Fragile Democracies: Argentina, Brazil, Peru, and Venezuela.* Princeton, NJ: Princeton Univ. Press

Whyte G, Levi AS. 1994. The origins and function of the reference point in risky group decision making: the case of the Cuban missile crisis. *J. Behav. Decis. Making* 7:243–60

Woodward B. 2004. *Plan of Attack.* New York: Simon & Schuster

Annu. Rev. Polit. Sci. 2005. 8:23–48
doi: 10.1146/annurev.polisci.7.012003.104904
First published online as a Review in Advance on Oct. 20, 2004

THE RELATIONSHIP BETWEEN THEORY AND POLICY IN INTERNATIONAL RELATIONS

Stephen M. Walt
*Kennedy School of Government, Harvard University, Cambridge, Massachusetts 02138;
email: Stephen_Walt@ksg.harvard.edu*

Key Words   policy relevance, academia, policy evaluation, prediction, social science

■ **Abstract**   Policy makers pay relatively little attention to the vast theoretical literature in IR, and many scholars seem uninterested in doing policy-relevant work. These tendencies are unfortunate because theory is an essential tool of statecraft. Many policy debates ultimately rest on competing theoretical visions, and relying on a false or flawed theory can lead to major foreign policy disasters. Theory remains essential for diagnosing events, explaining their causes, prescribing responses, and evaluating the impact of different policies. Unfortunately, the norms and incentives that currently dominate academia discourage many scholars from doing useful theoretical work in IR. The gap between theory and policy can be narrowed only if the academic community begins to place greater value on policy-relevant theoretical work.

INTRODUCTION

If the scholarly study of international relations—and especially work on IR theory—were of great value to policy makers, then those charged with the conduct of foreign policy would be in a better position today than ever before. More scholars are studying the subject, more theories are being proposed and tested, and outlets for scholarly work continue to multiply.[1]

The need for powerful theories that could help policy makers design effective solutions would seem to be apparent as well. The unexpected emergence of a unipolar world, the rapid expansion of global trade and finance, the challenges posed by failed states and global terrorism, the evolving human rights agenda, the spread of democracy, concerns about the global environment, the growing prominence of nongovernmental organizations, etc., present policy makers with

---

[1]One recent study reports that "there are at least twenty-two English-language journals devoted exclusively or largely to international relations, aside from the general politics and policy journals that also publish IR articles" (Lepgold & Nincic 2001, p. 15). IR scholars can also disseminate their work through weblogs, working papers, and outlets such as the Columbia International Affairs Online (CIAO) service.

problems that cry out for new ideas. These phenomena—and many others—have all been objects of sustained scholarly inquiry, and one might expect policy makers to consume the results with eagerness and appreciation.

Yet despite the need for well-informed advice about contemporary international problems, and the energy and activity being devoted to studying these questions, there has long been dissatisfaction with the contributions of IR theorists (Morgenthau 1958, Tanter & Ullman 1972). According to former diplomat David Newsom, "much of today's scholarship [on international issues] is either irrelevant or inaccessible to policymakers. . .much remains locked within the circle of esoteric scholarly discussion" (Newsom 1995–1996, p. 66). Another observer declares that "the higher learning about international relations does not loom large on the intellectual landscape. Its practitioners are not only rightly ignored by practicing foreign policy officials; they are usually held in disdain by their fellow academics as well" (Kurth 1998, p. 29). The veteran U.S. statesman Paul Nitze described theory and practice as "harmonic aspects of one whole," but he believed that "most of what has been written and taught under the heading of 'political science' by Americans since World War II. . .has also been of limited value, if not counterproductive as a guide to the conduct of actual policy" (Nitze 1993, p. 15). Similarly, George (2000) reports that policy makers' eyes "would glaze as soon as I used the word *theory*." Nor is the problem unique to the United States, as indicated by the Chief Inspector of the British diplomatic service's comment that he was "not sure what the academic discipline of IR—if indeed there be such a thing as an academic discipline of IR—has to contribute to the practical day-to-day work of making and managing foreign policy" (Wallace 1994).

A low regard for theory is also reflected in the organizations responsible for conducting foreign policy. Although academics do work in policy-making circles in many countries, a sophisticated knowledge of IR theory is hardly a prerequisite for employment. In the United States, for example, there is no foreign policy counterpart to the President's Council of Economic Advisors (which is staffed by Ph.D. economists), and being an accomplished IR scholar is neither necessary nor sufficient for appointment to the National Security Council or other similar bodies.[2] Instead, senior policy makers are more likely to be selected for their intelligence, loyalty, and/or intimate knowledge of a particular region or policy area. Nor is there much evidence that policy makers pay systematic attention to academic writings on international affairs.

Dissatisfaction with the limited influence of IR has inspired a small but growing literature that seeks to reconnect the worlds of theory and policy (George et al. 1971; George & Smoke 1974; Feaver 1999; Hill & Beshoff 1994; Kruzel 1994; Zelikow 1994; Lepgold 1998; Jentleson 2000, 2002; Lupia 2000; Nincic & Lepgold 2000;

---

[2]Several academics have served as U.S. National Security Advisor (e.g., Henry Kissinger, Zbigniew Brzezinski, Anthony Lake, Condoleezza Rice), but so have individuals with little or no formal training in IR (e.g., William Clark, Colin Powell, Sandy Berger, Robert McFarlane, and John Poindexter).

Lepgold & Nincic 2001; Siverson 2001). Taken as a whole, these works emphasize several key themes.

First, the literature sees a wide gap between academic theories of international relations and the practical conduct of foreign policy. Most works in this genre deplore this situation and offer various remedies for correcting it, although a few authors warn that greater emphasis on "policy relevance" might be detrimental (Hill & Beshoff 1994, Stein 2000).

Second, these works attribute the gap in part to the complexity of the policy maker's task and the limitations of existing social science theories, but also to the incentive structures and professional ethos of the academic world. In other words, IR theory is less relevant for policy makers because scholars have little incentive to develop ideas that might be useful.

Third, the literature tends to adopt a trickle-down model linking theory and policy. General or basic IR theory is seen as too abstract to influence policy directly, although it can provide overarching conceptual frameworks and thus influence scholars analyzing specific regional developments or applied "issue-oriented puzzles" (Lepgold 2000, Wilson 2000). These latter works will inform policy analyses of specific problems, thereby helping to shape the debate on specific actions and decisions. It follows that the current gap might be narrowed by strengthening the transmission belt linking these different activities, so that academic ideas reach the policy maker's desk more readily.

The present essay explores these themes in greater detail. Can theoretical IR work help policy makers identify and achieve specific foreign policy goals? What are the obstacles that limit its contribution? Given these obstacles, what should be done?

WHAT CAN THEORY CONTRIBUTE TO THE CONDUCT OF FOREIGN POLICY?

What Types of Knowledge Do Policy Makers Need?

Policy decisions can be influenced by several types of knowledge. First, policy makers invariably rely on purely factual knowledge (e.g., how large are the opponent's forces? What is the current balance of payments?). Second, decision makers sometimes employ "rules of thumb": simple decision rules acquired through experience rather than via systematic study (Mearsheimer 1989).[3] A third type of knowledge consists of typologies, which classify phenomena based on sets of specific traits. Policy makers can also rely on empirical laws. An empirical law is an observed correspondence between two or more phenomena that systematic inquiry has shown to be reliable. Such laws (e.g., "democracies do not fight each other"

---

[3]For example, someone commuting to work by car might develop a "rule of thumb" identifying which route(s) took the least time at different times of day, based on their own experience but not on a systematic study of traffic patterns.

or "human beings are more risk averse with respect to losses than to gains") can be useful guides even if we do not know why they occur, or if our explanations for them are incorrect.

Finally, policy makers can also use theories. A theory is a causal explanation— it identifies recurring relations between two or more phenomena and explains why that relationship obtains. By providing us with a picture of the central forces that determine real-world behavior, theories invariably simplify reality in order to render it comprehensible.

At the most general level, theoretical IR work consists of "efforts by social scientists...to account for interstate and trans-state processes, issues, and outcomes in general causal terms" (Lepgold & Nincic 2001, p. 5; Viotti & Kauppi 1993). IR theories offer explanations for the level of security competition between states (including both the likelihood of war among particular states and the war-proneness of specific countries); the level and forms of international cooperation (e.g., alliances, regimes, openness to trade and investment); the spread of ideas, norms, and institutions; and the transformation of particular international systems, among other topics.

In constructing these theories, IR scholars employ an equally diverse set of explanatory variables. Some of these theories operate at the level of the international system, using variables such as the distribution of power among states (Waltz 1979, Copeland 2000, Mearsheimer 2001), the volume of trade, financial flows, and interstate communications (Deutsch 1969, Ruggie 1983, Rosecrance 1986); or the degree of institutionalization among states (Keohane 1984, Keohane & Martin 2003). Other theories emphasize different national characteristics, such as regime type (Andreski 1980, Doyle 1986, Fearon 1994, Russett 1995), bureaucratic and organizational politics (Allison & Halperin 1972, Halperin 1972), or domestic cohesion (Levy 1989); or the content of particular ideas or doctrines (Van Evera 1984, Hall 1989, Goldstein & Keohane 1993, Snyder 1993). Yet another family of theories operates at the individual level, focusing on individual or group psychology, gender differences, and other human traits (De Rivera 1968, Jervis 1976, Mercer 1996, Byman & Pollock 2001, Goldgeier & Tetlock 2001, Tickner 2001, Goldstein 2003), while a fourth body of theory focuses on collective ideas, identities, and social discourse (e.g., Finnemore 1996, Ruggie 1998, Wendt 1999). To develop these ideas, IR theorists employ the full range of social science methods: comparative case studies, formal theory, large-N statistical analysis, and hermeneutical or interpretivist approaches.

The result is a bewildering array of competing arguments (Viotti & Kauppi 1993, Dougherty & Pfaltzgraff 1997, Walt 1997a, Waever 1998, Baylis & Smith 2001, Carlsnaes et al. 2002). With so many theories from which to choose, how do we know a good one when we see one?

What is a Good Theory?

First and most obviously, a good theory should be logically consistent and empirically valid, because a logical explanation that is consistent with the available evidence is more likely to provide an accurate guide to the causal connections that shape events.

Second, a good theory is complete; it does not leave us wondering about the causal relationships at work (Van Evera 1997). For example, a theory stating that "national leaders go to war when the expected utility of doing so outweighs the expected utility of all alternative choices" (Bueno de Mesquita & Lalman 1992) may be logically impeccable, but it does not tell us when leaders will reach this judgment. Similarly, a theory is unsatisfying when it identifies an important causal factor but not the factor(s) most responsible for determining outcomes. To say that "human nature causes war," or even that "oxygen causes war," is true in the sense that war as we know it cannot occur in the absence of these elements. But such information does not help us understand what we want to know, namely, *when* is war more or less likely? Completeness also implies that the theory has no "debilitating gaps," such as an omitted variable that either makes its predictions unacceptably imprecise or leads to biased inferences about other factors (Nincic & Lepgold 2000, p. 28).

A third desideratum is explanatory power. A theory's explanatory power is its ability to account for phenomena that would otherwise seem mystifying. Theories are especially valuable when they illuminate a diverse array of behavior that previously seemed unrelated and perplexing, and they are most useful when they make apparently odd or surprising events seem comprehensible (Rapaport 1972). In physics, it seems contrary to common sense to think that light would be bent by gravity. Yet Einstein's theory of relativity explains why this is so. In economics, it might seem counterintuitive to think that nations would be richer if they abolished barriers to trade and did not try to hoard specie (as mercantilist doctrines prescribed). The Smith/Ricardo theory of free trade tells us why, but it took several centuries before the argument was widely accepted (Irwin 1996). In international politics, it seems odd to believe that a country would be safer if it were unable to threaten its opponent's nuclear forces, but deterrence theory explains why mutual vulnerability may be preferable to either side having a large capacity to threaten the other side's forces (Wohlstetter 1957, Schelling 1960, Glaser 1990, Jervis 1990). This is what we mean by a powerful theory: Once we understand it, previously unconnected or baffling phenemona make sense.

Fourth, at the risk of stating the obvious, we prefer theories that explain an important phenomenon (i.e., something that is likely to affect the fates of many people). Individual scholars may disagree about the relative importance of different issues, but a theory that deals with a problem of some magnitude is likely to garner greater attention and/or respect than a theory that successfully addresses a puzzle of little intrinsic interest. Thus, a compelling yet flawed explanation for great power war or genocide is likely to command a larger place in the field than an impeccable theory that explains the musical characteristics of national anthems.

Fifth, a theory is more useful when it is prescriptively rich, i.e., when it yields useful recommendations (Van Evera 1997). For this reason, George advises scholars to "include in their research designs variables over which policymakers have some leverage" (George 2000, p. xiv; also Glaser & Strauss 1967, Stein 2000). Yet a theory that does not include manipulable variables may still be useful to policy makers. For example, a theory that explained why a given policy objective was impossible might be very useful if it convinced a policy maker not to pursue such an elusive goal. Similarly, a theory that accurately forecast the risk of war might provide a useful warning to policy makers even if the variables in the theory were not subject to manipulation.

Finally, theories are more valuable when they are stated clearly. *Ceteris paribus*, a theory that is hard to understand is less useful simply because it takes more time for potential users to master it. Although academics often like to be obscure (because incomprehensibility can both make scholarship seem more profound and make it harder to tell when a particular argument is wrong), opacity impedes scientific progress and is not a virtue in theoretical work. An obscure and impenetrable theory is also less likely to influence busy policy makers.

How Theory Can Aid Policy (in Theory)

Although many policy makers dismiss academic theorizing and many academics criticize the actions of government officials, theory and policy are inextricably linked. Each day, policy makers must try to figure out which events merit attention and which items or issues can be ignored, and they must select objectives and choose policy instruments that will achieve them. Whether correct or not, they do this on the basis of some sort of theory.

Furthermore, policy debates in both domestic and foreign affairs often hinge on competing theoretical claims, and each participant believes his or her preferred policy option will produce the desired result. For example, competing prescriptions for halting the ethnic conflicts in Bosnia and Kosovo rested in part on different theories about the underlying causes of these wars. Those who favored intervening to establish a multiethnic democracy in Bosnia (and Kosovo) tended to blame the fighting on the machinations of autocratic leaders such as Slobodan Milosevic, whereas those who favored ethnic partition blamed the conflict on a security dilemma created by intermingled populations (cf. Kaufmann 1996, Stedman 1997, Sambanis 2000). More recently, the debate over war against Iraq hinged in part on competing factual claims (did Iraq have weapons of mass destruction or not?) but also on competing forecasts about the long-term effects of the war. Advocates believed war would lead to a rapid victory, encourage neighboring regimes to "bandwagon" with the United States, hasten the spread of democracy in the region, and ultimately undermine support for Islamic terrorism. Their opponents argued that the war would have exactly the opposite effects (Sifry & Cerf 2003), and these disagreements arose in part because of fundamentally different views about the basic dynamics of interstate relations.

History also shows that bad theories can lead directly to foreign policy disasters. Prior to World War I, for example, Admiral Von Tirpitz's infamous "risk theory" argued that German acquisition of a large battle fleet would threaten British naval supremacy and deter Great Britain from opposing German dominance of the continent; in fact, the building of the fleet merely accelerated Britain's alignment with

Germany's continental opponents (Kennedy 1983). During the Cold War, Soviet policy in the Third World was justified by Marxist claims that the developing world was evolving in a socialist direction, and that this evolution would naturally incline these states to ally with the USSR. This theory of cooperation was flawed on both counts, which helps explain why Soviet efforts to build influence in the developing world were costly and disappointing (Rubinstein 1990). Similarly, U.S. intervention in Indochina and Central America was justified in part by the so-called domino theory, even though the logic and evidence supporting the theory were dubious at best (Slater 1987, 1993–1994). All of these examples show how bad IR theories can lead policy makers astray.

The converse is also true, however: Sometimes good theory leads to good policy. As discussed above, the Smith/Ricardo theory of free trade has for the most part triumphed over mercantilist thinking and paved the way for the rapid expansion of the world economy after World War II, thereby facilitating an enormous increase in global wealth and welfare. In the same way, the theory of deterrence articulated in the 1940s and 1950s informed many aspects of U.S. military and foreign policy during the Cold War, and it continues to exert a powerful impact today.[4]

The relationship between theory and policy is not a one-way street. Theory informs policy and policy problems inspire theoretical innovation (Jervis, 2004). For example, the development of the bureaucratic politics paradigm and the theory of nuclear deterrence illustrate how new political issues can spark theoretical developments, with implications that extend beyond the specific problems that inspired the theoretical innovation (Trachtenberg 1992). More recently, efforts to analyze the collapse of the Soviet empire (Kuran 1991, Lohmann 1994, Lebow & Risse-Kappen 1995, Evangelista 2002), the dynamics of unipolarity (Wohlforth 1999, Brooks & Wohlforth 2000–2001), or the origins of ethnic conflict (Posen 1993, Fearon & Laitin 1996, Lake & Rothchild 1998, Toft 2004) show IR theorists fashioning new theories in response to new concerns. Theory and policy form a web, even if the web has many gaps and missing strands. Despite these gaps, there are at least four ways that theoretical scholarship can help policy makers: diagnosis, prediction, prescription, and evaluation.

DIAGNOSIS   The first contribution that theory can make is diagnosis (Jentleson 2000). Like all of us, policy makers face a bewildering amount of information, much of it ambiguous. When seeking to address either a recurring problem or a specific event, policy makers must figure out what sort of phenomenon they are facing. Is expansionist behavior driven by a revolutionary ideology or individual megalomania, or is it rooted in legitimate security fears? Are trade negotiations in jeopardy because the participants' preferences are incompatible or because they do not trust each other? By expanding the set of possible interpretations, theories provide policy makers with a broader set of diagnostic possibilities.

---

[4]Of course, not all aspects of U.S. nuclear weapons policy conformed to the prescriptions of classic deterrence theory (Jervis 1984).

Diagnosis does not require a sophisticated theory, however; even simple typologies can help policy makers devise an appropriate response to a problem. In medicine, even if we do not know the exact mechanism that produces a disease, we may be able to treat it once the correct diagnosis is made (George 2000). Similarly, even if we cannot fully explain why certain international events occur, we may still be able to fashion a remedy once we have identified the problem.

Theory also guides our understanding of the past, and historical interpretations often influence what policy makers do later (May 1975, May & Neustadt 1984). Did the Cold War end because the Soviet economy was dying from "natural causes" (i.e., the inherent inefficiency of centrally planned economies), because Soviet elites were persuaded by norms and ideas imported from the West, or because the United States was putting greater pressure on its overmatched adversary? The question is not merely academic; it tends to shape attitudes on how the United States should use its power today. Hardliners tend to attribute the Soviet collapse to U.S. pressure, and they believe similar policies will work against contemporary enemies (e.g., Iraq, Iran, North Korea) and future "peer competitors" (Mann 2004). By contrast, if the Soviet Union collapsed because of its own internal contradictions, or because Western ideas proved contagious, then U.S. policy makers should consider whether future peer competitors might be more readily coopted than contained (cf. Wohlforth 1994–1995, Evangelista 2002).

The recent debate on war with Iraq offers an equally apt example. Analysts who focused primarily on Saddam Hussein's personality and the nature of the Ba'ath regime saw Hussein's past conduct as evidence that he was an irrational serial aggressor who could not be deterred and thus could not be permitted to acquire weapons of mass destruction (Pollock 2002). By contrast, scholars who focused on Iraq's external situation tended to see Hussein as a risk-acceptant but ultimately rational leader who had never used force in the face of a clear deterrent threat and thus could be deterred by superior force in the future (Mearsheimer & Walt 2003). Thus, interpretations about Iraq's past conduct were partly shaped by contrasting theoretical views and had a clear impact on contemporary policy recommendations.

Once a diagnosis is made, theory also guides the search for additional information. As discussed above, policy makers inevitably rely on different forms of knowledge—including purely factual information—but theory helps them decide what sort of information is relevant. To take a simple example, both policy makers and IR theorists know that power is an important concept, although there is no precise formula for measuring the relative power of different actors. We do not judge the power of nations by examining the quality of their opera productions, the average hair length of the citizenry, or the number of colors in the national flag. Why? Because there is no theory linking these measures to global influence. Rather, both policy makers and scholars generally use some combination of population, gross national product, military strength, scientific prowess, etc., because they understand that these features enable states to affect others (Morgenthau 1985,

Moul 1989, Wohlforth 1993, Mearsheimer 2001). That is why U.S. and Asian policy makers worry about the implications of China's economic growth but do not express similar concerns about Thailand or Brunei.

PREDICTION   IR theories can also help policy makers anticipate events. By identifying the central causal forces at work in a particular era, theories offer a picture of the world and thus can provide policy makers with a better understanding of the broad context in which they are operating. Such knowledge may enable policy makers to prepare more intelligently and in some cases allow them to prevent unwanted developments.

To note an obvious example, different theories of international politics offered contrasting predictions about the end of the Cold War. Liberal theories generally offered optimistic forecasts, suggesting that the collapse of communism and the spread of Western-style institutions and political forms heralded an unusually peaceful era (Fukuyama 1992, Hoffman et al. 1993, Russett 1995, Weart 2000). By contrast, realist theories of IR predicted that the collapse of the Soviet threat would weaken existing alliances (Mearsheimer 1989, Waltz 1994–1995, Walt 1997c), stimulate the formation of anti-U.S. coalitions (Layne 1993, Kupchan 2000), and generally lead to heightened international competition. Other realists foresaw a *Pax Americana* based on U.S. primacy (Wohlforth 1999, Brooks & Wohlforth 2000–2001), whereas scholars from different traditions anticipated either a looming "clash of civilizations" (Huntington 1997) or a "coming anarchy" arising from failed states in the developing world (Kaplan 2001). Some of these works were more explicitly theoretical than others, but each highlighted particular trends and causal relationships in order to sketch a picture of an emerging world.

Theories can also help us anticipate how different regions or states are likely to evolve over time. Knowing a great deal about a particular state's current foreign policy preferences can be useful, for example, but this knowledge may tell us relatively little about how this state will behave if its position in the world were different. For that task, we need a theory that explains how preferences (and behavior) will evolve as conditions change. For example, China's foreign policy behavior is virtually certain to change as its power grows and its role in the world economy increases, but existing realist and liberal theories offer sharply different forecasts about China's future course. Realist theories predict that increased power would make China more assertive, whereas liberal approaches suggest that increased interdependence and/or a transition to democracy is likely to dampen these tendencies significantly (cf. Goldstein 1997–1998, Mearsheimer 2001).

Similarly, there is a growing consensus that economic development is encouraged by competitive markets, the rule of law, education for both sexes, and government transparency. If true, then this body of theory identifies which regions or countries are likely to develop rapidly. In the same way, Hudson & Den Boer's (2002, 2004) work on the impact of "surplus males" may provide an early warning about particular regions or countries.[5] Dynamic theories of the balance of power offer similar warnings about effects of rapid shifts in relative power and thus can be used to identify potentially unstable regions (Gilpin 1981, Friedberg 1993–1994, Copeland 2000). In each of these cases, a theoretical argument carries important implications for future events.

The relationship between theoretical forecasting and real-world policy making is not straightforward, however (Doran 1999). Social science theories are probabilistic, and even a very powerful theory will make some false forecasts. Moreover, the objects of social science theory are sentient beings who may consciously adjust their behavior in ways that confirm or confound the theories on which they have based their decisions. In response to Huntington's forecast of a "clash of civilizations," a policy maker who concluded that the clash was inevitable would be inclined to adopt defensive policies that could easily make such a clash more likely, but someone who felt it was avoidable could take steps to minimize civilizational frictions and thus make Huntington's predictions appear false (Walt 1997b). In other cases, such as the Hudson & Den Boer study of "surplus males," the knowledge that certain countries were prone to conflict could enable policy makers to take preventive steps against anticipated problems.[6] In social science, in short, the observed validity of a theory may be affected by the degree to which it is accepted and acted on by policy makers.

PRESCRIPTION   All policy actions rest on at least a crude notion of causality. Policy makers select policies A, B, and C because they believe these measures will produce some desired outcome. Theory thus guides prescription in several ways.

First, theory affects the choice of objectives by helping the policy maker evaluate both desirability and feasibility. For example, the decision to expand NATO was based in part on the belief that it would stabilize the emerging democracies in Eastern Europe and enhance U.S. influence in an important region (cf. Goldgeier 1999, Reiter 2001–2002). Expansion was not an end in itself; it was a means to other goals. Similarly, the decision to establish the World Trade Organization arose from a broad multilateral consensus that a more powerful international trade regime was necessary to lower the remaining barriers to trade and thus foster greater global productivity (Preeg 1998, Lawrence 2002).

Second, careful theoretical work can help policy makers understand what they must do to achieve a particular result. To deter an adversary, for example, deterrence theory tells us we have to credibly threaten something that the potential

---

[5]Hudson & Den Boer argue that cultural preferences for male offspring produce a demographic bulge of "surplus males" with limited marriage prospects. This group generates high crime rates and internal instability, and their presence may also encourage states to adopt more aggressive foreign policies.

[6]As I have written elsewhere, this feature "is both the purpose and the paradox of social science: by gaining a better grasp of the causal forces that shape social phenomena, we may be able to manipulate them so as to render our own theories invalid" (Walt 1996, p. 351).

adversary values. Similarly, the arcane IR debate over the significance of absolute versus relative gains helped clarify the functions that international institutions must perform in order to work effectively. Instead of focusing on providing transparency and reducing transaction costs (as the original literature on international regimes emphasized), the debate on absolute versus relative gains highlighted the importance of side payments to eliminate gaps in gains and thus remove a potential obstacle to cooperation (Baldwin 1993).

Third, theoretical work (combined with careful empirical testing) can identify the conditions that determine when particular policy instruments are likely to work. As discussed above, these works focus on "issue-oriented puzzles" (Lepgold 1998), or what is sometimes termed "middle-range" theory, and such works tend to produce "contingent" or "conditional" generalizations about the effects of different instruments (George & Smoke 1974, George 1993). It is useful to know that a particular policy instrument tends to produce a particular outcome, but it is equally useful to know what other conditions must be present in order for the instrument to work as intended. For example, the theoretical literature on economic sanctions explains their limitations as a tool of coercion and identifies the conditions under which they are most likely to be employed and most likely to succeed (Martin 1992, Pape 1997, Haass 1998, Drezner 1999). Pape's related work on coercive airpower shows that airpower achieves coercive leverage not by inflicting civilian casualties or by damaging industrial production but by directly targeting the enemy's military strategy. The theory is directly relevant to the design of coercive air campaigns because it identifies why such campaigns should focus on certain targets and not others (Pape 1996, Byman et al. 2002).

Fourth, careful scrutiny of an alleged causal chain between actions and results can help policy makers anticipate how and why their policies might fail. If there is no well-verified theory explaining why a particular policy should work, then policy makers have reason to doubt that their goals will be achieved. Even worse, a well-established body of theory may warn that a recommended policy is very likely to fail. Theory can also alert policy makers to possible unintended or unanticipated consequences, and to the possibility that a promising policy initiative will fail because the necessary background conditions are not present.

For example, current efforts to promote democracy in the Middle East may be appealing from a normative perspective—i.e., because we believe that democracy leads to better human rights conditions—but we do not have well-verified theories explaining how to achieve the desired result. Indeed, what we do know about democracy suggests that promoting it in the Middle East will be difficult, expensive, and uncertain to succeed (Carothers 1999, Ottaway & Carothers 2004). This policy may still be the correct one, but scholars can warn that the United States and its allies are to a large extent "flying blind."

EVALUATION   Theory is crucial to the evaluation of policy decisions. Policy makers need to identify benchmarks that will tell them whether a policy is achieving the desired results. Without a least a sketchy theory that identifies the objectives to be sought, the definitions of success and failure, and the purported links between policy actions and desired outcomes, it will be difficult to know if a policy is succeeding or not (Baldwin 2000).

At the most general level, for example, a "grand strategy" based on liberal theory would emphasize the spread of democratic institutions within states or the expansion and strengthening of international institutions between states. Success would be measured by the number of states that adopted durable democratic forms, based on the belief that the spread of democracy would lead to other desirable ends (improved human rights performance, freer trade, decreased risk of international conflict, etc.) By contrast, a grand strategy based on realist theory would devote more attention to measuring the balance of power, and success might be measured by increases in one's own relative power, the successful courtship of powerful new allies, or the disruption of an opponent's internal legitimacy.

Similar principles apply in thinking about the role of external intervention in civil conflicts. If efforts to build democracy in a multiethnic society (such as Bosnia or Iraq) were based on the theory of consociational democracy advanced by Lijphardt (1969), then appropriate performance measures might include a success-ful census, high levels of voter turnout, the creation of institutions that formally allocated power across ethnic or other lines, etc. However, if the underlying theory of ethnic peace prescribed ethnic partition, then appropriate performance measures would focus on settlement patterns (Kaufmann 1996, Toft 2004). And theories of postwar peace that emphasize the enforcement role of third parties imply that we should try to measure the staying power of outside guarantors (Walter 2002).

EXPLAINING THE GAP: WHY THEORY AND POLICY RARELY MEET

If theory can do all these things for policy makers, and if it is impossible to formulate policy without a least a vague theory that links means and ends, then why doesn't theoretical IR scholarship play a larger role in shaping what policy makers do? Part of the explanation lies in the particular qualities of contemporary IR theory, and the remainder derives from the norms and incentives that govern the academic and policy worlds.

Is IR Theory Too General and Abstract?

A common explanation for the gap between theory and policy is that important works in the field operate at a very high level of generality and abstraction (George 1993, 2000; Jentleson 2000, p. 13). General theories such as structural realism, Marxism, and liberal institutionalism attempt to explain patterns of behavior that persist across space and time, and they use relatively few explanatory variables (e.g., power, polarity, regime type) to account for recurring tendencies. According to Stein (2000), "international relations theory deals with broad sweeping patterns;

while such knowledge may be useful, it does not address the day-to-day largely tactical needs of policymakers" (p. 56).

This criticism does not mean that general theories are of no value, however. General theories provide a common vocabulary with which to describe global issues (such terms as globalization, unipolarity, credibility, preemption, and free-riding) and create a broad picture of the context in which statecraft occurs. Moreover, some general theories do offer strategic prescriptions that policy makers can use to make choices. Abstract models can also help us understand many familiar features of international life, including the role of information asymmetries, commitment problems, and dilemmas of collective action. Thus, even abstract basic theory can help policy makers understand the context in which they are operating and suggest solutions to some of the challenges they face.

Nonetheless, many prominent works of general theory are simply not very relevant for informing policy decisions (and to be fair, they are not intended to be). For example, critics of Waltz's neo-realist theory of international politics have commonly complained that it is essentially a static theory that offers little policy guidance, a position reinforced by Waltz's own insistence that he did not assay a "theory of foreign policy" (Waltz 1979, 1997; George 1993; Kurth 1998). Although other scholars have found considerable policy relevance in Waltz's basic approach (e.g., Elman 1997), it is nonetheless true that *Theory of International Politics* offers only very broad guidelines for the conduct of statecraft. It provides a basic perspective on relations between states and sketches certain broad tendencies (such as the tendency for balances of power to form), but it does not offer specific or detailed policy advice.[7]

Similarly, Wendt's (1999) *Social Theory of International Politics* is an impressive intellectual achievement, and it has important implications for how scholars might study relations between states. But it does not offer even general prescriptions or insights concerning policy. Such works suggest that societies have greater latitude in constructing international reality than materialist conceptions imply, but they rarely offer concrete guidance for how policy makers might create a better world.

So Many Theories, So Little Time

A related problem arises from the limited explanatory power of the available theories. States' actions, and the effects of those actions, are the product of many different factors (relative power, domestic politics, norms and beliefs, individual psychology, etc.), and scholars have therefore produced a host of different theories employing many variables. Unfortunately, we do not have a clear method for combining these partial theories or deciding when to emphasize one over another. Policy makers can perhaps be forgiven for failing to embrace the theoretical scholarship in the field, when scholars of equal distinction offer radically different views.

---

[7]Waltz did offer specific policy recommendations in other works (e.g., Waltz 1967, 1981).

This problem is exacerbated by the nature of many policy problems. In general, social science theory offers the clearest advice when applied to situations with a well-defined structure: when the actors' preferences can be specified precisely, when the results of different choices are known, and when there are ample data with which to confirm and refine conjectures. For example, game theory and microeconomics are clearly useful—though not infallible—tools for analyzing public policy problems whenever these conditions are present (Stokey & Zeckhauser 1978, O'Neill 1994).[8]

Unfortunately, these conditions are often absent in the realm of foreign policy, where actors' preferences are frequently unknown, where each participant has many strategies available, and where the costs and benefits of different outcomes are uncertain. Nonlinear relationships and other systemic effects abound, and preferences and perceptions are constantly being revised (but not always according to Bayes' rule) (Jervis 1997). Scholars, as well as policy makers, often lack sufficient data for statistical analysis, and the data that are available are rife with endogeneity problems and other sources of bias (Przeworski 1995).

These problems may be less acute when scholars descend from the rarified heights of general theory to the level of specific policy instruments, where it is sometimes possible to devise convincing quasi-experiments that explain policy effects. Not surprisingly, therefore, the literature on the theory-practice gap tends to extol the virtues of middle-range theory. Such theory focuses on situations, strategies, or tools that are of direct concern to policy makers and can employ a more controlled, quasi-experimental assessment of the tools in question. Although these efforts often face a paucity of data (e.g., Pape's study of coercive airpower is based on a universe of only 33 cases, which is relatively large for an IR study), they can provide policy makers with at least a rough estimate of the effects of a given course of action.

These gains are bought with a price, however. Middle-range theory often sacrifices parsimony and generality, and it tends to produce contingent generalizations of the form, "if you do X, then Y will occur, assuming conditions a, b, c, and q all hold, and assuming you do X in just the right way." Indeed, prominent advocates of greater policy relevance see this feature as one of the main virtues of middle-range theory. It can sensitize decision makers to the contextual features that will affect the odds of success, and it emphasizes tailoring policy instruments to particular conditions (George 1993, Lepgold & Nincic 2001). The danger, however, is that the resulting generalizations become so heavily qualified that they offer little guidance beyond the original cases from which they were derived (Achen & Snidal 1989). This problem does not arise in all middle-range theory, but it is a legitimate criticism of much of it.

---

[8]Game theory and decision theory have been used to design public auctions of broadcasting licenses, for example, and decision theory has been used to develop more effective antisubmarine warfare strategies. Microeconomic models are commonly used to conduct cost-benefit analysis and to estimate the impact of rent control, health insurance, environmental regulations, insurance plans, and a host of other public policy initiatives.

Efforts to analyze the effects of different policy instruments are also bedeviled by complicated selection effects. No matter how large the universe of cases is, the observable connection between causes (i.e., policy actions) and effects is hard to measure with precision, because policy makers tend to choose the instruments that they deem most likely to work in a given situation. As a result, observed success or failure rates do not necessarily tell us which policies are "best" in any absolute sense. We can try to minimize these problems through appropriate research designs and control variables, but these biases can never be entirely eliminated. A particular policy instrument can fail quite often, for example, and still be the best available choice in certain circumstances.[9] These problems help explain why policy makers tend to view the results of even high-quality academic research with some skepticism.

Different Agendas

A recurring theme in the literature on theory and policy is the fact that scholars and policy makers have different agendas (Eckstein 1967, Rothstein 1972, Moore 1983). Social scientists (including IR theorists) seek to identify and explain recurring social behavior, but policy makers tend to be concerned with the particular problems they are facing today. Policy makers should be curious about general tendencies—if only to know whether their current goal is generally feasible—but knowing what happens most of the time may be less pertinent than knowing what will happen in the particular case at hand. Thus, a scholar might be delighted by a theory predicting that, on average, a 20% increase in X would produce a 25% decrease in Y, but a policy maker will ask whether the problem now occupying his inbox is an outlier or an exception to this general tendency. As a result, notes Stein (2000), "in-depth experiential knowledge dominates general theorizing and statistical generalizations for the formation of policy" (p. 60).

Furthermore, policy makers are often less interested in explaining a general tendency than in figuring out how to overcome it. A theorist might be content to explain why states are strongly inclined to form alliances against potential aggressors, or to demonstrate why economic sanctions rarely work, but a policy maker (e.g., Bismarck on the eve of the Franco-Prussian War) might be interested in how balancing tendencies might be impeded or how a particular sanctions campaign might be given sharper teeth.

A third contrast is the different attitudes that theorists and policy makers have toward time. Scholars want to make their work as accurate as possible, even if this takes longer, but policy makers rarely have the luxury of waiting. As Harvard professor and former State Department official Robert Bowie once put it, "the policymaker, unlike the academic analyst, can rarely wait until all the facts are in. He is very often under strong pressure to do something, to take some action" (quoted in May 1984). A policy maker who sought scholarly input, and was told that the

---

[9]For example, surgery to repair congenital heart defects in infants often fails, but alternative approaches (e.g., do nothing) are even less promising.

answer would require months of research and analysis, would be understandably reluctant to seek such advice again.

Finally, even a well-constructed and highly relevant theory may not help policy makers with a key aspect of their jobs: implementation. Theory can help diagnose the situation and identify the appropriate policy response, but the actual form of the response requires much more specific knowledge. First, the general decision (to seize foreign assets, declare war, reduce a tariff, issue a threat, etc.) must be fashioned into an action plan that identifies what government personnel will actually do (Zelikow 1994). And once the policy design is complete, the time-consuming work of overcoming bureaucratic resistance, legal constraints, fatigue, and partisan opposition still remains. Contemporary IR theory is largely silent on these problems, but they loom large in the life of any policy maker.

The Professionalization of the Discipline

The modest impact of contemporary IR theory on policy makers is no accident, because the creation of IR theory conforms to the norms and incentives of the academic profession rather than the needs of policy. IR scholarship is often impenetrable to outsiders, largely because it is not intended for their consumption; it is written primarily to appeal to other members of the profession. It is hard to imagine busy policy makers (or even their assistants) sitting down with a copy of *International Organization* or *World Politics* or devoting a weekend to perusing Waltz's *Theory of International Politics*, Wendt's *Social Theory of International Politics*, or Powell's (1999) *In the Shadow of Power*. Even when theorists do have useful ideas to offer, the people who need them will not know they exist and would be unlikely to understand them if they did.

This is not a new phenomenon; both scholars and policy makers have been complaining about it for decades (Rothstein 1972, Tanter & Ullman 1972, Wallace 1994). It is a direct consequence of the professionalization of the academic world and the specific incentives that scholars within the academy have established for themselves. The academic field of IR is a self-regulating enterprise, and success in the profession depends almost entirely on one's reputation among one's peers. There is therefore a large incentive to conform to the norms of the discipline and write primarily for other academics.

Over the past century, the prevailing norms of academic life have increasingly discouraged scholars from doing work that would be directly relevant to policy makers. Membership in the profession is increasingly dominated by university-based academics, and the discipline has tended to valorize highly specialized research (as opposed to teaching or public service) because that is what most members of the field want to do.[10] Younger scholars learn that the greatest

[10]In 1900, there were fewer than 100 full-time teachers of "political science" in the United States; by the late 1970s, the American Political Science Association (APSA) had over 17,000 members. In 1912, only 20% of APSA members were academics; by 1970, that

rewards go to those who can offer a new theory and that a careful policy analysis that offered valuable advice but broke no new theoretical ground would count for relatively little (Jentleson 2000). When success depends on the opinion of one's peers (rather than on the practical value of what one knows), and when those peers are all university-based scholars, there is a clear incentive to strive for novel arguments that will impress other scholars.

In the distant past, writers such as Machiavelli, Locke, Hobbes, Madison, Rousseau, and Marx were engaged in and inspired by the political events of their time. Similarly, the founders of modern political science in the United States consciously sought to use their knowledge to improve the world,[11] and the American Political Science Association was founded in part "to bring political science to a position of authority as regards practical politics." Not so very long ago, it was even common for prominent IR scholars to work in policy-making circles before returning to active (and prominent) academic careers.

This situation is quite different today. Although "in-and-outers" still exist, academics seem less interested in spending time in government even temporarily.[12] Prominent IR theorists rarely try to write books or articles that would be directly relevant to policy problems; policy relevance is simply not a criterion that the academy values. Indeed, there is a clear bias against it. Younger scholars are cautioned not to "waste" their time publishing op-eds, weblogs, or articles in general readership journals, and scholars who write for *Foreign Affairs*, *Foreign Policy*, or even peer-reviewed journals such as *Political Science Quarterly* or *International Security* run the risk of seeming insufficiently serious, even if they also publish in more rarified academic journals. According to Adam Przeworski, "the entire structure of incentives of academia in the United States works against taking big intellectual and political risks. Graduate students and assistant professors learn to package their intellectual ambitions into articles publishable by a few journals and to shy away from anything that might look like a political stance. ... We have the tools and we know some things, but we do not speak about politics to people outside academia" (quoted in Munck & Snyder 2004, p. 31). Given these biases—which are even more prevalent in other parts of political science—it is not surprising that academic research rarely has immediate policy impact.

---

percentage was over 75%. Since World War II, only one APSA President (Ralph Bunche) has been a nonacademic at the time of election (Ricci 1984, pp. 65–66).

[11]The extreme case, of course, is Woodrow Wilson, the president of APSA who became President of the United States—but the same is true of such men as Charles Merriam, Quincy Wright, and Hans Morgenthau.

[12]During the past five years, about one third (just under 37%) of International Affairs Fellowships at the Council on Foreign Relations were granted to academics on tenure track at universities, even though the original purpose of the fellowship was to provide academic scholars with an opportunity to get direct experience in government. Data from 2000–2001 to 2004–2005 are available at http://www.cfr.org/about/fellowship_iaf.php (accessed 9/2/2004).

Is a Division of Labor the Answer?

Most students of the theory-practice gap believe the chasm can be bridged by a division of labor between scholars and policy makers, because scholarly theorizing will eventually "trickle down" from the ivory tower into the mind-sets, in-boxes, and policy responses of policy makers.[13] In this knowledge-driven model of impact, general theory establishes the key concepts, methods, and principles that guide the analysis of specific empirical puzzles (such as alliance behavior, institutional effects, crisis behavior, and ethnic conflict), and these results are then used by policy analysts examining specific cases or problems (Weiss 1978). The latter works, in turn, provide the basis for advocacy and action in the public arena and in government (Lepgold 1998, Lepgold & Nincic 2001).

This is a comforting view insofar as it places academic theorists at the pinnacle of the status hierarchy, leaves scholars free to do whatever they want, and assumes that their efforts will eventually be of value. There is also much to be said for allowing scholars to pursue ideas that are not tied to specific policy problems, because wide-ranging inquiry sometimes yields unexpected payoffs. But there are also grounds for questioning whether the current division of labor is optimal.

First, the trickle-down model assumes that new ideas emerge from academic "ivory towers" (i.e., as abstract theory), gradually filter down into the work of applied analysts (and especially people working in public policy "think tanks"), and finally reach the perceptions and actions of policy makers (Haass 2002, Sundquist 1978). In practice, however, the process by which ideas come to shape policy is far more idiosyncratic and haphazard (Albaek 1995). An idea may become influential because of a single well-timed article, because its author happened to gain personal access to a key policy maker, or because its inventor(s) entered government service themselves. Alternatively, social science theory may exert its main impact not by addressing policy problems directly, but via the "long-term percolation of...concepts, theories and findings into the climate of informed opinion" (Weiss 1977).

Second, the gulf between scholars and policy makers may be getting wider as the links between theoretical research and policy problems grow weaker. As academic theory becomes increasingly specialized and impenetrable, even those scholars who are working on applied problems and other so-called research brokers (Sundquist 1978) may pay less and less attention to it. This is even more likely to be true in the world of policy-oriented think tanks, which are increasingly disconnected from the academic world. As is well known, in the 1950s and 1960s the RAND Corporation made seminal contributions to strategic studies and international security policy, as well as to social science more generally, and many RAND

---

[13]The classic expression of this view is Keynes' (1936) famous statement that "practical men, who believe themselves to be quite exempt from any intellectual influence, are usually the slaves of some defunct economist. Madmen in authority, who hear voices in the air, are distilling their frenzy from some academic scribbler of a few years back."

staff members had prominent careers in academe as well. Today, by contrast, a RAND analyst would be unlikely to be a viable candidate for an IR position at a major university, and RAND's research products do not exert much influence on the scholarly world. Similarly, in the 1970s and 1980s, the Foreign Policy Studies group at the Brookings Institution was not very different from an academic IR faculty, and publications by its staff were similar to works produced within prestigious departments.[14] Moreover, the director of the group, John Steinbruner, held a Ph.D. from MIT, had previously taught at Harvard, and was the author of several important theoretical works (Steinbruner 1974, 1976). Today, by contrast, the Foreign Policy Studies staff a Brookings writes relatively few refereed journal articles or scholarly books and concentrates primarily on producing op-eds and contemporary policy analyses (e.g., Daalder & Lindsay 2003, Gordon & Shapiro 2004). Consistent with this focus, the current director of Foreign Policy Studies is a lawyer and former government official with little or no scholarly training. My point is not to disparage the work done at Brookings (or at similar institutions); it is simply to note that the gulf between academic scholars and policy-oriented analysts is widening. One suspects that scholars in think tanks pay less attention to their academic counterparts than they did previously, and vice versa. This tendency is exacerbated by the emergence of "advocacy think tanks" (e.g., the Heritage Foundation, the American Enterprise Institute, the Cato Institute) in which analysis is driven by explicit ideological preferences (Wallace 1994, Weaver & Stares 2001, Abelson 2002). As connections between the ivory tower and more policy-oriented scholars become tenuous, the trickle-down model of scholarly influence seems increasingly questionable.

WHAT IS TO BE DONE?

The literature on the gap between theory and practice addresses most of its recommendations toward reforming the academic world, for two obvious reasons. First, scholars are more likely to read these works. Second, policy makers are unlikely to be swayed by advice to pay greater attention to academic theory. If scholars produce useful knowledge, policy makers will want to know about it. If academic writings are not useful, however, no amount of exhortation will persuade policy makers to read them.

What is needed, therefore, is a conscious effort to alter the prevailing norms of the academic IR discipline. Today's professional incentive structure discourages many scholars—especially younger scholars—from striving for policy relevance, but the norms that establish that structure are not divinely ordained; they are collectively determined by the members of the discipline itself. The scholarly community gets to decide what it values, and there is no reason why policy relevance cannot be

---

[14]I am thinking of the work of Richard Betts, John Steinbruner, Joshua Epstein, Bruce Blair, Paul B. Stares, Raymond Garthoff, Yahya Sadowski, William Quandt, and others.

elevated in our collective estimation, along with the traditional criteria of creativity, rigor, and empirical validity.

What would this mean in practice? First, academic departments could give greater weight to real-world relevance and impact in hiring and promotion decisions. When evaluating job candidates, or when considering someone for tenure, reviewers and evaluation committees could consider what contribution a scholar's work has made to the solving of real-world problems. Policy relevance would not become the only—or even the most important—criterion, of course, and scholars would still be expected to meet high scholarly standards. But giving real-world relevance greater weight would make it more likely that theory would be directed at real-world problems and presented in a more accessible fashion. "Should it really be the case," Jentleson (2000) correctly asks, "that a book with a major university press and an article or two in [a refereed journal]. . .can almost seal the deal on tenure, but books with even major commercial houses count so much less and articles in journals such as *Foreign Affairs* often count little if at all?. . . The argument is not about padding publication counts with op-eds and other such commentaries, but it is to broaden evaluative criteria to better reflect the type and range of writing of intellectual import" (p. 179). To put it bluntly: Should our discipline really be proud that relatively few people care about what we have to say?

Second, academic departments could facilitate interest in the real world of politics by giving junior faculty greater incentives for participating in it. At present, academic departments rarely encourage younger faculty to take time off to serve in government, and very few departments will stop the tenure clock for someone doing public service. A scholar who is interested in acquiring real-world experience (or in helping to shape policy directly) generally has to wait until after tenure has been granted. By allowing younger faculty to "stop the clock," however, academic departments would have more members who understood real-world issues and knew how to translate theoretical ideas into policy-relevant analyses. One suspects that such individuals would become better teachers as well, because students, unlike many scholars, do care about the real world and have little tolerance for irrelevant abstraction.

Third, academic journals could place greater weight on relevance in evaluating submissions,[15] and departments could accord greater status to journals that did this. Similarly, prize committees could consider policy relevance a criterion for awarding noteworthy books and articles, instead of focusing solely on contributions to narrow disciplinary issues. Finally, creating more outlets for work that translated "higher-end" theory into accessible form (as the *Journal of Economic Perspectives* does in economics) would strengthen the "transmission belt" from theory to policy.

The goal of such reforms is not to make the academic world a homogeneous mass of policy analysts or even worse, a community of co-opted scholars competing to win the attention of government officials. Rather, the purpose is to encourage a

---

[15]Some peer-reviewed journals do this (e.g., *International Security* and *Security Studies*), but it is hardly a widespread practice.

more heterogeneous community at all levels of academe: some scholars who do highly abstract work and others who do explicit policy analysis, but where both groups are judged according to their broad contribution to our understanding of critical real-world problems.

Is this vision a pipe dream? Perhaps not. Indeed, there are encouraging signs throughout the social sciences. In economics, for example, the awarding of the Nobel Prize to Douglass North, Amartya Sen, James Heckman, Amos Tversky, and Daniel Kahneman suggests a greater desire to valorize ideas and techniques that proved to be of value to public policy issues. In addition, a group of prominent economists has recently announced the creation of a new online journal (*The Economists' Voice*) to provide a more visible outlet for policy analysis informed by rigorous economic reasoning. Within political science, the perestroika movement arose partly in reaction to the formalism and irrelevance of recent scholarship, and the movement deserves partial credit for the creation of the journal *Perspectives on Politics* and the increased intellectual diversity and policy relevance of the *American Political Science Review*. These developments remind us that the criteria of merit used in academic fields are always subject to revision. In other words, IR scholars need not accept things as they are; we collectively determine how our field develops. IR theorists can provide valuable ideas for policy makers without sacrificing our integrity and objectivity, but only if we decide we want to.

The *Annual Review of Political Science* is online at
http://polisci.annualreviews.org

LITERATURE CITED

Abelson DE. 2002. *Do Think Tanks Matter? Assessing the Impact of Public Policy Institutes.* Montreal: McGill-Queen's Univ. Press. 251 pp.

Achen C, Snidal D. 1989. Rational deterrence theory and comparative case studies. *World Polit.* 41(2):143–69

Albaek E. 1995. Between knowledge and power: utilization of social science in public policy making. *Policy Sci.* 28:79–100

Allison GT, Halperin MH. 1972. Bureaucratic politics: a paradigm and some policy implications. *World Polit.* 24:40–79

Andreski S. 1980. On the peace disposition of military dictatorships. *J. Strat. Stud.* 3:3–10

Baldwin DA, ed. 1993. *Neorealism and Neoliberalism: The Contemporary Debate.* New York: Columbia Univ. Press. 377 pp.

Baldwin DA. 2000. Success or failure in foreign policy. *Annu. Rev. Polit. Sci.* 3:167–82

Baylis J, Smith S. 2001. *The Globalization of World Politics: An Introduction to International Relations.* New York: Oxford Univ. Press. 690 pp.

Brooks S, Wohlforth WC. 2000–2001. Power, globalization and the end of the Cold War: reevaluating a landmark case for ideas. *Int. Sec.* 25(3):5–53

Bueno de Mesquita B, Lalman D. 1992. *War and Reason.* New Haven, CT: Yale Univ. Press. 322 pp.

Byman D. 2002. *Keeping the Peace: Lasting Solutions to Ethnic Conflict.* Baltimore, MD: Johns Hopkins Univ. Press. 280 pp.

Byman D, Pollock K. 2001. Let us now praise great men: bringing the statesman back in. *Int. Sec.* 25:107–46

Byman D, Waxman MC, Wolf C. 2002. *The Dynamics of Coercion: American Foreign Policy and the Limits of Military Might.*

Cambridge, UK: Cambridge Univ. Press. 298 pp.

Carlsnaes W, Risse T, Simmons B, eds. 2002. *Handbook of International Relations*. Beverly Hills, CA: Sage. 572 pp.

Copeland D. 2000. *The Origins of Major War*. Ithaca, NY: Cornell Univ. Press. 322 pp.

Carothers T. 1999. *Aiding Democracy Abroad: The Learning Curve*. Washington, DC: Carnegie Endow. Int. Peace. 411 pp.

Daalder I, Lindsay J. 2003. *American Unbound: The Bush Revolution in Foreign Policy*. Washington, DC: Brookings Inst. 246 pp.

De Rivera J. 1968. *The Psychological Dimension in Foreign Policy*. Columbus, OH: CE Merrill. 441 pp.

Deutsch K. 1969. *Political Community in the North Atlantic Area: International Organization in the Light of Historical Experience*. New York: Greenwood. 228 pp.

Doran C. 1999. Why forecasts fail: the limits and potential of forecasting in international relations and economics. *Int. Stud. Rev.* 1:11–41

Dougherty J, Pfaltzgraff RL. 1997. *Contending Theories of International Relations: A Comprehensive Survey*. New York: Longman. 608 pp.

Doyle MW. 1986. Liberalism and world politics. *Am. Polit. Sci. Rev.* 80(4):1151–69

Drezner D. 1999. *The Sanctions Paradox: Economic Statecraft and International Relations*. Cambridge, UK: Cambridge Univ. Press. 362 pp.

Eckstein H. 1967. Political science and public policy. In *Contemporary Political Science: Toward Empirical Theory*, ed. ID Poole, pp. 121–65. New York: McGraw-Hill

Elman C. 1997. Horses for courses: Why not neorealist theories of foreign policy? *Sec. Stud.* 6:7–53

Evangelista M. 2002. *Unarmed Forces: The Transnational Movement to End the Cold War*. Ithaca, NY: Cornell Univ. Press. 416 pp.

Fearon J. 1994. Domestic audience costs and the escalation of international disputes. *Am. Polit. Sci. Rev.* 88:577–92

Fearon J, Laitin D. 1996. Explaining interethnic cooperation. *Am. Polit. Sci. Rev.* 90(4):713–35

Feaver P. 1999. The theory-policy debate in political science and nuclear proliferation. *Natl. Sec. Stud. Q.* 5(3):70–82

Finnemore M. 1996. *National Interests in International Society*. Ithaca, NY: Cornell Univ. Press. 154 pp.

Friedberg A. 1993–1994. Ripe for rivalry: prospects for peace in a multipolar Asia. *Int. Sec.* 18(3):5–33

Fukuyama F. 1992. *The End of History and the Last Man*. New York: Free. 418 pp.

George AL. 1993. *Bridging the Gap: Theory and Practice in Foreign Policy*. Washington, DC: U.S. Inst. Peace Press. 170 pp.

George AL. 2000. Foreword. See Nincic & Lepgold 2000, pp. ix–xvii

George AL, Hall D, Simons W. 1971. *The Limits of Coercive Diplomacy*. Boston: Little, Brown. 268 pp.

George AL, Smoke R. 1974. *Deterrence in American Foreign Policy: Theory and Practice*. New York: Columbia Univ. Press. 666 pp.

Gilpin R. 1981. *War and Change in World Politics*. Cambridge, UK: Cambridge Univ. Press. 272 pp.

Glaser BL, Strauss AL. 1967. *The Discovery of Grounded Theory*. Chicago: Aldine. 271 pp.

Glaser CL. 1990. *Analyzing Strategic Nuclear Policy*. Princeton, NJ: Princeton Univ. Press. 378 pp.

Goldgeier J. 1999. *Not Whether But When: The U.S. Decision to Enlarge NATO*. Washington, DC: Brookings Inst. 218 pp.

Goldgeier J, Tetlock P. 2001. Psychology and international relations theory. *Annu. Rev. Polit. Sci.* 4:67–92

Goldstein A. 1997–1998. Great expectations: intepreting China's arrival. *Int. Sec.* 22(3):36–73

Goldstein J. 2003. *War and Gender: How Gender Affects the War System and Vice Versa*. Cambridge, UK: Cambridge Univ. Press. 540 pp.

Goldstein J, Keohane RO, eds. 1993. *Ideas and*

Foreign Policy: Beliefs, Institutions, and Political Change. Ithaca, NY: Cornell Univ. Press. 308 pp.

Gordon P, Shapiro J. 2004. *Allies at War: America, Europe, and the Crisis Over Iraq*. New York: McGraw-Hill. 268 pp.

Haass RN. 1998. *Economic Sanctions and American Diplomacy*. New York: Counc. For. Relat. 222 pp.

Haass RN. 2002. Think tanks and U.S. foreign policy: a policy-maker's perspective. *U.S. For. Policy Agenda* 7:5–8

Halberstam D. 2001. *War in a Time of Peace: Bush, Clinton, and the Generals*. New York: Scribner. 543 pp.

Hall P, ed. 1989. *The Political Power of Economic Ideas: Keynesianism Across Nations*. Princeton, NJ: Princeton Univ. Press. 416 pp.

Halperin M. 1972. *Bureaucratic Politics and Foreign Policy*. Washington: Brookings Inst. 340 pp.

Hill C, Beshoff P, eds. 1994. *The Two Worlds of International Relations: Academics, Practitioners and the Trade in Ideas*. London: Routledge. 233 pp.

Hoffman S, Keohane RO, Nye J, eds. 1993. *After the Cold War: International Institutions and State Strategies in Europe, 1989–1991*. Cambridge, MA: Harvard Univ. Press. 481 pp.

Hudson V, Den Boer AD. 2002. A surplus of men, a deficit of peace: security and sex ratios in Asia's largest states. *Int. Sec.* 26(4):5–38

Hudson V, Den Boer AD. 2004. *Bare Branches: The Security Implications of Asia's Surplus Male Population*. Cambridge, MA: MIT Press. 275 pp.

Huntington SP. 1997. *The Clash of Civilizations and the Remaking of World Order*. New York: Touchstone. 367 pp.

Irwin DA. 1996. *Against the Tide: An Intellectual History of Free Trade*. Princeton, NJ: Princeton Univ. Press. 265 pp.

Jentleson BW. 2000. In pursuit of praxis: applying international relations theory to foreign policymaking. See Nincic & Lepgold 2000, pp. 129–49

Jentleson BW. 2002. The need for praxis: bringing policy relevance back in. *Int. Sec.* 26(4):169–83

Jervis R. 1976. *Perception and Misperception in International Politics*. Princeton, NJ: Princeton Univ. Press. 445 pp.

Jervis R. 1984. *The Illogic of U.S. Nuclear Strategy*. Ithaca, NY: Cornell Univ. Press. 203 pp.

Jervis R. 1990. *The Meaning of the Nuclear Revolution: Statecraft and the Prospect of Armageddon*. Ithaca, NY: Cornell Univ. Press. 266 pp.

Jervis R. 1997. *System Effects: Complexity in Political and Social Life*. Princeton, NJ: Princeton Univ. Press. 309 pp.

Jervis R. 2004. Security studies: ideas, policy, and politics. In *The Evolution of Political Knowledge: Democracy, Autonomy and Conflict in Comparative and International Politics*, ed. E Mansfield, R Sisson, pp. 100–26. Columbus: Ohio State Univ. Press

Kaplan R. 1993. *Balkan Ghosts: A Journey Through History*. New York: St. Martin's. 307 pp.

Kaplan R. 2001. *The Coming Anarchy: Shattering the Dreams of the Post Cold War*. New York: Vintage. 224 pp.

Kaufmann C. 1996. Possible and impossible solutions to ethnic civil war. *Int. Sec.* 20(4):136–75

Kennedy PM. 1983. Strategic aspects of the Anglo-German naval race. In *Strategy and Diplomacy 1870–1945: Eight Studies*, pp. 129–60. Boston: Allen & Unwin. 254 pp.

Keohane RO. 1984. *After Hegemony: Cooperation and Discord in the World Political Economy*. Princeton, NJ: Princeton Univ. Press. 290 pp.

Keohane RO, Martin LL. 2003. Institutional theory as a research program. In *Progress in International Relations Theory: Appraising the Field*, ed. C Elman, MF Elman, pp. 71–108. Cambridge, MA: MIT Press. 503 pp.

Keynes JM. 1936. *The General Theory of Employment, Interest, and Money*. London: Macmillan. 403 pp.

Kruzel J. 1994. More a chasm than a gap, but

do scholars want to bridge it? *Mershon Int. Stud. Rev.* 38:179–81

Kuran T. 1991. Now out of never: the element of surprise in the revolutions of 1989. *World Polit.* 44:7–48

Kurth J. 1998. Inside the cave: the banality of IR studies. *Natl. Interest* 53:29–40

Lake D, Rothchild D, eds. 1998. *The International Spread of Ethnic Conflict: Fear, Diffusion and Escalation.* Princeton, NJ: Princeton Univ. Press. 424 pp.

Lake D, Rothchild D. 1996. Containing fear: the origins and management of ethnic conflict. *Int. Sec.* 21(2):41–75

Lawrence R. 2002. International trade policy in the 1990s. In *American Economic Policy in the 1990s*, ed. JA Frankel, P Orszag, pp. 277–332. Cambridge: MIT Press

Layne C. 1993. The unipolar illusion: why new great powers will rise. *Int. Sec.* 17(4):5–51

Lebow RN, Risse-Kappen TW, eds. 1995. *International Relations Theory and the End of the Cold War.* New York: Columbia Univ. Press. 292 pp.

Lepgold J. 1998. Is anyone listening? International relations theory and policy relevance. *Polit. Sci. Q.* 113(3):43-62

Lepgold J. 2000. Scholars and statesmen: a framework for a productive dialogue. See Nincic & Lepgold 2000, pp. 75–106

Lepgold J, Nincic M. 2001. *Beyond the Ivory Tower: IR Theory and the Issue of Policy Relevance.* New York: Columbia Univ. Press. 228 pp.

Levy J. 1989. Domestic politics and war. In *The Origin and Prevention of Major Wars*, ed. R Rotberg, T Rabb, pp. 79–100. Cambridge, UK: Cambridge Univ. Press. 352 pp.

Lijphart A. 1969. Consociational democracy. *World Polit.* 21(2):207–25

Lohmann S. 1994. The dynamics of informational cascades: the Monday demonstrations in Leipzig, East Germany, 1989/1991. *World Polit.* 47(1):42–101

Lupia A. 2000. Evaluating political science research: information for buyers and sellers. *PS: Polit. Sci. Politics* 33(1):7–14

Lynn LE, ed. 1978. *Knowledge and Policy: The Uncertain Connection.* Washington, DC: Natl. Acad. Sci. 183 pp.

Mann J. 2004. *The Rise of the Vulcans: The History of Bush's War Cabinet.* New York: Viking Books. 400 pp.

Martin LL. 1992. *Coercive Cooperation: Explaining Multilateral Economic Sanctions.* Princeton, NJ: Princeton Univ. Press. 299 pp.

May ER. 1975. *"Lessons" of the Past: The Use and Misuse of History in American Foreign Policy.* New York: Oxford Univ. Press. 220 pp.

May ER. 1984. *Knowing One's Enemies: Intelligence Assessment Before the Two World Wars.* Princeton, NJ: Princeton Univ. Press. 561 pp.

May E, Neustadt RE. 1984. *Thinking in Time: The Uses of History for Decision-Makers.* New York: Free. 329 pp.

Mearsheimer JJ. 1989. Assessing the conventional balance: the 3:1 rule and the future of security studies. *Int. Sec.* 13(4):54–89

Mearsheimer JJ. 2001. *The Tragedy of Great Power Politics.* New York: WW Norton. 555 pp.

Mearsheimer JJ, Walt SM. 2003. An unnecessary war. *For. Policy* 134:51–61

Mercer J. 1996. *Reputation and International Politics.* Ithaca, NY: Cornell Univ. Press. 264 pp.

Moore MH. 1983. Social science and policy analysis: some fundamental differences. In *Ethics, the Social Sciences, and Policy Analysis*, ed. D Callahan, B Jennings, pp. 272–91. Kluwer Acad. 381 pp.

Morgenthau HJ. 1958. *Dilemmas of Politics.* Chicago: Univ. Chicago Press. 390 pp.

Morgenthau HJ. 1985. *Politics Among Nations: The Struggle for Power and Peace.* New York: Knopf. 688 pp.

Moul WB. 1989. Measuring the "balances of power": a look at some numbers. *Rev. Int. Stud.* 15:107–15

Munck G, Snyder R. 2004. What has comparative politics accomplished? *APSA-CP Newsl.* 15(2):26–31

Newsom D. 1995–1996. Foreign policy and academia. *For. Policy* 101:52–68

Nitze PH. 1993. *Tension Between Opposites: Reflections on the Practice and Theory of Politics.* New York: Scribner. 212 pp.

Nincic M, Lepgold J, eds. 2000. *Being Useful: Policy Relevance and International Relations Theory.* Ann Arbor: Univ. Mich. Press. 392 pp.

O'Neill B. 1994. Game theory models of war and peace. In *Handbook of Game Theory with Economic Applications,* ed. R Aumann, S Hart, 2:995–1053. Amsterdam: Elsevier

Ottaway M, Carothers T. 2004. *The Greater Middle East Initiative: Off to a False Start.* Washington, DC: Carnegie Endow. Int. Peace. Policy Brief 29:1–8

Pape R. 1996. *Bombing to Win: Airpower and Coercion in War.* Ithaca, NY: Cornell Univ. Press. 366 pp.

Pape R. 1997. Why economic sanctions do not work. *Int. Sec.* 22(2):90–136

Pollock K. 2002. *The Threatening Storm: The Case for Invading Iraq.* New York: Random House. 494 pp.

Posen B. 1993. The security dilemma and ethnic conflict. *Survival* 35(1):27–47

Powell R. 1999. *In the Shadow of Power: States and Strategies in International Politics.* Princeton, NJ: Princeton Univ. Press. 310 pp.

Preeg E. 1998. *From Here to Free Trade: Essays in Post-Uruguay Round Trade Strategy.* Chicago: Univ. Chicago Press

Przeworski A. 1995. Comment, in "The Role of Theory in Comparative Politics: A Symposium." *World Polit.* 48:1–49

Rapaport A. 1972. Explanatory power and explanatory appeal of theories. *Synthese* 10:341–42

Reiter D. 2001–2002. Why NATO enlargement does not spread democracy. *Int. Sec.* 26:230–35

Ricci D. 1984. *The Tragedy of Political Science: Politics, Scholarship, and Democracy.* New Haven, CT: Yale Univ. Press. 225 pp.

Rosecrance R. 1986. *The Rise of the Trading State: Commerce and Conquest in the Modern World.* New York: Basic Books. 268 pp.

Rothstein RL. 1972. *Planning, Prediction and Policymaking in Foreign Affairs: Theory and Practice.* Boston: Little, Brown. 215 pp.

Rubinstein A. 1990. *Moscow's Third World Strategy.* Princeton, NJ: Princeton Univ. Press. 329 pp.

Ruggie JG. 1983. International regimes, transactions, and change. In *International Regimes,* ed. S Krasner, pp. 195–232. Ithaca, NY: Cornell Univ. Press. 372 pp.

Ruggie JG. 1998. What makes the world hang together? Neo-Utilitarianism and the social constructivist challenge. *Int. Organ.* 52:887–917

Russett B. 1995. *Grasping the Democratic Peace: Principles for a Post-Cold War World.* Princeton, NJ: Princeton Univ. Press. 173 pp.

Sambanis N. 2000. Partition as a solution to ethnic war: an empirical critique of the theoretical literature. *World Polit.* 52(4):437–83

Schelling T. 1960. The reciprocal fear of surprise attack. In *The Strategy of Conflict,* ed. T Schelling, pp. 207–29. Cambridge, MA: Harvard Univ. Press. 309 pp.

Sifry M, Cerf C, eds. 2003. *The Iraq War Reader: History, Documents, Opinions.* New York: Touchstone. 715 pp.

Siverson R. 2001. A glass half-full? No, but perhaps a glass filling: the contributions of international politics research to policy. *PS: Polit. Sci. Politics* 33(1):59–63

Slater J. 1987. Dominos in Central America: Will they fall? Does it matter? *Int. Sec.* 12(2):105–34

Slater J. 1993–1994. The domino theory in international politics: the case of Vietnam. *Sec. Stud.* 3(2):186–24

Snyder JL. 1993. *Myths of Empire: Domestic Politics and International Ambition.* Ithaca, NY: Cornell Univ. Press. 344 pp.

Stedman S. 1997. Spoiler problems in peace processes. *Int. Sec.* 22(2):5–53

Stein A. 2000. Counselors, kings, and international relations: from revelation to reason, and still no policy-relevant theory. See Nincic & Lepgold 2000, pp. 50–74

Steinbruner J. 1974. *The Cybernetic Theory of Decision: New Dimensions of Political*

Analysis. Princeton, NJ: Princeton Univ. Press. 366 pp.

Steinbruner J. 1976. Beyond rational deterrence: the struggle for new conceptions. *World Polit.* 28(2):223–45

Stokey E, Zeckhauser R. 1978. *A Primer for Policy Analysis*. New York: WW Norton. 356 pp.

Sundquist J. 1978. Research brokerage: the weak link. See Lynn 1978, pp. 126–44

Tanter R, Ullman R, eds. 1972. *Theory and Policy in International Relations*. Princeton, NJ: Princeton Univ. Press. 250 pp.

Tickner J. 2001. *Gendering World Politics: Issues and Approaches in the Post-Cold War Era*. New York: Columbia Univ. Press. 200 pp.

Toft M. 2004. *The Geography of Ethnic Conflict: Identity, Interests, and the Indivisibility of Territory*. Princeton, NJ: Princeton Univ. Press. 226 pp.

Trachtenberg M. 1992. *History and Strategy*. Princeton, NJ: Princeton Univ. Press. 292 pp.

Van Evera S. 1984. The cult of the offensive and the origins of the First World War. *Int. Sec.* 9(1):58–107

Van Evera S. 1997. *Guide to Methods for Students of Political Science*. Ithaca, NY: Cornell Univ. Press. 136 pp.

Viotti P, Kauppi M. 1993. *International Relations Theory: Realism, Pluralism, Globalism*. New York: Macmillan. 613 pp.

Waever O. 1998. The sociology of a not-so international discipline: American and European developments in international relations. *Int. Organ.* 52:687–727

Wallace W. 1994. Between two worlds: think tanks and foreign policy. See Hill & Beshoff 1994, pp. 139–63

Walt SM. 1996. *Revolution and War*. Ithaca, NY: Cornell Univ. Press. 365 pp.

Walt SM. 1997a. International relations: one world, many theories. *For. Policy* 110:29–45

Walt SM. 1997b. Building up new bogeymen. *For. Policy* 106:176–90

Walt SM. 1997c. The ties that fray: why Europe and America are drifting apart. *Natl. Interest* 54:3–11

Walter B. 2002. *Committing to Peace: The Successful Settlement of Civil Wars*. Princeton, NJ: Princeton Univ. Press. 216 pp.

Waltz K. 1967. The politics of peace. *Int. Stud. Q.* 11(3):199–211

Waltz K. 1981. The spread of nuclear weapons: more may be better. Adelphi Pap. 171. London: Int. Inst. Strat. Stud. 32 pp.

Waltz KN. 1979. *Theory of International Politics*. New York: Random House. 251 pp.

Waltz KN. 1997. International politics is not foreign policy. *Sec. Stud.* 6:54–57

Weart SR. 2000. *Never at War: Why Democracies Will Not Fight One Another*. New Haven, CT: Yale Univ. Press. 432 pp.

Weaver RK, Stares PB, eds. 2001. *Guidance for Governance: Comparing Alternative Sources of Public Policy Advice*. Washington, DC: Brookings Inst. 240 pp.

Weiss C. 1977. Research for policy's sake: the enlightenment function of social research. *Policy Anal.* 3:531–45

Weiss C. 1978. Improving the linkage between social research and public policy. See Lynn 1978, pp. 23–81

Wendt A. 1999. *Social Theory of International Politics*. New York: Cambridge Univ. Press. 429 pp.

Wilson E. 2000. How social science can help policymakers: the relevance of theory. See Nincic & Lepgold 2000, pp. 109–28

Wohlforth WC. 1993. *The Elusive Balance: Power and Perceptions During the Cold War*. Ithaca, NY: Cornell Univ. Press. 317 pp.

Wohlforth WC. 1994–1995. Realism and the end of the Cold War. *Int. Sec.* 19(3):91–129

Wohlforth WC. 1999. The stability of a unipolar world. *Int. Sec.* 24(1):5–41

Wohlstetter A. 1957. The delicate balance of terror. *For. Aff.* 37(2):211–34

Zelikow P. 1994. Foreign policy engineering: from theory to practice and back again. *Int. Sec.* 18(4):143–71

Annu. Rev. Polit. Sci. 2005. 8:49–71
doi: 10.1146/annurev.polisci.8.032904.154633
First published online as a Review in Advance on Mar. 4, 2005

DOES DELIBERATIVE DEMOCRACY WORK?

David M. Ryfe

*School of Journalism, Middle Tennessee State University, Murfreesboro,
Tennessee 37132; email: dryfe@mtsu.edu*

Key Words   deliberation, deliberative democratic practice, political psychology,
civic engagement

■ **Abstract**   The growing literature on deliberative democratic practice finds that
deliberation is a difficult and relatively rare form of communication. Each moment of
a deliberative encounter raises significant obstacles in the path to stimulating greater
intentional reflection on public issues. I explore these obstacles in the context of other
empirical work in political and social psychology, small group communication, and
public opinion. Taken together, these literatures explain why deliberation is difficult
to achieve and sustain over time. They also suggest several rules that might assist
practitioners in making deliberative democracy work better. Many of the obstacles to
deliberative democracy raise questions about key theoretical constructs closely associated with deliberative democratic theory, including equality, legitimacy, autonomy,
and reason. I conclude by suggesting that deliberative practitioners, empirical scholars,
and theorists might gain from greater interaction.

INTRODUCTION

For most of its career, deliberative democracy has been something of a small,
rarefied subfield of political theory. This "phase" of deliberative democracy
(Chambers 2003) has not passed (see also Freeman 2000), but in recent years it has
been supplemented by a more pragmatic impulse. Empirically minded students of
deliberative democracy have turned to issues of implementation, institutional design, and evaluation (Abelson et al. 2002, 2003; Ackerman & Fishkin 2004; Bierle
1999; Denver et al. 1995; Dunkerly & Glasner 1998; Fishkin 1991, 1995; Gastil
2000; Gastil & Dillard 1999; Graham & Phillips 1998; Hibbing & Theiss-Morse
2000; Kim et al. 1999; Kraft & Clary 1991; Landeman 2002; Luskin & Fishkin
1998; Mackie 2002; Mansbridge 1980; Mullen 2000; Neblo 2000; Renn et al.
1995; Ryfe 2002; Simrell 1998; Smith & Wales 2000; Sulkin & Simon 2001).

These efforts do not supplant the need for normative theory. Indeed, to some
extent the empirical literature is driven by the passion and vision of deliberative theorists. Nonetheless, one cannot ignore the fact that the empirical findings
have been mixed. Under certain conditions, it appears that deliberation can produce
more sophisticated, tolerant, and participative citizens (Fung 2001, Fung & Wright
2001, Gastil & Dillard 1999, Gastil et al. 2002, Luskin & Fishkin 1998, Sulkin

& Simon 2001, Walsh 2003), but these outcomes are not automatic and in fact may be rare (Button & Mattson 1999, Hendriks 2002, Hibbing & Theiss-Morse 2000, Holt 1999, Kuklinski et al. 1993, Mendelberg & Oleske 2000). Combined with the fact that institutionalizing deliberation can be quite costly (Rossi 1997), this finding suggests a need for more reflection. Assuming for the moment that deliberation is a sensible and normatively preferable way of making decisions, why is it so difficult in practice? What does the empirical literature contribute to contemporary debates within deliberative democratic theory? What does the literature on deliberative practice tell us about the conditions most likely to promote deliberation? At bottom, of course, lies the fundamental question: As a practical matter, can deliberative democracy work?

The literature on deliberative practice is still in its infancy, and its answers to these questions are by no means definitive. However, even in its current state, it is suggestive. By linking its findings with other empirical and theoretical work, I tease out the broad outlines of the central issues. I divide my discussion into three moments of the deliberative process: the organization of a deliberative encounter; the practice of deliberation within an encounter, and finally, the product of deliberative talk. Each of these moments raises practical challenges for organizers of deliberative initiatives. Who should participate, and how should they be contacted? Once they meet face to face, how do and should participants talk to one another? That is, what does deliberative talk look like? And what should be done with the product of deliberative encounters once groups have met? Should public officials use the product as an expression of public opinion? Should they be bound by the conclusions reached by deliberative groups? The way in which these moments work themselves out tells us something about the possibilities for deliberative democracy in actual societies. It also illuminates key conceptual dilemmas in normative theory. As I weave together the empirical scholarship and normative theory, I assess where we are in answering the fundamental question of whether or not deliberative democracy can work.

WHO PARTICIPATES?

As Pratchett (1999) observes, "there is nothing particularly new about public participation as a supplement to representative democracy" (p. 616). Officials routinely solicit public comment, hold public hearings, and issue public reports on their activities. But the promise of deliberative democracy hinges on more than public consultation. Deliberative democrats believe that ordinary people ought not only to be consulted but also to have a hand in actual decision making. However that role is captured (a subject I take up later), the idea is that public decisions ought to be influenced in some way by the citizenry that will be affected by them. This assumption, of course, makes it vital that such citizens participate actively in the process of decision making.

With this goal in mind, it would seem to be a simple matter of opening the policy-making process to greater citizen input. In practice, however, it is not simple at all. Participation has long been a minor consideration in most liberal democracies (Barber 1984, Bobbio 1987, Macpherson 1977). Moreover, at least in the United States, the kinds of civic associations that once connected ordinary people to the political process have withered considerably (Putnam 2000, Skocpol & Fiorina 1999). This disconnect between citizens and public officials has led to great cynicism and distrust on both sides (Hibbing & Theiss-Morse 1995, Nye et al. 1997). Formidable psychological and structural barriers also impede public participation in policy making. People are, as cognitive psychologists like to call them, "cognitive misers." For everyday reasoning, people prefer to use cognitive heuristics (also called information shortcuts, discussed below) to make reasoning relatively efficient but unreflective (Kahneman & Tversky 1983, Kahneman et al. 1982, Lupia et al. 2001, Mondak 1994, Mutz et al. 1996, Nisbet & Ross 1980, Sniderman et al. 1991, Taber et al. 2001). Especially in the face of difficult, complex issues, people seek to "pass the buck" in an effort to avoid responsibility for decision making (Festinger 1964, Fiske & Taylor 1991, Janis & Mann 1977, Tetlock 2001). Further, as we have known for 50 years, choices about public goods tend to create "collective action" problems (Downs 1957). Their sheer extensiveness and complexity make them difficult issues amenable to no easy answers. Their extensiveness means that any rational individual will seek to forego the burden of participation because she is not likely to directly affect the result, yet will share in its benefits even if she refuses to participate. Organizing deliberative initiatives in the face of these historical, cognitive, and structural facts is a daunting enterprise indeed.

To overcome these impediments, organizers of deliberative initiatives have two basic options when inviting public participation: They may advertise their initiatives locally and allow individuals to self-select, or they may take more active and direct recruitment steps (Button & Mattson 1999, Leroux et al. 1998, Renn et al. 1995, Ryfe 2002). The first option typically produces a "snowball" sample, in which interested individuals recruit from their social networks, these individuals recruit from their social networks, and so on until a group is composed. The second option usually involves some kind of representative sampling procedure, in which organizers create a group with a demographic profile that reflects the community. In neither case is the resulting group very large. Most deliberative initiatives involve no more than 20–30 individuals talking directly to one another. A few try to link small groups into a larger conversation, often using information technologies such as the Internet, but for the most part the practice of deliberation is constrained to relatively small groups (Goodin 2000, 2004).

Each option has its pluses and minuses. The major benefit of the snowball method is that it makes recruitment relatively easy and inexpensive. Because organizers may find participants within their own social networks, they need not expend a great deal of time or resources recruiting beyond their immediate field of vision. However, this relative ease of access also marks the major drawback of this approach: Self-selection often makes for homogeneous groups. Other work on civic participation reveals why this is the case. Research shows that civic participation is strongly correlated with belonging to social networks that privilege civic identities and make access to the political process relatively easy and frequent (Burns et al. 2001, Verba et al. 1995). Further, civic participation is closely associated with education levels, and this variable correlates with other indicators such as race and class (Conway 2000, Nie et al. 1996). The upshot is that if participants are allowed to self-select, those who participate are very likely to be white, college-educated, and middle-class.

There are reasons to be concerned about this tendency toward homogeneity. Some are practical. Work on public talk and opinion shows that diversity can be a key indicator of a deliberative frame of mind (Huckfeldt & Sprague 1995; Knoke 1990; Krassa 1990; Leighley 1990; McLeod et al. 1999; Moscovici 1976, 1980; Mutz 2002a,b; Mutz & Martin 2001; Nemeth 1986; Nemeth & Kwan 1985; Turner 1991; Walsh 2003). Individuals confronted by a greater diversity of ideas, either in the context of their own social networks or in face-to-face discussions with strangers, tend to be more open-minded, to learn more from others, and to engage in a deeper consideration of issues—in short, to be more deliberative. In contrast, homogeneous groups tend to privilege more intimate kinds of talk that make open discussion of political conflict difficult (Eliasoph 1998).

Central deliberative principles are also at stake. It is difficult to see how equality—a key principle of deliberative democracy—is achieved when deliberative groups are largely white and middle-class. Although every person who is engaged in deliberation may have an equal opportunity to speak, not every person is so engaged when groups are self-selected. Deliberative theorists also argue that participation socializes individuals into being more civic-minded and trusting of others (Haney et al. 2002). But if self-selected members of deliberative groups are already predisposed to being participative and civic-minded, deliberation becomes more a consequence than a catalyst of democratic socialization. Finally, the idea that deliberation increases the legitimacy of outcomes also seems to be threatened by this tendency toward homogeneity. Legitimacy hinges on a belief that all views have been expressed and considered—an unlikely situation given the makeup of most self-selected deliberative groups.

These problems have led some architects of deliberative initiatives to favor random, representative sampling as a method of group formation (Fishkin 1995, Gastil 2000). This process seems to ensure that, even if every person in a community is not given an equal opportunity to deliberate, at least every point of view is included. If the literature is correct, such diversity ought to improve the quality of talk in these encounters. Further, the representativeness of these groups seems to allow a degree of legitimacy that is unattainable via the self-selection method. As Fishkin (1995) puts it, a random, representative sample of Americans should possess the "recommending force of the public's considered judgments" (p. 170). Finally, even though this method involves relatively few individuals and thus would seem limited in its capacity to socialize people into civic-mindedness, the participants might return to their social networks as catalysts for greater civic involvement (Huckfeldt & Sprague 1995, Knoke 1990).

However, there are reasons to be cautious about this method of selection. Most obviously, a small group of people—even if randomly selected—cannot represent the views of a community of any size. Random selection may ensure inclusivity, but it does not grant representativeness (Burnheim 1985). Without this latter quality, the legitimacy of the group is open to question. Moreover, a paradox lies at the core of sampling methodology when applied to deliberative conversations. When individuals represent others not present in a conversation, their views obviously precede participation in a deliberative encounter. Yet, deliberative democrats clearly wish and expect learning to take place. To the extent that learning takes place, individuals cease to represent the community from which they were drawn (Abramson 1994). Ironically, by fulfilling one deliberative principle (learning), the method short-circuits another (representativeness). There is also the question of which community to sample. The obvious answer is that the community consists of individuals who will be directly affected by a decision, but it is not always clear who those people are (Smith & Wales 2000). Moreover, there is little evidence that short-term participation in deliberative exercises—the preferred format of most initiatives that adopt random selection—spurs individuals to greater civic involvement (Kimmelman & Hall 1997, Delli Carpini & Keeter 1996). Thus far, the evidence indicates that such initiatives prompt short-term gains but little long-term civic activity. Finally, random selection can be dreadfully time-consuming and expensive. Fishkin (1995) reports that to get a woman in poverty to his 1996 National Issues Conference in Austin, Texas, he had to personally drive her to the local airport (p. 180). His more recent call for a national deliberation day includes paying participants $150.00 for their participation (Ackerman & Fishkin 2004). In short, random selection may be neither pragmatically feasible nor normatively preferable.

It is not clear what to make of the conundrum of participant selection. It appears that many of those who would be eager to deliberate already possess the motivation and civic skills to participate in public life. Random sampling may compensate for some of the deficiencies of self-selection, but it has significant drawbacks of its own. Clearer, however, is the fact that deliberative theorists have been content to ignore these pragmatic issues. They simply argue that, as a theoretical matter, deliberation requires equality, and that, once achieved, equality will produce legitimacy. Any difficulty in realizing this equation is an empirical matter having to do with society, not with deliberative theory. One other response has been to focus less on the participation of ordinary people and more on the promotion of deliberation within representative institutions, particularly within the legal system [see Chambers (2003) for a review, Schroeder (2002) for a criticism]. The idea seems to be that if equality and legitimacy cannot be achieved via greater public participation, perhaps already-existing institutions can be made more deliberative and thus more diverse and legitimate. There is a certain logic to this move. But it jettisons a primary catalyst of the movement, that is, to involve greater numbers of ordinary people in the policy-making process.

In the absence of conceptual assistance from the theorists, deliberative architects continue to experiment with new institutional designs (Ackerman & Fishkin 2004, Fung 2004, Fung & Wright 2001, Leib 2004). Perhaps their efforts might be enlivened and even emboldened by greater effort on the part of the theorists to resolve the riddle of participation.

WHAT DOES DELIBERATION LOOK LIKE?

In laboratory experiments, psychologists have shown that deliberation often reduces the consistency between attitudes and behavior among subjects. It can lead to decisions that not only conflict with expert opinion but also conflict with subjects' own opinions—that is, decisions they later regret (Holt 1993, 1999; Wilson et al. 1989; Wilson & Schooler 1991). Other studies have shown that deliberation can cause participants to doubt that a "correct" decision is available at all (Armor & Taylor 2003, Iyengar & Lepper 2000). And still others have found that participants may feel more anxious and frustrated about the issue under discussion after a deliberative encounter than before (Cook & Jacobs 1999, Button & Mattson 1999, Hendriks 2002, Kimmelman & Hall 1997).

Why should this be the case? We simply do not know. And we won't know, I think, until we learn more about how people actually deliberate with one another. Surprisingly, this issue remains something of a void in the literature. Deliberative theorists say quite a bit about what deliberation *ought* to look like. Following Habermas (1984, 1996), most assume that deliberation takes place through an exchange of reasons. A participant defends a view by providing reasons; others probe the usefulness of this view through criticism; by reflecting together on the evidence for and against various views, free and independent participants come to accept what Habermas calls "the force of the better argument." Other theorists challenge this picture of deliberation (Benhabib 1996, Moon 1991, Phillips 1999). They ask whether every individual must agree that one argument is better than all others. They wonder whether every individual must accept all of the reasons in support of an argument, or whether neutral standards even exist to allow individuals to make such a judgment. But in pursuing this debate, theorists remain silent about what deliberation looks like on the ground, where real people discuss concrete issues.

Perhaps more surprisingly, the empirical literature has not addressed the issue either. Researchers have been less interested in deliberation itself than in measuring its effects. Whether they use laboratory, survey, or participant-observation methods, the authors of most empirical studies assume that deliberation ensues when certain structural conditions (such as equality and autonomy) hold. By organizing interactions along these lines, they feel free to assume that deliberation takes place, thus allowing them to focus on measuring its effects. Typically, measurement takes the form of pre- and post-tests to ascertain changes in attitudes, beliefs, opinions, and learning. Findings such as more consistency in beliefs and opinions, or greater recall of factual information, are taken to indicate that deliberation has succeeded. In the process, however, deliberation itself remains essentially unexamined.

This area is ripe for greater investigation. As a start, a few scholars (Lupia 2002, Mendelberg 2002; Rosenberg 2002, 2003a,b) have called for linking the study of deliberation with the "cognitive revolution" that has occurred in the social sciences during the past 30 years (Baars 1986, Gardner 1985, Johnson & Ermeling 1997, Simon 1992). As applied to political psychology, the concept of heuristics is perhaps the most important idea to come out of this tradition. In a nutshell, the idea is that, in any given situation, individuals will reason by using information cues. Instead of taking in and evaluating all relevant information, individuals take an information shortcut, relying on some subset of information to make a judgment and discarding the rest.

Researchers have found this process at work in every level of choice making. For instance, research on mass opinion has shown that citizens make snap judgments on the basis of party identification, their liking for a candidate, group affiliation, personal ideology, media frames, elite cues, perceptions of likely winners and losers, and a host of other cues (Lupia et al. 2000, Mondak 1994, Mutz et al. 1996, Sniderman et al. 1991; for a review, see Lau & Redlawsk 2001). Several studies by Sears (1993, 2001) show that the mere presence of a symbol, notably race, can trigger reflexive, largely unconscious judgments. The mechanism of this process is in some dispute. Some heuristics appear to be attached to scripts stored in long-term memory: "I was raised Democratic and will always vote Democratic." Others seem to be stored in short-term or "on-line" memory (Taber et al. 2001). That is, as individuals encounter a new stimulus, they process it on the spot, revising calculations as they go. The difference between the two methods can be important. It can, for instance, determine whether and how much citizens are persuadable by immediate messages. For our purposes, the general point is key: As mass citizens, individuals rely on heuristics to unreflectively mobilize cognitive structures at their disposal.

Interestingly, a similar process has been observed in small group settings. Researchers have found that participants in small group interactions will work together to find some subset of information or cue that allows them to identify common knowledge. This information may be identified in several ways: through the influence of group leaders (Nye & Simonetta 1996, Ridgeway 1987), through the influence of individuals who have a strong motivation to achieve consensus (De Grada et al. 1999, Kruglanski 1996, Webster et al. 1997), through the acceptance of group stereotypes and identities (Giles et al. 1987, Haslam et al. 1996, Maass et al. 1989, Maas & Arcuri 1996, Messick & Mackie 1989), or through perceptions of group consensus (Sunstein 2002). However it is discovered, this subset of information becomes an information shortcut, providing the group with a basis on which to select subsequent information unconsciously but efficiently (Davis et al. 1989; Gigone & Hastie 1993, 1997; Kameda 1991; Kerr & Kaufman-Gilliland 1994; Nemeth & Rogers 1996; Orbell et al. 1988; Schulz-Hardt et al. 2000; Winquist & Larson 1998; Wittenbaum et al. 1999). Small groups arrive at these information cues in a slightly different manner than do mass societies. Mass-mediated cues require individuals to identify appropriate heuristics and personally mobilize pertinent scripts. In small groups, the same process occurs in social interaction. Individuals engage in microrituals of social behavior to avoid conflict, identify points of agreement, and reach consensus (Brown & Levinson 1987, Mulkay 1985, Pomerantz 1984, Schiffrin 1990, Sheldon 1992). The outcome is much the same: judgments based on information shortcuts that mobilize scripts and thus allow groups to reach unconscious rather than deliberate judgments.

This brings us to a key insight: Deliberation represents a disturbance of everyday reasoning habits. People prefer to rely on routine scripts to navigate through their social world. Being jolted out of these scripts is, generally speaking, a disconcerting experience. This directly implicates emotions in the process of deliberation. Marcus et al. (2000) elaborate this point in a theory of the role of emotions in political judgment. According to them, human judgment is regulated by two emotional systems, which they call, respectively, the dispositional and the surveillance systems. The dispositional system regulates the domain of habit and routine. Linked to conscious awareness and attached to procedural memory, the dispositional system monitors our interactions with familiar environments by adjusting emotional responses and calling up learned scripts in procedural memory. "Insofar as...behavior...falls within the realm of learned behaviors," they explain, "the disposition system...play[s] a role in the initiation, adaptation, and control of the plan of action. Moreover, reliance on habits, most of which are developed without explicit reasoning, provides efficient and therefore reasonable solutions to the recurring tasks of daily life" (Marcus et al. 2000, p. 52). In contrast, the surveillance system monitors novel or threatening environmental stimuli. It kicks in when habits are disrupted and routines break down. Associated with feelings of anxiety and unease, the surveillance system makes us more attentive to our environment and to assessing new information. "When activated," Marcus et al. (2000) conclude, "the surveillance system shifts our conscious state away from the task at hand and toward an explicit consideration of what we should choose as the best course of action" (p. 58).

This cognitive shift may or may not be natural, but ordinarily people are reluctant to make it, precisely because it involves frustration and anxiety. This helps us to understand why individuals tend to be hesitant deliberators, preferring to "pass the buck" when they can and to rely on information short cuts when they cannot. It also helps us to understand why participation in deliberation may produce greater anxiety and frustration than other choice-making processes. It is unsettling to have one's cognitive scripts disrupted, and it is even more frustrating to recognize that no new script is forthcoming, since decisions about public issues are necessarily complex and admit no easy answers. As the empirical research shows, this situation may engender greater sympathy for public officials, but it also often results in feelings of powerlessness and hostility toward ultimate decisions.

Why, then, should individuals let themselves be bothered enough to be jolted out of their everyday reasoning habits? This question highlights the crucial role of motivation in deliberative reasoning. A motivation is an incentive, or a drive, to do something. When we say that individuals succeed in deliberating, we mean that they have been motivated to overcome historical, structural, and psychological impediments to intentional reflection. Political scientists and psychologists have been interested in this subject, though not formulated in these terms, for some time [see Sorrentino & Higgins (1986) and Taber et al. (2001) for reviews]. They have shown, for instance, that individuals motivated to preserve prior beliefs are less willing to veer from conventional scripts (Festinger 1957). In recent years, the study of motivation has become more systematic (Kunda 1990). Psychologists have identified a continuum of motivational goals, ranging from maintaining prior beliefs to obtaining an accurate conclusion (Baumeister & Newman 1994, Kunda 1990). Within this continuum, deliberation is associated with accuracy goals. Individuals motivated to reach accurate conclusions are more likely to engage in an intentional consideration of symbolic stimuli. Thus, when we say that people deliberate, we assume that they are driven by a motivation to be accurate. What kinds of mechanisms might prompt this motivation?

Marcus et al. (2000) give the short answer: things that make us uncomfortable. Other empirical research provides a longer answer. So far, researchers have found three conditions that tend to motivate individuals to adopt a deliberative frame of mind: accountability, high stakes, and diversity. Experimental work has shown that individuals who are told that they will have to discuss their judgments publicly are more likely to process more information more objectively (Tetlock 1983, 1985). Related to this notion, but less well documented, is the idea that perceptions of consequences will also influence motivation (Taber et al. 2001). If consequences are perceived to be great and direct, then individuals ought to expend more energy to get decisions right. Finally, as discussed above, other work has shown that deliberation is more likely in diverse groups. Moscovici (1976, 1980) finds that, under some conditions, minority group members can offer novel views that spur majority members to learn—that is, to veer from established scripts toward a deeper consideration of new ideas (see also Nemeth 1986, Nemeth & Kwan 1985, Turner 1991). Similarly, Huckfeldt (1986) and Huckfeldt & Sprague (1995) argue that political participation increases the diversity of one's social networks. Moreover, there is some evidence that diversity of social networks prompts a more deliberative frame of mind (Mutz 2002a,b; Mutz & Martin 2001). By taking people out of their comfort zones, these conditions may instigate more considered judgment.

So far so good. But does being uncomfortable in and of itself prompt deliberation? Not quite. Even within such structurally promising situations, some individuals will express disappointment with a deliberative encounter while others will come away perfectly satisfied. Why should this be the case? As a way into this question, we might note that all three of our motivating prompts involve psychological assessments of self in relation to other people or to one's environment. One becomes motivated to deliberate when one is accountable to others; when one perceives oneself to be threatened by others or by one's environment; when one encounters others different from oneself. In other words, motivation is a culturally and socially constructed drive.

At first glance, this insight seems to violate the cognitive model of reasoning with which we began. As Gardner (1985) observes, for much of its career, the cognitive revolution has been spurred by an assumption that all humans reason in the same standard ways, regardless of context. "Nearly all cognitive scientists have conspired to exclude from consideration such nontrivial factors as the role of the surrounding context, the affect aspects of experience, and the effects of cultural and historical factors on human behavior and thought" (p. 387). And there is more than a grain of truth in this assumption. At least a basic structure of human reasoning is the birthright of every human [Hutchins (1980); for criticisms, see Bruner (1990), Putnam (1981)]. However, a growing body of work argues that more complex forms of reasoning are culturally and socially conditioned (Cole 1996, Conover & Searing 2002, D'Andrade 1995, Kuklinski 2001, Kuklinski & Hurley 1996, Nye & Brower 1996, Resnick et al. 1991, Shweder 1991, Sniderman et al. 2001). Mounting research suggests that the "mere presence" of others is enough to alter a person's cognitive activity (Levine et al. 1993). Other evidence shows that the way individuals mobilize and organize memory in complicated cognitive tasks differs across cultures (Cole & Scribner 1974, Scribner & Cole 1981, Shweder 1993, Stigler et al. 1990). Cognition, in other words, is not solely hard wired; it also involves cultural software. To accept this idea is not to enter a world of total cultural relativism. Remember, all humans share a basic architecture of the mind. Nor is it to lapse into a form of determinism in which individuals simply bear their inherited culture; after all, people must learn and adapt shared mental models to their own lives. Rather, it is to accept and perhaps deepen an image of culture offered by Geertz (1973) more than 25 years ago: Culture is a "web of significance," which people living in communities collectively spin, and which, we might add, is mapped onto the brains of its individual members (p. 5).

How ought this meeting of cognitive and cultural theory change our view of deliberation? Absent empirical research, it is difficult to know with any precision, but Bruner (1986) gives some helpful suggestions. As we know, deliberative theorists tend to conceive of deliberation as argument, a form of communication that Bruner describes as a "formal mathematical system of description and explanation." This view is based on a conceptual preference for argumentation and logic as legitimate forms of deliberative discourse. But of course political argument is never detached from its social and cultural circumstances (Laden 2001). Rather, as Bruner (1986) puts it, deliberation always "deals in human or human-like intention and action. . .[that] strives to put its timeless miracles into the particulars of experience, and to locate the experience in time and place" (pp. 12–13). To the extent that deliberation combines cognition (the act of making sense) with culture (the act of making meaning), it probably looks more like storytelling than argumentation. As Fisher (1999) puts it, "the idea of humans as storytellers indicates the general form of all symbol composition: it holds that symbols are created and communicated ultimately as stories meant to give order to human experience and to induce others to dwell in them to establish ways of living in common, in communities. . ." (p. 271). To the extent that narrative functions as a "metacode" (White 1980, p. 7), which organizes symbolic stimuli into recognizable patterns, it captures the sense of the terms script, schema, or model (see also Mink 1978). Stories bring order to human experience. But the notion of narrative connects cognition with other elements—norms and identity—that are also central to community. As Ricoeur (1980) observes, once organized, stories may be repeated; repeated often enough, they become tradition; and tradition is the basis of community. Put another way, beyond cognitive understanding, the ultimate force of storytelling is moral and constitutional. It is moral in the sense that stories tell us not only what happened but also what ought to have happened (White 1980). It is constitutional in the sense that it produces the conditions for self-identification (Somers 1994). Thus, stories place motivation—a central element in attaining and sustaining a deliberative mindset—into human experience; they provide a footing, to borrow a term from Goffman (1974), on which understanding and self-understanding might take place all at once.

If we grant that deliberation looks like storytelling, then we have to rethink the theoretical link between reason and autonomy. In deliberative theory, the use of reason is seen to promote autonomy to the extent that individuals freely and independently engage in an exercise of critical reflection. This assumption has led many empirical researchers to look skeptically at any outside influence on individual reflection (Bartels 1998, Edelman 1993, Manheim 1991, Parenti 1999). But this skepticism only makes sense if we assume that humans share basic cognitive structures that compel them to deliberate in the same ways regardless of context.

Research in social and cultural psychology does not support this view. Instead, it suggests that deliberation is associated at least as much with community as with autonomy. Recent work in deliberative theory has begun to develop this perspective (Connolly 2002, Devereaux 2000, Laden 2001, Mouffe 2000, Rosenberg 2002). It implies that for deliberation to be successful, motivating conditions such as accountability, high stakes, and diversity must be set in a cultural context that enables roles, identities, and norms compatible with a deliberative frame of mind. A literature on participation in social movements perhaps demonstrates this idea best. Gamson (1992) observes that groups motivated by stories of injustice develop a deeper, richer, more reflective texture of talk. They track arguments more closely, offer more of their own views for the group's consideration, and ultimately feel and act more connected to public life. In other words, such stories catalyze a sense of self that overcomes disincentives to participate in public life, and they form a barrier to disappointment about ultimate outcomes. As Mansbridge (1980) found in her study of Vermont town meetings, people are loath to participate in political conversations with their fellow citizens—so much so that, as one participant put it, "I wouldn't say a word...unless they got me madder'n hell" (p. 60). Being "madder'n hell" may motivate people to deliberate. But it is not enough to ensure that the subsequent interaction will be successful. Rather, the empirical literature on reason suggests that anger must be accompanied by a commonly shared narrative that promotes deliberative roles and norms.

What will we find when we devote greater attention to deliberation as a form of discourse? The cognitive literature suggests that we will find deliberation to be episodic, difficult, and tentative. Within any particular interaction, deliberation may ebb and flow as participants alternately resist and accept the challenge of deliberation. And we will find that deliberation sustains itself through these conversational eddies by means of the coconstruction of identities and values that keep people motivated and engaged. This picture of deliberation does not destroy the image proffered by deliberative theorists. It does, however, suggest some revisions. Habermas may be correct that deliberation is a natural human talent, but it is not easy to cultivate and maintain. The key to successful deliberation lies in the manner in which individuals collectively account for problems. As the initial studies show, it is as likely that groups will talk their way out of deliberating as it is that they will hunker down to do the difficult work of sifting through the choices that lie before them. Successful deliberation not only helps groups evaluate choices but also provides the cultural glue that keeps them engaged in the task. It is left to subsequent research to identify particular keys, strategies, or patterns of talk that assist in this outcome.

THE PRODUCT OF DELIBERATIVE TALK

Suppose for a moment that a deliberative initiative has overcome all the obstacles we have discussed so far. Its creators have devised a sampling procedure that ensures equality among its members and the legitimacy of its deliberations. It has facilitated conversations among its members in such a way that participants feel motivated to do the hard work of intentional reflection, cognitively able to handle its complexities, and culturally empowered to believe that their work can make a difference. Even after accomplishing all of this, the initiative can still go awry. Once a group has deliberated and reached its judgment, that choice must then enter the political system in which policy decisions are made. In the United States, this means that deliberative choices enter a pluralist system populated by, among others, elected officials, bureaucrats, and representatives of interest groups. The possibility of realizing a deliberative democracy depends in part on successfully linking deliberation to this political system.

Empirical researchers have examined three responses to this issue [see Leroux et al. (1998) and Rowe & Frewer (2000) for discussions]. First, a deliberative initiative may be designed to avoid an explicit linkage between deliberation and policy making. National Issues Forums (NIFs) take this form. NIFs invite participants to deliberate on an issue using materials provided by forum organizers. These materials are quite explicit that the goal of the discussion is education, not policy making. Participants are encouraged to see the process as an opportunity to learn and reflect, not to offer guidance to policy makers.

Second, in the consultative mode, representative bodies may be mandated to consult, but not abide by, the outcome of a deliberative initiative. Deliberative polls and citizens' juries are examples of this mode (Fishkin 1995, Gastil 2000). Typically, representative bodies use these formats to gauge public opinion. In this mode, a deliberatively made choice serves as one input among others for a policy maker's consideration.

Third, in the decision-making mode, policy officials are explicitly bound by the decisions of deliberative groups. When used, the decision-making mode usually involves the relevant "stakeholders" in a systematic process of reflection on a defined set of policy options (Button & Ryfe 2005, Ryfe 2002).

Interestingly, I have come across few examples of this last mode in the United States [but see Fung & Wright (2001) and Renn et al. (1995) on similar initiatives in other countries]. That is, the "ordinary citizen" representing only her views rarely makes an appearance in deliberative initiatives. Instead, most initiatives focus their efforts either on education or consultation. Put another way, most initiatives imagine that the ultimate impact of deliberation is on public opinion and not the policy-making process. This evident reluctance to incorporate citizen deliberation more fully into policy making indicates a structural ambivalence within deliberative democracy about the relationship between talk and action.

Warren's (2001) work on associations and democracy illuminates this ambivalence. We know that people prefer a psychological state in which they can rely on familiar cognitive routines and scripts. When dislodged from this condition, they will engage in more considered reflection, but they will also seek a return to equilibrium. Warren notes that different kinds of associations will help them achieve this goal in different ways. Some associations, such as social service providers, will simply take care of their problem without deliberation. Other advocacy groups will champion their cause in other venues. Deliberative associations—groups that foster and promote deliberation as a way to solve common problems—have a particular profile. They tend to be political groups; they are relatively easy to exit; and they favor talk as a medium of decision making (p. 65). This profile is difficult to maintain because an emphasis on deliberative talk can easily inhibit a desire for political action (and vice versa). On the one hand, because deliberative groups are easy to exit, those that stress action will tend to become cognitively homogeneous as those who think differently from the growing group consensus exit [on the psychology of this process, see Gollwitzer (1990) and Gollwitzer & Bayer (1999)]. On the other hand, groups that seek to preserve deliberative talk will either avoid "political" issues altogether or choose issues that allow a limited range of disagreement (Eliasoph 1998). Finally, a group may focus on process more than outcomes. And this is precisely what we see happening in the deliberative field. Along with NIFs, Warren (2001) observes that such foundations as the Pew Charitable Trusts and the Kaiser Family Foundation also fit this profile (p. 164). Each of these foundations dedicates itself to improving the critical skills of citizens. In so doing, however, they also work against the basic cognitive logic that motivates people to deliberate in the first place. Without feeling that the stakes are high, or that they are accountable for an outcome, individuals will be less willing to engage their critical faculties.

Warren's work shows, I think, that deliberative associations face a daunting challenge when seeking to link their efforts to the wider political system. To the extent that a group favors deliberation above all else, it will tend to avoid or constrain explicit linkages to the political system. By contrast, to the extent that a deliberative group seeks real political action, it risks losing its diversity of views. This is not to say that associations will necessarily fall into these traps, only that the structural conditions of conventional politics make such an outcome as likely as not.

One might suppose that the consultative mode, requiring policy officials to consult but not accept deliberatively made choices, can avoid these dilemmas. But this mode raises its own paradox. As Warren notes, deliberative groups tend to believe that political choices are legitimate only to the extent that they are made in a deliberative fashion, but this principle conflicts with the terms on which officials and policy experts evaluate public decisions. For members of these "strong publics" (Fraser 1989), decision making involves an artful compromise between the technicalities of issues and the politics of interest-group bargaining. Given this perspective, it is not surprising that they chafe at the values implicit in the deliberative model, i.e., that decisions are legitimate only if they arise from open discussion among equals. Consider how policy officials and experts might respond if a deliberative group came to a decision on where to put a waste-management facility, ignoring the political realities of a local community and overlooking a crucial technical detail of how waste-management systems work. In this situation, policy experts might rightly look on a deliberative outcome with suspicion and even contempt. Ironically, a choice that enjoys the legitimacy conveyed by a deliberative process may well lack political legitimacy. At the same time, were policy officials to summarily dismiss a deliberative group's judgment, one can understand why its participants might come away from the process more disenchanted with politics than ever. Observations of real deliberative initiatives find that these reactions are quite common (see Button & Mattson 1999, Hendriks 2002, Kimmelman & Hall 1997, Ryfe 2002). This work suggests that the term "consultation" elides important differences in the assumptions and expectations that deliberative groups and policy officials bring to public decision making. If these differences are not accounted for, a deliberative initiative can end unhappily for all involved.

These practical challenges raise the conceptual issue of how to coordinate deliberation with representative democracy. It is one thing to argue abstractly that contemporary politics might be reinvigorated with greater deliberation and participation. It is quite another to make interactions between ordinary people and policy makers actually work. As with the issue of participation, deliberative theorists sometimes respond to these difficulties by retreating into the abstractions of proceduralism or constitutionalism. But, just as practitioners of deliberative democracy would do well to buttress their conceptualization of what they do, it seems to me that deliberative theory can only be invigorated by closer contact with empirical realities.

CONCLUSION

Does deliberative democracy work? The empirical literature answers this question with a qualified yes. Even if it is a natural human capacity, deliberation is not easy. It seems to require a mixture of knowledge/skills, motivation, and civic identity. It is difficult to create conditions to bring these elements together. It is perhaps even more difficult to sustain them once they are created. At every step of this process, basic concepts such as equality, legitimacy, reason, autonomy, representation, and democracy are at stake. But although deliberation is difficult and fragile, it is not impossible. On my reading, five mechanisms seem to be particularly associated with successful deliberation: rules, stories, leadership, stakes, and apprenticeship.

1. *Rules.* "Fully public democratic conversation takes place," Schudson (1997) writes, "in settings where talk is bound to be uncomfortable. . . . Such talk is threatening enough to require formal or informal rules of engagement" (p. 306). Precisely because people seem disinclined to deliberate—and if at all, not for very long—explicit rules must prop up deliberative initiatives. Rules of equality, civility, and inclusivity may prompt deliberation even when our first impulse is to avoid it. They may institutionalize deliberation as a routine process. Once institutionalized, they ensure that deliberation continues over time, perhaps even across generations. Finally, during actual exchanges, rules help participants ensure that their judgments are reflective and based on a full range of information.

2. *Stories.* Deliberative theorists sometimes seem to adopt an "if we build it they will come" mentality. If we infuse a context with the right procedures, and organize an encounter to conform to the right norms (equality, civility, etc.), then deliberation ought to take place. But rules may mean little if individuals do not feel accountable for outcomes, and even less if participants are not imbued with a civic identity that harnesses them to the task even when the going gets tough. Successful deliberation seems to require a form of talk that combines the act of making sense (cognition) with the act of making meaning (culture). Storytelling is one such form of talk. Stories anchor reality by organizing experience and instilling a normative commitment to civic identities and values. Once set, stories function as a medium for framing discussions (Farr 1993).

3. *Leadership.* Leaders provide important cues to individuals in deliberative settings. They can steer small groups toward nondeliberative conversations by insisting on the salience of particular cues. Alternatively, they can keep groups on a deliberative track when their members prefer to slip into routine and habit. At the level of mass society, leaders often manipulate cues to achieve personal political goals. Indeed, Zaller (1992) argues that public opinion is largely a product of elite cues as they are transmitted by the news media. If this is the case, it stands to reason that leaders who engage in more thoughtful rhetoric may prime citizens to adopt a more deliberative posture. Like rules, leaders may act as sea walls against the tide of routine habits of reasoning.

4. *Stakes.* Individuals are more likely to sustain deliberative reasoning when outcomes matter to them. Tetlock's (1983, 1985) experimental work on accountability suggests as much. In a different way, Forester (1999) argues for

much the same principle. His work on deliberation and environmental planning finds that individuals who are included in a policy-making process from the beginning become more invested in the process than individuals brought in at the end to choose among a range of predetermined options. Put simply, deliberation works best when individuals are invested in the outcome.

5. *Apprenticeship.* Few people would characterize public life at any level of American society as "deliberative." Moreover, as I have been at pains to show, people tend to prefer nondeliberative forms of reasoning. Therefore, ordinary people have little experience with deliberation, and presumably little skill. This insight has prompted calls for renewed civic education. But what form should this education take? Basic political knowledge is necessary, but it is not a sufficient spur to deliberation. The arts of rhetoric are another obvious subject, but deliberation is a way of doing politics rather than a way of speaking about political subjects. We know that deliberation is shaped by culture and society. This implies that abstract forms of argument are not as central to deliberation as theorists sometimes imply. Instead, we might do well to imagine education as a form of apprenticeship learning (Lave 1988, Lave & Wenger 1991), in which individuals learn to deliberate by doing it in concert with others more skilled in the activity. In apprenticeship, new skills emerge from the sensuous but guided activity of deliberating in real contexts and not from the rote recall of information. One might enable such learning in any context of public decision making, simply by establishing deliberative mechanisms, providing effective leaders, and guiding ordinary people through the process.

These five mechanisms stand out as critical to the successful design of deliberative initiatives. There are probably more, and to discover them, a great deal more research remains to be done. Despite its breadth, the empirical study of deliberation is not yet very rich or deep. More integration across disciplinary boundaries would be useful. Political scientists have made great strides in recent years by linking the study of opinion formation to cognitive science and psychology. But other literatures—in communication, sociology, social psychology, linguistics, and anthropology—remain almost untapped. Moreover, the theory of deliberative democracy needlessly remains removed from its practice. Theorists and applied researchers alike would benefit from greater interaction. We need to know more about the specific political contexts in which deliberation is likely to succeed. Work by Fung (2004) in particular has begun to grapple with this question, but it is an area ripe for further investigation. Finally, and perhaps most importantly, we must learn more about what deliberation actually looks like. It simply will not do to place the very practice under investigation into a black box. Psychologists and small group communication scholars provide hints about the nature of deliberation as a form of communication. Political scientists might follow their lead by investigating deliberation in the natural political contexts in which it takes place (e.g., Walsh 2004). Extending our research agendas in these directions can only enhance our understanding of the possibilities and limitations of deliberative democracy.

The *Annual Review of Political Science* is online at
http://polisci.annualreviews.org

LITERATURE CITED

Abelson J, Eyles J, Smith P, Martin E, Martin FP. 2002. Obtaining public input for health systems decisionmaking: past experiences and future prospects. *Can. Public Admin.* 45: 70–97

Abelson J, Forest PG, Eyles J, Smith P, Martin E, Gauvin FP. 2003. Deliberations about deliberative methods: issues in the design and evaluation of public participation processes. *Soc. Sci. Med.* 57:239–51

Abramson J. 1994. *We, the Jury.* New York: Basic

Ackerman B, Fishkin J. 2004. *Deliberation Day.* New Haven, CT: Yale Univ. Press

Armor D, Taylor S. 2003. The effects of mindset on behavior: self-regulation in deliberative and implementational frames of mind. *Pers. Soc. Psychol. B* 29:86–95

Baars B. 1986. *The Cognitive Revolution in Psychology.* New York: Guilford

Barber B. 1984. *Strong Democracy: Participatory Politics for a New Age.* Berkeley: Univ. Calif. Press

Bartels L. 1998. *Democracy with attitudes.* Presented at Annu. Meet. Am. Polit. Sci. Assoc., Boston

Baumeister R, Newman L. 1994. Self-regulation of cognitive inference and decision processes. *Pers. Soc. Psychol. B* 20:3–19

Benhabib S, ed. 1996. *Democracy and Difference: Contesting the Boundaries of the Political.* Princeton, NJ: Princeton Univ. Press

Bierle TC. 1999. Using social goals to evaluate public participation in environmental decisions. *Policy Stud. Rev.* 16:75–103

Bobbio N. 1987. *The Future of Democracy: A Defense of the Rules of the Game.* Transl. R. Griffin (from Italian). Cambridge, UK: Polity

Brown P, Levinson S. 1987. *Politeness: Some Universals in Language.* Cambridge, UK: Cambridge Univ. Press

Bruner J. 1986. *Actual Minds, Possible Worlds.* Cambridge, MA: Harvard Univ. Press

Bruner J. 1990. *Acts of Meaning.* Cambridge, MA: Harvard Univ. Press

Burnheim J. 1985. *Is Democracy Possible? The Alternative to Electoral Politics.* Cambridge, UK: Polity

Burns N, Schlozman K, Verba S. 2001. *The Private Roots of Public Action: Gender, Equality, and Political Participation.* Cambridge, MA: Harvard Univ. Press

Button M, Mattson K. 1999. Deliberative democracy in practice: challenges and prospects for civic deliberation. *Polity* 31: 609–37

Button M, Ryfe D. 2005. What can we learn from deliberative democracy? In *Where the Public Meets: Assessing Innovative Methods for Promoting Citizen Deliberation and Dialogue Across the Globe,* ed. J Gastil, P Levine. Boston: Jossey-Bass. In press

Cole M. 1996. *Cultural Psychology: A Once and Future Discipline.* Cambridge, MA: Harvard Univ. Press

Cole M, Scribner S. 1974. *Culture and Thought: A Psychological Introduction.* New York: Wiley

Connolly W. 2002. *Neuropolitics: Thinking, Culture, Speed.* Minneapolis: Univ. Minn. Press

Conover P, Searing D. 2002. Expanding the envelope: citizenship, contextual methodologies, and comparative political psychology. See Kuklinski 2001, pp. 89–114

Conway M. 2000. *Political Participation in the United States.* Washington, DC: CQ Press. 3rd ed.

Cook FL, Jacobs LR. 1999. *Deliberative Democracy in Action: Evaluation of Americans Discuss Social Security.* Washington, DC: Pew Charit. Trust

D'Andrade R. 1995. *The Development of Cognitive Anthropology.* Cambridge, UK: Cambridge Univ. Press

Davis J, Kameda T, Parks C, Stasson M, Zimmerman S. 1989. Some social mechanics of group decision making: the distribution of opinion, polling sequence, and implications for consensus. *J. Pers. Soc. Psychol.* 57: 1000–12

De Grada E, Kruglanski A, Mannetti L, Pierro A. 1999. Motivated cognition and group interaction: need for closure affects the contents and processes of collective negotiations. *J. Exp. Psychol.* 35:346–65

Delli Carpini M, Keeter S. 1996. *What Americans Know About Politics and Why It Matters.* New Haven, CT: Yale Univ. Press

Denver D, Hands G, Jones B. 1995. Fishkin and the deliberative opinion poll: lessons from a study of the Granada 500 television program. *Polit. Commun.* 12:147–56

Devereaux M. 2000. *Cultural Pluralism and Dilemmas of Justice.* Ithaca, NY: Cornell Univ. Press

Downs A. 1957. *An Economic Theory of Democracy.* New York: Harper

Dunkerly D, Glasner P. 1998. Empowering the public? Citizens' juries and the new genetic technologies. *Crit. Public Health* 8:181–92

Edelman M. 1993. Contestable categories and public opinion. *Polit. Commun.* 10:231–42

Eliasoph N. 1998. *Avoiding Politics: How Americans Produce Apathy in Everyday Life.* New York: Cambridge Univ. Press

Farr J. 1993. Framing democratic discussion. In *Reconsidering the Democratic Public,* ed. G Marcus, R Hanson, pp. 379–91. University Park: Penn. State Univ. Press

Festinger L. 1957. *A Theory of Cognitive Dissonance.* Stanford, CA: Stanford Univ. Press

Festinger L. 1964. *Conflict, Decision, and Dissonance.* Stanford, CA: Stanford Univ. Press

Fisher W. 1999. Narration as a human communication paradigm: the case of public moral argument. In *Contemporary Rhetorical Theory,* ed. JL Lucaites, CM Condit, S Caudill, pp. 265–87. New York: Guilford

Fishkin J. 1991. *Democracy and Deliberation: New Directions for Democratic Reform.* New Haven, CT: Yale Univ. Press

Fishkin J. 1995. *The Voice of the People: Public Opinion and Democracy.* New Haven, CT: Yale Univ. Press

Fiske S, Taylor S. 1991. *Social Cognition.* New York: McGraw-Hill

Forester J. 1999. *The Deliberative Practitioner: Encouraging Participatory Planning Processes.* Cambridge, MA: MIT Press

Fraser N. 1989. *Unruly Practices: Power, Discourse, and Gender in Contemporary Social Theory.* Minneapolis: Univ. Minn. Press

Freeman S. 2000. Deliberative democracy: a sympathetic comment. *Philos. Public Aff.* 29: 371–419

Fung A. 2001. Accountable autonomy: toward empowered deliberation in Chicago schools and policing. *Polit. Soc.* 29:73–103

Fung A. 2004. *Empowered Participation: Reinventing Urban Democracy.* Princeton, NJ: Princeton Univ. Press

Fung A, Wright EO. 2001. Deepening democracy: innovations in empowered participatory governance. *Polit. Soc.* 29:5–41

Gamson W. 1992. *Talking Politics.* Cambridge, UK: Cambridge Univ. Press

Gardner H. 1985. *The Mind's New Science: A History of the Cognitive Revolution.* New York: Basic

Gastil J. 2000. *By Popular Demand: Revitalizing Representative Democracy Through Deliberative Elections.* Berkeley: Univ. Calif. Press

Gastil J, Deess EP, Weiser P. 2002. Civic awakening in the jury room: a test of the connection between deliberation and political participation. *J. Polit.* 64:585–94

Gastil J, Dillard J. 1999. Increasing political sophistication through public deliberation. *Polit. Commun.* 16:3–23

Geertz C. 1973. Thick description: toward an interpretive theory of culture. In *The*

Interpretation of Cultures, pp. 3–32. New York: Basic

Gigone D, Hastie R. 1993. The common knowledge effect: sharing information and group judgment. *J. Pers. Soc. Psychol.* 65:959–74

Gigone D, Hastie R. 1997. The impact of information on small group choice. *J. Pers. Soc. Psychol.* 72:132–40

Giles H, Mulac A, Bradac J, Johnson P. 1987. Speech accommodation theory: the first decade and beyond. *Commun. Yearb.* 10:13–48

Goffman E. 1974. *Frame Analysis: An Essay on the Organization of Human Experience.* Cambridge, MA: Harvard Univ. Press

Gollwitzer PM. 1990. Action phases and mindsets. In *Handbook of Motivation and Cognition: Foundations of Social Behavior*, ed. RM Sorrentino, ET Higgins, 2:53–92. New York: Guilford

Gollwitzer PM, Bayer U. 1999. Deliberative versus implemental mindsets in the control of action. In *Dual-Process Theories in Social Psychology*, ed. S Chaiken, Y Trope, pp. 403–22. New York: Guilford

Goodin R. 2000. Democratic deliberation within. *Philos. Public Aff.* 29:81–109

Goodin R. 2004. *Reflective Democracy.* New York: Oxford Univ. Press

Graham KA, Phillips SD, eds. 1998. Citizen engagement: lessons in participation from local government administration. *Monogr. Can. Public Admin.* No. 22. Toronto: Inst. Public Admin. Can.

Habermas J. 1984. *The Theory of Communicative Action.* 2 Vols. Transl. T McCarthy (from German). Boston: Beacon

Habermas J. 1996. *Between Facts and Norms: Contributions to a Discourse Theory of Law and Democracy.* Transl. W Rehg (from German). Cambridge, MA: MIT Press

Haney B, Borgida E, Farr J. 2002. Citizenship and civic engagement in public problem-solving. *Res. Micropolit.* 6:225–52

Haslam SA, Oakes P, Turner J, McGarty C. 1996. Social identity, self-categorization, and the perceived homogeneity of ingroups and outgroups: the interaction between social

motivation and cognition. See Sorrentino & Higgins 1986, pp. 182–222

Hendriks C. 2002. Institutions of deliberative democratic processes and interest groups: roles, tensions and incentives. *Austr. J. Public Admin.* 61:64–75

Hibbing J, Theiss-Morse E. 1995. *Congress as Public Enemy. Public Attitudes Toward American Political Institutions.* Cambridge, UK: Cambridge Univ. Press

Hibbing J, Theiss-Morse E. 2000. *Deliberation as a source of system delegitimation and popular disharmony.* Presented at Annu. Meet. Midwest Polit. Sci. Assoc., Chicago

Holt L. 1993. Rationality is hard work: an alternative interpretation of the disruptive effects of thinking about reasons. *Philos. Psychol.* 6:251–66

Holt L. 1999. Rationality is hard work: some further notes on the disruptive effects of deliberation. *Philos. Psychol.* 12:215–19

Huckfeldt R. 1986. *Politics in Context: Assimilation and Conflict in Urban Neighborhoods.* New York: Agathon

Huckfeldt R, Sprague J. 1995. *Citizens, Politics, and Social Communication: Information and Influence in an Election Campaign.* New York: Cambridge Univ. Press

Hutchins E. 1980. *Culture and Inference.* Cambridge, MA: Harvard Univ. Press

Iyengar SS, Lepper M. 2000. When choice is demotivating: can one desire too much of a good thing? *J. Pers. Soc. Psychol.* 79:995–1006

Janis IL, Mann L. 1977. *Decision Making: A Psychological Analysis of Conflict, Choice, and Commitment.* New York: Free

Johnson D, Ermeling C, eds. 1997. *The Future of the Cognitive Revolution.* New York: Oxford Univ. Press

Kahneman D, Slovic P, Tversky A, eds. 1982. *Judgment Under Uncertainty: Heuristics and Biases.* New York: Cambridge Univ. Press

Kahneman D, Tversky A. 1983. Choices, values, and frames. *Am. Psychol.* 39:341–50

Kameda T. 1991. Procedural influence in small-group decision making: deliberation style and assigned decision rule. *J. Pers. Soc. Psychol.* 61:245–56

Kerr N, Kaufman-Gilliland C. 1994. Communication, commitment, and cooperation in social dilemmas. *J. Pers. Soc. Psychol.* 66:513–29

Kim J, Wyatt R, Katz E. 1999. News, talk, opinion, participation: the part played by conversation in deliberative democracy. *Polit. Commun.* 16:361–85

Kimmelman D, Hall G. 1997. *A critical study of civic deliberation and the political process.* Walt Whitman Cent. Culture of Politics and Democracy. Rutgers Univ., New Brunswick, NJ

Knoke D. 1990. *Political Networks: A Structural Perspective.* New York: Cambridge Univ. Press

Kraft M, Clary B. 1991. Citizen participation and the NIMBY syndrome: public response to radioactive waste disposal. *West. Polit. Q.* 44:299–328

Krassa MA. 1990. Political information, social environment, and deviants. *Polit. Behav.* 12:315–30

Kruglanski A. 1986. A motivated gatekeeper of our minds: need-for-closure effects on interpersonal and group processes. See Sorrentino & Higgins 1986, pp. 465–96

Kuklinski J, ed. 2001. *Citizens and Politics: Perspectives from Political Psychology.* Cambridge, UK: Cambridge Univ. Press

Kuklinski J, Hurley N. 1996. It's a matter of interpretation. See Mutz et al. 1996, pp. 125–44

Kuklinski J, Riggle E, Ottati V, Schwarz N, Wyer R. 1993. Thinking about political tolerance, more or less, with more or less information. In *Reconsidering the Democratic Public*, ed. G Marcus, R Hanson, pp. 225–47. University Park: Penn. State Univ. Press

Kunda Z. 1990. The case for motivated reasoning. *Psychol. Bull.* 108:480–98

Laden A. 2001. *Reasonably Radical: Deliberative Liberalism and the Politics of Identity.* Ithaca, NY: Cornell Univ. Press

Landeman M. 2002. Opinion quality and policy preferences in deliberative research. *Res. Micropolit.* 6:195–221

Lau R, Redlawsk D. 2001. Advantages and disadvantages of cognitive heuristics in political decision making. *Am. J. Polit. Sci.* 45:951–71

Lave J. 1988. *Cognition in Practice: Mind, Mathematics and Culture in Everyday Life.* Cambridge, UK: Cambridge Univ. Press

Lave J, Wenger E. 1991. *Situated Learning: Legitimate Peripheral Participation.* Cambridge, UK: Cambridge Univ. Press

Leib P. 2004. *Deliberative Democracy in America: A Proposal for a Popular Branch of Government.* University Park: Penn. State Univ. Press

Leighley JE. 1990. Social interaction and contextual influences on political participation. *Am. Polit. Q.* 18:459–75

Leroux T, Hirtle M, Fortin LN. 1998. An overview of public consultation mechanisms developed to address the ethical and social issues raised by biotechnology. *J. Consum. Res.* 21:445–81

Levine J, Resnick L, Higgins ET. 1993. Social foundations of cognition. *Annu. Rev. Psychol.* 44:585–612

Lupia A. 2002. Deliberation disconnected: what it takes to improve civic competence. *Law Contemp. Probl.* 65:133–50

Lupia A, McCubbins M, Popkin S, eds. 2000. *Elements of Reason: Cognition, Choice, and the Bounds of Rationality.* Cambridge, UK: Cambridge Univ. Press

Luskin R, Fishkin J. 1998. *Deliberative polling, public opinion, and representative democracy: the case of the National Issues Convention.* Presented at Annu. Meet. Am. Assoc. Public Opin. Res., St. Louis, MO

Maass A, Arcuri L. 1996. Language and stereotyping. In *Stereotypes and Stereotyping*, ed. CN Macrae, C Stangor, M Hewstone, pp. 193–226. New York: Guilford

Maass A, Salvi D, Arcuri L, Semin GR. 1989. Language use in intergroup contexts: the linguistic intergroup bias. *J. Pers. Soc. Psychol.* 57:981–93

Mackie G. 2002. *Does deliberation change minds?* Presented at Annu. Meet. Am. Polit. Sci. Assoc., Boston

Macpherson CB. 1977. *The Life and Times*

of Liberal Democracy. Oxford, UK: Oxford Univ. Press

Manheim J. 1991. *All the People All of the Time: Strategic Communication and American Politics*. Armonk, NY: ME Sharpe

Mansbridge J. 1980. *Beyond Adversary Democracy*. New York: Basic

Marcus G, Neuman WR, Mackuen M. 2000. *Affective Intelligence and Political Judgment*. Chicago: Univ. Chicago Press

McLeod J, Scheufele D, Moy P, Horowitz E, Holbert R, et al. 1999. Understanding deliberation: the effects of discussion networks on participation in a public forum. *Commun. Res.* 26:743–74

Mendelberg T. 2002. The deliberative citizen: theory and evidence. *Res. Micropolit.* 6:151–93

Mendelberg T, Oleske J. 2000. Race and public deliberation. *Polit. Commun.* 17:169–91

Messick D, Mackie D. 1989. Intergroup relations. *Annu. Rev. Psychol.* 40:45–81

Mink L. 1978. Narrative form as cognitive instrument. In *The Writing of History: Literary Form and Understanding*, ed. RH Canary, H Kozicki, pp. 129–49. Madison: Univ. Wisc. Press

Mondak J. 1994. Cognitive heuristics, heuristic processing, and efficiency in political decision making. *Res. Micropolit.* 4:117–42

Moon JD. 1991. Constrained discourse and public life. *Polit. Theory* 19:202–29

Moscovici S. 1976. *Social Influence and Social Change*. New York: Academic

Moscovici S. 1980. Toward a theory of conversion behavior. *Adv. Exp. Soc. Psychol.* 13:209–39

Mouffe C. 2000. *The Democratic Paradox*. London: Verso

Mulkay M. 1985. Agreement and disagreement in conversations and letters. *Text* 5:201–27

Mullen P. 2000. Public involvement in health care priority setting: Are the methods appropriate and valid? In *The Global Challenge of Health Care Rationing*, ed. C Ham, A Coulter, pp. 163–74. Buckingham, UK: Open Univ. Press

Mutz D. 2002a. Cross-cutting social networks. *Am. Polit. Sci. Rev.* 96:295–309

Mutz D. 2002b. The consequences of cross-cutting networks for political participation. *Am. J. Polit. Sci.* 46:838–55

Mutz D, Martin P. 2001. Facilitating communication across lines of political differences. *Am. Polit. Sci. Rev.* 95:97–114

Mutz D, Sniderman P, Brody R, eds. 1996. *Political Persuasion and Attitude Change*. Ann Arbor: Univ. Mich. Press

Neblo M. 2000. *Thinking through democracy: deliberative politics in theory and practice*. PhD thesis. Univ. Chicago

Nemeth CJ. 1986. Differential contributions of majority and minority influence. *Psychol. Rev.* 93:23–32

Nemeth CJ, Kwan J. 1985. Originality of word associations as a function of majority and minority influence. *Soc. Psychol. Q.* 48:277–82

Nemeth CJ, Rogers J. 1996. Dissent and the search for information. *Br. J. Soc. Psychol.* 35:67–76

Nie N, Junn J, Stehlik-Barry K. 1996. *Education and Democratic Citizenship in America*. Chicago: Univ. Chicago Press

Nisbett R, Ross L. 1980. *Human Inference: Strategies and Shortcomings of Social Judgment*. Englewood Cliffs, NJ: Prentice Hall

Nye J, Brower A, eds. 1996. *What's Social About Social Cognition? Research on Socially Shared Cognition in Small Groups*. Thousand Oaks, CA: Sage

Nye J, Simonetta L. 1996. Followers' perceptions of group leaders: The impact of recognition-based and inference-based processes. See Nye & Brower 1996, pp. 124–53

Nye J, Zelikow P, King D, eds. 1997. *Why People Don't Trust Government*. Cambridge, MA: Harvard Univ. Press

Orbell J, van de Kragt A, Dawes R. 1988. Explaining discussion-induced cooperation. *J. Pers. Soc. Psychol.* 54:811–19

Parenti M. 1999. Methods of media manipulation. In *Impact of Mass Media: Current Issues*. ed. RE Hiebert, pp. 120–24. New York: Longman. 4th ed.

Phillips A. 1999. *Which Equalities Matter?* Cambridge, UK: Polity

Pomerantz A. 1984. Agreeing and disagreeing with assessments: some features of preferred/dispreferred turn shapes. In *Structures of Social Action*, ed. JM Atkinson, J Heritage, pp. 57–101. Cambridge, UK: Cambridge Univ. Press

Pratchett L. 1999. New fashions in public participation: towards greater democracy? *Parliament. Aff.* 52:616–33

Putnam H. 1981. *Reason, Truth, and History.* Cambridge, UK: Cambridge Univ. Press

Putnam R. 2000. *Bowling Alone: The Collapse and Revival of American Community.* New York: Simon & Schuster

Renn O, Webler T, Wiedelmann P, eds. 1995. *Fairness and Competence in Citizen Participation: Evaluating Models for Environmental Discourse.* Boston: Kluwer Acad.

Resnick L, Levine J, Teasley S, eds. 1991. *Perspectives on Socially Shared Cognition.* Washington, DC: Am. Psychol. Assoc.

Ricoeur P. 1980. Narrative time. *Crit. Inquiry* 7:169–90

Ridgeway C. 1987. Nonverbal behavior, dominance, and the basis of status in task groups. *Am. Sociol. Rev.* 52:683–94

Rosenberg S. 2002. *The Not So Common Sense: Differences in How People Judge Social and Political Life.* New Haven, CT: Yale Univ. Press

Rosenberg S. 2003a. *Reconstructing the concept of deliberation.* Presented at Annu. Meet. Am. Polit. Sci. Assoc., Philadelphia

Rosenberg S. 2003b. *Reason, communicative competence, and democratic deliberation: Do citizens have the capacities to effectively participate in deliberative decision-making?* Presented at Annu. Meet. Am. Polit. Sci. Assoc., Philadelphia

Rossi J. 1997. Participation run amok: the costs of mass participation for deliberative agency decision making. *Northwest. Univ. Law Rev.* 92:173–250

Rowe G, Frewer LJ. 2000. Public participation methods: a framework for evaluation. *Sci. Technol. Hum. Val.* 25:3–29

Ryfe D. 2002. The practice of deliberative democracy: a study of sixteen organizations. *Polit. Commun.* 16:359–78

Schiffrin D. 1990. The management of a cooperative self during argument: the role of opinions and stories. In *Conflict Talk: Sociolinguistic Investigations of Arguments in Conversations*, ed. AD Grimshaw, pp. 241–59. Cambridge, UK: Cambridge Univ. Press

Schroeder C. 2002. The law of politics: deliberative democracy's attempt to turn politics into law. *Law Contemp. Probl.* 65:95–127

Schudson M. 1997. Why conversation is not the soul of democracy. *Crit. Stud. Media Commun.* 14:297–309

Schulz-Hardt S, Frey D, Luthgens C, Moscovici S. 2000. Biased information search in group decision making. *J. Pers. Soc. Psychol.* 79:655–69

Scribner S, Cole M. 1981. *The Psychology of Literacy.* Cambridge, MA: Harvard Univ. Press

Sears DO. 1993. Symbolic politics: a sociopsychological theory. In *Explorations in Political Psychology*, ed. S Iyengar, W McGuire, pp. 113–49. Durham, NC: Duke Univ. Press

Sears DO. 2001. The role of affect in symbolic politics. See Kuklinski 2001, pp. 14–40

Sheldon A. 1992. Conflict talk: sociological challenges to self-assertion and how young girls meet them. *New Merrill-Palmer Q.* 38:95–117

Shweder R. 1991. *Thinking Through Cultures: Expeditions in Cultural Psychology.* Cambridge, MA: Harvard Univ. Press

Shweder R. 1993. Cultural psychology: Who needs it? *Annu. Rev. Psychol.* 44:497–523

Simon H. 1992. *Economics, Bounded Rationality, and the Cognitive Revolution.* Hants, UK: Edward Elgard

Simrell K. 1998. The question of participation: toward authentic public participation in public administration. *Public Admin. Rev.* 58:317–26

Skocpol T, Fiorina M, eds. 1999. *Civic Engagement in American Democracy.* Washington, DC: Brookings Inst.

Smith G, Wales C. 2000. Citizens' juries and deliberative democracy. *Polit. Stud.* 48:51–65

Sniderman P, Brody RP, Tetlock P, eds. 1991. *Reasoning and Choice: Explorations in Political Psychology.* Cambridge, UK: Cambridge Univ. Press

Sniderman P, Tetlock P, Elms L. 2001. Public opinion and democratic politics: the problem of nonattitudes and the social construction of political judgment. See Kuklinski 2001, pp. 254–88

Somers M. 1994. The narrative constitution of identity: a relational and network approach. *Theory Soc.* 23:605–49

Sorrentino R, Higgins ET, eds. 1986. *Handbook of Motivation and Cognition: The Interpersonal Context.* Vol. 3. New York: Guilford

Stigler JW, Shweder R, Herdt G, eds. 1990. *Cultural Psychology: Essays on Comparative Human Development.* Cambridge, UK: Cambridge Univ. Press

Sulkin T, Simon A. 2001. Habermas in the lab: a study of deliberation in an experimental setting. *Polit. Psychol.* 22:809–26

Sunstein C. 2002. The law of group polarization. *J. Polit. Philos.* 10:175–95

Taber C, Lodge M, Glathar J. 2001. The motivated construction of political judgments. See Kuklinski 2001, pp. 198–226

Tetlock P. 1983. Accountability and the perseverance of first impressions. *Soc. Psychol. Q.* 46:285–92

Tetlock P. 1985. Accountability: a social check on the fundamental attribution error. *Soc. Psychol. Q.* 48:227–36

Tetlock P. 2001. Coping with trade-offs: psychological constraints and political implications. See Lupia et al. 2001, pp. 239–63

Turner JC. 1991. *Social Influence.* Pacific Grove, CA: Brooks/Cole

Verba S, Schlozman K, Brady H. 1995. *Voice and Equality: Civic Voluntarism in American Politics.* Cambridge, MA: Harvard Univ. Press

Walsh KC. 2003. *The democratic potential of civic dialogue on race.* Presented at Annu. Meet. Midwest Polit. Sci. Assoc., Chicago

Walsh KC. 2004. *Talking About Politics: Informal Groups and Social Identity in American Life.* Chicago: Univ. Chicago Press

Warren M. 2001. *Democracy and Associations.* Princeton, NJ: Princeton Univ. Press

Webster D, Kruglanski A, Pattison D. 1997. Motivated language use in intergroup contexts: need-for-closure effects on the linguistic intergroup bias. *J. Pers. Soc. Psychol.* 72:1122–31

White H. 1980. The value of narrativity in the representation of reality. *Crit. Inquiry* 7:5–23

Wilson TD, Dunn D, Kraft D, Lisle D. 1989. Introspection, attitude change, and attitude-behavior consistency: the disruptive effects of explaining why we feel the way we do. *Adv. Exp. Soc. Psychol.* 22:287–343

Wilson TD, Schooler J. 1991. Thinking too much: introspection can reduce the quality of preferences and decisions. *J. Pers. Soc. Psychol.* 60:181–92

Winquist J, Larson J. 1998. Information pooling: when it impacts group decision making. *J. Pers. Soc. Psychol.* 74:371–77

Wittenbaum G, Hubbell A, Zuckerman C. 1999. Mutual enhancement: toward an understanding of the collective preference for shared information. *J. Pers. Soc. Psychol.* 77:967–78

Zaller J. 1992. *The Nature and Origins of Mass Opinion.* New York: Cambridge Univ. Press

Annu. Rev. Polit. Sci. 2005. 8:73–98
doi: 10.1146/annurev.polisci.8.082103.104930
Copyright © 2005 by Annual Reviews. All rights reserved
First published online as a Review in Advance on Mar. 4, 2005

CONSTITUTIONAL REFORM IN BRITAIN:
The Quiet Revolution

Vernon Bogdanor
Professor of Government, Brasenose College, Oxford University,
Oxford OX1 4AJ, United Kingdom

Key Words   devolution, federalism, human rights, second chambers

■ **Abstract**   Since 1997, Britain has been undergoing a period of constitutional reform. This reform has been radical and yet piecemeal. The process has been unique in
the democratic world, in that it has been converting an uncodified constitution into a
codified one, but by stages, there being neither the political will nor the consensus to
do more. Some of the contours of the new constitution will be familiar to Americans,
for Britain now enjoys a quasi-federal system of government, and, in effect, a Bill of
Rights. The creation of a more representative upper house is also part of the ongoing
process of reform. In consequence, Britain no longer lives under an organic "historic"
constitution but is in the process of fashioning one that is being created by deliberate
human agency.

THE END OF THE HISTORIC CONSTITUTION

"There is a great difficulty in the way of a writer who attempts to sketch a living
Constitution—a constitution that is in actual work and power. The difficulty is that
the object is in constant change" (Bagehot 1974 [1872], p. 165). The difficulty is
particularly acute in the case of the British Constitution. For, until very recently
at least, it was unique in the democratic world in being what Dicey[1] called a
"historic" constitution. By calling the British Constitution historic, Dicey meant
not just that it was very old, but that it was original and spontaneous, the product
not of deliberate design but of a long process of evolution. "Other constitutions
have been built," declared Sidney Low, an early twentieth century commentator on
British government; "that of England [sic] has been allowed to grow" (Low 1904,
p. 12). The constitution was based not on codified rules but on conventions, of which
the best modern account can be found in Marshall (1984) and in the reflections
of a former Cabinet Secretary (Wilson 2004). Low called these conventions "tacit
understandings," but went on ruefully to remark that "the understandings are not
always understood" (Low 1904, p. 12).

---

[1]Dicey AV. *Unpublished lectures on the comparative study of constitutions.* Codrington
Library, All Souls College, Oxford Univ., MS 323 LR 6 b 13, Oxford, UK.

Sidney Low's book, *The Governance of England*, appeared in 1904. An overview of Britain's constitutional evolution during the twentieth century can be found in the edited volume by Bogdanor (2003a). By the end of the twentieth century, it was by no means obvious that the British Constitution could still be described as historic, for it seemed to have been refashioned in a self-conscious and deliberate way to meet new exigencies. A new British Constitution seems about to evolve (see Bogdanor 2004). Since 1997, indeed, when a Labour government led by Tony Blair assumed office, Britain has been engaged in a process that seems quite unique in the democratic world—that of converting an uncodified constitution into a codified one by piecemeal means, there being neither the political will to do anything more, nor any consensus on where the final resting-place should be.

That the reforms are wide-ranging may be seen from the following list.

1. The constitutional independence of the Bank of England from government in monetary policy.

2. Referendums, under the Referendums (Scotland and Wales) Act, 1997, on devolution to Scotland and Wales.

3. The Scotland Act, 1998, providing for a directly elected Scottish Parliament.

4. The Government of Wales Act, 1998, providing for a directly elected National Assembly in Wales.

5. The Northern Ireland Act, 1998, providing for a referendum on a partnership form of devolution to Northern Ireland, following the Belfast or Good Friday Agreement. The terms of this Agreement—more properly two agreements, one between the parties in Northern Ireland (the multi-party agreement) and the other between the governments of Britain and Northern Ireland—can be found in Ruane & Todd (1999, pp. 171–201), and a pessimistic account of the British-Irish Council, established by the agreement, can be found in Bogdanor (1999b).

6. The establishment, under the Northern Ireland Act, 1998, following the successful outcome of the referendum, of a directly elected Assembly in Northern Ireland.

7. A referendum, under the Greater London Authority (Referendum) Act, 1998, on a directly elected mayor and assembly for London.

8. The introduction of proportional representation for the elections to the devolved bodies in Scotland, Wales, Northern Ireland, and the London Assembly.

9. The European Parliamentary Elections Act, 1999, providing for the introduction of proportional representation for elections to the European Parliament.

10. The requirement on local authorities, under the Local Government Act, 2000, to abandon the committee system and adopt a cabinet system, a city manager system, or a directly elected mayor. A local authority that wished to choose the directly elected mayor option, however, would be required, first, to hold

a referendum on this option. In addition, provision was made for 5% of registered electors to require a local authority to hold a referendum on a directly elected mayor—the first statutory provision for the use of the initiative in British politics. At the time of writing, however, there are only 11 directly elected mayors in England, and none in any large city, apart from London.

11. The Human Rights Act, 1998, requiring public bodies to comply with the provisions of the European Convention on Human Rights. The Act allows judges to declare a statute incompatible with Convention rights and provides for a fast-track procedure by which Parliament might repeal or amend such legislation.

12. The removal, under the House of Lords Act, 1999, of all but 92 of the hereditary peers from the House of Lords as the first phase of a wider reform of the Lords.

13. A Freedom of Information Act, 2000, most of whose provisions will not come into force until 2005 (for details, see Birkinshaw 2001).

14. The Political Parties, Elections and Referendums Act, 2000, registering political parties, controlling political donations and national campaign expenditure, and providing for the establishment of an Electoral Commission to oversee elections and to advise on improvements in electoral procedure. Ewing (2001) offers a valuable short analysis.

15. The abolition of the historic office of Lord Chancellor, the removal of the law lords from the House of Lords, and the establishment of a new Supreme Court, under the Constitutional Reform Act, 2004. The best account of the role of the Lord Chancellor—whose office involved a spectacular breach of the principle of the separation of powers, in that he was head of the judiciary, a member of the Cabinet, and the speaker of the upper house—appears in Woodhouse (2001). An analysis of the proposed changes can be found in a special issue of the journal *Legal Studies* (2004) and in Le Sueur (2004).

This process of constitutional reform is by no means complete. In November 2004, a referendum is due to be held, under the provisions of the Regional Assemblies (Preparations) Act, 2003, in the northeast region, on whether that region wishes to have a regional assembly. A nationwide referendum has been promised before Parliament ratifies the new European constitutional treaty. In addition, referendums have been promised on whether Britain should join the Eurozone, and whether the first-past-the-post electoral system should be retained for elections to the House of Commons.

The reader will find a useful overview, interpretation, and criticism of the program of reform in Johnson (2004), as well as some valuable essays in Jowell & Oliver (2004). In a previous edition of this latter work (Jowell & Oliver 2000, p. v), the reforms of the post-1997 period were said to "constitute hammer blows against our Benthamite and Diceyan traditions." There is also a highly polemical attack on the various reforms in Sutherland (2000), *The Rape of the Constitution?*

Margaret Thatcher is quoted on the dust-jacket as believing that the question mark was unnecessary.

This remarkable and wide-ranging program of constitutional reform has been carried out by a Labour government. That is in itself a matter for comment. Few analysts believe that constitutional reform had ever been a major priority for Labour before the 1980s [although Taylor (2000) seeks to show, through an analysis of the history of the Party, that reform of the constitution has always lain at the heart of its thinking]. Evans (2003) describes how Labour came to be committed to constitutional reform during the long years of Conservative rule between 1979 and 1997, the longest period of single-party government in Britain since the Napoleonic wars. Earlier works such as Jones & Keating (1985), as well as Foley (1999) and Bogdanor (1997b, 2001), take the view that constitutional reform was not, until recently, at the forefront of Labour's program, since the Party's mission was "to capture the main institutions of the state, not to transform them" (Bogdanor 2001, p. 140). There seemed, indeed, to be a peculiar affinity between the conceptual presuppositions of the British Constitution, which legitimized the power of the government of the day, and the ideals of Labour, a Party that sought, through the power of government, to transform society and the economy. Bogdanor (2001), indeed, saw a profound conflict between Labour's program of constitutional reform, in particular devolution, and its traditional ideals of social democracy, which presupposed a strong central government at Westminster able to redistribute resources in accordance with the canons of social justice. Others (for example, Griffith 1997, 2000) argued that constitutional reform would give too much power to the judges, who, being generally both individualist and liberal, had traditionally been hostile to Labour's aims. Bogdanor believed that "when a movement comes to be more concerned with. . .procedures than with substance, it has lost belief in its ultimate aims. . .a happy political party does not normally concern itself with the constitution. . .. Those who founded and fought for the Labour party when socialism seemed the wave of the future were concerned less with changing the rules by which governments were formed and power exercised, than with changing society" (Bogdanor 2001, pp. 154–55). He found the ideological origins of the Labour program of constitutional reform to lie, not in the history of the Labour Party, but in nineteenth-century liberalism, as mediated through reform organizations such as Charter 88.

Charter 88 was launched in 1988 to mark the 300th anniversary of the Glorious Revolution of 1688, which saw the deposition of James II and establishment of a parliamentary monarchy under William of Orange. The Charter was presented in the form of a petition with 10 demands including a written constitution, proportional representation, a reformed second chamber, a Bill of Rights, and freedom of information (Evans 1995). Dubbed by one Conservative minister "a loser's Charter," one of its supporters suggested that it was "a snowball that will hopefully become an avalanche." Its main purpose, a founder of the organization declared, was "to reawaken ideas of citizenship and democracy on the left and to show how they could rally a wide opposition to Thatcherism" (Evans 2003, p. 32). The Charter was to exert a significant impact on Labour's reform program. It was itself perhaps a legacy of the spirit of 1968, which, despite the *marxisant* language of many of its leaders, was concerned more with realizing the aspirations of nineteenth-century liberals such as John Stuart Mill toward greater participation and constitutional government, than with the social and economic aspirations of traditional socialists.

Political scientists are, of course, concerned to chart the consequences of reform as well as to explain why they occurred. This, however, is a task of peculiar difficulty in the case of the recent reforms. For constitutional changes do not yield their full effects for many years, sometimes for generations. The American Constitution was promulgated in 1787, but the Supreme Court did not strike down any federal statute until *Marbury v Madison* in 1803, and after that not until the *Dred Scott* case in 1857. An observer writing a decade after the constitution had been promulgated, therefore, would have obtained a quite false view of its significance. In France, similarly, the Conseil Constitutionnel was established by the Fifth Republic Constitution in 1958, but it did not seek to issue rulings on laws to determine whether they were in conformity with the constitution—something which would have appalled the Gaullist founding fathers—until 1971 (see Nicholas 1978).

In 1872, when he came to publish the second edition of *The English Constitution* [sic], Bagehot declared that it was

> too soon as yet to attempt to estimate the effect of the Reform Act of 1867.... The Reform Act of 1832 did not for many years disclose its real consequences; a writer in 1836, whether he approved or disapproved of them, whether he thought too little of or whether he exaggerated them, would have been sure to be mistaken in them. A new Constitution does not produce its full effect as long as all its subjects were reared under an old Constitution, as long as its statesmen were trained by that old Constitution. It is not really tested till it comes to be worked by statesmen and among a people neither of whom are guided by a different experience. (Bagehot 1974 [1872], p. 166)

The same warning should be borne in mind, surely, by anyone seeking to analyze the effects of the quiet revolution. Any conclusions concerning its significance must be both highly tentative and provisional.

Perhaps the main problem facing any analyst of the constitution is that of keeping up to date with the plethora of constitutional changes. For this reason alone, all writers on the constitution owe a massive debt to the Constitution Unit. This nonofficial and independent research body is based in the School of Public Policy at University College, London. It is involved in training, consultancy, and advice as well as research and performs a vital function in monitoring constitutional change through its *Constitutional Update*, which summarizes the main constitutional developments since 1997. In addition, it publishes a quarterly newsletter, *Monitor*. The Unit has also published more than 100 reports and seven books, including four volumes charting the progress of devolution (Hazell 2000, 2003; Trench 2001, 2004). The last of these volumes offers a particularly wide-ranging and comprehensive stock-taking of the effects of devolution during the first term of the Scottish Parliament and the National Assembly of Wales, from 1999 to 2004. A further volume in what promises to be a regular series is due to appear in 2005. The Unit has in addition published an exercise in futurology (Hazell 1999) entitled *Constitutional Futures: A History of the Next Ten Years*. The Constitution Unit's website, http://www.constitution-unit.ucl.ac.uk/, is a mine of information, indispensable for any serious student of constitutional change. In addition, the Parliament website—http://www.parliament.uk/—should be consulted. It contains not only parliamentary debates but also research papers as well as notes and commentaries on legislation written for the guidance of MPs.

THE REFERENDUM

The devolution reforms, including the mayor and assembly for London, have been validated by referendum. Moreover, Britain's adherence both to the Euro and to the European constitutional treaty will also require validation by referendum. Yet, until the 1970s, the referendum was widely regarded as unconstitutional. When, in 1945, Winston Churchill proposed putting to the people the question of the continuation of his wartime coalition government into peacetime, Clement Attlee, the Labour leader, declared the referendum to be a "device alien to all our traditions" and went on to say that it "has only too often been the instrument of Nazism and fascism. Hitler's practices in the field of referenda and plebiscites can hardly have endeared these expedients to the British heart" [*The Times*, May 22, 1945, cited in Bogdanor (1981), p. 35]. In 1964, a respected work on British government declared, "It has occasionally been proposed that a referendum might be held on a particular issue, but the proposals do not ever appear to have been taken seriously" (Birch 1964, p. 227). In her first speech as Conservative leader to the House of Commons, in February 1975, Margaret Thatcher—advised by the constitutional analyst, Nevil Johnson—opposed the proposal for a referendum on whether Britain should remain in the European Community (as it then was), on the grounds that the referendum was in conflict with the principle of parliamentary sovereignty. Arguments of this kind, as Johnson recognizes, now appear merely quaint (Johnson 2004, p. 316). For, if parliament is sovereign, if parliament can do what it likes, then surely it can call a referendum when it likes. In practice, it seems that referendums are called when it is being proposed that the powers of Parliament be transferred, either "upward" to Europe, or "downward" to devolved bodies. It may be indeed that a persuasive precedent, if not a convention, has been created such that a referendum is required on any proposal to transfer the powers of Parliament. A requirement of this kind would be in accord with the principles of liberal constitutionalism. For, as Locke declares in para. 141 of his *Second Treatise on Government*, "the Legislative cannot transfer the power of making laws to any other hands. For it being but a delegated power from the people, they who have it cannot pass it to others" (Locke 1960 [1690]). But, whether or not there are firm conventions regulating the use of the referendum, there can be no doubt that it has now become part of the British Constitution.

There is a useful comparative literature on the referendum—Butler & Ranney (1994) and Gallagher & Uleri (1996) on its use in Europe, and Magleby (1984) on its use in the United States, are particularly valuable. But relatively little has been written on the significance of the introduction of the referendum into British constitutional arrangements. Yet, were it not for the referendum, there can be little doubt that Britain would now be part of the Eurozone, since the Blair government favors entry. An account of the history of referendum proposals in Britain until 1981 can be found in Bogdanor (1981), updated in Bogdanor (1997b). There is also a discussion of when referendums should be used in Marshall (1997). However, the standard account of how referendums ought to be conducted is in the report of the independent Commission established by the Constitution Unit and the Electoral Reform Society in 1996, entitled "Commission on the Conduct of Referendums" (Constitution Unit 1996). This Commission recommended that the conduct of referendums be entrusted to a statutory independent body, accountable to Parliament, so as to secure confidence in the legitimacy of the results. The responsibilities of this independent body would include advising on the referendum question; liaising with and funding campaigning organizations; the fair presentation of public information; and organizing the poll. The Commission proposed the adoption of 20 guidelines to ensure that referendums were conducted efficiently, fairly, and consistently.

The government accepted the main recommendation of this Commission, and Parliament established an Electoral Commission in November 2000, with responsibilities to report on elections as well as referendums, to review electoral law and practice, and to promote public awareness of the electoral process (see http://www.electoralcommission.org.uk/). The Electoral Commission has taken an active approach to its work, producing regular reports on electoral matters and highlighting difficulties in the electoral process. Though in no sense a campaigning organization, it has taken a particular interest in combating political apathy and low turnout—turnout for the 2001 general election was, at 59.4%, the lowest since the first British general election under universal male suffrage in 1918. The Commission has published an official report on the conduct and results of the 2001 general election (Electoral Commission 2001), as well as numerous reports on other electoral matters, including use of the referendum and voting systems.

But, although the devolution reforms have been validated by referendum, it would be a mistake to conclude that constitutional reform, outside Northern Ireland, has aroused widespread public interest. One indication of the lack of interest can be found in the comparatively low figures for turnout in the referendums, except in Northern Ireland (see Table 1).

The director of Market and Opinion Research International, a polling organization, has shown that constitutional reform remains a low priority for most voters and that, even in Scotland, devolution was favored for instrumental reasons— that it was likely to make Scots richer, improve public services, etc.—rather than

TABLE 1   Voter turnout for devolution referendums

Referendum	Turnout
Scottish devolution, 1997	60.2%
Welsh devolution, 1997	50.1%
Northern Ireland—Belfast Agreement, 1998	80.0%
Directly elected London mayor and Authority, 1998	34.0%

for reasons of fundamental principle associated with the right to self-government (Worcester & Mortimore 1999, 2001). The British voter remains obstinately concerned with substance rather than procedure and remains profoundly indifferent to constitutional issues. Thus, if the reforms since 1997 amount to a constitutional revolution, the revolution has been a quiet one, albeit one whose consequences are likely to prove very profound.

THE CONSTITUTION AND LIMITED GOVERNMENT

All of the reforms listed on pp. 74–75 have the effect of limiting the power of the government of the day, of constraining what Lord Hailsham (1978) once memorably called the elective dictatorship. They are all examples of what might be called unilateral disempowerment, worth bearing in mind perhaps when the Blair government is accused, as it often is, of developing "presidential" tendencies. Perhaps the three reforms that pose the greatest threat to the ability of the government to secure its way are reform of the House of Lords, devolution, and the Human Rights Act.

A reformed House of Lords threatens the ability of the government of the day to secure passage of its legislation through Parliament. Since the Parliament Act of 1911, the Lords have been unable to reject money bills; their power over non-money bills was reduced to that of delay for three sessions, and further reduced to delay for just one session in the second Parliament Act of 1949. Moreover, the House of Lords, largely on account of its irrational and nonelected composition, can hardly hope to undermine the program of a confident government enjoying a secure majority. Wheeler-Booth (2003) provides a masterly analysis of recent developments, and the standard accounts of the working of the Lords are in Shell (1992) and Carmichael & Dickson (1999).

Britain, it is clear, has been able to combine a two-chamber legislature with an effectively unicameral system. The more, however, that the upper house is rationalized, the more likely it is to exercise its powers. Were the upper house to be wholly or even partially elected, an outcome desired by many reformers, then it might even seek an increase in its powers. There is perhaps some analogy with the history of the European Parliament, which, once it became directly elected in

1979, rapidly sought and obtained an increase in its powers. Whereas before 1979 it was a largely consultative body, it now enjoys power of codecision over a wide range of European legislation.

Devolution and the Human Rights Act seem to threaten the fundamental constitutional principle—perhaps the only constitutional principle that there is in Britain—of the sovereignty of Parliament.[2] Some would argue that this principle had already been undermined by Britain's entry in 1973 into the European Community (as it then was), for the Treaty of Rome proclaimed European law as a higher legal order than the law of the member states so that the laws of the Community would be superior to those of the member states and directly applicable to them. The government of the day, however, made heroic efforts in drafting the legislation to avoid conflict between the principle of parliamentary sovereignty and that of the superiority of European law by providing, in section 2(4) of the European Communities Act, that all future legislation should be interpreted by the courts as if Parliament intended it to conform with European legislation. Similar efforts have been made, as we shall see, to reconcile devolution and the Human Rights Act with the principle of parliamentary sovereignty. It is by no means clear, however, whether the attempt to reconcile seemingly conflicting principles will prove successful. The painter Wassily Kandinsky once predicted—wrongly—that the twentieth century would see the demise of "either/or" and the triumph of "and," something he would have regarded as a great achievement of civilization. It remains to be seen whether, in its constitutional reforms, Britain will now be successful in replacing what has hitherto been "either/or" by "and."

DEVOLUTION AND QUASI-FEDERALISM

The devolution program instituted in 1997 provided for different structures of government in the component parts of the United Kingdom. Scotland now enjoys a Parliament with legislative powers over a wide range of domestic affairs. The National Assembly of Wales, by contrast, enjoys powers not over primary legislation, but only over secondary legislation—orders, statutory instruments, and the like—with primary legislation remaining at Westminster. The Northern Ireland Assembly, like the Scottish Parliament, enjoys legislative powers, but the Northern Ireland Act of 1998 requires the executive in that province to contain representatives of each of the two warring communities, and the Assembly is required to operate in a consociational rather than a majoritarian fashion. These provisions were clearly much influenced by the well-known work of Lijphart (1975, 1977). The purpose of the consociational arrangement was, of course, to strengthen cooperation between the communities. The Northern Ireland Assembly was, however, after three earlier suspensions (two short and one long), once again suspended

---

[2]The history of this principle has been charted by Goldsworthy (1999); see also the typically acute commentaries by Bradley (2004) and Marshall (2003).

in 2002 precisely because it proved impossible to secure agreement between the communities. The elections of 2003 showed that the leading parties were the more intransigent parties—in the unionist community, the Democratic Unionist Party, led by Rev. Ian Paisley, and, in the nationalist community, Sinn Fein—rather than the more moderate Ulster Unionist Party and Social Democratic and Labour Party. Critics argued, therefore, that the Agreement had entrenched communalism rather than helping to ameliorate it. Nevertheless the remainder of this article assumes, perhaps overoptimistically, that devolution will be restored in Northern Ireland. Neither the National Assembly of Wales nor the Northern Ireland Assembly enjoy revenue-raising powers, not even the power to precept on Welsh or Northern Irish local authorities, while the Scottish Parliament enjoys merely the power to raise 3p in the pound in income tax, a negligible amount.

England, which is the largest component of the United Kingdom, containing around 85% of the population, has no devolved body, and calls for an English Parliament enjoy little resonance (see Chen & Wright 2000). There are, currently, proposals for regional assemblies in regions that indicate a significant level of support for them, as shown by a positive response in a referendum. At the time of writing, only one referendum is planned, in November 2004, in the northeast region. Regional assemblies, were they to come into existence, would have no legislative powers at all, not even powers over secondary legislation, and would be entrusted with only a severely limited range of functions, over such matters as economic development, transport, land use and regional planning, and environmental protection and public health. They would not have powers over such politically sensitive areas as the National Health Service, nor education, except possibly for some powers over further education. They would have no revenue-raising powers. Possibly, such assemblies, were they to come into existence, would gradually expand their powers. At present, however, they seem more in the nature of local authorities than genuinely devolved bodies. The same is true of the mayor of London and the London Assembly, whose functions lie primarily in the area of transport and who have no independent revenue-raising powers either, although the mayor can precept for funds from the London boroughs. The best account of the government of London is to be found in Travers (2004).

These variations between different parts of the United Kingdom may perhaps be defended as a response to dissimilar conditions in different parts of the country. The outcome, however, is, as former Home Secretary Douglas Hurd (2001) has pointed out, "a system of amazing untidiness—a Kingdom of four parts, of three Secretaries of State [for Scotland, Wales, and Northern Ireland] each with different powers, of two Assemblies and one Parliament, each different in composition and powers from the others."

Devolution poses once again two fundamental constitutional questions, first raised many years ago by Dicey (1887, 1889, 1893, 1912) in a series of polemics. The first question is whether devolution—or Home Rule as it was termed in the nineteenth century—is a constitutional category at all. Is there really a via media, other than federalism, between the unitary state and separatism? The second question is whether asymmetrical devolution, with its inevitable corollary of different rights and obligations in different parts of the polity, can yield a stable answer to "the British Question." Aughey (2001), in a most stimulating and insightful account of the challenges to the integrity of the United Kingdom posed by globalization, the European Union, and devolution, regards the British Question as "the central question at the start of the twenty-first century" just as the Irish Question was "the central question at the beginning of the twentieth century" (p. vii). Whether devolution will preserve the United Kingdom—or whether, alternatively, it should be characterized, as polemicist Tom Nairn (2000) suggests, as "Four Nations and a (British) Funeral"—is still very much an open question.

The Labour government adopted the policy of devolution to avoid separatism. The Dicey analysis, however, would hold that devolution is a mirage, which will lead inevitably to the breakup of the kingdom. On this basic issue, many journalists and others have rushed to judgment. It is, however, particularly difficult to make a judgment of any value at the present time because the Labour government at Westminster is dealing with politically congruent administrations in Scotland and Wales—a Labour/Liberal coalition in Edinburgh and a Labour administration, preceded by a Labour/Liberal coalition, in Cardiff. The true test of devolution will come when the devolved administrations find themselves in opposition to the government in London—that is, when a Labour administration in Scotland faces a Conservative government in London, or when a Labour administration in London faces a Scottish National Party administration in Scotland. Until then, judgments can be little more than guesswork. More than 20 years ago, Rose (1982) argued that the United Kingdom was held together by functional concerns, by a common approach to social and economic matters. It is by no means clear that these concerns are any less common in a postdevolution world. The devolved bodies, however, have already developed different policies to deal with these concerns. In Scotland, for example, there is a more generous system of student support than in England, and residential care for the elderly is, by contrast with England, free. Thus, devolution so far has threatened not so much the unity of the kingdom, but, as many socialists feared, the principle, fundamental to the British welfare state, that benefits and burdens should be distributed on the basis of need and not of geography (Bogdanor 2001).

At first sight, it may not be clear why the government adopted the policy of asymmetrical devolution, rather than implementing a tidy federal solution. The reason is that the English majority in the United Kingdom has always resisted federalism, there being little demand for an English Parliament and insufficient regional feeling in areas such as the populous southeast to make federalism on a regional basis appear a viable option. It is for this reason, the very considerable differences in the demand for devolution in different parts of the country, that the policy had to be an asymmetrical one. Moreover, the government decided that, even for those areas where it would establish devolved bodies— Scotland, Wales, and Northern Ireland—it would devolve power rather than divide it in a federal manner. But perhaps the difference between delegating or devolving power and dividing power may be less significant than at first sight appears.

The formal difference between devolution and federalism is of course perfectly clear. Federalism provides for a legal division of powers (Wheare 1963), whereas devolution provides for a mere handing down of power—a handing down that can in theory be revoked. In fact it was revoked, in the case of a previous experiment with devolution in Northern Ireland, in 1972, when the Northern Ireland Parliament, in the somewhat pathological circumstances of community breakdown, was prorogued and then abolished. Calvert (1968) offers an excellent account of that experiment—the most rigorous account of the constitutional aspects of devolution that has yet been written. The reasons for the breakdown of the experiment can be found in standard histories of the province (e.g., Bardon 1992, Hennessey 1997).

Yet, although the difference between federalism and devolution is perfectly clear in constitutional terms, Bogdanor (1979, 1999a, 2003b) has suggested that, in practical political terms, the categories almost merge. He suggested that the devolved bodies, and particularly the Scottish Parliament, would operate vis-à-vis Westminster so as to yield a "quasi-federal" system of government. He argued that devolution was similar to federalism in that both provided for the establishment of directly elected bodies, with a judicial body—in Britain the Judicial Committee of the Privy Council—as the final adjudicator on constitutional disputes. Moreover, the devolved bodies established in 1998, in contrast to the Northern Ireland Parliament established in 1921, were legitimized through referendums, and it would be difficult to abolish them against the wishes of the people in Scotland, Wales, or Northern Ireland. It would be difficult to abolish them without further referendums. So although, in theory, the devolved bodies could be unilaterally abolished by Westminster, in practice, they were probably entrenched politically. If that was so, then the devolution legislation was in the nature of a higher law, the basis perhaps for a codified constitution for the various territories of the United Kingdom.

An Oxford doctoral thesis prepared under Bogdanor's supervision (Horgan 2003), and using the framework of "executive federalism" derived from Watts (1999), found remarkable similarities between the position of a devolved Scotland in the United Kingdom and Quebec in federal Canada in terms of the machinery of intergovernmental relations. The brief experience of devolution seems to confirm that the sovereignty of the Westminster Parliament over domestic matters in Scotland and Wales is, at the very least, severely qualified. The sovereignty of Parliament has now come to mean something very different in Scotland, and even in Wales, from what it continues to mean in England. In England, the sovereignty of Parliament continues to correspond to a genuine supremacy over "all persons, matters and things." In Scotland, by contrast, it is coming to mean little more than a vague right of supervision over the Scottish Parliament, together perhaps with the power in a pathological situation, such as afflicted Northern Ireland in 1972, to abolish that Parliament. Thus, except perhaps during periods of crisis, the formal assertion of parliamentary sovereignty could easily become empty, since it will no longer be accompanied by the political supremacy that gives it life. If this argument is correct, then the term "devolution" may be misleading. It implies a mere delegation of powers, but in practice it divides the power to legislate, creating a quasi-federal relationship between the devolved bodies and Westminster.

Westminster itself has become, for Scotland, Wales, and Northern Ireland, a quasi-federal parliament. For MPs now play little part in legislating for the domestic affairs of Scotland and Northern Ireland, and their role with regard to Wales is confined to the scrutiny of primary legislation. Only with regard to England do MPs continue to enjoy the power, which hitherto they have enjoyed over the whole of the United Kingdom, of scrutinizing both primary and secondary legislation over all matters. Thus, Westminster is no longer a Parliament for the domestic and nondomestic affairs of the United Kingdom; it has been transformed into a parliament for England, a federal parliament for Scotland and Northern Ireland, and a parliament for primary legislation for Wales. Westminster has become the quasi-federal parliament of a quasi-federal state.

ELECTORAL REFORM AND PROPORTIONAL REPRESENTATION

The devolution legislation provided that the method of election to be used for the devolved bodies should be, not the traditional first-past-the-post system, but a variant of the German method of proportional representation. The same method is used in the election of the London Assembly, and it will also be used in the election of English regional assemblies, should any come into existence. It has probably come to be accepted that elections to any body other than the House of Commons or a local authority should be by proportional representation; moreover, the Scottish Parliament is currently proposing to introduce the single-transferable-vote method of proportional representation for elections to local authorities in Scotland, and this same system has been used for local elections in Northern Ireland since 1973.

In 1997, the Labour government established an Independent Commission on the Voting System to consider alternative systems for electing the House of Commons. It was chaired by Lord Jenkins, the Liberal Democrat leader in the House of Lords. This Commission reported in 1998 and recommended that Britain adopt the alternative vote to be topped up by list proportional representation on a county and city basis so as to secure greater proportionality [Independent Commission on the Voting System (1998), analyzed by McLean (1999) and Dunleavy & Margetts (1999), and criticized by Pinto-Duschinsky (1999)]. The government is committed to holding a referendum on reform of the electoral system for Westminster elections, but it proposes first to review the experience of the new voting systems. No date has been set for the referendum.

These are, nevertheless, remarkable developments. For, until the 1970s, it was generally assumed that the first-past-the-post electoral system was the natural one for Britain to use. Opposition to it was confined almost wholly to the Liberal Party, then in decline, and the arguments of Liberals could easily be dismissed as special pleading. In 1964, A.H. Birch fairly summed up the state of the argument by declaring that in Britain "the electoral system is no longer a bone of convention" (Birch 1964, p. 227). There are now, however, no fewer than four different electoral systems in operation in Britain in addition to the first-past-the-post system:[3]

1. The single-transferable-vote method of proportional representation used in all elections in Northern Ireland, except elections to the House of Commons, and currently being proposed for elections to local authorities in Scotland.

2. A system of proportional representation based on the German method, used for elections to the Scottish Parliament, the National Assembly of Wales, and the London Assembly.

3. The regional-list method of proportional representation used for elections to the European Parliament.

4. The supplementary vote—a variant of the alternative vote—used for elections for the mayor of London.

Thus, whereas at the beginning of the twentieth century Britain had enjoyed a uniform electoral system but a diversified franchise, by the century's end, the opposite was true. A uniform franchise was now accompanied by a diversity of electoral systems. A useful history of the British electoral system in the twentieth century can be found in Curtice (2003).

There have been just two elections to each of the devolved bodies, and it is, therefore, far too early to attempt to draw any general conclusions concerning the consequences of proportional representation. There have, however, been various attempts at an interim assessment. The most authoritative is a report of the Commission established by the Constitution Unit, *Changed Voting Changed Politics* (Constitution Unit 2004). The co-chairman of the Commission was the well-known political scientist David Butler, and the Commission included other experts on electoral matters. The Commission and various researchers (Cowley et al. 2001, Curtice & Steed 2000, Seyd 2004) have reached broadly similar conclusions. It was generally agreed that voters had no difficulty in understanding the mechanics of the new voting methods but were less informed on their systemic aspects, and in particular on how votes were actually translated into seats. Only a minority of voters understood that it was the second or list vote which determined the number of seats a party won, and not the first, constituency vote. Some voters believed that the second vote was a second *preference* vote rather than a list vote; similar findings have been reported in Germany. There was, however, evidence (albeit limited) that

---

[3]Bogdanor (1997a) and the Constitution Unit (2004) provide a standard account of the various voting systems. Analytical and comparative accounts of the effects of various electoral systems are available in well-known works by Taagepera & Shugart (1989) and Lijphart (1994).

some voters in Scotland and Wales were splitting their tickets, supporting Labour on the constituency vote but the Liberal Democrats on the list vote so as to signal a desire for a Labour/Liberal Democrat coalition—which was in fact the outcome in Scotland following the 1999 and 2004 elections, and in Wales from 2000 to 2004, after a brief and unconvincing experiment with minority government.

Coalition government in Scotland and Wales had proved fairly stable, and it had not proved very difficult to achieve acceptable compromises between the coalition partners. Yet there was no real evidence, in Scotland at least, of consensus building between the executive and the opposition parties, and so it did not seem that proportional representation had affected the working of the Scottish Parliament to the extent that a number of commentators—including the present writer—had predicted. Experience of proportional representation in Scotland and Wales, far from offering any definitive answers to the debate on proportional representation to Westminster, will therefore probably serve to entrench already existing attitudes. The debate will continue.

THE HUMAN RIGHTS ACT AND PARLIAMENTARY SOVEREIGNTY

The Human Rights Act, like devolution, posed the problem of how constitutional reform could be made compatible with the principle of parliamentary sovereignty. The European Convention of Human Rights was drawn up, in large part as a result of British influence, and signed in Rome in 1950. Britain was the first country to ratify it, in 1951, and it came into force in 1953. For a history of the drafting of the Convention, see the monumental work by Simpson (2001). The European Convention has nothing to do with the European Union, and it was drawn up not by the European Community, which did not exist in 1950, but by the Council of Europe, a purely intergovernmental organization. The institutions of the Convention—a Commission and a Court of Human Rights—are based in Strasbourg. The Court of Justice of the European Union, by contrast, is based in Luxembourg.

The Council of Europe, unlike the European Union, has no power to make laws. The Convention, therefore, unlike the law of the European Union, can have no direct effect on British law, nor can it be binding upon the member states. Nevertheless, many member states chose to incorporate it into their domestic law. In Britain, the Convention did not become part of British law and was not enforceable in the courts. But, in 1966, the government granted individuals the right to petition the Strasbourg court directly, and, where the Court has ruled in favor of the litigant, the government has agreed to amend the law accordingly. Nevertheless, the appeal to Strasbourg was both a lengthy and an expensive process. It seemed odd that British litigants had to appeal to a foreign court in order to secure their rights. To enable British citizens to avail themselves of Convention rights in British courts would not, therefore, mean creating new rights, but would rather involve, in the words of a Labour Party consultation document, *Bringing Rights Home* (Straw & Boateng 1996). The bill itself was accompanied by a government White Paper entitled *Rights Brought Home* (Home Office 1997), and the preamble to the Human Rights Act described it as an "Act to give further effect to rights and freedoms guaranteed under the European Convention of Human Rights."

The difficulty was that, were the Convention to be incorporated into British law, judges would be able to strike down Acts of Parliament that contravened it. Such a provision, although of course unexceptionable in the United States, would have amounted to a constitutional revolution in Britain. Moreover, it was alleged that British judges did not actually seek such a power, since they did not want to be put in a position of confronting the government. Thus, the government adopted a model for the protection of human rights that, although based in part on New Zealand experience, "is not (yet) replicated by any other state" (Klug 2000, p. 164). Klug provides a most valuable general introduction to the significance of the Human Rights Act. See also Lester & Clapinska (2004) for a balanced account of the Act. Lord Lester was one of Britain's leading campaigners for the incorporation of the European Convention. A more critical point of view can be found in Campbell et al. (2001).

British courts enjoy, under the Act, for the first time, the power to review Acts of Parliament for compliance with the standards of the Convention. When introducing legislation into Parliament, ministers are required to certify that, in their belief, it complies with the Convention. The courts are required to interpret all legislation, whether passed before or after the Human Rights Act, so that it is compatible with Convention rights. If, however, legislation cannot be so interpreted, then the courts in England and Wales—the situation in Scotland and Northern Ireland is somewhat different and is described in the next paragraph—must issue a declaration of incompatibility. The offending statute is not struck down, and it remains part of the law. But Parliament is given the power to amend or repeal it by a fast-track method, through secondary legislation, using a remedial order. Should Parliament fail to do so—and it is not difficult to imagine circumstances in which it might be unwilling, if, for example, a highly unpopular minority (e.g., suspected terrorists or pedophiles) were involved—the litigant could still appeal to Strasbourg with every hope that Strasbourg would confirm the verdict of the English or Welsh court. Even then, however, there would be no obligation on Parliament to accept the verdict of Strasbourg, although it has always done so in the past. It would thus be wrong to say that the European Convention has been incorporated into English law. It does not become part of the law, and the Convention is not directly justiciable. The Human Rights Act is in the nature of an interpretation clause, directing judges on how they should interpret legislation that might affect human rights. But there is no domestic remedy for anyone whose rights are infringed, and Article 13 of the European Convention, which declares that "Everyone whose rights and freedoms as set forth in this Convention are violated shall have an effective remedy before a national authority," is not part of the Human Rights Act. A senior American judge, to whom I described these provisions, expressed some astonishment, declaring that, if redress for violations of the Bill of Rights required endorsement by Congress, the Bill of Rights would not be worth very much. It seems, however, from preliminary analysis, that Parliament is in fact likely to give effect to the decisions of judges, except perhaps in highly pathological circumstances, and that there may be less difference in practice between the Bill of Rights as interpretation clause, as in Britain, and a statutory Bill of Rights in a country that nevertheless retains the doctrine of parliamentary sovereignty, as in New Zealand (see Allan 2001). To the extent that ministers and Parliament do uphold human rights, the Human Rights Act will, like the devolution legislation, take on the character of a higher law, something hitherto unknown in the British Constitution.

In Scotland and Northern Ireland, the situation is somewhat different because the devolved bodies (which are, of course, by contrast with Westminster, nonsovereign parliaments) are required by the devolution legislation—the Scotland Act 1998 and the Northern Ireland Act 1998—to observe the European Convention. It would be *ultra vires* for the Scottish Parliament or the Northern Ireland Assembly to legislate contrary to the Human Rights Act, and Scottish and Northern Irish judges are required to strike down law that is incompatible with it. The Convention has thus been incorporated into Scottish and Northern Irish law.

The Human Rights Act came into force in 2000, and it is far too early to form any genuine estimate of its long-term consequences. An early estimate of the likely impact can, however, be found in Markesinis (1998). Statistics on the working of the Act so far can be found on the website of the Department for Constitutional Affairs, http://www.dca.gov.uk/hract/statistics.htm, and details of declarations of incompatibility on http://www.dca.gov.uk/decihm.htm. Statistics from this latter site show that there have so far been 15 declarations of incompatibility, of which 5 have been overturned on appeal. Action has been taken by the government or Parliament on all of the remaining 10. More important, however, than this small number of declarations of incompatibility is the fact that the judges are now enjoined to interpret statutes in terms of the Human Rights Act.

The British courts, however, like the U.S. Supreme Court since 1937, have in general followed a doctrine of deference to the legislature. "It is...important," declared Lord Woolf, the Lord Chief Justice, in the case *R v Lambert, Ali and Jordan* [2000] 2 WLR 211, para. 17, "to bear in mind that legislation is passed by a democratically elected Parliament and therefore the Courts under the Convention should, as a matter of constitutional principle, pay a degree of deference to the view of Parliament as to what is in the interest of the public generally when upholding the rights of the individual under the Convention." The courts have generally adopted the doctrine of the "margin of appreciation" in considering legislation, accepting that there can, legitimately, be alternative interpretations of Convention rights. The U.S. Supreme Court similarly developed the doctrine of self-restraint during the New Deal. It is possible, however, that the courts may adopt a more stringent view when what judges regard as basic or fundamental rights are in question. In the case *R v DPP exp Kebilene* [1999] 3 WLR 972 at 994, Lord Hope of Craighead declared, "It will be easier for it [deference] to be recognized where the questions involve issues of social or economic policy, much less so where the rights are of high constitutional importance or are of a kind where the courts are especially well placed to assess the need for protection." Such a doctrine, of course, bears some similarity to the doctrine of preferred freedoms enunciated in Footnote Four—perhaps the most famous footnote in Supreme Court history—in *US v Carolene Products Co.* 304 US 144 1938.

It has been rightly said that the Human Rights Act will cause "a paradigm shift in the foundations of British constitutional law" (Edwards 2002, p. 866). For our traditional understanding of rights is that they derive from specific statutes and legal decisions; they have not been conceived of as deriving from any general principles. "There is," Dicey ([1885] 1959) wrote, "in the English [sic] constitution an absence of those declarations or definitions of rights so dear to foreign constitutionalists" (p. 144). Instead, the principles defining our civil liberties are "like all maxims established by judicial legislation, mere generalisations drawn either from the decisions or dicta of judges, or from statutes." By contrast, "most foreign constitution-makers have begun with declarations of rights. For this they have often been in no wise to blame."

The consequence, however, is that

> the relation of the rights of individuals to the principles of the constitution is not quite the same in countries like Belgium, where the constitution is the result of a legislative act, as in England, where the constitution itself is based on legal decisions—the difference in this matter between the constitutions of Belgium and the English constitution may be described by the statement that in Belgium individual rights are deductions drawn from the principles of the constitution, while in England the so-called principles of the constitution are inductions or generalisations based upon particular decisions pronounced by the courts as to the rights of given individuals. (Dicey [1885] 1959, p. 144)

The Human Rights Act, however, radically alters this situation, for our rights are in future to be derived not inductively but from "the principles of the constitution," i.e., the European Convention. The interpretation of these rights will increasingly be determined by judges, who will be interpreting legislation in the light of what a High Court judge, Sir John Laws, in *Thorburn v Sunderland City Council* [2002] 3 WLR 247, called a "constitutional statute," a form perhaps of higher law. Yet Dicey famously declared that there could be no higher law in the British Constitution. "There is no law which Parliament cannot change. There is no fundamental or so-called constitutional law," and no person or body "can pronounce void any enactment passed by the British Parliament on the ground of such enactment being opposed to the constitution" (Dicey [1885] 1959, pp. 88, 91). Formally, of course, these propositions remain true, since the Human Rights Act succeeds in preserving parliamentary sovereignty. Nevertheless, that sovereignty could, insofar as human rights are concerned, become little more than the grin on the Cheshire cat. For the Human Rights Act in effect makes the European Convention part of the fundamental law of the land and brings the modalities of legal argument into the politics of the British state.

REFORM OF THE HOUSE OF LORDS

The Labour Party has always been ambivalent about the House of Lords, which was until the introduction of life peers in 1958 a purely hereditary chamber, with the exception of the law lords and the bishops. Although the Party could not accept any justification for a nonelected second chamber, it appreciated that a more rationally composed upper house would be able to use its powers more forcefully to challenge a Labour government. In practice, therefore, until the late 1960s, Labour's policy toward the upper house was one of reducing its powers rather than rationalizing its composition. In 1968–1969, however, Harold Wilson's Labour government produced a complex and probably unworkable scheme of reform by which the government was given considerable, and some believed excessive, powers of patronage over appointments. The scheme, although supported by the official Conservative opposition, was defeated in the Commons by a back-bench combination of Right and Left, which was broad enough to include the Right-wing Conservative MP, Enoch Powell, who wanted the Lords preserved as it was, and the Left-wing Labour MP, Michael Foot, who wanted it abolished entirely [the story of this ill-fated piece of legislation is well told by Morgan (1975)].

By the time of the 1992 general election, however, which Labour lost, the Party had become committed to a directly elected second chamber. But it recoiled from implementing so drastic a solution immediately, and in 1994, Tony Blair, during his campaign for the Labour leadership, proposed a two-stage reform. The first stage would involve disenfranchising the hereditary peers, who comprised around two thirds of the House, "within months." This would be followed by some method of elucidating consensus on a second stage, such as a Royal Commission. Bogdanor (1997a) gives the details up to 1997 (see Ch. 4), and a book coauthored by a former Labour Leader of the House of Lords provides a good account of the arguments for reform (Richard & Welfare 1999).

Once Blair took office, the policy changed again, and an agreement was reached with the Conservatives, despite the opposition of that party's leadership, that 92 hereditary peers, to be elected from among their number, would remain until the second stage was actually carried out. Upon the death of a hereditary peer, a replacement would be elected from the hereditary peers as a whole, who would thus remain in existence as an electoral college. The Conservatives hoped that this peculiar arrangement would guarantee that a second stage of reform would actually be carried out, since Labour would not wish to countenance the continued existence of the hereditary peers in any form, even in the shadowy form of an electoral college. The House of Lords is currently composed of nearly 600 life peers and 92 hereditaries. It is perhaps a peculiarly British paradox that the hereditary peers are the only members of the upper house to be elected.

The Labour government established a Royal Commission chaired by the former Conservative minister, Lord Wakeham, to make recommendations for a second stage. The Royal Commission reported in 2000. It did not recommend a wholly elected chamber, but sought instead an evolutionary solution that would make the House of Lords more legitimate and therefore more generally acceptable.

The Royal Commission proposed, first, to disconnect the second chamber both from the honors system and from party patronage. Honors would continue to be granted to reward merit and achievement, but they would not entitle the holder to a seat in the second chamber. Patronage would be greatly limited because a statutory Appointments Commission would be created that would be required to nominate all appointed peers, and to ensure that the party composition of the Lords reflected the balance of votes—not of seats—cast at the most recent general election. The Appointments Commission would also be required to ensure that at least 20% of those appointed were cross-benchers; that at least 30% of those appointed were women; and that the second chamber represented effectively the main ethnic minorities and also religious faiths and denominations other than the established Church of England. Appointees would hold office for 15 years and would be ineligible to stand for the House of Commons for 10 years after retiring from the upper house, so preventing them using it as an apprenticeship for a career in professional politics.

The Royal Commission proposed that, in addition to the nominated members, there should be an elected element. Its members could not, however, agree on how large this element should be, although it was agreed that the elected members should comprise a minority of the whole. Under the most popular option, there would be 87 elected members (16% of the membership), but some members of the Royal Commission believed that the number should be 65 (12% of the membership), and others believed that it should be 195 (35%). Those who favored 87 or 195 elected members believed that they should be elected on a staggered basis at each round of European Parliament elections in one third of Britain's twelve nations and regions; those who favored just 65 elected members believed that they should be chosen from a list based on votes cast at the most recent general election. The reformed second chamber would be constructed so as to be dominated neither by the government, which would make it a compliant rubber-stamp, nor by the opposition, which could lead to endless constitutional conflict. Instead the balance would, almost always, be held by the nominated cross-bench peers (see Royal Commission 2000).

Not surprisingly, perhaps, this complex and artificial scheme found little favor. In 2003, the House of Commons was presented with various options but chose to reject them all, although opinion among Labour back-benchers seemed sympathetic to a chamber composed predominantly of elected members [see McLean et al. (2003) for an analysis of the vote]. Nevertheless, radical reform of the Lords now seems unlikely. The government, unsurprisingly, seems to have lost such appetite as it may have had for fundamental reform, and its policy, at the time of writing, is to propose legislation to remove the 92 remaining hereditary peers. The House of Lords would then be composed entirely of nominated members.

The failure to secure a radical reform of the House of Lords must be seen against the background of problems faced in other bicameral democracies. Most stable democracies of any size are bicameral. Among nations that have been democratic for more than 25 years, Portugal, with a population of around 10 million, is the largest unicameral state. Russell (2000) provides comprehensive information on seven second chambers—those of Australia, Canada, France, Germany, Ireland, Italy, and Spain. She lays out, in tabular form, comparative information on such matters as size, composition, method of election, and powers of the various second chambers, and she describes the procedures used for the resolution of disputes when the second chamber disagrees with the first. Her central conclusion is that, for a second chamber to be effective, it must be composed differently from the first, it must enjoy sufficient power to require a government to think again, and it must enjoy sufficient legitimacy in the eyes of the public so that it can actually use its powers.

In a valuable comparative survey of second chambers, Patterson & Mughan (1999) refer to upper houses as "essentially contested institutions." Few democracies are happy with them, and many are engaged "in an apparently incessant dialogue about how they should be reformed." Indeed, among the countries whose second chambers were considered, Germany and the United States appeared to be almost unique in having no campaign that seeks to reform the upper house. Since Patterson & Mughan wrote, however, Germany too has been considering whether to reform the Bundesrat, which seems to be making it increasingly difficult for government to operate effectively. The United States, then, may now be the only major democracy that is happy with its upper house.

The problem in any bicameral system is how to ensure that the upper house enjoys democratic legitimacy. An effective second chamber in a modern parliamentary democracy must exemplify an alternative principle of representation to that embodied in the first chamber. This is a problem that seems easier to resolve in a federal than in a unitary state, since in a federal state, an alternative to the principle of the representation of individuals immediately suggests itself—namely, the representation of territory. That is the logic which many would like Britain to follow, if it moves further toward federalism with assemblies in the English regions. In practice, however, the directly elected Senate in Australia represents less the interests of the territorial units, the states, than the interests of the state parties—an outcome that had been foreseen by one of Australia's founding fathers, Alfred Deakin, in the discussions on federation in Australia at the end of the nineteenth century. "The people," he predicted, "will divide themselves into two parties. The instant Federation is accomplished the two Houses will be elected on that basis. State rights and state interests...will never be mentioned" (Russell 2000, p. 210). Thus, even a directly elected second chamber in a federal state might, instead of yielding effective territorial representation, provide just another home for a second set of professional politicians, not differing in any significant respect from those elected to the first chamber. If the answer is more politicians, former British Prime Minister John Major is reputed to have said, you are asking the wrong question. The problem of finding an effective basis for a second chamber in a modern democracy remains as intractable now as it was at the beginning of Labour's term of office in 1997. For this reason, the House of Lords is likely to continue to fulfil the function it performed during the Napoleonic wars, if Gilbert and Sullivan's comic opera *Iolanthe* is to be believed.

> When Wellington thrashed Bonaparte,
> As every child can tell,
> The House of Peers throughout the war
> Did nothing in particular,
> And did it very well.

THE BRITISH CONSTITUTION AS A PUZZLE

Tocqueville famously remarked that there was no British constitution. "In England [sic], the Parliament has an acknowledged right to modify the constitution; as, therefore, the constitution may undergo perpetual change, it does not in reality exist; the Parliament is at once a legislative and constituent assembly" (Tocqueville 1835, Pt. 1, ch. 6, p. 169). It may be, however, that Tocqueville's remark is no longer true. It may be that Parliament is no longer a constituent assembly, insofar at least as devolution and human rights are concerned; although it retains, of course, the somewhat theoretical right of repealing the devolution legislation or the Human Rights Act.

Until 1973, when Britain entered the European Community, and perhaps even until 1997, the British Constitution could have been formulated in just eight words—what the Queen in Parliament enacts is law. If, however, statutes such as the European Communities Act of 1972, the devolution legislation of 1998, and the Human Rights Act of 1998 take on the function of higher laws, such a description may no longer be adequate. Yet Britain is still far from having a codified constitution, and it remains one of just three democracies, along with New Zealand and Israel, not to have one. The British, therefore, are living in a half-way house, suspended between the old "historic" constitution and a fully codified one, between a world that is dead and one that is waiting to be born. A member of the Committee on Standards in Public Life told historian Peter Hennessy that the British seemed actually to "like to live in a series of half-way houses" (Hennessy 1995, p. 184). It is possible, therefore, that the British will have to get used to living in a series of half-way houses for some considerable period of time until the foundations of these houses have been fully tested by experience. What is clear is that the British Constitution can no longer be described in straightforward or unambiguous terms—for an attempt at analyzing the broad direction of twentieth century experience, see Bogdanor (2004). The British Constitution has become a puzzle. Perhaps it always was one. There is at least one distinguished authority on the British Constitution who thinks so. The Queen, cited by Hennessy (1995), once declared, "The British Constitution has always been puzzling and always will be." That remark is even more true now than when it was made.

NOTE ADDED IN PROOF

In November 2004, proposals for a regional assembly in the northeast were defeated by a majority of around 4 to 1 on a turnout of 48%. The government responded by abandoning further plans for regional devolution in England.

ACKNOWLEDGMENT

I am grateful to my colleague, Anne Davies, Fellow in Law at Brasenose College, for her helpful comments on an earlier draft. But she is not to be implicated in my arguments or conclusions.

The *Annual Review of Political Science* is online at
http://polisci.annualreviews.org

LITERATURE CITED

Allan J. 2001. The effect of a statutory bill of rights where Parliament is sovereign: the lesson from New Zealand. See Campbell et al. 2001, pp. 375–90

Aughey A. 2001. *Nationalism, Devolution and the Challenge to the United Kingdom State*. London: Pluto

Bagehot W. (1872) 1974. *The English Constitution*. 2nd ed. Vol. 5 in *The Collected Works of Walter Bagehot*, ed. N St. John-Stevas. London: Economist.

Bardon J. 1992. *A History of Ulster*. Belfast: Blackstaff

Birch AH. 1964. *Representative and Responsible Government*. London: Allen & Unwin

Birkinshaw P. 2001. *Freedom of Information: The Law, the Practice and the Ideal*. London: Butterworths. 3rd ed.

Bogdanor V. 1979. *Devolution*. Oxford, UK: Oxford Univ. Press

Bogdanor V. 1981. *The People and the Party System: The Referendum and Electoral Reform in British Politics*. Cambridge, UK: Cambridge Univ. Press

Bogdanor V. 1997a. *Power and the People: A Guide to Constitutional Reform*. London: Gollancz

Bogdanor V. 1997b. Labour and the constitution. Part 1: the record. In *New Labour in Power: Precedents and Prospects*, ed. B Brivati, T Bale, pp. 111–20. London: Routledge

Bogdanor V. 1999a. *Devolution in the United Kingdom*. Oxford, UK: Oxford Univ. Press

Bogdanor V. 1999b. The British-Irish Council and devolution. *Gov. Oppos.* 34:287–98

Bogdanor V. 2001. Constitutional reform. In *The Blair Effect: The Blair Government 1997–2001*, ed. A Seldon, pp. 139–56. London: Little Brown

Bogdanor V, ed. 2003a. *The British Constitution in the Twentieth Century*. Oxford, UK: Oxford Univ. Press for Br. Acad.

Bogdanor V. 2003b. Asymmetric devolution: towards a quasi-federal constitution? In *Developments in British Politics 7*, ed. P Dunleavy, A Gamble, R Heffernan, G Peele, pp. 222–41. Basingstoke: Palgrave Macmillan

Bogdanor V. 2004. Our new constitution. *Law Q. Rev.* 120:242–62

Bradley A. 2004. In *The Changing Constitution*, ed. J Jowell, D Oliver, pp. 26–61. Oxford, UK: Oxford Univ. Press. 5th ed.

Butler D, Ranney A, eds. 1994. *Referendums Around the World: The Growing Use of Direct Democracy.* Basingstoke: Macmillan

Calvert H. 1968. *Constitutional Law in Northern Ireland.* London: Stevens

Campbell T, Ewing K, Tomkins A, eds. 2001. *Sceptical Essays on Human Rights.* Oxford, UK: Oxford Univ. Press

Carmichael P, Dickson B, eds. 1999. *The House of Lords: Its Parliamentary and Judicial Roles.* Oxford, UK: Hart

Chen S, Wright A. 2000. *The English Question.* London: Fabian Soc.

Constitution Unit. 2004. *Changed Voting Changed Politics: Lessons of Britain's Experience of PR Since 1997: Final Report of the Independent Commission to Review Britain's Experience of PR Voting Systems.* London: Constitution Unit

Constitution Unit and Electoral Reform Society. 1996. *Report of the Commission on the Conduct of Referendums.* London: Constitution Unit

Cowley P, Curtice J, Lochore S, Seyd B. 2001. *What We Already Know: Lessons on Voting Reform from Britain's PR Elections.* London: Constitution Unit

Curtice J. 2003. The electoral system. In *The British Constitution in the Twentieth Century*, ed. V Bogdanor, pp. 483–520. Oxford, UK: Oxford Univ. Press

Curtice J, Steed M. 2000. And now for the Commons? Lessons from Britain's first experience with proportional representation. *Br. Elect. Parties Rev.* 10:192–213

Dicey AV. (1885) 1959. *Introduction to the Study of the Law of the Constitution.* London: Macmillan. 10th ed.

Dicey AV. (1887) 1973. *England's Case Against Home Rule.* Richmond, UK: Richmond

Dicey AV. 1889. *Letters on Unionist Delusions.* London: Macmillan

Dicey AV 1893. *A Leap in the Dark.* London: John Murray

Dicey AV. 1912. *A Fool's Paradise.* London: John Murray

Dunleavy P, Margetts H. 1999. Mixed electoral systems in Britain and the Jenkins Commission on Electoral Reform. *Br. J. Politics Int. Relat.* 1:12–38

Edwards R. 2002. Judicial deference under the Human Rights Act. *Mod. Law Rev.* 65:859–82

Electoral Commission. 2001. *Election 2001: The Official Results.* London: Politico's

Evans M. 1995. *Charter 88: A Successful Challenge to the British Political Tradition?* Aldershot, UK: Dartmouth

Evans M. 2003. *Constitution-Making and the Labour Party.* Basingstoke: Palgrave Macmillan

Ewing K. 2001. Transparency, accountability and equality: the Political Parties Elections and Referendums Act, 2000. *Public Law* 542–57

Foley M. 1999. *The Politics of the British Constitution.* Manchester, UK: Manchester Univ. Press

Gallagher M, Uleri PV. 1996. *The Referendum Experience in Europe.* Basingstoke: Macmillan

Goldsworthy J. 1999. *The Sovereignty of Parliament: History and Philosophy.* Oxford, UK: Clarendon

Griffith JAG. 1997. *The Politics of the Judiciary.* London: Fontana. 5th ed.

Griffith JAG. 2000. The brave new world of Sir John Laws. *Mod. Law Rev.* 63:159–76

Hailsham Lord. 1978. *The Dilemma of Democracy: Diagnosis and Prescription.* London: Collins

Hazell R, ed. 1999. *Constitutional Futures: A History of the Next Ten Years.* Oxford, UK: Oxford Univ. Press

Hazell R, ed. 2000. *The State and the Nations: The First Year of Devolution in the United Kingdom.* Thorverton, UK: Imprint Acad.

Hazell R, ed. 2003. *The State of the Nations 2003: The Third Year of Devolution in the United Kingdom.* Exeter, UK: Imprint Acad.

Hennessey T. 1997. *A History of Northern Ireland 1920–1996.* London: Macmillan

Hennessy P. 1995. *The Hidden Wiring.* London: Gollancz

Home Office. 1997. *Rights Brought Home: The Human Rights Bill*, Cmnd. 3782. London: Stationery Off.

Horgan G. 2003. *Intergovernmental relations in the devolved Great Britain: a comparative perspective with particular reference to Canada*. D.Phil. thesis. Oxford Univ.

Hurd D. 2001. *On from the elective dictatorship*. First Hailsham Lecture to the Society of Conservative Lawyers. London: Soc. Conserv. Lawyers

Independent Commission on the Voting System. 1998. *Report*. Cm. 4090-I: Evidence Cm. 4090-II. London: Stationery Off.

Johnson N. 2004. *Reshaping the British Constitution: Essays in Political Interpretation*. Basingstoke: Palgrave Macmillan

Jones B, Keating M. 1985. *Labour and the British State*. Oxford, UK: Clarendon

Jowell J, Oliver D, eds. 2000. *The Changing Constitution*. Oxford, UK: Oxford Univ. Press. 4th ed.

Jowell J, Oliver D, eds. 2004. *The Changing Constitution*. Oxford, UK: Oxford Univ. Press. 5th ed.

Klug F. 2000. *Values for a Godless Age: The Story of the United Kingdom's Bill of Rights*. London: Penguin

Le Sueur A. 2004. *Building the United Kingdom's New Supreme Court: National and Comparative Perspectives*. Oxford, UK: Oxford Univ. Press

Legal Studies. 2004. Constitutional innovation: the creation of a Supreme Court for the United Kingdom: domestic, comparative and international reflections. *Legal Stud.* 24 (Spec. issue)

Lester A, Clapinska L. 2004. Human rights and the British Constitution. See Jowell & Oliver 2004, pp. 62–87

Lijphart A. 1975. *The Politics of Accommodation: Pluralism and Democracy in the Netherlands*. Berkeley: Univ. Calif. Press. 2nd ed.

Lijphart A. 1977. *Democracy in Plural Societies: A Comparative Exploration*. New Haven, CT: Yale Univ. Press

Lijphart A. 1994. *Electoral Systems and Party Systems*. Oxford, UK: Oxford Univ. Press

Locke J. (1690) 1960. *Two Treatises of Government*, ed. P Laslett. Cambridge, UK: Cambridge Univ. Press

Low S. 1904. *The Governance of England*. London: T. Fisher Unwin

Magleby D. 1984. *Direct Legislation: Voting on Ballot Propositions in the United States*. Baltimore, MD: Johns Hopkins Univ. Press

Markesinis B, ed. 1998. *The Impact of the Human Rights Bill on English Law*. Oxford, UK: Oxford Univ. Press

Marshall G. 1984. *Constitutional Conventions: The Rules and Forms of Political Accountability*. Oxford, UK: Clarendon

Marshall G. 1997. The referendum: What, when and how? *Parliam. Aff.* 50:307–13

Marshall G. 2003. The Constitution: theory and interpretation. See Bogdanor 2003a, pp. 29–68

McLean I. 1999. The Jenkins Commission and the implications of electoral reform for the UK. *Gov. Oppos.* 34:143–60

McLean I, Sperling A, Russell M. 2003. None of the above: the UK House of Commons vote on reforming the House of Lords. *Polit. Q.* 74(Feb.):293–310

Morgan J. 1975. *The House of Lords and the Labour Government* 1964–1970. Oxford, UK: Clarendon

Nairn T. 2000. *After Britain*. London: Granta

Nicholas B. 1978. Fundamental rights and judicial review in France. *Public Law* 82–101, 155–77

Patterson SC, Mughan A, eds. 1999. *Senates: Bicameralism in the Contemporary World*. Columbus: Ohio State Univ. Press

Pinto-Duschinsky M. 1999. Send the rascals packing: defects of proportional representation and virtues of the Westminster model. *Representation* 36:113–38

Richard I, Welfare D. 1999. *Unfinished Business: Reforming the House of Lords*. London: Vintage

Rose R. 1982. *Understanding the United Kingdom*. London: Longman

Royal Commission on the Reform of the House of Lords. 2000. *A House for the Future.* (Wakeham chairman) Cm 4354. London: Stationery Off.

Ruane J, Todd J. 1999. *After the Good Friday Agreement: Analysing Political Change in Northern Ireland.* Dublin: Univ. College Dublin Press

Russell M. 2000. *Reforming the House of Lords: Lessons from Overseas.* Oxford, UK: Oxford Univ. Press for Constitution Unit

Seyd B. 2004. *Coalition Government in Scotland and Wales.* London: Constitution Unit

Shell D. 1992. *The House of Lords.* London: Harvester Wheatsheaf. 2nd ed.

Simpson AWB. 2001. *Human Rights and the End of Empire: Britain and the Genesis of the European Convention.* Oxford, UK: Oxford Univ. Press

Straw J, Boateng P. 1996. *Bringing Rights Home: Labour's Plan to Incorporate the European Convention on Human Rights into United Kingdom Law.* London: Labour Party

Sutherland K, ed. 2000. *The Rape of the Constitution?* Exeter, UK: Imprint Acad.

Taagepera R, Shugart M. 1989. *Seats and Votes: The Effects and Determinants of Electoral Systems.* New Haven, CT: Yale Univ. Press

Taylor M. 2000. Labour and the Constitution. In *Labour's First Century*, ed. D Tanner, P Thane, N Tiratsoo, pp. 151–80. Cambridge, UK: Cambridge Univ. Press

Tocqueville A. 1835. *De La Démocratie en Amérique.* Paris: Garnier-Flammarion

Travers A. 2004. *The Politics of London: Governing an Ungovernable City.* London: Macmillan Palgrave

Trench A, ed. 2001. *The State of the Nations 2001: The Second Year of Devolution in the United Kingdom.* Thorverton: Imprint Acad.

Trench A, ed. 2004. *Has Devolution Made a Difference? The State of the Nations 2004.* Exeter: Imprint Acad.

Watts RL. 1999. *Comparing Federal Systems.* Montreal: McGill-Queen's Univ. Press. 2nd ed.

Wheare KC. 1963. *Federal Government.* London: Oxford Univ. Press. 4th ed.

Wheeler-Booth M. 2003. The House of Lords. In *Parliament: Functions, Practice and Procedures*, ed. R Blackburn, A Kennon, M Wheeler-Booth. London: Sweet & Maxwell. 2nd ed.

Wilson Lord. 2004. The robustness of conventions in a time of modernisation and change. *Public Law* 407–20

Woodhouse D. 2001. *The Office of Lord Chancellor.* Oxford, UK: Hart

Worcester R, Mortimore R. 1999. *Explaining Labour's Landslide.* London: Politico's

Worcester R, Mortimore R. 2001. *Explaining Labour's Second Landslide.* London: Politico's

Annu. Rev. Polit. Sci. 2005. 08:99–119
doi: 10.1146/annurev.polisci.8.082103.104854
Copyright © 2005 by Annual Reviews. All rights reserved
First published online as a Review in Advance on Oct. 29, 2004

IMMIGRATION AND POLITICS

Wayne A. Cornelius[1] and Marc R. Rosenblum[2]

[1]*Center for Comparative Immigration Studies, University of California–San Diego,
La Jolla, California 92093-0548; email: wcorneli@ucsd.edu*
[2]*Department of Political Science, University of New Orleans, New Orleans,
Louisiana 70148; email: Marc.Rosenblum@uno.edu*

Key Words   international migration, immigration policy, refugees, asylum,
sovereignty

■ **Abstract**   With nearly one in ten residents of advanced industrialized states now
an immigrant, international migration has become a fundamental driver of social,
economic, and political change. We review alternative models of migratory behavior
(which emphasize structural factors largely beyond states' control) as well as models of immigration policy making that seek to explain the gaps between stated policy
and actual outcomes. Some scholars attempt to explain the limited efficacy of control
policies by focusing on domestic interest groups, political institutions, and the interaction among them; others approach the issue from an international or "intermestic"
perspective. Despite the modest effects of control measures on unauthorized flows of
economic migrants and asylum seekers, governments continue to determine the proportion of migrants who enjoy legal status, the specific membership rights associated
with different legal (and undocumented) migrant classes, and how policies are implemented. These choices have important implications for how the costs and benefits
of migration are distributed among different groups of migrants, native-born workers,
employers, consumers, and taxpayers.

IMMIGRATION AND POLITICS

At the dawn of the twenty-first century, close to 200 million individuals lived as
migrants outside their birth countries, up from 154 million in 1990; and nearly
one in ten residents of advanced industrialized states was an immigrant (United
Nations 2002). These numbers reflect increasing population movements into and
out of almost every state within the global political economy. Just as the 1990s saw
global trade and investment approach their highest levels since the first great period
of globalization (i.e., 1870–1913), so too have recent years brought a second epoch
of radical growth in global population flows. And just as heightened economic
integration prompted backlashes against globalization at each century's turn, so
too has the recent surge in international migration provoked widespread public
opposition in industrialized countries—although effective immigration controls
have rarely been put in place.

This essay reviews political science explanations for unmet demands for immigration control, and for variations in immigration policy more generally. We begin by reviewing the assumptions on which most models of immigration and politics are built—assumptions about why people migrate and about the impacts of immigration (real and perceived) within migrant-sending and migrant-receiving states. We then turn to models of immigration policy making. Although the recent gap between formally restrictive policies and de facto permissiveness in the immigration domain partly reflects structural and technological obstacles to effective policy making, most models that seek to explain immigration policy outcomes focus on domestic interest groups, political institutions, and/or international-level determinants of immigration regulations. Finally, we argue that even though states' ability to control inflows is imperfect, migration policy affects both the nature of migration and the distribution of its costs and benefits. Political scientists should continue to analyze this important issue.

DETERMINANTS OF INTERNATIONAL MIGRATION

The political science literature on international migration and immigration policy draws heavily on work by economists, sociologists, and demographers concerning the determinants and consequences of migration (see, e.g., Hammar et al. 1997, Faist 2000). First, the act of migrating across international borders is usually costly in economic, cultural, and human terms. Along the U.S.-Mexico border and in the maritime passages from North Africa to Spain, thousands of unauthorized migrants die each year in illegal entry attempts (Cornelius 2001, 2004). What motivates individuals (or larger aggregations of people) to undertake these risky trips? Answers may be divided into rational actor approaches and those that emphasize deeper structural factors, and a separate distinction should be made between voluntary and forced (i.e., refugee) migration.

Traditional approaches to explaining migration decisions are rooted in neoclassical economic rational actor models. Just as individuals choose goods and services by maximizing their economic utility through market arbitrage, so too do they choose careers based on real wages. When the returns to labor are sufficiently high in foreign markets, such that the expected increase in wages exceeds the cost of migration, rational individuals choose migration. Thus, neoclassical economics generally predicts that labor flows from low-wage/labor-rich states to higher-wage/labor-poor states (Borjas 1989, Chiswick 2000). There is ample evidence that migrants are broadly motivated by such economic differentials. Hanson & Spilimbergo (1999), for example, cite evidence that the U.S.-Mexican wage gap outperforms a wide range of other independent variables as a predictor of undocumented migration from Mexico to the United States.

Yet as Massey et al. (1998) observe, the simple neoclassical model fails to account for a number of apparent anomalies. Why, for example, does field research reveal high levels of circular migration, with successful immigrants often returning to their low-wage countries of origin after brief periods of employment in high-wage states (see, e.g., Tsuda 2003)? And if financial returns to investment in migration are greatest among the poorest individuals, why do migrants disproportionately come from families at the median of the local income distribution? Why do middle-developed regions and states export more workers per capita than the least developed? To address these questions, the "new economics of labor migration" takes families or households—rather than individuals—as the unit of analysis (Stark 1991, Bailey & Boyle 2004). From this perspective, groups of moderately well-off individuals invest in emigration among other tools for diversifying income streams and improving living standards. Emigration is viewed as an especially attractive strategy for residents of states that typically lack other forms of social insurance. The same individual-level models account equally well for permanent and temporary (guestworker) migration. Developing unique models of these different types of flows is particularly difficult because many "temporary" migrants eventually change their plans and settle permanently in host states.

A second school of thought emphasizes the underlying global economic structures that motivate individual (or group) decision making. From this perspective, global economic integration and the commercialization of agricultural production encourage migration by undermining traditional family structures and lowering demand for rural labor in traditional areas (Hatton & Williamson 1997, Massey et al. 1998). Global economic integration also lowers the cost of migration by creating new linkages between migrant-sending and migrant-receiving states (Sassen 1996), including international people-smuggling networks and legal labor brokerage services (Kyle & Koslowski 2001, Tsuda 2003). Thus, counterintuitively, economic development increases migratory pressure, at least in the short term (Stalker 1994, Martin 2001, Cornelius 2002a).

These migration "pushes" are complemented by structural "pulls" within migration host states. In particular, "dual labor markets" in industrialized states mean that the least attractive jobs are often reserved for immigrants (Piore 1979, Tsuda et al. 2003). These labor demands have intensified in the past two decades, and the aging of many industrialized states—especially new immigration states such as Italy, Spain, and Japan—suggests that they will continue to do so (Calavita 2004). Once certain types of low-wage manual jobs become associated with migrant labor, even relatively high unemployment rates do not produce a return of native workers to these sectors, owing to a combination of social conditioning and path-dependent labor recruitment methods. Thus, whole sectors of advanced industrial economies become structurally dependent on immigrant labor (Cornelius 1998). From a Marxist perspective, owners of capital also benefit from maintaining a category of job characterized by a flexible labor supply, allowing layoffs to minimize losses to capital during economic downturns.

A third structural factor that promotes the continuation of migration once it begins is the presence of transborder social networks. When migrant communities become well established in the receiving country, residents of a labor-exporting community gain social capital in the form of migration-related knowledge and resources, which encourages further migration (Waldinger 1997). According to the theory of "cumulative causation," once a critical threshold is surpassed, migration becomes self-perpetuating because each migration decision helps to create the social structure needed to sustain subsequent migration (Massey et al. 1998, Fussell & Massey 2004). More generally, migration systems theory seeks to explain migration flows as regional phenomena that reflect long-standing migratory patterns, economic integration across multiple dimensions, the development of ethnic-specific commercial niches (Chinese laundries, Korean groceries, etc.), and the policies of migrant-sending and -receiving states (Castles & Miller 2003).

These alternative models of migration flows are not mutually exclusive but rather suggest an overdetermined model that strongly predicts continued migration within such well-established migration systems as the Mexico/United States, Turkey/Germany, and Brazil/Japan systems. In these and similar cases, the combination of gross demographic and economic imbalances and decades of migratory flows insures that all three structural determinants of migration are in place (i.e., pushes, pulls, and transborder social networks), and that rational migrants (at the individual or group level) have both cause and means to migrate. It is no small irony, in light of recent migration control efforts, that many of today's strongest migratory systems were initiated through deliberate, government-sponsored recruitment of "guestworkers" during the 1940–1970 period (Reisler 1976, Massey & Liang 1989, Martin 2004).

Regardless of the extent to which the structural factors discussed above may or may not limit the choice sets for would-be migrants, analysts and policy makers typically distinguish between voluntary and forced migration. Voluntary migration involves discretionary migrants motivated by economic or family considerations, and forced migration refers to refugees forced from their homes by natural or human-made disasters. The distinction is theoretically important because humanitarian refugees are (in principle) entitled to additional legal protections through a number of national and international institutions. Yet, in practice, forced migrants confront decision-making challenges similar to those of voluntary migrants, and structural pushes, pulls, and transborder social networks exert a strong influence on migration decisions when humanitarian "push factors" are controlled for (Stalker 1999, Tamas 2004). For this reason, the line between forced and voluntary migration is often hazy, and distinguishing between legitimate humanitarian migrants and those making humanitarian claims primarily for the sake of gaining access to otherwise closed destination states has become a highly controversial dimension of immigration policy making in Europe and the United States (Joppke 1998a, Loescher 2002, Gibney 2004).

CONSEQUENCES OF IMMIGRATION

If immigration policy makers seek to respond to these underlying causes of migration, they presumably do so because of the real or perceived consequences of migratory inflows. Evidence suggests that "real or perceived" is an important distinction, as public attitudes about immigration reflect substantial misconceptions—though at least some of these apparent misconceptions actually reflect citizens' tendency to respond to migration on emotional (or affective) levels rather than on the basis of objective self-interest or personal experience.

What are the actual effects of immigration within host states? The most basic approach to this question is at the demographic level: How does immigration change the size and structure of receiving-state populations (Keely 2000)? Migrants are younger and more likely to produce large families than host-state populations, but current immigration levels are not high enough to address the population-aging crises that threaten many advanced industrial societies, especially in Europe and Japan (United Nations 2000). International migrants also exhibit an hourglass-shaped educational distribution: Most recent South-North migrants have education levels significantly below host-state medians, but a minority of them—highly skilled/professional migrants—are more educated than host-state citizens (Cornelius et al. 2001). Although ethnic differences between migrants and host-state populations alarm nativists today as they have during previous migratory waves (Brimelow 1995, Huntington 2004), the historical record shows that immigrants typically become fully integrated within host states after two or three generations—more quickly if supported by proactive immigrant integration policies at the national and local levels (Alba & Nee 2003, Joppke & Morawska 2003, Ireland 2004).

A second approach to evaluating the impact of immigration on host states focuses on economic impacts, measured in various ways. First, what is the macroeconomic impact of international migration within destination states? In general, immigration expands the labor force and lowers prices, supporting economic growth. Nonetheless, economists consider these effects quite modest relative to total host-state economies. In the U.S. case, a panel of economists estimated that immigration was contributing only about $10 billion per year, or about 0.2% of the U.S. gross domestic product (Smith & Edmonston 1997).

More heated debates focus on distributive questions, including whether immigrants consume more in public services than they pay in taxes. Progressive taxation implies that immigrants will be net fiscal consumers, since immigrant earnings average well below natives' incomes. Immigrants are likely to represent a net fiscal burden to the localities in which they settle, especially given that they are more likely than natives to have young families with school-age children who require expensive social services such as education and health care. Yet immigrants are also less likely than natives to draw social security payments, and the record on usage of other income support programs is mixed. In the United States, estimates of immigrants' total net fiscal impact have ranged from +$1300 per immigrant household per year (Simon 1989) to –$2200 (Smith & Edmonston 1998). Regardless of their overall fiscal impact, there is no question that immigrants to the United States are a fiscal drain on states and localities with large immigrant communities but are net contributors to the federal treasury.

A final economic issue concerns the manner in which the costs of migration (e.g., downward pressure on wages, increased job competition) are distributed among different segments of the native-born population. The Heckscher-Ohlin model of international trade suggests that with abundant unskilled labor in the global South (i.e., migrant-sending states) and skilled labor in the global North, immigration—like trade—should benefit skilled workers in host states and unskilled workers in countries of origin, and that low-skilled workers in host states should see their wages fall (Borjas 1999, Scheve & Slaughter 2001). However, these assumptions ignore the possibility of positive externalities from immigration, including job creation and economic diversification (Nelson 2002). Empirical studies find a significant and substantively important link between U.S. immigration and falling wages during 1890–1910 (Goldin 1994, O'Rourke & Williamson 1999), and between contemporary immigration and falling European wages (Angrist & Kugler 2001). Yet negative wage effects in the U.S. case, like other economic impacts, are quite small (Hanson et al. 2001); and their scope is mainly limited to recent migrants, African-Americans, and workers who lack a high school education (Hamermesh & Bean 1998, Bean & Stevens 2003).

In addition to demographic and economic concerns, there is the issue of security. In principle, high levels of immigration may pose security threats to the extent that migrants overwhelm the integration capacity of host states and breed intergroup conflict (Teitelbaum & Weiner 1995). In practice, however, the security implications of large-scale international migration to industrialized states have been limited mainly to cultural issues (Rudolph 2003, Ireland 2004). These "security threats" have been balanced by periodic war-related demands for more foreign labor, exemplified by U.S. programs to import contract laborers from Mexico in World Wars I and II (Rosenblum 2003a). Only in the wake of the September 11, 2001 terror attacks have policy makers begun seriously to consider individual migrants as security threats.

Even if the actual effects of immigration on receiving countries are typically modest, many citizens of migrant-receiving states *perceive* negative consequences—economic and noneconomic—that lead them to prefer more restrictive immigration policies. A substantial body of political science literature examines general public responses to immigration, which are characterized throughout the industrialized world by opposition to existing immigration levels and negative feelings about the most recent cohort of migrants (Simon & Lynch 1999, Fetzer 2000, Saggar 2003, Cornelius et al. 2004). Partly in response to the coincidence after 1970 of surging global migration, global macroeconomic shocks, and growing concern about the sustainability of the welfare state, subsequent decades have been marked by the emergence of new anti-immigrant parties and movements throughout Europe and in some parts of the United States (Betz & Immerfall 1998, MacDonald & Cain 1998, Ono & Sloop 2002, Doty 2003, Givens 2005). Extremist anti-immigration parties have seldom had much electoral success (the exceptions are the National Front in France, which won 18% of the vote in the June 2002 presidential election, and the Freedom Party in Austria, which garnered 27% in a 1999 general election), but they have had disproportionate influence by nudging mainstream parties to adopt more restrictionist immigration policies. As

Layton-Henry (2004) has observed in the case of Britain, "Politicians firmly believe, despite the repeated failure of anti-immigration politics at the ballot box, that this issue has the potential to mobilize the electorate" (p. 332).

What explains popular anti-immigrant sentiment? Analysts have mainly focused on a pair of competing hypotheses: a class-based economic-threat hypothesis that draws broadly on Marxist thought, and an identity-based cultural-threat hypothesis derived from sociological group-threat theories. Fetzer (2000) further distinguishes between the concepts of "marginality" (hypothesizing that groups outside the mainstream are more receptive to newcomers than members of the dominant group) and "contact" (hypothesizing that meaningful contact with immigrants promotes tolerance but casual contact has the opposite effect) (also see Money 1999).

These competing hypotheses have been exhaustively analyzed at the individual, national, and cross-national levels making use of National Election Study, Eurobarometer, and similar poll data. The weight of the evidence favors individual-level noneconomic explanations of hostility to migration. Receptivity increases with years of education and more cosmopolitan cultural values (Fetzer 2000, Kessler 2001, Citrin & Sides 2004), personal contact with immigrants (Espenshade & Calhoun 1993), and positive anomic beliefs about migrants' personal characteristics (Burns & Gimpel 2000). Yet, as Fortin & Loewen (2004) observe, an inherent endogeneity problem makes some of this research problematic as anti-immigrant attitudes may themselves contribute to lack of contact, negative attitudes about migrant characteristics, etc. Other studies emphasize that both economics and cultural objections to immigration shape public attitudes (Espenshade & Hempstead 1996, Cornelius 2002b). Among economic factors, individuals' evaluations of national economic conditions and their employment status are robust predictors of attitudes about migration (Citrin et al. 1997, Kessler & Freeman 2004). Thus, the literature on anti-immigrant attitudes mirrors the political-behavior debate about symbolic racism: Does white racism reflect underlying "higher-order" values or abstract racial affect (Sears et al. 1979)? Do these abstract beliefs follow endogenously from racist attitudes (Schuman 2000), or do racism (and affect) reflect beliefs about race-related policies such as affirmative action (Sniderman & Carmines 1997)? Hostility to immigration is also correlated with the visibility of new migration inflows (Teitelbaum & Weiner 1995, Money 1999). The latter finding raises the issue of the political salience of migration, a promising area for additional research. The salience of immigration as a public policy issue has usually been low in the United States (Espenshade & Belanger 1998) but high in Britain and some other Western European countries (Lahav 2004), especially when publics focus on asylum seekers and their perceived abuse of welfare-state programs.

Finally, since migration represents an exchange between sending and receiving states, how are countries of origin affected by population outflows? On the economic side, emigration benefits source states by relieving employment pressures and raising wages (O'Rourke & Williamson 1999, Massey et al. 1998). Thus, emigration is a "safety valve" that provides flexibility in economic planning

(García y Griego 1992, Stepick 1992). Emigration is also a source of hard currency through remittances—indeed, the largest source of foreign exchange for many Caribbean Basin states. Official remittances to the five top Latin American labor-exporting countries (i.e., Mexico, the Dominican Republic, El Salvador, Guatemala, and Colombia) grew by 26% annually after 1980, exceeding $8 billion in 2000 (Lowell & de la Garza 2000). By 2003, Mexico alone received at least $14.5 billion in migrant remittances (Multilateral Investment Fund/Pew Hispanic Center 2003; Consesjo Nacional de Población, unpublished data).

But emigration also entails costs, especially the loss of human capital. Most attention to the "brain drain" problem has focused on efforts by China, India, and Canada to deter emigration of highly skilled workers (Cornelius et al. 2001). Both theoretical models and empirical evidence suggest that emigrants are more skilled than their conationals who fail to depart, even in Latin American countries where migration is predominantly low-skilled (A.E. Kessler, unpublished manuscript). Moreover, the emigration of individuals with *any* education means that sending states essentially subsidize economic growth in receiving states. Finally, migrant-sending countries may experience negative social consequences. The cumulative causation of migration means that whole regions of high-emigration countries are now structurally dependent on emigration, which distorts income distribution and arguably limits development possibilities in those regions (Asch & Reichmann 1994).

IMMIGRATION POLICY MAKING

A fundamental tension now characterizes immigration policy making in most of today's labor-importing states. Falling transportation costs, increasing economic integration, path-dependent migration linkages, structural demand for labor within host states, and global demographics all point to continued increases in immigration flows into the developed world. But many of these same features of contemporary immigration also generate public resistance to immigration in host states. Thus, much of the analytic attention to immigration policy has focused on the gaps between popular demands for tighter immigration control and limited (and/or ineffective) state responses (Joppke 1998b, Cornelius et al. 2004). Our discussion of the immigration policy-making process and policy outcomes focuses on domestic interest group politics, political institutions, and the relationship between immigration and international relations.

Domestic Interest Groups

The most common approach to explaining immigration policy making focuses on domestic interest groups. On the economic side, owners of land and capital benefit from the falling wages associated with migration inflows. Although labor unions have traditionally opposed new waves of immigrants (Goldin 1994), some major U.S. and European unions more recently have chosen to organize immigrants as new members rather than to persist with efforts to block their entry into the labor market (Haus 2002, Watts 2002). Extensive case study research documents aggressive lobbying by business and labor groups (Zolberg 1990, Calavita 1992), and analysis of roll call votes in the U.S. Congress shows that members vote on immigration legislation according to district-level economic interests (Gimple & Edwards 1999).

Noneconomic interest groups also care about immigration. Historically, these groups have included recently arrived immigrant/ethnic groups as well as nativist/ patriotic organizations (Fuchs 1990). Contemporary anti-immigration groups frequently emphasize ecological capacity and national-identity concerns (Reimers 1999, Huntington 2004). A broad array of civil liberties organizations have also entered the debate in support of proimmigration policies (Schuck 1998). Roll call and electoral analysis of U.S. and European policy making finds support for the influence of these noneconomic interest groups as well (Kessler 1999, Money 1999).

This diverse set of group demands produces cross-cutting cleavages (e.g., as business associations and civil libertarians line up against unions and cultural conservatives), which prevent the formation of stable partisan blocs on immigration policy (Hoskin 1991, Gimple & Edwards 1999, Tichenor 2002). Yet even though parties often resist classification on this issue, interest group dynamics are broadly predictable. Specifically, it is argued that the benefits of migration are concentrated and accrue to privileged groups with powerful peak associations, whereas the costs of migration are diffuse and its opponents divided. Thus, immigration policy is often described as a form of client politics, with policy makers being "captured" by proimmigration groups (Freeman 1995, 2001; Joppke 1998b).

Political Institutions

Although such interest group models are broadly descriptive of typical legislative outcomes in the post-1970 period, they do not explain variation over time or among migrant-receiving states. Thus, some recent efforts at theory building have grounded these widely held assumptions about interest group dynamics within a framework that emphasizes the mediating effects of political institutions. For example, Money (1999) argues that regional immigrant settlement patterns ensure that interest group disputes play out mainly at the level of gateway communities, whereas immigration policy making occurs at the national level. Thus, policy making may reflect either client politics or broader interest group demands, but policy shifts are likely only when immigrant communities become swing districts at the national level, causing national parties to pursue pro- or anti-immigration voters. [Money's book focuses exclusively on the British, French, and Australian cases; but Fuchs (1990) and Goldin (1994) make broadly similar arguments about migrant-settlement immigration policy making in the early twentieth-century United States.] Rosenblum (2004a) also seeks to explain the timing as well as the direction of policy shifts, focusing on how changes in the international and domestic salience of migration affect bargaining among Congress, the president, and migrant-sending states.

Whereas Money and Rosenblum adopt rational choice/institutionalist approaches, Fitzgerald (1996) and Tichenor (2002) examine the changing effectiveness of economic and noneconomic interest group demands through a historical-institutional lens. Tichenor also explains the timing and direction of U.S. immigration policy changes, emphasizing the interaction between evolving policy coalitions and legislative institutions, changes in the social construction of the immigration debate, and international events as catalysts for policy change. Fitzgerald focuses on U.S. interbranch relations, including the path-dependent evolution of congressional dominance in certain areas (e.g., allocation of permanent resident visas) and presidential dominance in others (e.g., regulation of refugee flows).

Other analysts treat institutions themselves as explanatory variables. Hollifield (1992) and Joppke (1998b) argue that liberal European and U.S. constitutions and judicial systems seriously constrain the ability of states to pass and enforce strong immigration control laws. Liberal institutionalists cite the U.S. Supreme Court's rejection of California's anti-immigrant Proposition 187 and recent steps by national courts and the European Court of Human Rights to overrule deportations in several European states as evidence that institutions matter. Yet there is also substantial evidence of states circumventing these judicial constraints, for example by delegating authority to sub- and supranational enforcement agents (Messina 1996, Guiraudon & Lahav 2000, Guiraudon 2001). And courts remain reluctant to overrule immigration legislation, although they have grown more willing to rule on its enforcement (Schuck 1998).

International Factors

Immigration is an inherently "intermestic" phenomenon (Manning 1977); accordingly, a final set of approaches to explaining variation in policy outcomes emphasizes international factors (alone or in combination with domestic politics) as determinants of migration policy (Hollifield 2000, Meyers 2004, Rosenblum 2004a). At least three distinct types of arguments are made about immigration policy and the international system. First, international migration now occurs within a more generalized process of global economic and political integration, and a number of analysts explain immigration policy making as a function of these broader changes. Sassen (1996) argues that the globalization of capital and the creation of global metropoles have empowered multinational corporations to successfully demand generous immigration policies from host states. Soysal (1994) and Jacobson (1996) focus on international humanitarian norms and regimes; they argue that the liberal domestic institutions discussed above are a product of emerging norms of personhood, which increasingly supersede traditional citizenship-based rights.

A second international-level argument about policy making concerns the complex relationship between population movements and national security. On one hand, many migration flows are the result of international conflict. Civil disputes in Central America and the Caribbean generated large refugee flows to the United States during the 1980s and 1990s, and conflicts in the former Yugoslavia and North Africa were major causes of migration to Western Europe in the 1990s. This pattern reflects structural changes in the nature of warfare in the post–Cold War period (Russell 1995, Helton 2002, Castles & Miller 2003). On the other hand, migration flows can also be a source of international conflict and insecurity. In such cases as the African Great Lakes region and the Balkans, whole regions have been destabilized by mass migration flows into weak states that are poorly equipped to handle them (Hollifield 2000, Helton 2002).

Given that the level and terms of international migration have important economic and sociopolitical implications for countries on both ends of the exchange, a third way in which international relations may influence immigration policy is at the diplomatic/economic level. Many sending states have strong preferences concerning receiving-state immigration policies (Mahler 1999, Rosenblum 2004b), and both sending and receiving states may seek to employ migration as a tool of foreign policy by linking cooperation on migration control and/or access to legal entry visas to other dimensions of bilateral relations, such as trade, investment, and security relations (Meyers 2004). More generally, numerous analysts writing within an international political economy tradition assume migration policy making reflects states' interests in regulating or permitting migration as an international factor flow, rather than (or in addition to) social and demographic considerations (Moehring 1988, Hollifield 1992, Haus 1999, O'Rourke & Williamson 1999, Rosenblum 2003b).

Empirically oriented work is skeptical about the constructivist argument that international norms are constraints on immigration policy making, in part because international migration regimes have notoriously weak enforcement provisions (Teitelbaum 1984, Gurowitz 1999, Hansen 1999, Guiraudon & Lahav 2000). Some analysts are optimistic that the severity of refugee crises in the post–Cold War period—as well as increased attention to such crises—will promote the development of stronger regimes to facilitate humanitarian burden-sharing (Helton 2002). Yet the absence of meaningful international migration regimes reflects a fundamental difference between migration and other types of international flows. Whereas international commercial regimes, for example, benefit states at both ends of the exchange by expanding gains from trade, strong migration institutions would primarily benefit poor sending states by regularizing outflows. Conversely, wealthy states under the status quo laissez faire regime operate in a "buyer's market," and the absence of migration institutions gives receiving states broad latitude to select immigrants and integrate them on their own terms (Rosenblum 2005). Thus, it is unsurprising that where international cooperation on migration exists it is overwhelmingly in the area of immigration control, not humanitarian or labor migration admissions (Koslowski 1998).

Nevertheless, there is substantial evidence that diplomatic and/or security considerations can shape immigration policy. For example, the removal of internal barriers to migration within Western European countries that adhere to the

Schengen agreement has been accompanied by substantial harmonization of external visa policies and cooperation on asylum adjudication (Koslowski 2000). In the case of the United States, the clearest recent example of migration-as-security-policy is the 1994 invasion of Haiti, in which 20,000 U.S. marines were deployed in large part to prevent additional asylum claims from that country (Newland 1995). Thus, even if political scientists continue to debate the extent to which immigration represents a fundamental threat to Westphalian sovereignty (Hollifield 2000, Shanks 2001), modern nation-states clearly view some types of migration flows through a national security optic.

The best-documented examples of immigration policy as diplomacy relate to the enforcement of refugee and asylum policy. The United States rewarded allies by refusing to admit asylum applicants fleeing these states' right-wing authoritarian regimes, and punished communist states during the Cold War by enforcing generous refugee provisions for those applicants (Loescher & Scanlan 1986, Russell 1995). Rosenblum & Salehyan (2004) demonstrate that differential standards were also applied after the Cold War, when trade relations and concerns about undocumented migration influenced enforcement patterns. Diplomatic considerations also inspired U.S. concessions to Mexico during the early years of the "bracero" temporary worker program, as part of an effort to repair strained relations with that state (García y Griego 1992, Rosenblum 2003a). Diplomacy may influence immigration control policies in addition to admissions. Important examples of negotiated control agreements include Germany's readmission treaties with all of its eastern neighbors, multilateral agreements between the Schengen countries and Poland, and the U.S.-Cuban readmission agreement of 1994.

DOES IMMIGRATION POLICY MATTER?

As noted above, a broad consensus exists that the determinants of international migration are overwhelmingly structural and path-dependent, and well-established migration systems are often deeply resistant to regulation. Indeed, some analysts question whether it is possible for labor-importing states to control their borders in the twenty-first century (Sassen 1996, Cornelius & Tsuda 2004). Others argue that immigration control policies are essentially symbolic (Andreas 2000).

Yet migration policy merits attention because different countries take disparate approaches to immigration control and immigrant integration. Among developed states, a distinction exists between "traditional" migrant-receiving countries (the United States, Canada, Australia) and those states for which immigration is mainly a late-twentieth-century phenomenon. The former have generally been more tolerant of legal permanent immigration, whereas most European states (as well as newer receiving states such as Japan and South Korea) have historically raised greater barriers to legal permanent settlement. Although most industrialized migrant-receiving states share a common toolkit (i.e., legal permanent admissions, guestworker admissions, humanitarian refugee and asylum policies, border and worksite enforcement), recent research emphasizes emerging intraregional similarities and inter-regional differences. EU members have moved toward common refugee and asylum policies and nationality laws, and most European states have liberalized their immigrant integration policies in an effort to incorporate immigrants into the body politic. But newer receiving states in East Asia are less generous in this regard, continuing to emphasize temporary guestworker programs without provisions for family reunification. Nonetheless, as Cornelius et al. (2004) observe, these broad patterns mainly hold at the macro level, and substantial variation exists between states (even within regions) in terms of specific admissions criteria, procedures, and policy implementation strategies. Finally, although most research has focused on developed-state immigration policies, a substantial majority of overall international migratory flows are within the global South (especially refugee movements); and many developing states have become important points of transmigration (e.g., Central American, South American, and Asian migration through Mexico to the United States; sub-Saharan migration through Morocco to Spain and other EU countries). These latter cases represent important opportunities for future research.

Moreover, even if the structural push-pull models of international migration flows are correct, immigration policy remains important for at least two reasons. First, all of the structural arguments described above assume that individuals (or families, or communities) believe that the expected benefits of migration outweigh its risks and known costs. Thus, on a theoretical level, it must be possible for receiving states to design policies that reduce unwanted flows by raising the expense of migration to the point at which deterrence is achieved.

Indeed, studies have found evidence that policy choices made by labor-importing countries have affected migration patterns. U.S. legislation passed between 1895 and 1924 was highly effective at restricting European immigration, and the expansion of inflows since the 1960s is directly rooted in additional legislative and regulatory changes passed between 1960 and 1980 (Zolberg 1999). Laws to limit inflows have also been sporadically effective since that time despite their often poor design.

The classic example of inefficient legislative design is the 1986 U.S. Immigration Reform and Control Act (IRCA), which penalized employers who "knowingly" hire unauthorized immigrants but failed to establish enforceable criteria for employment eligibility and thus enabled employers to continue their usual hiring practices (see Calavita 1994). Several quantitative studies found a significant drop in undocumented migration to the United States in the two years following passage of IRCA (Cornelius 1989, Bean et al. 1990), but these declines were offset by new inflows in the 1990s. U.S. immigration control efforts since 1993 have relied on an increasingly militarized U.S.-Mexican border (Andreas 2000, Nevins 2001), although the observable impact of tougher border enforcement has not been a decrease in the flow of unauthorized migrants but rather a rechanneling of the flow, an increase in migration-related deaths and in the fees paid to migrant smugglers, and a higher rate of permanent settlement in the United States (Massey et al. 2002, Cornelius 2005). Migration policy enforcement in the United States may have been further undermined by the fact that the U.S. Immigration and Naturalization Service (now reorganized as the Citizenship and Immigration Services) has been an exceptionally poorly controlled bureaucracy (Magaña 2003).

Another, more fundamental reason why immigration policy matters is that even though migrant-receiving states have imperfect capacity to determine the number of immigrants, policy choices perfectly define the conditions of migration. In particular, policy decisions classify migrants as legal permanent residents, temporary nonimmigrants, humanitarian migrants, or undocumented immigrants. Policy decisions determine the rights each class of migrant enjoys, as well as how aggressively those rights are enforced. The most important distinction is between legal and undocumented immigrants. The undocumented lack most rights associated with membership in an advanced industrial economy, including unionization and workplace safety rights, unemployment insurance, and programs to subsidize health care and home ownership. As a result, not only do unauthorized immigrants earn significantly less than legal immigrants (and natives) with similar skills, but they are also less likely to own houses, engage in entrepreneurial activity, and obtain preventive health care.

A second set of issues concerns legally admitted immigrants. Specifically, how are the rights of membership in the receiving society granted and enforced? Policies that limit immigrants' labor rights (e.g., limitations on a guestworker's ability to change employers, restrictions on the employment of asylum seekers) tend to have pernicious wage effects similar to those that affect unauthorized immigrants. Policies that impose additional limits on migrants' rights of membership and/or their ability to become citizens also exacerbate income inequality and more generally inhibit immigrant assimilation while promoting societal polarization (Schuck 1998, Koslowski 2000).

Legal access to the United States and other industrialized states is a scarce global resource, and policy makers have substantial discretion in how these precious visas are distributed (Shanks 2001). The distribution problem involves at least two questions: whether to discriminate among migrant-sending states, and how to allocate visas among nationals of a given sending state (on a first-come, first-served basis? on the basis of family ties? or occupational skills?). These decisions have obvious consequences for how the benefits of legal *emigration* are distributed among U.S. migration partners and for immigration's social and economic impacts on host states.

CONCLUSION

Contemporary international migration flows occur within migration systems in which pushes, pulls, and social networks make migratory pressures overdetermined. The macroeconomic impact of immigration is modest for most advanced industrialized states; its impact on host-state demographics is more significant. Distributive, security, and cultural impacts of immigration are harder to measure but increasingly drive public debate over immigration policy. General publics throughout the industrialized world typically desire lower levels of immigration than are currently being experienced.

Given the structural determinants of migration in both sending and receiving countries, the ability of host states to respond effectively to this desire is highly arguable. Yet even flawed control policies have at least a modest effect on flow levels, and immigration policy undoubtedly determines the proportion of migrants who enjoy legal status, the specific membership rights associated with different legal (and undocumented) migrant classes, and how policies are implemented. These choices have important implications for how the costs and benefits of migration are distributed among different groups of migrants, native-born workers, employers, consumers, and taxpayers.

For these reasons—and given the virtual demographic certainty that migratory pressures will continue to increase in the foreseeable future—developing better models for explaining immigration policy choices and policy outcomes has become a priority for political scientists in recent years. Much of this recent work seeks to explain the unmet demands for migration control (i.e., the "enforcement gap"), primarily by focusing on interest group dynamics and/or political institutions. A second line of analysis focuses on international models that emphasize security concerns, international institutions, and the role of migrant-sending states. While practitioners of these approaches have tended to focus on explaining modal policy outcomes, others have turned to more complex historical-institutional and cross-level models to explain historical variation in policy outcomes.

There is growing attention to cross-national analyses that seek to explain variance in immigration policy choices and outcomes among labor-importing countries by focusing on differences in regime type, national political cultures, and the distribution of power among governmental institutions. Indeed, the study of comparative politics in advanced industrial countries would benefit from more systematic attention to the ways in which these polities are being reshaped by, and responding to, the forces unleashed by contemporary immigration.

ACKNOWLEDGMENT

The authors thank Robert Jervis for helpful comments on an earlier draft of this article.

The *Annual Review of Political Science* is online at
http://polisci.annualreviews.org

LITERATURE CITED

Alba R, Nee V. 2003. *Remaking the American Mainstream: Assimilation and Contemporary Immigration*. Cambridge, MA: Harvard Univ. Press

Andreas P. 2000. *Border Games: Policing the U.S.-Mexico Divide*. Ithaca, NY: Cornell Univ. Press

Angrist J, Kugler A. 2001. *Protective or counter-productive? European labor market institutions and the effect of immigrants on*

EU natives. NBER Work. Pap. Ser. #8660. Cambridge, MA: Nat. Bur. Econ. Res.

Asch B, Reichmann C, eds. 1994. *Emigration and its effects on the sending country.* RAND Policy Rep. MR-244-FF. Santa Monica, CA: RAND Corp.

Bailey A, Boyle P, eds. 2004. Family migration and the new Europe: special issue. *J. Ethnic Migr. Stud.* 30(2):229–413

Bean FD, Edmonston B, Passel JS, eds. 1990. *Undocumented Migration to the United States: IRCA and the Experience of the 1980s.* Washington, DC: Urban Inst. Press

Bean FD, Stevens G. 2003. *America's Newcomers and the Dynamics of Diversity.* New York: Russell Sage Found.

Betz HG, Immerfall S, eds. 1998. *The New Politics of the Right.* New York: St. Martin's

Borjas G. 1989. Economic theory and international migration. *Int. Migr. Rev.* 23:457–85

Borjas G. 1999. *Heaven's Gate: Immigration Policy and the American Economy.* Princeton, NJ: Princeton Univ. Press

Brettel CB, Hollifield JF, eds. 2000. *Migration Theory: Talking Across the Disciplines.* New York: Routledge

Brimelow P. 1995. *Alien Nation.* New York: Random House

Burns P, Gimpel JG. 2000. Economic insecurity, prejudicial stereotypes, and public opinion on immigration. *Polit. Sci. Q.* 115 (2):201–25

Calavita K. 1992. *Inside the State: The Bracero Program, Immigration, and the I.N.S.* New York: Routledge

Calavita K. 1994. US immigration and policy responses: the limits of legislation. In *Controlling Immigration: A Global Perspective,* ed. WA Cornelius, PL Martin, JF Hollifield, pp. 55–82. Stanford, CA: Stanford Univ. Press

Calavita K. 2004. Italy: economic realities, political fictions, and policy failures. See Cornelius et al. 2004, pp. 345–80

Castles S, Miller MJ. 2003. *The Age of Migration: International Population Movements in the Modern World.* New York: Guilford. 3rd ed.

Chiswick B. 2000. Are immigrants favorably self-selected? See Brettell & Hollifield 2000, pp. 61–76

Citrin J, Green DP, Muste C, Wong C. 1997. Public opinion toward immigration reform: the role of economic motivations. *J. Polit.* 59(3):858–81

Citrin J, Sides JM. 2004. *The discreet charm of the bourgeoisie: why the educated favor immigration.* Presented at Annu. Meet. Am. Polit. Sci. Assoc., 100th, Chicago

Cornelius WA. 1989. Impacts of the 1986 U.S. immigration law on emigration from rural Mexican sending communities. *Popul. Dev. Rev.* 15 (4):689–705

Cornelius WA. 1998. The structural embeddedness of demand for Mexican immigrant labor. See Suárez-Orozco 1998, pp. 115–55

Cornelius WA. 2001. Death at the border: efficacy and unintended consequences of U.S. immigration control policy. *Popul. Dev. Rev.* 27(4):661–85

Cornelius WA. 2002a. Impacts of NAFTA on Mexico-to-U.S. migration. In *NAFTA in the New Millenium,* ed. EJ Chambers, PH Smith, pp. 287–304. Edmonton, Can./La Jolla, CA: Univ. Alberta Press/Cent. U.S.-Mex. Stud., Univ. Calif., San Diego

Cornelius WA. 2002b. Ambivalent reception: mass public responses to the "new" Latino immigration to the United States. In *Latinos: A Research Agenda for the 21ˢᵗ Century,* ed. M Suárez-Orozco, pp. 165–89. Berkeley: Univ. Calif. Press

Cornelius WA. 2004. Spain: the uneasy transition from labor exporter to labor importer. See Cornelius et al. 2004, pp. 388–429

Cornelius WA. 2005. Controlling "unwanted" immigration: lessons from the United States, 1993–2004. *J. Ethnic Migr. Stud.* 31(2): In press

Cornelius WA, Espenshade TJ, Salehyan I, eds. 2001. *The International Migration of the Highly Skilled.* La Jolla, CA: Cent. Comp. Immigr. Stud., Univ. Calif., San Diego

Cornelius WA, Tsuda T. 2004. Controlling immigration: the limits to government intervention. See Cornelius et al. 2004, pp. 3–48

Cornelius WA, Tsuda T, Martin PL, Hollifield JF, eds. 2004. *Controlling Immigration: A Global Perspective.* Stanford, CA: Stanford Univ. Press

Doty RL. 2003. *Anti-Immigrantism in Western Democracies: Statecraft, Desire, and the Politics of Exclusion.* New York: Routledge

Espenshade TJ, Belanger M. 1998. Immigration and public opinion. See M Suárez-Orozco 1998, pp. 361–408

Espenshade TJ, Calhoun C. 1993. An analysis of public opinion toward undocumented immigration. *Popul. Res. Policy Rev.* 12:189–224

Espenshade TJ, Hempstead K. 1996. Contemporary American attitudes toward US immigration. *Int. Migr. Rev.* 30(2):535–70

Faist T. 2000. *The Volume and Dynamics of International Migration and Transnational Social Spaces.* Oxford, UK: Clarendon/Oxford Univ. Press

Fetzer JS. 2000. *Public Attitudes toward Immigration in the United States, France, and Germany.* Cambridge/New York: Cambridge Univ. Press

Fitzgerald K. 1996. *The Face of the Nation: Immigration, the State, and the National Identity.* Stanford, CA: Stanford Univ. Press

Fortin J, Loewen PJ. 2004. *Two sides of the same coin? Measuring public support and opposition to immigration in Canada.* Presented at Annu. Meet. Am. Polit. Sci. Assoc., 100th, Chicago

Freeman G. 1995. Modes of immigration politics in liberal democratic states. *Int. Migr. Rev.* 29(4):881–902

Freeman G. 2001. Client politics or populism: immigration reform in the United States. See Guiraudon & Joppke 2001, pp. 65–95

Fuchs LH. 1990. *The American Kaleidoscope: Race, Ethnicity, and the Civic Culture.* Hanover, NH: Univ. Press New England

Fussell E, Massey DS. 2004. The limits to cumulative causation: international migration from Mexican urban areas. *Demography* 41(1):51–71

García y Griego M. 1992. Policymaking at the apex: international migration, state auton-

omy, and societal constraints. In *U.S.-Mexico Relations: Labor Market Interdependence,* ed. J Bustamante, C Reynolds, R Hinojosa-Ojeda, pp. 75–110. Stanford, CA: Stanford Univ. Press

Gibney MJ. 2004. *The Ethics and Politics of Asylum: Liberal Democracy and the Response to Refugees.* Cambridge/New York: Cambridge Univ. Press

Gimple JG, Edwards JR. 1999. *The Congressional Politics of Immigration Reform.* Boston: Allyn & Bacon

Givens T. 2005. *Voting Radical Right in Western Europe.* Cambridge/New York: Cambridge Univ. Press. In press

Goldin C. 1994. The political economy of immigration restriction in the United States, 1890–1921. In *The Regulated Economy: A Historical Approach to Political Economy,* ed. C Goldin, GD Libecap, pp. 223–57. Chicago: Univ. Chicago Press

Guiraudon V. 2001. De-nationalizing control: analyzing state responses to constraints on migration control. See Guiraudon & Joppke 2001, pp. 31–64

Guiraudon V, Joppke C, eds. 2001. *Controlling a New Migration World.* New York: Routledge

Guiraudon V, Lahav G. 2000. A reappraisal of the state sovereignty debate: the case of migration control. *Comp. Polit. Stud.* 33(2):163–95

Gurowitz A. 1999. Mobilizing international norms: domestic actors, immigrants, and the Japanese state. *World Polit.* 51(3):413–45

Hamermesh D, Bean FD. 1998. *Help or Hindrance? The Economic Implications of Immigration for African Americans.* New York: Russell Sage Found.

Hammar T, Brochmann G, Tamas K, Faist T, eds. 1997. *International Migration, Immobility, and Development: Multidisciplinary Perspectives.* Oxford/New York: Berg

Hansen R. 1999. Migration, citizenship, and race in Europe: between incorporation and exclusion. *Eur. J. Polit. Res.* 35(4):415–44

Hanson GH, Robertson R, Spilimbergo A. 2001. *Does border enforcement protect*

U.S. workers from illegal immigration? Cent. Comp. Immigr. Stud., Univ. Calif., San Diego, Work. Pap. 31, http://www.ccis-ucsd.org/PUBLICATIONS/wrkg31.PDF

Hanson GH, Spilimbergo A. 1999. Illegal immigration, border enforcement, and relative wages: evidence from apprehensions at the U.S.-Mexico border. *Am. Econ. Rev.* 89(5):1337–57

Hatton T, Williamson J. 1997. *The Age of Mass Migration: An Economic Analysis.* Oxford/New York: Oxford Univ. Press

Haus L. 1999. Integrated issues: migration and international economic interdependence. In *Free Markets, Open Societies, Closed Borders? Trends in International Migration and Immigration Policy in the Americas*, ed. M Castro, pp. 85–99. Miami, FL: Univ. Miami North-South Cent. Press

Haus L. 2002. *Unions, Immigration, and Internationalization: New Challenges and Changing Coalitions in the United States and France.* New York: St. Martin's/Palgrave

Helton A. 2002. *The Price of Indifference: Refugees and Humanitarian Action in the New Century.* Oxford/New York: Oxford Univ. Press

Hollifield JF. 1992. *Immigrants, Markets, and States: The Political Economy of Postwar Europe.* Cambridge, MA: Harvard Univ. Press

Hollifield JF. 2000. The politics of international migration: How can we "bring the state back in"? See Brettel & Hollifield 2000, pp. 137–85

Hoskin M. 1991. *New Immigrants and Democratic Society: Minority Integration in Western Democracies.* New York: Praeger

Huntington SP. 2004. *Who Are We? The Challenges to America's National Identity.* New York: Simon & Schuster

Ireland P. 2004. *Becoming Europe: Immigration, Integration, and the Welfare State.* Pittsburgh: Univ. Pittsburgh Press

Jacobson D. 1996. *Rights across Borders: Immigration and the Decline of Citizenship.* Baltimore, MD: Johns Hopkins Univ. Press

Joppke C. 1998a. Asylum and state sovereignty: a comparison of the United States, Germany, and Britain. See Joppke 1998c, pp. 109–52

Joppke C. 1998b. Why liberal states accept unwanted immigration. *World Polit.* 50:266–93

Joppke C, ed. 1998c. *Challenge to the Nation State: Immigration in Western Europe and the United States.* Oxford/New York: Oxford Univ. Press

Joppke C, Morawska E, eds. 2003. *Toward Assimilation and Citizenship: Immigrants in Liberal Nation-States.* Basingstoke, UK: Palgrave Macmillan

Keely CB. 2000. Demography and international migration. See Brettel & Hollifield 2000, pp. 43–60

Kessler AE. 1999. *Globalization, domestic politics, and the "curious coalitions" of postwar American immigration reform.* Presented at Annu. Meet. Am. Polit. Sci. Assoc., 95th, Atlanta, GA

Kessler AE. 2001. Immigration, economic insecurity, and the "ambivalent" American public. Cent. Comp. Immigr. Stud., Univ. Calif., San Diego, Work. Pap. 41, http://www.ccis-ucsd.org/PUBLICATIONS/wrkg41.PDF

Kessler AE, Freeman GP. 2004. *Political opportunism, social exclusion, and support for extremist parties in Europe.* Presented at Annu. Meet. Am. Polit. Sci. Assoc., 100th, Chicago

Koslowski R. 1998. European Union migration regimes, established and emergent. See Joppke 1998c, pp. 153–89

Koslowski R. 2000. *Migrants and Citizens: Demographic Change in the European State System.* Ithaca, NY: Cornell Univ. Press

Kyle D, Koslowski R, eds. 2001. *Global Human Smuggling: Comparative Perspectives.* Baltimore, MD: Johns Hopkins Univ. Press

Lahav G. 2004. *Immigration and Politics in the New Europe.* Cambridge/New York: Cambridge Univ. Press

Layton-Henry Z. 2004. Britain: from immigration control to migration management. See Cornelius et al. 2004, pp. 297–333

Loescher G. 2002. State responses to refugees and asylum seekers in Europe. In *West European Immigration and Immigrant Policy in the New Century*, ed. AM Messina, pp. 33–46. Westport, CT: Praeger

Loescher G, Scanlan JA. 1986. *Calculated Kindness: Refugees and America's Half-Open Door, 1945 to the Present*. New York: Free

Lowell LB, de la Garza RO. 2000. *The Developmental Role of Remittances in Latino Communities and in Latin American Countries: Final Project Report to the Inter-American Dialogue and Tomás Rivera Policy Institute*. Washington, DC: Inter-Am. Dialogue

MacDonald K, Cain B. 1998. Nativism, partisanship, and immigration: an analysis of Proposition 187. In *Racial and Ethnic Politics in California*, ed. MB Preston, B Cain, S Bass, II:277–304. Berkeley: Inst. Gov. Stud., Univ. Calif. Berkeley

Magaña L. 2003. *Straddling the Border: Immigration Policy and the INS*. Austin: Univ. Texas Press

Mahler SJ. 1999. Vested in migration: Salvadorans challenge restrictionist policies. In *Free Markets, Open Societies, Closed Border? Trends in International Migration and Migration Policy in the Americas*, ed. MJ Castro, pp. 157–74. Miami: North-South Cent. Press

Manning B. 1977. The Congress, the executive, and intermestic affairs: three proposals. *For. Aff.* 55(2):306–24

Martin PL. 2001. Trade and migration: the Mexico-to-U.S. Case. In *International Migration: Trends, Policies, and Economic Impact*, ed. S Djajic, pp. 89–109. London: Routledge

Martin PL. 2004. Germany: managing migration in the twenty-first century. See Cornelius et al. 2004, pp. 51–85

Massey DS, Arango J, Hugo G, Kouaouci A, Pellegrino A, Taylor EJ. 1998. *Worlds in Motion: Understanding International Migration at the End of the Millenium*. Oxford, UK: Clarendon

Massey DS, Durand J, Malone NJ. 2002. *Beyond Smoke and Mirrors: Mexican Immigration in an Era of Economic Integration*. New York: Russell Sage Found.

Massey DS, Liang Z. 1989. The long-term consequences of a temporary worker program: the U.S. bracero experience. *Popul. Res. Policy Rev.* 8:199–226

Messina A. 1996. The not-so-silent revolution: postwar migration to Western Europe. *World Polit.* 49:130–54

Meyers E. 2004. *International Immigration Policy: A Theoretical and Comparative Analysis*. Basingstoke, UK: Palgrave Macmillan

Moehring HB. 1988. Symbol versus substance in legislative activity: the case of illegal immigration. *Public Choice* 57:287–94

Money J. 1999. *Fences and Neighbors: The Political Geography of Immigration Control in Advanced Market Economy Countries*. Ithaca, NY: Cornell Univ. Press

Multilateral Investment Fund/Pew Hispanic Center. 2003. Remittance senders and receivers: tracking the transnational channels. Washington, DC: Inter-Am. Dev. Bank and Pew Hispanic Cent.

Nelson D. 2002. *Trade and migration policy in endogenous policy models: what works, what doesn't, and why*. Presented at Annu. Meet. Int. Stud. Assoc., 43rd, New Orleans, LA

Nevins J. 2001. *Operation Gatekeeper: The Rise of the "Illegal Alien" and the Remaking of the U.S.-Mexico Boundary*. New York: Routledge

Newland K. 1995. The impact of US refugee policies on US foreign policy: a case of the tail wagging the dog? See Teitelbaum & Weiner, pp. 190–214

Ono KA, Sloop JM. 2002. *Shifting Borders: Rhetoric, Immigration, and California's Proposition 187*. Philadelphia: Temple Univ. Press

O'Rourke K, Williamson J. 1999. *Globalization and History: The Evolution of a Nineteenth Century Atlantic Economy*. Cambridge, MA: MIT Press

Piore M. 1979. *Birds of Passage: Migrant*

Labor and Industrial Societies. Cambridge/New York: Cambridge Univ. Press

Reimers D. 1999. *Unwelcome Strangers.* New York: Columbia Univ. Press

Reisler MS. 1976. *By the Sweat of Their Brow: Mexican Immigrant Labor in the United States, 1900–1940.* Westport, CT: Greenwood

Rosenblum MR. 2003a. The intermestic politics of immigration policy: lessons from the bracero program. *Polit. Power Soc. Theory* 17:141–84

Rosenblum MR. 2003b. The political determinants of migration control: a quantitative analysis. *Migraciones Internacionales* 2(1):161–70

Rosenblum MR. 2004a. *The transnational politics of U.S. immigration policy.* La Jolla, CA: Cent. Comp. Immigr. Stud., Univ. Calif., San Diego, Monogr. No. 3

Rosenblum MR. 2004b. Beyond the policy of no-policy: emigration from Mexico and Central America. *Latin Am. Polit. Soc.* 4(1):91–125

Rosenblum MR. 2005. The price of indifference vs. the price of reform: review essay on Arthur Helton's *The Price of Indifference. Hum. Rights Rev.* In press

Rosenblum MR, Salehyan I. 2004. Norms and interests in U.S. asylum enforcement. *J. Peace Res.* 41(6):677–97

Rudolph C. 2003. Security and the political economy of international migration. *Am. Polit. Sci. Rev.* 97(4):603–20

Russell SS. 1995. Migration patterns of U.S. foreign policy interest. See Teitelbaum & Weiner 1995, pp. 39–87

Saggar S. 2003. Immigration and the politics of public opinion. In *The Politics of Migration,* ed. S Spencer, pp. 178–94. Malden, MA: Blackwell

Sassen S. 1996. *Losing Control? Sovereignty in an Age of Globalization.* New York: Columbia Univ. Press

Scheve KF, Slaughter MJ. 2001. Labor market competition and individual preferences over immigration policy. *Rev. Econ. Stat.* 83(1):133–45

Schuck PH. 1998. The re-evaluation of American citizenship. See Joppke 1998c, pp. 191–230

Schuman H. 2000. The perils of correlation, the lure of labels, and the beauty of negative results. In *Racialized Politics: The Debate about Racism in America,* ed. DO Sears, J Sidanius, L Bobo, pp. 302–23. Chicago: Univ. Chicago Press

Sears DO, Hensler CP, Speer LK. 1979. Whites' opposition to "busing": self-interest or symbolic politics? *Am. Polit. Sci. Rev.* 73:369–84

Shanks C. 2001. *Immigration and the Politics of American Sovereignty, 1890–1990.* Ann Arbor: Univ. Mich. Press

Simon JL. 1989. *The Economic Consequences of Migration.* Oxford, UK/Cambridge, MA: Basil Blackwell

Simon RJ, Lynch JP. 1999. A comparative assessment of public opinion toward immigrants and immigration policies. *Int. Migr. Rev.* 33(2):455–86

Smith JP, Edmonston B, eds. 1997. *The New Americans: Economic, Demographic, and Fiscal Effects of Immigration.* Washington, DC: Natl. Acad. Press

Smith JP, Edmonston B, eds. 1998. *The Immigration Debate: Studies on the Economic, Demographic, and Fiscal Effects of Immigration.* Washington, DC: Natl. Acad. Press

Sniderman PM, Carmines EG. 1997. *Reaching Beyond Race.* Cambridge, MA: Harvard Univ. Press

Soysal YN. 1994. *Limits of Citizenship: Migrants and Postnational Membership in Europe.* Chicago: Univ. Chicago Press

Stalker P. 1999. *Workers Without Frontiers: The Impact of Globalization on International Migration.* Boulder, CO: Lynne Rienner

Stalker P. 1994. *The Work of Strangers: A Survey of International Labour Migration.* Geneva: Int. Labour Organ.

Stark O. 1991. *The Migration of Labor.* Cambridge/New York: Cambridge Univ. Press

Stepick A. 1992. Unintended consequences: rejecting Haitian boat people and destabilizing

Duvalier, In *Western Hemisphere Immigration and United States Foreign Policy*, ed. C Mitchell, pp. 125–55. University Park: Penn. State Univ. Press

Suárez-Orozco M, ed. 1998. *Crossings: Mexican Immigration in Interdisciplinary Perspectives*. Cambridge, MA: David Rockefeller Cent. Latin Am. Stud., Harvard Univ.

Tamas K. 2004. *Mapping Study on International Migration*. Stockholm: Inst. Futures Stud.

Teitelbaum MS. 1984. Immigration, refugees, and foreign policy. *Int. Organ.* 38(3):429–50

Teitelbaum MS, Weiner M, eds. 1995. *Threatened Peoples, Threatened Borders: World Migration and U.S. Policy*. New York: Norton

Tichenor DJ. 2002. *Dividing Lines: The Politics of Immigration Control in America*. Princeton, NJ: Princeton Univ. Press

Tsuda T. 2003. *Strangers in the Ethnic Homeland: Japanese Brazilian Return Migration in Transnational Perspective*. New York: Columbia Univ. Press

Tsuda T, Valdez Z, Cornelius WA. 2003. Human versus social capital: immigrant wages and labor market incorporation in Japan and the United States. In *Host Societies and the Reception of Immigrants*, ed. JG Reitz, pp. 215–52. La Jolla, CA: Cent. Comp. Immigr. Stud., Univ. Calif., San Diego

Waldinger R. 1997. *Social capital or social closure? Immigrant networks in the labor market*. Work. Pap. 26. Lewis Cent. Reg. Policy Stud., Univ. Calif. Los Angeles

Watts J. 2002. *Immigration Policy and the Challenge of Globalization: Unions and Employers in Unlikely Alliance*. Ithaca, NY: Cornell Univ. Press

United Nations. 2000. *Replacement Migration: Is It a Solution to Declining and Aging Populations?* New York: Popul. Div., Dep. Econ. Soc. Aff., UN Secretariat

United Nations. 2002. *International Migration, 2002*. ST/ESA/SER.A/219. New York: Popul. Div., Dep. Econ. Soc. Aff., UN Secretariat

Zolberg A. 1990. Reforming the backdoor: the Immigration Reform and Control Act of 1986 in historical perspective. In *Immigration Reconsidered: History, Sociology, and Politics*, ed. V Yans-McLaughlin, pp. 315–38. Oxford/New York: Oxford Univ. Press

Zolberg A. 1999. Matters of state: theorizing immigration policy. In *The Handbook of International Migration*, ed. C Hirschman, P Kasinitz, J DeWind, pp. 71–93. New York: Russell Sage Found.

Annu. Rev. Polit. Sci. 2005. 8:121–43
doi: 10.1146/annurev.polisci.8.083104.163853
Copyright © 2005 by Annual Reviews. All rights reserved
First published online as a Review in Advance on November 1, 2004

MAKING SENSE OF RELIGION IN POLITICAL LIFE

Kenneth D. Wald,[1] Adam L. Silverman,[2] and Kevin S. Fridy[1]
[1]*Department of Political Science, University of Florida, Gainesville,
Florida 32611-7325; email: kenwald@polisci.ufl.edu, fridy@ufl.edu*
[2]*Department of Criminal Justice, Temple University, Philadelphia,
Pennsylvania 19122; email: adamsilv@temple.edu*

Key Words   social movements, culture, identity, resource mobilization, political
   opportunity structure

■ **Abstract**   After a long period of postwar neglect by mainstream scholars, religion
assumed a new prominence in political science during the late 1970s. Despite the latter-
day significance accorded religion by the discipline, the product of several unexpected
real-world events, much of the recent research has focused on specific episodes or
groups without drawing on or developing general theories. Social movement theory
(SMT), particularly in its most recent incarnation, offers a way to address the three
critical questions about religiously engaged political movements: What are the motives
for political activity by religious groups? By what means do these groups facilitate
political action? What features and conditions of the political system provide them
opportunities for effective political action? This review explores various expressions
of religiously based political action from the vantage point of SMT. We conclude that
the translation of religious grievances into political action is contingent on a string of
conditions that involve the interplay of motive, means, and opportunity. The implicit
message is that scholars should approach religiously engaged social movements with
the same theoretical frameworks used to understand secular political forces and that
focusing these interpretive lenses on religion will illuminate issues of general interest
to the discipline.

INTRODUCTION

Religious institutions are neither designed nor intended to mobilize political action. Yet, across the globe, they seem to have done precisely that (see, e.g., Marty
& Appleby 1992, Barkun 1994, Rudolph & Piscatori 1997, Hart 2001, Jelen &
Wilcox 2002). Rather than receding from the public square in blind obedience
to the dictates of secularization theory and the expectations of many social scientists, religion has instead increasingly engaged society and politics (Hadden
1987, Casanova 1994). Some recent agenda-setting works in political science—
Huntington's *Clash of Civilizations* (1996), Putnam's *Bowling Alone* (2001), Verba
et al.'s *Voice and Equality* (1995)—recognize the religious factor (in various guises)

as a major political force.[1] The American National Election Studies, the mother lode of data for many behavioralists, has repeatedly revised its interview schedule to help scholars get a better purchase on the electoral significance of the religious factor (Leege & Kellstdt 1993).

As much as we welcome the growth of disciplinary interest in the religious factor, the increased attention highlights the need for a stronger infusion of social science theory in this emerging subfield. Despite all the research generated by the relevant disciplines, neither political science nor religious studies has offered a comprehensive explanation for the genesis of religiously based political action. Case studies abound, but there is relatively little cumulative scholarly progress (Jelen 1998). Referring to an outburst of published studies about a social movement during the 1970s, a scholar jokingly suggested renaming the outlet for this research the *British Journal of National Front Studies*. In the same manner, considering much of the published work in recent years, one could justifiably refer to a subfield of Christian Right Studies or fill the pages of a journal devoted solely to fundamentalist Islam. When scholarly inquiry is walled off in specialized research outlets, its practitioners often cease drawing on larger scholarly currents and aiming at the development of general theory. We intend to offer scholars of religion and politics the opportunity to put their research in a framework that speaks to a wider audience of scholars, including many with only a peripheral interest in religion. Our framework also helps make clear that the study of religion in politics presents theoretical concerns similar to those that preoccupy scholars of other fields and subjects.

Specifically, this article draws on three important strands of social movement theory (SMT)—culture/identity, resource mobilization, and political opportunity structure—to identify the forces that account for political engagement by religious groups. Apart from constituting an important and intriguing phenomenon on its own, we argue, religiously based political action is a venue that can enhance our understanding of some perennial political issues.

BACKGROUND

Although religion has been a constant in human society, political scientists paid scant attention to it until about 20 years ago. Apart from normative theorists and comparativists, most scholars in the discipline regarded religion as too exotic or epiphenomenal to warrant sustained interest.[2] Even when religion was considered

---

[1]Upon close inspection, Huntington's civilizations are defined largely by their common religious heritage. Putnam argues that religious institutions are the major force that provides American society with social engagement, accounting for fully half the stock of social capital. Similarly, Verba et al. discover that religion is a powerful resource that promotes and encourages political participation, enabling some minorities to overcome deficits in tangible assets such as education and income.

[2]For example, Pals' (1996) account of classic approaches to religion includes profiles of psychologists (e.g., Freud), anthropologists (e.g., Levi Strauss, Geertz), sociologists (e.g., Durkheim), and economists (e.g., Marx), but not a single scholar with a direct link to

in systematic studies of political change, it was largely regarded as a problem in need of a solution. Consider the postwar comparative theorists who, preoccupied with the newly independent states carved out of colonial empires, identified modernization as the desired end product of political development. They defined modernization (in part) as the "separation of the polity from religious structures, substitution of secular modes of legitimation and extension of the polity's jurisdiction into areas formerly regulated by religion" (Smith 1974, p. 4). By definition, religion was placed in opposition to effective development.[3]

Not until the 1980s, when religion more or less forced itself back onto the mainstream scholarly agenda as a result of several real-world developments, did empirically minded political scientists begin to take seriously what William James once derided as "soul stuff." With a new appreciation for the political potency of religion, scholars convened specialized conferences and produced countless books, journal articles, and special issues of journals that ranged widely in their focus with regard to place, time, and form of political action.

This resurgence of scholarly interest in the 1980s owes much to an unlikely pair of sources: the late Ayatollah Khomeini of Iran and the Rev. Jerry Falwell of Lynchburg, Virginia. Both emerged in the 1970s as leaders of social movements that profoundly altered two of the largest subfields in political science—comparative and American politics, respectively. (We may yet come to regard Osama bin Laden as a comparable force for scholarly change in international relations.) The Islamic Revolution that Khomeini symbolized did not merely seize power in one nation; rather, it demonstrated the capacity of a movement rooted in "primordial" social forces to undermine what had been the very model of the modernizing state in the political development literature, the Shah's Iran. In much the same way, Falwell's emergence as the public symbol of what became known as the New Christian Right helped scramble the alignments in American party politics. The party system was shaken to its core by a force whose political salience was supposedly on the decline. Although both movements have generated their own Thermidorian reactions, each has left a profound imprint on the political system it challenged. Whatever their attitudes toward religion, political scientists could not avoid taking account of such major shifts in the subjects of their research.[4]

Scholars who approached these phenomena via the collective behavior paradigm, once the dominant approach to mass politics, were ill-prepared to make sense of politically engaged religion. Writing in this tradition, scholars tended to

---

political science. Although our discipline draws heavily on these thinkers for inspiration and understanding, it has been more a consumer than a producer of important theoretical frameworks. Even today, it is difficult to find a distinctively "political science" perspective on religion.

[3]Religion was not ruled off the research agenda entirely. It was recognized as a social force that might facilitate mass mobilization, another requisite of effective development.

[4]The strong religious motifs in the Sandinista uprising in Nicaragua and the overt piety of the Solidarity movement in Poland suggested that Iran and the United States were exemplars rather than outliers.

portray mass movements as irrational, dangerous, and socially marginal (Adorno et al. 1950, Kornhauser 1959, Smelser 1963). For example, although he recognized different forms of collective behavior, Smelser (1963) nonetheless found a common syndrome of panic, craze, and hostility at the core of all mass movements (p. 271). When this syndrome was married to the mystical and irrational connotations that religion carried for many social scientists, religiously based mass movements were seldom approached in a nonjudgmental way. Just as explanations of the anticommunist movement in the 1950s and 1960s had emphasized psychological disorders and sociological strains as the motivating force (Bell 1955), some early interpretations of fundamentalist political emergence in the 1980s called on similar dark impulses to account for the Christian Right (e.g., Crawford 1980, Lipset & Raab 1981; for a good summary of that literature, see Wilcox 1992).

The flowering of politically engaged religion coincided with the emergence of an alternative approach to mass politics, a perspective that drew on continental European traditions of social theory. Known generically as social movement theory (SMT), this new approach was deployed initially to account for the civil rights, student, antiwar, feminist, gay rights, and environmental campaigns (e.g., Morris et al. 1992, Meyer & Tarrow 1997). In contrast to the patronizing tone of the older collective behavior literature, SMT theorists generally empathized with their subjects and argued that the popular struggles added to the democratic character of society (Tesh 1984). By treating mass movements as legitimate political participants with reasonable perspectives, the SMT approach seemed better suited than its precursor to account for movements that were durable, rooted in middle-class social networks, highly institutionalized, committed to a range of action repertoires, and prone to making strategic choices from a cost-benefit perspective.

By now a well-established research tradition, SMT provides important clues to the mysteries of religiously based political activity.[5] Most important, the various approaches incorporated under the SMT rubric identify what we consider the central questions that need to be asked in order to account for religion as an idiom of political conflict and offer the potential to treat religiously based movements on their own terms. Like homicide detectives, scholars of religion and politics need to understand motive, means, and opportunity: the motives that draw religious groups into political action, the means that enable the religious to participate effectively, and the opportunities that facilitate their entry into the political system. These are precisely the domains addressed by SMT. To understand how religion influences individual and group preferences and how these preferences generate political grievances, we turn to cultural identity theory. How compelling is culture as a key to understanding why religious organizations engage the political system?

---

[5]Similar scholarship has more recently emerged under the rubric of contentious politics literature (e.g., Smith 1996, Aminzade & Perry 2001, McVeigh & Sikkink 2001). This similarity is no surprise given contentious politics' explicit annexation of SMT (McAdam et al. 1996). Because this paper focuses on religion's impact on social movements, we have chosen to situate our discussion in the more specific SMT literature.

After discussing motives, we examine theories of resource mobilization in search of religious organizations' means for political mobilization. What resources do religious organizations marshal that make political mobilization possible? The final ingredient in a comprehensive analysis of political mobilization by religious organizations is exogenous to religious organizations themselves. What types of opportunities must present themselves so that motive and means can congeal into an effective political mobilization? To address this question, the literature on political opportunity structure and contentious politics is consulted.

Despite this division of SMT into motive, means, and opportunity, we do not intend to suggest that the three domains are hermetically sealed. For instance, it is impossible to discuss political means of religious groups without invoking transcendental ideational forces that also serve as a key ingredient in the formation of motive. Moreover, the sacred nature of religious obligations secured through these otherworldly appeals alters the opportunity structures faced by religious groups in the public realm. As this overlap suggests, we believe that motive, means, and opportunity are both individually necessary and mutually sufficient to account for the political mobilization of religious organizations.[6]

MOTIVE: CULTURE AND IDENTITY

For Max Weber, individuals "undoubtedly act on the basis of their beliefs and ideas, and the ways in which they conduct themselves follow from the religious and political conceptions to which they subscribe" (Hughes 1995, p. 90). For Émile Durkheim, the "true purpose" of religion is to serve "as the carrier of social sentiments, providing symbols and rituals that enable people to express the deep emotions which anchor them to their community" (Pals 1996, p. 111). Despite their differences on whether religion should be understood as primarily mental (Weber) or communal (Durkheim), these two giants of social theory concurred that religion is a key determinant of one's "competing notions of how we should and should not live—the moral order" (Leege et al. 2002, p. 13). If religion shapes culture, or is shaped by culture, as Weber and Durkheim respectively suggest, then cultural theory offers an important insight into how religion shapes individual preferences. These preferences combine to form the motive for the political mobilization of religious organizations.

SMT theorists in the United States were relatively slow to focus on culture as the source of mobilization. Early work tended to discuss grievances without much concern about where they came from and to treat as exogenous the social identity

---

[6]Despite its explanatory potential, SMT was seldom invoked by the first generation of researchers, who seemed much more comfortable with what they perceived as liberation movements than seemingly reactionary crusades. That inattention to religion is slowly being rectified, but we believe that SMT still overlooks religious movements unless they are defined as progressive. For an exception, see Lo (1992).

that provided the cognitive glue for mass movements. Since the "cultural turn" in SMT research about a decade ago (Johnston & Klandermans 1995), these questions have bulked much larger and provide a take-off point for our discussion of the motives underlying mobilization. The concluding paragraph of this section points out the implications of training a cultural theoretical lens on religious organizations.

Wildavsky (1987) argues that in order to understand the cultural basis of social identity, one should define culture as a compilation of shared values and social relations (p. 5). Culture, as Wildavsky perceives it, performs three functions: it confers identity, prescribes behavioral norms, and maintains boundaries for relationships. That is, cultural identity tells us who we are, how we should behave, and how we should act toward those who are not part of us.[7] From the perspective of political science, it is most important that culture molds individual preferences. In understanding this, Wildavsky offers a useful menu metaphor. "Human beings do not choose what they want, like ordering *a la carte*," he contends. Rather, "[p]reference formation is much more like ordering *prix fixe* from a number of set dinners" (p. 4). A limited number of cultures exist in the real world. Once one has chosen a culture to join, or been chosen by one as the case may be, an infinite number of potential actions get whittled down to those that are culturally rational (p. 6). One's culture, though not taking away one's free will completely, directs one's preferences in such a way as to limit the range of acceptable choices in any given situation.

The intersection of culture with identity and grievance formation is apparent in Wood's (1999) instructive comparison of two small and homogeneous churches, St. Elizabeth and Full Gospel churches in Oakland, California. Emphasizing the contingent nature of identity formation, the author demonstrates concretely how culture, as conceptualized by Wildavsky, can produce political grievances (motive) in one religious organization while producing quiescence in another. Both churches have active congregations and provide a strong sense of community for their members, but St. Elizabeth's congregation sees active involvement in community politics as a religious virtue, whereas Full Gospel's leaders urge congregants toward the unambiguous pursuit of good, which does not readily translate into active involvement in the messy give-and-take of local politics (Wood 1999, pp. 316–21). A black and white moral universe does not provide the necessary cognitive tools to comprehend a political system painted in shades of gray. Because of these churches' different cultures, it is culturally rational for congregants of St. Elizabeth to show up *en masse* for protest marches to express their political grievances to local officials and for members of Full Gospel to direct "their calls for social change. . .largely at apolitical, other-worldly venues" (p. 327).

The concept of cultural rationality seems jarring, accustomed as we are to understanding rational behavior as instrumental, utility-maximizing action. But

---

[7]In emphasizing culture as a source of group boundaries, this approach differs from the classic anthropological understanding of culture as the force that unites society. Political conflict is often fueled by competition among subcultures in the same society.

Weber (1968) also spoke of value rationality, action that makes sense to people who are embedded in a subculture that places a premium on behavior that reflects the core norms and values of the group. The behavior of these two congregations is rooted in related but distinct religious subcultures that differ on what kinds of behavior are both appropriate and rewarding. The identity that has been created and fostered at St. Elizabeth's leads, in the right context, to very active forms of political participation. Conversely, the identity at Full Gospel promotes passive and otherworldly political responses, chiefly prayer. In both cases, the identity and context of the religious community has a direct and observable effect on behavioral options.

The larger temporal context also influences whether and how culturally based grievances are politicized. As Swidler (1986) argues, "[C]ulture is a 'tool kit' for constructing 'strategies of action rather than. . .a switchman directing an engine propelled by interests" (p. 277). Given the aforementioned example of St. Elizabeth and Full Gospel, Swidler would contend that St. Elizabethans can find a tool for stimulating political mobilization in their cultural kit whereas Full Gospelites' tools are unfit for the job. The latter church's symbols and strategies are better equipped for promoting acceptance of authority and creating a morally dichotomous universe. Swidler makes a distinct contribution to cultural theory by distinguishing culture's effects on what she calls settled and unsettled lives (p. 278). The causal connections between culture and action are much harder to deduce in settled cultural periods than in unsettled cultural periods (pp. 278–80).

For example, consider the reactions of church women to patriarchal beliefs, sacred images, language, and practices. Ozorak (1996) finds that common coping mechanisms of females in patriarchal churches in upper-middle-class America include rejection, translation, interpretation, and integration (pp. 17–19). Stated simply, women can leave the church, change the church behaviorally, change the church cognitively, or employ a combination of these latter two approaches. "Settled cultures," explains Swidler (1986), "support varied patterns of action, obscuring cultures' independent influence" (p. 280). It is because the upper-middle-class American women of Ozorak's study are living in a relatively settled culture that she can find a number of subjects who fit into each of her categories. Had the society in question been unsettled culturally, the ambiguity that allows women to comfortably report such things as "I don't say 'Our Father,' I say, 'Our Being, who art in Heaven. . .'" would be greatly diminished (Ozorak 1996, p. 23). In unsettled periods "doctrine, symbol, and ritual shape action" and it would be much harder, particularly in public, for women to reconcile a desire for gender equity with cherished symbols of male domination (Swidler 1986, p. 278).[8]

---

[8]Demonstrating that the dynamic is not confined to middle-class Protestants in the United States, Williams & Fuentes (2000) provide a rich account of how changes in the social environment affect the action repertoires of poor urban Catholics in Peru. They find that unsettled times encourage a resort to personal, self-help strategies and a turn away from collective, public solutions.

Grievances are infinite, whereas the number of social movements is finite. Hence, grievances cannot be taken for granted as the motive of collective action. Rather, we need to focus on the differential interpretation of culturally based grievances across individuals and, more importantly, across social groups. Borrowing from Snow et al. (1986), we use the language of framing to refer to "'schemata of interpretation' that enable individuals 'to locate, perceive, identify, and label' occurrences within their life space and the world at large" (p. 464). Their typology of cultural linkages between individuals and organizations recognizes four options, labeled as frame bridging, frame amplification, frame extension, and frame transformation (p. 467). These paths facilitate the transformation of individual grievances into collective action.

Frame bridging occurs when an organization recruits members whose individual cultural preferences resemble the organization's (Snow et al. 1986, p. 467). Organizations that use frame bridging solve their free-rider problem by offering members cultural, as opposed to material, goods. For example, when Jerry Falwell set out to enlist millions of culturally conservative Christians in his campaign of moral restoration in the late 1970s, he could simply tell them what they had already learned from fundamentalist churches: "[I]f Christ were to return today, he would find ample evidence of moral decay" (Liebman 1983, p. 52). Through grassroots campaigning and a multimedia enterprise, he offered his Moral Majority organization as a vehicle to combat the decay through political action and thus hasten the return of the Messiah. In so doing, Falwell extended an accepted motif from the social to the political realm.

The other three options, as their names imply, involve the amplification, extension, and transformation of motives (Snow et al. 1986, pp. 469–76) rather than a simple bridging between individuals and organizations with like motives. In these cases, organizations gerrymander their cultural message in order to attract a broader following. If successful, they will increase their membership base while pursuing the narrower cultural agenda of the organization's founders. If they are unsuccessful, membership will decline or stagnate and/or the organization's original political agenda will be replaced by one acceptable to the new adherents but unacceptable to the old (p. 476). Using the Moral Majority example, one can read between the lines to find potential examples of frame amplification, extension, and transformation. Frame amplification: The Moral Majority promoted Christian identity over class, racial, national, gender, and occupational identity because the Christian identity is more inclusive than the rich, white, American, male, Independent Baptist pastor identity. Frame extension: To attract a pool of racially conservative Americans who do not necessarily associate strongly with their religious identity, the Moral Majority encouraged the American government to support the Christian government of Rhodesia (whites) against the atheistic Marxist freedom fighters (blacks).[9] Frame transformation: The Moral Majority was a fundamentally right-wing organization that used the call of Christianity to inculcate and politicize a generation of

---

[9]On the power of race as a reference group in this context, see Hill (1993).

social conservatives. If any of these characterizations are accurate, one can make a compelling case that the Moral Majority motivated political action in individuals whose cultural values were not necessarily consonant with the organization's explicit religious mission.

Per the example of Falwell, elites are the critical actors in recontextualizing cultural components to allow for ideational mobilization. This observation draws heavily on the familiar political science understanding of elites as issue and interest entrepreneurs, a theme that recurs in a wide variety of political settings where religion has been politically mobilized. It makes sense to think of grievances as latencies, tools that are available for exploitation by strong or aspiring leadership. Three very different cases illustrate how elites facilitate the political expression of cultural values by deploying religious symbols and themes.

In stable polities, the politicization of group identity by elites has often driven partisan electoral strategies. Although culture, broadly speaking, may unite us, subcultures possess distinctive moral orders that help campaign organizations divide us (the electorate) into majority and minority coalitions. As Leege et al. (2002) document, the postwar electoral strategy of the major American parties was characterized by attempts to shape the electorate with appeals to deep-seated cultural values rooted in social group identifications. In their effort to build a new majority coalition, Republicans targeted various groups of wavering Democrats for both demobilization (abstention) and conversion (ticket splitting). They identified fault lines in society based on race, patriotism, gender, and religion; found symbols that appeared to demonstrate that the Democrats had abandoned core values; and created powerful emotional appeals that often bore impressive electoral fruit. Fears about "the other" in the form of communists, blacks, militant feminists, gays, and secularists became the late-twentieth-century equivalent of the Civil War era's "bloody shirt."

Recent tumult in Côte d'Ivoire provides another case in which elites effectively politicized religious and cultural grievances in the service of other goals. When Houphouët-Boigny, Côte d'Ivoire's leader since independence, died in the early 1990s, his successor began to enunciate the xenophobic theory of *Ivoirité* to justify his leadership. Initially this message implicitly aimed to unite "indigenous" groups loyal to the regime against "foreigners." By the time Laurent Gbagbo came to power, the dichotomy underlying *Ivoirité* was well understood as one pitting the predominately Christian south against the predominately Muslim north. By emphasizing north versus south and Christian versus Muslim, Gbago effectively undercut his most feared political rival, the Muslim Alassane Ouattara. When the Côte d'Ivoire's civil war broke out in late 2002, the head of state emphasized an explicit Us/Them rhetoric that caricatured Muslims in the north as *"talibans ivoiriens"* (Soudan 2003). Religious appeals were the idiom of a conflict that had multiple dimensions.

The same dynamic appears to operate when religion crosses state boundaries and becomes entwined with terrorist acts. The terrorist strikes of September 11, 2001, appear to be related to the identity-based grievances of the al Qaeda martyrs, which included the corruption of Islam, its siege by western powers, and the lack of an Islamically acceptable society and polity. Similarly, the terrorism of Eric Robert Rudolph, the presumed Centennial Park bomber also arrested for several abortion clinic bombings, drew on his immersion in Christian Identity, the American Patriot Movement, and the extremist wing of the prolife movement. This identity calls for the dismantling of the federal government; the social, political, and economic protection of white Christians; and the return of the majority of political power to the local level of government (Aho 1991, Barkun 1994). Moreover, it recontextualizes familiar parts of American social, religious, political, and economic culture in a manner that justifies white supremacy and antigovernment sentiment. The identity acquired from this milieu virtually forced on Rudolph a sense of responsibility and obligation to hold the government accountable for its actions (Silverman 2002a).

Elite-driven recontextualization is present in the *shahadat* and jihadist operations of reactionary Islamic revivalists and the Christian Identity behavior of Rudolph. Reactionary Islamic leaders, such as Osama bin Laden, Sheikh Omar Abdel Rahman, and many others, have argued in private and public statements that Islam is under attack, that Muslims are at risk, and that the behavior of the United States and other western/non-Muslim states recalls earlier episodes when Islam was threatened. From this context arise the references to westerners as "the Crusaders" and the lionization of "martyrs" who engage in behavior otherwise forbidden to Muslims. During his socialization, Rudolph was exposed to apocalyptic literature such as William Pierce's *The Turner Diaries*, a fictional account of a "patriot" revolution against the tyrannical U.S. government. In the same way that Hamas has made a cult of suicide bombing, Christian Identity and extremist prolife movements have used Rudolph as an exemplar. He is portrayed as a Christian patriot who is now the political prisoner of an ungodly state that butchers babies as part of Satan's plan to destroy America. By remaking Rudolph and numerous Islamically motivated terrorists as ideational examples to be emulated, the leadership of these movements helps motivate the next generation of actors.

By referring to grievances as the trigger for political mobilization, we mean to suggest that religious groups seldom enter the political realm driven primarily by abstract motivations to improve the world or otherwise achieve heaven on earth. No doubt such efforts exist—exemplified by Christian Reconstructionism, a movement that seeks to remake all of American society in its image of a biblical commonwealth (Barron 1992)—and groups may well understand and justify their political efforts in such spiritual terms. But we do not believe that the language of such movements accurately reflects the principal source of political engagement. As a rule, we believe, this kind of mobilization is reactive: Groups respond to what they perceive as social flaws, attacks on sacred values, and anti-religious practices. The tone is often defensive as religious elites declare that they are forced to intervene in politics so that their members can live godly lives. We sometimes forget that groups may suffer costs by virtue of political action and that it would often be easier to forego such action in favor of tending to hearth and home.

Typically, some trigger issue is required to overcome the tendency to focus on more immediate religious concerns.

Although it is certainly "*unreasonable* to neglect the study of why people want what they want," the level of abstraction involved in the study of preferences is far higher than that involved in the study of either organizational resource mobilization or political opportunity structures (Wildavsky 1987, p. 3). The above discussion began by linking religion to culture understood as shared values and social relations. Despite their differing conceptions of religion, both Weber and Durkheim make this connection in their work on religion. Cultures come with built-in moral orders and are sensitive to the violation of norms and mores. "Religion adds both a transcendent and immanent supernatural dimension to identity, norms, and boundaries," goes the recurring theme enunciated by Leege et al. (2002), "and is therefore a powerful instrument for persuasion" (p. 45). Alert to the mobilizing potential inherent in cultural tensions and conflicts, political elites may and often do exploit grievances as part of their quest for power and authority. In that process, the religious grievances amplified by religiopolitical entrepreneurs are constituted as the political motives of mobilized religious groups.

MEANS: RESOURCES

As we noted in the previous section, grievances are not automatically politicized, and an increase in the scope or intensity of dissatisfaction does not invariably translate into more active attempts at resolution. According to resource mobilization theory, the strength of the link between grievances and effective political action depends mainly on the organizational capacity of groups seeking change.[10] Resources are absolutely necessary for a successful social movement, religious or otherwise, and they vary in form, quality, and quantity from movement to movement. Labor unions, parent-teacher organizations, rebel armies, and local churches have all been mobilized politically in the past, but the resources each group marshaled have differed considerably. In the following discussion of resource mobilization in religious organizations, we emphasize five distinct modes of resource: culture, leadership, material resources, communication networks, and space. Although these categories are reminiscent of Zald & McCarthy's (1979) more generalized work on resource mobilization, we pay special attention to the unique access religious organizations have to these means. In stressing the resource advantages available to religious organizations, it is important to bear in mind that these assets

[10]SMT and resource mobilization are sometimes portrayed as contending approaches. SMT is often championed by scholars who feel that collective behavior research overemphasizes organizational resources. Nevertheless, we believe that resource mobilization, like political opportunity theory, should be considered a part of the SMT family, a specialized body of theory that helps explain the transformation of grievances into organizational form. We see the approaches as complementary rather than competitive.

may backfire and handicap movements as they engage society. Discussion of their utility must not overlook their nature as double-edged swords.[11]

The discussion of resources in SMT usually emphasizes tangible or material assets available to social groups. When the discussion turns to religiously based social movements, it is equally important to consider ideas as a means of mobilization. As discussed in the preceding section, religious organizations are both creators and maintainers of culture. In considering culture as a motive for political engagement, we focus on its capacity to define identity and provide meaning, frames of understanding, so that people interpret their situation in a certain way. Beyond providing a motive for political engagement, culture may enable religious organizations to exert on their members pressure unimaginable in most secular organizations. When culture legitimates shared values that claim divine origin, it drapes a powerful sacred canopy over the sometimes banal, sometimes brutal work involved in political mobilization. Describing the Iranian Revolution of the late 1970s, Salehi (1996) notes that "[t]he Islamic groups had thousands, even hundreds of thousands, of fully devoted individuals under their command." This devotion, Salehi continues, went so far as to incorporate martyrdom, "a concept that had become an internalized ideal" (p. 51). Although a social movement need not be religious for activists to be willing to lay down their lives in pursuit of its goals, divine sanction adds to these movements a transcendent nature. In a shared religious community, Leege & Kellsted (1993) contend, "[p]eople become empowered, they develop the capacity to *act* in concert" (pp. 9–10). Whereas individuals tend to be risk-averse about challenging the government in general, a sense of belonging to a sacred community can alleviate the free-rider problem and embolden individuals to act in ways that may appear individually irrational outside the religiocultural context.

Although culture is a resource that religious groups may exploit successfully, as the Ayatollah Khomeini and his Shia advisors did in Iran, it does have potential political drawbacks. In culturally and/or religiously diverse societies, cultural resources may be extremely divisive. The civil rights campaign in the 1960s illustrates this point well. For a brief period in the early 1960s, Rev. Martin Luther King, Jr. managed not only to incite members of his congregation to campaign for civil rights but also to draw a diverse group of individuals, white and black, into his movement. Among the most influential members of this coalition were the white leaders of the National Council of Churches, who cajoled midwestern

---

[11]In one of the very few attempts to balance the pros and cons of clerical influence on black politics, Reed (1986) emphasizes the down side to ministerial leadership in politics. He argues that ministers by their nature are given to an authoritarian leadership style that discourages the development of democratic habits and inhibits the emergence of other leadership sectors in the black community. The scandals that have engulfed a number of prominent political ministries, Jesse Jackson's included, also suggest that lack of accountability may encourage excess and redound against political movements that are hitched to religious stars.

legislators to support the Civil Rights Act of 1964 (Findlay 1990, p. 67). Later in the 1960s, James Foreman called on these same individuals to demand $500 million in "reparations." His demand was met with a terse rebuff as white mainline churches quickly retreated to their familiar, uninvolved stance on "race questions" (p. 92), where they remain more than a quarter century later. Certainly Foreman's move may have been politically beneficial in that it brought recognition to his cause, but it inhibited political mobilization by lopping off important components of what had been an effective coalition.

The most effective social movement organizations often owe their success to astute leadership. In their study of "Race, Ethnicity and Political Resources," Verba et al. (1993) discover statistically what observers of the American civil rights movement already knew well anecdotally: black Protestant churches can be remarkably effective incubators of political leadership (p. 482). Morris (1996) deduces two reasons for this state of affairs. First, he argues, blacks denied access to mainstream institutions turned to the church to fill a void. "Behind the church doors," Morris contends, "was a friendly and warm environment where black people could be temporarily at peace with themselves while displaying their talents and aspirations before an empathetic audience" (pp. 29–30). Motivated African-Americans saw, and continue to see, a relative dearth of role models in national and local government. Minority churches, however, provide a wealth of examples of African-American leadership. Because many of their congregations are predominately, if not exclusively, black, African-Americans fill every post from minister to choir director, from facilities manager to Sunday school teacher. Second, Morris contends, "[c]hurches, especially the prestigious or leading ones, demanded ministers who could command the respect, support, and allegiance of congregations through their strong, magnetic personalities" (p. 31). There is a great deal of overlap in the skill sets required behind the pulpit and the political podium. Church leaders are not only given a position of authority but also are forced to demonstrate a capacity to lead on a weekly basis.

Like culture, the resource of leadership in religious organizations is not unequivocally useful as a means of political mobilization. Two striking examples of the inability of religious leadership to translate itself into positive political resources are Jerry Falwell's infamous 9/11 comments (Harris 2001) and the Full Gospel pastor's attempt at community organization, discussed above. Used to speaking in terms of good and evil to a like-minded audience, the charismatic Falwell used the tragedy of September 11 to reiterate his familiar political mantra, namely that people who are not conservative Christians are ruining America. He held liberals, gays, prolife groups, civil libertarians, and others to blame for God's decision to withdraw the cloak of protection surrounding the United States, permitting the hijackers to do their work. His message not only fell on largely unsympathetic ears but also managed to push the Thomas Road Baptist Church further away from mainstream values. The leadership style that made him the master of a media empire proved an ineffective resource for political mobilization in that political climate. As for the pastor at Full Gospel, his message consistently urges his parishioners to fight off evil. This unwavering method confers job security, as evidenced by his long tenure, but leaves little room for the moral flexibility needed to mobilize politically on issues that are technical in nature and not clear cases of good versus evil. When it came time to "Tak[e] the City for Jesus Christ," Full Gospel's pastor was unable to lead his congregation into the political fray because his charismatic authoritarian style, well-suited for the pulpit, proved unable to deal with the arena's inherent ambiguity (Wood 1999, p. 319). Both of these styles of leadership are effective at promoting a certain type of in-group behavior. The identity-rooted messages are an excellent means of "boundary maintenance." The problem is that although the in-group may be mobilized and even attempt to take action, it is mobilized against several out-groups, which are put on guard by the original attempt at mobilization. The result is a draw at best, as out-group responses, not to mention the larger societal rejection, prevent the in-group from accomplishing its goals.[12]

Material resources are perhaps the type of resource least differentiated by the religious context. Regardless of the social movement, material resources are necessary to "pay organizers, rent office space, print flyers, make telephone calls, send direct mail appeals, construct banners and placards, transport protesters to protests, bail demonstrators out of jail, attract the attention of the media, and offset the costs of boycotts, strikes, and sanctions" (Smith 1996, p. 14). Although the millions of dollars donated to the Moral Majority by wealthy businessmen are certainly a striking example of a religious organization's capacity for accumulating wealth, that is far from the norm (Liebman 1983, p. 51). The example of the Anglican Church of Kenya (CPK) during the Moi regime is far more typical (Friedman 1996). Combining the tithing (both money and time) resources of thousands of relatively poor Kenyans with token support from the international Anglican Church, CPK managed to circumvent corrupt and often unaccommodating government channels to provide jobs, meeting places, education, health facilities, and a telephone to the residents of Murang'a in West Central Kenya (pp. 387–89). Because CPK Murang'a had a politically diverse congregation, these material resources were not applied in a unidirectional political movement. Nevertheless, political opposition groups found CPK Murang'a a safe place to recruit members because the government, which was not providing public services or jobs to many congregants, had little recourse within church walls (p. 392).

"[M]ovement success," as Liebman (1983) explains a lesson learned from the Moral Majority, "depends on an extensive network of communications between

---

[12]Religiously based social movements seem to have the greatest success when they persuade believers that political action is a religious duty, i.e., when they engage in successful frame bridging. Attempts to draw on religious legitimation for political ends may backfire when members of the religious community do not see the political program as a valid expression of religious purpose. When clergy from mainline Protestant denominations asserted a biblical basis for their positions on such disparate controversies as open housing, the Vietnam War, and farm worker rights in the 1960s and 1970s, many parishioners rejected the linkage and drove the social justice advocates from the pulpit (Hadden 1969).

organizers and constituents" (p. 56). Compared to nonreligious social movements, religious organizations have a real organizational advantage in communication. "Scholars of the church have consistently noted," for example, "how rapidly and efficiently information is transmitted to the black community from the pulpit" (Morris 1996, p. 33). At least at the level of congregation, churches have regular weekly meetings to disseminate information from the leadership to the masses. Even if this information is not overtly political, latent political messages creep into sermons, and occasionally less covert messages work their way into services. An example of this latter tendency arises in the case of the Anglican church of Kenya. Through subversive songs referring to the "glorious days of the past" when Kenyatta was president and the Mau Mau were waging war from the hills, Kikuyu speakers managed to vocalize their political discontent through worship (Friedman 1996, p. 391).

Although still a useful means for political mobilization, religious communication networks may begin to lose their potency beyond the congregational level. The functioning of the Moral Majority provides an example of this diminished capacity. Using interpersonal relationships within the Baptist Bible Fellowship, the movement cobbled together a number of influential Independent Baptist churches from across the country. Initially, this amalgamation of mega-churches cut an impressive figure on the national political scene with its 2.5-million-member mailing list (Liebman 1983, p. 61). Soon, however, the autonomy of the Moral Majority's member institutions began to show. State chapters and even individual churches readily expressed their independence when congregations called for one issue or another to gain ascendance on the local political agenda. Undoubtedly the Moral Majority represents the extreme case in that it was constructed of congregations with a long history of independence, but the diminished capacity of communication networks when one moves from the congregation level to national bodies is a reality even for religions with a hierarchical tradition (see Byrnes 1991, p. 50).

Of all the resources discussed in this section, political "space" most strikingly differentiates religiously oriented political movements from their secular counterparts. "[C]hurches," notes Gautier (1998), "have probably the greatest possibility of autonomous existence in civil society, outside the realm of direct influence by the state" (p. 291). In the months leading up to the Iranian revolution, Shiia leaders were on the front lines of antigovernment protests, and mosques served as the meeting place for government opposition (Salehi 1996, p. 51). Just prior to the dismantling of South Africa's apartheid state, Archbishop Desmond Tutu and Reverend Frank Chikane were firing verbal salvos at the Nationalist Party's legitimacy and Anglican churches were serving as de facto opposition headquarters (Borer 1996, p. 137). Why, one might ask, in such diverse contexts, were religious leaders and buildings spared the harshest treatment of oppressive regimes? Space is the answer.

Had either the Shah or De Klerk brought the full brunt of their security apparatuses to bear on the aforementioned religious institutions, they would have faced an almost certainly fatal backlash. If the military had not turned their weapons on their leaders, the masses likely would have. One cannot attack a people's God without incurring their fiercest wrath. All but the most desperate governments grant a certain leeway to religious leaders, a freedom that is not afforded their secular equivalents. Religious organizations can use this leeway, as the Ayatollah and South African Council of Churches did, to act politically where few others dare tread. Similarly, by bombing churches in an attempt to forestall the civil rights movement, white racists instead provided an otherwise unenthusiastic federal government a reason to intervene in southern politics (Chalmers 2003).

Space is likely to be particularly critical when religiously based social movements can draw on an international civil society for legitimacy and more tangible forms of support. The churches that led the way in challenging apartheid could draw on a global network of allies to put additional pressure on the regime when it trespassed on sacred space (Warr 1999). Through the antiracism programs of the National and World Councils of Churches, parishioners in North America were enlisted (not always willingly) in the struggles of black South Africans. Elsewhere in Africa, local clerics who battled oppressive states on behalf of parishioners received important support from the human rights campaign championed by the Vatican (Hanson 1987). On the other side of the political spectrum, the anticommunist movements associated with evangelical Protestantism in places such as Nicaragua and the People's Republic of China benefited from the moral and material support provided by their coreligionists in North America (Buss & Herman 2003).

OPPORTUNITY

Social movements do not exist in a political vacuum where range of motion is unobstructed and all choices are equally sound. Instead, they arise and act in a political environment full of formal and informal structures that provide both incentives and disincentives for political mobilization. Not surprisingly, political scientists have made their greatest contribution to SMT by highlighting the importance of the state and political conditions to the emergence and success of movements (McAdam 1982, Tarrow 1994). Rather surprisingly, students of religiously based political mobilization have not rushed to apply the insights of this literature to their subjects. This section illustrates the potential contribution of this research to help us understand which movements flourish and which languish.

Contingencies of time and place matter greatly for the evolution of social movements with a religious base. Drawing on Tarrow (1994), scholars have suggested that collective mobilization is most likely when (a) access to institutional participation has begun to open up, (b) political alignments are in disarray and new realignments have not yet been formed, (c) challengers can take advantage of major conflicts within the political elite, and (d) challengers are aided by influential allies within or outside of the system (Steigenga & Coleman 1995, p. 467).

The remainder of this section addresses each of these criteria in turn and describes their impact on the role of Chilean Protestants in the Allende and Pinochet regimes (Steigenga & Coleman 1995), U.S. Catholic voting patterns in the 1960s (Byrnes 1991), abortion politics in the United States and Canada (Tatalovich 1995), and black South Africans' struggle to abolish apartheid (Borer 1996), respectively.

Given the same sets of motives and means in different contexts, religious organizations are more apt to mobilize politically in a democratic and open political system than in a closed, authoritarian system. Although this antecedent stipulation is admittedly artificial in that motives and means of organizations are likely to differ significantly between these regime types, the point remains valid. Here the case of Protestant mobilization in Chile between 1972 and 1991 is instructive. Steigenga & Coleman (1995) find that "[l]ower class Protestants moved leftward when opportunities for political participation opened up in the late 1960s, and retreated into conservatism or quiescence during the repressive Pinochet period" (p. 465). This thesis is consistent with Tarrow's hypothesis. When Chile was a democracy, religious groups, including Protestants, mobilized to address political concerns with government officials. They found "ways to attend to material concerns on this earth via political action, while waiting for the imminent return of Jesus Christ" (Steigenga & Coleman 1995, p. 480). When Chile was a military dictatorship, religious groups, especially Protestants, acquiesced. This reaction to the change in political opportunity structure, according to Steigenga & Coleman, "appears to represent one logical strategy for survival in the face of a highly repressive regime" (p. 481).

Uncertain political alignments produce situations ripe for political mobilization. Opposing political camps jockey for support wherever they can find it when constituencies once considered unattainable or solidly supportive are perceived as up-for-grabs. In such a scenario, religious groups seeking to have grievances addressed are more likely to find political accommodation. Such was the case for American Catholics in the late 1960s and early 1970s. During this period, with prodding from the Church hierarchy in the form of the Second Vatican Council, American priests went out into their communities to speak to the broader American public about the legal and moral failings of a national policy legalizing abortion (Byrnes 1991, pp. 56–57). Given the centrality of the issue of abortion on the Vatican's political agenda, certainly many of these priests would have championed the "right-to-life" cause regardless of whether politicians took them seriously. Yet without the political fluidity that made Catholics a target for political conversion, their religiopolitical movement would have been conducted in relative obscurity.

Seeing potential weaknesses in the Democrats' New Deal coalition, Republicans were able to pick off Southerners in the 1968 presidential elections and set their sights on Catholics in 1972 (Byrnes 1991, p. 63). They needed Catholic support, one theory goes, "in order to refute the notion that Nixon had formed his new coalition by cynically appealing to the baser motives of Southern whites" (p. 65). Preaching to congregations that strongly supported the Democratic Party despite its ardently prochoice stance on abortion, the Catholic hierarchy was not averse

to political wooing. The Republican Party capitalized on uncertain political alignments by pushing an antiabortion program to the center of its socially conservative
agenda. At least partially as a result of these efforts, Catholic voters gave Nixon
a comfortable majority of their vote in 1972 (p. 65). To summarize, the disarray
of political alignments in the late 1960s allowed Republicans to capture a base of
political support (Catholics) that had once been solidly Democratic. These uneasy
alignments also allowed the Catholic hierarchy to move a nationally unpopular
platform (the right-to-life cause) onto a major party's agenda.

As illustrated by comparative analysis of abortion politics in the United States
and Canada (Schwartz 1981, Tatalovich 1995), the root of elite conflict may be
structural in nature. In Canada's parliamentary system, where parties have significantly more formal and informal powers of persuasion than their American
counterparts have, there are fewer points of view showcased on the national political scene (Tatalovich 1995, p. 7). Prolife and prochoice groups have found much
more support on Capitol Hill than on Parliament Hill. The evidence suggests that
electoral and legislative structures in the United States encourage a divided elite
whereas Canadian structures diminish elite conflict. In the United States, junior
representatives and backbenchers may find it politically desirable to champion
emotionally charged, unbargainable religious issues supported by small minority
groups. Such a move will not only bring publicity and name recognition but may
also be seen by constituents as a moral local politician standing up to an amoral
and unwieldy leviathan in Washington. In Canada, parliamentarians interested in a
political career are encouraged to toe the company line and avoid taking politically
costly zero-sum stances. Social movements that champion nationally unpopular
causes find few, if any, politically elite supporters in such a setting. This reinforces
the prediction that conflicts within the political elite will provide opportunities for
social movements to act politically.[13]

The final piece of the political opportunity structure to be discussed here is
the assistance of influential allies. This type of political opportunity can easily
be misconceptualized as a political resource or means: the commodity of friends
in high places. Such a conception would, however, be missing an important distinction. Political means are endogenous resources to a social movement. Political
opportunities are exogenous resources. Although the support and encouragement
of allies may contribute greatly to an organization's ability to collectively mobilize,
allies no more belong to politically mobilized organizations than do openings in
participation, alignments in disarray, or elite conflicts.

---

[13]Moreover, the lack of opportunity for dealing with the issue of abortion in Canada has
resulted in significantly lower levels of abortion-related violence there. It seems that the
frustration that results from the U.S. prolife movement's inability to effectively capitalize
on the political opportunity surrounding the issue of abortion, a frustration that seems to
lead to fairly high levels of political violence, does not exist in Canada. In this instance,
lack of opportunity means lack of frustration at the failure to bring about effective change
on the issue. This seems to inhibit extreme behavior.

Consider the case of religious leaders' roles in South Africa's antiapartheid movement. By the time the apartheid oligarchy was finally toppled in 1994, black residents of South Africa had been fighting an oppressive and racist state apparatus for centuries. For most of this period, these freedom fighters had few influential allies either domestic or international. The political opportunity structure changed dramatically in the 1980s, however, when such groups as the South African Council of Churches (SACC) and South African Catholic Bishops Conference (SACBC) openly joined the antiapartheid campaign alongside social movement organizations such as the African National Congress (Borer 1996, p. 125). Previously, many religious leaders in these two institutions had found the segregationist policies of the South African government morally distasteful, but they remained politically inactive. Increasing intensity of opposition to the government and a reciprocal intensification of state oppression made this silence untenable (p. 126). By the mid-1980s, South African clergy and their transnational support agencies were regularly publishing antiapartheid statements, traveling the world to seek international condemnation of apartheid, and calling for a regime change (pp. 131–35). Many factors eventually undermined apartheid, but South Africa's clergy were essential to the cause of the black majority.

Like the famous dog that did not bark, enabling Sherlock Holmes to solve a mystery, the importance of the opportunity structure may be most evident in cases when religious groups fail to mobilize politically despite propitious motives and resources. In the case of Mexico's Catholic Church, anticlerical provisions of the Mexican Constitution of 1917 firmly closed the opportunity structure for confessional politics (Metz 1992). Punished for its long-time alliance with the landholding oligarchy, the Church was expressly forbidden to engage in political life by a series of draconian enactments that disenfranchised the clergy, appropriated all church property to the state, prohibited church operation of schools, and otherwise narrowed the permissible scope of church involvement with society. More than half a century passed before most of these provisions were relaxed, facilitating a political witness by the Church. The salience of opportunity for successful mobilization is made even clearer by the fate of Algeria's Islamist movement, the Islamic Salvation Front (FIS). Since the beginning of democratization in the late 1980s, the social movement represented by the FIS had quietly built up a strong base of popular support by providing a broad array of social services and addressing human needs far more effectively than the sagging state bureaucracy (Entelis 2001). The initial round of voting in parliamentary elections late in 1991 suggested the FIS would soon emerge as the majority party and take the reins of central government, displacing the secular regime that had governed Algeria since independence. Unwilling to accept a religious state, the military stepped in with a coup d'etat on behalf of the secular political elites who were on the verge of dispossession by the Islamic movement. The elections were canceled, a civilian government was installed, and all traces of political Islam were ruthlessly suppressed. When the guarantors of the election, France and the United States, refused to intervene, the FIS had lost its opportunity. With the political opening now firmly closed, the FIS split into the mainstream religious opposition movement and the Armed Islamic Group (GIA), a full-fledged insurgent/terrorist movement. As Mexico and Algeria attest, the degree of political openness contributes to shaping both the degree and form of religiously based political mobilization.

CONCLUSION

The sheer diversity of religious expression in politics precludes any single-factor model of broad applicability. Over the past two decades, we have witnessed religiously based political action overthrow seemingly entrenched dictatorial regimes, impose theocratic states, seek freedom for oppressed minorities, and reinforce the dominance of specific social groups. Virtually every major and many minor religious traditions have been mined for their political utility in nations old and new, economically advanced and desperately poor, core and peripheral to the global order. The mode of this action has varied from quiet and worshipful petitioning of the state to violent terrorist assaults that left thousands dead and wounded.

This explosion of interest in religion contrasts sharply with its long neglect by the discipline of political science. Although we believe this attention is warranted and long overdue, the new attentiveness brings challenges of its own. In particular, we have argued, the ubiquity of religion as a political force may convey the impression that religious engagement with politics is the norm, natural or, at least, unproblematic. In fact, there is no necessary linkage between religious communities and political action. For that linkage to be forged, three conditions must be satisfied. Religious groups must come to consider political action as a sacred obligation, draw on various internal resources to prosecute that action, and confront a political environment that may hinder such efforts. Because of their comprehensive nature, we argue, the various branches of social movement theory (SMT) offer a unique framework by which to understand how religiously based organizations negotiate the steps that lead to political engagement.

SMT is particularly well suited to emphasize the contingency of the nexus between religion and politics. Although each major component of the theory may help us comprehend a different dimension of mobilization, all three are required to transform religious sentiment into an effective political presence. Mobilization is not guaranteed by the existence of grievances, by organizational capacity, or by a political system that invites groups into the zone of contention. Rather, all three must be present before religiously grounded grievances are translated into effective political action.

We hope this sense of contingency will guide subsequent work on the political activity of religious groups. There is nothing natural or inevitable about religious activity in political life or about the manner in which religion expresses itself politically. Religion may be active or quiescent, supportive or subversive of the dominant order. The path depends on the contingent conditions we have identified throughout this essay. Religious activists often assert with naive self-confidence that their faith dictates a certain political stance. In truth, most religious traditions contain rich and nuanced bodies of doctrine that can be mined to support a wide variety of political positions. What interests us is not the political message supposedly embedded in a religious tradition—a construct whose innate existence we doubt—but rather the inherently subjective social processes that prompt people to understand their tradition in a certain way. The Exodus metaphor of the Hebrew Bible can be invoked as a call to challenge society, the predominant motif encountered in Christian tradition (Walzer 1985), or, as one of us once heard in a Baptist congregation, as a justification for building a physical wall around the church grounds. Jihad may be understood either as a call for self-purification, a struggle between the solitary believer and Allah, or as the rationale for a crusade against unbelievers (Eickelman & Piscatori 1996, Silverman 2002b). Religious traditions are interpreted, contextualized, framed, and taught in the service of many political goals. Ideas matter, but the manner in which they are understood, acted on, and received by the broader society is the critical problem for social scientists who want to grasp the political dimension of religion.

ACKNOWLEDGMENTS

Without in any way implicating them, we thank our colleagues Philip J. Williams and Jennifer Hochschild for helping us sharpen our focus.

The *Annual Review of Political Science* is online at
http://polisci.annualreviews.org

LITERATURE CITED

Adorno TW, Frenkel-Brunswik E, Levinson DJ, Sanford RN. 1950. *The Authoritarian Personality.* New York: Harper

Aho JA. 1991. *The Politics of Righteousness: Idaho Christian Patriotism.* Seattle, WA: Univ. Washington Press

Aminzade R, Perry EJ. 2001. The sacred, religious, and secular in contentious politics: blurring boundaries. In *Silence and Voice in the Study of Contentious Politics*, ed. RR Aminzade, JA Goldstone, D McAdam, EJ Perry, WH Sewell Jr, et al., pp. 155–78. New York: Cambridge Univ. Press

Barkun M. 1994. *Religion and the Racist Right.* Chapel Hill, NC: Univ. North Carolina Press

Barron B. 1992. *Heaven on Earth? The Social and Political Agendas of Dominion Theology.* Grand Rapids, MI: Zondervan

Bell D, ed. 1955. *The New American Right.* New York: Criterion

Borer TA. 1996. Church leadership, state repression, and the "spiral of involvement" in the South African anti-apartheid movement, 1983–1990. See Smith 1996, pp. 25–43

Buss D, Herman D. 2003. *Globalizing Family Values: The Christian Right in International Politics.* Minneapolis: Univ. Minn. Press

Byrnes TA. 1991. *Catholic Bishops in American Politics.* Princeton, NJ: Princeton Univ. Press

Casanova J. 1994. *Public Religions in the Modern World.* Chicago: Univ. Chicago Press

Chalmers DM. 2003. *Backfire: How the Ku Klux Klan Helped the Civil Rights Movement.* Lanham, MD: Rowman & Littlefield

Crawford A. 1980. *Thunder on the Right.* New York: Pantheon

Eickelman DF, Piscatori J. 1996. *Muslim Politics.* Princeton, NJ: Princeton Univ. Press

Entelis J. 2001. Religion and politics in Algeria: conflict or consensus. *Islam Christian-Muslim Relat.* 12:417–34

Findlay JF. 1990. Religion and politics in the sixties: the churches and the Civil Rights Act of 1964. *J. Am. Hist.* 77:66–93

Friedman GS. 1996. The power of the familiar: everyday practices in the Anglican Church of Kenya (CPK). *J. Church State* 38:377–96

Gautier ML. 1998. Church elites and restoration of civil society in the communist societies of Central Europe. *J. Church State* 40:289–318

Hadden JK. 1969. *Gathering Storm in the Churches.* Garden City, NY: Doubleday-Anchor

Hadden JK. 1987. Toward desacralizing secularization theory. *Soc. Forces* 65:587–611

Hanson EO. 1987. *Catholic Church in World Politics.* Princeton, NJ: Princeton Univ. Press

Harris JF. 2001. God gave U.S. "what we deserve," Falwell says. *Wash. Post* Sept. 14:1

Hart S. 2001. *Cultural Dilemmas of Progressive Politics.* Chicago: Univ. Chicago Press

Hill KA. 1993. The domestic sources of foreign policymaking: congressional voting and American mass attitudes toward South Africa. *Int. Stud. Q.* 37:195–214

Hughes JA. 1995. *Understanding Classical Sociology.* Thousand Oaks, CA: Sage

Huntington SP. 1996. *The Clash of Civilizations and the Remaking of World Order.* New York: Simon & Schuster

Jelen TG. 1998. Research in religion and mass political behavior in the United States: looking both ways after two decades of scholarship. *Am. Polit. Q.* 26:110–34

Jelen TG, Wilcox CC, eds. 2002. *Religion and Politics in Comparative Perspective: The One, the Few, and the Many.* New York: Cambridge Univ. Press

Johnston H, Klandermans B, eds. 1995. *Social Movements and Culture.* Minneapolis: Univ. Minn. Press

Kornhauser W. 1959. *The Politics of Mass Society.* Glencoe, IL: Free

Leege DC, Kellstedt LA, eds. 1993. *Rediscovering the Religious Factor in American Politics.* Armonk, NY: M.E. Sharpe

Leege DC, Wald KD, Krueger BS, Mueller PD. 2002. *Politics of Cultural Differences: Social Change and Voter Mobilization Strategies in the Post-New Deal Period.* Princeton, NJ: Princeton Univ. Press

Liebman RC. 1983. Mobilizing the moral majority. In *The New Christian Right*, ed. RC Liebman, pp. 50–73. New York: Aldine

Lipset SM, Raab E. 1981. The election and the evangelicals. *Commentary* 71:25–31

Lo CYH. 1992. Communities of challengers in social movement theory. In *Frontiers in Social Movement Theory*, ed. AD Morris, CM Mueller, pp. 224–47. New Haven, CT: Yale Univ. Press

Marty ME, Appleby RS. 1992. *The Glory and the Power: The Fundamentalist Challenge to the Modern World.* Boston: Beacon

McAdam D. 1982. *Political Process and the Development of Black Insurgency, 1930–1970.* Chicago: Univ. Chicago Press

McAdam D, Tarrow S, Tilly C. 1996. To map contentious politics. *Mobilization* 1:17–34

McVeigh R, Sikkink D. 2001. God, politics, and protest: religious beliefs and the legitimation of contentious tactics. *Soc. Forces* 79:1425–58

Metz A. 1992. Mexican church-state relations under President Carlos Salinas de Gortari. *J. Church State* 34:111–30

Meyer DS, Tarrow S, eds. 1997. *The Social Movement Society: Contentious Politics for a New Century.* New York: Oxford Univ. Press

Morris AD. 1996. The black church in the civil rights movement: the SCLC as the decentralized, radical arm of the black church. See Smith 1996, pp. 29–46

Morris AD, Mueller CM, eds. 1992. *Frontiers in Social Movement Theory.* New Haven, CT: Yale Univ. Press

Ozorak EW. 1996. The power but not the glory:

how women empower themselves through religion. *J. Sci. Stud. Relig.* 35:17–29

Pals D. 1996. *Seven Theories of Religion.* New York: Oxford Univ. Press

Putnam RD. 2001. *Bowling Alone.* New York: Simon & Schuster

Reed AL Jr. 1986. *The Jesse Jackson Phenomenon: The Crisis of Purpose in Afro-American Politics.* New Haven, CT: Yale Univ. Press

Rudolph SH, Piscatori J, eds. 1996. *Transnational Religion and Fading States.* Boulder, CO: Westview

Salehi MM. 1996. Radical Islamic insurgency in the Iranian Revolution of 1978–1979. See Smith 1996, pp. 47–63

Schwartz M. 1981. Politics and moral causes in Canada and the United States. In *Comparative Social Research*, ed. RF Tomasson, pp. 65–90. Greenwich, CT: JAI

Silverman AL. 2002a. *An exploratory analysis of an interdisciplinary theory of terrorism.* Ph.D. thesis, Dep. Polit. Sci., Univ. Florida

Silverman AL. 2002b. Just war, Jihad, and terrorism: a comparison of Western and Islamic norms for the use of political violence. *J. Church State* 44:73–92

Smelser NJ. 1963. *Theory of Collective Behavior.* New York: Free

Smith C, ed. 1996. *Disruptive Religion: The Force of Faith in Social-Movement Activism.* New York: Routledge

Smith DE. 1974. Religion and political modernization: comparative perspectives. In *Religion and Political Modernization*, ed. DE Smith, pp. 3–28. New Haven, CT: Yale Univ. Press

Snow DE, Rochford EB Jr, Worden SK, Benford RD.1986. Frame alignment processes, micromobilization, and movement participation. *Am. Sociol. Rev.* 51:464–81

Soudan F. 2003. French, go home? *Jeune Afrique Intelligent* Feb. 8:61

Steigenga TJ, Coleman KM. 1995. Protestant political orientations and the structure of po-

litical opportunity: Chile, 1972–1991. *Polity* 27:465–82

Swidler A. 1986. Culture in action: symbols and strategies. *Am. Sociol. Rev.* 51:273–86

Tarrow S. 1994. *Power in Movement: Social Movements, Collective Action and Politics.* New York: Cambridge Univ. Press

Tatalovich R. 1995. *Abortion Politics in the United States and Canada.* Armonk, NY: M.E. Sharpe

Tesh S. 1984. In support of "single-issue" politics. *Polit. Sci. Q.* 99:27–44

Verba S, Schlozman KL, Brady H. 1995. *Voice and Equality: Civic Voluntarism in American Politics.* Cambridge, MA: Harvard Univ. Press

Verba S, Schlozman KL, Brady H, Nie NH. 1993. Race, ethnicity and political resources: participation in the United States. *Br. J. Polit. Sci.* 23:453–97

Walzer M. 1985. *Exodus and Revolution.* New York: Basic

Warr K. 1999. The normative promise of religious organizations in global civil society. *J. Church State* 41:499–524

Weber M. 1968. *Economy and Society: An Outline of Interpretive Sociology*, ed. G Roth, C Wittich. Trans. E Fischoff (from German). New York: Bedminster

Wilcox C. 1992. *God's Warriors: The Christian Right in Twentieth-Century America.* Baltimore, MD: Johns Hopkins Univ. Press

Wildavsky A. 1987. Choosing preferences by constructing institutions: a cultural theory of preference formation. *Am. Polit. Sci. Rev.* 81: 3–21

Williams PJ, Fuentes V. 2000. Catholic responses to the crises of everyday life in Lima, Peru. *J. Church State* 42:89–114

Wood RL. 1999. Religious culture and political action. *Sociol. Theory* 17:307–32

Zald MN, McCarthy JD. 1979. *The Dynamics of Social Movements: Resource Mobilization, Social Control, and Tactics.* Cambridge, MA: Winthrop

Annu. Rev. Polit. Sci. 2005. 8:145–70
doi: 10.1146/annurev.polisci.8.082103.104927
Copyright © 2005 by Annual Reviews. All rights reserved
First published online as a Review in Advance on Nov. 11, 2004

STRATEGIC SURPRISE AND THE SEPTEMBER 11 ATTACKS

Daniel Byman

*Edmund A. Walsh School of Foreign Service at Georgetown University,
Washington, DC 20057; email: dlb32@georgetown.edu*

Key Words   terrorism, intelligence, al Qaeda, organization theory

■ **Abstract**   This essay examines the failure to anticipate the terrorist attacks of September 11 from four perspectives: cognitive biases of government analysts and policy makers concerned with terrorism, organizational pathologies of key bureaucracies such as the CIA and the FBI, political and strategic errors of senior government officials, and the unusual nature of al Qaeda. Drawing on past studies of strategic surprise, it argues that agencies such as the CIA at times did impressive work against the terrorist organization, but that in general the U.S. government, and the U.S. intelligence community in particular, lacked a coherent approach for triumphing over the skilled terrorists it faced. In hindsight, it is clear that numerous mistakes at all levels of the U.S. government and the broader U.S. analytic community made strategic surprise more likely.

INTRODUCTION

The quest to understand, and to lay blame for, the terrorist attacks on September 11, 2001 began even before the fires stopped burning. Pundits, policy makers, and analysts alike have cast the net of responsibility widely. Presidents Clinton and Bush are excoriated for letting bin Laden slip through their fingers. The Central Intelligence Agency and Federal Bureau of Investigation are lambasted for dithering in the face of a looming threat. Other analysts look outside the United States, painting a picture of al Qaeda as a formidable adversary against which even the most robust counterterrorism program would fail.

Of the many troubling features of the attacks, their sheer surprise was most disturbing to many Americans. The attacks shattered U.S. complacency and replaced it with fears of a new and menacing organization that seemed to threaten our very survival (Byman 2003). As journalist Peter Bergen notes, "Suddenly, the blithe days of dot-com billionaires, Puff Daddy's legal problems, and Gary Condit's evasions about the missing Chandra Levy had disappeared like a delightful mirage" (Bergen 2002, p. 226).

This essay focuses on understanding the September 11 attacks and, more broadly, the U.S. response to the emergence of al Qaeda, within the context of strategic surprise. Strategic surprise encompasses both warnings of a threat and the response to it (Betts 1982, p. 87).[1] This focus on surprise is essential not only for understanding what allowed the September 11 attacks to happen, but also for prevailing against terrorism. Terrorists depend on secrecy and surprise to conduct successful operations (and indeed to survive) against a far stronger state (Bell 1994; Hoffman 1998, pp. 170–71; McCormick & Owen 2000; Crenshaw 2002, p. 57).

Although September 11 has few parallels, the problem of strategic surprise is not new. This essay first probes the scholarship on strategic surprise and organizational learning for insights into the question of warning. This probe offers four frames for understanding difficulties in providing warning: cognitive failures by analysts and policy makers; bureaucratic pathologies that inhibit an effective response; the tradeoffs and limits policy makers face; and the nature of the adversary. The remainder of the essay uses these four analytic frames in a detailed look at September 11 and the U.S. government response to the rise of al Qaeda.

ARE SURPRISE ATTACKS REALLY SURPRISING?

Warning failures, including catastrophic ones, are not new for those concerned with national security. Betts (1978, 1982) has even argued that intelligence failures are natural, as well as inevitable. Pearl Harbor is perhaps the most notorious of surprises for Americans, but other notable surprise attacks include the Egyptian crossing of the Suez Canal at the onset of the Yom Kippur War in 1973, the German attack on France through the Ardennes forest in 1940, and the German invasion of Russia in 1941, all of which caught the victims flat-footed (Wohlstetter 1962; Chan 1979; Betts 1982; Stein 1982; May 1986, 2001; Levite 1987; Cohen & Gooch 1991).[2]

Scholars have turned to the study of individual psychology, small group behavior, organizational theory, and bureaucratic politics, among other disciplines, to understand why seemingly competent intelligence organizations and sensible policy makers are surprised by events that, in hindsight, seem obvious (Allison 1971, Janis 1972, Halperin 1974, Jervis 1976). Perhaps more troubling, some policy makers heard the warning but nevertheless did little to stave off disaster. In the case of September 11, it is essential to know the particular characteristics of al Qaeda that made surprise more attainable for the organization.

---

[1]Levite (1987) defines strategic surprise at length with a different emphasis on the response to warning. In contrast to Betts, he contends that if the policy maker recognizes the problem but does not prepare properly, the resulting crisis is not strategic surprise but unpreparedness (pp. 1–3).

[2]Most assessments of strategic surprise, however, focus on surprise in war—traditionally the most important national security concern. Pearl Harbor, the Yom Kippur War, intelligence weaknesses before the two world wars, and the potential of the Soviet Union to conduct a surprise nuclear attack during the Cold War have received particular scrutiny.

Cognitive Problems for Analysts and Policy Makers

Discerning a looming danger can be exceptionally difficult. Analysts and policy makers must transform fragmented and weak data into a coherent vision of the future—a task that challenges even the best minds. Their imaginations must leap, discerning a future threat where none existed in the past.

Analysts' and policy makers' biases and preconceptions shape how information is received and analyzed. Such a framework is necessary; information cannot be interpreted in an analytic void (Betts 1978, p. 63). At times, however, the framework indiscriminately filters out contradictory information, leading to disaster. Cohen & Gooch (1991), for example, contend that Israeli intelligence (and policy makers) clung to "the Concept"—the belief that the militarily inferior Egypt would not start a war unless it had the means of striking Israel proper and neutralizing the Israeli Air Force—despite evidence of Egyptian preparations to attack (Cohen & Gooch 1991, pp. 114–15; Jervis 2002). Similarly, Snook (2000) contends that one of the reasons for the tragic friendly-fire incident that led to the downing of two U.S. Black Hawk helicopters over Iraq in 1994 was that the F-15 pilots expected, and wanted, to engage the enemy and incorrectly "saw" the Black Hawks as Iraqi Hind helicopters. Thus "they created the two Hinds; then they shot them down" (p. 98).

Analysts may seek consensus rather than appraising alternative explanations. This problem, often particularly acute in small groups, has been labeled "groupthink" (Janis 1972), and it often inhibits effective analysis by discouraging reappraisal or any other challenge to the existing wisdom. In 2004, members of the Senate Select Committee on Intelligence blamed "groupthink" as one reason why the intelligence community did not properly assess Iraq's weapons of mass destruction program (U.S. Senate Select Committee on Intelligence 2004).

One of the most common problems when trying to tease out a new pattern of behavior and thus prevent surprise is the "signal to noise ratio." Wohlstetter's *Pearl Harbor: Warning and Decision*, one of the first and best looks at the question of surprise attack, famously found that the "noise" of irrelevant information drowned out the "signal" of a looming threat for analysts looking at the question of where Japan might attack (Wohlstetter 1962, pp. 1–2, 111–12; Chan 1979). Only in hindsight was the true signal clear.[3] Wohlstetter contends, "In short, we failed to anticipate Pearl Harbor not for want of relevant materials, but because of a plethora of irrelevant ones" (p. 387).

---

[3] At times, intelligence agencies may "successfully" collect the wrong information. In Vietnam, the CIA made methodologically sound estimates of the Viet Cong's order of battle based on information captured from the enemy—information that enemy commanders had distorted in order to deceive their own superiors about how well they were doing. Similarly, Israel's interpretation of "the Concept" came in part from excellent intelligence on senior Egyptian officials who believed it. Israel, however, failed to recognize that the dismissal of these individuals meant the Concept might not hold (Cohen & Gooch 1991, p. 116; Wirtz 1991).

Even when the signal can be discerned with some certainty, it is often presented in a way that inhibits effective warning. At times, intelligence is politicized and presented to policy makers in a way that justifies their preconceptions and preferred policies. Overwarning is another problem. Intelligence assessments often overreact to previous errors that underestimated a threat but do not correct sufficiently when a threat is overestimated (*Report of a Committee of Privy Counsellors* 2004, p. 112, para. 456). The intelligence community may cry wolf so often that policy makers become inured to the danger and dismiss reports of a looming crisis (Betts 1978).

Intelligence analysts and policy makers at times do not understand all the dimensions of the threat they face, and this lack can cause a "failure to anticipate" (Cohen & Gooch 1991, pp. 95–131). For example, in 1973, Israel analysts assumed that Israel's tactical superiority made an attack from its neighbors inconceivable; they ignored the strategic and political logic of such an attack. As a result, Israel suffered a near-disastrous surprise (Levite 1987; Cohen & Gooch 1991, pp. 95–131). Often, this inability to anticipate occurs because of changes in the adversary's capabilities and procedures. The French, for example, were caught off-guard in 1940 partly because they did not recognize that new German tactics and organizational concepts would enable an armored breakthrough.

At times, intelligence analysts may correctly identify a problem but policy makers' own biases do not change sufficiently for them to address the new problem. In his classic book on strategic surprise, Betts (1982) declares that "*the primary problem in major strategic surprises is not intelligence warning but political disbelief*" (p. 18, author's italics). Like intelligence analysts, policy makers have biases and see only part of the overall picture. This limited view leads to many mistakes.[4]

Bureaucratic Pathologies

Even if individuals can overcome data weaknesses and their own cognitive limits to sound an alarm, the institution as a whole may not fully recognize the problem

---

[4]It is always easiest, and most politically rewarding, to blame disaster on the men (and, more rarely, women) at the top. After September 11, a cottage industry of finger-pointing sprang up, with book after book blaming one leader or another. President Clinton, for example, is blamed for obstructing the FBI and the CIA, ignoring opportunities to seize bin Laden from the Sudan, refusing to authorize military force against al Qaeda after numerous attacks, and in general fiddling while al Qaeda plotted to burn down America (Miniter 2003, Bossie 2004). President Bush, of course, did not escape unscathed. Making much of the Bush family's business and personal ties to the Saudi royal family, journalist Craig Unger contends that the September 11 disaster began in the 1970s, when the Saudis began their successful courtship of the Bush family—a courtship that, according to Unger, led the Bush administration to ignore Saudi complicity in the rise of al Qaeda (Unger 2004). However, studies of strategic surprise have shown that almost never is a single leader the real problem (Cohen & Gooch 1991).

and shift its procedures and resources accordingly. Once some members of an organization know about a threat, why would the organization as a whole not incorporate this knowledge into its procedures? Organization theory offers insights into this knotty question.

Different organizations have different cultures, a generalization as true for intelligence and national security agencies as it is for businesses. Knowledge is transmitted and the task at hand approached in highly different ways, with profound implications for overall performance. The "rules" in an organizational handbook or a doctrine manual may be far from the practice on the ground (Snook 2000, pp. 190–92). A particular concern of many organizational cultures facing a new situation is whether change is in keeping with the institution's current identity (Cook & Yanow 1996, p. 451). Submarine warfare, for example, was a clear possibility before both world wars. However, no major navy prepared for antisubmarine warfare, because they saw their mission and identity as linked to large surface-unit action. As a result, they were unprepared for what in hindsight was an obvious development (Herwig 1998).

Organizations and their procedures often remain constant despite mounting problems with the task at hand. Cohen & Gooch (1991) depict the British Gallipoli campaign in this light, arguing that the failure of British commanders to correct the disastrous actions (and, most important, inactions) of their subordinates led to an overall failure at Suvla Bay (Cohen & Gooch 1991, pp. 156–63). More broadly, institutions often do not change their approaches to problem solving— their "organizational frames" (Eden 2004, p. 50)—despite the inadequacy of their current approach. At times, responsibility may be too diffuse; everyone has some share of the overall problem, so no particular person considers it his or her job to act (Snook 2000, pp. 135–36).

Political Limits on Effective Policy

Warning occurs in a policy context, which depends on politics. Information provided by intelligence agencies is an important factor in shaping policy, but it is only one of many (Herman 2004). The presidency is only one element of government, and it must accommodate as well as attempt to shape such diverse actors as the Congress, the media, the bureaucracies, and public opinion (Neustadt 1991, Howell 2003, Pfiffner 2004). Important decisions such as going to war or making a major shift in foreign policy can be particularly problematic (Lian & Oneal 1993).

In addition to the need to work with many actors with different agendas, another common problem is competing priorities that divert attention and resources. Policy makers must choose their battles, and they often have limited resources. They cannot solve every problem or mitigate every risk. Moreover, policy makers' attention often gyrates wildly from crisis to crisis, giving them little time to study long-term trends (Blackwill & Davis 2004).

Policy makers also have limited abilities to redirect bureaucracies. In the United States, intelligence agencies are often criticized for not respecting civil liberties. These concerns led Congress and the executive branch to monitor and limit the agencies' power, and several scholars contend these restrictions have limited the agencies' effectiveness (Hitz 2004, Johnson 2004).

The Nature of the Adversary

Some intelligence challenges are more demanding than others, and this difficulty affects the collection and use of intelligence. For example, Lord Butler's investigation into the British government's use of intelligence on Iraq's weapons of mass destruction program found that many problems arose in the handling and interpretation of intelligence owing to "the difficulty of achieving reliable human intelligence on Iraq" (*Report of a Committee of Privy Counsellors* 2004, p. 109, para. 443).

The warning problem of terrorism is exceptionally difficult, compounding the challenges that individual analysts, bureaucracies, and policy makers face with regard to strategic surprise. As Pillar argues,

> The basic problem that terrorism poses for intelligence is as simple as it is chilling. A group of conspirators conceives a plot. Only the few conspirators know of their intentions, although they might get help from others. They mention nothing about their plot to anyone they cannot absolutely trust. They communicate nothing about their plans in a form that can be intercepted. . . . They live and move normally and inconspicuously, and any preparations that cannot be done behind closed doors they do as part of those movements. The problem: How do we learn of the plot? (Pillar 2004b, p. 115)

Moreover, as Pillar contends, "The target for intelligence is not just proven terrorists; it is anyone who *might* commit terrorism in the future" (p. 115, author's italics).

The problem of tactical warning is particularly vexing. Investigations of attacks before September 11 emphasized that tactical warning may be lacking even though strategic warning was sound. In 1985, the "Report of the Secretary of State's Advisory Panel on Overseas Security" (the "Inman Report") examined the bombings of the U.S. Embassy and Marine barracks in Lebanon and concluded, "If determined, well-trained and funded teams are seeking to do damage, they will eventually succeed." The inquiry into the 1996 Khobar Towers attack and the investigation of the 1998 embassy bombings both found strategic warning was sound even though tactical warning was lacking (Pillar 2004b, p. 125). In January 1999, the "Report of the Accountability Review Boards on the Embassy Bombings in Nairobi and Dar es Salaam" (better known as the "Crowe Commission") contended that "we cannot count on having such intelligence to warn us of such attacks."

Deception and denial compound the problem of surprise. Skilled adversaries do their best to counter intelligence gathering. Encryption, limits on the dissemination of sensitive information, and other means are used to inhibit standard means of intelligence collection. Adversaries also scheme to mislead each other (Shulsky 2002, pp. 116–25). Famously, British intelligence during World War II successfully fed false information to German agents on British shores to mislead them as to the location of Allied landings on the French coast, a deception operation vital to the success of the Normandy landings. Ironically, fear of deception can also lead to failures, as suspicions of deception may lead intelligence agencies to discount true information (Betts 1982, p. 109). Fear of deception also reinforces the importance of existing analytic biases. Contrary information may be suspected of being "disinformation" whereas confirming information may wrongly be treated as accurate.

The above four perspectives are analytically distinct, but in practice interact. It is best to view the components of surprise and warning as a system, as it is often characteristics of the system rather than any particular component of it that lead to mistakes and disaster (Perrow 1999, p. 66.).

A CLOSER LOOK AT SEPTEMBER 11

September 11 represents a failure, but the nature of the failure is unclear. Many things went wrong in many places and at many levels, making the exact problems hard to pinpoint, diffusing responsibility, and obscuring the path ahead. This section discusses whether an alarm was sounded and then notes various opportunities that analysts and policy makers missed.

Was the Alarm Sounded?

The intelligence community, particularly the CIA, did well in providing strategic warning of an al Qaeda threat. The identity of the foe, the scale of its ambitions, and its lethality were known and communicated in a timely manner. The CIA had begun its warning about al Qaeda even before the simultaneous attacks on two U.S. embassies on August 7, 1998 made the danger clearer to many observers (Coll 2004, p. 383). After the embassy bombings, warning with regard to al Qaeda became a top priority, and even weak pieces of intelligence led to the sounding of the alarm. In journalist Steve Coll's description, "It was a vast, pulsing, self-perpetuating, highly sensitive network on continuous alert" (Coll 2004, p. 417).

By 2001, the system was on high alert, and any policy maker (or member of the general public) who cared to look could see the CIA's concern. In February 2001, Director of Central Intelligence (DCI) George Tenet testified publicly that bin Laden and his organization posed "the most immediate and serious threat" to the United States (Tenet 2001)—a clarion example of strategic warning. Senior policy makers from both the Clinton and Bush administrations have testified that Tenet and other CIA officials warned that al Qaeda was planning lethal "spectaculars" against Americans (Woodward 2002, p. 34). The FBI also added its voice to the warning. Louis Freeh, then FBI Director, testified on May 10, 2001 that a primary objective of al Qaeda "is the planning and carrying out of large-scale, high-profile, high-casualty terrorist attacks against U.S. interests and citizens and those of our allies, worldwide" (Freeh 2001).

This strong strategic warning, however, was accompanied by a failure to learn clues about the specifics of the attack on the U.S. homeland, which led to a devastating failure of tactical warning. If policy makers listened to intelligence, they would know al Qaeda was coming, but they would not know when, where, or how.

Missed Opportunities for Intelligence

Even though the plotters made several mistakes and "the system was blinking red," in the words of the 9/11 Commission's report, much of the plotters' activity went on undetected (National Commission 2004, pp. 254–77). The missed opportunities include the following:

- Working with Malaysian internal security forces, the CIA covered a meeting of key operatives, several of whom were involved in the September 11 plot, but lost track of them when the meeting ended.

- The CIA did not "watchlist" two key plotters, Khalid al-Midhar and Nawaf al-Hazmi, to prevent them from entering the United States, despite learning that they had U.S. visas and were traveling to the United States. Nor did the CIA pass this or related information to the FBI promptly.

- Several suggestive leads were not pursued. For example, in July an alert FBI agent in the Phoenix, Arizona office noted in an electronic communication that an "inordinate number of persons of investigative interest" (*Report of the Joint Inquiry* 2002, pp. 2–3) were seeking flight training in the area and called for a more comprehensive investigation into the matter—a warning ignored by FBI headquarters.

- The jihadist Zacarias Moussaoui fell into the hands of the FBI in Minnesota because of suspicions that he might be trying to hijack a plane. Moussaoui had links to several of the plotters, including Ramzi Binalshibh, one of the masterminds. This information was not briefed up the chain of command at the FBI (though DCI Tenet was briefed!), despite the high level of threat being communicated in general.

- During their time in the United States, the hijackers had contacts with several Islamist radicals whom the FBI already was monitoring.

- The CIA scrapped a plan to kidnap bin Laden that some experts believe had a reasonable chance of success. Several military strikes against bin Laden were also called off because of concerns about intelligence of uncertain reliability (Coll 2004, pp. 484–85, 564; National Commission 2004, pp. 181–82, 267–75).

Policy Mistakes

In hindsight, U.S. policy toward al Qaeda also had several fatal flaws that allowed the organization to flourish. Perhaps most important, U.S. policy left the issue of terrorist sanctuary unresolved. In Afghanistan, al Qaeda was allowed to build an army of like-minded radicals outside the reach of the United States and its allies. Richard Clarke, the senior counterterrorism official for the Clinton administration and for the Bush administration through September 11, notes to his dismay that the United States allowed "the existence of large scale al Qida bases where we know people are trained to kill Americans" (National Commission 2004, p. 213). Even more troubling, al Qaeda enjoyed a permissive environment in the West, where it could recruit, raise money, and otherwise sustain its cause.

Before September 11, the United States had no coherent counterterrorism policy with regard to Pakistan and a vague policy with regard to Saudi Arabia, although both were central to the effort against al Qaeda. Pakistan was the Taliban's primary sponsor, and it also backed jihadist groups as part of its campaign against India in Kashmir. The Saudi regime did not directly back al Qaeda itself, but it often turned a blind eye as its citizens bankrolled and swelled the ranks of affiliated jihadist groups. The result was stagnation in policy even as the threat metastasized (Coll 2004, p. 571).

The United States also relied too heavily on law enforcement tools such as trials and arrests to fight al Qaeda before September 11. Law enforcement has several weaknesses as a counterterrorism instrument. Even successful law-enforcement measures often fail to nab the terrorist masterminds. In addition, trials place considerable demands on the resources of the intelligence community, which might otherwise be spent disrupting future attacks (Pillar 2001, pp. 80–89). Arrests and trials did little against the army being built in the haven in Afghanistan, which was perhaps the biggest challenge for fighting al Qaeda.

WHY WERE THE OPPORTUNITIES MISSED?

The four frames derived from various social science literatures offer insights into why analysts and policy makers missed these potential opportunities to disrupt the plot and to tailor U.S. policy to counter al Qaeda.

Cognitive Failures

Even those most concerned with al Qaeda failed to grasp the dimensions of the threat. Former New Jersey Governor Thomas Kean, the Chairman of the 9/11 Commission, reports a vast "failure of imagination" (http://www.cnn.com/2004/ALLPO LITICS/07/22/911.report/).[5] Policy makers often failed to recognize that, unlike past terrorist groups, al Qaeda had both the capability and intention of inflicting mass casualties on America (Benjamin & Simon 2002). President Bush at first

---

[5] Ironically, with regard to Iraq, intelligence analysts and policy makers are accused of having their imaginations run away with them. Analysts and policy makers did not sufficiently scrutinize many facts about Iraq's programs, and they even extrapolated on them with little reason, all to support the idea that Iraq had a massive but concealed weapons of mass destruction program. I thank Robert Jervis for pointing out this contrast.

thought the first plane strike on the North Tower of the World Trade Center may have been due to a pilot's heart attack (Woodward 2002, p. 15). Even Clarke, one of the most perspicacious observers of al Qaeda, underestimated the threat; he had gloomily predicted an attack in which "hundreds" of Americans would die (National Commission 2004, p. 344).

But the "failure of imagination" was in practice more complex. The problem for officials such as Tenet, Berger, and Clarke was not in failing to imagine that al Qaeda could and would kill thousands. Indeed, they devoted considerable attention to the possibility that al Qaeda would acquire and use a chemical, biological, or nuclear weapon or agent to this end. However, their imaginations did not transform their day-to-day actions. As Deputy Secretary of State Richard Armitage noted after the attacks, "I don't think we really had made the leap in our mind that we are no longer safe behind these two great oceans" (Coll 2004, p. 542). Their minds often soared, but their guts did not clench.

For analysts looking at al Qaeda, the signal-to-noise problem was immense. In 2001, CIA analysts tracked possible al Qaeda plots in Europe, Africa, and the Middle East. The U.S. homeland was also of concern, but it was lost in the data swamp of information related to overseas attacks. These overseas threats, moreover, were not always pure noise but rather were often signals of other attacks. Al Qaeda was indeed plotting attacks in Europe and the Middle East, as later events would show.

The FBI suffered from a bias in assuming that the threat would focus outside the United States. The Bureau's analysts did not challenge their own preconceptions, even though by 1998 it was clear that bin Laden was seeking recruits to attack the United States and developing an infrastructure here (Coll 2004, p. 420). In part, this bias existed because of how the FBI viewed Islamist terrorist groups. The Bureau correctly recognized that Hizballah, Hamas, and other religio-nationalist groups primarily operate in the United States to raise money. Conducting an attack here would be illogical, killing the golden goose. Al Qaeda, however, had in the past proved willing to jeopardize its logistics and fundraising bases in pursuit of a successful attack.

The CIA also had its set of blinders to the danger at home, in part because of its successful collection of the wrong information. The CIA collected considerable intelligence on the danger of al Qaeda attacks overseas, which led to warnings in Italy, the Persian Gulf, and elsewhere in 2001. More general indications of a major attack were interpreted in the light of this information that pointed to an attack overseas.

Another problem for warning was the shift in adversary tactics. Using airplanes as weapons was innovative, and there was relatively little intelligence suggesting al Qaeda would do this. Its use of different types of attack platforms (truck bombs in Africa, a boat bomb in Yemen, and so on) did not lead analysts to anticipate that the organization would innovate yet again.

The tremendous sensitivity to any potential threat led to overwarning. Any mention of al Qaeda activity was conveyed to senior policy makers, and indeed often to the President himself. The result was a "warning fatigue" with regard to al Qaeda—a problem that only grew after September 11 (Posner 2003; Anonymous 2004, p. 84).

The cognitive failures were perhaps even worse among policy makers than among intelligence analysts. Despite the repeated warnings of Tenet and others, it is not clear where terrorism was on the overall U.S. priority list. Many former and current U.S. officials claim that terrorism was "a top priority" well before September 11, but for both the Clinton and Bush administrations, so too were Iraq, China, the Balkans, missile defense, military reform, and other foreign policy issues (Coll 2004, p. 541). Policy makers "knew" al Qaeda was a growing danger, but they were not able to shift their attention sufficiently to reflect this.

As a result of this lack of prioritization, each agency focused on the issues of greatest importance to them. The CIA was responsible for supporting war-fighting in Iraq and the Balkans, monitoring China and other potential rivals, providing economic analyses, and so on. For the FBI, deadbeat dads, drug running, and infrastructure protection demanded resources. There was no single plan everyone followed, and counterterrorism was at times neglected or not given enough money or manpower.[6]

Neglect and confused priorities characterized U.S. policy toward Afghanistan for many years. Before the embassy bombings in 1998, Afghanistan was neglected (Coll 2004, pp. 5–6, 15). In its regional policy, the State Department focused on issues ranging from a possible nuclear exchange between India and Pakistan to the disruption of democracy in Nepal. When Afghanistan came on the radar screen, it was usually with regard to narcotics or human rights violations, not terrorism (Coll 2004, p. 383; Albright 2003, p. 363). Although the United States focused far more on terrorism as the decade went on, these other concerns did not go away and greatly complicated efforts to press the Taliban on terrorism issues. As Clarke notes, the Taliban knew that it would not escape U.S. pressure by surrendering bin Laden; the United States would still harp on women's rights, narcotics, and other issues (Clarke 2004, p. 208).

Another indicator of a cognitive disjuncture between the knowledge of individuals and the logical actions that should flow from that knowledge is the limited attention given to defensive measures against terrorism, particularly in the United States itself. Despite the finding of various commissions that specific tactical intelligence is *likely* to be lacking when we face a skilled adversary—and the intelligence community's warning that al Qaeda was planning lethal attacks—policy

---

[6]Even today, prioritizing terrorism is exceptionally difficult because its lethality is quite low although its psychological impact is high. The number of deaths from terrorism is minuscule compared to other sources of death, such as traffic accidents, heart disease, and cancer. As John Mueller (unpublished manuscript) notes, "Even with the September 11 attacks included in the count, the number of Americans killed by international terrorism since the late 1960s...is about the same as the number killed over the same period by lightning—or by accident-causing deer or by severe allergic reaction to peanuts" (p. 1).

makers initiated few defensive measures in the United States. They relied on intelligence for defense even though they knew intelligence (particularly at home) was flawed.

Bureaucratic Pathologies

Part of the reason for the lack of tactical warning was that the intelligence community and other institutions did not respond to the strategic warning and sufficiently strengthen their ability to collect, analyze, and disseminate information or act on what they did know. In addition, some institutions, including the U.S. military, did not embrace counterterrorism as a mission despite the high level of strategic warning.

CONTINUED CIA WEAKNESSES   On December 4, 1998, George Tenet declared: "We are at war. I want no resources or people spared in this effort" (Coll 2004, p. 435). Yet despite this rhetoric and Tenet's strenuous effort to warn policy makers of the danger, the CIA did not significantly shift resources from other priorities to counterterrorism or change its culture and focus. As one intelligence officer long involved in assessing al Qaeda lamented, lower-level intelligence officers "knew a runaway train was coming at the United States, documented that fact, and then watched helplessly—or were banished for speaking out—as their senior leaders delayed action, downplayed intelligence, ignored repeated warnings. . ." (Anonymous 2004, p. ix).

Resource allocation is one primary area where action did not match the level of threat (Coll 2004, p. 435). How much can Tenet be faulted? The DCI's lack of budget authority contributes to this problem (Scowcroft 1996, p. 143; Johnson 1996, p. 35). Because the DCI controlled only perhaps 15% of the pre–September 11 intelligence budget, much of the intelligence community felt no compulsion to observe the DCI's directives if they ran counter to their own bureaucratic imperatives. Consequently, even though the DCI "declared war" on al Qaeda, no agency dramatically changed its priorities.

If the DCI had controlled more of the intelligence community's budget and people, it is plausible that far more money could have been devoted to counterterrorism. The evidence from Tenet's track record at the CIA, however, suggests that changes would have been limited. Before the attacks, when pressed by policy makers to transfer more money to the al Qaeda effort, the CIA claimed that none of its other programs could be ended or curtailed to free up resources (Clarke 2004, p. 210). Nevertheless, under Tenet the CIA expanded counterterrorism efforts even as intelligence budgets for other programs declined (*Report of the Joint Inquiry* 2002, pp. 250–69). This indicates that other agencies, too, might have increased spending on counterterrorism. Conceivably, much of the money that went to support military programs through technical means, which dwarfs the amount spent on human intelligence, could have been transferred to beef up the CIA's human intelligence programs.

Operational weaknesses compounded the budget problems. The CIA also did not penetrate al Qaeda's upper echelons. As discussed below, this failure was partly due to the nature of the adversary, and it is clear that by the late 1990s such a penetration was a priority target for the CIA [*Report of the Joint Inquiry* (2002), pp. 387–88; for an incorrect contrary claim, see Bamford (2004), p. 156]. However, some critics maintain that the Agency did not have the proper approach for targeting jihadists—a fault of institutional response, not just of intelligence collection in general. In part, this was because the Agency continued to operate its personnel out of U.S. government buildings, and even its "nonofficial cover" (NOC) officers tended to be fake businessmen. None of these could operate in a mosque without giving themselves away. One former CIA officer claimed, "The CIA probably doesn't have a single truly qualified Arabic-speaking officer of Middle Eastern background who can play a believable Muslim fundamentalist who would volunteer to spend years of his life with shitty food and no women in the mountains of Afghanistan" (Gerecht 2001).[7]

Analysis on al Qaeda was also often weak. Despite the CIA's awareness of the danger, it often lacked detailed knowledge of the enemy. Clarke, for example, criticized the CIA for not recognizing the importance of Khalid Shaykh Mohammad, the mastermind of September 11, claiming that he could have been snatched in Qatar had this been known (Clarke 2004, p. 153). This problem was not simply due to the difficulty of gaining information on al Qaeda. Rather, the CIA's emphasis was on operations against al Qaeda, and efforts to build a full picture of the organization did not receive sufficient support. Indeed, no comprehensive intelligence assessment of al Qaeda was drafted until after September 11. This lack of an estimate appears to go against the traditional CIA emphasis on detailed analysis, one of its core missions. However, in the CIA most of the detailed, long-term analysis was done by the area divisions of the Directorate of Intelligence, whereas the primary emphasis of the CIA's Counterterrorist Center (CTC) was on operations (it reports to the DCI through the Deputy Director of Operations), which made it less likely to focus on analysis. Most of the CTC's "analysis" focused on collection issues linked to operations rather than on broader estimates and strategic assessments (National Commission 2004, pp. 118, 342).

Risk aversion was another problem for the CIA. As the 9/11 Commission contended, the CIA was "an organization capable of attracting extraordinarily

---

[7]The emphasis on the "super spy," however, may be misguided. Although many critics of the CIA grouse that it lacks individuals who can directly penetrate an organization like al Qaeda, such an expectation ignores how the terrorist organization itself vets candidates, preserves operational security, and otherwise screens for penetration. Indeed, as Pillar (2004b) contends, "Terrorist operations that are funded on one continent, planned on another continent, and carried out on a third by perpetrators of multiple nationalities (as was true of the attacks of September 11) are unlikely to reveal their entire shape to even the most skilled local collection effort. Living where the water is bad, by itself, is apt to yield more stomach ailments than insights about terrorism—insights that are just as likely to be gleaned in the papers being pushed at Langley" (pp. 128–29).

motivated people but institutionally averse to risk" (National Commission 2004, p. 93.) Director of Operations James Pavitt, for example, questioned whether the effort to work with the Northern Alliance against the Taliban was worth the high possibility that a case officer might die in an accident in a rickety helicopter en route—an instance of what other critics have called a general risk aversion to physical danger (Coll 2004, pp. 519, 524; Gerecht 2001).

This risk aversion, however, was sensible from an institutional perspective. As Coll notes, the CIA was "conditioned by history to recoil from gung-ho 'allies' at the National Security Council." The institution had learned that these allies often turned to covert action in lieu of making tough policy decisions and—when things went poorly—hung the CIA out to dry (Coll 2004, p. 395).

Culturally and procedurally, the CIA was focused on the threat overseas. The CIA, of course, is prohibited from running operations on U.S. soil, and in the wake of several scandals revealed in the 1970s, the Agency is exceptionally sensitive to the charge that it might be spying on Americans. As a result, its resources, collection capabilities, and analysis are focused on the overseas threat. Not surprisingly, even when it identified the possible "signal" of an attack on U.S. soil, its activities were focused on gathering "noise" (or, more accurately, other signals) related to al Qaeda activities overseas.

The above problems reflect how the broader institutional mission interfered with successful counterterrorism. The CIA's reluctance to divert resources from other concerns, change collection platforms to emphasize NOCs, focus on dangers at home rather than overseas, and engage in politically risky covert action reflected the institution's history and identity rather than the threat of al Qaeda.

WAS THE FBI ASLEEP AT THE SWITCH?   The list of FBI shortcomings revealed after September 11 is long. The FBI not only failed to intercept the plotters, but more generally did not appreciate the danger the country faced—in sharp contrast to the CIA. Before September 11, the FBI was not properly structured or oriented for counterterrorism or, more broadly, for intelligence work. This failure occurred in part because of the FBI's culture, but also because the organization did not learn and respond properly as information about al Qaeda grew.

Prior to September 11, the Bureau often failed to collect information relevant to counterterrorism. For example, when Abdul Hakim Murad was interviewed in connection with his participation in a plot to bomb as many as 12 airplanes over the Pacific in 1995, the FBI did not devote attention to his possible plans to crash an airplane into CIA headquarters—a harbinger of the September 11 plot. Nor did the FBI place opportunities for collection in context; for example, it failed to link suspicious flight-training activity in Arizona or the arrest of an Islamic extremist (Moussaoui) in Minnesota to the heightened national threat level. In general, the FBI did not train its operatives sufficiently in intelligence collection or provide collectors with sufficient resources, particularly with regard to surveillance and translation (National Commission 2004, p. 77).

Often what information the FBI did collect was not disseminated, even internally. The FBI's antediluvian computer system and case-file approach to holding information meant that information was not regularly passed from the field to headquarters, nor to other FBI agents and analysts who might be working on similar problems. The FBI did not see itself as part of the national security apparatus and did not share information with the national security community (Benjamin & Simon 2002, p. 298; National Commission 2004, p. 358).

As a result, the FBI did not inform policy makers of the jihadist threat at home. Two former White House officials working on counterterrorism in the National Security Council wrote about learning FBI information from trial transcripts of al Qaeda suspects, noting, "In many instances, we discovered information so critical that we were amazed that the relevant agencies did not inform us of it while we were at the NSC" (Benjamin & Simon 2002, pp. xii–xiii). It is not surprising that policy makers, agencies, and analysts outside the FBI never learned of this information—most of the FBI did not know of it either.

Nor did the FBI conduct strategic analysis. Clarke (2004) depicts the FBI as plodding and hidebound, comfortable in its ignorance of al Qaeda (p. 192). The office created to do strategic analysis atrophied. The FBI had only two analysts looking at information on the bin Laden threat, and it did not prepare a document like the National Intelligence Estimate to assess the al Qaeda threat to the United States or the radical Islamic presence in this country (National Commission 2004, pp. 93, 265).

The Bureau's culture and organization fostered these problems. Before September 11, the FBI was primarily a law enforcement agency, and it was probably the world's best. But law enforcement focuses on prosecuting a case, not on understanding a broader network. Law enforcement emphasizes gathering specific evidence, not collecting and sharing possibly relevant information. Given this organizational ethos, it is not surprising that terrorism was viewed as a criminal matter and treated accordingly. In addition, FBI leaders emphasized finding the perpetrators of the last attack rather than stopping the next one (Watson 2002).

The FBI's organizational structure both reflected this culture and worsened it. The decentralized field-office structure allowed offices to set their own priorities, few of which focused on terrorism or al Qaeda. The 56 FBI field offices in the United States were all independent fiefdoms in which local priorities took precedence (Clarke 2004, p. 219; Kessler 2002, p. 432).

The FBI also faced many restrictions—and tremendous political scrutiny—on its functions related to counterterrorism. For example, in 1996, right-wing conservatives joined liberal civil libertarians to block legislation that would allow multipoint wiretaps, which are useful for tracking terrorists who change phones or use multiple phones. In addition to restricting the tools the FBI could use, this odd alliance made the FBI exceptionally sensitive to investigating religious-based terrorism in the United States (Benjamin & Simon 2002). Congressional investigations into deaths at Ruby Ridge and Waco further increased FBI sensitivity. In general, the FBI preferred to err on the side of respect for civil liberties, setting a high bar for surveillance.

FBI procedures separating intelligence from law enforcement cases—the so-called "Wall"—reflected the Bureau's problems on this issue. The rules were confusing and were often interpreted in the most restrictive way, which hindered efforts to track al Qaeda activities in the United States (National Commission 2004, pp. 78–80, 271). However, given the FBI's law enforcement culture, the inherent problems of the Wall were not as troubling as they would be for an intelligence organization. Moreover, because the Bureau did not appreciate the growing danger, it felt little need to change course. Thus, despite grumbling among the ranks, FBI leaders did not press hard to lower the Wall.

The problems of the Wall stemmed from leadership. Former FBI Director Louis Freeh reportedly disdained technology and thus did not invest in systems to improve data storage, retrieval, and sharing (Kessler 2002, p. 422). Much of Freeh's attention on counterterrorism was related to investigating attacks that had happened overseas, such as the Khobar Towers bombing (Walsh 2001). Freeh also worsened the problem of local fiefdoms, cutting staff at headquarters and placing the lead in the field for operations (National Commission 2004, p. 76).

THE MISSING MILITARY   The CIA, the FBI, and other members of the intelligence community are not the only institutions in the line of fire. The military is also often criticized for not having embraced the counterterrorism mission (Coll 2004, p. 572; Benjamin & Simon 2002, pp. 292–96). Policy makers turned to the military for help against al Qaeda but went away empty-handed. In addition to not preparing an outright invasion plan, the military opposed using special operations forces to snatch al Qaeda operatives in countries such as Afghanistan, Sudan, and Qatar (Clarke 2004, pp. 143, 152–53). The military also rebuffed President Clinton's suggested use of a special operations force raid as one way to intimidate al Qaeda. More generally, the military resisted NSC requests for military options. Clark contends, "The White House wanted action. The senior military did not and made it almost impossible for the President to overcome their objections" (p. 145). Clinton himself notes, "It was clear to me that the senior military didn't want to do this. . ." (Clinton 2004, p. 804).

A particular military concern appears to have been the inappropriate use of limited force against al Qaeda (National Commission 2004, pp. 120–21). General Henry Shelton, then the Chairman of the Joint Chiefs of Staff, believed that the deployment of special operations forces or other "boots on the ground" missions would probably fail, since intelligence was poor and they lacked a secure base of operations. In his view, any military mission should involve thousands of soldiers or else it risked turning into a humiliating operational disaster (Coll 2004, p. 497) like the ill-fated "Desert One" hostage rescue mission in 1980.

Shelton's view has a point. The military has a role to play in counterterrorism, but barring outright invasion, that role is quite different from the military's normal function, which is to literally interpose itself between the American people and their enemy. Limited uses of military force make a poor deterrent, seldom inflict meaningful damage that reduces terrorists' capabilities, anger allies, and may rally supporters for the terrorists (Pillar 2001, pp. 102–9; Jervis 2002, p. 39).

The military, like the CIA, sought to minimize risk with regard to counterterrorism. Using special operations forces or even launching cruise missiles had a high risk of failure given the hostile operating environment and the lack of precise intelligence. But these risks would have been more acceptable if military leaders had considered the problem a grave one. They did not. Moreover, the military did not take steps to improve its capabilities significantly, either by gathering its own intelligence to improve the likely success of a special operations force mission or by arranging bases in nearby staging areas. Even while threat warnings grew, the military did not adapt.

NO DOMESTIC RESPONSE   There is little to report on the responses of other agencies linked to homeland security with regard to al Qaeda. Only those in the corridors of power in Washington heard the steady drumbeat of strategic warning that al Qaeda was coming. Nor did the day-to-day threat reporting or even the public testimony make a strong impression, as state and local officials and noncore national security agencies such as the Immigration and Naturalization Service did not see terrorism as their concern. The 9/11 Commission reported, "In sum, the domestic agencies never mobilized in response to the threat. They did not have direction, and they did not have a plan to institute. The borders were not hardened. Transportation systems were not fortified. Electronic surveillance was not targeted against a domestic threat. State and local law enforcement were not marshaled to augment the FBI's efforts. The public was not warned" (National Commission 2004, p. 265).

LIMITED INSTITUTIONAL MANAGEMENT   Many of the problems of the CIA, the FBI, the military, and other institutions involved in counterterrorism can be laid, at least in part, at the feet of policy makers. It is the duty of elected officials to impose their will on unelected elements of the government, and they have the authority to do so. Policy makers, however, did a poor job imposing their will on various bureaucracies that were not aggressive in counterterrorism. The FBI's investigation of President Clinton for various scandals gave it effective immunity from White House oversight (Benjamin & Simon 2002, pp. 298–306). Nor did the President impose his will on the military, perhaps because of widespread distrust of his credentials on security in the military and among the public.

Despite its often frantic engagement on counterterrorism issues, the Clinton administration suffered from an unwillingness to place counterterrorism in the context of overall U.S. foreign policy. As Pillar (2001) has argued, "Terrorism is primarily a foreign policy issue, as well as a national security issue" (p. 9). Key decision makers, including the President, Vice President, National Security Advisor, and Attorney General, paid little attention to integrating counterterrorism into relations with such countries as Afghanistan, Pakistan, or Saudi Arabia, or to broader issues such as terrorism fundraising, popular hostility to the United States in the Middle East, or other long-term counterterrorism concerns. The activities of Clarke's Counterterrorism Support Group were often independent of the regular policy and agency meetings related to foreign relations (Coll 2004, p. 407; National Commission 2004). The result was repeated surges in action, but only limited sustained institutional change.

Resources were another issue. Neither administration provided a massive resource boost to key counterterrorism agencies; nor did they ensure that the existing budgets of those agencies were devoted appropriately to counterterrorism. The FBI budget grew considerably in the mid-1990s, and so did the CIA's resources for counterterrorism. The FBI, however, spent much of its money on concerns unrelated to al Qaeda (National Commission 2004, pp. 76–77). The CIA also tried to use spending increases to preserve many of its other programs rather than diverting resources to counter al Qaeda.

The White House did not provide clear authorities, particularly with regard to the assassination of bin Laden. Directing the CIA to kill him through covert action would have required a significant change in the CIA's rules for covert action, which in general prohibited assassination (Fredman 1997). Not surprisingly for a bureaucracy burned by accusations of "rogue" behavior in the past, the CIA sought to have its authorities made crystal clear. The White House, on the other hand, preferred to give more general guidance, retaining deniability, and the Justice Department wanted to avoid giving the CIA unfettered authority to kill (Coll 2004, pp. 423–24; National Commission 2004). Each institution followed its own political and bureaucratic imperatives, and the result was the worst of all worlds—a disjuncture between senior policy makers and the operators on the ground. Senior aides to Clinton recall that the President's desire to kill bin Laden and his associates "was very clear to us early on" (Coll 2004, p. 426). In the absence of clear authority, however, the CIA told its Afghan clients, "You are to capture him [bin Laden] alive" (Coll 2004, p. 378).[8]

Limits on Policy Makers

Policy problems often stemmed from legitimate political limits or tradeoffs that made it difficult for senior leaders to focus on al Qaeda. Moreover, even those policy makers most concerned with al Qaeda had to contend with the ignorance, indifference, or conflicting preferences of other political actors. Many of the

---

[8]This debate took on an aspect of unreality, as both policy makers and CIA operatives knew that their Afghan agents would probably disregard any instructions to exercise restraint. Afghans were not used to "any culture of nitpicking lawyers" (Coll 2004, p. 378), and both the White House and the CIA believed they would just shoot everyone in an attempt to "capture" bin Laden. Moreover, the CIA lacked the information on bin Laden's location that was necessary to make an assassination probable.

"obvious" responses to the rise of al Qaeda only became politically feasible after the carnage of the attacks generated the political will.[9]

Policy makers often had priorities other than counterterrorism. President Clinton, for example, met with Pakistan's Prime Minister Sharif several times in the years before September 11; Pakistan's nuclear program often headed the list of topics to discuss, as did the related problem of an Indo-Pak war over Kargil (Reidel 2002). The problem of Saudi Arabia also proved difficult for policy makers to address. When counterterrorism specialists criticized the kingdom, its defenders in the State Department and the Pentagon responded that other, more vital interests were at stake. As a result, the massive Saudi financial support to radical causes did not receive sufficient attention (Coll 2004, p. 512).[10]

The problems were interrelated, but a clear solution (even in hindsight) was evasive (Posner 2004). Bush administration policy makers saw the al Qaeda problem as tied to the Afghanistan problem, which was in turn tied to Pakistan. Developing a policy toward one required developing a policy toward all—a logical point, but one that slowed down efforts to confront al Qaeda even as threat reporting was increasing (Coll 2004, pp. 559–60; Clarke 2004, p. 232). When pressing both countries, moreover, the United States had few levers. Sanctions already in place because of Pakistan's nuclear programs meant that commercial incentives or threats were not available, as there were no real economic ties. Military-to-military relations had deteriorated as well (Kux 2001, Benjamin & Simon 2002, Griffin 2003). Saudi Arabia, of course, was a key ally on whom the United States depended for many of its vital interests, particularly with regard to Iraq, the Middle East peace process,

---

[9]This essay does not address the important issue of whether U.S. foreign policy contributed to the rise of al Qaeda by fomenting anger around the world. Chomsky, for example, contends that U.S. support for the *mujahedin* in Afghanistan, U.S. support for Israeli atrocities, and U.S. involvement in oppression in general led to the September 11 attacks (Chomsky 2001). Nor does the essay address policy toward the "root causes" of terrorism. Policy makers of all stripes are often chided for not attacking the root causes of terrorism and the grievances that make terrorists sympathetic—a seemingly obvious recommendation (Hitz 2004, p. 160). Unfortunately, neither policy makers nor academics know what the root causes are. Poverty, oppression, and other ills are often mentioned, but there seems little indication that such problems are motivating al Qaeda. Indeed, when radical jihadist organizations affiliated with al Qaeda are included, the number of motivations becomes staggering (Jervis 2002, pp. 41–42; Kepel 2002; Pillar 2004a, p. 31). In my judgment, the effort to find root causes ignores much of the logic of terrorism—that it is a tactic used by people who feel they have few other means for achieving their ends.

[10]An ignorance of events in Pakistan and Saudi Arabia made it even more difficult to craft an effective policy. Because shaping internal politics in these countries was not a policy priority, little intelligence was collected. For many years, the United States did not see Islamic extremism in Pakistan as an independent policy problem. The CIA in the 1980s focused on gathering information about the Afghan insurgency and the nuclear program, not on Pakistani politics (Coll 2004, p. 57). Similarly, U.S. intelligence on developments in Saudi Arabia was always limited.

and oil price stability. Standard forms of military or economic pressure thus were not available and almost certainly would have backfired (Lippman 1994; Gause 1995, 2002).

Dramatic change with regard to homeland defense or going to war against the Taliban was also politically difficult. As the 9/11 Commission contends, "It is hardest to mount a major effort while a problem still seems minor. Once the danger has fully materialized, evident to all, mobilizing action is easier—but it then may be too late" (National Commission 2004, p. 350). It is striking that no political leaders of either party were calling for a dramatic change with regard to homeland defense, U.S. policy toward Afghanistan or Pakistan, or other tectonic shifts that seem obvious only in hindsight.

Policy makers keenly felt the limits of the possible and thus turned to law enforcement measures because they were feasible and would demonstrate responsiveness to the various attacks. They knew covert action had at best a limited chance of success, even under favorable conditions. Clinton's National Security Advisor Sandy Berger and Secretary of State Madeleine Albright have contended that Congress, the American people, and U.S. allies would have opposed the use of ground forces in Afghanistan against al Qaeda before the September 11 attacks (Albright 2003, p. 375; Coll 2004, p. 408; National Commission 2004, p. 349). Because the military option was apparently off the table, law enforcement remained one of the most important means of fighting terrorism, along with using the CIA and allied intelligence agencies to disrupt activities abroad. The Congressional 9/11 Inquiry found that this reliance was really a default decision rather than a strategic one, with many law enforcement officials themselves seeing their role as an adjunct to other measures such as military action (Hill 2002).

Policy makers also had to balance risk, particularly when using the military. There were several instances when the CIA may have had information on bin Laden's location (or, more meaningfully, his future location), which made him vulnerable to cruise missile strikes. This information, however, usually came from one source whose accuracy was dubious at best. Failure could prove disastrous. The 1998 missile strikes on Afghanistan had lionized bin Laden, and a subsequent miss would further enhance his stature. In addition, if the strike killed any of the women and children at the target site it would further damage America's reputation. Other officials feared that the United States was already being painted as a "Mad Bomber" because of its attacks in Iraq and Serbia and that the strikes might destabilize Pakistan. One strike was called off in part because it might kill members of the United Arab Emirates royal family who may have been hunting with bin Laden. Even in hindsight, it is hard to judge the right course here. The CIA later found that bin Laden was present at only one of the three supposed sightings (Clarke 2004, pp. 20, 201–2, 422, 448). Had policy makers been risk acceptant, the errant strikes might have elevated bin Laden's status, jeopardized relations with a key ally in the Gulf, and made the United States look foolish and brutal in attacking noncombatants.

The Nature of the Adversary

Too often, assessments of failure focus on the mistakes of the victim rather than on the skill of the adversary. Most terrorist groups fall into the intelligence category of "hard targets." Their members are difficult to identify, their actions difficult to anticipate, and their organizations difficult to infiltrate. Only 50% of terrorist groups survive a year, and only 5% survive a decade; those that endure generally are skilled at minimizing their exposure to government law enforcement and intelligence agencies (Hoffman 2002b, p. 84). Typically, terrorist groups are composed of small cells, where ties of kinship and neighborhood often cement a strong ideological commitment. Frequently, they blend into sympathetic, or often intimidated, local communities that are not willing to cooperate with security services. Much of the stock in trade of standard intelligence analysis, such as imagery analysis, is of little help in counterterrorism.

Even within the rarified world of terrorism, al Qaeda is an exceptionally difficult target to counter. Al Qaeda is also large by the standards of terrorist organizations, and its ties to other radical groups make it even larger. The hard core of terrorists who have sworn loyalty to bin Laden probably numbers in the hundreds, and the organization has helped train and support tens of thousands of insurgents who passed through its camps in Afghanistan. Al Qaeda is also tied to radical groups as far afield as South Africa, the Philippines, Mauritania, Uzbekistan, and dozens of other countries. Globalization has increased the organization's potency, both by helping it unite its operatives and preach its message from the remote confines of Afghanistan and by increasing resentment of the United States (Anonymous 2002, p. 179; Bergen 2002, p. 35; Cronin 2002/2003; Gunaratna 2002, pp. 8, 95; Hoffman 2002a, p. 307).

The survival or collapse of a terrorist group depends on its ability to maintain operational security. Al Qaeda's inner core is extremely sensitive to this issue. For example, the instructions of the "jihad manual" that al Qaeda has circulated focus on blending in and ensuring that the overall organization is not disrupted. bin Laden himself employed only trusted Arabs as bodyguards and avoided using cell phones (Coll 2004, p. 492). The September 11 plotters also tried, at times unsuccessfully, to preserve operational secrecy.

Al Qaeda has demonstrated an ability to revise its methods and structure in response to setbacks or failures. Its operatives regularly review lessons learned in order to improve the chances of success for future attacks (Hoffman 2002a, p. 307). This gives the organization the ability to recuperate quickly from disaster or successful countermeasures.

Before September 11, al Qaeda had also forged an unprecedented relationship with a state. The organization had an exceptionally close relationship with the Taliban regime, bound by a shared ideology, close friendships, and al Qaeda's provision of manpower and financial support to the regime. The United States' failures to persuade and coerce the Taliban into giving up al Qaeda gave the organization a secure base (Anonymous 2002, Bergen 2002, Burke 2003, Griffin 2003).

For U.S. intelligence and policy makers, the nature of the adversary had tremendous consequences for the resulting failures to stop the attacks. The safe haven in Afghanistan made collection far more difficult and required that the United States remove a regime from power in order to disrupt al Qaeda's activities there. Al Qaeda was also hard to disrupt because of its transnational nature and large size, both of which enabled it to lose a cell or skilled operatives yet continue operations elsewhere. Finally, the organization's professionalism made collection and disruption difficult because, unlike many terrorist groups, it made relatively few mistakes.

RESPONDING TO THE NEXT FAILURE

When we examine the failures of counterterrorism before September 11, it is clear that no single measure, by itself, would have made America safe. Although this essay breaks down the weaknesses that contributed to al Qaeda's successful attacks on September 11 into several categories, these problems are highly interdependent. A simple change at one level or another would have had profound repercussions, but more comprehensive changes were necessary to tackle the broader danger of al Qaeda.

After September 11, policy makers tried to solve many of these problems. Terrorism, of course, became a top priority for the Bush administration, with the full support of the Congress and the American people. On an institutional level, the military, the CIA, the FBI, and the various agencies involved in homeland security made numerous changes designed to help them better fight al Qaeda. U.S. foreign policy also changed dramatically, with the United States overthrowing the Taliban and making al Qaeda a priority in many of its bilateral relations.

Although these steps have led to considerable progress, new problems have emerged. Support for jihadism has risen, even as al Qaeda as a discrete organization appears under siege. Anti-Americanism in particular is rife (Anonymous 2004, Pillar 2004a). Stopping "the next 9/11" will require not only avoiding the mistakes that allowed the first attack but also adapting to the changing strategic environment.

Yet we must recognize that when dealing with terrorist organizations in general, and when confronting such a skilled organization as al Qaeda in particular, some attacks will inevitably succeed. Indeed, more than three years after the attacks, warnings that another catastrophic strike is imminent remain constant. Policy makers thus must focus not only on preventing the next attack but on ensuring the proper response should an attack nevertheless occur. This effort includes consequence management, making sure that hospitals, fire fighters, and other emergency personnel have the proper procedures, training, and resources. Just as important, however, is expectations management. Terrorists "win" through the psychological damage they spread, not through the physical carnage they inflict (Hoffman 1998). Leaders who dampen rather than feed this panic will do far more to defeat terrorists than would any particular covert-action measure or military strike.

ACKNOWLEDGMENTS

I thank Andrew Amunsen, David Edelstein, Lynn Eden, and Robert Jervis for their help and comments on earlier versions of this essay.

The *Annual Review of Political Science* is online at
http://polisci.annualreviews.org

LITERATURE CITED

Albright M. 2003. *Madam Secretary.* New York: Miramax Books

Allison G. 1971. *Essence of Decision.* Boston: Little Brown

Anonymous. 2002. *Through Our Enemies' Eyes: Osama bin Laden, Radical Islam, and the Future of America.* Washington, DC: Brassey's

Anonymous. 2004. *Imperial Hubris: Why the West is Losing the War on Terror.* Washington, DC: Brassey's

Bamford J. 2004. *A Pretext for War: 9/11, Iraq, and the Abuse of America's Intelligence Agencies.* New York: Doubleday

Bell JB. 1994. The armed struggle and underground intelligence: an overview. *Stud. Confl. Terrorism* 17:115–50

Benjamin D, Simon S. 2002. *The Age of Sacred Terror.* New York: Random House

Bergen PL. 2002. *Holy War, Inc.: Inside the Secret World of Osama bin Laden.* New York: Simon & Schuster

Betts R. 1978. Analysis, war, and decision: why intelligence failures are inevitable. *World Polit.* 21:61–89

Betts R. 1982. *Surprise Attack: Lessons for Defense Planning.* Washington, DC: Brookings Inst.

Blackwill RD, Davis J. 2004. A policymaker's perspective on intelligence analysis. See Johnson & Wirtz 2004, pp. 112–19

Bossie DN. 2004. *Intelligence Failure: How Clinton's National Security Policy Set the Stage for 9/11.* Nashville, TN: WND Books

Burke J. 2003. *Al-Qaeda: Casting a Shadow of Terror.* New York: I.B. Tauris

Byman D. 2003. Al Qaeda as an adversary:

Do we understand the enemy? *World Polit.* 56(1):139–63

Chan S. 1979. The intelligence of stupidity: understanding failures in strategic warning. *Am. Polit. Sci. Rev.* 73(1):171–80

Chomsky N. 2001. *9–11.* New York: Seven Stories

Clarke R. 2004. *Against All Enemies.* New York: Free

Clinton WJ. 2004. *My Life.* New York: Knopf

Cohen EA, Gooch J. 1991. *Military Misfortunes: The Anatomy of Failure in War.* New York: Vintage

Coll S. 2004. *Ghost Wars: The Secret History of the CIA, Afghanistan, and bin Laden, from the Soviet Invasion to September 10, 2001.* New York: Penguin

Cook SDN, Yanow D. 1996. Culture and organizational learning. In *Organizational Learning,* ed. MD Cohen, LS Sproull, pp. 430–59. London: Sage

Crenshaw M. 2002. The logic of terrorism: terrorist behavior as a product of strategic choice. In *Terrorism and Counterterrorism: Understanding the New Security Environment,* ed. RD Howard, RL Sawyer, pp. 55–67. Guilford, CT: McGraw Hill

Cronin AK. 2002/2003. Behind the curve: globalization and international terrorism. *Int. Sec.* 27(3):30–58

Eden L. 2004. *Whole World on Fire: Organizations, Knowledge, & Nuclear Weapons Devastation.* Ithaca, NY: Cornell Univ. Press

Findings of the Final Report of the Senate Select Committee on Intelligence and the House Permanent Select Committee on Intelligence Joint Inquiry into the Terrorist Attacks of September 11, 2001. December 10,

2002. U.S. Senate Select Committee on Intelligence and U.S. House Permanent Select Committee on Intelligence. http://intelligence.senate.gov/findings.pdf

Fredman J. 1997. Covert action, loss of life, and the prohibition on assassination. *Stud. Intel.* 15–25

Freeh LJ. 2001. *Statement for the Record on the Threat of Terrorism to the United States.* U.S. Senate Committees on Appropriations, Armed Services, and Select Committee on Intelligence (May 10)

Gause FG III. 1995. *Oil Monarchies.* New York: Counc. For. Relat. Press

Gause FG III. 2002. Be careful what you wish for: the future of U.S.-Saudi relations. *World Polit. J.* Spring:37–50

Gerecht RM. 2001. The counterterrorist myth. *Atlantic Monthly* July/August. http://www.theatlantic.com/cgi-bin/send.cgi?page=http%A//www.theatlnatic.com/issues/. Downloaded July 19, 2004

Gertz B. 2003. *Breakdown: How America's Intelligence Failures Led to September 11.* New York: Plume

Goodson LP. 2001. *Afghanistan's Endless War: State Failure, Regional Politics, and the Rise of the Taliban.* Seattle, WA: Univ. Washington Press

Griffin M. 2003. *Reaping the Whirlwind: Afghanistan, Al Qa'ida and the Holy War.* Sterling, VA: Pluto

Gunaratna R. 2002. *Inside Al Qaeda.* New York: Columbia Univ. Press

Halperin M. 1974. *Bureaucratic Politics and Foreign Policy.* Washington, DC: Brookings Inst.

Herman M. 2004. Intelligence and national action. See Johnson & Wirtz 2004, pp. 224–33

Herwig HH. 1998. Innovation ignored: the submarine problem—Germany, Britain, and the United States, 1919–1939. In *Military Innovation in the Interwar Period*, ed. W Murray, AR Millet, pp. 227–64. New York: Cambridge Univ. Press

Hill E. 2002. *Joint Inquiry Staff Statement. Hearing on the Intelligence Community's Response to Past Terrorist Attacks Against the United States from February 1993 to September 2001.* http://intelligence.senate.gov

Hitz FP. 2004. Unleashing the rogue elephant: September 11 and letting the CIA be the CIA. See Johnson & Wirtz 2004, pp. 390–96

Hoffman B. 1998. *Inside Terrorism.* New York: Columbia Univ. Press

Hoffman B. 2002a. Rethinking terrorism and counterterrorism since 9/11. *Stud. Confl. Terrorism* 25:303–16

Hoffman B. 2002b. The modern terrorist mindset. In *Terrorism and Counterterrorism: Understanding the New Security Environment*, ed. RD Howard, RL Sawyer, pp. 75–95. Guilford, CT: McGraw Hill

Hopple GW. 1984. Intelligence and warning: implications and lessons of the Falkland Islands War. *World Polit.* 36(3):339–61

Howell WG. 2003. *Power without Persuasion: The Politics of Direct Presidential Action.* Princeton, NJ: Princeton Univ. Press

Janis I. 1972. *Victims of Groupthink.* Boston: Houghton Mifflin

Jervis R. 1976. *Perception and Misperception in International Politics.* Princeton, NJ: Princeton Univ. Press

Jervis R. 2002. An interim assessment of September 11: What has changed and what has not? *Polit. Sci. Q.* 117(1): 37–54

Johnson L. 1996. *Secret Agencies: U.S. Intelligence in a Hostile World.* New Haven, CT: Yale Univ. Press

Johnson L. 2004. Covert action and accountability: decision-making for America's secret foreign policy. See Johnson & Wirtz 2004, pp. 370–89

Johnson LK, Wirtz JJ. 2004. *Strategic Intelligence: Windows Into a Secret World.* Los Angeles: Roxbury

Kepel G. 2002. *Jihad: The Trail of Political Islam*, transl. AF Roberts (from French). Cambridge, MA: Harvard Univ. Press

Kessler R. 2002. *Bureau: The Secret History of the FBI.* New York: St. Martin's

Kux D. 2001. *The United States and Pakistan, 1947–2000: Disenchanted Allies.* Baltimore, MD: Johns Hopkins Univ. Press

Levite A. 1987. *Intelligence and Strategic Surprises*. New York: Columbia Univ. Press

Lian B, Oneal J. 1993. Presidents, the use of military force, and public opinion. *J. Confl. Resolut.* 37(2):277–300

Lippman TW. 1994. *Inside the Mirage: America's Fragile Partnership with Saudi Arabia*. Boulder, CO: Westview

May E. 2001. *Strange Victory: Hitler's Conquest of France*. New York: Hill & Wang

May ER, ed. 1986. *Knowing One's Enemies: Intelligence Assessment before the Two World Wars*. Princeton, NJ: Princeton Univ. Press

McCormick GH, Owen G. 2000. Security and coordination in a clandestine organization. *Math. Comput. Model.* 31:175–92

Miller J. 2002. *The Cell: Inside the 9/11 Plot and Why the FBI and the CIA Failed to Stop It*. New York: Hyperion

Miniter R. 2003. *Losing Bin Laden: How Bill Clinton's Failures Unleashed Global Terror*. Washington, DC: Regnery

National Commission on Terrorist Attacks Upon the United States. 2004. *The 9/11 Commission Report: Final Report of the National Commission on Terrorist Attacks Upon the United States*. New York: W.W. Norton

Neustadt RE. 1991. *Presidential Power and Modern Presidents: The Politics of Leadership from Roosevelt to Reagan*. New York: Free

Perrow C. 1999. *Normal Accidents: Living with High-Risk Technologies*. Princeton, NJ: Princeton Univ. Press

Pfiffner JP. 2004. *The Modern Presidency*. Lexington, KY: Wadsworth

Pillar P. 2001. *Terrorism and U.S. Foreign Policy*. Washington, DC: Brookings Inst.

Pillar P. 2004a. Counterterrorism after Al-Qaeda. *Washington Q.* 27(3):101–13

Pillar P. 2004b. Intelligence. In *Attacking Terrorism: Elements of a Grand Strategy*, ed. AK Croning, JM Ludes, pp. 115–39. Washington, DC: Georgetown Univ. Press

Posner GL. 2003. *Why America Slept: The Failure to Prevent 9/11*. New Home: Random House

Posner R. 2004. The 9/11 report: a dissent. *N.Y. Times Book Rev.* Aug. 29. http://www.nytimes.com/2004/08/29/books/review/29postnerl.html?

Reidel B. 2002. *American diplomacy and the 1999 Kargil summit at Blair House*. Cent. Advanced Study of India. http://www.sas/upenn.edu/casi/reprots/RiedelPaper051302.htm

Report of a Committee of Privy Counsellors. 2004. *Review of Intelligence on Weapons of Mass Destruction*. London: Stationery Off.

Report of the Joint Inquiry Into Intelligence Community Activities before and after the Terrorist Attacks of September 11, 2001. 2002. Washington, DC: U.S. Gov. Printing Off.

Scowcroft B. 1996. *Statement before the Permanent Select Committee on Intelligence, House of Representatives*. Reprinted in *IC21: The Intelligence Community in the 21st Century*. Washington, DC: U.S. Gov. Printing Off.

Shulsky A. 2002. *Silent Warfare: Understanding the World of Intelligence*. Washington, DC: Brassey's

Snook SA. 2000. *Friendly Fire: The Accidental Shootdown of U.S. Black Hawks Over Northern Iraq*. Princeton, NJ: Princeton Univ. Press

Stein JG. 1982. Military deception, strategic surprise, and conventional deterrence: a political analysis of Egypt and Israel, 1971–73. *J. Strat. Stud.* 5(1):94–121

Tenet G. 2001. *Worldwide Threat 2001: National Security in a Changing World*. Statement before the U.S. Senate Select Committee on Intelligence. http://www.cia.gov/cia/public_affairs/speeches/2001/UNCLASWWT_02072001.html

Unger C. 2004. *House of Bush, House of Saud: The Secret Relationship between the World's Two Most Powerful Dynasties*. New York: Scribner

U.S. Senate Select Committee on Intelligence. 2004. *Report of the Senate Select Committee on Intelligence on the U.S. Intelligence Community's Prewar Intelligence Assessments on*

Iraq. Washington, DC: U.S. Gov. Printing Off.

Walsh E. 2001. Louis Freeh's last case. *New Yorker* May 14. http://newyorker.com/archive/content/?010924fr_archive06

Watson D. 2002. *Testimony before the House and Senate Intelligence Committees*. http://intelligence.senate.gov/0209hrg/020926/watson.pdf

Wirtz J. 1991. Intelligence to please? The order of battle controversy during the Vietnam War. *Polit. Sci. Q.* 106(2):239–63

Wohlstetter R. 1962. *Pearl Harbor: Warning and Decision.* Stanford, CA: Stanford Univ. Press

Woodward B. 2002. *Bush at War.* New York: Simon & Schuster

Annu. Rev. Polit. Sci. 2005. 8:171–201
doi: 10.1146/annurev.polisci.7.012003.104851
Copyright © 2005 by Annual Reviews. All rights reserved

UNPACKING "TRANSNATIONAL CITIZENSHIP"*

Jonathan Fox

Latin American and Latino Studies Department, University of California,
Santa Cruz, Santa Cruz, California 95064; email: Jafox@ucsc.edu

Key Words   civil society, globalization, rights, migrants

■ **Abstract**   What "counts" as transnational citizenship? Like the related notions of global or transnational civil society, the term's appeal to internationalists is greater than its conceptual precision. However, a wide range of empirical trends do raise questions about the nation-state-based approach to the concept of citizenship. In an effort to avoid conceptual stretching, this essay assesses the degree to which the concept of transnational citizenship helps to address issues raised by "globalization from below." Because many approaches to citizenship focus on the dynamics and texture of participation, this review incorporates recent findings in sociology, anthropology, and geography into the political science discussion. The essay is organized by propositions that bring together analysis of two distinct empirical literatures, on transnational civil society and on migrant civic and political participation. The review concludes by contrasting two cross-cutting sets of definitional choices. The discussion is framed by a recognition that definitions of citizenship vary along two main dimensions: in their emphasis on rights versus membership, and in high versus low intensity. Only a very bounded definition of transnational citizenship holds up under conceptual scrutiny, limited to what is also called dual or multiple citizenship for migrants.

INTRODUCTION

Diverse patterns of "globalization from below" are both claiming rights across borders and constructing transnational political communities. As our analytical frameworks try to catch up with these new empirical trends, the concept of transnational citizenship resonates with those who want to extend rights and principles of political and social equality beyond nation-state boundaries. Yet normative appeal

---

*This is a substantially revised and expanded version of a paper first presented at the workshop on "The Rights and Responsibilities of Transnational Citizenship," Kennedy School of Government, Harvard University, March 11–12, 2004. The essay is informed by recent collaborative studies of three different sets of transnational civil society actors: U.S.-Mexico civil society coalitions (Brooks & Fox 2002), campaigns seeking World Bank accountability (Clark et al. 2003, Fox & Brown 1998), and cross-border indigenous Mexican migrant organizations (Fox & Rivera-Salgado 2004).

is no substitute for a precise definition. Is "transnational citizenship" just a rhetorical tool to encourage globalization from below, or can it be defined with sufficient precision to add analytical value?

Applying the concept of transnational citizenship with analytical consistency requires making explicit definitional choices that specify both what kinds of rights and what kinds of membership are involved. Otherwise, transnational citizenship is a "you know it when you see it" term that is difficult to distinguish from other kinds of civic or political relationships and blurs the conceptual edge of citizenship itself. To focus the discussion, "transnational" will be defined here in common sense terms as "cross-border" (and therefore, technically, "trans-state").[2]

In response to these dilemmas, this essay spells out some of the conceptual challenges that any definition of transnational citizenship would have to address in order to be analytically useful. In the process, the review addresses a series of more general questions about both citizenship and globalization from below. The discussion begins by framing some definitional choices, followed by propositions that emerge from the literatures on transnational civil society and migrant collective action. The essay concludes that the concept's usefulness—so far—is limited to those migrant civic and political rights and memberships that could also be described, perhaps more precisely, as "dual" or "multiple" citizenship. The rest of what might look like transnational citizenship turns out to consist primarily of genres of civic and political participation and membership that fall short of the category of citizenship.

This review crosses three sets of intellectual boundaries. First, the discussion explores the still-underdeveloped interface between international relations, comparative politics, and normative political theory. Second, because so many approaches to citizenship are informed by analysis of collective action and the political construction of rights and membership, the essay draws from relevant research in political sociology, anthropology, and geography. Third, the essay weaves together dilemmas and propositions that emerge from the literatures on migration and transnational civil society—two fields of study that rarely intersect.[3] Seen from a different angle, cross-border rights and membership can be framed either as the civil society dimension of the broader process of nonstate actor involvements in international relations, on the one hand, or as the transnational extension of the national construction of rights and political inclusion, on the other (see, e.g., Josselin & Wallace 2001 on nonstate actors more generally).

---

[2]The existence of states that include more than one nation raises issues for defining transnational citizenship that will not be addressed here. Some states recognize their multinational character institutionally through various autonomy and power-sharing relationships (e.g., Belgium, Canada, Spain, Russia, and the former Yugoslavia). A consistent definition of the concept of transnational citizenship would need to address this dimension of the distinction between trans- and multinational (Bauböck 2003).

[3]For exceptions to this generalization, see Brysk (2003), Yashar (2002), and Tarrow (2005).

Empirically, at least four very distinct trends are raising questions about classic nation-state-based models of citizenship. First, in some cases, globalization from above is undermining national and local rights, as in the widely debated case of the tension between "investor rights" and international trade and financial institutions, on the one hand, and citizen-based national efforts to defend social rights and environmental standards, on the other. This is the "mirror image" of the emergence of transnational rights and membership and will not be addressed in this review (see Fox 2003). Second, the widespread entry of transnational migrant communities into the public sphere, long-distance nationalism, and the rise of dual national identities are provoking sustained debate about distinctions between national identities and civil-political rights (e.g., Faist 2000, Jacobson 1996, Soysal 1994). Third, the rise of transnational civil society and an associated public sphere is extending claims to membership in cross-border civic and political communities grounded in rights-based worldviews, such as feminism, environmentalism, indigenous rights, and human rights. Fourth, within multilateral institutions, regional integration in Europe and broader international "soft law" reforms are recognizing individuals' standing and "proto-rights" vis-à-vis transnational authorities.[4]

As Bauböck (2003) put it, "the new challenge for political theory is to go beyond a narrow state-centered approach by considering political communities and systems of rights that emerge at levels of governance above or below those of independent states or that cut across international borders" (p. 704). Can these incipient processes of cross-border inclusion be understood in terms of transnational citizenship, at a historical moment that might turn out to be comparable to the early stages of the construction of national citizenship? After all, it took centuries to construct and expand national citizenship (Tilly 1998). Today, something *is* going on across borders that requires new conceptual categories—the question here is whether (and how) the concept of transnational citizenship might shed light on it.

The rest of this essay is organized into five sections. The first asks what "counts" as transnational citizenship and cautions against "conceptual stretching." The second section raises questions for the agency-based approach to citizenship by exploring the distinction between claiming rights and actually gaining rights. The third section searches for possible emerging forms of cross-border citizenship relations within the broader trends in transnational civil society. The fourth section turns to migrant civic and political practices, to assess the degree to which forms of cross-border citizenship are developing within what are widely recognized as "transnational communities." The fifth section briefly proposes a conceptual framework for mapping possible forms of transnational citizenship. This framework

---

[4]In one paradigm case, the multilateral development banks have responded to local/global protest by creating a set of ostensibly mandatory minimum social and environmental standards for institutional behavior, reinforced by the right of affected people to appeal directly to semiautonomous investigative bodies (Clark et al. 2003, Fox & Brown 1998).

returns to the distinction between state- and society-based definitions, cross-cut by the distinction between thick and thin genres of citizenship.

WHAT "COUNTS" AS TRANSNATIONAL CITIZENSHIP?

When one tries to define transnational citizenship with any degree of precision, the most challenging question is, "What counts?" After all, not all migrant political participation involves crossing borders, and not all transnational public interest campaigning leads to the construction of citizenship. Keck & Sikkink's (1998) now-classic analysis of transnational advocacy networks detailed the "boomerang" approach, through which civil society campaigns outflank authoritarian regimes by reaching out across borders to use international pressure to open up domestic political space.[5] Although transnational action can influence the balance of power between civil society actors and states, this process does not necessarily create transnational citizenship. Influence is not the same as rights, and not all rights are citizenship rights. For example, human rights are not equivalent to citizenship rights. In addition, networks may or may not constitute political communities, and not all forms of community involve citizenship.

Any attempt to pin down the concept of transnational citizenship raises all the contested issues that are associated with the term citizenship itself.[6] Some approaches are defined primarily in reference to the state, with citizenship grounded in rights that are strong enough to constitute "enforceable claims on the state" (Tilly 1998, pp. 56–57). In contrast, diverse communitarian conceptions of citizenship are grounded in membership in civic or political communities.[7] In other words, approaches to citizenship that depend on institutionally guaranteed rights are quite different from those defined by collective action and shared identities. These two different dimensions of citizenship can be described in shorthand as state-based and society-based. Though conceptually distinct, in practice they are interdependent. A long tradition of comparative historical-sociological analysis, associated most notably with Barrington Moore, shows how waves of collective action made individual rights possible (e.g., Tilly 1998). As Foweraker & Landman

---

[5]Most of the relevant literature about the influence of cross-border campaigning focuses on the global south, but the process is relevant for the global north as well. For a revealing analysis of a native Canadian campaign experience, see Jenson & Papillon (2000).

[6]Jones & Gaventa (2002) provide a useful overview of the recent literature on citizenship, which focuses on agency-based approaches. From a different tradition of political theory, Schuck & Smith (1985) distinguish between "ascriptive" (based on circumstances such as birthplace) and "consensual" bases of citizenship (based on "free individual choices").

[7]Johnston (2001) tries to transcend this dichotomy. His definition, which is applied to politically empowered migrants, regardless of official citizenship status, "include[s] the citizenries of multiple nationalities within a single state, citizenries of single nations that straddle state borders, and citizenries that simultaneously belong to more than one national polity" (p. 256). See also Johnston (2003).

(1997) put it, "almost paradoxically, the essentially *individual* rights of citizenship can only be achieved through different forms of *collective* struggle" (p. 1, italics in original).

In other words, if the core criteria of rights and membership mean that citizenship is a relational concept—between citizens and a state and/or a political community—then what would transnational citizenship relate to? In the context of liberal democratic states, the relationship is vertical, between the individual and the state, mediated by the rule of law and formal political equality. Some analysts deploy a more horizontal approach, focusing on power relations within society. In the case of transnational citizenship, however, the reference point is not as clear—citizen power in relation to what? If one extends the vertical citizen-state relationship transnationally, then the analogous reference point would be multilateral public authorities, such as the European Union, the United Nations, and the international financial and trade institutions, as well as new bodies such as the International Criminal Court. If one extends the more society-based approach to citizenship horizontally across borders, then the focus would be on membership in transnational civic or political communities. These conceptual choices between state- versus society-based definitions of citizenship are each path-dependent, ultimately determining what counts as citizenship according to a given set of assumptions. In an actor-based approach, membership in a political community is the key criterion. In a rights-based approach, the establishment of enforceable access to rights marks the threshold that determines citizenship.

If, as the actor-based approach might suggest, the process of claiming rights across borders were to generate transnational citizenship, then the citizenries that are empowering themselves should be clearly identifiable. If citizenship is about membership in a polity, in addition to claims about rights, then how is that polity defined? Baubök (1994) defines a polity as "an inclusive community or association of equal members that extends basic rights to everybody subject to its collective decisions" (p. viii). The key questions for defining a transnational polity, then, are (*a*) what are the criteria for membership? and (*b*) how are the boundaries delineated? Transnational civil society actors are constructing new kinds of membership, but do they involve rights and responsibilities that are sufficiently clear to count as transnational citizenship? Or are the boundaries of both the concept and the actors themselves so difficult to pin down that transnational citizenship is watered down by its very breadth—a case of conceptual stretching (Collier & Mahon 1993, Sartori 1980)?

A narrow approach would limit the definition of transnational citizenship to those migrants who manage to create or sustain dual or multiple national identities (Baubök 1994). A broad approach would refer to those multi-level processes through which social, civic, and political actors claim rights in the transnational public sphere. For example, in "the age of globalization," Yuval-Davis (1999) speaks of "citizenship as a *multi-layered* construct in which one's citizenship in collectivities—local, ethnic, national, state, cross or trans-state and suprastate—is affected and often at least partly constructed by the relationships and positionings of each layer" (p. 119, emphasis added). Both these approaches evoke an agency-based notion of citizenship, as distinct from a primarily state-focused rights-based approach.

CLAIMING RIGHTS VERSUS GAINING CITIZENSHIP

One of the problems that arises when we look for citizenship in the transnational public sphere is that claiming rights is not the same as gaining citizenship. Most claims are not enforceable, which underscores the big difference between the widely resonant notion of the "right to have rights" and the actual winning of those rights. The first idea is primarily normative, whereas the second is empirically tangible. This distinction suggests that the society-based or agency-driven concept of citizenship is problematic. Though normatively appealing, it is difficult to define with precision. Yes, in practice, rights are constituted by being exercised, but only some attempts actually win respect for rights.

This leads to the following puzzle: Are those who consider themselves to have rights, but are denied them with impunity, citizens of anything? Imagine the case of a frontline grassroots organizer who is treated as a full participant in international civil society or United Nations forums but is abused with impunity once she gets back home (whether by governments, local political bosses, or her husband). How would the concept of transnational citizenship apply? Can one be a "citizen" while abroad but not at home? Here Yuval-Davis' (1999) concern for disentangling the interaction between levels of "multi-layered citizenship" is relevant. Painter (2002), a geographer focused on the EU experience with multi-layered citizenship, notes that empirical research on actual practices lags behind the conceptual discussion. The right to be heard in international forums does matter, but it falls short of transnational citizenship. Other terms to describe cross-border recognition of human rights and excluded voices are more precise, such as the notion of standing.

In summary, the claiming of rights is necessary but not sufficient to build citizenship. Along the lines of the state- versus society-based dimensions of citizenship described above, one could pose a distinction between a rights-based approach and an empowerment-based approach. Empowerment, in the sense of actors' capacity to make claims, is distinct from rights, defined as institutionally recognized guarantees and opportunities. They do not necessarily go together. Institutions may nominally recognize rights that actors, because of a lack of capacity to make claims, are not able to exercise in practice. Conversely, actors may be empowered in the sense of having the experience and capacity to demand and exercise rights, while lacking institutionally recognized opportunities to do so. Rights and empowerment can each encourage the other, and indeed they overlap in practice, but they are analytically distinct. In other words, some must act like citizens (claim rights) so that others can actually be citizens (have rights), but acting like a citizen is not the same as being a citizen. If this distinction makes sense, then most of transnational civil society falls far short of transnational citizenship.

LOOKING FOR CITIZENS IN TRANSNATIONAL CIVIL SOCIETY

The term transnational citizenship is less expansive than its apparent synonyms, world citizenship and global citizenship, and is more clearly cross-border than the term cosmopolitan citizenship. A longstanding normative theoretical tradition calls for "global" or "world" citizenship.[8] In contrast, the term transnational citizenship can refer to cross-border relations that are far from global in scope. This is analogous to the distinction between the concepts of global versus transnational civil society (i.e., Edwards & Gaventa 2001, Florini 2000, Kaldor et al. 2003, Keane 2003, Lipschutz & Mayer 1996, Tarrow 2001, Walzer 1995, Wapner 1996). Critics of the concept of global civil society argue that it implicitly overstates the degree of cross-border cohesion and joint action in civil society (Laxer & Halperin 2003). In the context of this debate, the term transnational citizenship would apply most clearly to membership in the EU—a political community that is clearly cross-border yet certainly not global.[9] Yet Bauböck (2003), one of the leading proponents of the concept of transnational citizenship, suggests that the EU is better understood instead as "supranational," meaning that individual membership requires citizenship in an EU nation-state. Indeed, it is not at all clear whether the EU's transnational political experiment is the leading edge of a growing trend or is the exception that proves the rule in terms of the persistent grip of nation-states on political sovereignty. So far, the latter seems more likely. Either way, analysts agree that EU citizenship is still both "thin" and fundamentally grounded in national citizenship.

Transnational citizenship could also refer more narrowly to strictly *bi*national relationships that are limited to specific political communities (not necessarily nation-states) and are therefore considerably less than global in scope. In contrast, the idea of cosmopolitan citizenship, although it refers to freedom from national limitations, does not necessarily have a cross-border dimension in terms of community membership or rights (Hutchings & Dannreuther 1999). The term cosmopolitan citizenship is close to a synonym for multicultural citizenship, which

---

[8]Comprehensive normative discussions include Delanty (2000), Heater (2002), and Hutchings & Dannreuther (1999), as well as Bowden's (2003) critique. Bowden observes that "the idea of global citizenship is inextricably linked to the West's long and torturous history of engaging in overzealous civilising-cum-universalising missions in the non-Western world" (p. 350). From a Chinese perspective, however, He (2004) defends the concept of world citizenship and Henderson & Ikeda (2004) offer a distinctly non-Western (Buddhist-inspired) approach.

[9]A serious discussion of changes in rights, membership and sovereignty in the EU would require a separate review (see, e.g., Bauböck 2003, Bellamy & Warleigh 2001, Jacobson 1996, Jacobson & Benarieh Ruffer 2004, Østergaard-Nielsen 2003a,b, Painter 2002, Schmitter 2000, Soysal 1994). Bellamy & Warleigh (2001) are not very sanguine: "[T]he scope and character of the equality conferred by EU citizenship is more akin to that of the subjects of a common ruler than of citizens capable of being both rulers and ruled in turn" (p. 3).

recognizes and respects multiple identities (Kymlicka 1995). From the field of Latino Studies, the term cultural citizenship has come to refer to a similar inclusionary respect for difference, but without specific reference to a cross-border dimension (Flores & Benmayor 1997).

Tarrow (2005) shifts the concept of cosmopolitan citizenship from a multicultural stance toward cross-border engagements with his broad definition of "rooted cosmopolitans" as "people and groups who are rooted in their specific national contexts, but who engage in regular activities that require their involvement in transnational networks. . . ." In contrast with the term transnational citizenship, "rooted cosmopolitan" is broader, not limited to civic-political engagements, and the threshold of transnational engagement is lower than the full membership in a community that one associates with citizenship.

Transnational Civil Society is Necessary but not Sufficient for Transnational Citizenship

Within the arenas of transnational civil society that do not involve migrants, nongovernmental organizations that are active across borders include both idea-based and interest-based groups (difficult to disentangle as those collective identities may be). Some share normative principles, as in the case of human rights, environmental, and feminist "principled issue networks" (Keck & Sikkink 1998). Others are based on counterpart class locations, as in the case of the multiplicity of cross-border business associations (Sklair 2001), as well as labor union federations and coalitions within shared industries (Levi & Olson 2000, Waterman 1998, Waterman & Wills 2001) and emerging peasant movement networks (Edelman 2003).

Not all cross-border collective action takes the form of processes that claim rights. Where then does one draw the line between transnational citizenship and other kinds of cross-border collective action? Most transnational civil society strategies lead to a presence in the public sphere that often involves voice and sometimes extracts concession but usually falls short of either rights vis-à-vis powerful institutions or membership in a transnational polity. In the words of a key proponent of the notion of global citizenship, "Citizenship is tied to democracy, and global citizenship should in some way be tied to global democracy, at least to a process of democratization that extends some notion of rights, representation and accountability to the operations of international institutions, and gives some opportunity to the peoples whose lives are being regulated to participate in the selection of leaders" (Falk 1994, p. 128). Muetzelfeldt & Smith (2002) also make the case that "to analyze global civil society and global citizenship it is necessary to focus on global governance" (p. 55). This approach refers to the specific subset of transnational civil society that relates to transnational institutions, but even then citizenship will have to wait until they are (somehow) democratized. Note that the widely-used related term "democratization of global governance" has yet to be defined with any precision. It usually refers to reforms of multilateral institutions that would provide greater North-South balance between nation-states (see, e.g., Aksu & Camilleri 2002), regardless of their political regimes, an approach that is unrelated to one-person/one-vote definitions to democracy.

As a final caveat here, the growing literature on transnational civil society focuses primarily on those organizations that pursue certain values: gender, ethnic, and racial equality, political freedom, defense of the environment, and public accountability for powerful institutions. Just as in the case of national civil societies, however, much of existing transnational civil society reinforces the status quo or promotes conservative change that could roll back rights. Are these other civil society actors generating transnational citizens as well?

Most Cross-Border Networks and Coalitions do not Constitute Transnational Movements[10]

The construction of a transnational public sphere involves a wide range of face-to-face encounters, information sharing, exchanges of experiences, and expressions of solidarity. Sometimes these exchanges generate networks of ongoing relationships. Sometimes these networks in turn lead to coalitions and generate the shared goals, trust, and understanding needed to collaborate on specific campaigns. Yet most encounters do not generate ongoing networks, and most networks do not produce sustained active coalitions. As Keck put it (personal communication), "coalitions are networks in action mode." Networks, unlike coalitions, do not necessarily coordinate their actions, nor do they come to agreement on specific joint actions. In addition, neither networks nor coalitions necessarily involve significant horizontal exchange between their respective bases. Indeed, many rely on a handful of interlocutors to manage relationships between broad-based social organizations that have relatively little awareness of the nature and actions of their counterparts. The concept of transnational social *movement* organizations, in contrast, implies much higher density and much more cohesion than networks or coalitions have. The term transnational movement organizations suggests a collective actor that is present in more than one country. Classic cases include migrant groups that have organized membership in more than one country, or transnational environmental organizations that have organized social bases (not just employees) in multiple countries, such as Greenpeace and Friends of the Earth.[11] In short, transnational civil society exchanges *can* produce networks, which *can* produce coalitions, which *can* produce movements—but not necessarily.

Distinguishing between networks, coalitions, and movements helps to avoid blurring political differences and imbalances within so-called transnational movements, which may appear homogeneous from the outside. As Keck & Sikkink

---

[10]These two paragraphs draw on Fox (2002). For a similar approach, see Khagram et al. (2002).

[11]Despite their apparent similarities, these two groups have very different transnational structures. Greenpeace is a single organization with national branches, whereas Friends of the Earth is a coalition of distinct and more autonomous national affiliates.

(1998) point out, transnational networks face the challenge of developing a "common frame of meaning" despite cross-cultural differences (p. 7). In practice, however, such shared meanings are socially constructed through joint action and mutual understanding rather than through shared intentions or professed values and goals. And political differences within transnational networks, despite apparently shared goals, should not be underestimated. Even those transnational networks that appear to share basic political-cultural values, such as environmental, feminist, indigenous, or human rights movements, often consist of actors who have very different, nationally distinct political visions, goals, and styles. At the same time, national borders may not be the most important ones here. For example, ecologists or feminists from different countries who share systemic critiques may have more in common with their cross-border counterparts than with the more moderate wings of their respective national movements in each country (Fox 2002).

These networks and coalitions create a transnational public sphere from which shared ideas of membership, rights, and mutual responsibility *can* emerge, but only in cases and under conditions that have yet to be specified. In this context, it is useful to distinguish the broad "social field" within which transnational civil society actors operate from the actual relationships between specific actors and their widely varying degrees of cross-border density, cohesion, and balance (Alvarez 2005).[12]

Shared Targets may not Generate Shared Political Community

Some mobilizations that look transnational are really more international. People in different countries may have common enemies without necessarily experiencing membership in a shared community. For example, wars of aggression can provoke resistance in many countries, but that does not mean that participants identify either with each other or with the target of the aggression. Recall the mobilizations in the 1960s against the U.S. war in Indochina, or in the 1980s against nuclear weapons—protest was very international but not very transnational. Even when there is some degree of coordination among protesters in different countries, that could be purely instrumental, without a shared transnational political community.

Some mobilizations that are widely presented as transnational are in practice more international. For example, campaigns against probusiness trade and investment liberalization, such as those against the North American Free Trade Agreement, the Multilateral Investment Agreement, and the World Trade Organization,

---

[12]One way to unpack cross-border civil society relationships without assuming high levels of cohesion and mutual understanding is to keep in mind Tsing's notion of "the 'friction' of global activism." As she puts it, "friction here refers to the sticky materiality of worldly encounters. Aspirations for global connection come to life in friction. Universal dreams and schemes become practical and engaged in friction. A friction-oriented approach allows *ethnographic* engagement with universals and global packages. We can trace what happens to them as they move—and are transformed through engagement" (Tsing 2004a, p. 4; 2004b).

have not necessarily generated a transnational political community that shares more than instrumental goals (Fox 2002, Laxer 2003). Some would argue similarly regarding a case that seems a paradigm of successful transnational advocacy, the campaign for an international treaty against land mines (Mekata 2000). Only the handful of cross-border campaigners who become the "synapses" and "relays" that stitch together coalitions of primarily locally and nationally grounded movements are plausible candidates for transnational citizenship (Fox & Brown 1998; Tarrow 1995, 2001). These strategic bridge-builders have been called "rooted cosmopolitans" (Tarrow 2005), "citizen pilgrims" (Falk 1994, pp. 138–39, cited in Heater 2002, p. 13) and "grassroots globalists" (Henderson & Ikeda 2004).

Rethinking Past Internationalisms Sheds Light on What "Counts" as Transnational Citizenship

If, following an agency-based approach, transnational citizenship refers to cross-border collective civic or political identities that are rooted in more than one society, then it could provide a way to rethink historical experiences with classic internationalist social and political movements. Keck & Sikkink (1998) pioneered the historical contextualization of contemporary transnational activist networks. Throughout history, individuals have crossed borders and described one society to another—including "explorers," traders, and fellow travelers from Marco Polo to John Reed. They are distinct, however, from the cross-border campaigners described above, who more strategically strive to construct collective political identities that are shared across borders. For example, the First International was the first transnational workers' political coalition (Nimtz 2002). Other historical examples of deeply rooted cross-border political identities arise from the spread of anarcho-sindicalism through Europe and the Americas as part of a massive wave of migration. Marcus Garvey's pan-Africanist movement was widely felt in the United States and throughout the Caribbean (Campbell 1987). The Mexican revolution incorporated U.S. participants and sent internationalist exiles who joined the U.S. left, and revolutionary leader Ricardo Flores Magón pioneered "full" political binationality in both countries (MacLachan 1991). Were the internationalists who fought to defend Republican Spain transnational citizens? Clearly, transnational collective political identities have a long history—the question is whether they add up to a kind of citizenship.

Fast-forward later into the twentieth century and one can ask, where does the tradition of international solidarity with "national liberation movements" fit into the current discussion of transnational citizenship? Strongly influenced by movements against colonial and neocolonial legacies, these international solidarity movements could also be considered fellow travelers of long-distance nationalism—though their cross-border constituencies and partners included internationalists of diverse nationalities as well as diasporic nationalists. At least since the 1960s, the national boundaries of these movements have been quite porous, allowing nationals of one Latin American country to join movements in other countries. Based on shared regional transnational collective identities organized around class struggle and anti-imperialism, nationals of one Latin American country could even reach leadership positions across borders. Che Guevara was a paradigm case, an internationalist who became a national icon.

In the 1970s, southern African revolutionaries helped to inspire the U.S. branch of the transnational antiapartheid movement with their call to join the fight from "within the belly of the beast" (e.g., Seidman 2000). U.S. movements in solidarity with Central American revolutionary movements in the 1970s and 1980s followed two parallel tracks, one targeting Central American refugee communities in the United States, the other reaching out to U.S. civil society organizations. These consciously constructed South-North transnational political communities involved U.S. supporters "taking direction" from the South and encouraged an unprecedented degree of people-to-people exchange among religious congregrations, trade unions, women's organizations, and civil rights leaders. By the late 1980s, these networks had gained significant influence in mainstream civil society institutions and the U.S. Congress (e.g., Gosse 1988, 1995). Such international-solidarity activism did involve a kind of cross-border membership, at least for a handful of cultural-political interlocutors, who often had some voice though no vote. They gained a form of internationalist membership by choosing to take on responsibilities, but they rarely gained rights within these political communities.

International Solidarity: Ideological Affinity Versus Counterpart-Based Coalitions

What has long been called international solidarity was firmly grounded in nationalism as the dominant ideological framework for understanding the struggle for self-determination. More recently, the widespread disillusionment with vanguard political-party-led approaches to national liberation, together with internationalist civil society ideologies, has led to a shift away from implicitly statist "long-distance nationalist" approaches to national liberation. The paradigm case is the Zapatista rebellion, which, despite the "national" and "army" in its name, did not pursue a classic statist approach and instead focused on energizing and mobilizing other civil society actors. Its main focus was on the rest of Mexican civil society, although the Zapatistas soon discovered that their message resonated internationally.[13] Their movement became the "shot heard round the world" against top-down globalization. Their claim to authenticity, their performance and communicative strategies, and their very limited use of violence grounded a vision of changing power relations through participation from below, instead of the classic revolutionary attempt to administer power from above. Their rights discourse reached out to disparate social movements around the world that felt excluded by globalization and disil-

---

[13]There is a fascinating debate over the relative weight of international factors and actors in the Zapatista rebellion (see, e.g., Cleaver 2000, Hellman 2000, Oleson 2003, Paulson 2001, Stephen 2002). For an analysis that emphasizes their communicative strategies in terms of "marketing," see Bob (2001).

lusioned with political parties, helping to construct the ideological foundation for what later became known as the global justice movement. However, although this broad "we're all excluded together" approach can build cross-border solidarities, it does not necessarily generate enough density and cohesion for us to be able to speak of membership in a shared cross-border political community, much less to mention citizenship.

Another important shift away from classic cross-border solidarities based on ideological affinities is less discursive and more grounded in the practical challenges faced by local and national civil society organizations that had not looked across borders until globalization pushed them to. This is the shift toward the construction of networks and coalitions based on shared status as "counterparts." The concept of cross-border counterparts among social actors does not imply similarity or agreement but rather analogous roles in their respective societies (Brooks & Fox 2002). For example, the notion of counterparts could apply to antitoxics campaigners dealing with the same corporation or pesticide, workers in the same industry or sector, women's reproductive freedom campaigners, or indigenous rights activists. One cannot assume that they share ideologies, and their politics are not necessarily internationalist—but their analogous locations in their respective national societies create at least an incentive to share experiences. If counterparts share more than related challenges, if they also share cultures or languages, then there is a much greater possibility of going to the next stage and forging a shared collective identity. For example, in the U.S.-Mexico setting, worker-to-worker exchanges that bring together Mexican workers from both countries are much more likely to generate a shared identity than are exchanges that must confront deep language and cultural differences. For another example, reproductive rights activists who share a cross-border movement culture as well as a cause have a much stronger basis for a sense of common membership. Note, for example, the case of shared feminist Catholicism in the Latin American and U.S. branches of the advocacy group Catholics for the Right to Choose (Fox 2002). Here, a shared collective identity has been constructed in the overlapping space between two clearly delineated communities: the transnational feminist community and the one constructed by the transnational institution of the Catholic Church. However, the rights and responsibilities of membership in this transnational community are still highly contingent, certainly falling short of thicker notions of citizenship.

CROSS-BORDER MIGRANT POLITICS

Insofar as the most clear-cut manifestation of citizenship involves actual political enfranchisement, emerging patterns of transnational voting rights merit review here.

Direct Transnational Political Enfranchisement

The direct genre of transnational voting rights takes four principal forms: cross-border voting rights for migrant citizens, migrants' right to vote in polities where they are not citizens, legislative representation of expatriates, and the election of transnational authorities.

CROSS-BORDER VOTING RIGHTS   The number of countries that allow migrants to vote from abroad is increasing, but the actual terms of engagement between polities and migrant citizens vary widely. The devil is often in the details: the conditions for the exercise of the rights (which migrants can vote, under what administrative requirements); the degree to which the rights are exercised (degree of expatriate voter turnout); and the relative weights of migrants in the national polity—measured both by their share of the potential electorate and by their presence in the national imagination (Aleinikoff 2001, Aleinikoff & Klusmeyer 2000, Aleinikoff et al. 2003, Castles & Davidson 2000).

So far, the political symbolism of migrant voting appears to outweigh its actual electoral significance. Turnout is driven down by extensive lags in implementation and administrative obstacles. In the Philippine case, for example, 16 years passed between legislative approval and implementation, and voting rights were conditional on the voting migrant's permanent return to the Philippines within three years (Landigin & Williamson 2004). So far, the Mexican and Turkish experiences seem likely to follow similar paths.[14] Given the conflicting incentives that domestic political leaders face when deciding whether and how to grant voting rights to migrants, one could hypothesize that the larger the emigrant share of the national population, the more likely politicians are to promise them political inclusion while making the actual exercise of political rights as narrow and difficult as possible.

MIGRANTS VOTING WHERE THEY ARE NOT CITIZENS   The second form of direct transnational enfranchisement takes the form of migrants voting in polities in which they are not citizens, as in the case of local elections in several European countries, New Zealand, and even some U.S. localities.[15] For those migrants who become naturalized citizens where they settle, the question of transnational membership becomes ambiguous, insofar as some migrants actively retain home country identities, loyalties, and sometimes rights, whereas others follow the path of "don't look back" assimilation. Until recently, at least in the United States, belonging to two distinct national polities at once was widely seen as difficult or impossible, with the partial exception of Israel (e.g., Renshon 2000). It turns out, however, that continued engagement with home country politics does not necessarily

---

[14]An added complication is posed by the distinction between nationality and citizenship, since not all nation-states consider the two to be equivalent. For the case of Mexico, see Calderon & Martínez Saldaña (2002), Castañeda (2003, 2004), and Martínez-Saldaña & Ross (2002).

[15]See Bauböck's (2003) useful discussion as well as Waldrauch's (2003) detailed review of migrant voting regulations in 36 countries. On the emerging debate in the United States, see Swarns (2004).

conflict with incorporation into the U.S. political system. Migrants from countries that recognize dual nationality are more likely to become naturalized U.S. citizens than are those from other countries (Jones Correa 2001a,b). This finding is consistent with the findings of Guarnizo et al. (2003) and Escobar (2004). At the same time, at least for Latinos in the United States, it is likely that U.S. cultural, political, and legal factors are also powerful determinants of the propensity to become naturalized citizens. For example, a longitudinal cross-state comparative study clearly shows how naturalization rates change in response to anti-immigrant political campaigns (Pantoja et al. 2001). Naturalization decisions should also be understood against the contradictory backdrop of a dominant U.S. political culture that tends to treat Latinos and Asian-Americans as permanent foreigners, even after many generations as citizens (Rocco 2004). New comparative research in developing countries also suggests that some undocumented immigrants also manage to gain voting rights without going through the conventional process of naturalization associated with Europe and the United States (Sadiq 2003).

LEGISLATIVE REPRESENTATION OF EXPATRIATES   The third kind of direct cross-border electoral participation involves the right to be voted for, though not necessarily the right to vote. Some nation-states, such as Italy and Colombia, assign legislative seats to represent expatriate constituencies. In other countries, migrants can run for office—examples include mayoral races and party lists for state and federal Congress in Mexico.

ELECTED TRANSNATIONAL AUTHORITIES   The paradigm case of an elected transnational authority is the European parliament. As in many political systems, there appears to be a chicken-and-egg relationship between the European parliament's perceived institutional relevance and levels of voter engagement (Minder 2004).

Indirect Transnational Political Enfranchisement

Transnational electoral enfranchisement can be indirect in at least two ways. First, migrants can participate in home country elections without voting, both by influencing their family and social networks and through campaigns, fund-raising, and media action (Fitzgerald 2004). Second, they can participate electorally in their country of residence without actually voting by encouraging sympathetic citizens to vote, as in the notable case of campaigns by Los Angeles' mobilized trade unions that actively include noncitizens—"voting without the vote" (Varsanyi 2004). The question of migrant suffrage raises the broader issue of the relationship between citizenship and voting rights. Today voting rights are seen as inherent in (democratic) citizenship, yet in historical terms this convergence is relatively recent. Before World War I, the majority of U.S. citizens could not vote, whereas alien suffrage was widespread for men of European origin (Varsanyi 2004).

Transnational Citizenship Versus "Long-Distance Nationalism"

Organized social, civic, and political participation by migrants, often grounded in transnational communities, provides the strongest set of cases for both conceptually clarifying and empirically documenting processes of transnational citizenship. Transnational communities are groups of migrants whose daily lives, work, and social relationships extend across national borders. The existence of transnational communities is a precondition for, but is not the same as, an emerging migrant civil society, which also involves the construction of public spaces and representative social and civic organizations.[16]

As Fitzgerald (2004) has pointed out, much of the literature on transnationalism conflates two distinct forms of nationalism: "(1) the trans-state *long-distance nationalism* of identification with a 'nation' despite physical absence from the homeland and (2) the *dual nationalism* of political identification with two distinct 'nations'" (emphasis in original).[17] Although some individuals may participate in both forms of nationalism, they are analytically distinct. Long-distance nationalists are not necessarily dual nationalists.[18] Another important distinction is that

---

[16]For reviews of the flourishing sociological literature on transnational communities, see, among others, Fletcher & Margold (2003), Guarnizo et al. (2003), Levitt (2001a,b), Portes (2001, 2003), Portes et al. (1999), Smith & Guarnizo (1998), and Waldinger & Fitzgerald (2004). Much of this debate is framed in the broader context of "transnationalism." Some, like Portes, use survey methods in which the individual is the unit of analysis. He and his colleagues find that only a minority of migrant populations participates intensively in collective transnational activities, while a larger group participates intermittently. Compared to romanticized expectations of very broad-based transnational communities, these levels of reported participation appear low. However, if one compares reported participation levels to the degree to which members of most other social groups engage in sustained social or civic collective action, then they do not seem so low.

[17]On long-distance nationalism more generally, see Anderson (1998). Space does not permit a full examination of the literature on diasporic nationalism; Hanagan's (1998) history of the Irish experience is especially useful. For comprehensive overviews of dual nationality, see Bosniak (2003), Hansen & Weil (2002), and Martin & Hailbronner (2003).

[18]Waldinger & Fitzgerald (2004) also make the stronger claim that long-distance nationalism is inherently "particularistic." For them, transnationalism does not refer to "trans-state" relationships. Instead they define it much more subjectively as "extending *beyond* loyalties that connect to any specific place of origin or ethnic or national group" (p. 1178, emphasis in original). By definition, this excludes most of what other sociologists consider to be transnational civic or political identities and collective action. For example, on Turkey, see Østergaard-Neilsen (2003a); on Mexico, see Goldring (2002), Smith (2003a), and Orozco (2004); on the Dominican Republic, see Levitt (2001a) and Itzigsohn et al. (1999); on Colombia, see Escobar (2004); on El Salvador, see Landholdt et al. (1999); on Guatemala, see Popkin (1999); and on Haiti, see Francois (2001) and Glick-Schiller & Fouron (1999). Comparative approaches include Itzigsohn (2000) and Østergaard-Neilson (2003b). On the role of "sending" nation-states in this process, see footnote 19 and Levitt & de la Dehesa (2003).

long-distance nationalism has a much longer history—only relatively recently have changes in political cultures created the space needed for dual nationalisms to be tolerated.

Historically, the dominant national political cultures in both societies obliged migrants to choose one polity or the other. As Jones-Correa (1998) put it, "loyalties to different territorial political communities are often seen as irreconcilable" (p. 5). Nevertheless, in practice, migrant social and civic actors try to escape this dichotomous choice and are increasingly constructing both the practice of and the right to binationality. In the United States, for example, Latino civil rights activists debate whether migrant cross-border organizing will contribute to the fight for empowerment (Fox 2002). Until recently, there was a notable disconnect between U.S. Latino political representatives and migrant membership organizations, such as hometown clubs and their federations. For example, during the 1994 campaign against California's infamous anti-immigrant ballot initiative, Prop. 187, Mexican migrant and U.S. Latino organizations had little contact, even if their offices were located across the street from one another. More recently, however, Mexican migrant hometown federations have worked closely with U.S. civil rights organizations and trade unions in Los Angeles to campaign and lobby for undocumented migrants' right to drivers' licenses (Rivera-Salgado & Escala-Rabadán 2004, Seif 2003, Varsanyi 2004). Meanwhile, at the other end of the ideological spectrum, other Mexican migrants are active in the Republican Party while campaigning for migrant voting rights in Mexico (Najar 2004).

Transnational Versus Translocal Membership

In the context of what are increasingly called transnational migrant communities, sometimes what seem to be transnational collective identities may be more precisely understood as translocal identities. For many migrants, their strongest cross-border social ties link specific communities of origin and settlement, without necessarily relating to national social, civic, or political arenas in either country. Translocal relationships are community-based social, civic, and family ties that cross borders despite being geographically dispersed, or "deterritorialized" as the anthropologists say (see Besserer 2002, 2004 for examples of multi-sited ethnography of dispersed communities).

However, "long-distance localism" is often treated as transnational, and the former does not necessarily imply the latter—depending on how one defines transnational (Fitzgerald 2004). In this view, translocal and transnational are analytically and empirically distinct. The additional claim that localistic cross-border identities inherently *inhibit* broader identifications is overstated, however (e.g., Waldinger 2004, Waldinger & Fitzgerald 2004). In practice, translocal and transnational identities often overlap and may well reinforce each other (Castañeda 2003, 2004), as exemplified by the annual Easter festival in the town of Jeréz, Zacatecas. Its combination of regionally specific customs with the intense involvement of returning migrants would appear to be a paradigm case of translocal, not transnational, collective identity. However, both U.S. and Mexican national flags are prominently displayed, and crowds joyfully burn effigies of both national presidents as part of the mass celebration (Moctezuma 2004, p. 37).

The distinction between transnational and translocal membership becomes clearest when the boundary between community insiders and outsiders is drawn with precision by community members themselves. This self-definition helps to answer the concerns of some anthropologists about the ambiguity inherent in the concept of "local." Many Mexican indigenous communities explicitly use the term citizenship to refer to community membership, which requires high levels of responsibility to sustain the rights and standing involved in their participatory self-governance structures. Their definition of community membership, highly regulated by customary law, would meet any criteria for high-intensity, thick citizenship. Many of these communities have been experiencing out-migration for decades and as a result have experimented with a wide range of approaches to permit migrants to retain their community membership, depending on their long-distance contributions and/or their return to fulfill rotating service requirements. Some communities have remained firm, in an effort to address the loss of local leadership by requiring migrants to return to perform the obligatory unpaid leadership service required of all local citizens (e.g., Mutersbaugh 2002). Other communities, especially those with a longer tradition of migration, have redefined membership in an effort to reconcile both local leadership and migrant needs (Robles 2004). In this context, indigenous migrants who do not comply with community membership requirements become lapsed local citizens, though without becoming less (nationally) Mexican.

Three Main Forms of Transnational Citizenship

One could argue that full transnational citizenship, if it were defined as participation in more than one national political community, could follow at least three distinct paths. "Parallel" transnational participation refers to individuals who are active in more than one political community but whose organized communities do not themselves come together. The individuals may have multiple national identities, but the different organizations in which they participate do not.

"Simultaneous" transnational participation refers to collective actions that in themselves cross borders. For example, indigenous Mexican farmworkers in Oregon engage in parallel transnational organizing: They participate both in a mainly U.S.-focused farmworker union and in a mainly Mexico-focused hometown association with multiple branches throughout the United States. The same people defend their class and migrant interests through one organization while defending their ethnic and translocal identities through another (Stephen 2004). Yet the two kinds of organizations do not come together. In contrast, in the case of the Oaxacan Indigenous Binational Front (FIOB), migrants use the same membership organization to fight for human rights vis-à-vis local, state, and national governments. Thousands of families identify as members, participating through local committees in both countries while reaching out to civil society organizations and policy makers in both countries (Fox & Rivera-Salgado 2004). This example demonstrates simultaneous binational participation as distinct from parallel involvement (see Levitt & Glick-Schiller 2005 for a related approach to simultaneity).

"Integrated" transnational participation involves multiple levels and arenas, as in the cases of the cross-border coalition builders mentioned above, the FIOB's trajectory, or the application of the concept of multi-level citizenship to describe membership in local, regional, national, and transnational polities in Europe (Painter 2002). In spatial terms, parallel and simultaneous kinds of membership are solely horizontal; integrated participation is also vertical, crossing levels as well as borders. In terms of cross-border public interest campaigning, vertical integration describes strategic efforts to bring together civil society actors from local, regional, national and international levels to be more effective counterweights to the often vertically well-integrated powers that be (Fox 2001).

The dynamics of integrated transnational participation raises an issue about the study of local-global linkages more generally. Few studies analyze the dynamic interactions across levels and sectors with a full command of what makes each set of actors tick. Analysts often know one sector or issue area, one set of actors, or one level of analysis well, but then skate out onto thinner ice when discussing others, imputing decisions and motivations by reading them off of externally observable behavior. A synthesis of the subnational comparative method with anthropology's "multi-sited ethnography" or sociology's "global ethnography" can help us understand how very different actors strategize in practice (Burowoy 2000, Snyder 2001).

Flexible Forms of Transnational Citizenship

Anthropologists use the concept of flexible citizenship to refer to a specific genre of transnational citizenship. Flexible citizenship "refers to the cultural logics of capitalist accumulation, travel and displacement that induce subjects to respond fluidly and opportunistically to changing political-economic conditions" (Ong 1999, p. 6). Ong's influential and revealing study focuses on diasporic Chinese entrepreneurs' cross-border "repositioning in relation to markets, governments and cultural regimes." The diasporic foundation for these transnational identities and communities is clear and confers a strong sense of belonging. The subjects are what Ong calls "ethnically marked class groupings," and their cross-border flexibility depends heavily on their class location (p. 7). However, the specific relevance of the concept of citizenship to this group is not clearly defined; it remains implicit rather than explicit in the study. These diasporic entrepreneurs are clearly members of a sustained social and cultural community—but they do not appear to be members of a shared civic or political community. This raises questions about whether the term citizenship applies at all.

Another kind of flexible membership in national societies involves the ways in which migrants frequently develop more pronounced national or ethnic identities in the diaspora than they experienced before leaving their homelands, in cases where local or regional rather than national loyalties had been primary. The migration literature has produced an ongoing debate about what precisely is new about transnational communities, but one point is clear: In at least some cases, national identities emerged from transnational migration. Notably, the idea of being Italian was created partly in the diaspora (Smith 2003b, p. 746) and Polish peasants became Polish in the diaspora (Burowoy 2000).

Frey (2003) offers a dramatically different approach to "flexible citizenship." His normative perspective, grounded in an economist's deductive approach, develops the concept of "organizational and marginal" citizenship, in an effort to account for multiple and partial kinds of rights and obligation-based participation in a wide range of formal institutions. In the process, however, the concept of citizenship becomes nearly synonymous with membership more generally. This conceptual exercise would be enriched by more empirical reflection. For example, Tilly (1998) recalls that early French revolutionary citizenship was defined incrementally, separating passive citizens from active citizens (those who paid three or more days' wages in taxes and could vote) and second-degree active citizens (who paid at least ten days' wages in taxes and could be elected).

Power Relationships between Organized Migrants and At-Home Civil Society Actors

On the one hand, migrant civil society appears to be the paradigm case for transnational citizenship, including both the possibility of binational political rights and a common sense of membership in a shared political community. On the other hand, relationships between migrant organizations and civil society in the home country may or may not be balanced. Organized migrant civil society may or may not overlap or engage with organized civil society back home. The concept of counterparts is useful here. To what degree are migrant organizations engaged in balanced partnerships with counterparts in their countries of origin? In the Mexican context, many migrant organizations have won recognition as interlocutors with national and local governments, as they leverage and administer community development matching funds, but relatively few migrant organizations actually constitute the U.S.-based branch of an organized social actor based in both countries. For example, the Zacatecan federations in the United States are the largest and most consolidated Mexican migrant groups there, but their civil society partnerships in their home state are incipient at best (Goldring 2002). Indeed, civil society in some high-out-migration communities can be quite thin—not surprisingly, given the loss of enterprising young people. In contrast, some of the Oaxacan migrant organizations, many of which are based on broader regional and ethnic identities as well as hometowns, have organized branches not only in California and Oaxaca but also in Baja California, in between. This transnational political space constitutes the imagined community of "Oaxacalifornia" (Fox & Rivera-Salgado 2004).

It is also important to recognize that transnational migrant political mobilization may be undemocratic. This point is especially obvious in the case of authoritarian transnational political projects, whether based on diasporic nationalism, the Third International, or religious fundamentalism, but the problem can also involve competitive electoral politics. Specifically, cross-border electoral mobilization can reproduce clientelistic practices within transnational families and communities that are inconsistent with democratic citizenship. Three main points are relevant here. First, the outreach strategies of home country political parties and states have had a major influence on patterns of migrant political action, and there is a substantial comparative literature on migrant relations with home country governments.[19] Second, migrants who support families in their home country by sending remittances may try to use that power to tell family members how they should vote, and trading money for votes is a defining feature of clientelism.[20] Third, claims to voting rights and political representation for migrants in their home country are often based on the legitimacy and membership that are associated with their economic contribution through remittances.[21] If cross-border economic investments were a sufficient basis for claiming citizenship and political rights, however, then transnational corporations could also claim membership, and if they were a necessary condition, then those migrants who could not afford to send remittances would be excluded. The implication of the remittance-based argument for cross-border voting rights is that national citizenship is not sufficient to justify the right to vote from abroad. In short, although basing claims for political rights on remittances has obvious instrumental political advantages, it risks contradicting such basic democratic principles as birthright citizenship and freedom of movement.

MAPPING TRANSNATIONAL RIGHTS AND MEMBERSHIP

Having reviewed some of the key empirical issues that emerge in the search for possible forms of transnational citizenship, let's return to the question of how to define citizenship more generally. Our definitional choices about this term will inform the final assessment of whether transnational citizenship works conceptually.

---

[19] See, among others, Goldring (2002), Guarnizo (1998), Guarnizo et al. (2003), Levitt & de la Dehesa (2003), Østergaard-Neilsen (2003a,b,c), Smith (2003a,b), and Waldinger & Fitzgerald (2004).

[20] As Carlos Villanueva, a leader of a Mexican migrant organization campaigning for the right to vote abroad, put it, "one in four households received remittances. They are our militants." He is both a convener of the National Convention of Mexican Organizations Abroad and a Bush Republican liaison with the Mexican migrant community (Najar 2004).

[21] For a pioneering discussion of "market membership," see Goldring (1998). The National Convention of Mexican Organizations Abroad recently proposed that migrants' political representation be "at least proportional to the annual level of remittances" Najar (2004). For analyses of remittances and Mexican migrant organizations more generally, see Goldring (2002) and Orozco (2004), among others.

TABLE 1   Domains and intensities of transnational rights and membership

Domains	Intensities	
	Thick	**Thin**
Rights vis-à-vis public authorities	Full cross-border political standing, equal political and civil rights (including migrant rights in host societies and/or in home societies) Membership rights in a supranational public body, such as the European Union	Recognition of basic human rights, regardless of citizenship status Recognition of subnational rights for migrants (e.g., drivers' licenses, police acceptance of consular IDs, noncitizen voting rights for local government) Nominal standing and voice, including the right to self-representation in international forums—the right to be heard, but not necessarily listened to (e.g., International Criminal Court, World Bank Inspection Panel, NAFTA labor and environmental commissions)
Societal membership	Full membership in a civic or political community that is rooted in more than one state, or in more than one nation within a state, usually based on shared cultures (nationality, ethnicity, religion and/or language) Clear minimum conditions for membership in a cross-border political community, with explicit rights and responsibilities	Shared political ideals and/or ideologies (e.g., democracy, transparency, accountability, gender and racial equality, environmental sustainability, peace, national self-determination) Mutual affinity, shared targets, joint action

As illustrated in Table 1, these choices can be mapped along two distinct axes: state- versus society-based definitions of citizenship and degrees of intensity (thick versus thin). The first dimension contrasts different frames of reference, whether defined primarily in terms of *rights* as enforceable claims on public authorities (national or international) or in terms of *membership* in society-based political communities (i.e., those defined by ethno-national identities or transformative ideologies, which in turn could be civic or religious).[22] The second dimension distinguishes between different degrees of "thickness," that is, the varying *intensities* of rights (how broad and deep the rights are vis-à-vis public authorities) and membership (how active it is within society-based transnational political communities). This thick/thin approach is analogous to the distinction between "narrow and broad transnationality" made by Itzigsohn et al. (1999) but adds the distinction between rights and membership.

The sense of citizenship based on active participation and the struggle for equality could be considered "high-intensity citizenship," whereas a minimum set of rights linked to membership, without necessarily requiring agency, could be seen as "low-intensity."[23] The two are related—the more the first kind of citizenship raises the ceiling, the more the standards for the floor can go up. So the actual "height" of the high-intensity approach clearly matters. However, high-intensity citizenship rarely reaches more than a small fraction of a given polity, so the "height of the floor" of low-intensity citizenship is what determines most people's rights, most of the time. Identifying the causal pathways through which the ceiling for the empowered few can raise the floor for the rest is easier said than done. Rights for some citizens may conflict directly with rights for others (as in the case of racialized voting rights or certain property rights). More generally, many national experiences have shown that the widely studied horizontal expansion of citizenship rights from empowered subgroups to encompass entire societies is usually very slow and highly discontinuous, and can be reversible. This point would apply to transnational civil society as well, since there is no clear secular trend toward ever-broader inclusion.

Examples of varying degrees of thickness of rights include the growing array of less-than-full forms of recognition, such as the growing body of international "soft law" (Abbot & Snidal 2000). This discussion quickly leads to the international relations discussion of norms, which has gone furthest in the case of human rights (e.g., Risse et al. 1999, Hawkins 2003). The arena of soft law consists of the international agreements and institutional reforms that grant some degree of recognition or standing to people without requiring the explicit permission of nation-states. These "thin" transnational rights vis-à-vis public authorities range from international agreements on the rights of indigenous peoples, migrants, and refugees, to international multisectoral-stakeholder standard-setting bodies (such as those that propose standards with which to regulate dams or extractive industries), to the right to use national law to sue torturers or corporate abusers across borders, to the unusual degree of "standing" that the World Bank's Inspection Panel extends

---

[22]Translocal Mexican indigenous communities complicate this implicitly dichotomous approach to rights- and membership-based domains, since their participatory approach to community self-governance blurs the boundary between local state and society.
[23]"Low-intensity citizenship" has its analogue in "low-intensity democracy" (see, e.g., Gills et al. 1993, O'Donnell 1993).

to affected people who make formal claims (e.g., Fox & Brown 1998, Clark et al. 2003, Khagram 2004, Rajagopal 2003). These soft law provisions begin to institutionalize the "boomerang" pattern of bypassing unresponsive nation-states, but the rights remain thin because they are not enforceable. Within nation-states, examples of thin rights include forms of recognition granted by subnational governments to migrants—for example, through acceptance of home country identification documents, the right to vote in local elections, the right to "in-state resident" tuition in state universities, or the right to drivers' licenses (e.g., Seif 2003, Waslin 2002). Arguably, these subnational measures are forms of "paralegalization."

On the society side, thick and thin membership are mainly differentiated by culturally rooted forms of collective identity, such as national, ethnic, linguistic, or religious identities. By comparison, the ties that bind ideologically based communities across borders tend to be thin. However, when combined, those different bases for identity—culture, ideology, and counterpart status—can create an especially strong sense of shared collective identity. Smith's work on the political construction of peoples is relevant here. He defines a "political people" as a form of imagined community that can impose binding obligations and duties, the scope of which varies along two dimensions: (*a*) the range of issues involved, which may be broad, intermediate, or narrow; and (*b*) "the potency of peoplehood," the intensity of the claims, which may be weak, moderate, or strong (Smith 2003c, pp. 20–21). Table 1 maps analogous variation in relationships to authorities and societies across borders, but it does not yet answer the key question: Does any of this add up to transnational citizenship, conceptually or in practice?

CONCLUSIONS

Whenever a concept varies greatly in the eye of the beholder—as in the case of citizenship—the risk of conceptual stretching is high. This risk is accentuated when a contested adjective is applied. As a result, the concept of transnational citizenship raises expectations that are difficult to meet. Perhaps the actual processes that the concept tries to capture are still too incipient. In another decade or two, we will know much more about whether current processes of globalization from below will intensify, erode, or evolve in an unforeseen direction. In the meantime, however, most of the transnational civic and political communities discussed here involve boundaries, rights, and responsibilities that are too amorphous to warrant the term citizenship, especially when ideas such as membership, standing, or human rights will do.

This review has addressed both rights-based and membership-centered definitions of the term, focusing on the conceptual challenges posed by the definitional choices. These choices involve tradeoffs. Given these dilemmas, illustrated in Table 1, only a high-intensity, rights-based definition of transnational citizenship holds up well. By this definition the term refers to dual or multiple citizenships that are grounded both in enforceable rights and in clearly bounded membership(s). For the sake of precision, therefore, the terms dual or multiple citizenship are preferable to the more open-ended concept of transnational citizenship. Multi-layered citizenship is evocative and captures meaningful new trends, but there is nothing necessarily cross-border about it.

The most powerful evidence in favor of taking notions of multiple or multi-layered citizenship seriously is in the EU. Europeans' thin form of transnational individual membership can be dismissed as less than transnational citizenship because it is derived from their national citizenship. Skeptics may ask, what rights do "EU citizens" get—really—beyond what their states already provide? One answer is the right to move and work freely across national borders, a right that most migrants can only dream of. Whether one finds the term transnational citizenship evocative or too fuzzy, it is clear that the increasing significance and complexity of migrant-state-society relations leave the conceptualization of citizenship with some catching up to do.

ACKNOWLEDGMENTS

Thanks very much to John Gershman, Walter Goldfrank, Margaret Keck, Peggy Levitt, Sidney Tarrow, Anna Tsing, and especially Margaret Levi for useful comments on earlier versions.

The *Annual Review of Political Science* is online at
http://polisci.annualreviews.org

LITERATURE CITED

Abbott K, Snidal D. 2000. Hard and soft law in international governance. *Int. Org.* 54(3): 241–76

Aksu E, Camilleri JA, eds. 2002. *Democratizing Global Governance*. Houndsmills, UK: Palgrave Macmillan

Aleinikoff TA, ed. 2001. *Citizenship Today: Global Perspectives and Practices*. Washington, DC: Carnegie Endow. Int. Peace

Aleinikoff TA, Klusmeyer D, eds. 2000. *From Migrants to Citizens: Membership in a Changing World*. Washington, DC: Carnegie Endow. Int. Peace

Aleinikoff TA, Martin DA, Motomura H, eds. 2003. *Immigration and Citizenship: Process and Policy*. St. Paul, MN: Thomson/ West

Alvarez S. 2005. *Feminism in Movement: Cultural Politics, Policy Advocacy, and Transnational Organizing in Latin America*. Durham, NC: Duke Univ. Press

Anderson B. 1998. *The Spectre of Comparisons: Nationalism, Southeast Asia, and the World*. London: Verso

Bauböck R. 1994. *Transnational Citizenship: Membership and Rights in International Migration*. Aldershot: Edward Elgar

Bauböck R. 2003. Towards a political theory of migrant transnationalism. *Int. Migr. Rev.* 37(3):700–23

Bellamy R, Warleigh A, eds. 2001. *Citizenship and Governance in the European Union*. London: Continuum

Besserer F. 2002. *Contesting community: cultural struggles of a Mixtec transnational community*. Ph.D. thesis, Anthropol. Dep., Stanford Univ.

Besserer F. 2004. *Topografías transnacionales. Hacia una geografía de la vida transnacional*. Mexico City: UAM-Iztapalapa and Plaza y Valdes Ed.

Bob C. 2001. Marketing rebellion: insurgent

groups, international media and NGO support. *Int. Polit.* 38:311–34

Bosniak L. 2003. Multiple nationality and the postnational transformation of citizenship. In *Rights and Duties of Dual Nationals*, ed. DA Martin, K Hailbronner, pp. 27–48. The Hague/London: Kluwer Law Int.

Bowden B. 2003. The perils of global citizenship. *Citizenship Stud.* 7(3):349–62

Brooks D, Fox J, eds. 2002. *Cross-Border Dialogues: US-Mexico Social Movement Networking*. La Jolla: Univ. Calif. San Diego, Cent. US-Mexican Stud.

Brysk A, ed. 2003. *Globalization and Human Rights*. Berkeley: Univ. Calif. Press

Brysk A, Shafir G, eds. 2004. *People Out of Place: Globalization, Human Rights and the Citizenship Gap*. New York: Routledge

Burawoy M, ed. 2000. *Global Ethnography: Forces, Connections and Imaginations in a Postmodern World*. Berkeley: Univ. Calif. Press

Calderon Chelius L, ed. 2003. *Votar en la distancia: La extension de los derechos politicos a los migrantes, experiencias comparadas*. Mexico City: Instituto Mora

Calderon Chelius L, Martínez Saldaña J. 2002. *La dimensión política de la migración mexicana*. Mexico City: Instituto Mora

Campbell H. 1987. *Rasta and Resistance: From Marcus Garvey to Walter Rodney*. Trenton, NJ: Africa World Press

Castañeda A. 2003. *The politics of citizenship: Mexican migrants in the U.S.* Ph.D thesis, Anthropol. Dep., Univ. Calif. Santa Cruz

Castañeda A. 2004. Roads to citizenship: Mexican migrants in the United States. *Latino Stud.* 2(1):70–89

Castles S, Davidson A. 2000. *Citizenship and Migration: Globalization and the Politics of Belonging*. New York: Routledge

Clark D, Fox J, Treakle K, eds. 2003. *Demanding Accountability: Civil Society Claims and the World Bank Inspection Panel*. Lanham, MD: Rowman & Littlefield

Cleaver H. 2000. The virtual and real Chiapas Support Network: a review and critique of Judith Adler Hellman's "Real and Virtual Chiapas: Magic Realism and the Left." *Socialist Reg.* July, http://www.eco.utexas.edu/faculty/Cleaver/anti-hellman.html

Collier D, Mahon JF. 1993. Conceptual "stretching" revisited: adapting categories in comparative analysis. *Am. Polit. Sci. Rev.* 87(4):845–55

Delanty G. 2000. *Citizenship in a Global Age: Society, Culture and Politics*. Buckingham, UK: Open Univ.

Edelman M. 2003. Transnational peasant and farmer movements and networks. In *Global Civil Society 2003*, ed. M Kaldor, H Anheier, M Glasuis, pp. 185–220. Oxford, UK: Oxford Univ. Press

Edwards M, Gaventa J, eds. 2001. *Global Citizen Action*. Boulder, CO: Lynne Reinner

Escobar C. 2004. Dual citizenship and political participation: migrants in the interplay of United States and Colombian politics. *Latino Stud.* 2:45–69

Faist T. 2000. Transnationalization in international migration: implications for the study of citizenship and culture. *Ethnic Racial Stud.* 23(2):189–222

Falk R. 1994. The making of global citizenship. In *The Condition of Citizenship*, ed. B van Steenbergen, pp. 127–40. London: Sage

Fitzgerald D. 2004. Beyond "transnationalism": Mexican hometown politics at an American labor union. *Ethnic Racial Stud.* 27(2):228–47

Fletcher P, Margold J. 2003. Transnational communities. *Rural Mexico Res. Rev.* Vol. 1. http://www.reap.ucdavis.edu/rural_review.html

Flores WV, Benmayor R, eds. 1997. *Latino Cultural Citizenship: Claiming Identity, Space, and Rights*. Boston: Beacon

Florini A, ed. 2000. *The Third Force: The Rise of Transnational Civil Society*. Washington/Tokyo: Carnegie Endow. Int. Peace/Jpn. Cent. Int. Exchange

Foweraker J, Landman D. 1997. *Citizenship Rights and Social Movements: A Comparative and Statistical Analysis*. Oxford, UK: Oxford Univ. Press

Fox J. 2001. Vertically integrated policy monitoring: a tool for civil society policy advocacy. *Nonprofit Voluntary Sector Q.* 30(3): 616–27

Fox J. 2002. Lessons from Mexico-US civil society coalitions. See Brooks & Fox 2002, pp. 341–418

Fox J. 2003. Introduction: framing the panel. In *Demanding Accountability: Civil Society Claims and the World Bank Inspection Panel,* ed. D Clark, J Fox, K Treakle, pp. xi–xxxi. Lanham, MD: Rowman & Littlefield

Fox J, Brown LD, eds. 1998. *The Struggle for Accountability: The World Bank, NGOs and Grassroots Movements.* Cambridge, MA: MIT Press

Fox J, Rivera-Salgado G, eds. 2004. *Indigenous Mexican Migrants in the United States.* La Jolla: Univ. Calif. San Diego, Cent. Comp. Immigr. Stud. & Cent. US-Mex. Stud.

Francois PL. 2001 *Transnational organizations and citizen participation: a study of Haitian immigrants in New York City.* PhD thesis, Grad. Faculty Polit. Sci., City Univ. NY

Frey BS. 2003. Flexible citizenship for a global society. *Polit. Phil. Econ.* 2(1):93–114

Gills B, Rocamora J, Wilson R, eds. 1993. *Low Intensity Democracy: Political Power in the New World Order.* London: Pluto

Glick-Schiller N, Fouron GE. 2001. *Georges Woke Up Laughing: Long Distance Nationalism and the Search for Home.* Durham, NC: Duke Univ. Press

Goldring L. 1998. From market membership to transnational citizenship? The changing politicization of transnational social spaces. *L'Ordinaire Latino-Americaine* 173–74, July–Dec.

Goldring L. 2002. The Mexican state and transmigrant organizations: negotiating the boundaries of membership and participation. *Latin Am. Res. Rev.* 37(3):55–99

Gosse V. 1988. "The North American Front": Central American solidarity in the Reagan era. In *Reshaping the US Left: Popular Struggles of the 1980s*, ed. M Davis, M Sprinker, pp. 11–50. London: Verso

Gosse V. 1995. Active engagement: the legacy of Central America solidarity. *NACLA Rep. Americas* 28(5), Mar./Apr.

Guarnizo L. 1998. The rise of transnational social formations: Mexican and Dominican state responses to transnational migration. *Polit. Power Soc. Theory* 12:45–96

Guarnizo L, Portes A, Heller W. 2003. Assimilation and transnationalism: determinants of transnational political action among contemporary migrants. *Am. J. Sociol.* 108(6):1211–48

Hanagan M. 1998. Irish transnational social movements, deterritorialized migrants, and the state system: the last one hundred and forty years. *Mobilization* 3(1):107–26

Hansen R, Weil P, eds. 2002. *Dual Nationality, Social Rights and Federal Citizenship in the US and Europe: The Reinvention of Citizenship.* New York: Berghahn

Hawkins D. 2003. Universal jurisdiction for human rights: from legal principle to limited reality. *Global Governance* 9:347–65

He B. 2004. World citizenship and transnational activism. In *Transnational Activism in Asia*, ed. N Piper, A Uhlin, pp. 78–93. London: Routledge

Heater D. 2002. *World Citizenship: Cosmopolitan Thinking and Its Opponents.* London: Continuum

Hellman JA. 2000. Real and virtual Chiapas: magic realism and the Left. *Socialist Register 2000*, ed. L Panitch. New York: Mon. Rev.

Henderson H, Ikeda D. 2004. *Planetary Citizenship.* Santa Monica, CA: Middleway

Hutchings K, Dannreuther R, eds. 1999. *Cosmopolitan Citizenship.* New York: St. Martin's

Itzigsohn J. 2000. Immigration and the boundaries of citizenship. *Int. Migr. Rev.* 34(4): 1126–54

Itzigsohn J, Dore Cabral C, Hernández Medina E, Vásquez O. 1999. Mapping Dominican transnationalism: narrow and broad transnational practices. *Ethnic Racial Stud.* 22(2):316–39

Jacobson D. 1996. *Rights Across Borders:*

Immigration and the Decline of Citizenship. Baltimore, MD: Johns Hopkins Univ. Press

Jacobson D, Benarieh Ruffer G. 2004. Agency on a global scale: rules, rights and the European Union. In *People Out of Place: Globalization, Human Rights and the Citizenship Gap*, ed. A Brysk, G Shafir, pp. 73–86. New York: Routledge

Jenson J, Papillon M. 2000. Challenging the citizenship regime: the James Bay Cree and transnational action. *Polit. Soc.* 28(2):245–64

Johnston P. 2001. The emergence of transnational citizenship among Mexican immigrants in California. In *Citizenship Today: Global Perspectives and Practices*, ed. T Alexander, D Klusmeyer, pp. 253–77. Washington, DC: Carnegie Endow. Int. Peace

Johnston P. 2003. Transnational citizenries: reflections from the field in California. 7(2):199–217

Jones E, Gaventa J. 2002. Concepts of citizenship. *IDS Dev. Bibliogr.* 19, Feb.

Jones-Correa M. 1998. *Between Two Nations: The Political Predicament of Latinos in New York*. Ithaca, NY: Cornell Univ. Press

Jones-Correa M. 2001a. Under two flags: dual nationality in Latin America and its consequences for naturalization in the United States. *Int. Migr. Rev.* 35(4):997–1032

Jones-Correa M. 2001b. Institutional and contextual factors in immigrant naturalization and voting. *Citizsh. Stud.* 5(1):41–56

Josselin D, Wallace W, eds. 2001. *Non-State Actors in World Politics*. Houndsmills, UK: Palgrave Macmillan

Kaldor M, Anheier H, Glasuis M, eds. 2003. *Global Civil Society 2003*. Oxford, UK: Oxford Univ. Press

Keane J. 2003. *Global Civil Society?* Cambridge, UK: Cambridge Univ. Press

Keck M. 2004. Governance regimes and the politics of discursive representation. In *Transnational Activism in Asia*, ed. N Piper, A Uhlin, pp. 43–60. London: Routledge

Keck M, Sikkink K. 1998. *Activists Beyond Borders*. Ithaca, NY: Cornell Univ. Press

Khagram S, Riker JV, Sikkink K 2002. From Santiago to Seattle: transnational advocacy groups restructuring world politics. In *Restucturing World Politics: Transnational Social Movements, Networks and Norms*, ed. S Khagram, JV Riker, K Sikkink, pp. 3–23. Minneapolis: Univ. Minn. Press

Khagram S. 2004. *Dams and Development: Transnational Struggles for Water and Power*. Ithaca, NY: Cornell Univ. Press

Kymlicka W. 1995. *Multicultural Citizenship: A Liberal Theory of Minority Rights*. Oxford, UK: Clarendon

Landholt P, Autler L, Baires S. 1999. From hermano lejano to hermano mayor: the dialectics of Salvadoran transnationalism. *Ethnic Racial Stud.* 22(2):291–315

Landigin R, Williamson H. 2004. Overseas Filipinos put off by rigid rules in their first chance to vote. *Financ. Times* May 8/9, p. 8

Laxer G. 2003. The defeat of the multilateral agreement on investment: national movements confront globalism. See Laxer & Halperin 2003, pp. 169–88

Laxer G, Halperin S, eds. 2003. *Global Civil Society and Its Limits*. London: Palgrave

Levi M, Olson D. 2000. The battles in Seattle. *Polit. Soc.* 28(3):309–29

Levitt P. 2001a. *Transnational Villagers*. Berkeley: Univ. Calif. Press

Levitt P. 2001b. Transnational migration: taking stock and future directions. *Global Netw.* 1(3):195–216

Levitt P, de la Dehesa R. 2003. Transnational migration and the redefinition of the state: variations and explanations. *Ethnic Racial Stud.* 26(4):587–611

Levitt P, Glick-Schiller N. 2005. Conceptualizing simultaneity: theorizing society from a transnational social field perspective. *Int. Migr. Rev.* In press

Lipschutz R, Mayer J. 1996. *Global Civil Society and Global Environmental Governance: The Politics of Nature from Place to Planet*. Albany, NY: State Univ. NY Press

MacLachlan C. 1991. *Anarchism and the Mexican Revolution: The Political Trials of*

Ricardo Flores Magón in the United States. Berkeley: Univ. Calif. Press

Martin DA, Hailbronner K, eds. 2003. *Rights and Duties of Dual Nationals.* The Hague/London: Kluwer Law Int.

Martínez Saldaña J, Ross R. 2002. Suffrage for Mexicans residing abroad. See Brooks & Fox 2002, pp. 275–92

Mekata M. 2000. Building partnerships toward a common goal: experiences with the international campaign to ban landmines. In *The Third Force: The Rise of Transnational Civil Society*, ed. A Florini, pp. 143–76. Washington, DC: Carnegie Endow. Int. Peace/Jpn. Cent. Int. Exchange

Muetzelfeldt M, Smith G. 2002. Civil society and global governance: the possibilities for global citizenship. *Citizsh. Stud.* 6(1):55–75

Minder R. 2004. Turnout low among new member states. *Financ. Times* June 14, p. 2

Moctezuma M. 2004. Simbolismo de un encuentro donde los ausentes de Jeréz, Zacatecas se hacen presentes. *MX Sin Fronteras* May(5):34–37

Mutersbaugh T. 2002. Migration, common property and communal labor: cultural politics and agency in a Mexican village. *Polit. Geogr.* 21(4):473–94

Najar A. 2004. Cero, calificación de migrantes a Fox. *Jornada* Jan. 30, p. 14

Nimtz A. 2002. Marx and Engels: the prototypical transnational actors. In *Restructuring World Politics: Transnational Social Movements, Networks and Norms*, ed. S Khagram, JV Riker, K Sikkink, pp. 245–68. Minneapolis: Univ. Minn. Press

O'Donnell G. 1993. On the state, democratization and some conceptual problems: a Latin American view with some glances at post-Communist countries. *World Dev.* 21(8):1355–69

Olesen T. 2003. The transnational Zapatista solidarity network: an infrastructure analysis. *Global Netw.* 4(1):89–107

Ong A. 1999. *Flexible Citizenship: The Cultural Logics of Transnationality.* Durham, NC: Duke Univ. Press

Orozco M, LaPointe M. 2004. Mexican home-town associations and development opportunities. *J. Int. Aff.* 57(2):31–51

Østergaard-Nielsen E. 2003a. *Transnational Politics: Turks and Kurds in Germany.* London: Routledge

Østergaard-Nielsen E, ed. 2003b. *International Migration and Sending Countries: Perceptions, Policies and Transnational Relations.* Houndsmills, UK: Palgrave Macmillan

Østergaard-Nielsen E. 2003c. The politics of migrants' transnational political practices. *Int. Migr. Rev.* 37(3):760–86

Painter J. 2002. Multi-level citizenship, identity and regions in contemporary Europe. In *Transnational Democracy: Political Spaces and Border Crossings*, ed. J Anderson, pp. 93–110. London: Routledge

Pantoja AD, Ramirez R, Segura GM. 2001. Citizens by choice, voters by necessity: patterns in political mobilization by naturalized Latinos. *Polit. Res. Q.* 54(4):729–50

Paulson J. 2001. Peasant struggle and international solidarity: the case of Chiapas. In *Socialist Register 2001*, ed. L Panitch, C Leys, with G Albo, D Coates. New York: Mon. Rev.

Popkin E. 1999. Guatemalan Mayan migration to Los Angeles: constructing transnational linkages in the context of the settlement process. *Ethnic Racial Stud.* 22(2):268–89

Portes A. 2001. Introduction: the debates and significance of immigrant transnationalism. *Global Netw.* 1(3):181–93

Portes A. 2003. Conclusion: theoretical convergences and empirical evidence in the study of immigrant transnationalism. *Am. J. Sociol.* 37(3):874–92

Portes A, Guarnizo L, Landholt P. 1999. The study of transnationalism: pitfalls and promise of an emergent research field. *Ethnic Racial Stud.* 22(2):481–507

Rajagopal B. 2003. *International Law from Below.* Cambridge, UK: Cambridge Univ. Press

Renshon SA. 2000. Dual citizens in America: an issue of vast proportions. *Cent. Immigr. Stud. Backgr.* July, http://www.cis.org

Risse T, Ropp S, Sikkink K, eds. 1999. *The Power of Human Rights: International*

Norms and Domestic Change. Cambridge, UK: Cambridge Univ. Press

Rivera-Salgado G, Escala Rabadán L. 2004. Collective identity and organizational strategies among indigenous and mestizo Mexican migrants. See Fox & Rivera-Salgado 2004, pp. 145–78

Robles S. 2004. Migration and return in the Sierra Juárez. See Fox & Rivera-Salgado 2004, pp. 467–82

Rocco R. 2004. Transforming citizenship: membership, strategies of containment and the public sphere in Latino communities. *Latino Stud.* 2:4–25

Sadiq K. 2003. *Redefining citizenship: illegal immigrants as voters in India and Malaysia.* PhD thesis, Univ. Chicago, Polit. Sci. Dep.

Sartori G. 1984. *Social Science Concepts.* Beverly Hills, CA: Sage

Schmitter P. 2000. *How to Democratize the European Union—and Why Bother?* Lanham, MD: Rowman & Littlefield

Schuck PH, Smith RM. 1985. *Citizenship Without Consent: Illegal Aliens in the American Polity.* New Haven, CT: Yale Univ. Press

Seidman G. 2000. Adjusting the lens. In *Globalizations and Social Movements: Culture, Power, and the Transnational Public Sphere,* ed. JA Guidry, MD Kennedy, MB Zald, pp. 339–57. Ann Arbor: Univ. Mich. Press

Seif H. 2003. *"Estado de oro" or "Jaula de oro"? Undocumented Mexican workers, the drivers license and subnational illegalization in California.* Cent. Comp. Immigr. Stud. Work. Pap. No. 86, http://www.ccis-ucsd.org/publications

Sklair L. 2001. *The Transnational Capitalist Class.* Oxford, UK/Malden, MA: Blackwell

Smith MP, Guarnizo LE, eds. 1998. *Transnationalism from Below.* New Brunswick, NJ: Transaction

Smith R. 2003a. Migrant membership as an instituted process: transnationalization, the state and the extra-territorial conduct of Mexican politics. *Int. Migr. Rev.* 37(2):297–343

Smith R. 2003b. Diasporic memberships in historical perspective: comparative insights from the Mexican, Italian and Polish cases. *Int. Migr. Rev.* 37(3):724–59

Smith R. 2003c. *Stories of Peoplehood: The Politics and Morals of Political Membership.* Cambridge, UK: Cambridge Univ. Press

Snyder R. 2001. Scaling down: The subnational comparative method. *Stud. Comp. Int. Dev.* 36(1):93–110

Soysal YN. 1994. *Limits of Citizenship: Migrants and Postnational Membership in Europe.* Chicago: Univ. Chicago Press

Stephen L. 2002. In the wake of the Zapatistas: US solidarity work focused on militarization, human rights and democratization in Chiapas. See Brooks & Fox 2002, pp. 303–28

Stephen L. 2004. Mixtec farmworkers in Oregon: linking labor and ethnicity through farmworker unions and hometown associations. See Fox & Rivera-Salgado 2004, pp. 179–204

Swarns RL. 2004. Immigrants raise call for right to be voters. *NY Times* Aug. 9, p. A13

Tarrow S. 1995. *Fishnets, internets and catnets: globalization and transnational collective action.* Occ. Pap. Madrid: Juan March Found., Cent. Adv. Study Soc. Sci.

Tarrow S. 2001. Transnational politics: contention and institutions in international politics. *Annu. Rev. Polit. Sci.* 4:1–20

Tarrow S. 2005. *The New Transnational Activism.* New York/Cambridge, UK: Cambridge Univ. Press

Tilly C. 1998. Where do rights come from? In *Democracy, Revolution and History,* ed. T Skocpol with G Ross, T Smith, J Eisenberg Vichniac, pp. 55–72. Ithaca, NY: Cornell Univ. Press

Tsing A. 2004a. *Thoughts on the workshop: the rights and responsibilities of transnational citizenship.* Prepared for presentation to "The Rights and Responsibilities of Transnational Citizenship," Kennedy School Gov., Harvard Univ., Cambridge, MA, March 11–12

Tsing A. 2004b. *Friction.* Princeton, NJ: Princeton Univ. Press

Varsanyi MW. 2004. *Stretching the boundaries of citizenship in the city: undocumented migrants and political mobilization in Los*

Angeles. PhD thesis, Geography Dep., Univ. Calif. Los Angeles

Waldinger R. 2004. Immigrant "transnationalism" and the presence of the past. Pap. 15, *Theory and Research in Comparative Social Analysis*. Dep. Sociol., Univ. Calif. Los Angeles, http://repositories.cdlib.org/uclasoc/trcsa/15

Waldinger R, Fitzgerald D. 2004. Transnationalism in question. *Am. J. Sociol.* 109(5): 1177–95

Waldrauch H. 2003. *Electoral rights for foreign nationals: a comparative overview of regulations in 36 countries*. Natl. Eur. Cent. Pap. No. 73. Presented at Univ. Sydney, Sydney, Aust., http://www.anu.edu.au/NEC/waldrauch_paper.pdf

Walzer M. 1995. *Toward a Global Civil Society*. Providence, RI/Oxford: Berghahn Books

Wapner P. 1996. *Environmental Activism and World Civic Politics*. Albany, NY: State Univ. NY Press

Waslin M. 2002. *Safe roads, safe communities: immigrants and state driver's license requirements*. Iss. Brief No. 6. Washington, DC: Natl. Counc. La Raza, http://www.nclr.org/policy/briefs

Waterman P. 1998. *Globalization, Social Movements, and the New Internationalisms*. London: Mansell

Waterman P, Wills J, eds. 2001. *Place, Space and New Labour Internationalisms*. Oxford, UK: Blackwell

Yashar D. 2002. Globalization and collective action. *Comp. Polit.* 34(3):355

Yuval-Davis N. 1999. The 'multi-layered citizen:' citizenship in the age of globalization. *Int. Femin. J. Polit.* 1(1):119–36

Annu. Rev. Polit. Sci. 2005. 8:203–25
doi: 10.1146/annurev.polisci.8.082103.104840
First published online as a Review in Advance on Mar. 4, 2005

THE POLITICAL EVOLUTION OF PRINCIPAL-AGENT MODELS

Gary J. Miller
*Department of Political Science, Washington University in St. Louis,
St. Louis, Missouri 63130; email: gjmiller@artsci.wustl.edu*

Key Words   information asymmetry, incentives, oversight, credible commitment

■ **Abstract**   With tools borrowed from the economic analysis of insurance, principal-agency theory has allowed political scientists new insights into the role of information asymmetry and incentives in political relationships. It has given us a way to think formally about power as the modification of incentives to induce actions in the interests of the principal. Principal-agency theory has evolved significantly as political scientists have sought to make it more applicable to peculiarly political institutions. In congressional oversight of the bureaucracy, increasing emphasis has been placed on negotiation of administrative procedures, rather than the imposition of outcome-based incentives, as originally conceived. Awareness of the problem of credible commitment has impelled more dramatic reformulations, in which agents perform their function only when their interests conflict with those of the principal, and they are guaranteed some degree of autonomy.

> *The 'political master' finds himself in the position of the 'dilettante' who stands opposite the 'expert,' facing the trained official who stands within the management of administration.*

> (Weber 1958)

INTRODUCTION

Weber identified a relationship that is common to many aspects of politics—an asymmetric relationship in which authority is located on one side and informational advantage on the other. Much of the time, Weber suggested, the power lies with the expert; but is that the case? What resources are available to the master versus the expert? How can one assess the relative impact of authority versus expertise? An answer to this question seems essential for understanding not only Weberian bureaucracies but also the relation between elected officials and their constituencies, or party leaders acting for their caucuses. These relationships exemplify what I refer to as Weber's asymmetry.

Principal-agency theory (PAT) is one modeling technique that specifically addresses various manifestations of Weber's asymmetry. Like Weber, PAT assumes a relationship in which the agent has an informational advantage over the principal and takes actions that impact both players' payoffs. The principal has the formal authority, but in PAT, the attention is on a particular form of formal authority: the authority to impose incentives on the agent. Unlike Weber, PAT focuses on the leverage that these incentives give the informationally disadvantaged principal. In particular, the question is whether the principal can induce the more expert agent to take those actions that the principal would take if the principal had the same information as the agent. By manipulating the agent's incentives, the principal seeks to minimize shirking, or agency costs—the losses imposed on the principal by an inability to align the agent's self-interest with that of the principal. This is the motivational question for the mathematical analysis of what PAT calls "the principal's problem."

This essay begins with a review of the principal's problem as formulated by economists in the 1970s. It then discusses several illustrative applications in political science. The latter half of the paper, however, argues that principal-agency has been substantially challenged, modified, and even turned upside down in order to accommodate the distinctly political aspects of several key Weberian asymmetries.

PRINCIPAL-AGENCY THEORY AS RECEIVED FROM ECONOMICS: THE PRINCIPAL'S PROBLEM

Several articles written in the 1970s did much to define the theory of principal-agency in the field of economics. In the first article (Spence & Zeckhauser 1971), the theory was framed as a question about insurance, but it turned out to be central to understanding the effects of information asymmetries in other settings.

The Trade-off in Risk and in Incentives

A risk-averse automobile driver would be willing to pay a premium for insurance from a risk-neutral insurance company. The risk of an accident is determined jointly by the driver's behavior and by actions beyond her control. Because the driver is more risk-averse than the insurance company, the only efficient outcome would be full insurance for the driver at an appropriate premium. This would be possible, Spence & Zeckhauser (1971) point out, if the insurance company could monitor the driver's behavior directly (for instance, by a device that records the automobile's speed at all times). With no "hidden action," the company could write a contract that fully insures the driver as long as she obeys the rules set out in the contract.

However, the information asymmetry between insurer and driver does not allow such a solution. Because there is no feasible way for the insurance company to monitor the driver's behavior, full insurance will invite her to take risks that she would not take if she were uninsured. The unmonitored driver may well break the speed limit, talk on the cell phone, and run red lights (all at the same time!). This tendency to take actions that increase the insurance company's risk is "moral hazard," a recurring concern in PAT.[1]

Is there any way to induce the driver to drive safely without constant monitoring? Can incentives substitute for a coercive system of rules and supervision? Spence & Zeckhauser (1971) show that appropriate incentives can reduce moral hazard—but only if the driver is not fully insured. If the driver has to pay a large enough deductible, she will engage in less morally hazardous behavior, as a result of her self-interest, even without being monitored. The manipulation of the driver's incentives is sufficient to overcome (partially) the problem caused by information asymmetry.

Although the insurance company's use of incentives makes it possible to take over part of the driver's risk, use of the deductible is definitely second-best. The risk-averse driver (by definition) is uncomfortable with the deductible and would like to be able to promise not to drive hazardously—and the insurance company would like to believe her. Because of moral hazard, incentives offer only a partial correction for the problem of information asymmetry.

The Canonical Principal-Agent Model

By 1980, economists working from the insurance model had defined the issues, concerns, and canonical results of PAT (Holmstrom 1979, Shavell 1979). To be defined as a principal-agency model, a model must have the following features, which I subsequently refer to as its core assumptions:

1. Agent impact. The agent takes an action that determines (along with a risky variable) a payoff to the principal. For instance, an auto salesman's monthly sales are determined in part by factors beyond his control, but in part by the energy, personality, and effort of the agent himself.

2. Information asymmetry. The principal can readily observe the outcome but not the action of the agent. Monitoring of agent actions may be theoretically possible, but gathering complete information is regarded as prohibitively expensive. The owner of the car lot may not be able to tell whether the salesman's bad sales in a given month are due to the economy, bad luck, or the agent's own inadequate effort. The employer's problem is the same as the insurance company's in the previous example. Given the information asymmetry, can incentives substitute for monitoring?

3. Asymmetry in preferences. The agent's preferences are assumed to differ from the principal's. For example, the actions that benefit the principal's well-being may be costly to the agent, resulting in a preference for shirking.

---

[1]Owing to space considerations, this paper does not address the related issue of "adverse selection," which leads to another rich literature on bureaucratic appointments, for instance.

Another key difference is that the agent is assumed to be more risk-averse than the principal.

4. Initiative that lies with a unified principal. The principal acts rationally based on a coherent set of preferences, and is able to move first by offering a contract.

5. Backward induction based on common knowledge. Principal and agent share knowledge about the structure of the game, effort costs, probability distribution of outcomes, and other parameters. Just as important, they share common knowledge of the agent's rationality; both know that the agent will prefer any incentive package with an expected utility slightly more than the agent's opportunity cost. This leads to backward induction by the principal. The principal can infer the agent's best response function from known parameters and use backward induction to identify the best possible outcome, subject to that function.

6. Ultimatum bargaining. The principal is presumed to be able to impose the best possible solution from the agent's correctly inferred best response function. Or as Sappington (1991) says, "The principal is endowed with all of the bargaining power in this simple setting, and thus can make a 'take-it-or-leave-it' offer to the agent" (p. 47).

These six core assumptions lead to two primary results:

1. Outcome-based incentives. The principal chooses to use outcome-based incentives to overcome in part the problems of moral hazard, despite operating at an informational disadvantage with the agent. This necessarily transfers risk to the risk-averse agent.

2. Efficiency tradeoffs. Moral hazard limits both the benefits to the principal and the efficiency of the transaction as a whole. The risk-averse salesman will demand a higher average compensation package to compensate for her extra risk, and the owner's profits will therefore suffer. Just as in the insurance problem, efficiency in incentives must be traded off against efficiency in risk-bearing, and the second-best solution (i.e., the best trade-off) must involve paying the risk-averse agent a risky, outcome-based bonus (Shavell 1979).

A few of the canonical model's applications to PAT maintain all six of these assumptions and result in some form of outcome-based incentives. These applications have also provided the basis for understanding persistent and puzzling inefficiencies in bureaucracy and other forms of political hierarchy.

Many more political science applications have relaxed one or more assumptions. The result has been a flowering of insight about informational asymmetries and incentives that has made enormous contributions to various subfields of political science. At the same time, PAT has itself been modified in ways that are inconsistent with the original formulations, but often in ways that are distinctly advantageous for progress in political science.

A Canonical Application to Political Science

The relationship between a state's chief executive (as agent) and the executive's constituency (as principal) may seem to be one of the more unlikely political relationships to which to apply the received economic theory of agency. Chief executives tend to be such powerful figures in politics that it is initially unsettling to think of them as agents. Further, the executive's constituency is so diffuse as to be subject to extreme rational ignorance and collective action problems, so it is unlikely that the public will be able to control the executive.

Downs & Rocke (1994) provide perhaps the most convincing application of canonical PAT to a political science setting. They conceive of the chief executive as being the agent of the public, though potentially having different foreign policy preferences than the public. The public's control over the chief executive is the probability of his being removed from power. The public is unable to monitor the chief executive's actions but can readily monitor the success or failure of his decisions—for example, the success or failure of a war.

Certainly, the chief executive takes foreign policy actions that result in salient consequences for the electorate (Assumption 1). Furthermore, the public normally has an enormous informational disadvantage, made worse by collective action problems among the electorate (Assumption 2). The executive may well be either more or less aggressive than is in the public's interest (Assumption 3). At least as regards issues of war and peace, the constituency has relatively homogeneous preferences (Assumption 4). The public, despite the information asymmetry, knows whether or not it likes the results of the executive's war-or-peace decisions. It can use backward induction to determine the best contract, and offer that contract as a take-it-or-leave-it deal (Assumptions 5 and 6). The question is, what is that best contract?

Given the impossibly large costs of monitoring the executive, the constituency must contract on outcomes rather than on the executive's actions—just as argued by principal-agency theorists. If a war goes badly, the executive must be kicked out of office, even if his actions were in the public's best interests. As Downs & Rocke (1994) point out, this is not done out of vindictiveness, but as an incentive for future executives operating under the same outcome-based contract and information asymmetry. Conversely, if the war goes well, the executive must be rewarded, even if he went to war for the wrong reasons and was successful out of sheer luck.

Further, Downs & Rocke (1994) note that the other standard conclusion of PAT applies: There is an inevitable residual of inefficiency. Even though the contract succeeds (despite a considerable information asymmetry) in decreasing the executive's moral hazard problem, it does so by recognizing the inevitability of certain inefficiencies. As they say, "Second-best solutions to agency problems are not infrequently costly from the agent's perspective as well as from that of the principal" (1994, p. 373). The constituency must punish the losing but well-intentioned executive, even though this action makes both executive and public worse off; otherwise, future executives will be freed of the incentive effect and things will be worse yet.

Another form of inefficiency (not mentioned by Downs & Rocke, but general to principal-agent problems) is the fact that a risk-averse agent would demand a higher risky compensation package than he would have accepted in a risk-free environment; one can readily envision what forms this compensation might take, in the case of a chief executive who has an enormous but temporary capacity to exploit economic and political primacy.

Most interestingly, Downs & Rocke (1994) contribute to the theory of principal-agency by noting a form of inefficiency that is perfectly general to principal-agent relationships but was not previously discussed in the literature. Picture a sharecropper who will lose his position with a poor crop—even if he has supplied the best possible effort. If, at a certain point in the summer, the crop looks bad, the sharecropper may be driven to extreme measures (say, expenditures on unproven and risky cloud-seeding for rain), simply because he has nothing to lose. As Downs & Rocke argue, the same thing is true of an executive with a war that is going badly. Prolonging the war on the increasingly thin chance of a surprise victory is in the executive's interest (although not the constituency's), given the inevitability of being kicked out of office when failure becomes evident to the constituency. Paradoxically, even risk-averse executives may be forced to take more and more unattractive gambles in hopes of saving their position. This phenomenon, which the authors aptly term "gambling for resurrection," is an excellent example of a discovery of an unanticipated agency cost that results from the stubborn problems caused by PAT.

Although Downs & Rocke do not discuss it, both executive and constituency could be made better off by improvements in the technology of monitoring (Holmstrom 1978). That is, if the constituency could verify that the executive was going to war in violation of the public's best interest, then the constituency would not be forced to punish well-intentioned executives—and the executive would be less likely to "gamble for resurrection" in the face of a losing war. Everyone would be better off. Unfortunately, the debate in 2004 with respect to the U.S. attack on Iraq (regarding weapons of mass destruction, links to al Qaeda, and possible pressure from the Bush administration on the CIA) demonstrates how unlikely the "better monitoring" solution is. The information asymmetry between executive and public is too profound to be resolved by better monitoring.

PRINCIPAL-AGENCY THEORY EXTENDED AND CHALLENGED: CONGRESSIONAL OVERSIGHT

The most extensive and influential application of PAT was initiated with two articles on, respectively, the Federal Trade Commission (Weingast & Moran 1983) and the Securities and Exchange Commission (Weingast 1984). Weingast, like Downs & Rocke, was at pains to explore the implications of information asymmetry and the possibilities of outcome-based incentives. The result sparked an immediate and creative reformulation of the study of congressional oversight and bureaucratic politics—two topics that had not previously been successfully penetrated by rational choice theory. The extensive empirical literature initiated by Weingast's principal-agency perspective on bureaucracies has been enormously valuable. For the first time, the field of public bureaucracy had a research agenda that was based on deductive theory and demanded the highest level of methodological competence. At the same time, the empirical results suggested a more complicated story—one that led to challenges to the canonical model and opened the door to reformulations of PAT that better fit this important political relationship.

Congressional Control Through Incentives

Prior to Weingast's work, the most common perspective on congressional oversight was that it was ineffectual. The evidence for this was the small fraction of resources going into congressional oversight, the haphazard nature of the oversight activities that did take place, the lack of expertise by members of Congress and their staffs, and the disregard of bureaucrats for members of Congress.

Weingast used PAT to provide a different interpretation of these same empirical facts. The evidence documented lack of congressional monitoring—not an absence of control. If Congress does not spend much time monitoring and reprimanding bureaucrats, then that may mean the bureaucrats are adequately motivated by incentives to act in Congress's best interests—just as a hefty commission can keep a sales agent performing well with virtually no intervention by the car lot owner.

In the first article, "Bureaucratic Discretion or Congressional Control," Weingast & Moran (1983) claim that congressional committees "possess sufficient rewards and sanctions to create an incentive system for agencies" (p. 768). Congressional committees may be totally ignorant of bureaucratic behavior because bureaucratic behavior is irrelevant to Congress; Congess doesn't care how the bureaucrats sell cars, it just wants the cars to be sold. In effect, members of Congress shape bureaucratic behavior without monitoring it, by offering implicit contracts based on the observable effects of that behavior.

The threat of ex post sanctions creates ex ante incentives for the bureau to serve a congressional clientele. "This has a striking implication: the more effective the incentive system, the less often we should observe sanctions in the form of congressional attention through hearings and investigations. Put another way, direct and continuous monitoring of inputs rather than of results is an inefficient mechanism by which a principal constrains the actions of his agent" (Weingast & Moran 1983, p. 769).

In the 1984 paper, Weingast is precise about the nature of the incentives available to congressional committees: bureaucratic competition for (ultimately) limited budgetary appropriations, congressional influence over the appointment of top bureaucratic officials, and the threat of ex post sanctions in the form of congressional hearings and investigations (Weingast 1984).

If Congress does not hold hearings, how does it measure outcomes? McCubbins & Schwartz (1984) solve this part of the puzzle. Members of Congress are interested only in the bottom line—whether their constituents are getting what they want from bureaucrats. Constituents are normally uninformed about the bureaucrats' behaviors, but they do know whether they are getting the services they want. When bureaucrats fail to supply those services, constituents "pull the fire alarm"—complain loudly to their member of Congress. Legislators are able to economize on oversight resources by ignoring all those bureaucratic services about which they hear no fire alarms (McCubbins & Schwartz 1984).

For principal-agency theorists, bureaucratic independence and congressional "dominance" are observationally equivalent as far as monitoring and sanctions are concerned. We should see little of either if bureaucrats are independent; but we should also see little if bureaucratic behavior is shaped by congressionally imposed incentives. Therefore, it is necessary to look beyond monitoring and sanctions to bureaucratic outputs, to determine if they can be shown to vary with congressional preferences. In the case of the Securities and Exchange Commission, Weingast argues that its imposition of deregulation was in response to congressional representation of the interests of large institutional investors. With respect to the Federal Trade Commission (FTC), Weingast & Moran (1983) show more convincingly that the ideological preferences of the Senate and the subcommittee chairman (as measured by Americans for Democratic Action scores) were significantly associated with the FTC's emphasis over time on consumer-oriented credit (p. 789). In other words, a more conservative Senate led to a less consumer-oriented FTC.

Although neither of these empirical forays could be regarded as the final word on the subject, Weingast's articles constitute an enormous contribution to the study of congressional oversight and public bureaucracy by exemplifying quantitative research directed at precise questions (e.g., what are the political and other determinants of bureaucratic outputs?) derived from rigorous theory. Almost single-handedly, these articles raised the bar for academic research in the area of bureaucracy. Weingast (1984) offers the "congressional dominance" hypothesis: "The mechanisms evolved by Congress over the past one hundred years comprise an ingenious system for control of agencies that involves little direct congressional monitoring of decisions but which nonetheless results in policies desired by Congress" (p. 148).

Weingast specifically acknowledges that congressional oversight is not perfect. He cites Holmstrom (1979) on the inevitability of agency costs, which in this context he interprets as equivalent to "bureaucratic discretion." However, he notes that the existence of bureaucratic discretion "does not imply that the system fails to serve congressional interests. If creating too many agencies implied that congressmen lost control over the policy decisions valuable for reelection, then they would not do so" (p. 154). The ultimate indicator of whether members of Congress are getting what they need out of bureaucracies is the incumbent reelection rate. The high rate of incumbent reelection (over 90% in the House) is the result of many factors, but it is consistent with the conclusion that legislators are able to shape bureaucratic outputs to their purposes—hence they must control bureaucrats.

Multiple Principals

But does the assumption of a unified principal acting on coherent preferences (Assumption 4) really apply to oversight? What difference would it make if it didn't? Moe (1984) expresses several doubts, chiefly the problem of multiple principals.

As Moe (1984, 1987a) observes, separation of powers and highly competitive partisan politics guarantee that bureaucratic agencies will be in a contentious environment of warring principals. Interest groups are pitted against each other, both parties strive for majority status, oversight committees compete with appropriations committees, and Congress jealously vies with the President. "In fact, politicians impose constraints on one another in a competitive effort to see to it that their own interests are protected from the intrusions of politician-opponents" (Moe 1984, p. 769). And in the context of warring principals, the ability of bureaucratic agents to use information asymmetries to their own advantage is enhanced.

In an obvious example, congressional committees must compete with the White House for control of bureaucracies. Moe (1985) reports a significant influence of the presidency on the decisions of the National Labor Relations Board (NLRB). Moe (1987b) gives a detailed account of the fine-tuned interaction of interest groups, president, and Congress as regards the NLRB. Over time, the institutional compromise has been for interest groups, and Congress, to limit themselves to a competition over appointments of bipartisan commissioners to the NLRB. Because neither labor nor business could dominate, given the partisan competitiveness and separation of powers, a procedural deal was struck. Business and labor each use their influence to veto commissioners who strongly favor the other party. The result of this stalemate is that "the two sides have a common interest in ensuring that labor law is in the hands of experienced, knowledgeable people who understand the issues" (p. 261). The competition between "principals" inevitably results in the appointment of relatively centrist, pragmatic commissioners dedicated to professionalism of the Board and its staff.

The bureaucratic professionals of the NLRB realize that the legalistic, quasi-judicial procedure by which the NLRB makes its most important decisions protects them from partisan political storms and provides them a stable career—as long as they follow the procedures in a neutral, professional way. The result is a high degree of autonomy for the professional staff at the NLRB. "Professionals are difficult to control, but their behavior is fairly easy to predict. . . . A professional, if given total autonomy and insulated from external pressures, can be counted on to behave in a manner characteristic of his type. This is what true professionalism is all about. This very predictability ensures business and labor that their mutual interests in stability, clarity, and expertise will be protected" (Moe 1987b, p. 261).

Moe's portrayal is one in which legislators have limited control over the NLRB—at the margins, through the stylized negotiations with the President over the appointments process. Congressional committees have almost no control of the NLRB through budgetary competition or the prospect of ex post hearings. No one—business or labor—has a strong vested interest in cutting the NLRB's funds; and following legalistic procedure is a defense that renders NLRB lawyers virtually immune to sanctions from unhappy legislators. The separation of powers arguably insulates bureaucrats from the outcome-based incentives that are the hallmark of the economic theory of agency.

Although Congress's influence is marginal, stylized, and shared with the President, that does not mean that lack of control carries large reelection risks for legislators. If a labor constituency, for example, objects to the trend of NLRB decisions under a Republican president, the member of Congress has only to prove that he is doing the best he can: lobbying (often symbolically) for good pro-labor members of the NLRB. But what can a Democratic legislator do when the president is a Republican? And what other tools are available to the member of Congress? The legislator's obvious powerlessness is itself a defense against constituency dissatisfaction. Lack of control over the bureaucracy can be as effective as complete control in a legislator's reelection strategy. If the reelection needs of members of Congress are not very tightly linked with the performance of a particular agency, then we can expect that congressional "dominance" will not be a very tight constraint on that bureaucracy. The problem of observational equivalence reappears in a different guise: High rates of reelection for members of a particular oversight committee might mean that the committee has gained control over the agencies it monitors, or it might mean that the bureaucracy is simply irrelevant to the reelection strategy of those legislators.

The Limited Impact of Incentives

The message of the multiple-principals argument is the opposite of the message of congressional dominance models: Incentivizing bureaucrats is an activity with limited scope. The empirical literature has identified some of these limits, as well.

RESISTANCE AT THE EPA   For example, Wood (1988) has looked beyond a simple correlation between agent actions and legislative ideology. Wood examines how the U.S. Environmental Protection Agency (EPA) responded to the change in partisan control of White House and senatorial oversight committees that resulted from the 1980 election. He found that, far from being responsive to this change, the EPA defied rather stringent attempts by the White House, supported by the Republican Senate, to lower the level of clean air enforcement. "All of the available tools of administrative control were applied toward moving EPA away from vigorous implementation of the law. But the data analysis shows that in the end EPA's revealed preferences were completely opposite from what the model predicted" (Wood 1988, p. 227).

In response to a suggestion that he specifically consider the role of Senate oversight committees on clean air enforcement, Wood subsequently pointed out that the chairs of the oversight committee and subcommittee were both less supportive of enforcement than preceding Democratic chairs, as was the Senate as a whole

(Cook & Wood 1989). Although it may be that public opposition to the Reagan initiatives encouraged Congress to be more supportive of the EPA, Cook &Wood (1989) pointed to the EPA's role in sparking interest group response and noted that "this explanation reverses the hierarchical model by suggesting that strategic bureaucrats can manipulate Congress through mobilized support" (p. 973).

STRUCTURE AND THE LIMITS OF INCENTIVES   Whitford (2002) has studied bureaucratic structure as a key variable mediating the importance of incentives and the limits of control. His case study was of the Nuclear Regulatory Commission (NRC). In response to an initiative by President Reagan, the NRC decentralized decision making. As a result of the decentralization, each newly empowered Regional Office could make its own enforcement decisions, independent of the Commission. This decentralization occurred without changes in other bureaucratic incentives or staffing.

Whitford's careful empirical analysis shows that the NRC's enforcement decisions were not particularly responsive to congressional preferences either before or after the new decision structure. Ironically, the NRC had been noticeably responsive to presidential ideology before the decentralization, but was no longer responsive after decentralization. "After decentralization, finding themselves insulated from national control, bureaucrats became more task-oriented" (Whitford 2002, p. 185). This may have been a consequence unanticipated by Reagan.

Most importantly, the results indicate a dependence of control on structural variables, "which means that principal-agency theory is limited as an organizing framework for the study of Congressional and presidential oversight of the bureaucracy. When bureaucratic agents implement policy, monitoring, incentives and selection are never as effective as political principals would hope and only as effective as structure allows" (Whitford 2002, p. 186).

MODELING "MULTIPLE PRINCIPALS"   The political science discipline has taken to heart Moe's point about multiple principals. The result is a rather large literature on multiple principals—a literature that is grounded more in agenda control models than in PAT.

Shipan (2004) proposes a model of the regulatory activity of the U.S. Food and Drug Administration (FDA) that uses the gatekeeping power of the oversight committee. Shipan describes a game in which the agency determines policy subject to the committee's decision to acquiesce (and make no legislative proposals) or to propose a bill that will be amended to the floor median's preferred alternative. He considers a committee ideal point C; a floor ideal point F to the right of C; and the point an equal distance to the left of C, given by $C(F)$, where the committee is indifferent to the floor's ideal point F. The agency then has discretion in the range of outcomes (centered at C) between F and $C(F)$. As long as the agency chooses to locate at any point in that range, the bureaucratic-autonomy range, then the committee will prefer to protect the agency's decision rather than introduce a bill that will be replaced (through amendments) by F.

If the agency's ideal point is outside of that range, then the agency should respond strategically by introducing either $C(F)$ or F. In this case, the committee's gatekeeping power will be binding on the agency, and changes in the committee's preferences should change the agency's proposed policy. Shipan's estimate of FDA regulatory activities provides evidence that the agency's actions are impacted by the committee's power when the agency's ideal point is outside that range of bureaucratic autonomy. However, when the agency's ideal point is inside that range, Shipan finds statistical evidence that legislative preferences have no impact on the agency's choice.

The Shipan model is a much more complex and contingent story about bureaucratic accountability than that offered by the original formulation of PAT. By adding two chambers to the model, Shipan enhances the possibilities for bureaucratic discretion. Legislative interactions, especially the checks and balances between chambers, and between chamber and floor, provide a discretionary range for bureaucrats. With moderate preferences, bureaucratic action is unconstrained by congressionally imposed incentives.

Congressional Control Without Incentives

Responding in part to the weak evidence for links between congressionally imposed incentives and bureaucratic behavior, McCubbins et al. (1987) moved the principal-agency literature in a new direction, featuring congressionally imposed procedure rather than congressionally imposed incentives.

The authors expressed doubt that congressional incentives were as powerful as they had seemed in earlier papers. Indeed, "a system of rewards and punishments is unlikely to be a completely effective solution to the control problem. This is due to the cost of monitoring, limitations in the range of rewards and punishments, and for the most meaningful forms of rewards and punishments, the cost to the principals of implementing them" (McCubbins et al. 1987, pp. 251–52). For example, exposing and punishing bureaucratic noncompliance may cause the electorate to doubt the effectiveness of legislators.

In place of incentives, McCubbins et al. (1987) adopt a highly influential and distinctly political approach to the information asymmetry between legislators and bureaucrats. They claim that members of Congress control the bureaucracy by imposing bureaucratic procedures that "stack the deck" in favor of congressionally favored constituencies.

The motivation for the argument is once again informational asymmetry. "The most subtle and, in our view, most interesting aspect of procedural controls is that they enable political leaders to assure compliance without specifying, or even necessarily knowing, what substantive outcome is most in their interest. By controlling processes, political leaders assign a relative weight to the constituents whose interests are at stake in an administrative procedure" (McCubbins et al. 1987, p. 243). For example, the legislature can benefit privileged interest groups by an appropriate assignment of the burden of proof, as well as by procedural rules that require consultation with those groups. Additionally, McCubbins et al. refer to public disclosure and other transparency requirements that make it difficult for bureaucrats secretly to "mobilize a new constituency" that may upset Congress's political calculations.

This is a distinctly political view because it assumes, in addition to political principals and bureaucratic agents, a court system that is capable of enforcing due process and legislative procedural mandates. It also assumes interest groups that, if satisfied, will advance the reelection goals of legislators. PAT, designed to explain relationships within the firm, has no analogous concepts. The directors of a firm clearly specify to the CEO that they expects profits—but they do not constrain the CEO by specifying a particular procedure, especially one that may benefit a single subset of investors. Any such procedure would only constrain the profit-maximizing activities of the CEO, and would require constant monitoring either by the board (which is unlikely) or by an external court system (equally unlikely). As a result, the procedural-control argument, although it has been extremely productive of innovative research in political science, represents a discontinuity with PAT, rather than a simple extension of it.

The subsequent literature on administrative procedures has not been uniformly supportive of the original procedural-control hypothesis. Mashaw (1990) notes that procedural statutes do not stack the deck very seriously because both winning and losing interest groups are given procedural status. Furthermore, legislative mandates presumably designed to help particular congressionally favored interest groups do not always have the intended effect. Balla (1998) shows that low-income medical specialties were not benefited by stipulations about their participation in the early-comment stage of rule making at the Health Care Financing Administration. Balla concludes that legislatively mandated procedures "did not operate as an instrument of political control in the manner posited by the deck-stacking thesis" (p. 671).

An alternative view is that procedural requirements represent a procedural bargain on the part of concerned political interests—and an abdication of control by legislators. Spence (1997) claims that legislators cannot well foresee the policy outcomes of alternative procedural requirements, and that without this foresight, administrative procedures fall short of yielding the kind of congressional control envisioned by principal-agency theorists. Procedural requirements are of use to legislators, but more because they guarantee a procedure that interest groups can regard as fair. Procedures yield more legitimacy than control.

Administrative procedures provide a clear demarcation of steps to follow—independently of outcome. The rules of baseball may be said to constrain the umpire, but they still give him enormous discretion in calling strikes and outs. As long as the umpire calls the batter out after three strikes, not two or four, then nothing he does in the way of calling the pitches can get him in too much trouble. Similarly, the bureaucrat's compliance with the procedural mandates constitutes the ideal defense against subsequent congressional criticism of any policy decision the bureaucrat chooses to reach at the end of the process. For this reason, we can expect risk-averse bureaucrats to demand procedural guidance from the legislature. More than being a congressional control technique, legislative procedural mandates constitute a clarification of the rules of the game that create the confidence that allows bureaucratic delegation to take place.

PRINCIPAL-AGENCY THEORY REEXAMINED

In the last half of this paper, I examine explicit attempts to test and/or modify basic assumptions of PAT, especially the assumptions of common-knowledge and ultimatum bargaining. First, I argue that PAT has been structured as a form of ultimatum game, and that this provides a clue to empirical limitations of principal-agency models. Second, I argue that an awareness of credible commitment problems and moral hazard call for paradoxical reformulations of PAT.

From Ultimatum Bargaining to Bilateral Bargaining

Principal-agency models are based on a set of assumptions that make the principal-agency relationship a special case of an ultimatum game. The ultimatum game is a simple one in which Player 1 decides how to divide $10 between herself and Player 2, subject only to Player 2's approval. Player 2 can make no counterproposals, and so once Player 1 has made a decision, Player 2 can choose only between accepting Player 1's proposal and vetoing—which results in zero for both players.

The assumption of common knowledge of rationality allows Player 1 to "know" how Player 2 will respond: Player 2 should always accept any proposal that gives him more than zero. Knowing this, Player 1 can choose an allocation that gives herself virtually all of the $10. This outcome is the only subgame-perfect equilibrium of the ultimatum game.

The subgame-perfect equilibrium prediction of the ultimatum game is possibly the most famous falsified prediction in game theory. It is virtually never observed (Camerer 2003, pp. 48–59). In dozens of experiments in many cultural and economic settings, Player 1 almost never offers anything close to the minimum share of the prize, and when she does, Player 2 is likely to reject the offer, resulting in a zero payoff for both. The typical Player 1 will choose an allocation that gives Player 2 a significant share of the prize, often approaching or equaling an equal split.

The reason for this lies squarely with violations of the common knowledge of rationality. Contrary to that assumption, Player 1 is *not* certain that Player 2 will choose a dime over nothing. Each Player 1 believes that Player 2 could be vindictive—and the impressive number of rejections of unequal splits validates that belief. Without that common knowledge, various radical reformulations of noncooperative game theory are required (see Camerer 2003, p. 110–12).

The similarities between the ultimatum game and the principal-agent problem are striking. The principal, like Player 1 in the ultimatum game, moves first, with knowledge of the agent's effort costs. As Sappington (1991) says, "The principal is endowed with all of the bargaining power in this simple setting, and thus can make a 'take-it-or-leave-it' offer to the agent" (p. 47). The common-knowledge assumption once again does a lot of the work. It implies that the principal can offer an incentive package that gives the agent nothing more than his opportunity costs, with perfect confidence that it will be accepted. This guarantees that the principal can guarantee for herself the lion's share of the resources, subject only to the agent's rationality constraint.

Laboratory experiments do not support this or other basic predictions from canonical PAT (Fehr et al. 1997, Miller & Whitford 2002). The reasons for this failure seem to be related to the failure of the ultimatum game predictions: a failure of the common-knowledge assumption.

Fehr et al. (1997) ran experiments in which principals were allowed to set various levels of a flat wage. Because payment is not contingent on outcome, it theoretically should not motivate agent effort. Yet participants assigned the role of principal typically offer a considerably higher than predicted wage, and in return they receive higher than predicted levels of effort. The authors' explanation is that many agents feel an obligation to reciprocate sizable risk-insuring flat wages with high effort as a form of "gift exchange." Principals evidently count on that sense of reciprocity.

Unlike Fehr et al. (1997), Miller & Whitford (2002) allow their principals to offer contracts featuring outcome-contingent bonuses if they choose. This should make it possible for principals to shift to agents a sufficient amount of risk that agents find it in their interest to supply high effort, even if the result is that the principal claims most of the rents. Instead, a majority of the principals offer too small a bonus to eliminate the moral hazard. Their contracts transfer significant amounts of the surplus to the agents, and most of the agents who receive such contracts provide high effort despite moral hazard.

Miller & Whitford (2002) show that contrary to the common-knowledge assumption, principals do not expect agents to behave rationally, and many of the agents in fact do not. Ironically, because of the irrational actions of the agents, the exchange is much more efficient than it should be; the dire trade-off between efficiency in risk sharing and incentives is bypassed.

Principal-Agency Theory and Cooperation

Experimental evidence of a more meaningful negotiation process than that presumed by the ultimatum game is not necessarily surprising. After all, the subgame-perfect equilibrium of the principal-agent game is inevitably Pareto-suboptimal—meaning that it leaves money on the table. In fact, the more profound the information asymmetries, and the more risk-averse the agent, the more money is left on the table. Reaching a more efficient outcome is sufficiently motivating to generate a meaningful discussion between principal and agent.

Furthermore, the conditions for effective negotiation are often met in the case of political actors. For instance, members of congressional committees and bureaucrats are generally in their roles for long periods of time. It is reasonable to assume that they would be at least as open to mutually beneficial negotiation as would two undergraduate experimental subjects who communicate anonymously by computer.

Cooperation is often modeled by means of a repeated prisoners' dilemma game. Radner (1985) noticed that the principal-agency game (like a prisoners' dilemma) has a unique, suboptimal outcome as a one-shot game, and asked what would happen if the game were repeated. The conclusion, consistent with the Folk Theorem, is that an infinite number of outcomes, including efficient outcomes, are sustainable if the shadow of the future is sufficiently large.

Cooperation is easy to visualize with a trigger strategy. The principal adopts the strategy, "Pay the agent the flat wage that he prefers as long as there is no evidence of shirking; if there is such evidence, always insist on a risky output-based compensation scheme." The agent responds with, "Always supply a generous high effort with a flat wage; but give the self-interested minimum to any risky compensation plan."

Scholz (1991) is one of the few political scientists to take seriously the possibility of cooperation in a principal-agent relationship. In the relationship that Scholz studies, the principal is the occupational safety regulatory agency, and the agent is the regulated firm. Consistent with PAT, Scholz argues that the one-shot game between the two results in the "deterrence equilibrium," in which the firm offers minimal compliance and the agency provides maximal, inflexible enforcement. This is a Nash equilibrium because each side's choice is the best response to the other's choice: The agency doesn't want to provide any flexibility to a firm that is exhibiting minimal compliance, and the firm doesn't want to be more cooperative (responding to hazards not clearly defined in the laws, making hidden information available, etc.) with an agency that is showing every disposition to use all such concessions punitively.

However, as Scholz argues, both could be better off if both were more cooperative. The firm could make an honest effort to comply in exchange for an agency that was willing to overlook minor technical violations. The firm would find itself in less legal trouble, and the agency could report more real improvement in safety conditions.

PRINCIPAL-AGENCY THEORY REFORMULATED: CREDIBLE COMMITMENT PROBLEMS

One universally applied aspect of PAT is that the principal's problem consists of inducing the agent to act in the principal's interests. Clearly, the problem of inducing the agent *not* to act in the principal's interests is not "the principal's problem" as conventionally conceived. Yet, in credible commitment models, the principal's self-interest is the problem, and the solution is to ensure that the agent is unresponsive to those interests.

Credible Commitment: The Principal's Other Problem

Writing two years before the Cuban missile crisis, Schelling (1960) was concerned with making nuclear deterrence believable. In a simple game-tree version of the problem, the Soviet Union can either invade Europe or not. In response to an invasion, the U.S. can either use its nuclear weapons or not. The problem is that the former course of action would result in the worst case for the United States. For that reason, the Soviet Union can use backward induction to conclude that self-interest would prevent the United States from using its nuclear deterrent. The subgame-perfect equilibrium of the game is for the Soviet Union to invade and for the U.S. to acquiesce. Nuclear deterrence, in the hands of any reasonable individual, is a hollow threat.

The solution that Schelling proposed was to hire an agent—but not an agent who would be easily recognized as such by advocates of the economic theory of agency. Schelling's agent must have preferences entirely different from those of the principal—in particular, a willingness to use nuclear weapons and thereby engender nuclear holocaust. But finding such a person is only half the solution. The agent must be insulated from pressure from the principal, so that the principal's last-minute (postinvasion) attempts to prevent the agent from wreaking havoc are powerless. The useful agent must be out of the principal's control, and prefer mutual annihilation to acquiescence.

A person with the right preferences was in fact the Chairman of the Joint Chiefs of Staff at that time: Curtis "Boom-boom" LeMay. During the Cuban missile crisis, his was the voice that was most insistent on an air attack, presumably ending in a nuclear exchange.

After the crisis, when Premier Khrushchev had backed down and the missiles were returning to the Soviet Union, LeMay argued for an air strike against Cuba anyhow. While President Kennedy was experiencing enormous relief at the termination of the immediate threat of nuclear annihilation, LeMay was demanding exactly the nuclear exchange that Kennedy had been working so hard to avoid.

From the standpoint of PAT, it was insanity for Kennedy to keep an agent who had such strikingly different preferences and possibly enough autonomy to bring on the crisis that Kennedy was trying to prevent. But that merely shows the theoretical limitations of canonical PAT.

From Schelling's standpoint, LeMay's usefulness was precisely that his preferences were perverse enough and his authority great enough to make U.S. use of nuclear weapons a credible threat. The Soviet Union had sufficient intelligence to know that LeMay and other hardliners were arguing for the use of nuclear weapons during the crisis. They also knew that civilian control of the military was a question, not a certainty. This knowledge made the Kennedy bargaining posture (blockade followed by threat of attack) more effective with Khrushchev and induced him to withdraw the missiles. As Schelling (1960) said, "The sophisticated negotiator [Kennedy] may find it difficult to seem as obstinate as a truly obstinate man [LeMay]. If a man knocks at a door and says that he will stab himself on the porch unless given $10, he is more likely to get the $10 if his eyes are bloodshot" (p. 22).

The point is that this problem is not comprehensible in terms of conventional PAT, which has the sole avowed purpose of finding incentives that align the agent's actions with the principal's preferences and eliminate shirking. For Schelling, the problem is finding someone with the appropriate nonaligned preferences; but having perverse incentives is not enough. The principal must convincingly give up some of his control to the agent with the bloodshot eyes. To be credible, the use of such an agent must involve "some voluntary but irreversible sacrifice of freedom of choice" by the principal (Schelling 1960, p. 22). In this view of the Weberian asymmetry, agent responsiveness would paradoxically destroy the agent's value to the principal.

The Principal's Moral Hazard

In the case of nuclear deterrence, credible commitment through delegation plays a role even when the principal has laudable and reasonable preferences. Credible commitment becomes the more desirable when the principal is plagued by moral hazard—preferences that, when acted on, diminish social efficiency.

In PAT, only the agent can exhibit moral hazard, because the formal responsibility is strictly unidirectional—from the agent to the principal. The phrase "principal's moral hazard" makes no sense, since the principal's proclivity to follow her own interests is presumed to be natural and legitimate. However, from the perspective of the overall efficiency of the relationship between principal and agent, it is possible for the principal's pursuit of her own self-interest to be self-destructive.

INVESTORS, BANKERS, AND CREDIBLE COMMITMENT   Consider a game between an investor and a ruler. The investor can either take her gold out of her mattress and invest it in the ruler's economy or not. If not, the normalized payoff to each is $1. If she does invest it, the investment generates $10 worth of benefit. The ruler can either steal the $10, leaving the investor with nothing, or tax the investor $5, leaving the investor with $5. In the backward-induction equilibrium of the game, the investor, anticipating that the ruler will choose $10 over $5, leaves her gold in her mattress, and both are worse off than if the ruler could be counted on to constrain his self-interest.

In this game, the ruler's self-interest is a form of moral hazard. If the ruler could commit not to pursue his own self-interest at the only point in the game in which he has a choice to make, everyone would be better off.

Because the problem is the ruler's moral hazard, one solution is delegation. Suppose the ruler hires an agent and yields decision authority to the agent at the ruler's decision node. This will induce the investor to make an investment, but only if the investor believes that the agent will defy the ruler's best interests. This would be the case if the agent were known to have contrary interests—for example, if the agent would receive a fee if and only if she defies the ruler. Credible commitment of the ruler is established by the agent's nonresponsiveness to the ruler's interests (North & Weingast 1989).

As simple as this model of credible commitment is, it corresponds in several ways to our best understanding of the political economy of central banking (Jensen 1997). Elected officials will always find advantage in providing public expenditures, tax cuts, and other benefits to their constituents. These benefits, however, generate inflationary tendencies. Investors and other economic agents adjust their actions accordingly, and eventually such governmental actions generate inflation with little impact on unemployment. A government that campaigned on promises not to provide such inflationary shocks would not be believed. Credible constraint of the government is the key to controlling inflation.

The governments that are so constrained are those that have tied their hands by creating independent central banks. Studies have shown that independent central bank decision making has an impact on lowering the inflation rate (Franzese 1999). The central bank's credibility is enhanced when private economic actors perceive that the bank's decisions are irrevocable. In contrast, if private actors perceive that partisan administrations influence the decisions of the central bank, then the credibility of a nominally independent bank is undermined.

How are investors convinced of the independence of the central bank? Part of the answer comes in the form of the multiple-principals argument (Moe 1984). Morris (1999), for example, pictures monetary policy alternatives as a one-dimensional space. A variety of political actors, including the President, members of both houses of Congress, and the Chairman of the Federal Reserve Board, all have single-peaked preferences in that space. A coalition of the President and a majority of both chambers is decisive, so a Fed chairman who enacts a policy that is, say, to the right of the ideal points of the President and the median voter in both chambers can be overturned by the normal legislative procedure. However, there is normally a range of outcomes between the President's ideal point and the ideal point of the more distant chamber median that cannot be upset by a normal coalition. (A slightly more complicated model incorporates legislative override coalitions, with similar results.) Although Morris does not identify them as such, this range of points is the "core" of the monetary policy game, the size of which increases with increasing preference conflict between the President and the members of the two chambers (Hammond & Knott 1996).

The amount of the Fed chairman's discretion is given by the size of the core, since (by definition) no legislative coalition can upset any policy enacted by the Fed chairman inside the core. This is a novel and useful conceptualization of congressional oversight, but one of its paradoxical messages is that the ability to control bureaucrats by the use of incentives is limited by the system of separation of powers. As long as the Fed chairman chooses a policy within the core, his policies cannot be overturned; nor would the legislature ever agree to impose any legislative sanctions on a Fed chairman who chooses a policy in this range.

At any given time, a strategic bureaucrat should be able to make choices from his or her discretionary zone with no fear of reprisals. This results in an interesting reversal of Weingast's (1984) point about "observational equivalence." The reason we virtually never see successful legislative sanctions of the Fed is not because the Fed is so well-tamed by the Congress but because the Fed chairman should be able to avoid reprisals by choosing policies in the legislative core.

Investors perceive the Fed as independent of the political ambitions of politicians precisely because the joint action of both chambers of Congress and the President is required to reverse its decisions—and joint action is not likely, given their distinct goals and the likelihood of strategic behavior by the Fed chairman (Keefer & Stasavage 2003). From the perspective of credible commitment, the loss of control implied by its multiplicity of principals is not an efficiency loss, as argued by the original advocates of congressional control. On the contrary, the loss of political control is the prerequisite for effective performance of the Fed's function.

PARTY CAUCUSES AND PARTY LEADERS   Kiewiet & McCubbins (1991) provide another principal-agent model in which the principal's moral hazard is the primary problem to be solved. Their starting point is a study of collective action dilemmas in legislatures. Other things being equal, legislators would like to vote in ways that maximize their chance of reelection from their particular district. In the limit, this could result in chaos, as it may be very difficult to coordinate on major pieces of legislation that affect national constituencies. Just as important, if someone goes to the trouble of organizing such a coalition, individual legislators will have a hard time taking credit for the legislation or even informing their constituencies that they voted for it. In particular, party coalitions will be unable to compete effectively without constraining their own members.

Party labels, Kiewiet & McCubbins suggest, are public goods. They allow a group of legislators to claim credit for party-based coalitions that pass major legislation, and they enable legislators in that party to inform constituents of their role in that legislation. In order to be effective, however, parties need some way of inducing members to vote for party-label legislation, even at times when individual legislators would prefer to oppose it. Party caucuses hire "agents" (party leaders) and give them the means of coordinating or disciplining the members of the caucus. It is the moral hazard of the collective principal (the caucus) that is the problem to be solved, not moral hazard on the part of the agent (the party leader).

Lyndon Johnson, as majority leader, was the expert "agent" of the Democratic caucus in the Senate. His expertise, ironically, was in methods of political control—of the principal. This provides an entirely different perspective on the Weberian asymmetry, in which the agent's expertise generates significant political power and significant rents (Caro 2002).

BASE-CLOSING COMMISSION   A striking example of the principal's moral hazard (in the legislative context) is the creation of the base-closing commissions in 1988 and 1990. Despite petitions from the Defense Department and the President, Congress had refused to allow numerous inefficient military bases to be closed, thereby diverting valuable resources away from better military uses. In 1988 and again in 1990, Congress delegated authority to a base-closing commission that was expected to close bases that Congress did not want closed.

From the standpoint of conventional PAT, this is an anomaly. Congress is not supposed to create agencies with the purpose of defying the dearest reelection aspirations of its members. "The conventional wisdom holds that base closures end congressional careers, and few legislators are willing to sacrifice themselves" (Mayer 1995, p. 396). This was a case in which Congress itself recognized that its reelection desires were at war with its institutional responsibilities. Congress would look irresponsible, during a period of record-breaking and destructive deficits, if it allowed the reelection goals of its members to waste defense resources.

The solution was to delegate away their ability to protect their parochial interests in outdated military bases. "Legislators agreed to restrict their own parochial tendencies by delegating authority to the Independent Commission and granting it the power to make and effectively enforce decisions on the group (saying, in effect, 'stop us before we vote again')" (Mayer 1995, p. 394). The commission had the power to make proposals to the secretary of defense, which individual members of Congress could subsequently protest but not prevent.

From the congressional perspective, this was a success. Individual members had adequate opportunity to attempt to save bases in their districts—an electorally essential losing battle—and Congress as a whole was able to contribute to the more effective use of military appropriations. No member of Congress lost his or her seat because of the closing of the military bases. This outcome was accomplished, not by creating the kind of ideal agent visualized by the "congressional dominance" approach—one that is demonstrably responsive to the incentives created by Congress and ultimately to Congress's every reelection-motivated demand—but rather by creating a kind of perverse agent who was designed to be insulated from Congress and to deny the particular reelection demands of its members.

CONCLUSION: CONTRIBUTIONS OF POLITICAL SCIENCE TO PRINCIPAL-AGENCY THEORY

The economic theory of agency provided the first formal technique for investigating the Weberian asymmetry. However, it questioned the conclusion that the advantage is always with the expert against the rulers; sometimes, subtle incentives may trump considerable informational advantages. Furthermore, principal-agency modeling encouraged a whole generation of political scientists to think seriously about incentives and their effect on actors who were previously viewed as unconstrained and isolated. PAT has thus considerably aided the awareness of institutional interdependence.

At the same time, a healthy skepticism about PAT has encouraged the evolution of a flock of related models for studying the Weberian asymmetry from other perspectives. The examination of multiple principals has allowed us to place bureaucratic discretion within a better understanding of a system of checks and balances. The examination of the negotiation process has allowed us to soften the assumption that the principal can impose incentives unilaterally on a passive agent. And the examination of credible commitment models allows us to understand settings in which the agent's contribution is constraint of the principal's moral hazard.

ACKNOWLEDGMENTS

The author acknowledges the contributions of Gerhard Loewenberg, William Lowry, Michael Lynch, Jack Knott, Andrew Whitford, and the members of the political science department at the University of California, Davis, as well as the research assistance of Tasina Nitzschke.

**The *Annual Review of Political Science* is online at
http://polisci.annualreviews.org**

LITERATURE CITED

Balla SJ. 1998. Administrative procedures and the political control of the bureaucracy. *Am. Polit. Sci. Rev.* 92:663–73

Camerer CF. 2003. *Behavioral Game Theory.* New York: Russell Sage

Caro RA. 2002. *Master of the Senate.* New York: Alfred Knopf

Cook BJ, Wood BD. Principal-agent models of political control of bureaucracy. *Am. Polit. Sci. Rev.* 83:965–78

Downs GW, Rocke DM. 1994. Conflict, agency, and gambling for resurrection: the principal-agent problem goes to war. *Am. J. Polit. Sci.* 38:362–80

Fehr E, Gachter S, Kirchsteiger G. 1997. Reciprocity as a contract enforcement device. *Econometrica* 65:833–60

Franzese R. 1999. Partially independent central banks, politically responsive governments, and inflation. *Am. J. Polit. Sci.* 43:681–706

Hammond TH, Knott JH. 1996. Who controls the bureaucracy? *J. Law Econ. Org.* 12:119–66

Holmstrom B. 1979. Moral hazard and observability. *Bell J. Econ.* 10:74–91

Jensen H. 1997. Credibility of optimal monetary delegation. *Am. Econ. Rev.* 87:911–20

Keefer P, Stasavage D. 2003. The limits of delegation: veto players, central bank independence, and the credibility of monetary policy. *Am. Polit. Sci. Rev.* 97:408–23

Kiewiet DR, McCubbins MD. 1991. *The Logic of Delegation.* Chicago: Univ. Chicago Press

Knott JH. 1986. The Fed chairman as a political executive. *Admin. Soc.* 18:197–232

Mashaw JL. 1990. Explaining administrative process: normative, positive, and critical stories of legal development. *J. Law Econ. Org.* 6:267–98

Mayer KR. 1995. Closing military bases (finally): solving collective dilemmas through delegation. *Legis. Stud. Q.* 20:393–413

McCubbins MD, Noll RG, Weingast BR. 1987. Administrative procedures as instruments of political control. *J. Law Econ. Org.* 3:243–77

McCubbins MD, Schwartz T. 1984. Congressional oversight overlooked: police patrols versus fire alarms. *Am. J. Polit. Sci.* 28(1):165–79

Miller GJ, Whitford AB. 2002. Trust and incentives in principal-agent negotiations. *J. Theor. Polit.* 14:231–67

Moe TM. 1984. The new economics of organization. *Am. J. Polit. Sci.* 28:739–77

Moe TM. 1985. Control and feedback in economic regulation: the NLRB. *Am. Polit. Sci. Rev.* 79:1094–16

Moe TM. 1987a. An assessment of the positive theory of congressional dominance. *Legis. Stud. Q.* 12:475–520

Moe TM. 1987b. Interests, institutions and positive theory. In *Studies in American Political Development*, ed. K Orren, S Skowronek, 2:236–99. New Haven, CT: Yale Univ. Press

Morris IL. 1999. *Congress, the President, and the Federal Reserve*. Ann Arbor: Univ. Mich. Press

North D, Weingast BR. 1989. Constitutions and commitment: the evolution of institutions governing public choice in seventeenth century England. *J. Econ. Hist.* 49:803–32

Radner R. 1985. Repeated principal-agent games with discounting. *Econometrica* 53:1173–98

Sappington DE. 1991. Incentives in principal-agent relationships. *J. Econ. Persp.* 5:45–66

Schelling TC. 1960. *The Strategy of Conflict.* London: Oxford Univ. Press

Scholz JT. 1991. Cooperative regulatory enforcement and the politics of administrative effectiveness. *Am. Polit. Sci. Rev.* 85:115–36

Shavell S. 1979. Risk sharing and incentives in the principal and agent relationship. *Bell J. Econ.* 10:55–73

Shipan C. 2004. Regulatory regimes, agency actions, and the conditional nature of congressional influence. *Am. Polit. Sci. Rev.* 98:467–80

Spence DB. 1997. Agency policy making and political control: modeling away the delegation problem. *J. Public Admin. Res. Theory* 2:199–219

Spence M, Zeckhauser R. 1971. Insurance, information, and individual action. *Am. Econ. Rev.* 61:380–87

Weber M. 1958. *From Max Weber: Essays in Sociology.* New York: Oxford Univ. Press

Weingast BR. 1984. The congressional-bureaucratic system: a principal-agent perspective (with applications to the SEC). *Public Choice* 44:147–88

Weingast BR, Moran MJ. 1983. Bureaucratic discretion or congressional control? Regulatory policymaking by the Federal Trade Commission. *J. Polit. Econ.* 91:765–800

Whitford AB. 2002. Decentralization and political control of the bureaucracy. *J. Theor. Polit.* 14:167–94

Wood D. 1988. Principal, bureaucrats, and responsiveness in clean air enforcement. *Am. Polit. Sci. Rev.* 82:213–37

Annu. Rev. Polit. Sci. 2005. 8:227–49
doi: 10.1146/annurev.polisci.8.082103.104829
First published online as a Review in Advance on Dec. 8, 2004

CITIZENSHIP AND CIVIC ENGAGEMENT

Elizabeth Theiss-Morse and John R. Hibbing

*Department of Political Science, University of Nebraska, Lincoln, Nebraska
68588-0328; email: etheissmorse@unl.edu, jhibbing@unl.edu*

Key Words   civic participation, voluntary associations, political participation,
social capital, group heterogeneity

■ **Abstract**   Is it possible for people to join their way to good citizenship? Contemporary thinking, both academic and popular, often leaves the impression that it is, but a careful investigation of the evidence raises serious doubts. In actuality, belonging to voluntary associations is a woefully inadequate foundation for good citizenship for three primary reasons: People join groups that are homogeneous, not heterogeneous; civic participation does not lead to, and may turn people away from, political participation; and not all groups promote democratic values. Good citizens need to learn that democracy is messy, inefficient, and conflict-ridden. Voluntary associations do not teach these lessons.

INTRODUCTION

The prevailing view of good citizenship holds that people should be actively involved in politics, they should be knowledgeable, and they should hold strong democratic values, such as tolerance (see, e.g., Almond & Verba 1963; Barber 1984; Berelson et al. 1954; Conover et al. 1991; Mill 1910, 1962; Thompson 1970). At the heart of virtually all strategies for achieving these objectives is some form of participation. Active participation in society presumably encourages citizens to participate further, boosts their knowledge of society and its issues, and makes them more tolerant of and attached to their fellow citizens. But a successful approach for securing public participation in the first place has not been conceived.

Not for want of effort. Scholars and observers have devised inventive ways for people to become involved, including citizen juries, policy forums (Dahl 1970), coffee klatches (Mathews 1994), electronic town hall meetings (Etzioni 1972), deliberative opinion polls (Fishkin 1995), people's courts, issue caucuses, grassroots opinion columns in newspapers, "confessional talk shows" (Eliasoph 1998, p. 260), telepolls, national issue referenda (Cronin 1989), full-fledged teledemocracy (Becker & Slaton 2000), neighborhood assemblies of 5000 people meeting weekly, and a civic videotex service (Barber 1998). The most recent proposal, offered by Ackerman & Fishkin (2004), is to have a national holiday every presidential election year on which Americans would gather in public spaces to deliberate on the major issues of the election.

The problem is that all of these perfectly well-intentioned recommendations involve somewhat artificially structured efforts to get people to deliberate. As we have described elsewhere (Hibbing & Theiss-Morse 2002), securing broad-based, meaningful deliberation on contentious issues from ordinary citizens, most of whom have little desire to engage in public policy discussions, is next to impossible no matter how creative the contrived forum may be.

But there is another popular strategy for securing citizen engagement. We speak of efforts to get citizens to join the many civic and voluntary organizations that already exist, to band together with acquaintances and neighbors for whatever purpose they might choose. The issues need not be contentious or national in scope, and the participants need not be randomly selected or primed with customized information. People simply need to meet face to face and the rest will fall into place.

Putnam unleashed a storm of approving excitement when he documented a sharp decline in associational life in the United States and elsewhere and described the improvements that would accompany a reversal of that sorry trend (Putnam 2000, Putnam et al. 2003). Enthusiasm for redressing deficiencies in citizenship through a renewed involvement in voluntary associational life—what came to be termed civic participation[1]—was widespread and intense. Many scholars jumped at the prospect of rejuvenating citizenship through voluntary association membership. The added allure was that citizens would not need to do anything particularly distasteful in the process, such as becoming involved in politics. The idea that civic engagement and therefore good citizenship could be achieved so painlessly seemed too good to be true. Indeed, in this review essay we argue it *is* too good to be true.

Like deliberation theorists, proponents of civic participation make broad, sweeping claims concerning the beneficent effects of community and group involvement on the development of good citizenship. We begin by discussing these claims before turning to the three key limitations on the potential of civic participation to inspire good citizenship:

1. The voluntary associations people are most likely to join are decidedly homogeneous and therefore incapable of generating the benefits claimed.

2. Civic participation in some circumstances actually turns people off of politics, leaving them less, not more, politically engaged.

3. Many groups do not pursue the kinds of goals that would be necessary for promoting democratic citizenship.

For true civic engagement to be achieved, a more realistic view is necessary.

---

[1]Civic participation, according to Campbell (2004), consists of "nonremunerative, publicly spirited collective action that is not motivated by the desire to affect public policy" (p. 7). As such, it forms a sharp contrast with political participation, which consists of "those activities by private citizens that are more or less directly aimed at influencing the selection of governmental personnel and/or the actions they take."

CIVIC PARTICIPATION AS A CURE-ALL

Civic participation is all the rage. If we could just get people engaged in their communities, the argument goes, many of society's ills would vanish. Supporters of civic participation believe it would lead to reduced crime rates (McCarthy et al. 2002, Rosenfeld et al. 2001), more efficient and responsive democratic governments (Putnam et al. 1993, Ch. 4; Ray 2002), and an empowered and vibrant citizenry, including young people (Youniss et al. 2001). On the basis of this positive and appealing message, foundations and institutes have poured hundreds of millions of dollars into the study of civic participation. Academic communities have supported it through scholarship, required volunteering, and service-learning programs. In the political arena, the perception of voluntary associations as a cure-all for democratic societies is embraced by both the right and the left.

The right sees voluntary associations as a means of devolving power to local communities and as an alternative to government-sponsored programs. George H.W. Bush's "thousand points of light" and George W. Bush's "faith based and community initiatives" are clear examples. Don Eberly, who served as the deputy director of the White House Office of Faith Based and Community Initiatives, claims:

> The voluntary sector...often prompts us toward acts of generosity, mutual assistance, self-sacrifice, and compassion—which we would not otherwise undertake in the workplace or during the course of an average day. American greatness hangs not only upon a successful market and a strong government but upon the cultivation of humane and moral habits in the voluntary sector.... The voluntary sector, more than any other sector in society, possesses the capability to train our moral sensibilities and develop in us an active respect for the dignity of others. (Eberly & Streeter 2002, pp. ix–x)

The left views voluntary associations as a means of fostering grassroots politics and increasing the voice of ordinary people. Bill Clinton, through his national service program AmeriCorps, was no less eager than the Bushes to promote voluntary activity. Turning to Tocqueville, Galston makes strong social and political claims for voluntary associations:

> They can serve as sites of resistance against tyranny and oppression. By strengthening social bonds, they can reduce the dangers of anomie. They can foster the bourgeois virtues that modern democratic societies need, and they can nourish the habits of civic engagement. They can help form opinions that shape deliberation in democratic public institutions. They provide vehicles for the noninstrumental expression of moral convictions as norms for the wider society. And of course, they offer opportunities for groups of citizens to conduct important public work through collective action outside the control of government. (Galston 2000, p. 69)

Of the many claims about the positive effects of civic participation, we focus on three claims about voluntary associations that are prevalent in the recent academic literature. Volunteering is said to instill civic values, enhance political behavior, and improve democracy and society.

Impact on Civic Values and Attitudes

According to the proponents of voluntary associations, interacting with others for a broader cause than one's own selfish interests pushes people to shift their attitudes. They learn to appreciate differences and they acquire basic democratic values. One of the most important of these values is tolerance. In a democratic society where freedom of speech and association are so important, the willingness to grant basic civil liberties to people whose views are abhorrent is essential. The argument for the positive effects of associational life on tolerance goes like this. People join groups for a variety of reasons and interact with others in pursuit of the group's goals. Since most people do not automatically talk about politics when in a nonpolitical group, and often actively avoid it (see, e.g., Eliasoph 1998, Ch. 2), they become friends with fellow members before learning that these new friends hold different political views. Since they now like these people, they become more tolerant of these different views. This tolerance then spreads to people who are not members of the group (see Mutz 2002b for an excellent overview of cross-cutting networks and tolerance). And research shows that indeed people involved in civic participation are more tolerant (Hooghe 2003), although there are disagreements over the specific mechanisms that lead to this increased tolerance.

Improved civic values do not stop with tolerance. A primary argument in the social capital literature is that civic participation increases interpersonal trust. "Trustworthiness lubricates social life. Frequent interaction among a diverse set of people tends to produce a norm of generalized reciprocity" (Putnam 2000, p. 21). People come to believe that if they do a good deed for someone or for their community, that action will be reciprocated. When people distrust others, they will not assume that a good deed will someday be reciprocated, and they will be less likely to do the good deed at all. A great deal has been written on trust (e.g., Braithwaite & Levi 1998, Fukuyama 1995, Jackman & Miller 1998, Levi & Stoker 2000, Uslaner 2002), so we will not review this area in depth. Suffice it to say that research confirms the correlation between civic participation and interpersonal trust: People who are involved in voluntary associations are more likely to trust people than those who are not involved (Brehm & Rahn 1997, Claibourn & Martin 2000, McLaren & Baird 2003). Some scholars also argue that involvement in voluntary associations increases trust in government (Joslyn & Cigler 2001), although others find that it decreases government approval (Brehm & Rahn 1997).

There is evidence that civic participation improves other attitudes. Joslyn & Cigler (2001) find that participation in voluntary associations increases members' sense of political efficacy and decreases the polarization of their evaluations of the candidates running for president. People involved in associations may experience first-hand the effect they can have as a group, and this sense of efficacy may then be generalized to the political arena. As far as the decreased polarization of opinions is concerned, research has shown that through interaction in voluntary associations, members share information that they can then use when making political judgments (Ray 2002). In addition, members of voluntary associations are more likely to watch television news and to read newspapers, which increases the breadth of information available for discussion (Norris 1996). This sharing of information could contribute to moderating evaluations as people hear from trusted others that the opposing candidate is not as horrible as some might think.

Impact on Political Behavior

Proponents of civic participation contend that voluntary association involvement not only improves attitudes but also enhances political behavior. People who join voluntary associations are more likely to participate in politics (Teorell 2003, Verba et al. 1995), especially time-based and volunteer-oriented activities (Ayala 2000). One argument put forward to explain this phenomenon is that people learn civic skills in voluntary associations, such as how to lead a meeting or write an effective letter, and they can transfer these skills to the political realm (Verba et al. 1995, 309–17). Once people have these skills in their behavioral repertoire, they feel more comfortable using them in different realms.

A problem with the civic skills argument is that even passive members in groups increase their political participation, though it is hard to imagine that passive members improve their civic skills nearly as much as active members do. An alternative argument is that voluntary group membership, even if passive, increases the opportunity to be recruited to participate more broadly in politics (Teorell 2003; Verba et al. 1995, p. 144). In essence, the more people you know, the more people there are who might get you to sign up for some political activity.

It is likely that both arguments are correct: group members learn civic skills and they are more likely to be recruited. The main point, though, is that civic participation is related to political participation. People who are active in voluntary associations also tend to be active in politics. It is not just group participation that increases, though. An in-depth study of the relationship between voluntary association involvement and turnout found that group involvement increases the likelihood of voting (Cassel 1999). Part of the reason for this link is that group membership increases participatory predispositions, civic skills, and the likelihood of being recruited. Much of the relationship, however, remained unexplained.

Impact on Democracy and Society

Supporters believe voluntary association membership not only helps the individual members, it also helps society more broadly. Voluntary associations strengthen social bonds and develop a sense of community (Dekker & van den Broek 1998, Galston 2000, Ray 2002); they breed cooperation and ease coordination to help solve collective action problems in communities (Brehm & Rahn 1997); and they increase social capital in communities (Wollebaek & Selle 2002). Democracy is also strengthened when civil society is strong. The primary argument is that democratic institutions must be more effective, responsive, and accountable when citizens are highly involved in groups (Dekker & van den Broek 1998, Galston 2000, Ray 2002). And because power is more broadly distributed, freedom and liberty are safeguarded (Ray 2002). Indeed, a major contention of Tocqueville was that a strong associational life prevented government from becoming too strong, because although individuals can be ignored, groups cannot be (Tocqueville [1840] 1969, pp. 513–17). There is power in numbers.

WHY CIVIC PARTICIPATION IS NOT A PANACEA

Who could possibly be opposed to the idea of people working together to better their community? Virtually no one. The concerns expressed about civic partic- ipation have not been attached to the typically laudable immediate community outcomes but rather to proponents' optimistic claims for the positive effects of civic participation. Does involvement in community organizations and voluntary associations really make people better citizens and make democracies stronger?

We take aim at the three central claims outlined above: that interaction among di- verse people will automatically enhance democratic values, that civic participation fosters political participation, and that democracy is strengthened by widespread involvement in voluntary associations. A significant array of recent research calls into question the beneficial effects of civic participation, and in some cases even raises the specter of decidedly negative effects.

Diversity and the Enhancement of Citizen Values

Putnam (2000) draws a crucial distinction between "bonding" and "bridging" so- cial capital. Bonding activities are "inward looking and tend to reinforce exclusive identities and homogeneous groups," whereas bridging activities are "outward looking and encompass people across diverse social cleavages" (p. 22). Most scholars believe bridging groups are far more likely to have a positive effect on interpersonal trust (McLaren & Baird 2003) and other important personal and societal traits, although not everyone agrees that groups must be heterogeneous. Those in the latter group claim that multiple association memberships even in ho- mogeneous groups can increase political activity (Teorell 2003) and social capital formation (Wollebaek & Selle 2002). Regardless, the general argument is still the same: When people come into contact with those who are different, they become better citizens, as indicated in their values and their behavior.

But involvement in heterogeneous (or multiple homogeneous) groups is not the nostrum some scholars hope it is. Social capital theorists assume that through face-to-face interaction with diverse people, group members develop ingroup trust that is then generalized to the broader community. Membership in a homogeneous group would not improve the extent to which trust is generalized to people outside the group. The social psychology research on groups, however, shows how difficult it can be to get people involved in heterogeneous groups, and even if they do join a heterogeneous group, they are likely to gravitate toward and interact with fellow group members who are similar to them.

Study after study shows that people are attracted to those who are similar to them (e.g., Berscheid & Reis 1998, Byrne 1997). People choose friends who resemble them in their demographics, attitudes, values (Newcomb 1961), personality (Boyden et al. 1984), interpersonal style, and communication skills (Burleson & Samter 1996). Although proximity is important initially, it is similarity that really matters over the long haul.

Similarity is not limited to the interpersonal level. Research shows that group members tend to be similar in terms of age, sex, beliefs, and opinions (see, e.g., George 1990, Levine & Moreland 1998, Magaro & Ashbrook 1985). Popielarz (1999), for example, found that women tend to belong to gender-segregated groups and that women's groups tend to be homogeneous in terms of age, education level, marital status, and work status as well. Beyond women's groups, evidence suggests that civic groups are becoming more homogeneous over time. It certainly appears to be the case that group membership is more stratified by class now than in the past (Skocpol 2002, Costa & Kahn 2003). And when income inequality increases, it is the lower classes whose group involvement is most likely to diminish (Brown & Uslaner 2002), meaning not only that the membership within a given group becomes more homogeneous but that on the aggregate level the membership across all groups becomes more homogeneous. Voluntary association members tend to be better educated and wealthier than nonmembers (Hooghe 2001; Oxendine 2004; Verba et al. 1995, pp. 190, 432), and those who are most active in organizations overwhelmingly come from a higher socioeconomic status. In Canada, 6% of adults account for 35%–42% of all civic involvement (Reed & Selbee 2001). The same people tend to be active across a variety of organizations.

Groups tend to be homogeneous for two reasons. First, groups attract people who are similar to the existing group members, both because people like to be around people like themselves and because people who are similar are more likely to be recruited into the group. Second, groups encourage similarity among members (Moreland 1987) by shunning those who break the norms too often and pressuring the repeat offenders to leave the group (Schachter 1951). Campbell (2004) argues convincingly that homogeneous groups can more easily reach a consensus on the norms that guide behavior. They are also better able to enforce the norms and to sanction those who defy them. It is no accident, then, that people tend to be members of homogeneous groups. They are drawn to them, recruited into them, and pressured to conform within them. Breaking out of this pattern is not easy (Eliasoph 1998).

Work on social identity offers a compelling explanation for why adhering to group norms is so important to people. According to social identity theory, people who are members of a group easily come to identify with the group, characterize fellow group members in a positive way, and like fellow group members (Tajfel 1982,

Turner 1999). Because they like and identify with the group, they want to be good group members, which means that they want to behave the way a good member behaves. This entails following the group norms and fitting the stereotype they hold of the group (Hogg & Abrams 1988, Ellemers et al. 1999). People who strongly identify with the group tend to see themselves as prototypical members of the group and to behave as prototypical members. They also see consensus in their group (Turner 1999) and perceive it as homogeneous and cohesive (Branscombe et al. 1999).

Homogeneous groups can therefore offer their members a relatively conflict-free environment. When someone does raise an issue likely to create conflict, association leaders quickly let him or her know that the group is not interested in discussing it (Eliasoph 1998, p. 33; Mansbridge 1983, Chs. 6, 13). Group members feel uncomfortable when conflict arises and quickly want to return to the warm feelings generated by consensus. Conflict avoidance is not uncommon. As Mutz (2002a) points out, conflict threatens social relationships, and people use a variety of avoidance techniques to remove the conflict situation. People do not want to feel uncomfortable and tense among those in their social network. It is easier simply to disengage.

It is this tendency to disengage that reveals a problem with the heterogeneous versus homogeneous group argument. To get the full benefits of associational involvement, the groups must be diverse so that people interact with others who hold different opinions. But what if heterogeneous groups dampen civic participation?[2] Researchers have found that heterogeneous communities have significantly lower civic participation rates than homogeneous communities (Alesina & La Ferrara 2000, Campbell 2004, Costa & Kahn 2003). Conflicting viewpoints can dampen the desire to become involved in civic participation. People from heterogeneous communities are less likely to want to attend a voluntary association meeting only to have fellow members get upset with each other. When people have to interact face to face, consensus becomes very desirable.

At the group level, researchers tend to focus not on diversity's effects on civic participation but on its effects on particularized and generalized trust (see, e.g., Fukuyama 1995, Putnam 2000, Uslaner 2002). Heterogeneous groups, these researchers argue, are much more likely to generate generalized trust than are homogeneous groups. However, comparative research on the relationship between

---

[2]The nature of existing research makes it somewhat difficult to address this possibility definitively. Researchers have used various combinations of civic and political activities in their participation measures, which have led to mixed results. For example, when looking at community-level heterogeneity, Oliver (1999) measures civic engagement by using four variables: voting in local elections, contacting locally elected officials, attending community board meetings, and attending voluntary association meetings. Costa & Kahn (2003) examine volunteering, group membership, trust, and voter turnout. Campbell (2004) carefully distinguishes between the two types of participation and finds that community heterogeneity increases political participation but decreases civic participation. As political scientists have long recognized, conflicting viewpoints can increase excitement about politics, thereby increasing the desire to participate in politics.

group diversity and trust has generated mixed findings at best. McLaren & Baird (2003) find that, among Italians, heterogeneous group members have higher generalized trust than homogeneous group members; however, Stolle (2001) finds that this relationship obtains only in certain countries. In Sweden, group diversity (defined as involvement of foreigners in the groups) was significantly and positively related to generalized trust, but in the United States, group diversity (defined as racial diversity) was significantly and *negatively* related to generalized trust.

Because people are unlikely to be involved in heterogenous groups, the more important concern is what happens to homogeneous group members. The prospects are not positive. People involved in homogeneous associations do not learn generalized trust, do not learn how to cooperate with people who are different, and do not confront a wide array of information from many different perspectives. Homogeneous group members develop "strong" trust (Granovetter 1973), but this acts to exclude those who are different and to turn group members inward.

Indeed, some evidence indicates that group homogeneity increases participation directed toward helping group members but diminishes participation directed toward bettering the community as a whole. Uslaner (2001)[3] studied fundamentalist religious groups in the United States, which are homogeneous. He reports, "Religion leads people to do good deeds, but generally only for their own kind" (p. 28), although mainline churches sometimes promote outgroup helping behaviors (see also Cassel 1999). Wuthnow (1998, p. 148) quotes a woman named Mary who volunteers at a church-based center. When Wuthnow asks about diversity at the center, Mary "says church people are often interested in helping the needy, but hold back because the needy are not like them or because they fear the needy may become involved in their church: 'It's very hard for them to embrace someone who maybe doesn't look like them or doesn't look like they would like to be a part of their relationships.'"

The evidence that joining voluntary associations, whether homogeneous or heterogeneous, increases civic values is decidedly weak. The claim, made by proponents of civic participation, that participation in bridging groups increases social capital and civic participation is a hard one to sell. People rarely become involved in heterogeneous groups, and even when they do, they tend to interact with those members who are similar to them. And although some scholars argue that involvement in heterogeneous groups increases generalized trust (Brehm & Rahn 1997), others point out that it is those people who are trusting in the first place who tend to join heterogeneous groups (Stolle 1998, 2001; Stolle & Rochon 1998).

The Civic versus Political Divide

Aside from the problems introduced by people's attraction to homogeneous groups, some scholars worry that placing a strong emphasis on civic participation could

---

[3]See also Uslaner's unpublished manuscript, *Civic engagement in America: why people participate in political and social life* (University of Maryland, College Park, MD).

actually make people *less* likely to become politically involved. Walker (2002) relates her experiences with the Center for American Women and Politics' National Education for Women leadership program: "The participants, students from colleges and universities across the country, were actively engaged in volunteer and service learning activities. But any talk of political engagement—voting, running for office, lobbying—and they recoiled with disgust. Service was a friendly, morally pure alternative to the messy, dirty, compromise-filled world of politics" (p. 183).

Arguments abound for why voluntary association activity might not increase political activity. We focus on four of these arguments: (*a*) Associations increasingly limit members' participation; (*b*) the federal government's role is less likely to stimulate political participation; (*c*) civic participation leads to negative views of democratic governance; and (*d*) increased generalized trust enables more free riders.

First, Putnam (2000, p. 51) and Skocpol (2003) suggest that as associations moved from membership-directed organizations with face-to-face interactions to Washington-based organizations with elites making all of the decisions, association members lost the opportunity to learn the civic skills necessary for participating in politics and the connections with the political sphere that more grassroots associations offered them. Writing a check to an organization, whether it be the National Rifle Association, the Environmental Defense Fund, or the American Association of Retired Persons, does not have the same political engagement benefits for members as does regular interaction with fellow members of community-based groups.

Others go further and argue that membership in associations harms political activity, perhaps because of shifts in the government's role in society. Berry and his fellow working group members state that, "as the nonprofit sector has grown and increasingly taken over a wide range of social service delivery, the concomitant increase in civic indicators such as volunteering and charitable fundraising may have come at the expense of political voice" (Berry et al. 2003, p. 6). If federal, state, and local governments were providing the services that are now offered by many nonprofit organizations, people would be motivated to become politically involved in these various levels of government to have a say in how the money was spent and to try to influence policies related to these programs. When many of the services are handled by private, nonprofit organizations, whose boards are not elected by the general populace, there is little incentive for people to become involved in politics, since governments seemingly have little to do with them.

Tocqueville, the presumed intellectual forebear of the associational life advocates, takes a less than benign view of government's role in fostering associational membership (see McLean et al. 2002). According to Tocqueville ([1840] 1969, p. 523),

> the governments of today look upon [political] associations much as medieval
> kings regarded the great vassals of the Crown; they feel a sort of instinctive

abhorrence toward them and combat them whenever they meet. But they bear a natural goodwill toward civil associations because they easily see that they, far from directing public attention to public affairs, serve to turn men's minds away therefrom, and getting them more and more occupied with projects for which public tranquillity is essential, discourage thoughts of revolution.

Politicians are free to do what they want to do while the public, disengaged from politics, tranquilly pursues its interests in civic organizations.

The third argument points out that people are disgusted with politics in the United States. People view democratic processes as messy, inefficient, unprincipled, and filled with conflict (Hibbing & Theiss-Morse 2002). Voluntary associations offer an alternative that provides a conflict-free environment. "For young people eager to make a difference, but living in a culture that regards politics with distrust and disgust, service may present a welcome way of 'doing something' without the mess and conflict of politics" (Walker 2002, p. 187). People can feel good about doing something to help their community even as they disengage from the political system itself.

The problem is that reinforcing the message that consensus and harmony are good whereas conflict and disagreements are bad undermines what democracy is all about.

> The focus on consensus and helping implies that citizens should get along because of a shared base of interests and needs. But, in a diverse, pluralistic society, citizens often do not share similar interests or needs. Democratic institutions exist not to level out differences between citizens, but to find ways to bring competing needs to the table and make difficult decisions about the allocation of resources and the production of values. Democracy does not demand that citizens like each other. The process is supposed to be messy, conflictual, and difficult. . ... This is a very different message than the one that is conveyed by most of the service rhetoric and research, and by a culture that seeks to avoid or denigrate politics. (Walker 2002, p. 187)

Because younger people are the ones who are especially pressed into volunteering and service—what with service learning programs, "volunteering" required by their schools, and national programs such as AmeriCorps—they are the ones who are learning that politics is bad, and this bodes ill for their participation rates in the future. Keeter et al. (2002) note a disturbing finding: "While the country has succeeded in transmitting the value of civic engagement to successive generations, there is strong evidence that it has failed in keeping the chain of political engagement unbroken" (p. 2). Youth who are engaged in political groups at school tend to be politically active, but most student groups are nonpolitical in nature. Indeed, volunteers in general consider their volunteer work to be nonpolitical (Keeter et al. 2002, p. 19). But it is in the political realm where important policy decisions are made that will have a fundamental effect on people, young and old. Volunteering in a soup kitchen will help hungry individuals in a town but will do nothing to address broader problems of homelessness and poverty. These issues need government.

Adherents of the final argument start with the premise proposed by social capital theorists that voluntary association membership increases generalized trust. People learn to trust the members of their associations, and this trust then gets generalized to the population as a whole. It is this generalized trust, according to social capital theorists, that ultimately makes the economy and the democratic system run smoothly. Some scholars argue, though, that this generalized trust might actually diminish political participation because those who trust political and community leaders may not see a need to participate (Claibourn & Martin 2000, Muhlberger 2003). Participating in politics incurs costs, including the costs of gaining political knowledge and spending time on politics, so it makes sense to become a free rider if others can be trusted to make the right decisions. When people's varying general tendencies to join groups are controlled for, it is the distrustful who are more likely to feel compelled to participate (Hibbing & Theiss-Morse 2001).

No matter who is right (and the four arguments are not mutually exclusive, so they may all be right), it is important to reiterate that there is a positive, though not robust, relationship between voluntary association membership and political participation (Campbell et al. 2003, Jenkins et al. 2003, Keeter et al. 2002). Generally, people who participate in voluntary associations are also likely to participate in politics. The relationship holds true for heterogeneous (Oliver 1999) and homogeneous (Hero & Tolbert 2004, Hill & Leighley 1999, Mutz 2002a, Rubenson 2003) communities. Among Chinese-Americans with high levels of generalized trust, Uslaner & Conley (2003) found that large social networks, membership in ethnically homogeneous groups, and participation in politics went hand in hand. The political participation of blacks and Hispanics also appears to be unharmed by their involvement in homogeneous groups. Ayala & Benavides (2003) found that the homogeneity of an association's membership did not negatively affect political participation, and, even among whites, group homogeneity actually increased political participation rates.

Age groups, however, may be a different matter. Scholars have been particularly concerned about the effects of civic participation on political participation among the young. Older people are more likely to be active both politically and civically. Younger people, however, often find civic participation more appealing than political participation, and the percentage of young people who are involved in both is significantly lower (11%) than the percentage of people aged 38 and older (~18%) (Jenkins et al. 2003). What remains unclear is whether young people's appreciation for civic participation will continue as they age. For many young people, volunteering in the community is not a choice but a school requirement. Campbell et al. (2003) note that making political participation mandatory decreases people's internal motivation to participate in other ways. Students who are forced to be involved in civic activities might well lose their intrinsic motivation to be involved in the future and may find themselves even less likely to participate in civic or political activities.

Nonetheless, the relationship between civic and political participation leads some to believe that getting people involved in voluntary associations will lead to their increased political involvement. But clearly there is a self-selection bias that makes it difficult to determine the effect of voluntary association membership on political participation rates (Stolle 2003). People who join voluntary associations are by nature active people. Research has shown convincingly that active people tend to join groups of whatever stripe and they also tend to participate in politics (Keeter et al. 2002, Jenkins et al. 2003). Joiners participate in politics because it is another form of joining; therefore, it is a mistake to assume a causal relationship between voluntary association membership and political participation. Further, the more active people are, the more likely they are to have large social networks, which McClurg (2003) has shown is more strongly related to political participation than group membership per se.

The Importance of Group Goals

Scholars have increasingly recognized that not all groups are created equal. There is a "dark side" to civic participation (Fiorina 1999) that can create "unsocial" capital (Levi 1996). The effects of group membership, according to these scholars, depend on the group's goals and values. If the group's goals are democratic, politically oriented, and tolerant of others, then its members will learn democratic values and become politically active as a benefit of being involved in the group. If, however, the group is antidemocratic, disdainful of politics, and intolerant of outsiders, then its members will learn undemocratic values and probably become disengaged from the political system. "We might be right to be wary about too much bonding among people who disdain others" (Uslaner & Dekker 2001, p. 181).

Armony (2004, p. 20), drawing on an article by Michael Berryhill in *The New Republic*, dramatically illustrates the problem.

> Members of the Aryan Brotherhood, the Aryan Circle, the Texas Syndicate, the Crips, the Bloods, and the Confederate Knights of America—all prison gangs in Texas—attend meetings, elect officers, have a system of rules and sanctions, exercise internal accountability, make the bulk of their decisions democratically, distribute benefits according to merit, and write their own constitutions. Members learn to trust each other and thus discover the benefits of cooperation and reciprocity. They develop organizational skills by handling paperwork and taking responsibility for specific tasks. They also learn to exercise their rights. . . .

Indeed, upon leaving prison, one member of the Knights, John King, decided to start a chapter of the Knights in his home town and brutally murdered an African-American, James Byrd, presumably to gain credibility for his new group among the Knights (Armony 2004). These groups are voluntary associations that develop many of the citizenship virtues extolled by those who promote civic participation, yet no one argues that this type of voluntary association is positive for democracy or for good citizenship.

Part of the problem is that not all groups are formed for positive reasons, and some groups are formed for decidedly negative ones. Rosenblum (1998) argues, "Insulated from government, people form associations to meet all sorts of emotional and ideological needs, amplify selfish interests, and give vent to exclusionary impulses" (p. 14). Kohn (2002) contends that "the protection of status is among the core purposes of association" (p. 296). There is no guarantee that groups will be tolerant or actively democratic, so voluntary association membership will not necessarily enhance democracy. A common example offered by critics of civic participation is Nazi Germany. Associational life was rich and vibrant, yet clearly many of the German people were not tolerant toward those who were different, nor did they exhibit key democratic attitudes and behaviors: "active associational life worked to reinforce rather than overcome narrow particularistic interests" (Knack 2002, p. 773; see also Armony 2004).

Activists tend to be drawn from a higher socioeconomic status, and higher-status individuals tend to hold most strongly the dominant cultural values of their time and place. Therefore, associational values may simply reflect the dominant cultural values (Rossteutscher 2002). If these are democratic and civil, then group members will exhibit higher levels of democratic and civil values than nonmembers, not because of their associational experiences but because they are more likely to have held the dominant values in the first place.

Undemocratic and intolerant groups have constituted an undeniable component of associational life in the United States. Kaufman (2002) argues persuasively, drawing on historical evidence, that when association life is particularly vibrant and growing, "competitive voluntarism" takes hold. The growth of associations sets off competition among the numerous groups for "members, money, institutional legitimacy, and political power" (p. 7). Group members more actively than ever try to recruit new members into the association. These associations become more homogeneous and segregated by demographic characteristics because of recruitment practices and pressures to adhere to group norms. People who do not fit the group often quit, "further reinforcing the selection pressures incumbent on the membership-attainment process" (p. 7).

In the heyday of voluntary associations in the United States (between the Civil War and World War I), competitive voluntarism increasingly differentiated society along gender, ethnic, and racial lines. The outcome of this segregation was not benign. Kaufman (2002, p. 9) contends that

> by encouraging Americans to bond together along gender, ethnonational, and ethnoreligious lines, associationalism further disposed them to fear one another and thus to fear government itself—particularly any government program that might require the redistribution of income or collectivization of risk. The result was a nation with a rather bizarre sense of self, one rooted not in the benefits of citizenry or in the value of inclusion but in libertarian paranoia and mutual distrust.

He further argues that many of the problems deplored by many Americans today are the result of this group segregation: racial prejudice, special-interest politics, a love of guns, a fear of government, a weak labor movement, and limited government-based social services and welfare provisions.

Armony (2004) similarly argues that associations can serve undemocratic ends, especially when people in dominant positions in society feel threatened. Armony's in-depth case study of the Citizens' Councils, a prosegregationist group, shows how associations can actively pursue undemocratic ends in an attempt to shore up the status quo against the threat of change. To help with recruitment, the segregationist Citizens' Councils often worked with associations that Putnam (2000) and others have held up as exemplars of civic participation, such as the Rotary Club, Kiwanis, Lions, and American Legion. Clearly, "the 'dark side' of civil society may not be easily set apart from the 'bright side'" (Armony 2004, p. 80). The Citizens' Councils, with the aid of allied organizations, could effectively impose economic sanctions against people who favored integration. Because of the social networks created by these associations, word spread quickly and efficiently that anyone who supported integration should be denied jobs, service, and credit. The social networks were highly effective, especially in smaller towns. In America's cities, middle- and upper-class homeowners formed associations to defend their property and to lobby local governments to influence zoning and incorporation. As Berman (1997) notes, one "factor to examine in determining when civil society activity will bolster or weaken a democratic regime. . .is the political context within which that activity unfolds" (p. 567). When the political context is uncivil, including when political elites join with associations to maintain the status quo against democratic change, the outcome of civic participation will be negative.

A separate, although clearly related, issue is the extent to which the processes used by the associations are democratic. The common argument is that organizations run democratically will help create better democratic citizens than will organizations run in an authoritarian fashion. Putnam's (1993) work on Italy showed that vertical and hierarchical organizations, such as the Catholic Church, are less likely to foster social capital and civic engagement than horizontal and voluntary organizations. In vertical organizations, subordinates can shirk, bosses can exploit, and norms of reciprocity and trust never develop. Additionally, social networks are denser in horizontal organizations as people interact as equals.

A related argument is that members of democratic organizations are more likely than members of undemocratic organizations to learn civic skills that can then be transferred to the political realm (Verba et al. 1995). Horizontal organizations, such as many Protestant churches, allow many members to obtain important civic skills (e.g., letter writing and meeting organization) because a wide range of members are involved in decision making. Vertical organizations, such as the Catholic Church, limit this skill development to a select few. Workplace democracy similarly gives workers an opportunity to learn how to make decisions in a democratic fashion (see, e.g., Witte 1980, Greenberg 1986). Organizational democracy empowers members.

These arguments presume that people generalize to other settings what they have learned in civic associations or democratic workplaces. Rosenblum (1998), however, is highly critical of what she calls the "transmission belt" model of civil society, the idea that "the beneficial formative effects of association spill over from one sphere to another" (p. 48). She adds, "As if we can infer enduring traits from behavior in a particular setting. As if moral dispositions shaped in one context, public or private, are transferable to dissimilar ones. The 'transmission belt' model is simplistic as a general dynamic." Rosenblum doubts that "the habits of trust culti-vated in one social sphere are exhibited in incongruent groups in separate spheres" (p. 48), as the model's proponents contend. Empirical support for her skepticism comes from Carlson (2003), who finds that organizational democracy is unrelated to members' democratic attitudes and behaviors. Indeed, he concurs with Rosen-blum that "citizens are quite capable of distinguishing the grounds for associational autocracies from the philosophy that undergirds democratic government" (p. 47).

CIVIC ENGAGEMENT AND THE GOOD CITIZEN

Disputes over the view that civic participation invariably makes people better citizens ultimately rest on our understanding of human behavior. We conclude this review with a plea that researchers make explicit their assumptions regarding human nature in order to strengthen theories and research. Proponents of civic par-ticipation, and social capital in particular, tell a comforting tale, one that promises better citizens, a healthier community, and a stronger democracy with little hard work involved. But this is not a realistic tale.

> Social capital is an undemanding master...social capital is fundamentally about how we conduct our everyday life. . . . It does not take years of pushing hard for structural reforms. It does not involve upsetting the political coalitions that have strong stakes in existing institutions. It does not require the painful choices that economists...say that poor countries must make in the transition to free markets. Instead, we can mobilize people to do what they would do naturally—join with others in pleasurable activities. (Uslaner & Dekker 2001, p. 178)

The problem, as we have seen, is that the evidence does not clearly support the contention that associational activity leads to more democratic citizens and polities. Some research even suggests such activity leads to less democratic citizens and polities.

Where did proponents go wrong? The error was probably in their implicit theory of human behavior. Participatory democrats and advocates of civic participation often assume that people want to be involved in politics. They believe that many more people would participate if only the right conditions were created. For ex-ample, Ackerman & Fishkin (2002; see also 2004) recognize that not all of the American voting population would participate in the first Deliberation Day, a day set aside as a national holiday to bring people together to deliberate about the major issues of the election, but they still expect that fully half of the electorate would participate. Since approximately 100 million Americans typically vote in presidential elections, this means that about 50 million would be involved in Deliberation Day (Ackerman & Fishkin 2002, p. 139). But people's willingness to participate in exchange for a substantial monetary payment ($150 has been mentioned) should not be confused with good citizenship. We think it highly unlikely that there would be a great outpouring of interest in spending a national holiday deliberating about politics with a bunch of strangers for purposes other than acquiring $150. Aside from those who need the money, the people most likely to show up are those who would have voted anyway. And participants who attend Deliberation Day for the money are unlikely to deliberate much, feeling cowed by those more loquacious and better informed.

Our own experience with running numerous focus groups around the country is telling. These sessions lasted less than two hours. Participants volunteered and were paid for their time. We served refreshments and tried to make everyone feel comfortable and welcome. Yet almost invariably, one or two of the focus group participants refused to say a word throughout the whole discussion. When asked by other participants to say something, the nontalkers would either shrug and not respond or they would say they did not know anything about politics. Throughout the discussion, they frequently doodled on a piece of paper or looked dreadfully bored. The nontalkers were there because another participant had dragged them along or because they wanted the money. They were clearly uncomfortable and wanted to leave.

As we have argued elsewhere (Hibbing & Theiss-Morse 2002), many people are not interested in politics. Americans are busy. "The demands of job and family, not to mention the appeal of sports, movies, TV, and a host of other things that compete with politics for the public's attention, all tend to make politics a fairly low priority for the average voter" (Donovan & Bowler 2004, p. 35). It is not helpful to imagine people to be something they currently are not and have no desire to become. To assume that people would ever flock voluntarily (i.e., without monetary incentive) to Deliberation Day, or any other political event, is simply wrong. If they are interested, they will come. If not, they won't. In 2004, the war in Iraq and the polarizing candidacy of George W. Bush overcame many citizens' preference to stay away from politics. When these or comparable factors are absent, that motivation will be gone.

Those committed to promoting civic engagement typically believe that current governmental institutions and societal arrangements conspire to dull people's innate desire to engage. They note problems such as prejudicial barriers to engagement, unstimulating political choices, biased media, and elites who prefer to be undisturbed by the hoi polloi. As real as these problems may be, acknowledging them does nothing to support the claim that if they were removed people would be civically engaged. Instead, the belief that civic engagement is the default behavior is simply an article of faith, and advocates apparently see little need for empirical tests of it. They so enjoy politics and civic life themselves that they are unable to fathom the possibility that others do not share their "curious passion" (Mueller 1999, p. 185).

But a careful review of the empirical evidence suggests that many people lack the motivation to engage in civic life generally and politics specifically. In those political contexts where institutions are absent, such as town hall meetings, participants' reactions are cynical and negative (see Mansbridge 1983, Ch. 6). Less articulate people feel belittled, the decision-making process is roundly ridiculed by participants, and many people quit going or advocate that decisions be made in other forums (see Hampson 1996). Institutions cannot really be the problem in town hall meetings; there are no parties, media, interest groups, or elaborate rules, only dozens of neighbors meeting to discuss shared problems. And still the people are disgusted. In fact, comments subsequent to participation in a town hall meeting are interchangeable with the comments people make about Congress, indicating that the problem runs much deeper than institutions. Making collective decisions in the context of heterogeneous opinions is a challenging and frustrating experience, one that many people could do without.

Faced with the realization that politics is inherently distasteful to many ordinary people, civic engagement advocates have been eager to believe that belonging to self-selected, homogeneous, service-oriented organizations could substitute. As we have documented in this review, despite the prevalence of this belief in recent decades, it is open to empirical challenge. Voluntary groups perform wonderful services and have undeniable value to society, but their effect on democratic politics is tenuous and possibly negative. If these groups teach something other than democratic values or if they serve to weaken ties among diverse people by strengthening ties among those who are similar, then the effects of voluntary associations are not just irrelevant to democracy, they are deleterious. The real nature of voluntary groups is rarely investigated. The most detailed effort is that of sociologist Nina Eliasoph, who, after describing the recruitment, socialization, norms, procedures, and discussions of numerous voluntary groups, concludes that "in an effort to appeal to regular, unpretentious fellow citizens without discouraging them, [groups] silence public-spirited deliberation" (Eliasoph 1998, p. 63). Instead of discussing "potentially upsetting issues," groups confine their concerns to "practical fundraising projects" that support noncontroversial goals (p. 31). To be sure, more needs to be learned about the nature and specific political consequences of voluntary associations, but the empirical literature currently available is not a source of consolation for believers. Even group sympathizers such as Eliasoph, when they analyze the subject, realize that joining groups is not a way of embracing politics but rather a way of avoiding politics.

The message for students of empirical democratic theory is that there is no shortcut to true civic engagement. Neither tweaking institutions nor promoting volunteerism is likely to help. Ordinary people understandably do not want to get involved in politics, and most voluntary group activity is essentially apolitical. Although this conclusion may seem depressing, it does not have to be. We firmly believe that by starting from the empirical realities, social scientists can reach a new, more appropriate, and therefore more useful set of recommendations for improving civic engagement. The key is letting people know that becoming active in their favorite clubs does not fulfill their citizenship obligations. The route to enhancing meaningful civic life is not badgering people to become engaged because politics is fun and easy; it is asking people to become engaged because politics is dreary and difficult.

The *Annual Review of Political Science* is online at
http://polisci.annualreviews.org

LITERATURE CITED

Ackerman B, Fishkin JS. 2002. Deliberation Day. *J. Polit. Philos.* 10:129–52

Ackerman BA, Fishkin JS. 2004. *Deliberation Day.* New Haven, CT: Yale Univ. Press

Alesina A, La Ferrara E. 2000. Participation in heterogeneous communities. *Q. J. Econ.* 115:847–904

Almond GA, Verba S. 1963. *The Civic Culture: Political Attitudes and Democracy in Five Nations.* Princeton, NJ: Princeton Univ. Press

Armony AC. 2004. *The Dubious Link: Civic Engagement and Democratization.* Stanford, CA: Stanford Univ. Press

Ayala LJ. 2000. Trained for democracy: the differing effects of voluntary and involuntary organizations on political participation. *Polit. Res. Q.* 53:99–115

Ayala LJ, Benavides E. 2003. *Diversity, civic engagement, and the social capital debate.* Presented at Annu. Meet. Am. Polit. Sci. Assoc., Philadelphia

Barber BR. 1984. *Strong Democracy: Participatory Politics for a New Age.* Berkeley: Univ. Calif. Press

Barber BR. 1998. *A Passion for Democracy.* Princeton, NJ: Princeton Univ. Press

Becker TL, Slaton CD. 2000. *The Future of Teledemocracy.* Westport, CT: Praeger

Berelson BR, Lazarsfeld PF, McPhee WN. 1954. *Voting: A Study of Opinion Formation in a Presidential Campaign.* Chicago: Univ. Chicago Press

Berman S. 1997. Civil society and political institutionalization. *Am. Behav. Sci.* 40:562–74

Berry J, Reich R, Levi M, Levinson M, Brintnall M. 2003. *APSA Standing Committee on Civic Education and Engagement: report of the Working Group on the Nonprofit, Voluntary, and Philanthropic Sectors.* Presented at Annu. Meet. Am. Polit. Sci. Assoc., Philadelphia

Berscheid E, Reis HT. 1998. Attraction and close relationships. In *The Handbook of Social Psychology,* ed. DT Gilbert, ST Fiske, G Lindzey, pp. 193–281. New York: McGraw-Hill. 4th ed.

Boyden T, Carroll JS, Maier RA. 1984. Similarity and attraction in homosexual males: the effects of age and masculinity-femininity. *Sex Roles* 10:939–48

Braithwaite V, Levi M, eds. 1998. *Trust and Governance.* New York: Russell Sage Found.

Branscombe NR, Ellemers N, Spears R, Doosje B. 1999. The context and content of social identity threat. See Ellemers et al. 1999, pp. 35–58

Brehm J, Rahn W. 1997. Individual-level evidence for the causes and consequences of social capital. *Am. J. Polit. Sci.* 41:999–1023

Brown M, Uslaner EM. 2002. *Inequality, trust, and civic engagement.* Presented at Annu. Meet. Am. Polit. Sci. Assoc., Boston

Burleson BR, Samter W. 1996. Similarity in the communication skills of young adults: foundations of attraction, friendship, and relationship satisfaction. *Commun. Rep.* 9:127–39

Byrne D. 1997. An overview (and underview) of research and theory within the attraction paradigm. *J. Soc. Pers. Relat.* 14:417–31

Campbell DE. 2004. *What you do depends on where you are: community heterogeneity and participation.* Presented at Annu. Meet. Midwest Polit. Sci. Assoc., Chicago

Campbell DE, Galston W, Niemi R, Rahn W. 2003. *APSA Standing Committee on Civic Education and Engagement: report of the Working Group on Electoral Processes.* Presented at Annu. Meet. Am. Polit. Sci. Assoc., Philadelphia

Carlson N. 2003. *Testing the transmission belt: Do internal associational institutions affect national political attitudes and behaviors in the United States?* Presented at Annu. Meet. Am. Polit. Sci. Assoc., Philadelphia

Cassel CA. 1999. Voluntary associations, churches, and social participation theories of turnout. *Soc. Sci. Q.* 80:504–17

Claibourn MP, Martin PS. 2000. Trusting and joining? An empirical test of the reciprocal nature of social capital. *Polit. Behav.* 22:267–91

Conover PJ, Crewe IM, Searing DD. 1991. The nature of citizenship in the United States and Great Britain: empirical comments on theoretical themes. *J. Polit.* 53:800–32

Costa DL, Kahn ME. 2003. Civic engagement and community heterogeneity: an economist's perspective. *Perspect. Polit.* 1:103–11

Cronin T. 1989. *Direct Democracy: The Politics of Initiative, Referendum, and Recall.* Cambridge, MA: Harvard Univ. Press

Dahl RA. 1970. *After the Revolution: Authority in a Good Society.* New Haven, CT: Yale Univ. Press

Dekker P, Uslaner EM, eds. 2001. *Social Capital and Participation in Everyday Life.* London: Routledge

Dekker P, van den Broek A. 1998. Civil society in comparative perspective: involvement in voluntary associations in North America and Western Europe. *Voluntas* 9:11–38

Donovan T, Bowler S. 2004. *Reforming the Republic: Democratic Institutions for the New*

America. Upper Saddle River, NJ: Pearson Prentice Hall

Eberly DE, Streeter R. 2002. *The Soul of Civil Society: Voluntary Associations and the Public Value of Moral Habits.* Lanham: Lexington Books

Eliasoph N. 1998. *Avoiding Politics: How Americans Produce Apathy in Everyday Life.* Cambridge, UK: Cambridge Univ. Press

Ellemers N, Spears R, Doosje B, eds. 1999. *Social Identity: Context, Commitment, Content.* Oxford: Blackwell

Etzioni A. 1972. Minerva: an electronic town hall. *Policy Sci.* 3:457–74

Fiorina MP. 1999. Extreme voice: a dark side of civic engagement. In *Civic Engagement in American Democracy*, ed. T Skocpol, MP Fiorina, pp. 395–426. Washington, DC: Brookings Inst.

Fishkin JS. 1995. *The Voice of the People.* New Haven, CT: Yale Univ. Press

Fukuyama F. 1995. *Trust: The Social Virtues and the Creation of Prosperity.* New York: Free

Galston WA. 2000. Civil society and the "art of association." *J. Democr.* 11:64–70

George JM. 1990. Personality, affect, and behavior in groups. *J. Appl. Psychol.* 75:107–16

Granovetter MS. 1973. The strength of weak ties. *Am. J. Sociol.* 78:1360–80

Greenberg ES. 1986. *Workplace Democracy: The Political Effects of Participation.* Ithaca, NY: Cornell Univ. Press

Hampson R. 1996. Decline of the town meeting. *Lincoln J. Star*, Oct. 14, p. 2A

Hero RE, Tolbert CJ. 2004. *Community, race, and political participation in America: examining social capital and social diversity.* Presented at Annu. Meet. Midwest Polit. Sci. Assoc., Chicago

Hibbing JR, Theiss-Morse E. 2001. *Do uncaring politicians make people want to get involved or drop out of politics?* Presented at Annu. Meet. Am. Polit. Sci. Assoc., San Francisco

Hibbing JR, Theiss-Morse E. 2002. *Stealth Democracy: Americans' Beliefs about How*

Government Should Work. Cambridge, UK: Cambridge Univ. Press

Hill KQ, Leighley JE. 1999. Racial diversity, voter turnout, and mobilizing institutions in the United States. *Am. Polit. Q.* 27:275–95

Hogg MA, Abrams D. 1988. *Social Identifications: A Social Psychology of Intergroup Relations and Group Processes.* London: Routledge

Hooghe M. 2001. "Not for our kind of people": the sour grapes phenomenon as a causal mechanism for political passivity. See Dekker & Uslaner 2001, pp. 162–75

Hooghe M. 2003. Value congruence and convergence within voluntary associations: ethnocentrism in Belgian organizations. *Polit. Behav.* 25:151–75

Jackman RW, Miller RA. 1998. Social capital and politics. *Annu. Rev. Polit. Sci.* 1:47–73

Jenkins K, Andolina M, Keeter S, Zukin C. 2003. *Is civic behavior political? Exploring the multidimensional nature of political participation.* Presented at Annu. Meet. Midwest Polit. Sci. Assoc., Chicago

Joslyn MR, Cigler A. 2001. Group involvement and democratic orientations: social capital in the postelection context. *Soc. Sci. Q.* 82:357–68

Kaufman J. 2002. *For the Common Good? American Civic Life and the Golden Age of Fraternity.* New York: Oxford Univ. Press

Keeter S, Zukin C, Andolina M, Jenkins K. 2002. *The civic and political health of the nation: a generational portrait.* http://www.puaf.umd.edu/CIRCLE/research/products/Civic_and_Political_Health.pdf

Knack S. 2002. Social capital and the quality of government: evidence from the states. *Am. J. Polit. Sci.* 46:772–85

Kohn M. 2002. Panacea or privilege? New approaches to democracy and association. *Polit. Theory* 30:289–98

Levi M. 1996. Social and unsocial capital: a review essay of Robert Putnam's *Making Democracy Work. Polit. Soc.* 24:45–55

Levi M, Stoker L. 2000. Political trust and trustworthiness. *Annu. Rev. Polit. Sci.* 3:475–507

Levine JM, Moreland RL. 1998. Small groups. In *The Handbook of Social Psychology*, ed. DT Gilbert, ST Fiske, G Lindzey, pp. 415–69. New York: McGraw-Hill. 4th ed.

Magaro PA, Ashbrook RM. 1985. The personality of societal groups. *J. Pers. Soc. Psychol.* 48:1479–89

Mansbridge JJ. 1983. *Beyond Adversary Democracy.* Chicago: Univ. Chicago Press

Mathews D. 1994. *Politics for People: Finding a Responsible Public Voice.* Urbana: Univ. Ill. Press

McCarthy B, Hagan J, Martin MJ. 2002. In and out of harm's way: violent victimization and the social capital of fictive street families. *Criminology* 40:831–65

McClurg SD. 2003. Social networks and political participation: the role of social interaction in explaining political participation. *Polit. Res. Q.* 56:449–64

McLaren LM, Baird VA. 2003. *Growing trust: the role of communal participation in the creation of interpersonal trust.* Presented at Annu. Meet. Am. Polit. Sci. Assoc., Philadelphia

McLean SL, Schultz DA, Steger MB, eds. 2002. *Social Capital: Critical Perspectives on Community and "Bowling Alone."* New York: NY Univ. Press

Mill JS. 1910. *Utilitarianism, Liberty, and Representative Government.* London: Everyman's Library, Dent, Dutton

Mill JS. 1962. *Essays on Politics and Culture.* Garden City, NY: Doubleday

Moreland RL. 1987. The formation of small groups. In *Review of Personality and Social Psychology*, ed. C Hendrick, pp. 80–110. Newbury Park, CA: Sage

Mueller JE. 1999. *Capitalism, Democracy, and Ralph's Pretty Good Grocery.* Princeton, NJ: Princeton Univ. Press

Muhlberger P. 2003. *Political trust vs. generalized trust in political participation.* Presented at Annu. Meet. Am. Polit. Sci. Assoc., Philadelphia

Mutz DC. 2002a. The consequences of cross-cutting networks for political participation. *Am. J. Polit. Sci.* 46:838–55

Mutz DC. 2002b. Cross-cutting social networks: testing democratic theory in practice. *Am. Polit. Sci. Rev.* 96:111–26

Newcomb TM. 1961. *The Acquaintance Process.* New York: Holt, Rinehart, Winston

Norris P. 1996. Does television erode social capital? A reply to Putnam. *PS: Polit. Sci. Polit.* 29:474–80

Oliver JE. 1999. The effects of metropolitan economic segregation on local civic participation. *Am. J. Polit. Sci.* 43:186–212

Oxendine AR. 2004. *Inequality and isolation: the impact of economic stratification on bridging and bonding social capital.* Presented at Annu. Meet. Midwest Polit. Sci. Assoc., Chicago

Popielarz PA. 1999. (In)voluntary association: a multilevel analysis of gender segregation in volunteer organizations. *Gender Soc.* 13:234–50

Putnam RD. 2000. *Bowling Alone: the Collapse and Revival of American Community.* New York: Simon & Schuster

Putnam RD, Leonardi R, Nanetti R. 1993. *Making Democracy Work: Civic Traditions in Modern Italy.* Princeton, NJ: Princeton Univ. Press

Ray MR. 2002. *The Changing & Unchanging Face of U.S. Civil Society.* New Brunswick, NJ: Transaction

Reed PB, Selbee LK. 2001. The civic core in Canada: disproportionality in charitable giving, volunteering, and civic participation. *Nonprof. Volunt. Sec. Q.* 30:761–80

Rosenblum NL. 1998. *Membership and Morals: the Personal Uses of Pluralism in America.* Princeton, NJ: Princeton Univ. Press

Rosenfeld R, Messner SF, Baumer EP. 2001. Social capital and homicide. *Soc. Forces* 80: 283–309

Rossteutscher S. 2002. Advocate or reflection? Associations and political culture. *Polit. Stud.* 50:514–28

Rubenson D. 2003. *Community heterogeneity and political participation in American cities.* Presented at Annu. Meet. Am. Polit. Sci. Assoc., Philadelphia

Schachter S. 1951. Deviation, rejection, and communication. *J. Abnorm. Soc. Psychol.* 46:190–207

Skocpol T. 2002. United States: from membership to advocacy. In *Democracies in Flux*, ed. RD Putnam, pp. 103–36. New York: Oxford Univ. Press

Skocpol T. 2003. *Diminished Democracy: from Membership to Management in American Civic Life.* Norman: Univ. Okla. Press

Stolle D. 1998. Bowling together, bowling alone: the development of generalized trust in voluntary associations. *Polit. Psychol.* 19: 497–525

Stolle D. 2001. "Getting to trust": an analysis of the importance of institutions, families, personal experiences and group membership. See Dekker & Uslaner 2001, pp. 118–33

Stolle D. 2003. The sources of social capital. In *Generating Social Capital: Civil Society and Institutions in Comparative Perspective*, ed. M Hooghe, D Stolle, pp. 19–42. New York: Palgrave Macmillan

Stolle D, Rochon TR. 1998. Are all associations alike? Member diversity, associational type, and the creation of social capital. *Am. Behav. Sci.* 42:47–65

Tajfel H. 1982. *Social Identity and Intergroup Relations.* Cambridge, UK: Cambridge Univ. Press

Teorell J. 2003. Linking social capital to political participation: voluntary associations and networks of recruitment in Sweden. *Scand. Polit. Stud.* 26:49–66

Thompson DF. 1970. *The Democratic Citizen: Social Science and Democratic Theory in the Twentieth Century.* London: Cambridge

Tocqueville A. (1840) 1969. *Democracy in America.* New York: Anchor

Turner JC. 1999. Some current issues in research on social identity and self-categorization theories. See Ellemers et al. 1999, pp. 6–34

Uslaner EM. 2001. Volunteering and social capital: how trust and religion shape civic participation in the United States. See Dekker & Uslaner 2001, pp. 104–17

Uslaner EM. 2002. *The Moral Foundations of Trust*. Cambridge, UK: Cambridge Univ. Press

Uslaner EM, Conley RS. 2003. Civic engagement and particularized trust: the ties that bind people to their ethnic communities. *Am. Polit. Res.* 31:1–30

Uslaner EM, Dekker P. 2001. The "social" in social capital. See Dekker & Uslaner 2001, pp. 176–87

Verba S, Schlozman KL, Brady HE. 1995. *Voice and Equality: Civic Voluntarism in American Politics*. Cambridge, MA: Harvard Univ. Press

Walker T. 2002. Service as a pathway to political participation: what research tells us. *Appl. Dev. Sci.* 6:183–88

Witte JF. 1980. *Democracy, Authority, and Alienation in Work: Workers' Participation in an American Corporation*. Chicago: Univ. Chicago Press

Wollebaek D, Selle P. 2002. Does participation in voluntary associations contribute to social capital? The impact of intensity, scope, and type. *Nonprof. Volunt. Sec. Q.* 31:32–61

Wuthnow R. 1998. *Loose Connections: Joining Together in America's Fragmented Communities*. Cambridge, MA: Harvard Univ. Press

Youniss J, McLellan JA, Yates M. 2001. A developmental approach to civil society. In *Beyond Toqueville: Civil Society and the Social Capital Debate in Comparative Perspective*, ed. B Edwards, MW Foley, M Diani, pp. 243–53. Hanover, NH: Univ. Press New England

Annu. Rev. Polit. Sci. 2005. 8:251–70
doi: 10.1146/annurev.polisci.7.090803.161841

THE DEVELOPMENT OF INTEREST GROUP POLITICS IN AMERICA: Beyond the Conceits of Modern Times

Daniel J. Tichenor[1] and Richard A. Harris[2]

[1]Department of Political Science and Eagleton Institute of Politics, Rutgers University, New Brunswick, New Jersey 08901-8557; email: tichenor@polisci.rutgers.edu
[2]Department of Political Science, Rutgers University, Camden, New Jeresey; email: raharris@camden.rutgers.edu

Key Words   interest groups, lobbying, representation, development, parties

■ **Abstract**   Research on interest groups today neglects the important task of analyzing historical patterns and secular, long-term changes. We note critical measurement errors in how contemporary political science has assessed the origins and development of interest group politics in the United States. Interest group scholars lack the reliable longitudinal data available to such fields as electoral or congressional studies. We suggest multidimensional means of recovering the "lost years" of interest group research, compensating for the absence of comprehensive and systematic data on U.S. organized interests before the 1960s. In order to generate empirical and theoretical insights that are not constrained by a particular historical context, we propose a conceptual framework for studying "interest group systems" across time. We also examine the rich possibilities of investigating the interest group and party systems as interacting and autonomous vehicles of representation in American political development. Only by broadening the time horizons of research will scholars be able to develop reliable insights about patterns and transformations of American interest group politics.

INTRODUCTION: INTEREST GROUP STUDIES AND THEIR DISCONTENTS

Few areas of scholarship in political science have a more central, though checkered, lineage than the study of interest groups in the United States. Long after the celebrated writings of James Madison and Alexis de Tocqueville underscored the fundamental importance of organized interests to American political life, the discipline's earliest and most influential practitioners argued for groups as a crucial focus of investigation and analysis (Wilson 1885, Bentley 1908, Herring 1929, Merriam 1934, Key 1942). For all of the normative debate about whether interest groups facilitate or bedevil representative democracy, virtually no one has questioned their importance in American politics.

1094-2939/05/0615-0251$20.00   **251**

At its zenith a half-century ago, the "group basis of politics" emerged as the cornerstone of a modern political science that sought to liberate the discipline from formal constitutional-legalist traditions deemed irrelevant for understanding the authentic, informal workings of the political system. The activities of organized interests seemed to promise a more accurate view of political reality, and the "modernized theory of political pluralism" served as a powerful model of American democracy. Yet even as Truman (1951), Latham (1952a,b), Dahl (1961) and Lindblom (1963) breathed life into a pluralist tradition that defined American politics as the outcome of group struggle, critics justly noted that interest group scholars had produced "little real research" to vindicate their powerful theoretical speculations (Eldersveld 1958, Garceau 1958). In retrospect, one of the most glaring limitations of interest group studies in its heyday was the enormous gap between ambitious theory building and decidedly modest empirical findings.

During the 1960s, the discipline tired of the group approach as its theoretical claims grew increasingly strained, if not tautological, and as new research programs shifted attention from groups to individuals. More specifically, interest group studies were whipsawed in this decade by a fierce normative debate initiated by pluralists such as Dahl (1961), who saw the salutary democratic role of interests, and elite theorists like Mills (1956) and Schattschneider (1960), who attacked what they considered a representational bias embedded in interest group politics. Significantly, the extensive case study literature produced since the 1950s failed to resolve this fundamental theoretical dispute (Griffith 1939, Maass 1951, Bernstein 1955, Cater 1964, Freeman 1965, McConnell 1966, Redford 1969, Greenstone 1969, Fritschler 1975). Careful reviews of the pluralist-elitist donnybrook underlined how difficult it would be to measure group power (Bachrach & Baratz 1962, McFarland 1969). Subsequent work (Milbrath 1963, Bauer et al. 1963, Olson 1965, Lowi 1969, Salisbury 1969) transformed interest group studies during the decade, yet political science continued to lack systematic data on which to test its leading interest group theories. Like an exiled monarch, the study of interest groups was marginalized by the discipline during the 1970s. As the 1980s began, several scholars lamented that interest group research had essentially lain fallow for more than a decade and noted the irony that political scientists were looking away from organized interests precisely when they were becoming more significant in American politics (Wilson 1981, Arnold 1982). However, a resuscitation of interest group studies was already under way.

Reviving Interest Group Research

The past quarter century has seen a rebirth of interest group scholarship, including new, large-scale surveys of interest group behavior and other ambitious data collection efforts (Walker 1983, 1991; Schlozman & Tierney 1983, 1986; Knoke 1990; Baumgartner & Jones 1993; Heinz et al. 1993; Gray & Lowery 1996; Berry 1999). Such scholars as Baumgartner & Leech (1998) rightly worry that the hundreds of carefully circumscribed studies of group lobbying in recent decades rarely speak to one another, enervate cumulative science, and edge the field toward "elegant irrelevance." But they also recognize that contemporary political scientists have accumulated unprecedented amounts of reliable new data on group activities and that this information enables important advances in collective knowledge about organized interests in American politics. For Baumgartner & Leech, the Achilles' heel of today's interest group research is that its reaction against the all-encompassing and unscientific approach of earlier group scholars has produced too many investigations that offer clear and quantitatively sophisticated answers to overly narrow questions.

Rescuing interest group studies from the periphery of the discipline will require more cumulative research and a shared agenda that addresses important issues at the heart of American politics and contemporary political science. However, modern-day scholars would be mistaken to assume that empirical gaps are primarily the shortcoming of a bygone era when the interest group literature was "theory rich and data poor" (Arnold 1982). As we argue in this essay, one of the most profound challenges that confronts interest group studies today is the absence of systematic historical data on organized interests in American politics. Even when scholars have developed provocative hypotheses about historical cycles of American interest group politics (e.g., McFarland 1991), little or no effort has been to test them empirically.

Indeed, political scientists know precious little about the contours of interest group politics in the United States before the 1960s. Past theoretical work draws almost entirely on a relatively modest number of case studies that focus on a particular group or on a small set of groups active in a specific area of public policy. More recent comprehensive accounts of the world of interest groups in American politics are exceptions to the norm, and their earliest point of departure is the 1960s (Schlozman & Tierney 1986, Walker 1991). The relatively shallow historical baseline of contemporary empirical investigations of organized interests, however, has its own significant theoretical limitations, especially in terms of analyzing transformations and continuities in the interest group system over time (Petracca 1982a). Consider, for example, that students of American parties and elections have reliable data stretching back at least to the early nineteenth century, allowing for ambitious theory building and empirically rooted debate about topics such as electoral realignments and party systems over the course of U.S. history (see Burnham 1970, Mayhew 2002). By contrast, interest group scholars have little more than four decades of systematic, large-scale empirical data to analyze.

Unfortunately, contemporary interest group researchers in political science have neglected the important task of analyzing historical patterns and secular changes in American interest group politics over time. This shortcoming creates critical measurement errors in the assessment of the origins and development of interest group politics in America. In response, we suggest multidimensional means of recovering the "lost years" of interest group research, compensating for the absence of comprehensive and systematic data on U.S. organized interests before the 1960s. In order to generate empirical and theoretical insights that are not constrained by a particular historical context (including our own era), we then propose a conceptual framework for studying interest group systems across American political history. Finally, we consider the rich possibilities of investigating the interest group and party systems as interacting and autonomous vehicles of representation in American political development. Unless interest group scholars broaden the time horizons and analytic dimensions of their research, they will remain hamstrung in their efforts to generate empirical findings and theoretical insights that transcend a particular historical context or inform those outside the field.

STUDYING CHANGE AND CONTINUITY: EMPIRICAL DILEMMAS

One of the great ironies of the study of organized interests in America is that although its origins reach back to the birth of political science, the field has produced little systematic knowledge about long-term changes and continuities in the interest group system. As Petracca (1982b) wryly observes, nearly every generation of researchers has seen their own time as *the* critical juncture in remaking American interest group politics. Early in the twentieth century, the first ambitious empirical study of lobbying organizations in Washington noted a dramatic expansion of interest group mobilization, activity, and influence in the national policy-making process (Herring 1929). Every few decades since then, interest group scholars have heralded a momentous "explosion" or "dramatic transformation" of the Washington lobbying community (Crawford 1939, Turner 1958, Mahood 1967, Knoke 1986, Schlozman & Tierney 1986, Berry 1989a). Indeed, each wave of researchers, including the current one, has demonstrated little or no interest in seismic shifts described in previous decades and has trained a spotlight on what they perceived as unprecedented changes in their own day. This recurrent scholarly amnesia reflects the fact that interest group researchers have never had at their disposal the same reliable historical data available to fields such as congressional or electoral studies (Salisbury 1984, Crotty 1994, Baumgartner & Leech 1998, Berry 1999).

The foremost challenge to developing systematic historical data is the methodological predilection of interest group scholars to rely on survey instruments, field interviews, or contemporary reference works such as the *Encyclopedia of Associations, Washington Information Directory*, or *Washington Representatives*. Although these data sources have yielded important results in terms of quantifying the population of lobbying organizations at particular times, they impose serious limitations on how far back we can measure the scope and activities of interest groups. Interest group surveys have been conducted at irregular intervals, have posed varied sets of questions, have employed disparate categorization schemes, and have provided only a handful of reliable snapshots of the world of organized interests in the United States from the 1980s to the present (Schlozman &

Tierney 1986, Walker 1991). Although Herring (1929) pioneered field interviewing of lobbyists not long after World War I, several decades passed before political scientists once again talked to large numbers of interest group representatives. As one might expect, contemporary reference sources do not permit us to examine the long-term development of the national lobbying community. The oldest of the reference works regularly consulted by interest group researchers, the *Encyclopedia of Associations*, first appeared in 1959 and fails to provide crucial information across volumes about such issues as whether an organization is politically active or not. *Washington Representatives* and *Washington Information Directory* offer more data on the political activities of interest groups, but they are both younger and less comprehensive than their older counterpart.

At the end of the day, the preferred methods and data sources of the field do not permit us to analyze the origins and development of American interest group politics. They also tell us woefully little about attrition rates among organized interests over long periods of time. Attrition, as we discuss below, is a critical measure of representational bias that is rarely, if ever, adequately addressed in the literature.

Underestimating Group Mobilization in the Progressive Era

Given these constraints, it is little wonder that quantitative research on interest groups in national public life before the past half-century is hard to find. Walker's (1983, 1991) path-breaking work on interest group origins and maintenance is a notable exception. Determined to gather comprehensive evidence on group formation and mobilization in the United States, Walker turned to the *Washington Information Directory* to draw a representative sample of organized interests engaged in national politics from the nineteenth century to the present. He ultimately identified 913 lobbying organizations from this source, 564 of which completed the survey he administered. On the basis of survey reports from these organizations about when they were founded, Walker offered evidence that a relatively small number of organized interests comprised the Washington lobbying community before the 1950s and that the wellsprings of modern interest group politics could be traced to the post–World War II decades.

Two key elements of Walker's research design and historical analysis should give us pause (Tichenor & Harris 2002/2003). First, his survey focuses on existing associations from a contemporaneous reference source to calculate the aggregate number and variety of lobbying organizations that emerged in national politics over time. As Walker himself acknowledges, such a source obviously excludes interest groups that were once active in national policy making but have become inactive or no longer exist. Second, he omits several significant kinds of interest groups from his analysis, such as trade associations and labor unions.

To illustrate the limitations of looking at existing groups for information about long-term mobilization trends, we compiled a list of all interest groups printed in the *Washington Information Directory*. Instead of employing a survey instrument to determine the founding dates for our sample population of organized interests, we turned to the *Encyclopedia of Associations* for information on group origins. The *Encyclopedia* yielded founding dates for 71.2% of the groups in our sample (higher than the 64.8% response rate elicited in Walker's survey). Consistent with standard accounts and Walker's original findings, our results from these contemporary reference sources suggest that a comparatively modest number of interest groups emerged in national politics before the 1920s.

To test these findings, we collected fresh data from the Congressional Information Service's *U.S. Congressional Committee Hearings Index* (hereafter *CIS Index*). The *CIS Index* tracks congressional hearings since 1833 and identifies every organization that testified at these hearings. It offers one of the best available sources of systematic data on the number, variety, and issue attention of groups engaged in national affairs during years that interest group scholars recognize as a significant empirical blind spot. It allows us, moreover, to examine the same measures across time. Careful analysis of when interest groups first appear at congressional hearings also can serve as a proxy measure for the early mobilization of new groups. For hearings conducted between 1833 and 1917, we were able to track 10,656 appearances of 5372 organized interests. Of course, data collected from the *CIS Index* have their own limitations. One of the most prominent constraints is that the list of organizations derived from it excludes groups that were never invited or refused to testify before Congress. Interest group testimony undoubtedly was influenced by momentous changes in Congress, such as the number of standing committees and subcommittees, the relative professionalism of lawmakers, partisan control, and new policy agendas. However, the inability of the *CIS Index* to identify organized interests that never testified could only underestimate the number of lobbying organizations engaged in national politics. That is, the bias of the data should favor standard accounts by undercounting the number of organized interests in the nineteenth and early twentieth centuries.

Even with the conservative bias of this measure of how many interest groups participated in national politics before 1920, our findings from the *CIS Index* data suggest a far greater number than previous studies recognized. Figure 1 illustrates how dramatically the *Washington Information Directory* and the nature of Walker's survey-based measurements understate the emergence of new organized interests in national politics during the early twentieth century. Our findings from the *CIS Index* data highlight a substantial increase in the number of interest groups that first appeared at congressional hearings in the Progressive Era. Between 1890 and 1899, 216 interest groups testified for the first time at a congressional hearing. Almost three times as many groups (622) did so in the first decade of the twentieth century. During the following decade, more than 1000 new interest groups appeared before Congress. Moreover, there is considerable evidence of growing diversity, centralization, and professionalism of lobbying organizations in these years (Tichenor & Harris 2002/2003). In short, a decidedly modern and national interest group system emerged during the Progressive Era, one that has been either overlooked or underestimated by contemporary interest group scholars.

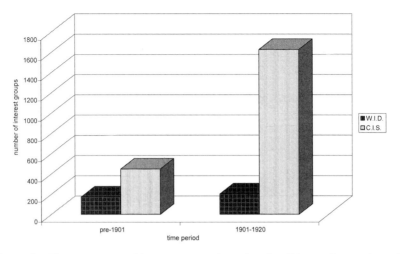

Figure 1   The emergence of interest groups in national politics: estimates from the *Washington Information Directory*, CQ Press, 2000 (dark grey) versus estimates from the *Congressional Committee Hearings Index, 23rd–64th Congresses*, U.S. General Printing Office, 1985 (light grey).

"Doing History" and Employing Multidimensional Methods

Walker's survey-based research, published between 1983 and 1991, devotes far more attention to the origins and development of American interest group politics than the work of nearly all his colleagues during those years. His work remains exceptional in this regard within a largely ahistorical field today. Our test of his methods against fresh *CIS Index* data underscores the extent to which contemporary interest group studies underestimate the past, both in terms of the scale and activity of organized interests and in terms of the empirical and theoretical payoffs of expanding research time horizons. Yet whereas Walker saw the absence of a reliable data base on lobbying organizations before the 1960s as a disquieting liability, most of today's interest group scholars routinely minimize the importance of earlier periods. Many subscribe to what might be called the interest group field's own Big Bang theory—a claim that the size, scope, and character of the modern interest group system were born of the advocacy explosion of the late 1960s and 1970s. Earlier developments are assumed to be so dissimilar from contemporary forms as to be of little or no theoretical utility (see, e.g., Berry 1999). Historically rooted quantitative work concerning voluntary associations, an admittedly narrow slice of the interest group universe, has done little to alter this view (Gamm & Putnam 1999, Skocpol 2004, Skocpol et al. 2000). Not unlike Neustadtian analysis of presidential leadership, this approach relegates organized interests and lobbying activities that precede the Big Bang of the 1960s to a quaint and irrelevant premodern category.

Political scientists who study lobbying organizations all but ignore the work of historians who see the first decades of the twentieth century as the pivotal period in which modern interest group politics emerged in America (Galambos 1970, Wiebe 1980, Link & McCormick 1983). They also routinely neglect significant and historically sophisticated qualitative research on social movements and interest groups in recent years (e.g., Clemens 1997, Sanders 1999). The turn away from history profoundly undermines the field's ability to develop meaningful insights about the evolution and tempos of our interest group system. To recover the lost years of American interest group politics will require a new generation of interest group scholars to recognize the value of richer longitudinal data and to embrace fresh methods of overcoming barriers to the accumulation of reliable historical evidence.

One way to address this problem is to develop multidimensional research strategies that are attentive to long-term processes of change and continuity. For example, the methodological strategy we have employed in our work involves three layers of historical research on organized interests in American political development (Tichenor & Harris 2005). The first layer is a comprehensive data base on interest groups, social movements, and private firms that have lobbied in Washington since the early nineteenth century. This data set tracks lobbying of roughly 100,000 organized interests over the years, drawing from a variety of archival collections, Washington directories, and the *CIS Index*. Building data sets from reliable reference works with broad time horizons, rather than contemporary sources inattentive to past groups, has been rarely undertaken by the field despite the obvious empirical and theoretical value of this approach (Baumgartner & Jones 1993, Tichenor & Harris 2002/2003). Still fewer interest group scholars today have experience conducting historical archival research, even though other vineyards of the discipline have benefited enormously by investigating records of the past (see, e.g., Skowronek 1982, Skocpol 1992, Weir 1992, Milkis 1993, Shefter 1994, King 1995, Clemens 1997, Sanders 1999, Smith 1999, Kryder 2000, Lieberman 2001, Tichenor 2002a, McMahon 2003).

This large data base provides a valuable view of the topography of Washington's lobbying community over time. Still, it leaves significant questions unanswered about why organized interests form and mobilize, how and why their goals and activities take a particular shape and why they change, what techniques and strategies they employ, what relationships they have with other organized interests, why they succeed or fail in gaining access or securing desired policy outcomes, and why they may disappear. The second layer of our research helps remedy these shortcomings by developing more fine-grained, middle-range data on the origins, activities, and attrition of 750 organized interests distributed across U.S. history. The final layer of research develops case studies that provide "thick" descriptions of the network and interactions of organized interests engaged in a given policy arena over time. These three layers of investigation have proven synergistic, not only for creating a broader and deeper portrait of organized interests in American political development, but in highlighting the limitations of any one measurement alone (Tichenor & Harris 2005).

PERIODIZING INTEREST GROUPS
IN AMERICAN POLITICS

In order to address gaps in the literature, we propose a new research agenda that investigates and compares distinctive periods of interest group mobilization, political activity, and attrition in U.S. history. Political scientists long have been drawn to the definition of historical periods and the study of regime transformation (Burnham 1970, Huntington 1981, Skowronek 1982, Harris & Milkis 1989, Morone 1990, Skocpol 1992, Shefter 1994, Smith 1999). Establishing periodization schemes imposes a theoretical order on the profound shifts that occur in political culture, institutions, and public policy. Equally important, analyzing regime transformation provides theoretical rigor for the normative comparison of different periods. From its inception, political analysis has sought to assess the values of democracy—participation, accountability, and popular sovereignty—across regimes. In contemporary American politics, it is clear that organized interests offer one of the most significant institutional opportunities for those values. We suggest that the study of interest group systems will provide important theoretical insights into the development of American politics—insights that have been conspicuously absent from the study of regime transformation in the United States.

Sources of Dynamism

We define an interest group system in terms of five key variables: the aggregate number of organized interests, the variety of organized interests, the nationalization of organized interests, the professionalism of organized interests, and the structural opportunities and barriers that confront organized interests. The first three of these variables are fairly straightforward quantitative measures of the level and kind of organized interest activity. The latter two are more complex indicators of the character of interest group systems and react on each other as groups develop resources to take best advantage of the structural milieu in which they operate. Together, these variables will enable us to distinguish systems of interest group politics in different historical periods.

NUMBER   Beginning with Herring's salutary efforts to quantify the Washington lobbying community in the 1920s, interest group theorists episodically have sought to estimate the overall size of the interest group universe (Herring 1929, Crawford 1939, Truman 1951, Salisbury 1984, Schlozman & Tierney 1986, Walker 1991, Petracca 1982b, Baumgartner & Leech 1998). At the most elemental level, aggregate population figures for organized interests provide a useful benchmark of growth and change in American interest group politics over time. Not only is the development of reliable data on aggregate numbers of politically active organized interests a logical first step in empirical analysis of interest group behavior, but it also has theoretical implications for understanding broader shifts in American politics. Recent studies have attempted to gauge the population of national lobbying groups since 1959 based on listings in the *Encyclopedia of Associations* (Baumgartner & Leech 1998, Skocpol 2004). These statistical summaries, however, exemplify two important empirical limitations. First, they leave us in the dark concerning group population dynamics in earlier decades. Second, they fail to distinguish organized interests that are in fact politically active and engaged in lobbying from those that are not. That is, the population totals developed in these studies reflect aggregations of both political and relatively apolitical associations—from business groups, environmental organizations, and unions to fan clubs, hobby associations, and Greek societies. If developed with reliable historical sources, longitudinal data on overall group numbers and formation rates since the nineteenth century offer a valuable means of demarcating interest group systems.

VARIETY   Scholarly efforts to categorize organized interests and to compare their proportions of the population and relative influence have been driven primarily by the long-standing pluralist/elitist debate. On the one hand are those who believe, with Mills (1956) and Schattschneider (1960), that the heavenly chorus sings with an upper-class accent or, with Lindblom (1963), that business enjoys a privileged position. On the other hand are those who maintain, like Bauer et al. (1963), that even if business groups are more numerous than others, they are hardly monolithic (Harris 1989, Vogel 1989, Hart 2004). Still others have adduced evidence to show that the influence of citizen groups has been severely underestimated (McFarland 1976, McCann 1986, Berry 1999). By periodizing American interest group politics, analysts are better positioned to assess representational bias by tracking across time differential rates of growth and changing proportions of citizen groups, trade associations, professional organizations, farm groups, labor unions, peak business associations, and other lobbying organizations.

NATIONALISM AND PROFESSIONALISM   Consistent with recurrent claims of an "explosion" of lobbying organizations in Washington, DC, different generations of political scientists have described interest group politics of their own time as undergoing unprecedented shifts toward greater nationalization and professionalism (Herring 1929, Crawford 1939, Truman 1951, Schlozman & Tierney 1986, Berry 1989a, Walker 1991). One of the empirical advantages of identifying distinct interest group regimes or systems in American political history is that it allows us to sort out these rival accounts by comparing relative levels of centralization and professionalism over time. Of course, professionally managed organizations need not confine their lobbying efforts to the national level. As Gray & Lowery (1996) found in their analysis of interest group populations in six states from 1980 to 1990, highly professional lobbying organizations are not confined to the Washington community; more than a few seek to influence the policy process in various states. Still, it is useful to classify systems based on the shifting number of organized interests with staff and offices in Washington and on the changing amount and kind of human, financial, and technological assets mobilized by lobby groups.

OPPORTUNITIES AND CONSTRAINTS   Although organized interests seek to transform political institutions to create a more hospitable policy environment, they also are influenced by the nature of the governing structures that confront them. As these institutions change over time, so too does interest group politics (and vice versa). Studies of interest group lobbying in the legislative and bureaucratic settings are most common in the field, but there is a growing literature on the involvement of interest groups in the courts and presidential politics (O'Connor & Epstein 1982, Pika 1984, Caldeira & Wright 1988, Peterson 1982, McGuire & Caldeira 1993, Tichenor 2002b). The relationship between organized interests and legislative, judicial, and executive politics has changed markedly over time and captures an important source of dynamism in the lobbying behavior and political influence of American interest groups since the nineteenth century.

New Leverage on the Mobilization, Bias, Policy Networks, and Attrition of Interest Groups

Analysis of distinct interest group regimes in American political history promises special empirical and theoretical leverage on many significant issues ranging from interest group mobilization to representational bias.

The political science literature on mobilization largely turns on the question of why new organized interests emerge as active participants in the policy-making process. Herring (1929) pointed to World War I and the government's need to coordinate industry to meet wartime production imperatives. While recognizing government sponsorship of interest group mobilization during times of war, Truman (1951) perceived the interest group mobilization that accompanied the Great Depression as a generalizable example of how economic crises and social disturbances can spur the creation of new lobbying organizations. Numerous scholars of the postwar decades focused on new government programs of the New Deal and subsequent reform periods as the major impetus for the political mobilization of new groups (see Truman 1951, Lowi 1969). According to Walker (1991), social movements—from the civil rights campaign to environmental activism—served as a powerful catalyst for the emergence of citizens groups and other organized interests. He also emphasized the role of financial support from patrons and government grants in facilitating the growth of various interest groups after the 1960s.

Clearly, each of these causal arguments is deeply informed by the most prominent forces and events of the historical period in which it was advanced. Attending to the history of American interest group politics paradoxically enables us to build empirical and theoretical insights that are not confined to particular moments in history. Recent scholarship on American political development suggests that interest group mobilization has preceded, accompanied, and followed significant policy innovation and state building in American politics (Clemens 1997, Sanders 1999, Tichenor & Harris 2002/2003). To develop stronger theories that explain these distinctive waves of mobilization, the field of interest group studies would do well to investigate the lost years.

Drawing analytical comparisons across distinct periods of American interest group politics also may contribute to a more robust treatment of the classic bias question. As noted above, the study of interest group systems allows careful examination of differential rates of growth and influence over long periods of time. However, it also raises questions about the limitations of familiar categories of organized interests. One of the strongest tendencies of the interest group literature is to evaluate bias in terms of the aggregate size of organized business interests (trade associations, firms, and peak associations) in relation to citizen groups (Baumgartner & Leech 1998). More nuanced studies look beyond population totals to assess whether citizen groups can marshal enough influence to serve as a legitimate countervailing power to organized business interests (McFarland 1976, Berry 1999). Yet, the historical approach to studying interest group politics complicates traditional views of business advantage by highlighting the enormous diversity of organizational types, tactics, and policy goals among business associations (Harris 1989, Vogel 1989, Hart 2004) and citizen groups (Tichenor & Harris 2005) both within specific periods and across American political development. More specifically, the historical approach may find evidence of increased diversity among these interests from the nineteenth century to the present. The empirical elusiveness of unified business and citizen group sectors underscores the need for richer theoretical understandings of biases in American interest group politics that transcend the familiar strictures of the pluralist-elitist debate that have pervaded the field since the 1950s. Periodizing interest group politics enables us to examine such crucial issues as whether the policy agendas of citizen groups have shifted over time from primarily industrial to postindustrial concerns (Inglehart 1977, Berry 1999). This sort of research agenda casts the upper-class biases that haunted Mills (1956) and Schattschneider (1960) in a decidedly new light, wresting the field from its routine focus on what proportions of the lobbying population are composed of business associations versus citizen groups.

Recent work on popular participation in voluntary associations since the earliest days of the American republic provides a fresh view on the dynamics of bias in national interest group politics (Gamm & Putnam 1999, Skocpol 2004). Lowi (1969) aptly characterized U.S. interest group politics after the New Deal as "socialism for the organized and capitalism for the unorganized." Offering a different perspective on emergent bias, Skocpol (2004) chronicles the post-1960s demise of mass-membership voluntary associations in favor of professionally managed lobbying organizations all but disengaged from ordinary citizens. The empirical roots of this research stretch deep into American history, but her research is trained on a very narrow—though important—slice of the total array of organized interests: voluntary associations with a mass membership of 1% or more of the population. Not surprisingly, this high membership threshold excludes the vast majority of voluntary citizen groups, not to mention other politically active membership groups, and has enabled Skocpol (2004) to focus on 42 exceptionally large voluntary associations. A broader assessment of the hypothesized decline of membership groups might take stock of vast numbers of farmer, labor, public interest, occupational and trade, and peak business associations that emerged since the early nineteenth century. Systematic research of organized interests in eras neglected by most political scientists could yield richer evidence about long-term trends concerning grassroots membership groups and centralized nonmembership organizations and about their meaning for democratic engagement in America.

One of the oldest traditions in interest group research is the study of so-called policy subgovernments or "iron triangles." As elucidated in numerous case studies of particular policy arenas, this model emphasizes insulated policy-making subsystems in which a few key interest groups share a symbiotic relationship with certain congressional committees and bureaucratic agencies and exercise enormous influence over outcomes (Griffith 1939, Maass 1951, Bernstein 1955, Cater 1964, Freeman 1965, Fritschler 1975). A quarter-century ago, the central tenets of the subgovernment model came under attack when Heclo (1978) argued that iron triangles were being supplanted by "issue networks" that drew greater public attention, provided opportunities for a larger and more diverse set of organized interests to participate, made policy knowledge the coin of the realm, and often led to conflict between rival coalitions (Berry 1989b). Scholarship on contemporary policy making, however, suggests that the death of subgovernments may be greatly exaggerated. Indeed, this work indicates considerable variation across policy arenas and describes a national policy-making process littered with a broad array of high-visibility issue networks and low-profile issue niches (see, e.g., Laumann & Knoke 1987, and Heinz et al. 1993).

For our purposes, it is revealing that scholars who examine the activities and relative influence of interest groups in a policy area over a long period tend to gain more theoretical leverage than those who do not (Bosso 1987, Hansen 1991). Moreover, our case study research on interest group politics and immigration reform suggests that the concept of issue networks is highly relevant to historical periods as early as the Progressive Era. Our findings challenge standard accounts of a secular shift in recent decades from iron triangles to issue networks. Instead, we discern a number of nascent issue networks emerging in the early twentieth century that evolved into subgovernments in later decades and then became issue networks again in recent decades (Tichenor & Harris 2002/2003, 2005). The relative openness of specific policy domains is of fundamental importance for democratic representation, and its variation over time merits careful investigation.

Studying interest group systems in American political development also may illuminate processes too often obscured by short time horizons. Consider, for example, the field's remarkably scant attention to interest group attrition. Walker (1983, 1991) understood that the disappearance of certain groups dramatically affected the contours of the Washington lobbying community but saw no easy way to quantify past attrition. Data analysis based on lobbying registrations at the state level (Gray & Lowery 1996) in the 1980s stands as a very significant exception to the standard neglect of group attrition. Yet, our macro-level research of the Washington lobbying community suggests that tens of thousands of organized interests either became politically disengaged or perished altogether over the course of American political development (Tichenor & Harris 2005). Explaining how and why particular sets of organized interests disappeared from the political process is at least as important as theorizing about mobilization. Attrition levels, moreover, may reveal a great deal about biases in the system. If citizen groups rise and fall in the policy-making process at a swifter pace than trade associations, for instance, the bias in outcomes might be profound. Analysis of attrition among various lobbying organizations grows richer and more reliable by developing systematic longitudinal data.

PARTIES AND INTEREST GROUPS: INTERWOVEN SYSTEMS OF REPRESENTATION

If the study of organized interests in American politics has been bedeviled by a somewhat cavalier ahistoricism, it is also impoverished by its disconnection with the study of political parties. It was not always thus, however. The architects of the American Constitution generally viewed political parties and interest groups with equal contempt and viewed the creation of a strong central government as a necessary, though problematic, objective to suppress their negative effects. To the extent that parties and interest groups were apt to promote their own partial or narrow interests over the common good, the founders viewed them as cut from the same cloth. Tellingly, in his famous tenth Federalist Paper, Madison used "faction" and "party" interchangeably to denote either citizen minorities or majorities impelled, by a common interest, to act against other citizens or the body politic. Clearly, for the founders, factions or parties were organizational embodiments of the "assertive selfishness of human nature," and devising methods for controlling their mischief—whether by increasing the geographical scope of the republic or by infusing the central government with requisite energy—ranked as a high priority for the fledgling nation if liberty and republican governance were to flourish (Ramney 1975). Thus began the now familiar antipathy in American political thought toward political parties and organized interests.

Subsequent generations of political scientists have rendered a decidedly different verdict about the role of interest groups and political parties in American political life. To be sure, the political science community has produced its share of Madisonian laments about parties and interest groups and offered hopeful prescriptions for resisting their ill effects. Yet, whereas most American leaders, pundits, reformers, and ordinary citizens have perceived these informal organizations as inevitable sores on the body politic, more than a few political scientists have recognized that interest groups and parties may serve as significant vehicles of political representation. Since the early twentieth century, political scientists have noted the capacity of interest groups and parties to establish crucial linkages between citizens and government. Key (1942) believed that it was crucial for his colleagues to study the relationship between interest groups and parties precisely because both were "informal and extraconstitutional" institutions that breathed democratic life into the formal constitutional system. A failure to research the reciprocal relations of parties and interest groups, he warned, would lead political scientists to the mistaken belief that these representative organizations were independent and unrelated. Truman (1951) later sounded similar themes in pointing to the profound importance of interactions between interest groups and parties for representative democracy in the United States. He called on the discipline to investigate carefully what he described as an evolving "interdependence" between these institutions. For the most part, these admonitions fell on deaf ears.

Few speculative claims have gained more currency in political science absent empirical evidence than Schattschneider's (1948) provocative assertion that an adversarial relationship exists between the American party and interest group systems. More precisely, he argued that expanding the political power of interest groups enervates that of parties and that the empowerment of parties directly hurts interest groups. The logic of this zero-sum model has appealed to countless scholars over the years, despite the lack of effort by Schattschneider (1942, 1948) or his later admirers to test it with systematic qualitative or quantitative longitudinal data. Schlozman & Tierney (1986), for example, note that the notion that party and organized interest strength are inversely proportional has become "common wisdom" in political science. The conflict between this zero-sum model and the interdependence arguments of Key and Truman has never been adequately examined or resolved.

Building in part on the work of Schattschneider (1948) and Key (1964), Lowi (1969) called attention to an ominous sign in the evolving relationship between political parties and organized interests. Lowi agreed with Schlessinger (1960) that political parties ought to include the "leading interests" in society in order to insure robust and representative policy debate. However, he decried the fact that the relationship had slipped into a distinctly corporatist mode, in which society's leading interests circumvented parties as an institution of interest aggregation. As Lowi wryly noted, it is one thing to extol pluralism within a political party, and quite another to accept pluralism embedded directly in the government's administrative apparatus. As troubling as this development was to Lowi, it should not have been surprising. Both Truman and Key noted the ambition of interest groups to directly affect the decisions of government officials. It is clearly more effective for groups to interact directly with governmental administrators and congressional overseers than to have their preferences filtered through the parties, where policy outcomes are the product of compromise. In their treatises on American democracy, Key, Truman, Schattschneider, and Lowi all provide interesting and provocative general commentary on the important historical relationship of parties to organized interests, but none truly develops a careful analysis of that relationship or its historical development.

Today, students of political parties and organized interests essentially have created two distinct subfields in political science, each with its own vast literature. Frankly, the ahistoricism of interest group scholarship may have contributed to this disconnect insofar as students of organized interests have never produced an empirical analysis of interest group politics that could match the depth or sophistication found in the theoretical work on the history of party systems. Contrary to the typical compartmentalization that defines the study of American politics, contemporary political science would benefit enormously by taking up Key and Truman's charge to systematically investigate the complex and shifting relationship between political parties and interest groups. This will require political scientists to transcend the comfortable isolation of distinct subfields and institutional specializations. The history of parties and organized interests reveals that they constitute two distinct elements in a wider system of representation, a system whose character has developed as a consequence of the changing relationship between the two. It makes sense, in our estimation, to think of parties and interest groups as intimately connected and interacting subsystems whose joint evolution has largely defined that wider system. Investigating the relationship between these critical extraconstitutional institutions over the course of American political development is sure to yield path-breaking results, given that the subject remains one of the most glaring lacunae of the discipline. More specifically, new research in this area may help resolve such theoretical controversies as whether the interaction between interest groups and political parties is fundamentally adversarial or symbiotic. It also enables us to examine what Orren & Skowronek (2004) describe as multiple orderings in American political development, providing a window onto how the interest group and partisan orders have collided and become entangled as they have moved through time.

CONCLUSION: RECOGNIZING PATTERNS AND TRANSFORMATIONS

The central aim of this essay is to underscore the empirical and theoretical payoffs of studying the long-term development of interest group politics in America. It is telling that Walker, one of the first political scientists to launch a comprehensive quantitative study of lobbying organizations, never doubted the potential theoretical value of longitudinal data. While he conducted pioneering surveys of organized interests and drew additional data from modern organizational directories and encyclopedias, Walker acknowledged the limitations of his methods for understanding earlier lobbying behavior. Indeed, he bemoaned the absence of comprehensive data on interest groups before the 1960s as an important empirical blind spot. In a similar vein, Petracca warned interest group scholars that the historical thinness of their research presented an enormous liability.

Unfortunately, most of today's interest group specialists have reified the lack of comprehensive and systematic data before the 1960s. Many believe that the opportunity to collect reliable quantitative or qualitative data on interest group mobilization, influence, or bias in earlier periods passed us by long ago. Others too quickly assume that the organized interests of earlier periods are politically so distinct from our own that they are of little or no theoretical value. However, these dissimilarities or variations over more than a century could prove to be of enormous theoretical and empirical utility in themselves. The fact that successive generations of political scientists have heralded unprecedented "explosions" of lobbying organizations in their own time, each said to mark the dawn of modern interest group politics in America, suggests that there are equally intriguing historical patterns to be studied. In short, this august field all but eschews history to its own detriment.

In fairness, American interest group scholars have never had at their disposal the kind of systematic longitudinal data that animate such enterprises as congressional or electoral studies. Nonetheless, we have pointed to multidimensional research methods by which interest group studies might develop fresh and reliable evidence about organized interests in historical periods long considered lost to social scientific analysis. Even if one has little use for historical theories of politics associated with sequencing, path dependence, critical junctures, intercurrence, or other temporal variables, simply turning to "history as data" will produce enormous benefits for interest group studies. In this spirit, we have proposed a conceptual framework for studying interest group systems across U.S. political history that promises to enrich existing theory concerning such essential issues as group mobilization, attrition, mass membership, and representational bias. To understand significant patterns and transformations in American interest group politics over time, scholars must build theory and data that are not overdetermined by the contemporary setting. This transition will require specialists in the field to acknowledge that often the past has as much to teach us as the present.

ACKNOWLEDGMENT

The authors thank Byron Shafer for his helpful comments on an earlier draft of this manuscript.

The *Annual Review of Political Science* is online at
http://polisci.annualreviews.org

LITERATURE CITED

Arnold RD. 1982. Overtilled and undertilled fields in American politics. *Polit. Sci. Q.* 97: 91–103

Bachrach P, Baratz M. 1962. The two faces of power. *Am. Polit. Sci. Rev.* 56:947–52

Bauer RA, De Sola Pool I, Dexter LA. 1963. *American Business and Public Policy: The Politics of Foreign Trade.* New York: Atherton

Baumgartner FR, Jones BD. 1993. *Agendas and Instability in American Politics.* Chicago: Univ. Chicago Press

Baumgartner FR, Leech BL. 1998. *Basic Interests: The Importance of Groups in Politics and in Political Science.* Princeton, NJ: Princeton Univ. Press

Bentley AR. (1908) 1967. *The Process of Government.* Cambridge, MA: Belknap Press of Harvard Univ. Press

Bernstein MH. 1955. *Regulating Business by*

Independent Commission. Princeton, NJ: Princeton Univ. Press

Berry JM. 1989a. *The Interest Group Society.* Glenview, IL: Scott, Foresman/Little Brown. 2nd ed.

Berry J. 1989b. Subgovernments, issue networks, and political conflict. See Harris & Milkis 1989, pp. 239–60

Berry JM. 1999. *The New Liberalism: The Rising Power of Citizen Groups.* Washington, DC: Brookings Inst.

Bosso CJ. 1987. *Pesticides and Politics: The Life Cycle of a Public Issue.* Pittsburgh, PA: Univ. Pittsburgh Press

Burnham WD. 1970. *Critical Elections and the Mainsprings of American Politics.* New York: Norton

Caldeira GA, Wright JR. 1988. Organized interests and agenda-setting in the U.S. Supreme Court. *Am. Polit. Sci. Rev.* 82:1109–27

Cater D. 1964. *Power in Washington.* New York: Random House

Clemens ES. 1997. *The People's Lobby: Organizational Innovation and the Rise of Interest Group Politics in the United States, 1890–1925.* Chicago: Chicago Univ. Press

Crawford KG. 1939. *The Pressure Boys.* New York: Julian Messner

Crotty W, Schwartz MA, Green JC, eds. 1994. *Representing Interests and Interest Group Representation.* Lanham, MD: Univ. Press Am.

Dahl R. 1961. *Who Governs?* New Haven, CT: Yale Univ. Press

Eldersveld SJ. 1958. American interest groups: a survey of research and some implications for theory and method. In *Interest Groups on Four Continents,* ed. HW Ehrmann, pp. 122–56. Pittsburgh, PA: Univ. Pittsburgh Press

Freeman JL. 1965. *The Political Process: Executive Bureau-Legislative Committee Relations.* New York: Random House. Rev. ed.

Fritschler AL. 1975. *Smoking and Politics.* Englewood Cliffs, NJ: Prentice-Hall 2nd ed.

Galambos L. 1970. The emerging organizational synthesis in modern American history. *Bus. Hist. Rev.* 44:279–90

Gamm G, Putnam R. 1999. The growth of voluntary associations in America. *J. Interdiscip. Hist.* 29:511–57

Garceau O. 1958. Interest group theory in political research. In *Unofficial Government: Pressure Groups and Lobbies, the Annals of the American Academy of Political and Social Sciences,* ed. DC Blaisdell, pp. 104–12

Gray V, Lowery D. 1996. *The Population Ecology of Interest Representation.* Ann Arbor: Univ. Mich. Press

Greenstone JD. 1969. *Labor in American Politics.* New York: Knopf

Griffith ES. 1939. *The Impasse of Democracy.* New York: Harrison-Hilton

Hansen JM. 1991. *Gaining Access: Congress and the Farm Lobby, 1919–1981.* Chicago: Univ. Chicago Press

Harris RA. 1989. Politicized management: the changing face of business in American politics. See Harris & Milkis 1989, pp. 261–92

Harris RA, Milkis SM, eds. 1989. *Remaking American Politics.* Boulder, CO: Westview

Hart DM. 2004. "Business" is not an interest group: on the study of companies in American national politics. *Annu. Rev. Polit. Sci.* 7:47–69

Heclo H. 1978. Issue networks and the executive establishment. In *The New American Political System,* ed. A King, pp. 87–125. Washington, DC: Am. Enterprise Inst.

Heinz JP, Laumann EO, Nelson RL, Salisbury RH. 1993. *The Hollow Core: Private Interests in National Policymaking.* Cambridge, MA: Harvard Univ. Press

Herring EP. 1929. *Group Representation Before Congress.* Baltimore, MD: Johns Hopkins Univ. Press

Huntington SP. 1981. *American Politics: The Promise of Disharmony.* Cambridge, MA: Belknap Press of Harvard Univ. Press

Inglehart R. 1977. *The Silent Revolution: Changing Values and Political Styles Among Western Publics.* Princeton, NJ: Princeton Univ. Press

Key VO Jr. (1942) 1964. *Politics, Parties, and Pressure Groups.* New York: T.J. Crowell. 4th ed.

King DS. 1995. *Separate and Unequal: Black*

Americans and the U.S. Federal Government. New York: Oxford Univ. Press

Knoke D. 1986. Associations and interest groups. *Annu. Rev. Sociol.* 12:1–21

Knoke D. 1990. *Organizing for Collective Action: The Political Economy of Associations.* Hawthorne, NY: Aldine de Gruyter

Kryder D. 2000. *Race and the American State During World War II.* New York: Cambridge Univ. Press

Latham E. 1952a. *The Group Basis of Politics.* Ithaca, NY: Cornell Univ. Press

Latham E. 1952b. The group basis of politics: notes for a theory. *Am. Polit. Sci. Rev.* 46:376–97

Laumann EO, Knoke D. 1987. *The Organizational State: Social Choice in National Policy Domains.* Madison: Univ. Wisc. Press

Lieberman RC. 2001. *Shifting the Color Line: Race and the American Welfare State.* Cambridge, MA: Harvard Univ. Press

Lindblom CE. 1963. *The Intelligence of Democracy.* New York: Free

Link A, McCormick RL. 1983. *Progressivism.* Arlington Heights, IL: Harlan Davison

Lowi TJ. 1969. *The End of Liberalism.* New York: Norton

Maass A. 1951. *Muddy Waters: Army Engineers and the Nation's Rivers.* Cambridge, MA: Harvard Univ. Press

Mahood HR. 1967. Pressure groups: a threat to democracy? In *Pressure Groups in American Politics,* ed. HR Mahood, pp. 72–97. New York: Charles Scribner's Sons

Mayhew DR. 2002. *Electoral Realignments: A Critique of an American Genre.* New Haven, CT: Yale Univ. Press

McCann M. 1986. *Taking Reform Seriously: Perspectives on Public Interest Liberalism.* Ithaca, NY: Cornell Univ. Press

McConnell G. 1966. *Private Power and American Democracy.* New York: Knopf

McFarland A. 1969. *Power and Leadership in Pluralist Systems.* Stanford, CA: Stanford Univ. Press

McFarland A. 1976. *Public Interest Lobbies.* Washington, DC: Am. Enterprise Inst.

McFarland A. 1991. Interest groups and political time: cycles in America. *Br. J. Polit. Sci.* 21:257–84

McGuire KT, Caldeira GA. 1993. Lawyers, organized interests, and the law of obscenity: agenda setting and the Supreme Court. *Am. Polit. Sci. Rev.* 87:746–55

McMahon K. 2003. *Reconsidering Roosevelt on Race: How the Presidency Paved the Road to Brown.* Chicago: Univ. Chicago Press

Merriam CE. (1934) 1964. *Political Power.* New York: Collier Books

Milbrath LW. 1963. *The Washington Lobbyists.* Chicago: Rand McNally

Milkis SM. 1993. *The President and the Parties: The American Party System Since the New Deal.* New York: Oxford Univ. Press

Mills CW. 1956. *The Power Elite.* New York: Oxford Univ. Press

Morone JA. 1990. *The Democratic Wish: Popular Participation and the Limits of American Government.* New York: Basic Books

O'Connor K, Epstein L. 1982. Amicus curiae participation in U.S. Supreme Court litigation: an appraisal of Hakman's "Folklore." *Law Soc. Rev.* 16:311–20

Olson M Jr. 1965. *The Logic of Collective Action.* Cambridge, MA: Harvard Univ. Press

Orren K, Skowronek S. 2004. *The Search for American Political Development.* New York: Cambridge Univ. Press

Peterson MA. 1982. Interest mobilization and the presidency. See Petracca 1982c, pp. 345–62

Petracca MP. 1982a. The future of an interest group society. See Petracca 1982c, pp. 221–41

Petracca M. 1982b. The rediscovery of interest group politics. See Petracca 1982c, pp. 3–31

Petracca MP. 1982c. *The Politics of Interests.* Boulder, CO: Westview

Pika JA. 1984. Interest groups and the executive: presidential intervention. In *Interest Group Politics,* ed. AJ Cigler, BA Loomis, pp. 298–323. Washington, DC: C.Q. Press

Ramney A. 1975. *Curing the Mischiefs of Faction.* Berkeley: Univ. Calif. Press

Redford ES. 1969. *Democracy in the Administrative State.* New York: Oxford Univ. Press

Salisbury RH. 1969. An exchange theory of interest groups. *Midw. J. Polit. Sci.* 13:1–32

Salisbury RH. 1984. Interest representation: the dominance of institutions. *Am. Polit. Sci. Rev.* 78:64–76

Sanders E. 1999. *Roots of Reform: Farmers, Workers, and the American State, 1877–1917*. Chicago: Univ. Chicago Press

Schattschneider EE. 1942. *Party Government*. New York: Farrar & Rinehart

Schattschneider EE. 1948. Pressure groups versus political parties. *Ann. Am. Acad. Polit. Soc. Sci.* 29:11–32

Schattschneider EE. 1960. *The Semi-Sovereign People*. New York: Holt, Rinehart & Winston

Schlessinger A Jr . 1960. *Kennedy or Nixon— Does It Make Any Difference?* New York: Macmillan

Schlozman KL, Tierney JT. 1983. More of the same: Washington pressure group activity in a decade of change. *J. Polit.* 45:351–77

Schlozman KL, Tierney JT. 1986. *Organized Interests and American Democracy*. New York: Harper & Row

Shefter M. 1994. *Political Parties and the State: The American Historical Experience*. Princeton, NJ: Princeton Univ. Press

Skocpol T. 1992. *Protecting Soldiers and Mothers: The Political Origins of Social Policy in the United States*. Cambridge, MA: Belknap Press of Harvard Univ. Press

Skocpol T. 2004. *Diminished Democracy: From Membership to Management in American Civic Life*. Norman: Univ. Okla. Press

Skocpol T, Ganz M, Munson Z. 2000. A nation of organizers: the institutional origins of civic voluntarism in the United States. *Am. Polit. Sci. Rev.* 94:527–46

Skowronek S. 1982. *Building a New American State: The Expansion of National Administrative Capacities, 1877–1920*. New York: Cambridge Univ. Press

Smith R. 1999. *Civic Ideals: Conflicting Visions of Citizenship*. New Haven, CT: Yale Univ. Press

Tichenor DJ. 2002a. *Dividing Lines: The Politics of Immigration Control in America*. Princeton, NJ: Princeton Univ. Press

Tichenor DJ. 2002b. The presidency and interest groups: programmatic ambitions and contentious elites. In *The Presidency and the Political System*, ed. M Nelson, pp. 329–54. Washington, DC: C. Q. Press

Tichenor DJ, Harris RA. 2002/2003. Organized interests and American political development. *Polit. Sci. Q.* 117:587–612

Tichenor DJ, Harris RA. 2005. *Evolving Interests: Political Mobilization, Attrition, and Bias*. New York: Cambridge Univ. Press

Truman DB. 1951. *The Governmental Process: Political Interests and Public Opinion*. New York: Knopf

Turner HA. 1958. How pressure groups operate. *Ann. Am. Acad. Polit. Soc. Sci.* 319:63–72

Vogel DJ. 1989. *Fluctuating Fortunes: The Political Power of Business in America*. New York: Basic Books

Walker JL Jr. 1983. The origins and maintenance of interest groups in America. *Am. Polit. Sci. Q.* 77:390–406

Walker JL Jr. 1991. *Mobilizing Interest Groups in America*. Ann Arbor: Univ. Mich. Press

Weir M. 1992. *Politics and Jobs: The Boundaries of Employment Policy in the United States*. Princeton, NJ: Princeton Univ. Press

Wiebe R. 1980. *The Search for Order*. Westport, CT: Greenwood

Wilson GK. 1981. *Interest Groups in the United States*. New York: Oxford Univ. Press

Wilson W. 1885. *Congressional Government*. Boston: Houghton, Mifflin

Annu. Rev. Polit. Sci. 2005. 8:271–96
doi: 10.1146/annurev.polisci.8.082103.104843
Copyright © 2005 by Annual Reviews. All rights reserved
First published online as a Review in Advance on Dec. 16, 2004

TRANSFORMATIONS IN WORLD POLITICS:
The Intellectual Contributions of Ernst B. Haas*

John Gerard Ruggie,[1] Peter J. Katzenstein,[2]
Robert O. Keohane,[3] and Philippe C. Schmitter[4]
[1] *John F. Kennedy School of Government, Harvard University, Cambridge, Massachusetts
02138; email: john_ruggie@harvard.edu*
[2] *Department of Political Science, Cornell University, Ithaca, New York 14853;
email: pjk2@cornell.edu*
[3] *Department of Political Science, Duke University, Durham, North Carolina 27708;
email: rkeohane@duke.edu*
[4] *Department of Political and Social Sciences, European University Institute,
Florence 50016, Italy; email: Philippe.Schmitter@IUE.it*

Key Words   international transformation, European integration, global
governance, nationalism, constructivism in international relations theory

■ **Abstract**   For half a century, Ernst B. Haas was an extraordinarily prolific contributor to theoretical debates in international relations. His work focused on the question of continuity and transformation in the system of states. His substantive writings are extremely diverse and can be difficult, so no overall appreciation has ever been attempted. This essay pulls together the major strands of Haas' theoretical work into a coherent whole and seeks to make it accessible to the broadest possible audience of IR scholars. The first section locates Haas in the overall theoretical milieu in which his thinking evolved, and it identifies some core intellectual choices he made. The next three sections summarize Haas' main theoretical contributions to the fields of European integration, the study of change at the level of the world polity, and nationalism.

If there were a Nobel Prize for contributions to the study of international relations, Ernst B. Haas surely would have won it. He was a giant in the IR field, almost from the day he arrived on the Berkeley campus as an Instructor in 1951 to his death 52 years later, at the age of 79—still writing, and still teaching his immensely

---

*This article is based on the authors' presentations at the Roundtable on "The Contributions of Ernst B. Haas to the Study of Politics," American Political Science Association, Philadelphia, August 30, 2003. Ruggie and Schmitter were students of and coauthors with Haas; Ruggie went on to become Haas' junior colleague on the Berkeley faculty, where they codirected a research project on international cooperation in scientific and technological domains. Katzenstein and Keohane did not study with Haas formally but were drawn into his invisible college early in their careers and consider him to have been a close mentor.

popular and demanding course, Political Science 220: Theories of International Relations. Within a decade of entering the profession, Haas had accomplished the following:

- written two widely reprinted critiques of the wooliness, internal incoherence, and contradictory policy implications of balance-of-power theory, to which only Waltz (1979), more than a quarter century later, provided an adequate response;
- helped invent the study of European integration and devised a novel theoretical framework, termed neofunctionalism, for understanding its dynamics and consequences;
- helped place the field of international organization on a more sound social scientific footing, rescuing it from legal prescriptions and institutional descriptions; and
- coauthored a moderately successful textbook.

Needless to say, he got tenure. Subsequently, Haas was deeply engaged in every major debate in the IR field well into the 1990s, including transnationalism, interdependence theory, regime theory, the role of ideas and knowledge in international policy making, and the ascendancy of neorealism and neoliberalism as well as the social constructivist rejoinder to them. He advanced our understanding of epistemological and ontological issues in IR theory. And he topped it all off with a two-volume study of nationalism, culminating more than half a century of teaching and research on that subject.

Yet, beyond the field of regional integration studies, Haas' work is not well known in the United States and is barely known at all elsewhere. This neglect of such immense contributions is a great pity. But it is also an interesting chapter in the sociology of knowledge in our discipline. Part of the problem is that Haas' work is difficult. His writing can be quite opaque; here, for example, is his preferred selection from the menu of systems theories that he surveyed as possible frameworks for analysis in *Beyond the Nation State*: "A dynamic system capable of linking Functionalism with integration studies is a concrete, actor-oriented abstraction on recurrent relationships that can explain its own transformation into a new set of relationships" (Haas 1964, p. 77). He also had a habit of sharing with the reader his step-by-step assessment of every one of the voluminous literatures he drew upon in formulating his own thinking, even when they had led him to intellectual dead ends. But he was hardly alone in either of these practices.

The bigger part of the problem, we suspect, is that Haas swam against so many currents in the field while constructing his own intellectual terrain, including realism, idealism, the penchant for grand theory, neorealism and neoliberalism, most forms of rational choice theory, and positivism. As a result, he had relatively few natural allies in the discipline beyond the circle of his students and others who were drawn into personal contact with him. All within that circle were transformed by the experience of engaging with a truly learned, disciplined yet imaginative scholar of the highest intellectual caliber and integrity—and a deeply caring person with an infectious laugh.[1]

Thus, our objective in this article, as honored members of that circle, is simple yet challenging: not so much to praise Haas' work or to assess it critically as to make it accessible to the broadest possible audience of IR scholars. We do so in four parts. The first section locates Haas in the overall theoretical milieu in which his thinking evolved, and it identifies some core intellectual choices he made. The next three sections summarize Haas' main theoretical contributions to the fields of European integration, the study of change at the level of the world polity, and nationalism. A brief reprise concludes the article.

INTELLECTUAL ORIENTATION

When Haas entered the discipline, the reigning approaches to international relations were realism and idealism, though idealism—for example, the movement to achieve world peace through world law, divorced from power—was being slain by realism. The brutal reality of World War II and the growing recognition that life hinged on a balance of nuclear terror saw to that. Haas, it goes without saying, was no idealist. As his students well remember, of all intellectual frailties, none earned greater disdain than being "a mush head"—and idealists topped this category for him.[2] Realists were another matter. They never thought much (if at all) about Haas' work, but Haas did think about theirs. As already noted, he wrote trenchant critiques of balance-of-power theory early in his career (Haas 1953b,c). And he stated explicitly that his own theoretical work "takes for granted—even capitalizes on—certain Hobbesian aspects of international life" (Haas 1970, p. viii). So what was the problem?

For one thing, Haas questioned the core assumption of realism. A democratic and pluralistic society, he wrote, simply "is not keyed to external dangers on a

---

[1]Haas' lack of interest in coalition building within the discipline is best illustrated by a letter he wrote to Peter Katzenstein, in which he chastised him for going too easy, in a recent paper, on intellectual currents dissenting from the IR mainstream. In this letter, dated July 10, 1995, Haas wrote: "I don't share your tolerance for anyone who is disgusted—as we both are—with the primitivism of our rationalist colleagues, economists, IR people, and (in my case) the 'new institutionalists' in sociology. Just because we have a common enemy, do we have to be in bed with each other? In fact, the common enemy is also elusive because I have considerable tolerance for positivism (in nuances) even while detesting its manifestations in neorealism and neoliberalism in our profession. I guess what I am telling myself, in arguing with you, is not to trim my own work as counterpunching against the work of our friends and colleagues, but to tell our tales as plausibly as we can just to make the point that the same story can be told plausibly in a number of ways."

[2]Although Haas strongly supported the promotion and protection of human rights, he remained cautious throughout his career about the best means by which to pursue these goals (see Haas 1986, 1993).

full-time basis and. . .is not organized so as to make one single conception of the national interest assert itself vigorously and consistently" (Haas 1953c, p. 398). Therefore, assuming the existence of a singular national interest, as realists do, becomes a matter of analytical choice. But analytical choices are driven by research agendas—not by existential necessity, as many realists claimed. So Haas made his choice based on his research priorities. More serious for Haas was his perception that realists' analytical choices lead them to recapitulate endlessly why change in international politics is impossible, whereas the puzzle that interested him was how and why it happens. Indeed, he described neofunctionalism as a theoretical tool "to get us beyond the blind alley" and to "break away from the clichés" of realist analysis (Haas 1964, p. 24). The stakes were high, Haas maintained, because the cost of the realists' choices is spent not only in theoretical coin. For example, none of the major realists of his day believed that the project of European unification could succeed, so if political leaders and policy makers had acted on the basis of those realist analyses, they would not have undertaken what turned out to be one of the most significant initiatives in the history of the modern system of states. Indeed, roads theoretically proscribed by realists are many, and others, too, have led to profound change in the actual practice of international politics.[3] Haas had that hunch early and pursued it for half a century.

But if neither realist nor idealist, who was Haas, intellectually speaking? This article aims to answer that question. The present section concerns the fundamental tenets of Haas' thinking that shaped all of his work, leaving it to later sections to address the specific theoretical orientations he brought to his major strands of research.

Haas' most enduring premises and approaches are essentially Weberian. We say "essentially" because some of these postures were adopted not directly from the grand master himself but through the writings of contemporary sociologists, including Reinhard Bendix, Philip Selznick, Peter Blau, and Daniel Bell, several of whom were Berkeley colleagues. Be that as it may, the following core elements of Haas' overall theoretical orientation may be described as Weberian.[4]

First, as the following three sections demonstrate, the meta-trend or axial principle around which Haas' theoretical reflections revolved was the process of rationalization—that is to say, the gradual elimination of such traditional factors as status, passions and prejudices from the organization of public life and determinants of public policy, coupled with an ever expanding role of systematic calculation and evidence-based reflection (Weber 1947, ch. 1). As seen in Weber's

---

[3]Even the North Atlantic Treaty Organization provides an example. Leading realists, including George Kennan, who first defined and helped formulate the postwar strategy of containing the Soviet Union, opposed framing NATO around indivisible security guarantees (Article 5 of the treaty), which arguably turned out to be the very foundation of NATO's durability through and beyond the Cold War (see Ruggie 1995).

[4]The following discussion of Weber's approach to the social sciences and its implications for IR theorizing draws in part on Ruggie (1998).

analysis of the evolving bases of legitimate authority toward the legal and bureaucratic, this development had profound effects on the structure and functioning of institutions—including, Haas took for granted, international institutions and the modern system of states itself. Over time, Haas came to ascribe to human agency considerably greater control over the unfolding of rationalization than Weber had done, especially over the construction of shared meanings and consensus-based truth through social learning. Thus, in direct contrast to realism, a driver of change was at the very core of Haas' work—not linear, not immutable, but ever-present as a force to be reckoned with.

Second, Haas believed deeply in the possibility of a social science but, like Weber, only in one that expressed the distinctive attributes of social action and social order. For Weber, none was more foundational than the human capacity and will "to take a deliberate attitude towards the world and lend it *significance*" (Weber 1949, p. 81, emphasis in original). Ernst and Peter Haas put it more simply. In the natural sciences, they quipped, units of analysis "don't talk back" and they "lack free will; at least, none has been empirically demonstrated in atoms, molecules and cells" (Haas & Haas 2002, p. 583). A viable social science, Haas believed, must accommodate—indeed, thrive on—the reflective and reflexive nature of human beings.

Third, despite being one of the most sophisticated theorists in the field, Haas protested throughout his career that none of his intellectual formulations constituted a theory as such. This was no mere quirk, fetish, or false humility. It followed directly from the Weberian understanding of the differences in concept formation and explanation between the natural and social sciences. Because human beings are reflective and reflexive, concepts in the social sciences must aid in uncovering the meaning of specific actions and in demonstrating their significance within a particular social context, or risk becoming mere reifications. In Weber's words, "We wish to understand on the one hand the relationships and the cultural significance of individual events in their contemporary manifestations, and on the other the causes of their being historically *so* and not *otherwise*" (Weber 1949, p. 56, emphasis in original). Haas described his objective in *The Uniting of Europe* in similar terms: "My aim is merely the dissection of *the actual* 'integration process' in order to derive propositions about its nature" (Haas 1958, p. xii, emphasis added). If the purpose of social science is to demonstrate why things are historically *so* and not *otherwise*, then it follows that the appropriate cruising altitude is middle-range theory—a term Haas borrowed from Merton (1957)—grounded in actor-oriented processes, both intentional and unintended. Grand theory was a chimera, or worse.

Fourth, like Weber, Haas adhered to an ontology that included not only material but also ideational factors, and he paid particular attention to the interaction between the two. Here is how Haas (2004) summarized his understanding in 2004:

> [S]ocial actors, in seeking to realize their value-derived interests, will choose whatever means are made available by the prevailing democratic order. If thwarted they will rethink their values, redefine their interests, and choose

new means to realize them. The alleged primordial force of nationalism will be trumped by the utilitarian-instrumental human desire to better oneself in life, materially and in terms of status, as well as normative satisfaction. It bears repeating that the ontology is not materialistic: values shape interests, and values include many nonmaterial elements. (p. xv)

Haas also drew from Weber his extensive use of typologies, explicitly conceived as ideal types, to illuminate *possible* modes of behavior, against which actual behavior could be assessed. An ideal type of political community is at the center of the analysis in *The Uniting of Europe* (Haas 1958, pp. 5–6). In *Beyond the Nation State* he uses a method he terms "contextual analysis" and states that it belongs to the same family as Weberian ideal types, "more ambitious than historical narration and more modest than the effort at deductive 'science.' It seeks the general within the more confined context of a given historical, regional, or functional setting." The investigator selects and arranges the facts of actor conduct by using his own capacity "to identify himself with human motives that all of us accept as 'real' and relevant to the study of politics" (Haas 1964, pp. viii–ix). In an influential article on "issue linkages and international regimes," Haas (1980) elaborates a fourfold ideal type of regimes, organized according to the capabilities that organizers of a regime might seek to create (p. 397). Haas never viewed ideal types as generating testable generalizations. That simply was not their purpose. "The best service to be expected from an ideal-typical discussion of regimes," he declared, "is to make people pause and think" (Haas 1980, p. 405).

It follows that Haas had grave doubts about the entire positivist project in international relations—and political science as a whole. He was not data-shy and was willing to use quantitative indicators. Although his statistical skills were limited, he coded and updated thousands of labor standards issued by the International Labor Organization (ILO) since its origin in 1919 (Haas 1964, 1970); he constructed and maintained a data base of United Nations peacekeeping missions (Haas 1972, 1983, 1986); and he coded indicators of the evolution of various forms of nationalism in five industrialized countries over two centuries (Haas 1997). So quantification was not the issue; it was ontology and epistemology.

The covering law model of explanation, to which the mainstream of the discipline aspires, is ruled out by Haas' Weberian commitment. Causality remains concrete and is anchored in historically contingent meaning. The purpose of the various analytical tools that Weber used was not to subsume specific social actions or events under putative deductive laws, of which he believed few existed in the social world, but to establish links between them and concrete antecedents that most plausibly had causal relevance for real social actors within the social collectivity at hand. And so it was with Haas: "It is difficult to formulate universal claims over time and across cultures because of the mutable nature of institutions and the potential role of free will (that is, of actors' ability to change their minds and pursue new goals)" (Haas & Haas 2002, p. 584). Or, as Ernst Haas wrote to Peter Katzenstein in 1995, "You cannot 'test' theories in such a way as to discard the worse for the better as our colleagues seek to do. Not even real scientists do it that way very often."[5] Let us be clear: Haas did not reject rigor; his own work was a very model of it. But he insisted on a rigor that was relevant to the object under study, and thus he contested the claim that a valid social science must pass positivism's natural-science-based truth tests.

Besides adhering to positivist fallacies, neorealism and neoliberalism premised their approach on the notion of exogenous and fixed interests—adding insult to injury, as far as Haas' entire research agenda was concerned. Haas considered these assumptions not only implausible but also of little use to him, as a scholar who had spent a lifetime studying the processes whereby actors come to define and redefine the ends they pursue in international politics, not just the means of pursuit. But, contrary to his admonition to Katzenstein in 1995 (see footnote 1), Haas did go relatively easy, at least in print, on neorealism and (even more so) neoliberalism, counting several of their leading practitioners among his closest professional friends.

One of Haas' last publications, coauthored with his son Peter Haas (who has contributed significantly to the study of social learning in the area of environmental policy and governance), describes the Haases' preferred methodological posture as "pragmatic constructivism" (Haas & Haas 2002).[6] This approach emphasizes the role of human consciousness in the social reality that we study and relies on a consensus theory of truth to support interpretations and explanations. Its practitioners believe that progress in achieving a shared understanding of international institutions is possible, but only through "interparadigm mid-level discussions that try to resolve different interpretations of similar phenomena and conceptual applications that may lead, ultimately, to some degree of provisional closure and dispute resolution between paradigms" (Haas & Haas 2002, p. 595).

Having established Haas' overall point of departure, let us turn now to the subfields of the discipline in which he made his most important theoretical contributions, beginning with the study of European unification.

EUROPEAN INTEGRATION

"Two events of great importance in the history of European integration happened in 1958," writes Dinan (2004). "One was the launch of the European Economic Community (EEC); the other was the publication of Ernst Haas' *The Uniting of Europe*" (p. ix). As far-fetched as it may seem to put the two on par, Dinan continues, they were in fact inextricably linked. Not only did Haas help to invent the academic field of integration studies, but practitioners also frequently invoked his work as they devised their strategies for advancing this historic project. Haas' students, when conducting interviews in Brussels, often heard responses to their questions framed in Haas' analytical categories. In 1997, *Foreign Affairs* selected *The Uniting of Europe* as one of the most important IR books of the twentieth century.

---

[5]The same letter cited in footnote 1.
[6]Adler (1991) had earlier described Haas' thinking in terms of "evolutionary epistemology."

Haas was among the first to realize that by liberalizing flows of trade, investment, and persons across previously well-protected borders, regional integration might transform the traditional interstate system that had characterized European politics for three centuries—the system whose failure had caused two world wars in a single generation. But he departed significantly from classical liberalism in his understanding of how this transformation could occur. He was the founder of neofunctionalism as an approach to the study of integration—insisting vigorously that it was not a "theory." This represented a novel synthesis of Mitrany's theory of functionalism and Monnet's pragmatic strategy for operating the European Coal and Steel Community and developing it into the EEC—both forerunners of the present European Union.

Mitrany (1943, 1966) believed that an expanding system of functionally specialized international organizations run by experts could become a transformative force in world politics. Haas reformulated this technocratic vision into a more political conception in which international cooperation was based on competing and colluding subnational interests that might be reconciled by the creative interventions of supranational technocratic actors. Jean Monnet, a leading French economic planner, was devoted to eliminating the risk of war in Europe, and that meant defusing the antagonism between France and Germany above all else.[7] After trying and failing to promote direct routes to this end—federalism and military unification— he hit upon a second-best indirect solution: integrate the coal and steel sectors. These would be necessary to fuel any future conflict. And they had the additional "virtue" (given Monnet's objective) of being in decline, thus imposing economic as well as political adjustment costs on national political systems that international collaboration might help reduce. With the Marshall Plan and the Organization for European Economic Cooperation (the OECD's precursor) behind him, and the U.S. government beside him, Monnet managed to cajole six countries into forming the European Coal and Steel Community, and also endowing its Secretary-General (a position he subsequently occupied) with modest supranational powers. What Haas did in *The Uniting of Europe* was to explore the dynamics, unanticipated consequences, and limits of this second-best strategy—nicely summarized in Monnet's phrase *"petits pas, grand effets."*

It has always been difficult to classify neofunctionalism in disciplinary terms because it intersects the usual assumptions of international relations and comparative politics. Neofunctionalism recognizes the importance of national states, especially in the foundation of regional organizations and at subsequent moments of formal refoundation by treaty. Yet it also emphasizes the roles of two sets of nonstate actors in providing the dynamic for further integration: (*a*) the interest associations and social movements that form at the regional level, and (*b*) the secretariat of the organization involved. Member states may set the terms of the initial

---

[7]Monnet's (1978) memoirs were published two decades after *The Uniting of Europe*; Haas relied on the public record and interviews.

agreement and strive to control subsequent events, but they do not exclusively determine the direction, extent, and pace of change. Rather, regional bureaucrats in league with actors whose interests and values are advanced by a regional solution to a concrete task at hand seek to exploit the inevitable "spillover" and unintended consequences that occur when states agree to some degree of supranational responsibility for accomplishing that task but then discover that success also requires addressing related activities.

According to this approach, regional integration is an intrinsically sporadic and conflictual process. But under conditions of democracy and pluralistic interest representation, national governments will find themselves increasingly entangled in regional pressures and end up resolving their conflicts of interest by conceding a wider scope, and devolving more authority, to the regional organizations they have created. Eventually, their citizens will begin shifting more and more of their expectations to the region, and satisfying them will increase the likelihood that economic-social integration will spill over into political integration.

Neofunctionalism as articulated by Haas had no specific temporal component. How long it would take for these functional interdependencies to become manifest, for affected interests to organize themselves across national borders, and for officials in the regional secretariats to come up with projects that would expand their tasks and authority was left undetermined. Unfortunately for the academic reception of neofunctionalism, many scholars presumed that spillovers would occur "automatically" and "in close, linear sequence to each other" (Saeter 1993). Even a cursory reading of Haas, however, especially of his more systematic presentation in *Beyond the Nation State*, demonstrates these to be fallacious inferences. But when the integration process in Europe proved to be more controversial and to make less continuous progress than expected, the theory was repeatedly declared "disconfirmed."

The irony of this tale is that Haas himself contributed substantially to the demise of interest in his own theory. By declaring in print on two separate occasions (Haas 1971, 1975b) that neofunctionalism had become "obsolescent," he made it virtually impossible for any other scholar to take the approach seriously. Who would dare to contradict its founder? Moreover, in the early 1970s, the process of European integration itself seemed stagnant, if not moribund. Lindberg & Scheingold (1970) concluded that although the (then) EEC had accomplished much, by the end of the 1960s it had settled into a sluggish equilibrium from which it was unlikely to escape for some time. Indeed, of the 10 contributors to a *magnum opus* of theorizing about regional integration (Lindberg & Scheingold 1971), only one (Donald Puchala) was still writing on the subject 10 years later.

Why did Haas lose faith in neofunctionalism? The simple answer was Charles De Gaulle—a living embodiment of the *realpolitik* backlash against integration. Not only did De Gaulle put a sudden stop to the gradual expansion of tasks and authority by the Commission and to the prospective shift to majority voting in the Council, but he also made a full-scale effort to convert the EEC/EC into an instrument of French foreign policy. By the time it became clear that, however much

De Gaulle and his successors desired these outcomes, they were not to happen, Haas was deeply engaged in research on transformation at the global level.

But, to borrow Adler's (2000) characterization, Haas turned out to be wrong about being wrong. When interest in European integration picked up smartly in the mid-1980s, with the unanticipated breakthrough of the signature and easy ratification of the Single European Act, interest in neofunctionalism also revived and blossomed in Europe—although not in the United States, where scholarly work on European integration as a whole has lagged seriously behind (one obvious exception being Moravcsik 1998). Indeed, with the fall of the Berlin Wall and the end of the Cold War, American realists declared that the entire *raison d'être* of European integration had collapsed and that its nation-states would inexorably restore their previous interstate system (Mearsheimer 1990). But thus far the opposite has happened. The calculation that German reunification made it more urgent than ever to bind Germany firmly to the rest of Western Europe undoubtedly played a major role in ensuring agreement on the Maastricht Treaty in 1991. But rather than confirming realism, this move demonstrates Haas' argument that even core realist imperatives can be resolved through broader integrative measures, once the process of integration has reached a certain level. Maastricht committed its signatories to establishing a common currency, the Euro, an idea that had been proposed on several occasions but always rejected as intruding too far, materially and symbolically, into the sovereignty of member states. To the surprise of almost everyone, the introduction of the new common currency produced relatively little resistance, and this "mother of all spillovers," as it became known, has been a quiet yet historic success.

Haas was quite skeptical about broadening the analysis of integration to other regions. In 1961 he concluded that integration is a "discontinuous process," and he declared that "if regional integration continues to go forward in these areas [outside of Europe], it will obey impulses peculiar to them and thus fail to demonstrate any universal 'law of integration' deduced from the European example" (Haas 1961).

So what is Ernst Haas' European legacy? His work on regional integration continues to be read and cited—with increasing frequency since the 1990s. At the same time, by now almost everyone recognizes that no single theory or approach can explain everything one would like to know or predict about the EU. The process has already generated the world's most complex polity, and despite the Convention's "Constitutional Treaty," there is every indication that it will become even more complex now that it has 10 new members and has been taking on new tasks.[8]

---

[8] A very important limitation of neofunctionalism should be noted. It focuses exclusively on the extension of the integrative process to new tasks and on the expansion of common authority. It says nothing about the incorporation of new members, which has been a major dynamic feature of the EU. How, when, why, and under what conditions a regional organization will expand territorially is simply not contemplated by the neofunctionalist approach.

Moreover, the entire logic of spillover based on underlying and unanticipated functional interdependencies may have exhausted itself. On the one hand, the EU is already involved in some fashion in almost all policy domains. On the other hand, if monetary union is any indication of the future, the designers of the European Central Bank were very careful to insulate it from any relation with the Commission or with organized interests. The same seems likely to occur in the cases of police cooperation and foreign policy coordination. Only a common energy policy and certain aspects of transport infrastructure seem capable of igniting latent functional linkages and generating the unintended consequences on which neofunctionalism thrived. Moreover, the expansion to 25 members of much greater heterogeneity of interests and values means that it will become much more difficult to respond with an expansive package deal that will have something in it for everyone. Given such diversity, it is much less likely that actors will recognize a common need, that experts will agree on what to do, that lessons will be transferred from one experience to another, and that citizens will mobilize in order to demand that the good, service, or regulation they desire be supplied by the EU rather than their national state or subnational region.

But the real impediment to a revived neofunctionalist dynamic comes from something Haas long ago anticipated yet which was slow in coming to the European integration process: its growing politicization (Schmitter 1971). When citizens begin to pay attention to how the EU affects their daily lives, when political parties and large social movements begin to include "Europe" in their platforms, and when politicians begin to realize that they can win or lose votes by addressing policy issues at the regional level, then the entire neofunctionalist strategy becomes much less viable. Discreet regional officials and invisible interest representatives in league with national civil servants can no longer monopolize the decision-making process in Brussels (known in Euro-speak as "comitology"). Integration starts to generate winners and losers within member states, and its aura of being an all-winners game fades. Haas (1976) had an idiosyncratic term for this: he called it "turbulence." There is no question that the process of integration in Europe has become turbulent and that neofunctionalism, therefore, no longer captures many of its main drivers.

Yet in his last published work, an introduction to a reissue of *The Uniting of Europe*, Haas (2004) began to sort through the many bodies of institutionalist theory that now seek to explain European integration. His aim was to identify how neofunctionalism itself needed to be updated and modified. Nothing conveys Haas' enduring commitment to scholarship more clearly than this effort, completed only weeks before his death.

INTERNATIONAL CHANGE

When Haas (temporarily, as it turned out) abandoned European integration studies in the 1970s, he turned his attention full-time to exploring processes of change at the level of the world polity. *Beyond the Nation State*, published in 1964, had set the stage but also altered it permanently. It was Haas' only sustained study of integration at the global level. However, he found that the record of more than 40 years of ILO conventions on labor standards, which he coded carefully, yielded few of the predicted consequences. As a result, he expanded his analytical focus considerably beyond integration to examine different patterns of international cooperation and their potential long-term effects on the structure and conduct of international politics.

At this point, we encounter a problem. Whereas Haas' contributions to the study of European integration comprise a coherent whole and are readily assessed against actual developments, it is far more difficult even to summarize, let alone evaluate, his work on global cooperation and its transformative potential. One impediment is that the subject matter itself is so vast, and Haas' voluminous writings left virtually no aspect of it untouched. At the same time, though, he produced no single, definitive piece of work in this area, but rather a series of plausibility probes— some in hefty book form, to be sure—that comprise successive approximations of the reality he was trying to grasp and elucidate.

Nevertheless, a good place to begin is with the realization that, although Haas viewed the European integration experience as unique, it was for him but a special or extreme case of a more general phenomenon. "The study of integration is a step toward a theory of international change at the macrolevel" (Haas 2004, p. xv). So the puzzles that animated his curiosity and drove his research in the two areas were in some ways similar, but the processes and forms of cooperation at the global level would differ because the world polity differed from the European regional system. Therefore, his analytical apparatus would have to be modified accordingly and parts jettisoned entirely. Haas' work in this area is a moving target because it represents an ongoing, systematic effort at reflection and reformulation. His quest reached closure of any sort only in 2002, when Haas endorsed what he called "pragmatic constructivism" as the theoretical orientation best equipped to capture international change at the macro level, and acknowledged that he had been speaking its prose all along (Haas & Haas 2002). In his introduction to the reissued *Uniting of Europe* (Haas 2004), he reached the same conclusion with regard to the study of European integration. At least in overall approach, then—including their ontology and epistemology—his "special theory" and "general theory" (to use the terms metaphorically) had become unified.

Thus, rather than engaging individual pieces of Haas' work that often were superseded in their specifics by subsequent writings, we take a twofold tack. First, we identify and discuss briefly the distinctive and enduring questions that drove Haas' inquiries into the processes of change in the world polity, wherever possible using his own words. Then we offer our own synthesis of his endeavor in this domain, which we believe to be consistent with his thinking.[9]

---

[9]Some of Haas' former students and collaborators contributed to a *Festschrift* dedicated to Haas, building on his insights on progress in international policy and politics; see Adler & Crawford (1991).

Strategic Questions

What were the core questions that drove Haas' studies of international change? Without claiming to be exhaustive, we have selected five questions that seem central to his evolving research program.

HOW DOES VOLUNTARY COOPERATION OCCUR?   The first and most general question Haas addressed was: How does voluntary cooperation, not involving the use of force, take place in international politics (Haas 1970, p. 608)?

He did not take the easy way out by assuming altruism or commitment to principle on the part of the major actors. On the contrary, he insisted consistently that states act "on their perceived interests" (Haas 1990, p. 6). "Major interest groups as well as politicians determine their support of, or opposition to, new central institutions and policies on the basis of a calculation of advantage" (Haas 1958, p. xiv). Indeed, he held that even "learning is based on the perception of self-interest displayed by the actors" (Haas 1964, p. 48).

Moreover, he rejected the idea that formal structures or treaty texts were a good guide to what international organizations end up doing or making possible. Even in *The Uniting of Europe*, he argued that cooperation depends more on people's perceptions and attitudes than on formal structures. Contrary to some advocates of supranationalism, for example, Haas did not assume that "an intergovernmental structure automatically guarantees the prevalence of diplomatic decision-making techniques and thereby controls [in the sense of limiting] integration." Instead, he believed (Haas 1964, p. 487):

> It is impossible to assess the role of the Council in European integration merely...on the basis of treaty texts. If the operational code habitually employed by the people who compose the Council can be demonstrated to result in further integration, then plainly the general level of argumentation described [in treaty texts] is beside the point. The corollary would be that institutions of a federal type do not necessarily guarantee integration, while organs of a diplomatic character may actually aid it, depending on the techniques of decision-making used.

Haas' approach to resolving the puzzle of cooperation was sociological, behavioral, and cognitive. Broadly speaking, cooperation occurs in situations where domestic welfare concerns dominate considerations of national power, and where groups exist that can articulate those welfare concerns within national decision-making structures. Thus, capitalist social democracies and pluralism are fertile grounds for cooperation, but functional equivalents can exist in other political systems. Beyond that background condition, cooperation requires some convergence of actors' interests, which can be helped along by international institutional actors with appropriate problem-solving orientations. Success in meeting initial interests on one round may produce incremental shifts in expectations among the actors, and begin to create habits of practice that reinforce cooperation. By employing creative bargaining styles, key elites can upgrade conceptions of individual interests into some acceptable formulation of a common interest, thereby leading at least to a partial redefinition of the separate self-interests (Haas 1958, pp. xv, xvi; 1964, p. 111). A second question followed closely on the first.

WHAT KINDS OF INSTITUTIONAL ARRANGEMENTS FOSTER COOPERATION?   Under what conditions is cooperation fostered by institutional arrangements focused on specific tasks that do not directly involve the interstate politics of peace and security?

All of Haas' work was based on the premise that "international organizations are designed by their founders to 'solve problems' that require collaborative action" (1990: 2)—and not for their own sake. But not all such efforts were equally successful. The ability to solve problems, he believed, was related to the "functional specificity" of tasks the organization was assigned, or their "separability" from core issues related to national power and status (Haas 1964, pp. 47–52).

Again, European integration represented one end of the spectrum. There, certain kinds of organizational tasks most intimately related to functionally specific group and national aspirations—beginning with rationalizing the coal and steel sectors—resulted in integration, even though the actors responsible for this development may not have deliberately worked toward it (Haas 1964, p. 35). In contrast, when Haas (1983) examined the evolution of UN peacekeeping, he saw "regime decay" occurring over time. In a superficial sense, the neofunctionalist expectation is borne out: Functionally specific tasks promote intense cooperation, whereas matters more centrally related to national security exhibit the limits imposed on it. However, most areas of international cooperation examined by Haas fell in between those two extremes and remained "encapsulated," showing few if any signs of contributing to learning or to an overall expansion of cooperation. This puzzle led to still another question.

WHAT IS THE ROLE OF ACTOR COGNITION?   In successful instances of international cooperation, when and how do actors' key cognitions change to reinforce cooperation? Haas kept asking this question—almost alone among students of world politics—for 40 years. But the types of cognition he focused on changed over time.

He began by considering possible shifts in loyalty, which was central to the process of political integration as explored in *The Uniting of Europe* and subsequent articles. Shifts in loyalty did not travel beyond the European context, however, and produced complex results even there. Haas also was critically attuned to changing actor expectations about who can best deliver the goods, a concern that foreshadowed the emphasis on expectations both in the literature on regimes and more generally in contemporary game theory (Haas 1961, 367). In *Beyond the Nation State*, he examined different bargaining styles that promote or limit cooperation, as well as actor learning, particularly whether lessons learned in one functional context are transferred to others (Haas 1964, p. 48).

In his long and complex essay, "Is there a Hole in the Whole" (1975a), Haas first addressed in some depth the issue that would become the hallmark of his subsequent intellectual agenda: the role of consensual knowledge in organizational learning that results in expanding the domain of cooperative action. By 1990 he considered such knowledge, or self-consciousness, to involve questioning "basic beliefs underlying the selection of ends," and not merely of means (Haas 1990, p. 36). In this line of research, he sought to elaborate "a notion of organizational decision making in which knowledge, consensual or not, deflects raw interest. I am not here interested," he declared, "in goals based on interests uninformed by knowledge" (Haas 1990, p. 75), because such conventional cases would entail none of the potential for international change that he sought to discern.

In his contribution to the famous *International Organization* special issue on international regimes, Haas (1982) emphasized the differences between the mechanical metaphors of mercantilism and liberalism, on the one hand, and the organic metaphors of ecologically minded analysts, on the other, and suggested that the latter held far greater potential to expand cooperation. In *When Knowledge is Power* (Haas 1990), self-reflective learning took center stage: learning based on consensual causal knowledge—in other words, on physical and social science—and its ability to inform the definition of the means and ends of policy.

IS ORGANIZATIONAL LEARNING PROMOTED BY SCIENTIFIC KNOWLEDGE AND BY THE INVOLVEMENT OF EXPERTS?   In key articles of the 1970s and 1980s, culminating in *When Knowledge is Power*, Haas answered, "It can be." He differentiated learning, which involves changes in causal beliefs, from mere adaptation, which does not. Adopting a concept introduced by Ruggie (1975) in a special issue of *International Organization* they coedited, Haas articulated the idea of "epistemic communities" of professionals "who shared a commitment to a common causal model and a common set of political values" (Haas 1990, p. 41)—the epistemic community comprised of practitioners of Keynesian economics, for example, or of various branches of ecology. He expressed the belief that "the language of science is becoming a world view that penetrates politics everywhere" (p. 46), and therefore would affect the way in which states' interests are defined.

This proposition seemed truer in some areas than others. "The more dependent an issue area becomes on technical information, the greater the likelihood that epistemic communities gain in influence" (Haas & Haas 2002, p. 592). At the same time, there must be a growing demand for such knowledge on the part of policy makers: "Consensual knowledge that is not acknowledged by government remains irrelevant, though the demand can sometimes be stimulated by enterprising knowledge brokers"—international institutional actors being key among them.

Haas' emphasis on epistemic communities and socially influenced learning made him identify, during his last decade, with constructivism as an approach to understanding international relations. "Pragmatic constructivism" was the label he and Peter Haas applied to their favored approach to social science, in particular the study of international institutions.

ARE THERE ALTERNATIVES TO REALISM AND IDEALISM?   Finally, from the start, Haas asked different versions of a fundamental normative question: Are there "other ways to peace than either power [realism] or law [idealism]?" (Haas 2004, p. xiv). He saw his own work as providing a tentative "yes" for an answer. Neo-functionalism, he wrote in 2004, "was developed explicitly to challenge the two theories of IR dominant in the 1950s, classical realism and idealism" (Haas 2004, p. xiv).

Haas sometimes seemed reticent about addressing normative issues explicitly; indeed, on occasion he wrote as if he studied international cooperation merely out of intellectual curiosity. This comes as little surprise when we recall that, when Haas started his long scholarly career, the mere accusation of being an "idealist" could marginalize a scholar within the discipline. And so, in the original *Uniting of Europe*, he disclaimed interest in evaluating whether a United Europe would be good or bad and said he saw it as akin to a laboratory experiment in voluntary cooperation (Haas 1958, p. xi). In *Beyond the Nation State* he wrote that "even chaos becomes bearable when its constituents and their movements are understood" (Haas 1964, p. 497). And in *When Knowledge is Power* he declared, "states, not scholars writing books, are the architects that will design the international organizations of the future" (Haas 1990, p. 6).

But he let the cat out of the bag in 1970 when he admitted that "the main reason for studying regional integration is normative"—the opportunity to "study the peaceful creation of possible new types of human community" (Haas 1970, p. 608). One of his most explicit normative statements came in "Is there a Hole in the Whole?" (Haas 1975a), where he grappled with the role of science in politics. Haas was deeply committed to the proposition that scientific knowledge could contribute to a social learning, which in turn could generate better-informed conceptions of the public interest. Yet he was resolutely opposed to deterministic or totalizing notions of science, in which scientific knowledge would provide moral purposes as well as the means of their realization. For Haas, human purposes had to remain primary, and they had to be determined through political participation. In using knowledge, "all groups making a claim to having studied the issue must be included" (Haas 1975a, p. 850), and conceptions of knowledge must remain open-ended, subject to debate and change. In that article, he declared his commitment to "informed incrementalism as a way to approach the construction of wholes, as resulting from a better understanding of the parts and their linkages" (p. 851).

In his later work, Haas became interested in deliberate learning strategies, through consensual knowledge and epistemic communities. He cited as one example the UN Global Compact's efforts to develop and apply consensual knowledge about best corporate practices in promoting human rights, labor standards, and environmental sustainability at the global level (Haas & Haas 2002, p. 597). Consensual knowledge and the raising of consciousness had the potential, he thought, for helping to transform political life. Throughout his career, Haas used his methodology of ideal types to imagine transformative possibilities, rather than simply to analyze world politics as it is. But he never permitted his normative interests or commitments to get in the way of the evidence, frequently reaching conclusions—as with the entire integration project in the 1970s—that were uncongenial to his own preferences.

The last chapter of *When Knowledge is Power* is a profession of Haas' personal commitment to progress, defined in terms of more holistic, but still human-centered, ways to manage interdependence better. His normative view is expressed on the last page: "One can think about human progress as an open-ended groping for self-improvement, without a final goal, without a transcendent faith, but with frequent reverses and sporadic self-questioning about the trajectory of change" (Haas 1990, p. 212).

A Synthesis

If we combine these core animating questions and Haas' evolving answers into a coherent whole, what is the resulting model—or ideal type, to be precise—of international change at the macro level?

It is important to stress again that he assumed "certain Hobbesian aspects of international life" (Haas 1970, p. viii). But he also assumed domestic pluralism and interest group competition, or some functional equivalents. And he stipulated that international actors—typically leaders of international institutions—served as norm entrepreneurs as well as potential allies of domestic groups who saw that their interests could be, or even must be, pursued beyond the confines of their own national state. So to the "certain Hobbesian aspects" Haas added both push and pull factors inclined toward some measure of internationalizing policy processes.

Next, Haas expected that certain kinds of issues would bias the process in favor of actors who perceived internationalization to be in their interest, because it helped them meet their objectives. Over the years, as we have seen, he explored a number of such "strategic items," as he once called them (Haas 1964, p. 83), which might have this "expansive" potential: (*a*) the emergence of domestic economic and social welfare as the universal measures of political legitimacy, so that national decision makers faced higher costs if they opposed internationalization of policy processes when it advanced those goals; (*b*) the emerging concept of human rights, which by definition claims universality and addresses the most intimate of relations between citizens and their state; (*c*) the human environment, which embodies intrinsic natural connectivities that respect no political boundaries; and more generally, (*d*) what we might call the growing demand-capacity gap that results from the increased complexity and mobilization of modern society, coupled with the proliferation and escalation of diverse objectives that policy makers consequently must consider—which Haas (1976) described as "turbulent fields."

Haas' research suggested that greater international cooperation, at least on early iterations, did not necessarily trigger transformation. There was just more of it: in the forms of international regimes, institutions, and norms. And so, as a second-order question, he explored how the growing role of scientific knowledge and scientists in policy making changed the picture. Why would it? Because, he presumed, natural scientists would be more likely than politicians or bureaucrats to push consensual knowledge about, say, environmental degradation, and social scientists would add both a reflective and a reflexive element to the policy-making mix.[10]

Along the way, Haas also gradually modified what he meant by international change. His first inclination was to extend into the global arena his original template for regional integration: "the process whereby political actors in several distinct national settings are persuaded to shift their loyalties toward a new center, whose institutions possess or demand jurisdiction over the pre-existing national states" (Haas 1958, p. 16; 1961). He quickly abandoned this model of supranationality even for the case of Europe and realized that it had no relevance globally. In *Beyond the Nation State*, the definition of international transformation was modified to "the process of increasing the interaction and the mingling [between states and international organizations] so as to obscure the boundaries [between them]" (Haas 1964, p. 29). But it was still expected to involve a shift from unit to system. By the time he got to "Is there a Hole in the Whole?" (Haas 1975a), that notion, too, was abandoned, and transformation itself was transformed. In that essay, "transformation" refers to state actors learning to manage problems collectively that exceed the grasp of any one, by constantly aggregating and reaggregating issue bundles into temporary wholes that they agree to govern collectively. In this account, successive rounds of that process, over the long term, come to approximate more closely the consensual knowledge about underlying cause/effect relations in the issue areas in question, as well as the substantive values at stake in them—be they human rights, environmental sustainability, or a measure of distributive justice via development assistance. Judging from the 2002 article Ernst Haas coauthored with Peter Haas, he seems to have concluded that the empirical processes of international cooperation that he had studied for so long at least modestly conformed to and explained this outcome.

But by the 1990s Haas also seems to have concluded that, in terms of fundamental international transformation, at least outside the EU, the transformative potential of action at the international level would continue to be both modest and incremental, as his most recent work had recorded. And so he turned his attention back to the source where, in a certain sense, the challenge had begun: back to the phenomenon of nationalism.

ON NATIONALISM

As a Jew, Haas was forced to leave Germany with his parents in 1938, at the age of 14, having experienced first-hand a virulent and intolerant nationalism that detested difference in the German *Volk*. In the United States, in contrast, he found

---

[10]Thus, it was a moment of professional pride for Haas when UN Secretary-General Kofi Annan was awarded the Nobel Peace Prize in 2001 for "bringing new life to the organization," in the words of the Nobel citation. Although he and Annan never met, for Haas it was enough that Ruggie was Annan's chief advisor for strategic planning, and that, as a former Haas student, Ruggie was attempting to practice what Haas had long preached.

a liberal nationalism that was tolerant of a great variety of differences. His work on nationalism undoubtedly had emotional roots in these early personal experiences. But there is nothing emotional or personal about the work itself.

Haas' two-volume study on nationalism, published in 1997 and 2000, totals over 800 pages. Whatever else critics may say of these books, they are not "scholarship lite" parading stylized facts. They exude the signs of elbow grease and many years of hard yet joyous research informed by an evolving, open-ended intellectual agenda. At the end of an illustrious career exploring patterns of transformation in the traditional conduct of international politics, Haas returned to liberal nationalism as the political force that he thought still promised the greatest potential for creating human progress at the outset of the twenty-first century—more than regional integration, more than international organizations and global regimes, and more than expert knowledge; more, that is, than all the other preoccupations of his rich intellectual life. In 1964, in Part III of *Beyond the Nation State* Haas had laid out a typology of different kinds of nationalism. After 40 years (like Goethe's long hiatus between the first and second parts of *Faust*), Haas articulated his position fully and magisterially. The first and last chapters of the two volumes are in fact nothing less than the summation of a lifetime of learning.[11]

Volume 1, *Nationalism, Liberalism and Progress* (Haas 1997), analyzes the five major advanced industrial states: Great Britain, the United States, France, Germany, and Japan. Haas argues that nationalism, liberalism, and progress can go hand in hand. Nationalism is neither historically regressive nor morally misleading. It is an instrument, not a structure. It is political, not primordial. It is behavioral, not imaginary. And it is designed to make life better for societies that have to cope with the consequences of modernization. Race, religion, and language are cultural building blocks of national identity. They permit leaders to articulate a collective national vision.

Haas rejected the distinction between good, Western, civic nationalism and bad, Eastern, ethnic nationalism, which from Kohn (1944) to Greenfeld (1992) has been a staple in the scholarship on nationalism. He also rejected imbalanced conceptions of nationalism that focus too much on elites (intellectuals in Kohn's massive study) or too much on mass publics [as in Deutsch's (1953) theory of social mobilization and cultural assimilation]. Haas saw little merit in overly structural macrohistorical arguments of state building, such as those by Tilly (1975) and Rokkan (Flora et al. 1999). At the same time, he had little patience for overly voluntaristic accounts that conceive of nations as imagined communities, like the work of Anderson (1983). As in the story of the three bears, Haas' conceptual schemes and taxonomic distinctions aim for the "just right" balance in between.

---

[11]Haas taught a course on nationalism and imperialism throughout his academic career at Berkeley. But with the exception of one section of *Beyond the Nation State*, he wrote relatively little on nationalism until late in life. Privately he described the two-volume study as his retirement project, though he never fully retired even from teaching.

The story of liberal nationalism starts in the eighteenth century, with the rise of the idea of progress and the very possibility for a public policy that incorporates scientific reasoning and evidence. Liberal nationalism could be defeated temporarily by other types of nationalism—for example, the integral nationalism that Haas experienced as a boy in Nazi Germany. Whereas liberal, progressive nationalism is affirming and open to change, Nazi-style integral nationalism lacks self-examination and acts out only one political repertoire of action. More than half of the songs in the Horst Wessel songbook, for example, sung by millions of young Germans in the 1930s, reportedly dealt with death. It was a nationalism that celebrated the prospect of marching itself and tens of millions into the grave. Among all the different kinds of nationalism, over the long term, liberal nationalism alone holds forth the promise of bringing about reciprocal exchanges in society, of sustaining formal rationality and self-examination based on adaptation or learning.

For each of the five societies, Haas collected systematic data on 16 indicators, such as official language, conscription rules, popular acceptance of state taxation, and the like. The consensual degree of acceptance of each indicator was ranked in ordinal terms and the scores were summed for each of seven years over the course of two centuries. Across the seven data points, the acceptance scores increase for all five societies, indicating that over time substantial social learning occurred. But they also reflect movement at different speeds and temporary reversals. The Anglo-Saxon countries evolved differently from France and Germany, for example, not only until World War II but also between 1950 and 1990. France and Germany appear to have attained in the recent past a higher degree of internal reciprocity and procedural liberalism, as well as a greater awareness of the inevitability of nesting their liberal nationalism in Europe-wide political arrangements, than Britain has. The United States, like Britain, shows signs of growing social divisions in recent decades, and a growing resistance to governance beyond the nation-state. In the long run, however, liberal nationalism clearly is progressive. Indeed, Haas anticipated that it eventually will transform itself, at least in part, into new forms of multilateral cosmopolitanism.

The analysis of eight latecomers to nationalism is the subject of the second volume, subtitled *The Dismal Fate of New Nations* (Haas 2000). The analysis includes China, India, Iran, Egypt, Brazil, Mexico, Russia, and the Ukraine. Nation-building leaders in the Third World and transition states use nationalism as a rationalizing and progressive formula. Modernization can occur under the banners of different syncretist nationalisms in which religion continues to play a large role. Even among latecomers to nationalism, strategy and choice matter more to outcomes than structure does, and they reflect the different pressures of ideology, adaptation (the choice of new means), and, occasionally, social learning (the choice of new ends). Yet only four of the eight countries—Brazil, China, Mexico, and Russia (until 1991)—have experienced successful rationalization.

Haas concluded that only social learning leads to lasting societal integration and that this outcome is due to the self-examination that it permits. So here, too, liberal nationalism is found to be the most progressive type of nationalism. It alone is open to continuous compromise between changing perceptions of interest and values, on the one hand, and newly acquired knowledge, on the other. It should be noted that for Haas the triumph of liberalism is procedural rather than substantive. He rejected fixed liberal dogmas in favor of liberal rules that remain devoid of moral content and that permit vigorous debate and conflict among competing interests and values, none of which can claim inherent superiority. Diffuse reciprocity and compromise, not moral ends, are at the core of his procedural understanding of liberal, progressive nationalism.

Haas' theory of nationalism is distinctive and yet deeply influenced by the work of Karl Deutsch, a fact freely acknowledged in the preface of the first volume, where he wrote that Deutsch's work persuaded him "at the very beginning of my academic life that history can be formally analyzed, not merely told as stories" (Haas 1997, p. ix). For both Deutsch and Haas, modernization and social mobilization are crucial forces driving the spread of nationalism. And these processes are amenable to quantitative estimates: in Haas' case to measurements of the degree of consensual rationalization, and in Deutsch's to measurements of the balance between the nationally assimilated and unassimilated shares of the population. Haas saw and hoped for an open-ended process in which liberal nationalism would eventually prevail and then transform itself into variants of multilateral cosmopolitanism; Deutsch, in contrast, predicted a century or more of fragmenting empires and polities, accompanied only in a few instances by the emergence of pluralistic security communities. Still, there exists a remarkable similarity in their overall assessment of the future of nationalism and in the empirical methods they used for coming to a reasoned assessment of trend lines that connect the past to the future. Moreover, their scholarship stands up extremely well in comparison to the best classical work of scholars like Kohn, who preceded them during the interwar years, and to the most recent scholarship on the subject, such as Anderson's. Haas and Deutsch were frequently on opposite sides of arguments about the future of regional integration. But on the question of nationalism they shared intellectual orientations and were politically committed to a somewhat technocratic, progressive notion of achieving social change.

This is not to argue that Haas was propounding the message of modernization theory 1960s- or 1990s-style. No End of History here. The data in Volume 2 suggest that the continued salience of religion is the main reason why modernization does not automatically yield a progressive liberal nationalism. Significant rationalization can be achieved through nonliberal forms of nationalism that mobilize religion in support of governance. Indeed, integral—not liberal—nationalism is the most effective modernizer, although sustainable progress thereafter is best served by liberal nationalism.

Volume 2 thus links directly to a line of reasoning developed in the 1990s by Eisenstadt and historians working under the label of "multiple modernities." Like Haas, these scholars think in long time periods and put religion at a central place. Modern societies are not converging around common patterns of capitalist industrialization, political democratization, and secularism. Rather, "the idea of multiple modernities presumes that the best way to understand the contemporary world...is to see it as a story of continual constitution and reconstitution of a multiplicity of cultural programs" (Eisenstadt 2000, p. 2). Different civilizational or religious cores continuously reinfuse culturally different programs in creating the antinomies of modernity. Modernizing non-Western societies and modern Western societies thus display different patterns of modernity. The cultural core of West European modernity offers a specific "bundle of moral-cognitive imperatives under the premises of the rationalization of the world" (Spohn 2001, p. 501), and a secularizing reconstruction of religious traditions that radiates outward to other parts of Europe as well as North and South America through imposition, emulation, and incorporation.

Because Western modernity is adopted selectively and transformed in widely differing political and cultural contexts, however, it does not create a common global standard. Indeed, Western modernity is sufficiently broad to allow for tensions, even contradictions, between orthodox and heterodox orientations and identities, and ineluctable conflicts between geographic and socioeconomic centers and peripheries. Even among advanced industrial societies, such as Germany and Japan, the ability of modernity to accommodate the vast differences in religious traditions confirms its political plasticity and institutional plurality (Eisenstadt 1986, 1996, 1998). Yet Haas and Eisenstadt did part company on the crucial case of Japan. For Haas, Japan ends up in the liberal nationalist camp, whereas Eisenstadt would code it as a case of syncretist nationalism. That disagreement cuts to a question at the very core of Haas' enterprise: Does liberal nationalism win out in his formulation simply because of his prior, strong ontological commitment to open-ended learning that, by the author's fiat, only liberal (not syncretist) nationalism can embody? Going well beyond the Japanese case, the answer to this question is of fundamental importance to the political evolution of nationalism in this century. While Eisenstadt's work is rooted in Weber on world religions, Haas' draws from Weber on bureaucratic rationality. And whereas Eisenstadt is willing to accept antinomies that are perpetually recreated and that make even traditional fundamentalism modern, Haas held with determination to the idea that in the long term the self-reflexivity, open-endedness, and procedural thinness of liberal nationalism give it a decisive edge over all other forms of nationalism.

Finally, at least on the surface, there is nothing that connects Haas' work to the recent and highly innovative combinations of rational choice and anthropology, and of computer simulation based on agent-based modeling, which have begun to make important inroads in the analysis of national identity. Because of his profound interest in social learning and knowledge rather than mere interest and information, Haas kept his distance from strong—he might even have said "dogmatic"—versions of rational choice. But surface appearances can be somewhat misleading. The boost that complexity theory is getting from the microelectronic revolution might have tempted Haas were he to start his academic career now. For him, words always were imperfect instruments for catching deeper theoretical insights. He always struggled to express holistic thinking in analytical language. Whereas analytic thought dissects the world into a limited number of discrete objects that can be captured by language, holistic thought responds to a much wider array of objects and their complex relations, and is less well suited to linguistic representation. Haas' taxonomies, piled on top of each other in dizzying cascades, were an effort to recreate holistic thought out of atomistic categories and concepts. Thus, he surely would explore the relevance of computer simulations based on complexity theory.

There is also a deeper connection between Haas' work on nationalism and recent approaches that take us into entirely new realms of theory and data. Important advances at the intersection of rational choice and anthropology, as well as in agent-based modeling, have been made by some of Haas' former students, Laitin (1998) and Lustick (2000) being among the best known. Haas' two-volume study resulted from decades of teaching, but in turn also learning from, students in his ever-popular seminar on nationalism and imperialism. Though solitary at the moment of creation, the production of all knowledge was for Haas an inherently social enterprise. Indeed, he encouraged his students to explore frontiers of learning that he was eager to hear about, even though for his own good reasons he did not choose to visit all those places himself.

CONCLUSION

Haas was preparing for his professional career at one of those rare foundational moments in the history of world politics: the reconstruction of the international order after World War II. While he was studying at Columbia University on the GI Bill, the UN General Assembly and Security Council began to meet at nearby Lake Success, the World Bank and International Monetary Fund got under way, the General Agreement on Tariffs and Trade was established, NATO was founded—and the European Coal and Steel Community was created. He also witnessed, and wrote his dissertation on, early moves towards decolonization and the role of the UN in facilitating the process (Haas 1952, 1953a). For Haas, these were all clear signals of a world being remade, potentially offering new possibilities for reordering the relations among states that had not existed in the past. And he wanted better to understand them.

Others in that same period—and at the same graduate school—developed different professional preoccupations, including Kenneth Waltz, Haas' future Berkeley colleague, who was a few years behind him but overlapped briefly with him at Columbia. (The two even had the same dissertation adviser, William T.R. Fox, but never met.) For Waltz, the emerging bipolarity and the nuclear balance of terror stood out as the most distinctive features of the new era, drawing his professional attention and theoretical acumen. Who could argue that they did not both make sound choices? But the interparadigmatic dialogue for which Haas pleaded at the end of his career never came. It is our hope that a new generation of young scholars will advance that cause. We have sought to contribute to it by summarizing Haas' voluminous and sometimes difficult work, making it more readily accessible and clarifying why he took the analytical positions he did.

Haas' special contribution was to push us beyond the limits of the mundane, observable, contemporary realities of world politics, including "certain Hobbesian aspects." He presented us with enduring questions about, and brilliant insights into, the relationships among the universal desire for human betterment, the unintended consequences of self-interested behavior on the part of states and other actors, and social learning and transformations in the practices and institutions of world politics. Those who believe in the possibility of progress in the relations among states without succumbing to illusions about its immanence—or imminence—are permanently in his debt.

The *Annual Review of Political Science* is online at
http://polisci.annualreviews.org

LITERATURE CITED

Adler E. 1991. Cognitive evolution: a dynamic approach for the study of international relations and their progress. See Adler & Crawford 1991, pp. 43–88

Adler E. 2000. *Ernst Haas' theory of international politics. Remarks presented on the occasion of Ernst Haas' retirement celebration*, Univ. Calif., Berkeley

Adler E, Crawford B, eds. 1991. *Progress in Postwar International Relations*. New York: Columbia Univ. Press

Anderson B. 1983. *Imagined Communities: Reflections on the Origin and Spread of Nationalism*. London: Verso

Deutsch K. 1953. *Nationalism and Social Communication*. Cambridge and New York: MIT Press and Wiley

Dinan D. 2004. Foreword. *The Uniting of Europe*. South Bend, IN: Notre Dame Univ. Press

Eisenstadt SN. 1986. *The Origins and Diversity of Axial-Age Civilizations*. Albany, NY: SUNY Press

Eisenstadt SN. 1996. *Japanese Civilization: A Comparative View*. Chicago: Univ. Chicago Press

Eisenstadt SN. 1998. Axial and non-axial civilizations: the Japanese experience in comparative perspective the construction of generalized particularistic trust. In *Japan in a Comparative Perspective*, ed. H Sonoda, SN Eisenstadt, pp. 1–17. Kyoto: Int. Res. Cent. Jpn. Stud.

Eisenstadt SN. 2000. Multiple modernities. *Daedalus* 129(1):1–29

Flora P, Kuhnle S, Urwin D, eds. 1999. *State Formation, Nation-Building, and Mass Politics in Europe: The Theory of Stein Rokkan—Based on His Collected Works*. Oxford, UK: Oxford Univ. Press

Greenfeld L. 1992. *Nationalism: Five Roads to Modernity*. Cambridge, MA: Harvard Univ. Press

Haas EB. 1952. The reconciliation of conflicting colonial policy aims: acceptance of the League of Nations mandate system. *Int. Organ.* 6(4):521–36

Haas EB. 1953a.The attempt to terminate colonialism: acceptance of the United Nations trusteeship system. *Int. Organ.* 7(1):1–21

Haas EB. 1953b. The balance of power as a guide to policy-making. *J. Polit.* 15(3):370–98

Haas EB. 1953c. The balance of power: prescription, concept or propaganda? *World Polit.* 5(4):442–47

Haas EB. 1958. *The Uniting of Europe*. Stanford: Stanford Univ. Press

Haas EB. 1961. International integration: the European and the universal process. *Int. Organ.* 15(3):366–92

Haas EB. 1964. *Beyond the Nation State*. Stanford: Stanford Univ. Press

Haas EB. 1970. *Human Rights and International Action*. Stanford: Stanford Univ. Press

Haas EB. 1971. The study of regional integration: reflections on the joy and anguish of pretheorizing. In *Regional Integration: Theory and Research*, ed. LN Lindberg, SA Scheingold, pp. 3–44. Cambridge, MA: Harvard Univ. Press

Haas EB, Butterworth RL, Nye JS. 1972. *Conflict Management by International Organizations*. New York: General Learning Press

Haas EB. 1975a. Is there a hole in the whole? Knowledge, technology, interdependence, and the construction of international regimes. *Int. Organ.* 29(3):827–76

Haas EB. 1975b. *The Obsolescence of Regional Integration*. Inst. Int. Stud. Monogr. Ser. Berkeley, CA: Inst. Int. Stud.

Haas EB. 1976. Turbulent fields and the theory of regional integration. *Int. Organ.* 30(2):173–12

Haas EB. 1978. *Global Evangelism Rides Again: How to Protect Human Rights Without Really Trying*. Univ. Calif. Policy Pap. No. 5, Berkeley, CA

Haas EB. 1980. Why collaborate? Issue-linkage and international regimes. *World Polit.* 32(3):357–405

Haas EB. 1982. Words can hurt you; or, who said what to whom about regimes. *Int. Organ.* 36(2):207–43

Haas EB. 1983. Regime decay: conflict management and international organizations, 1945–1981. *Int. Organ.* 37(2):189–56

Haas EB. 1986. *The United Nations and Collective Management of International Conflict*. United Nations: UN Inst. Train. and Res.

Haas EB. 1990. *When Knowledge is Power: Three Models of Change in International Organizations*. Berkeley: Univ. Calif. Press

Haas EB. 1993. *Beware the Slippery Slope:*

Notes Toward the Definition of Justifiable Intervention. Univ. Calif., Inst. Int. Stud. Policy Pap. No. 42, Berkeley, CA

Haas EB. 1997. *Nationalism, Liberalism and Progress*. Vol. 1. *The Rise and Decline of Nationalism*. Ithaca, NY: Cornell Univ. Press

Haas EB. 2000. *Nationalism, Liberalism and Progress*. Vol. 2. *The Dismal Fate of New Nations*. Ithaca, NY: Cornell Univ. Press

Haas EB. 2004. Introduction: institutionalism or constructivism? In *The Uniting of Europe*. South Bend, IN: Univ. Notre Dame Press

Haas EB, Haas PM. 2002. Pragmatic constructivism and the study of international institutions. *Millennium J. Int. Stud.* 31(2):573–601

Kohn H. 1944. *The Idea of Nationalism.* New York: Macmillan

Laitin DD. 1998. *Identity in Formation: The Russian-speaking Populations in the Near Abroad.* Ithaca, NY: Cornell Univ. Press

Lindberg LN, Scheingold SA. 1970. *Europe's Would-be Polity:* Patterns of Change in the European Community. Englewood Cliffs, NJ: Prentice-Hall

Lindberg LN, Scheingold SA, eds. 1971. *Regional Integration: Theory and Research.* Cambridge, MA: Harvard Univ. Press

Lustick I. 2000. Agent-based modeling of collective identity: testing constructivist theory. *J. Artif. Soc. Social Simul.* 3(1): http://jasss. soc.surrey.ac.uk/5/3/7.html

Mearsheimer JJ. 1990. Back to the future: instability in Europe after the Cold War. *Int. Sec.* 15(1):5–56

Merton R. 1957. *Social Theory and Social Structure.* New York: Free

Mitrany D. (1943) 1966. *A Working Peace System.* London: R. Inst. Int. Aff.; Chicago: Quadrangle Books

Monnet J. 1978. *Memoirs.* Garden City, NY: Doubleday

Moravcsik A. 1998. *The Choice for Europe: Social Purpose and State Power From Messina to Maastricht.* Ithaca, NY: Cornell Univ. Press

Ruggie JG. 1975. International responses to technology: concepts and trends. *Int. Organ.* 29(3):557–83

Ruggie JG. 1995. The false premise of realism. *Int. Sec.* 20(1):62–70

Ruggie JG. 1998. What makes the world hang together? Neo-utilitarianism and the social constructivist challenge. *Int. Organ.* 52(4):855–85

Saeter M. 1993. *Democracy, Sovereignty and Supranationality: Institution-Building and the European Union—A Neofunctionalist Perspective*. Work. Pap. 497, Nor. Inst. Int. Aff., Oslo

Schmitter PC. 1971. A revised theory of regional integration. See Lindberg & Scheingold 1971, pp. 232–65

Spohn W. 2001. Eisenstadt on civilizations and multiple modernity. *Eur. J. Soc. Theory* 4(4):499–508

Tilly C, ed. 1975. *The Formation of National States in Western Europe*. Princeton, NJ: Princeton Univ. Press

Waltz K. 1979. *Theory of International Politics*. Reading, MA: Addison-Wesley

Weber M. 1947. *The Theory of Social and Economic Organization*, ed. T Parsons. New York: Free

Weber M. 1949. *The Methodology of the Social Sciences*. Transl. E Shils, HA Finch (from Ger.). Glencoe, IL: Free

Annu. Rev. Polit. Sci. 2005. 8:297–333
doi: 10.1146/annurev.polisci.8.090203.103000
First published online as a Review in Advance on Jan. 24, 2005

THE GLOBALIZATION OF PUBLIC OPINION RESEARCH

Anthony Heath, Stephen Fisher, and Shawna Smith

*Department of Sociology, University of Oxford, Oxford OX1 3UQ, United Kingdom;
email: anthony.heath@sociology.ox.ac.uk, stephen.fisher@sociology.ox.ac.uk,
shawna.smith@sociology.ox.ac.uk*

Key Words   survey methodology, cross-national research, comparative research, survey history

■ **Abstract**   As globalization has opened up channels of communication between different countries and increased interest in cross-national analysis, public opinion survey research has expanded its reach in the world. This article examines both the breadth and the depth of the globalization of public opinion research. First, we discuss the growth of cross-national surveys such as the World Values Survey, the International Social Survey Program, the European Social Survey, and the various Global Barometers. We then turn to the issues of data quality and comparability. Has the globalization of survey research meant the spread of a standard "product" of known and equivalent quality to diverse countries? Can survey research in diverse countries and contexts deliver meaningful comparisons of public opinion? Has globalization led to the dominance of an intellectual framework and set of assumptions that may not be quite appropriate outside their original homes? Finally, the article suggests a new standard for "grading" cross-national programs of survey research, inspired by debates in evidence-based medicine.

INTRODUCTION

If globalization is "the emergence of a global culture system. . .brought about by a variety of social and cultural developments" (Marshall 1998, p. 258), these social and cultural developments connote a number of processes specific to public opinion and survey research. For one, the greater ease and speed of communication between countries, seen in the close collaboration between national teams, makes these cross-national programs of survey research feasible. Another connotation of globalization is the export of Western technology and practices to less developed countries, seen in the export of survey research methodologies across the globe. And a third is the penetration of global brands to markets around the world. This article explores the extent to which a global "brand" or "product" of public opinion research has spread across the world, and what the current limitations and intellectual assumptions of such a brand might be.

We begin with a brief history of the spread of public opinion surveys, particularly noting growth among commercial, government, and academic surveys, and most specifically the growth of cross-national survey endeavors, around the world. We then turn to the issues of data quality and comparability. Has the globalization of survey research meant the spread of a standard "product" of known and equivalent quality to diverse countries? Can survey research in diverse countries and contexts deliver meaningful comparisons of public opinion? And finally, has globalization led to the dominance of a particular intellectual framework and set of assumptions that may not be quite appropriate outside their original homes?

In this review, we focus largely on academic survey research rather than on government or commercial opinion polls, and we focus particularly on the widely used and highly regarded cross-national survey programs. However, a great deal of what we say will also apply to academic surveys (and indeed to government and commercial ones) that are not part of these cross-national programs.

A BRIEF HISTORY

Commercial Polls

Although roots of the survey method can be traced back to the nineteenth century (see, e.g., Marsh 1982, Converse 1987), the start of systematic public opinion research is usually taken to be the work of George Gallup in the United States during the interwar years (Worcester 1987, Bulmer 1998, Rose & Osborne 1999). Although there were opinion polls before Gallup's, his contribution was the use of systematic samples of the population:

> If a sample is accurately selected, it represents a near replica of the entire population. It is a miniature electorate with the same proportion of farmers, doctors, lawyers, Catholics, Protestants, old people, young people, business-men, laborers and so on, as is to be found in the entire population. (Gallup 1948, pp. 22–23)

The key features of survey research established by Gallup—and followed ever since—were the use of random samples from a defined population (typically quota rather than probability samples), the use of standardized "closed" questions to measure subjective attitudes and demographic characteristics of respondents, the administration of face-to-face surveys by trained interviewers, and the quantitative analysis of the results. The focus of these early surveys was on political attitudes and behavior; most famously, Gallup successfully predicted Roosevelt's win in the 1936 presidential election (in contrast to the *Literary Digest*, whose predic-tion of an Alf Landon victory relied on a nonrepresentative sample) (Rose & Osborne 1999). Gallup exported his approach and methods to Britain in 1937 and France in 1938, and commercial public opinion research rapidly spread during the war years to other wealthy industrialized countries, reaching Australia, Canada,

Denmark, Switzerland, the Netherlands, West Germany, Finland, Norway, and Italy by 1946 (Worcester 1987). In nearly all of these countries, Gallup polls (and others) continue to thrive, although telephone interviewing has gradually replaced face-to-face interviews, mainly owing to cost concerns.

A continuing theme has been the political opinion poll, for which commercial sponsors (such as the mass media) can readily be found. By the beginning of the 1980s, commercial political polls were being conducted in nearly all Western democracies and in a growing number of Communist and less-developed nations (Crespi 1989). Today that number is even larger; Gallup's most recent survey, The Voice of the People (http://www.voice-of-the-people.net), drew respondents from 51 countries in 2003, including a number of Middle Eastern, West Asian, and African countries. It is now rare to have a general election in a democracy without a pre-election poll [although, as Smith (2004) notes, bans on polls during the immediate run-up to an election still exist in some countries].

Government-Sponsored Polls

A second broad category of polls, government-sponsored surveys, began to grow at around the same time that Gallup's methods were being exported. Government polls, however, were designed to meet governments' needs for knowing about (and perhaps influencing) their citizens, and had the potential to be somewhat less benign than commercial polls. One of the earliest examples is the "survey" of each British county demanded by the Defense of the Realm Act of April 1798, conducted by the British government to ascertain the willingness of the (male) public to fight against the French in the event of an invasion (Colley 1992). More contemporarily, however, Samuel Stouffer and his team in the Research Branch of the Information and Education Division of the U.S. War Department conducted surveys of the U.S. armed forces between 1942 and 1945. These studies, collectively known as The American Soldier, used polling techniques to examine the attitudes and morale of soldiers, injecting for the first time social psychological questions and questioning subjective opinions and preferences (Stouffer et al. 1949a,b, 1950; Hovland 1950; Kuechler 1998; Rose & Osborne 1999). Interestingly, nondemocratic governments also have a history of carrying out opinion polls. When Khrushchev came to power in the Soviet Union, his criticisms of the lack of reliable information on his publics led to the formation of the Institute for Concrete Social Research and the appointment of Boris Grushin as the head of a center for studying public opinion in 1969 (Worcester 1987). And in the former Czechoslovakia, although the previously established Institute for Public Opinion Research was abolished and condemned as "bourgeois pseudoscience" by the Communist Party in 1948, it was re-established in 1965 within the newly formed Institute of Sociology. As Otava (1988) notes, however, the "empirical" results of these studies were not always used in good faith:

> [I]n the first issue of the *Sociological Journal* for 1987, a regular feature entitled "Empirical Surveys" presented the results of an investigation called

"Public Opinion on Questions of War and Peace". . . . It begins with the sentence: "The empirical results confirm a positive evaluation of the foreign-policy orientation of the USSR. The opinion that the USSR is working for peace was unanimous. . . ." (pp. 252–53)

At best, government polls can give citizens a voice—although at worst they can be a source of political manipulation. The growing need to obtain the assent of the governed in an advanced society means that such government surveys have also become more global. Most recently, for example, the Coalition Provisional Authority in Iraq commissioned public opinion surveys to help formulate its policy.

An additional weakness of government-sponsored opinion surveys is that they are rarely available for secondary academic analysis. One important exception, however, is the Eurobarometer (http://europa.eu.int/comm/public_opinion/) sponsored by the European Commission. In 1962, the then EEC (European Economic Community) commissioned the "Attitudes to Europe" survey of Germany, France, and the Benelux counties. This was a prelude to the Eurobarometer, a biannual survey that started in 1970 and has included all European member states since 1973. Its coverage has expanded as the European Union has grown, and it has recently been supplemented by the Candidate Countries Eurobarometer (CC-EB; http://europa.eu.int/comm/public_opinion/), which was launched in 2001 as a replacement for the Central and Eastern Eurobarometer. As both of these surveys have EU funding, their primary purpose has been meeting the needs of the EU; however, the Eurobarometers have also had substantial academic input, notably collaboration with the Inter-University Consortium for Political and Social Research at the University of Michigan and the ZUMA (Zentrum für Umfragen, Methoden und Analysen) Center for Survey Research and Methodology at the University of Mannheim. These two institutes have also made the data available for secondary analysis, and the data have been widely used in academic research (see Inglehart 1990, 1997).

Academic Surveys

The main focus of this review is on a third category of surveys, namely academic surveys, funded by research councils or charities and directed by independent research institutes. Some of the earliest academic surveys of public opinion were again in the United States but were based on local samples. The Columbia studies of Erie County, OH in 1940 and Elmira County, NY in 1948, funded initially by the Rockefeller Foundation and guided by Berelson and Lazarsfeld, examined individuals in these two communities to study how voters made up their minds during presidential election campaigns. Both studies were panel studies, and attention was given to several individual variables as well as contextual variables, such as the mass media (largely in the Erie study) and interpersonal associations (in Elmira) (Lazarsfeld et al. 1948, Rossi 1964, Berelson et al. 1954).

Published several months before the Elmira study, but examining the 1952 election, was another study of the American electorate conducted by the Survey

Research Center (SRC) at the University of Michigan. The SRC's Michigan Studies, later the American National Election Studies (ANES; http://www.umich.edu/~nes/), differed from the Columbia studies by using relatively small but nationally representative probability samples and by focusing on individual motivations for party preferences. Campbell developed the sociopsychological intellectual framework embodied by the Michigan Studies in the classic works *The Voter Decides* and *The American Voter* (Campbell et al. 1954, 1960). The Michigan Studies shortly became the gold standard in electoral research and have conducted studies of every presidential and congressional election since 1948. The National Science Foundation (NSF) took over funding the studies in 1977, formally establishing the ANES.

After their establishment in the United States, the Michigan Studies were exported, not unlike Gallup's export, via links with scholars in other countries. The model was first exported to Britain, with the famous collaboration between Donald Stokes (part of the *American Voter* team) and the British psephologist David Butler. They began with a 1963 pre-election survey and instituted panel studies of electoral behavior and opinion. This led to the classic work on British politics and public opinion, *Political Change in Britain* (Butler & Stokes 1974), and helped to establish the British Election Studies (BES; http://www.essex.ac.uk/bes/index.html/), in which panel research continues to play a large role. The Michigan Studies were also exported in rather similar fashion to India with a 1967 survey (Eldersveld & Ahmed 1978), and they established what remains a notable tradition of Indian electoral research.

Many other wealthy societies now have regular election surveys funded by national science foundations and intellectually independent of national governments or other interested bodies; however, only a few have long histories like the ANES or BES. France, for example, has still to acquire a series of this kind, and although a series of German election surveys can be constructed going back to 1949, it is not a formal series in the American or British sense. However, over the past 20 years or so there has been a rapid spread of election studies around the world, and the Comparative Study of Electoral Systems (CSES, http://www.umich.edu/~cses), a cross-national collaboration that includes a standardized "add-on" module to individual country election surveys, now covers more than 50 states. The first module, running from 1996 to 2001, was completed in more than 30 diverse countries, including the Ukraine, Israel, Korea, Thailand, and Peru.

In addition to the ANES, a second widely copied model has been the American General Social Survey (GSS; http://www.norc.uchicago.edu/projects/gensoc.asp/), which began in 1972, funded by the Russell Sage Foundation and the NSF. The GSS has a broader remit than the election survey and includes standardized, closed questions on social attitudes and values as well as political issues; the survey was annual until 1994 and has been biennial since. Like the ANES, it uses a nationally representative probability sample with face-to-face interviewing. The British Social Attitudes survey, which started in 1983, is largely the British equivalent of the GSS and holds a similar remit. In Germany, the Allgemeinen Bevölkerungsumfrage der

Sozialwissenschaften (ALLBUS), begun in 1980, also serves as a biennial survey of social behaviors and attitudes.

Collaboration between the ALLBUS and the GSS occurred as early as 1982. In 1984 these three social surveys, in conjunction with representatives from the Research School of the Social Sciences at the Australian National University, agreed to a further and more developed program of cross-national collaboration, eventually in the form of the International Social Survey Program (ISSP; http://www.issp.org). The founding countries—the United States, Britain, Germany, and Australia—devised the format of add-on modules of standardized closed questions, designed by the cross-national team, with identical wording in each participating country. The ISSP continues to conduct annual surveys, investigating a new topic each year. It now surveys 38 countries, predominantly Western but including Bangladesh since 1996 and South Africa since 2001, as well as Japan, Chile, Venezuela, and several former communist countries. Table 1 gives details of the countries that have been included in the ISSP (and in other major cross-national programs) since inception.

Most extensive of the academic survey programs has been the World Values Survey (WVS; http://www.worldvaluessurvey.org), which can make some claims to being global. It began in 1981 as the European Values Survey (EVS, http://www.europeanvalues.nl/), which covered 10 West European societies. The funding for the initial survey was provided by a private foundation, and the focus of the research was on changing moral and social values, particularly Christian values and "alternative" meaning systems (see Halman 2001). The EVS has now completed three rounds of surveys, the latest of which commenced in 1999, and continues to focus on values and value systems among European countries. The WVS grew out of the EVS; after the successful completion of the 1981 EVS, the survey was replicated in 12 non-European countries. Following the success of this wave, subsequent waves were conducted in 1990–1993 (42 countries), 1995–1997 (54 countries), and 1999–2001 (60 countries). Surveys have now taken place in almost 80 societies that represent all major regions of the world, although, as WVS documentation notes, illiterate rural respondents have been underrepresented. All WVS surveys are carried out in face-to-face interviews, using a standardized sampling universe of adult citizens aged 18 and over. Fieldwork in each country is typically supported by funding from that country, and although the WVS has a relatively stable questionnaire, since the 1990 survey, participants from all six continents have been involved in design, fieldwork, analysis, and interpretation.

Akin to the WVS in some respects (although consciously modeled on the Eurobarometer) are the instruments now known as the Global Barometers (http://www.globalbarometer.org). The New Europe Barometer (http://www.cspp.strath.ac.uk; formerly New Democracies Barometer) series was founded by Richard Rose at Strathclyde University "to monitor mass response to the transformation of polity, economy and society in post-Communist countries." The study has regularly surveyed the eight new EU countries and three applicant countries (Croatia, Bulgaria, and Romania), and has conducted intermittent surveys in Serbia, Moldova, and, for

TABLE 1 Country coverage in cross-national research programs

	ISSP[a]	WVS/EVS[b]	Global Barometers[c]	CSES[d]	ESS[e]	Eurobarometers[f]
Albania		WVS: '95				CC-EB: '91–'96
Algeria		WVS: '00				
Argentina		WVS: '81, '90, '95, '00	Lat: '88, '95–'04			
Armenia		WVS: '95				CC-EB: '92–'96
Australia	'85–'88, '90–'02	WVS: '81, '95		'96		
Austria	'85–'89, '91–'95, '98–'02	WVS: '90 EVS: '90, '99	NE: '91, '98, '04		'02	EB: '94–'04
Azerbaijan		WVS: '95				
Bangladesh	'96–'97, '99–'00	WVS: '95, '00				
Belarus		WVS: '90, '95 EVS: '99	NE: '92–'93, '95, '98, '04	'01a		CC-EB: '92–'96
Belgium	'00, '02	WVS: '81, '90 EVS: '81, '90, '99		'99	'02	EB: '74–'04
Bolivia			Lat: '96–'04			
Bosnia-Herzegovina		WVS: '95				
Botswana			Afro: '99, '03, '05			
Brazil	'00–'02	WVS: '90, '95	Lat: '88, '95–'04			
Bulgaria	'92–'00, '02	WVS: '81, '90 EVS: '99	NE: '91–'95, '98, '01, '04	'01b		CC-EB: '90–'97, '01–'03

(Continued)

TABLE 1 (*Continued*)

	ISSP[a]	WVS/EVS[b]	Global Barometers[c]	CSES[d]	ESS[e]	Eurobarometers[f]
Canada	'92–'01	WVS: '81, '90, '00		'97		
Cape Verde			Afro: '02, '05			
Chile	'98–'02	WVS: '90, '95, '00	Lat: '88, '95–'04	'99		
China		WVS: '90, '95, '00	EAsia: '94, '02			
Colombia		WVS: '95	Lat: '96–'04			
Costa Rica			Lat: '96–'04			
Croatia		WVS: '95 EVS: '99	NE: '92–'93, '95, '98, '04			CC-EB: '95–'96
Cyprus	'96–'02					CC-EB: '01–'03
Czech Republic	'93–'02	WVS: '90, '95 EVS: '99	NE: '91–'95, '98, '01, '04	'96	'02	CC-EB: '90–'97, '01–'03 EB: '02
Denmark	'98–'02	WVS: '81, '90 EVS: '81, '90, '99		'98	'02	EB: '74–'04
Dominican Republic		WVS: '95	Lat: '02, '04			
Democratic Republic of the Congo		WVS: '95				
Ecuador			Lat: '96–'04			
Egypt		WVS: '00				
El Salvador		WVS: '95	Lat: '96–'04			
Estonia		WVS: '90, '95 EVS: '99	NE: '98, '01			CC-EB: '91–'97, '01–'03

Finland	'00–'02	WVS: '81, '90, '95 EVS: '81, '90, '99			'02	EB: '93–'04
France	'96–'02	WVS: '81, '90 EVS: '81, '90, '99		'02	'02	EB: '74–'04
Georgia		WVS: '95				CC-EB: '92, '94–'96
Germany^g	'85–'02	WVS: '81, '90, '95 EVS: '81, '90, '99	NE: '04	'98, '02	'02	EB: '74–'04
Great Britain	'85–'02	WVS: '81, '90, '95 EVS: '81, '90, '99		'97	'02	EB: '74–'04
Ghana		WVS: '95	Afro: '97, '99, '02, '05			
Greece		EVS: '99			'02	EB: '80–'04
Guatemala			Lat: '96–'04			
Honduras			Lat: '96–'04			
Hong Kong			EAsia: '94, '01	'98, '00		
Hungary	'86–'02	WVS: '81, '90, '95 EVS: '81, '99	NE: '91–'95, '98, '01, '04	'98, '02	'02	CC-EB: '90–'97, '01–'03 EB: '02
Iceland		WVS: '81, '90 EVS: '81, '90, '99		'99		EB: '03
India		WVS: '90, '95, '00	EAsia: TBC			
Indonesia		WVS: '00				
Iran		WVS: '00				

(*Continued*)

TABLE 1 (*Continued*)

	ISSP[a]	WVS/EVS[b]	Global Barometers[c]	CSES[d]	ESS[e]	Eurobarometers[f]
Ireland	'86–'96, '98–'00, '02	WVS: '81, '90 EVS: '81, '90, '99		'02	'02	EB: '74–'04
Israel	'89–'91, '93–'94, '96–'02	WVS: '00		'96	'02	
Italy	'85–'01	WVS: '81, '90 EVS: '81, '90, '99			'02	EB: '74–'04
Japan	'93–'02	WVS: '81, '90, '95, '00	EAsia: TBC	'96		
Jordan		WVS: '00				
Kazakhstan						CC-EB: '94–'96
Kenya			Afro: '03, '05			
Latvia	'95–'02	WVS: '90, '95 EVS: '99	NE: '98, '01			CC-EB: '91–'97, '01–'03
Lesotho			Afro: '00, '03, '05			
Lithuania	'94	WVS: '90, '95 EVS: '99	NE: '98, '01	'97		CC-EB: '91–'97, '01–'03
Luxembourg		EVS: '99			'02	EB: '74–'04
Macedonia		WVS: '95				CC-EB: '93–'96
Malawi			Afro: '99, '03, '05			
Mali			Afro: '01, '02, '05			
Malta		EVS: '99				CC-EB: '01–'03
Mexico	'00, '02	WVS: '81, '90, '95, '00	Lat: '95–'04	'97, '00		
Moldova		WVS: '95	NE: '04			CC-EB: '92
Mongolia			EAsia: TBC			

Montenegro		WVS: '95, '00	NE: '98			CC-EB: '96
Morocco		WVS: '00				
Mozambique			Afro: '02, '05			
Namibia			Afro: '99, '02, '03, '05			
Netherlands	'87–'89, '91, '93–'95, '97–'00, '02	WVS: '81, '90; EVS: '81, '90, '99		'98	'02	EB: '74–'04
New Zealand	'91–'02	WVS: '95		'96, '02		
Nicaragua			Lat: '96–'04			
Nigeria		WVS: '90, '95, '00	Afro: '00, '01, '03, '05			
Northern Ireland	'01–'02	WVS: '81, '90; EVS: '81, '90, '99			'02	EB: '75–'04
Norway	'89–'02	WVS: '81, '90, '95; EVS: '81, '90		'97	'02	EB: '90, '92–'04
Pakistan		WVS: '95, '00				
Panama			Lat: '96–'04			
Paraguay			Lat: '95–'04			
Peru		WVS: '95, '00	Lat: '95–'04	'00, '01a		
Philippines	'91–'02	WVS: '95, '00	EAsia: '02			
Poland	'87, '91–'02	WVS: '90, '95; EVS: '99	NE: '91–'95, '98, '01, '04	'97, '01b	'02	CC-EB: '90–'97, '01–'03
Portugal	'97–'00, '02	WVS: '90; EVS: '90, '99		'02	'02	EB: '85–'04

(Continued)

TABLE 1 (*Continued*)

	ISSP[a]	WVS/EVS[b]	Global Barometers[c]	CSES[d]	ESS[e]	Eurobarometers[f]
Puerto Rico		WVS: '95, '00				
Romania		WVS: '90, '95 EVS: '90, '99	NE: '91–'95, '98, '01, '04	'96		CC-EB: '91–'97, '01–'03
Russia	'91–'02	WVS: '90, '95 EVS: '99	NE: '04	'99		CC-EB: '90–'96
Senegal			Afro: '02, '05			
Serbia		WVS: '95, '00	NE: '98, '04			CC-EB: '96
Slovakia	'96, '98–'00, '02	WVS: '90, '95 EVS: '99	NE: '91–'95, '98, '01, '04			CC-EB: '92–'97, '01–'03
Slovenia	'91–'02	WVS: '90, '95 EVS: '90, '99	NE: '91–'95, '98, '01, '04	'96	'02	CC-EB: '92–'97, '01–'03
South Africa	'86, '01	WVS: '81, '90, '95, '00 EVS: '81, '90, '99	Afro: '94, '95, '97, '98, '00, '02, '05			
South Korea		WVS: '81, '90, '95, '00	EAsia: '94, '96, '98, '99, '01	'00		
Spain	'92–'02	WVS: '81, '90, '95, '00 EVS: '81, '90, '99	Lat: '01–'04	'96, '00	'02	EB: '85–'04
Sweden	'92, '94–'00, '02	WVS: '81, '90, '95, '00 EVS: '81, '90, '99		'98	'02	EB: '94–'04
Switzerland	'87, '93, '98–'02	WVS: '90, '95 EVS: '90		'99	'02	

Taiwan	'02	WVS: '95	EAsia: '94, '98, '01	'96	
Tanzania		WVS: '00	Afro: '01, '03, '05		
Thailand			EAsia: '01	'01a	
Turkey		WVS: '90, '95, '00 EVS: '99			CC-EB: '01–'03
Uganda			Afro: '00, '02, '05		
Ukraine		WVS: '95 EVS: '99	NE: '92–'93, '95, '98, '04	'98	CC-EB: '92–'96
United States	'85–'02	WVS: '81, '90, '95, '00		'96	
Uruguay		WVS: '95	Lat: '88, '95–'04		
Valencia		WVS: '95			
Venezuela	'99–'00	WVS: '95, '00	Lat: '95–'04		
Vietnam		WVS: '00			
Zambia			Afro: '93, '96, '99, '03, '05		
Zimbabwe			Afro: '99, '04, '05		

[a] Annual waves, reported 1985–2002; date listed is date of wave, not necessarily of fieldwork [source: http://www.issp.org (1985–2000) and http://www.gesis.org/en/data_service/issp/index.htm (2001–2002)].

[b] WVS, four waves: 1981–1984, 1990–1993, 1995, 2000; EVS, three waves: 1981–1984, 1990–1993, 1999 (source: http://www.worldvaluessurvey.org).

[c] Afrobarometer (Afro): round 1, 1999–2001; round 2, 2002–2004; round 3, 2005 (planned); plus additional time series in some countries (source: http://www.afrobarometer.org). East Asia (EAsia): no systematic waves (source: http://www.eastasiabarometer.org). Latinobarómetro (Lat): 1988 pilot, annual since 1995 (except 1999) (source: http://www.latinobarometro.org). New Europe (NE): annual 1991–1995, 1998 (as New Democracies Barometer), 2001, 2004 (source: http://www.cspp.strath.ac.uk).

[d] Module 1: 1996–2001a; Module 2: 2001b–2005 (source: http://www.umich.edu/~cses/).

[e] Round 1, 2002 (source: http://www.europeansocialsurvey.org).

[f] Candidate Countries Eurobarometer, formerly Central and Eastern Eurobarometer (CC-EB): annual 1990–1997, biennial 2001–2003. Eurobarometer (EB): biennial 1985–2004 (sources: http://europa.eu.int/comm/public_opinion/ and http://www.gesis.org/en/data_service/eurobarometer/).

[g] Prior to 1990, typically West Germany only.

comparison, Austria and reunified Germany. The Latinobarómetro (http://www.latinobarometro.org) was established next in 1995, following a four-country pilot study in 1988. It initially covered eight countries in Latin America (excluding the Caribbean) but expanded to 17 countries in 1996. The Latinobarómetro is designed as a time series with a rotation of topics included in the survey, such as attitudes toward international trade and the environment, patterns of political participation, and gender and discrimination. Funding for this series has been provided by the Corporación Latinobarómetro, a private, nonprofit initiative, and a large international board of notable academics oversees the project. The Afrobarometer (http://www.afrobarometer.org) completed its first round of studies covering 12 countries in 2001 and commenced a second wave in 2002. The Afrobarometer has been funded by a number of African and non-African governmental agencies, including the NSF and the U.S. Agency for International Development. From round two, an identical survey instrument has been used in all countries, and sample sizes within countries range from 1200 to 2400. Finally, the East Asia Barometer (http://www.eastasiabarometer.org), the newest of the Global Barometers, began surveys in late 2001 with funding from the Ministry of Education of the Republic of China. To date, surveys have been conducted in Taiwan, South Korea, Hong Kong, Thailand, the Philippines, mainland China, and Mongolia, with additional fieldwork in Indonesia and Japan pending. However, no results are yet available publicly, nor is technical information about the fieldwork. A new five-nation "State of Democracy in South Asia" survey (http://www.lokniti.org/projects.htm#sdsa), organized by the Center for the Study of Developing Societies in Delhi, is now under way; this survey could be thought of as a South Asian Barometer, and may perhaps be the next to join the conglomerate of Global Barometers.

Whereas most cross-national surveys, such as the ISSP and WVS, are administered by different organizations in different countries with different sampling and fieldwork methodologies, the European Social Survey (ESS; http://www.europeansocialsurvey.org/) was established in 2002 with an emphasis on methodological rigor and uniformity. Twenty-two nations participated in the first round, namely the then 15 member states of the EU plus four accession states (the Czech Republic, Hungary, Poland, and Slovenia) and three non-EU members (Israel, Norway, and Switzerland). All ESS surveys are based on face-to-face probability samples, and detailed rules are provided in all participating countries, including study-wide targeted response rates of 70% and strict rules regarding sampling (Lynn et al. 2004). Overall the ESS aims to be a cross-national social survey that achieves "uniform methodological standards that make it at least as rigorous as the very best national surveys within Europe."[1]

The most recent foray into cross-national survey research has been the Pew Global Attitudes Project (http://people-press.org/pgap), started in 2002. This

---

[1]R. O'Shea, C. Bryson, R. Jowell. Undated. *Comparative attitudinal research in Europe.* http://www.europeansocialsurvey.org/

survey, funded by the Pew Charitable Trusts, lacks the academic oversight of previously discussed surveys, but is far reaching in coverage. The 2002 survey included 44 nations and involved more than 38,000 people. Of particular interest in this first wave of studies were global attitudes about America, particularly in light of the 9/11 attacks, and particularly among Muslim communities. The Global Attitudes Surveys mark some of the first large-scale survey experience in the Middle East, including samples from Egypt, Pakistan, Jordan, Lebanon, Turkey, and Uzbekistan. Subsequent waves have included individuals from 50 populations.

Table 2 summarizes the characteristics of these main cross-national survey programs.

Of course there have also been many academic social surveys that have been part of neither a regular national series nor a cross-national survey program. Particularly notable is Almond & Verba's (1963, 1989) pioneering five-nation civic culture study of 1959, which covered the United States, Britain, Italy, Germany, and Mexico. The civic culture studies were unusual for their extensive use of open-ended questions, and this has not become the norm in cross-national research. The eight-nation *Political Action* surveys, conducted between 1973 and 1975 in Britain, West Germany, the Netherlands, Austria, the United States, Italy, Switzerland, and Finland, were similarly purpose-built; they examined forms of political participation in industrialized countries (Barnes & Kaase 1979). It is, however, beyond the scope of this paper to document or discuss these.

As this section has shown, the expansion of survey research throughout the world has been to date rapid and relatively far reaching. Whereas in the 1950s and 1960s academic public opinion research was largely relegated to a handful of wealthy, industrialized Western countries, by the early 1980s this tradition had grown to include most of North America and Europe, although the majority of these countries were still predominantly wealthy. Coverage of Latin America and Asia began during the 1990s, and systematic public opinion research has been undertaken in Africa and the Middle East only over the past five years. Thus, although public opinion research has clearly been affected by the pursuits of globalization, only very recently could it be considered a global phenomenon.

Even now it is not yet completely global. Certain areas of the world, particularly the Middle East and sub-Saharan Africa, are still underrepresented within large cross-national programs, and illiterate and rural populations are underrepresented in nearly all parts of the world. And although recognition of the value of public opinion research and cross-national comparisons has grown since the 1950s, Smith (2004) notes that independent surveys are still banned in a number of nations (including Burma, Cuba, Laos, North Korea, and Turkmenistan), and in other countries (such as China, Venezuela, and Iran), polling topics and/or the publication of results are restricted (Rohme 1997, Spangenberg 2003).

This section has focused on the breadth of cross-national research, but understanding the extent to which public opinion research has been globalized also requires an understanding of the depth of the research. In other words, how does the quality of public opinion research in newly defined markets compare to standards

TABLE 2 Features of cross-national survey programs[a]

Series	Inception[b]	Countries covered[c]	Frequency	Survey type	Mode of data collection	Available data	Website
Comparative Study of Electoral Systems (CSES)	1996	36	Module every 5 years	Module	Face-to-face, telephone, and self-completion	Public archives	www.umich.edu/~cses
Eurobarometers:							
Candidate Countries Eurobarometer (CC-EB)	1990	24	Annual	Standalone	Face-to-face	Public archives	http://europa.eu.int/comm/ public_opinion/
Eurobarometer	1973	19	Bi-annual	Standalone	Face-to-face[d]	Public archives	http://europa.eu.int/comm/ public_opinion/
European Social Survey (ESS)	2002	22	Biennial	Standalone	Face-to-face	Public archives	www.europeansocialsurvey.org
European Values/World Values Surveys (EVS/WVS)	1981/1983	33/77	~5 years	Standalone	Face-to-face	Public archives	www.worldvaluessurvey.org www.europeanvalues.nl/index2.htm
International Social Survey Program (ISSP)	1985	39	Annual	Module	Face-to-face and self-completion	Public archives	www.issp.org

Gallup Int'l Voice of the People Survey	2002	60	Standalone	Annual	Telephone and face-to-face	Tables only	www.voice-of-the-people.net/
Global barometers:							
Afrobarometer	1999	16	Standalone	Annual	Face-to-face	Public archives	www.afrobarometer.org
East Asia Barometer	2001	9	Standalone	Annual	Face-to-face	None to date	www.eastasiabarometer.org
Latinobarómetro	1995	19	Standalone	Annual	Face-to-face	Tables only	www.latinobarometro.org
New Europe Barometer	1991	18	Standalone	Annual	Face-to-face	Tables only	www.cspp.strath.ac.uk/
Pew Global Attitudes Survey	2002	49	Standalone	Annual	Telephone	Tables only	http://people-press.org/pgap

[a]This table is an expansion of the table presented by Norris (2004).

[b]In all cases but the CC-EB and the New Europe Barometer, pilot studies and forerunners (such as the European Community Study which preceded the Eurobarometer) have been excluded. As the CC-EB replaced the Central and Eastern Eurobarometer (CEEB), the CEEB's date of inception is listed; similarly the New Democracies Barometer preceded the New Europe Barometer and thus its date of inception is listed.

[c]Number of countries included in at least one survey.

[d]Interviews in Sweden for survey 42 were carried out by telephone.

for research in established markets; or, more importantly, how comparable are the surveys undertaken by cross-national survey programs? The following section explores these methodological issues.

METHODOLOGICAL ISSUES IN CROSS-NATIONAL RESEARCH

Although there is no strict division, cross-national survey research can be thought of as being affected both by general methodological issues relevant to any survey (survey quality) and by the comparability of responses from different countries (equivalence of meaning). The spread of public opinion research to a greater number and diversity of countries almost certainly entails greater problems of equivalence of meaning and consistency of survey quality. Harkness (1999) argues that, in the cross-national context, discussions of quality are rare compared with discussions of equivalence of meaning. This section examines both issues. We begin with survey quality because it is, in a sense, prior.

We recognize that our terminology here is somewhat different from the usual one, which would treat issues such as equivalence of meaning as one aspect of data quality. We draw a pragmatic distinction between the quality of the surveys implemented by the separate national teams and the problems of the questionnaire content designed by the central coordinating committee of the cross-national program.

Quality Issues

Data quality is an issue with all surveys, including those in the affluent democratic societies, but there are particular issues with the extension of survey research to countries outside the traditional core. The GSS may be considered the gold standard of survey research, but the extension of such research has by no means spread the application of the same survey methods used in the GSS. In short, surveys have not been a standard product exported across the world.

There are many reasons why different survey methods are used in different countries, even if they are part of the same cross-national project. Different countries and survey research institutions have different kinds of sampling frames, legislation regarding survey practice, traditions of how to pick samples, technical expertise, methods of recruiting and training interviewers, access to experienced interviewers and supervisors, access to computer equipment for computer assisted personal/telephone interviewing (CAPI/CATI), and practices of using call-backs and/or conversion techniques for nonrespondents and refusals. Populations differ in the extent of their experience with survey research and their levels of willingness to participate in it.

Groves (1987, 1989) distinguishes the following components of survey quality: coverage error, nonresponse error, sampling error, and measurement error. We examine each of these in turn.

COVERAGE   Coverage error refers to "the discrepancy between sample survey results and the results of a full enumeration of the population under study which arises because some members of the population are not covered by the sampling frame" (Groves 1987, p. S159). Lynn et al. (2004) also argue that equivalent study populations are one of two fundamental criteria for comparable sample design (the other being similar precision of sample-based estimates, which we examine below). Usually in public opinion research the population is taken to be the adult population, although the definition of when adulthood starts is far from clear cross-nationally. The ESS, for example, takes the target population to be all residents in private households 15 years or older, whereas the sampling universe for the WVS is all citizens aged 18 and older.

The true level of coverage, however, tends to depend on the nature of the sampling frame and on the cost of reaching some of the groups included in the frame. Sample frames might be drawn from complete records of the resident population (e.g., the Danish Central Person Register), lists of households (e.g., the SIPO database in the Czech Republic), registers of addresses (e.g., the Postcode Address File in the United Kingdom), electoral registers (e.g., in India), or no records at all (e.g., in Bosnia-Herzegovina) (Lynn 2003a,b). Complete registers of the population are valuable as sample frames because they enable researchers to pick equal-probability samples; but even when they exist, the availability of registers to academic researchers varies, and they are sometimes restricted for use by the national statistics institute only. Coverage problems can also arise from parochial practices. Park & Jowell (1997) note that in the 1995 ISSP, five countries (mostly European) imposed an upper age cut-off for the sample at 74. Institutional populations in many countries (e.g., the United Kingdom) are also often overlooked in sampling designs.

Problems of coverage have been growing even in the affluent West, where cost issues have driven the growth of telephone interviewing and the consequent restriction of the sample to individuals with access to telephones. Cost has also tended to limit coverage of face-to-face surveys to accessible areas, e.g., exclusion of the highlands north of the Caledonian Canal in many British surveys because of the expense of reaching potential respondents.

Not surprisingly, coverage is likely to be a particular issue in less developed countries with less urbanized populations and with greater difficulties of access to much of the rural population. Inglehart (1997), writing about the 1991 WVS, is admirably frank about the problems:

> In Chile, the sample covers the central portion of the country, which contains 63% of the total population; the income level of this region is about 40% higher than the national average. In Argentina, sampling was limited to the urbanized central portion of the country...which also has above-average incomes. In India, the sample was stratified to allocate 90% of the interviews to urban areas and 10% to rural areas, and to have 90% of the [interviews] with literate respondents (who are slightly less than 50% of the population). In Nigeria,

the fieldwork was limited to urban areas plus a sample of rural areas within 100 kilometers of an urban center. In China the sample is 90% urban. The samples have been weighted accordingly to make the samples replicate the national population parameters more closely. (p. 346)

The Afrobarometer Sampling Protocol (2002, http://www.afrobarometer.org/SamplingProtocol.pdf) also notes that areas experiencing armed conflict are excluded from sampling, and case-by-case judgments are made as to whether to include areas experiencing political unrest. The Pew Global Attitudes survey restricted areas even further, limiting its surveys in some countries to major cities—e.g., Luanda in Angola and Cairo in Egypt.

The extent to which weighting can deal with the problem of lack of coverage is an unresolved (and in many cases perhaps an irresolvable) question. The crucial issue is whether the opinions of the nonsampled population are in fact similar to those of their notional equivalents in the sampled population. For example, are rural Nigerians who live more than 100 km from an urban center similar in their opinions to rural Nigerians who live within 100 km? In other words, does public opinion show an interaction effect between rural residence and distance from an urban center?

This is in principle a researchable question. For example, in India, the National Election Survey is a probability sample of the adult population (drawn from the electoral register and hence with some problems of coverage); it could be used to explore whether such interactions are present and whether weighting of India's WVS survey, with its more limited coverage, would be sensible. However, in general, such research has not been carried out, and users of cross-national datasets need to be warned of the potential problems of differing coverage.

NONRESPONSE   Nonresponse error has been a major concern of Western survey research organizations, and there appears to be a widespread decline in response rates in affluent, urbanized countries. For example, according to the GSS website (http://www.norc.uchicago.edu/projects/gensoc3.asp), GSS response rates have fallen from just under 80% in the 1980s to 70% in 2002. Even the most methodologically rigorous of the cross-national programs, the ESS, with a target response rate of 70% for all countries, experienced considerable variation in response rates during its first round; five countries had response rates below 50%, the lowest being 33.5% for Switzerland (Lynn et al. 2004). Add-on modules favored by the ISSP may well have lower response rates than the main survey.

The identification of low response rates is difficult because the globalization of survey research has not led to the globalization of good survey documentation. As Harkness (1999) points out, documentation about details such as response rates is often unavailable, or inaccessible without considerable detective work. We believe that it should be the responsibility of the cross-national programs themselves to provide this documentation for the participant surveys.

The problem is compounded further by differing usages of sampling methods. Cross-national programs often use quota samples, random-route methods, or sampling methods that permit substitution—particularly in less developed countries, which have little infrastructure for survey research. In such cases, response rates cannot be calculated. Although the ESS strictly forbids both substitution and quota sampling, other survey programs continue to make use of these methods. During the 2001 ISSP, three countries reported using quota sampling at different stages, and 12 reported some level of substitution (Klein & Harkness 2003). However, as Groves (1987) points out, nonresponse bias is not simply a matter of nonresponse rates but also of the difference of means for respondents and nonrespondents; thus, bias is ultimately the key issue—not the response rate per se.

Checks on the size of the bias can sometimes be carried out directly for public opinion surveys—especially electoral surveys, for which the official records of aggregate vote will be available. Where an up-to-date and accurate census is available, the demographic profile of respondents can be checked against census figures. It is not known how nonresponse bias varies across countries (or indeed across surveys within a country), but clearly it could be a significant problem in cross-national research. Given the problem of declining response rates in the case of probability samples, methodologists should perhaps pay more attention to estimating the extent of nonresponse bias that arises from different sampling procedures.

SAMPLING   In contrast to coverage error and nonresponse error, the principles of sampling error are well understood, at least in the case of probability samples. However, some issues in the spread of survey research need more investigation. The standard of academic acceptability has been a probability sample with a sample size of $\sim$1000 (assuming population estimates with a confidence interval of $\pm3\%$ are required). Most cross-national surveys programs, including the EVS/WVS, the ISSP, the Eurobarometer, and the CC-EB, tend to target samples of this size.

There are several problems, however, with this standard. Clustering is often used (for cost reasons), and this tends to reduce the effective sample size. Many of the highest-quality surveys report design effects—the ratio of the variance of a variable to that which would have been obtained under simple random sampling (see Kish 1965 and Lynn et al. 2004 for more on design effects). Because a clustered design increases the variance, design effects are nearly always greater than one but tend to be relatively low in Western Europe. Modern software allows one to take the clustering into account in the analysis stage; however, because of ethical concerns about disclosure, it is becoming increasingly rare for the datasets released to investigators to identify the cluster of a particular respondent. Most analysts therefore tend to ignore the sampling error due to clustering, either because it is small or because they do not have the information to do so.

However, it is not clear that design effects are always small. They may generally be small in a relatively homogeneous West European society (e.g., in the ESS, the average predicted design effects were calculated as $\sim$1.5 in Great Britain, Germany, and France), but even in these countries we find that ethnic groups tended to be geographically concentrated, and much larger design effects are associated with variables strongly related to ethnicity. This may also be true for ethnically diverse societies, such as India or many African countries, and may be both a methodological and a substantive problem. The precision of sample estimates may therefore vary across countries in unknown ways, and the substantive influence of local contexts on public opinion may be neglected. A practice that in the past was broadly acceptable in Western Europe may not be a good model for more heterogeneous societies.

It is also unclear that the standard sample of 1000 found in many cross-national programs is equally appropriate everywhere. This depends in part on the purpose of the survey. We are not always interested in simple population estimates of public opinion, as in the typical opinion poll of government popularity. We may also be interested in relations between variables; for example, in Northern Ireland, polarized between Catholics and Protestants, a larger sample size will be needed in order to provide sufficient power to determine the extent of difference between Catholic and Protestant public opinion. Divided societies need much larger sample sizes than homogeneous ones, and a target sample of 1000 may be quite misleading. The surveys may simply lack the power to detect differences in public opinion, and these differences may be the most important aspect of public opinion(s) in that country. In principle, there is no technical difficulty in designing appropriate sample sizes for diverse or divided societies. The Afrobarometer, for example, has set larger sample sizes ($N = 2400$) for those countries it considers "extremely heterogeneous," namely South Africa and Nigeria, and this must be considered the correct strategy.

MEASUREMENT   Measurement error—the discrepancy between respondents' attributes and their survey responses—is perhaps the largest topic of all. It has been extensively studied, particularly in the United States by scholars such as Groves (see also Schumann & Presser 1981, Lyberg et al. 1997). Groves (1987) distinguishes the measurement errors that arise from "the influence of the interviewer, the weakness of the survey questions, failures of the respondent to give appropriate answers to the questions, and effects of the mode of data collection on survey answers" (p. S162). We deal with some aspects of the weakness of survey questions in the next section on equivalence of meaning, but a few observations relevant to the globalization of survey research may be in order.

It is perhaps most useful to distinguish between what we might call noise and bias. In countries with shorter traditions of survey research and a less well-trained field force, there may be greater interviewer variability in the conduct of the interview (e.g., in how strictly they adhere to the interviewer instructions), and there may be less supervision of interviewers to weed out "bad practice." (As with most issues that we cover, we must emphasize that there will also be important within-country variations—a cheaper survey in an affluent Western society may well involve a trade-off with measurement error.) This variability could lead to greater noise, which in turn could lead to weaker observed relationships between variables. If we are simply interested in population estimates, this may not be important, since it may not affect the mean. However, noise clearly could be important if our interest is in studying relationships between variables, as in most academic research on public opinion. If we discover, for example, that social class is less strongly associated with socialist versus free-market values in developing countries than in developed ones, we cannot be sure whether this is because the values (or, indeed, social class) have been measured with more error or whether the relationship is actually weaker. Interviewer assessment of social class or self-coded measures of class, for example, will almost certainly have greater noise than more expensive office-coded measures based on details of occupation. This strikes at the heart of a great deal of cross-national research.

Bias is a separate matter. Whereas noise is of particular concern when one is looking at relationships between variables, bias becomes a central concern in estimating population means, proportions, or other quantities of interest. Differences in methods of survey administration, such as different modes or different sorts of interviewers, can lead to bias, but perhaps the main sources of bias arise from questionnaire content, to which we turn in the next section.

SUMMARY   Globalization has not meant the spread of a standard social survey methodology across the world. The gold standard may be achieved by the GSS and some (but by no means all) European surveys with complete coverage, high response rates and low nonresponse bias, known and appropriate precision of sample estimates, and minimal measurement error; however, it is clear that survey research often falls short of this standard both within and between countries. Although we have highlighted the problems of coverage in developing countries, the wide variety of response rates—even in such a methodologically rigorous program as the ESS—indicates that major problems exist even in the developed world despite its relatively long tradition of survey research.

To be sure, the imposition of the same standard of survey methods in different countries, with their differing traditions of survey research, may not be possible or desirable. For example, different modes of survey administration (CATI, CAPI, etc.) may be appropriate in different countries with different histories and problems. Random-route or quota samples may be quite acceptable alternatives in a country where probability samples could not be implemented effectively, provided they do not involve excessive nonresponse bias.

However, the requisite information to enable one to judge the quality of surveys or the appropriateness of the method to the particular country is not always available cross-nationally. The documentation for cross-national survey research needs to be especially thorough but is rarely available (Harkness 1999). Requirements include (a) standard documentation on methods in each country; (b) meta-documentation for the program as a whole, highlighting and explaining the differences in the methods and contexts for the surveys; (c) translation notes, with guidance on the use of functional equivalence; and (d) indications of the implications for analysis. Perhaps the biggest problem is the difficulty of finding the technical details of the surveys in order to make an informed judgement. The ESS is a model; its website offers information about most aspects of fieldwork, including response rates, as well as some assessment of measurement error. The ISSP, although it falls far short of the strict ESS methodology (likely because of a lack of central organization and funding), is to be commended for including regular reports monitoring the study (see Park & Jowell 1997, Sinnott 1998, Klein & Harkness 2003).

In summary, the consumer of cross-national research (whether the secondary data analyst or the reader) is often ignorant of the extent to which the quality of the "product" varies and how this might affect the results and interpretation.

Equivalence of Meaning

While survey design and implementation remain far from standardization, questionnaire content is much closer. Although some early surveys (such as Almond & Verba's civic culture project) made great use of open-ended questions, which allow respondents to articulate their opinions using their own concepts and language, usual survey practice has favored closed questions that can be asked in identical format in different surveys. However, these questions are often "decontextualized" in order to achieve identical wording.

Several different, albeit related, issues are relevant to the study of equivalence of meaning across countries. Perhaps most fundamentally, there may simply not be common concepts to measure (e.g., the concept of God may be specific to certain religious traditions). Second, there may be common concepts whose interpretation varies in different contexts. Third, poor translation may introduce errors. We deal with these issues in reverse order.

Translation of questions into different languages is inevitably fraught with problems, and in some surveys translation has not received enough attention. Sinnott (1998), for example, demonstrated that the Eurobarometer question on party identification had a systematically different meaning if it was derived from the English-language version rather than the French-language version of the original questionnaire. Whereas the English version asked the equivalent of "Are you close to a political party?" the French version asked, "Are you closer to one party than the others?" As Sinnott (1998) notes, "An individual who is only moderately or weakly aligned with a party could well answer no to the English version...and yes to the French version" (p. 631). And indeed, Sinnott's results reflect this disparity: More individuals answered yes to the relative (French) version of the question, and more answered no to the absolute (English) version.

The standard method of improving the quality of translation is to use "back translation"—the translation of a question from one language into another and then back again by a separate translator. By comparing the original with the doubly translated question, it should be clear whether there are any problems. However, Harkness & Schoua-Glusberg (1998) argue that in practical and theoretical terms (results, effort, costs, reliability, viability), back translation is one of the less recommendable procedures. Harkness (1999) describes it as merely a procedure for checking translations. Warwick & Osherson (1973) similarly argue that back translation is a method of achieving linguistic equivalence and does not take account of more contextual factors.

Translation problems can often be solved, as for example in the Eurobarometer case described by Sinnott (1998), where a revision of the questionnaire appears to have led to greater comparability. They are probably not, in themselves, major sources of lack of comparability. Different interpretations of the same appropriately translated question can raise more difficult problems. For example, in its module on migration, the ESS has a question asking whether more individuals from "poorer countries outside Europe" should be allowed to enter. This is a question that can be asked in all countries with the same wording, but will it be interpreted in the same way in the different countries? In Israel, for example, migrants from poorer countries may be taken to mean Jewish migrants from North Africa and the Middle East, but in Britain the same phrase may be interpreted to refer to migrants from South Asia or the Caribbean. The question has been decontextualized in a way that permits standardization of wording (and accurate translation) but can lack equivalence of meaning. One simple (but expensive) way of dealing with this particular question would be to add an open-ended follow-up asking respondents to name those groups they were thinking of when answering the question.

Other solutions to this problem of contextualization have also been suggested. Przeworski & Teune (1967) recommend building scales composed of answers to several different questions to measure each concept. For each concept there needs to be a set of positively correlated questions that are valid in every country and can thus be used to measure the concept everywhere. They call these questions "identities." In addition to identities, some culturally specific items may be asked in a particular country, which are positively correlated with the identities and which can thus contribute to the scale for that country. Items like these are referred to as "equivalents." A good example of an equivalent for political participation might be voting in elections, which is impossible (and thus irrelevant) in nondemocratic countries but a good measure of participation in democratic countries. Thus, Przeworski & Teune recommend an "identity-equivalence" procedure for measurement, in which the same concept is measured with different scales in different countries, but each scale includes a common core of identities and possibly some culturally specific equivalents.

This kind of approach might be particularly useful if we are interested (as Przeworski & Teune are) in investigating relationships between variables in different countries. What we want, it could be argued, is the best measure of the concept in question for a particular country rather than a standard measure that is more appropriate in some countries than in others (and will therefore show weaker relationships in some countries than in others). The export of a standard measuring instrument, which was appropriate in the country of origin, may give an illusory appearance of comparability. A simple example is that of educational level. Number of years of completed education may well be an excellent measure in some countries (e.g., the United States) where it is isomorphic with the educational system, but less appropriate in European systems with their selective educational systems. In Europe, respondents with a similar number of years of completed education may have had very different educational experiences, and measures of education that focus on qualifications achieved may be much more appropriate.

The difficulty with "functional equivalence," however, is the absence of any clear guidelines to indicate when equivalence has been achieved. These methods have not, therefore, acquired general support, nor are they useful for making population estimates.

King et al. (2004) have recently proposed a novel method of dealing with this problem using vignettes. Their starting point is Sen's (2002) observation that subjective assessments of health status may be highly context-dependent:

> The state of Kerala has the highest levels of literacy...and longevity...in India. But it also has, by a very wide margin, the highest rate of reported morbidity among all Indian states.... At the other extreme, states with low longevity, with woeful medical and educational facilities, such as Bihar, have the lowest rates of morbidity in India.... In disease by disease comparison, while Kerala has much higher reported morbidity than the rest of India, the United States has even higher rates for the same illnesses. If we insist on relying on self-reported morbidity as the measure, we would have to conclude that the United States is the least healthy in this comparison, followed by Kerala, with ill-provided Bihar enjoying the highest levels of health. In other words, the most common measure of the health of populations is negatively correlated with actual health. (Sen 2002, pp. 860–61)

As Sen explains, respondents in Bihar judge their health according to different yardsticks than do respondents in Kerala or the United States, thus leading to the paradoxical results.

King et al. (2004) attempt to build-in this subjectivity by establishing what responses probably mean in different contexts. Their approach is best illustrated by their main example. The ordinal question "How much say do you have in getting the government to address issues that interest you?" has been used to measure political efficacy in different countries. But it is not clear that similar answers mean the same thing in different political contexts. King et al. show that when the answers are taken at face value, political efficacy is greater in China (a country that has never had a democratic election) than in Mexico (a country that has had several elections, one of which recently removed a long-standing government). However, when respondents are asked to assess the level of political efficacy of characters in a set of fictional vignettes (see Table 3), it becomes clear that the Chinese are much more likely to ascribe greater political efficacy to the characters in the vignettes than are the Mexicans. Most strikingly, >40% of the Chinese respondents assessed their own level of political efficacy below that of the vignette character who "suffered in silence."

TABLE 3   Political efficacy vignettes (King et al. 2004)

1	[Alison] lacks clean drinking water. She and her neighbors are supporting an opposition candidate in the forthcoming elections that has promised to address the issue. It appears that so many people in her area feel the same way that the opposition candidate will defeat the incumbent representative.
2	[Imelda] lacks clean drinking water. She and her neighbors are drawing attention to the issue by collecting signatures on a petition. They plan to present the petition to each of the political parties before the upcoming election.
3	[Jane] lacks clean drinking water because the government is pursuing an industrial development plan. In the campaign for an upcoming election, an opposition party has promised to address the issue, but she feels it would be futile to vote for the opposition since the government is certain to win.
4	[Toshiro] lacks clean drinking water. There is a group of local leaders who could do something about the problem, but they have said that industrial development is the most important policy right now instead of clean water.
5	[Moses] lacks clean drinking water. He would like to change this, but he can't vote and feels that no one in the government cares about this issue. So he suffers in silence, hoping something will be done in the future.

King and his colleagues claim that vignettes can be used to "anchor" various survey questions, and they propose both a simple and a more sophisticated method for using the information from the vignettes to rescale self-assessment responses. For the simple method, they assume only (*a*) consistency of response over the vignettes and self-assessment question and (*b*) vignette equivalence across societies. This method has two particularly attractive aspects. First, it is not necessary to administer the vignettes in conjunction with the self-assessment question every time the question is asked; rather, the vignettes can be used to establish a rule for rescaling a particular question for a particular society, and that rule could be applied to earlier or later surveys (although the extent to which rescaling rules are stable over time has yet to be established). Second, it is not limited to tackling issues of comparability between societies; it could also be used to identify and tackle instances of questions and concepts being interpreted differently by different groups within the same society.

This method does seem to be one of the most promising for dealing with equivalence of meaning, but it is not yet clear whether appropriate vignettes can be developed to study other concepts of interest in public opinion research. To satisfy the assumption of vignette equivalence across societies, one needs to be able to construct a set of vignettes that are ranked in the same order in the different societies. This may prove to be a rather demanding requirement.

Cross-national differences in social desirability bias may also lead to problems for equivalence of meaning. For instance, Jones (1963) suggests that acquiescence bias (a tendency to agree with whatever proposition the interviewer poses) is greater in Southeast Asia than elsewhere. Acquiescence bias can often be dealt with through good design, with measuring instruments that include questions with reverse wording. But this technique will not necessarily deal with social acceptability bias. If voting in elections is socially desirable, replacing the item "Do you agree that it is everyone's duty to vote?" with "Do you agree that it does not matter whether people turn out to vote or not?" is unlikely to get rid of social acceptability bias. Rather than treating social acceptability bias as a problem, we might regard it as a real difference between societies in their expression of public opinion. It would, however, be important to know if the relation between opinion and behavior varied systematically in more or less "courteous" societies. The inclusion of some behavioral items is therefore important for gaining a fuller understanding of public opinion.

The most severe difficulties in equivalence occur when the concept that a question is trying to tap into is less appropriate, or even nonexistent, in some contexts. Jowell (1998) gives the example of the difficulties that the cross-national ISSP team faced when developing their module on religion:

> [T]he Japanese delegation eventually came to the reluctant conclusion that there was no appropriate word or phrase in Japanese that approximated the concept of God. In the end, of course, they managed to come up with a doubtless somewhat tortuous circumlocution designed to get across the basic meaning of the Judaeo-Christian-Islamic concept of God. But beware of data that depend on such contrivances based on collegiality. (Jowell 1998, p. 172)

However, limiting a survey to concepts that can be measured in all countries could result in a set of anodyne questions that necessarily focus on common features of belief systems rather than on the distinctive features that have no cross-national equivalents. This point was made almost 40 years ago by Hodge and his colleagues in their classic comparative study of occupational prestige:

> It is quite possible that much genuine diversity in occupational-prestige systems not captured by our analysis is reflected in the relative placement of occupations that are not comparable across societies, or even across subsectors of any given society. In Tiryakian's study of the Philippines, for example, only a small number of occupations could be found about which it was sensible to ask both peasants in remote villages and the residents of Manila. (Hodge et al. 1966, p. 311)

The globalization of public opinion research does seem, therefore, to have led to the use of standardized closed questions around the world—something of a standard global product. The strong assumptions underlying this product are well known, but the alternatives, such as the use of supplementary open-ended questions or the vignette method, are likely to be time-consuming and expensive. A program of methodological work to determine which measuring instruments are particularly prone to problems of "equivalence of meaning" appears overdue.

THE INTELLECTUAL ASSUMPTIONS
OF CROSS-NATIONAL SURVEYS

Rather broader intellectual questions should also be asked about the globalization of public opinion research. It could be argued that standardized questions are not the West's only global export; there is also (perhaps in consequence) the export of a broader intellectual understanding of public opinion and of the appropriate concepts for describing public opinion. Particular questions also embody particular intellectual traditions.

This can perhaps be seen most clearly in the 1960s export of the Michigan model of election studies, with its sociopsychological intellectual framework, rather than the Columbia model, with its more sociological framework. Currently dominant intellectual approaches for understanding electoral behavior tend to be individualistic, often based on rational choice theory. The questions asked, for example, in the CSES module cover the kinds of concepts (such as attitudes toward leaders, the left-right domain, and judgments of economic performance) that have been associated with this type of intellectual framework.

We do not mean to suggest that attitudes toward leaders or the left-right dimension are unimportant aspects of public opinion; however, we can question whether the intellectual framework implicit in this particular battery of questions is as appropriate for, say, India (not actually a member of CSES) as it is for the United States or Britain. An emphasis on attitudes toward issues or the national economy may well be appropriate in countries with literate electorates who read newspapers or view televised debates about key issues, but in other parts of the world—such as India—the group processes of the sort investigated originally by the Columbia school [and more recently by Huckfeldt (1984) and Huckfeldt & Sprague (1995)] might be equally valuable in understanding public opinion.

Nor do we wish to be critical of the Michigan model and its export, which was at the time a highly progressive development. However, since many cross-national series (rightly) aim to chart change over time, there is a tendency to maintain previous questions. This has perhaps led to an institutional conservatism in questionnaire content and, hence, in intellectual approach.

A second, related concern is the notion of public opinion itself. In the United States, Converse (1964), one of the key members of the Michigan team, raised the fundamental issue of attitudes and nonattitudes. It is beyond the scope of this review to discuss the enormous debate that ensued, but it may be of particular contemporary relevance with the globalization of attitude research. There is clearly a risk that the administration of standard questions in surveys across the world might give a misleading impression that publics in different countries do vary in their attitudes toward the topics posed. The various barometers, for example, will often tabulate mean scores toward a topic, e.g., international trade relations, by country. But is there a danger that these findings are in part an artifact of the survey method? Might it not be the case that in some countries there is no public debate about international trade relations, and thus no good grounds for supposing public opinion is more or less supportive of this issue than in other countries?

An empirical example of this kind of problem can be seen with the measurement of economic left-right values. We can ask the same battery of questions that tap this dimension across the world (and there are questions in the WVS that can be used for this purpose) and then calculate mean scores on a scale derived from this battery. However, the more instructive finding may not be the calculated mean scores but rather the finding that the internal reliability of the scale is almost meaninglessly low in some countries. Tilley (2002), for example, shows that a scale of economic left-right values makes much better sense (as judged by internal reliability) in Northwestern Europe than it does in Latin America or Eastern Europe. This suggests that in these latter areas, either people do not respond to different economic issues in a way that is consistent with a unifying ideological position, as in Northwestern Europe, or there are problems with the applicability of the questions in the different contexts there.

This is not, in itself, a criticism or limitation of cross-national survey research, as checking internal reliability of scales is routine. Indeed, one important task of cross-national research could be to detect how far there actually is public opinion on certain domains.

But even if the problem of nonattitudes has been addressed, a national mean score may not be appropriate in a divided society. We referred above to the problem of divided societies such as Northern Ireland in the context of fixing sample sizes. In such cases, it is quite conceivable that no one in the society actually holds the national mean-score opinion, because public opinion is polarized rather than normally distributed. This calls into question the idea of a single measure of national public opinion and suggests that the relevant unit of analysis may not be the state but some subunit. This may be particularly important in multination states, such as the many countries in which nations and states are truly misaligned. Because the state is the usual administrative unit (both for sampling frames and for political decisions), it is understandable that public opinion research has tended to take the state, rather than the nation, as the unit of analysis. The subjective quality of "the nation" makes it perhaps more appropriate as the subject matter of public opinion research than as the basis of its conduct. However, there are many cases, such as Canada, Belgium, and several Indian states, where territorial subunits of the overall state make both effective administrative units and meaningful linguistic or ethnic groupings.

CONCLUSIONS

As the overview of cross-national survey programs presented at the beginning of this paper showed, globalization of academic public opinion research has indeed been occurring—but it is still far from complete. Although the number of countries included in the major cross-national programs continues to grow, there is still a predominance of the core established democracies of North America, Western Europe, and Australia. In addition, globalization of public opinion surveys has not entailed a straightforward spread of a standardized "product" throughout the world in terms of survey conduct. Some key features—systematic sampling and standardized questionnaires administered by trained interviewers—have been present in virtually all the surveys included in the various cross-national programs, but sample designs and fieldwork methods remain highly diverse. To a degree, this reflects the diversity of survey research methods in the core countries, but inevitably it also reflects the varying conditions under which survey research has to be conducted in different parts of the world. These differences can give rise to large, but often unknown, differences in quality between surveys and between countries. The World Association for Public Opinion Research has suggested rules of practice regarding the documentation of surveys (http://www.unl.edu/WAPOR/ethics.html), but these rules are all too rarely followed.

Globalization has tended to lead to a more standardized product with respect to questionnaire content, but this may itself be another source of noncomparability if the same questions are interpreted differently in different contexts. There has also perhaps been a globalization of intellectual assumptions and frameworks, which partly reflects the assumptions and theories of the questionnaires' originators. Intellectual frameworks developed to understand public opinion in urbanized, literate, and relatively homogeneous societies should not be assumed to be appropriate for other contexts.

A number of writers have suggested rules for the conduct of cross-national research designed to address some technical aspects of noncomparability (e.g., Scheuch 1968; Kuechler 1987, 1998; Jowell 1998), and the ESS is a particularly impressive example of the implementation of rules designed to secure high-quality surveys in all participating countries. Other scholars, however, suggest that if a country is of particular theoretical interest, even low-quality data might be acceptable if nothing better is available (e.g., Inglehart 1997, p. 347).

This debate is, in some ways, akin to debates in evidence-based medicine. One could insist on the "gold standard"—in the medical case, double-blind placebo-controlled experiments. However, because experiments of this sort are often hard to come by, current medical practice is to consider results from other, less rigorous research designs as well when deciding on treatment, although these are given less weight. Grading systems have been developed to aid in this delineation. Table 4 shows one such grading system (Eccles et al. 1998). (For more details on evidence-based medicine, see http://www.cochrane.dk/cochrane/handbook/hbook.htm.)

Our own sympathies are with the evidence-based medicine approach. We agree with the medical guidelines that the most weight should be given to meta-analyses of high-quality data and that the least weight should be given to nonsystematic research. It may be more difficult than in the medical case to achieve consensus on the intermediate grades, but for the sake of argument, we propose a scheme along the lines of Table 5. We suspect that the great majority of the surveys involved in the cross-national programs described in this paper fall into the proposed categories II

TABLE 4   Categories of evidence about treatment (Eccles et al. 1998)

Ia	Evidence from meta-analysis of randomized controlled trials
Ib	Evidence from at least one randomized controlled trial
IIa	Evidence from at least one controlled study without randomization
IIb	Evidence from at least one other type of quasi-experimental study
III	Evidence from nonexperimental descriptive studies, such as comparative studies, correlation studies, and case-control studies
IV	Evidence from expert committee reports or opinions and/or clinical experience of respected authorities

and III. Although we sympathize with the aim of the ESS to drive up standards so that they all come into our top category, we believe the reality is that most surveys will continue to be in category II at best, and that public opinion analysts need to adjust to this reality. We consider it a priority, therefore, for methodologists to establish empirically whether findings from random-route samples, for example, show different patterns from those obtained by strict probability samples with high response rates. (In the evidence-based medicine field, methodologists have been at pains to emphasize that scales of data quality have to be assessed empirically in just the same way as other measuring instruments, and our proposed grading ought also to be validated by empirical research.)

The need for schemes of this kind arose in medicine because of the sheer volume of research, of highly uneven quality, which the individual practitioner could not hope to study in the required depth. Because public opinion research does not have the same volume of studies as medicine, the need for meta-analyses may not be so evident. However, as Table 1 showed, many countries now participate in several different cross-national programs, and so the possibility of meta-analysis is there. Moreover, the unevenness of quality is certainly an issue, and where studies fall short of the gold standard (as the great majority do), it becomes all the

TABLE 5   Proposed weighting of sample surveys

Ia	Evidence from meta-analysis of systematic samples with full documentation
Ib	Evidence from at least one probability sample with response rate of 70% or above and full documentation following WAPOR[a] rules of practice
II	Evidence from at least one systematic representative survey (including random route or quota methods or probability samples with response rate below 70%) with full documentation following WAPOR rules of practice
III	Evidence from at least one systematic survey lacking full documentation
IV	Evidence from nonsystematic nonrepresentative studies, such as "snowball" samples

[a]WAPOR, World Association for Public Opinion Research.

more important to compare results from several different studies rather than to rely solely on the one that happens to have participated in the particular cross-national program. In short, data of lower than ideal quality should be checked against the results of other surveys that cover the same topics.

To be sure, one reason why meta-analysis is rarely carried out is that the very standardization of questions within cross-national programs tends to lock the user into one particular program, making it difficult or impossible to compare findings with those of other programs. Each program tends to have developed its own, idiosyncratic questions and question wording even when it is studying a relatively common concept, such as left-right values. Again, public opinion researchers may have something to learn from medicine, where there tend to be many standardized (and validated) measuring instruments that can be used in any study on the topic. Inglehart's postmaterialism index is one of the few such instruments in public opinion research. King's political efficacy vignettes deserve to become another. Although there have been many criticisms of the postmaterialism index, the advantage of such a widely used index is that its properties are now well known. The wider use of such instruments in public opinion research would certainly aid meta-analysis.

We have raised several serious caveats about the use of standardized measures in different cultural contexts, and these caveats would necessarily apply to the use of standard instruments such as the postmaterialism index as well as to the standardized questions favored by cross-national programs. (However, we must emphasize that our main reason for advocating standard instruments is to permit cross-checking of results *within* a given country, not necessarily to aid cross-national comparison.) Given the current state of uncertainty about the equivalence of standard items across cultural contexts, we advocate the use of a range of methods and the evaluation of these methods by systematic methodological research. We have, for example, advocated the use of supplementary open-ended material [as recommended by Schumann & Presser (1981) in their classic work on questions and answers] and the use of King's vignette method. Przeworski & Teune's method of identities and equivalences also deserves to be revived; we believe that, in addition to the common questions designed by the central coordinating committee of the national program, individual participating countries should be encouraged to include their own questions that are faithful to the local context.

Comparisons of public opinion between countries at a single point in time are the most vulnerable to problems of survey quality and comparability, even if their findings are statistically significant according to standard tests. The claim that Country X has greater support for democracy than Country Y could be misleading for numerous reasons; by contrast, a claim (supported by significance tests) that over the past five years support for democracy has increased in Country X but declined in Country Y is likely to be more robust. If there is continuity of methodology, the analysis of change in public opinion over time within countries and the comparison of trends across countries are much safer than single-time-point comparisons, since context-specific interpretations of questions and idiosyncrasies in sample design are likely to be relatively stable and should effectively cancel out when the difference between two time points is calculated within a country.

Repeated cross sections are valuable (though vulnerable to differences in survey quality over time given declining response rates), but change is best calculated with a panel study in which the same individuals are interviewed more than once. It is unfortunate that no cross-national panel studies carry a substantial number of social attitude items of interest to political scientists. Although we began our discussion by presenting the GSS as our gold standard in survey research, there is a growing tendency in social science to see the cross-section survey as second-best to a well-conducted panel. Perhaps a new process of the globalization of panel studies ought to begin.

Finally, cross-national survey researchers need to pay more attention to the unit of analysis. The state is the usual unit, and there are some good, practical reasons for this. But the nature of states is often contested by independence movements, and it is not always clear that the state is sociologically the most appropriate unit, especially in diverse or divided multination states. To take an extreme example, Czechoslovakia was a single state at the time of the 1991 WVS and was covered with a single survey, but now there would be separate surveys in the independent states of the Czech Republic and Slovakia. However, the "velvet divorce" between the two parts of Czechoslovakia was presumably related to cultural and social differences of exactly the sort that public opinion research addresses. Similarly, Quebec almost certainly warrants a separate survey from the rest of Canada, Flanders from Wallonia, and Scotland from England. To accept the state as the unit of analysis is to accept a questionable normative position.

We recognize that many of our suggestions for larger samples, panel studies, vignettes, and open-ended and country-specific questions are expensive. However, the Afrobarometer and the new State of Democracy in South Asia program indicate that there are practicable alternative ways forward. Rather than a simple export of Western methods, assumptions, and intellectual frameworks to nonwestern societies, public opinion research might benefit from imports in the reverse direction.

APPENDIX: SURVEY-RELATED WEB SITES

Afrobarometer: http://www.afrobarometer.org/

- ■ Sampling Protocol: http://www.afrobarometer.org/SamplingProtocol.pdf

American National Election Studies: http://www.umich.edu/~nes/

British Election Studies (University of Essex): http://www.essex.ac.uk/bes/index.html/

Candidate Countries Eurobarometer: http://europa.eu.int/comm/public_opinion/

- Data Archive: http://www.gesis.org/en/data_service/eurobarometer/cceb/index.htm

Comparative Study of Electoral Systems: http://www.umich.edu/~cses/

East Asia Barometer. http://www.eastasiabarometer.org/

Eurobarometer. http://europa.eu.int/comm/public_opinion/

- Data Archive: http://www.gesis.org/en/data_service/eurobarometer/

European Social Survey: http://www.europeansocialsurvey.org/

European Values Survey: http://www.europeanvalues.nl/

Gallup Voice of the People Survey: http://www.voice-of-the-people.net/

General Social Survey: http://www.norc.uchicago.edu/projects/gensoc.asp/

Global Barometer: http://www.globalbarometer.org/

International Social Survey Programme: http://www.issp.org/

Latinobarómetro: http://www.latinobarometro.org/

New Europe Barometer: http://www.cspp.strath.ac.uk/

Pew Global Attitudes Project: http://people-press.org/pgap/

State of Democracy in South Asia: http://www.lokniti.org/projects.htm#sdsa

World Association of Public Opinion Research: http://www.unl.edu/WAPOR/

- Code of Professional Ethics and Practices: http://www.unl.edu/WAPOR/ethics.html

World Values Survey: http://www.worldvaluessurvey.org/

The *Annual Review of Political Science* is online at
http://polisci.annualreviews.org

LITERATURE CITED

Almond GA, Verba S. 1963. *The Civic Culture: Political Attitudes and Democracy in Five Nations.* Princeton, NJ: Princeton Univ. Press

Almond GA, Verba S. 1989. *The Civic Culture Revisited.* Newbury Park, CA: Sage

Barnes SH, Kaase M, Allerbeck KR, Farah BG, Heunks F, et al. 1979. *Political Action.* Beverly Hills, CA: Sage

Lazarsfeld P, Berelson B, Gaudet H. 1948. *The People's Choice.* New York: Columbia Univ. Press

Berelson BR, Lazarsfeld PF, McPhee WN. 1954. *Voting: A Study of Opinion Formation in a Presidential Campaign.* Chicago: Univ. Chicago Press

Bulmer M. 1998. The problem of exporting social survey research. *Am. Behav. Sci.* 42:153–67

Butler D, Stokes D. 1974. *Political Change in Britain.* London: Macmillan

Campbell A, Gurin G, Miller WE. 1954. *The Voter Decides.* Evanston, IL: Row, Peterson

Campbell A, Converse PE, Miller WE, Stokes DE. 1960. *The American Voter.* Chicago: Univ. Chicago Press

Colley L. 1992. *Britons: Forging the Nation: 1707–1827.* New Haven, CT: Yale Univ. Press

Converse PE. 1964. The nature of belief systems in mass publics. In *Ideology and*

Discontent, ed. DE Apter, pp. 206–61. New York: Free

Converse PE. 1987. *Survey Research in the United States: Roots and Emergence 1890–1960*. Berkeley: Univ. Calif. Press

Crespi I. 1989. Public opinion. In *International Encyclopedia of Communications*, ed. E Barnouw, 3:386–91. New York: Oxford Univ. Press

Eccles M, Freemantle N, Mason J 1998. North of England evidence based guidelines development project: methods of developing guidelines for efficient drug use in primary care. *Br. Med. J.* 316:1232–35

Eldersveld SJ, Ahmed B. 1978. *Citizens and Politics: Mass Political Behaviour in India*. Chicago: Univ. Chicago Press

Gallup G. 1948. *A Guide to Public Opinion Polls*. Princeton, NJ: Princeton Univ. Press

Groves RM. 1987. Research on survey data quality. *Public Opin. Q.* 51:S156–72

Groves RM. 1989. *Survey Errors and Survey Costs*. New York: Wiley

Halman L. 2001. The European Values Study: a third wave. *Source Book of the 1999/2000 European Values Study Surveys*. Tilburg, The Netherlands: EVS, WORC, Tilburg Univ.

Harkness J. 1999. In pursuit of quality: issues for cross-national survey research. *Int. J. Soc. Res. Methodol.* 2:S125–40

Harkness J, Schoua-Glusberg A. 1998. Questionnaires in translation. In *Cross-Cultural Survey Equivalence*. Mannheim, Ger.: Zentrum für Umfragen, Methoden und Analysen

Hodge RW, Treiman DJ, Rossi PH. 1966. A comparative study of occupational prestige. In *Class, Status, and Power: Social Stratification in Comparative Perspective*, ed. R Bendix, SM Lipset, pp. 309–21. New York: Free. 2nd ed.

Hovland CI, Lumsdaine AA, Sheffield FD. 1950. *The American Soldier, Volume III: Experiments in Mass Communication*. New York: Wiley

Huckfeldt RR. 1984. Political loyalties and social class ties: the mechanisms of contextual influence. *Am. J. Polit. Sci.* 78:399–417

Huckfeldt RR, Sprague J. 1995. *Citizens, Politics and Social Communication: Information and Influence in an Election Campaign*. Cambridge, UK: Cambridge Univ. Press

Inglehart R. 1990. *Culture Shift in Advanced Industrial Society*. Princeton, NJ: Princeton Univ. Press

Inglehart R. 1997. *Modernization and Postmodernization: Cultural, Economic and Political Change in 43 Societies*. Princeton, NJ: Princeton Univ. Press

Jones EL. 1963. The courtesy bias in Southeast Asian surveys. *Int. Soc. Sci. J.* 15:70–76

Jowell R. 1998. How comparative is comparative research? *Am. Behav. Sci.* 42:168–77

King G, Murray CJL, Salomon JA, Tandon A. 2004. Enhancing the validity and cross-cultural comparability of measurement in survey research. *Am. Polit. Sci. Rev.* 94:191–207

Kish L. 1965. *Survey Sampling*. New York: Wiley

Kish L. 1994. Multipopulation survey designs: five types with seven shared aspects. *Int. Stat. Rev.* 62:167–86

Klein S, Harkness J. 2003. *ISSP Study Monitoring 2001: Report to the ISSP General Assembly on Monitoring Work Undertaken for the ISSP by ZUMA, Germany*. Mannheim, Ger.: Zentrum für Umfragen, Methoden und Analysen

Kuechler M. 1987. The utility of surveys for cross-national research. *Soc. Sci. Res.* 16:229–44

Kuechler M. 1998. The survey method: an indispensable tool for social science research everywhere? *Am. Behav. Sci.* 42:178–200

Lyberg L, Biemer P, Collins M, de Leeuw E, Dippo C, et al. 1997. *Survey Measurement and Process Quality*. New York: Wiley

Lynn P. 2003a. Developing quality standards for cross-national survey research: five approaches. *Int. J. Soc. Res. Methodol.* 6:323–36

Lynn P. 2003b. *Development of a sampling method for household surveys in post-war Bosnia and Herzegovina*. Work. Pap., Inst. Soc. Econ. Res., Univ. Essex, Colchester, UK

Lynn P, Hader S, Gabler S, Laaksonen S. 2004. *Methods for achieving equivalence of samples in cross-national surveys: the European Social Survey experience*. Work. Pap., Inst. Soc. Econ. Res., Univ. Essex, Colchester, UK

Marsh C. 1982. *The Survey Method*. London: Allen and Unwin

Marshall G. 1998. *Oxford Dictionary of Sociology*. Oxford, UK: Oxford Univ. Press

Norris P. 2004. From the civic culture to the Afrobarometer. *APSA-CP Newsl.* 15:2

Otava J. 1988. Public opinion research in Czechoslovakia. *Soc. Res.* 55:247–60

Park A, Jowell R. 1997. *Consistencies and Differences in a Cross-National Survey*. London: Social and Community Planning Research

Przeworski A, Teune H. 1967. Equivalence in cross-national research. *Public Opin. Q.* 30:551–68

Rohme N. 1997. *The Freedom to Publish Opinion Polls: Report on a Worldwide Study*. Amsterdam: ESOMAR

Rose N, Osborne T. 1999. Do the social sciences create phenomena? The case of public opinion research. *Br. J. Sociol.* 50:367–96

Rossi P. 1964. Four landmarks in voting research. In *Readings in Political Parties and Pressure Groups*, ed. F Munger, D Price, pp. 304–47. New York: Thomas Y. Crowell

Scheuch EK. 1968. The cross-cultural use of sample surveys: problem of comparability. In *Comparative Research Across Cultures and Nations*, ed. S Rokkan, pp. 176–209. Paris: Mouton

Schumann H, Presser S. 1981. *Questions and Answers in Attitude Surveys: Experiments on Question Form, Wording, and Context*. New York: Academic

Sen A. 2002. Health: perception versus observation. *Br. Med. J.* 324:860–61

Sinnott R. 1998. Party attachment in Europe: methodological critique and substantive implications. *Br. J. Polit. Sci.* 28:627–50

Smith TW. 2004. Freedom to conduct public opinion polls around the world. *Int. J. Public Opin. Res.* 16:215–23

Spangenberg F. 2003. *The Freedom to Publish Opinion Polls: Report on a Worldwide Update*. Amsterdam: ESOMAR

Stouffer SA, Suchman EA, DeVinney LC, Star SA, Williams RM Jr. 1949a. *The American Soldier, Volume I: Adjustment During Army Life*. New York: Wiley

Stouffer SA, Lumsdaine AA, Lumsdaine MH, Williams RM J Jr, Smith MB, et al. 1949b. *The American Soldier, Volume II: Combat and Its Aftermath*. New York: Wiley

Stouffer SA, Guttman L, Suchman EA, Lazarsfeld PF, Star S, Clausen JA. 1950. *The American Soldier, Volume IV: Measurement and Prediction*. New York: Wiley

Tilley J. 2002. Is youth a better predictor of sociopolitical values than is nationality? *Ann. Am. Acad. Polit. Soc. Sci.* 580:226–56

Warwick DP, Osherson S. 1973. Comparative analysis in the social sciences. In *Comparative Research Methods: An Overview*, ed. DP Warwick, S Osherson, pp. 3–41. Englewood Cliffs, NJ: Prentice-Hall

Worcester RM. 1987. The internationalization of public opinion research. *Public Opin. Q.* 51:S79–85

Annu. Rev. Polit. Sci. 2005. 8:335–56
doi: 10.1146/annurev.polisci.8.081404.075608
Copyright © 2005 by Annual Reviews. All rights reserved
First published online as a Review in Advance on Mar. 17, 2005

RISK, SECURITY, AND DISASTER MANAGEMENT

Louise K. Comfort

*Graduate School of Public and International Affairs, University of Pittsburgh, Pittsburgh,
Pennsylvania 15260; email: comfort@gspia.pitt.edu*

Key Words   uncertainty, resilience, networks, information asymmetry, adaptive
learning

■ **Abstract**   This review examines the policies and practices that address the evolving conditions of risk, security, and disaster management in U.S. society. Although each condition presents particular challenges to public agencies and the communities they serve, all represent varying states of uncertainty and require different approaches for informed action. This analysis reframes the issue of managing risk by focusing on the distinction between policies and practices developed in reference to natural and technological hazards and those developed to enhance security from hostile acts. The author concludes that building networks of organizations committed to a process of continual inquiry, informed action, and adaptive learning is a more flexible, robust strategy than the standard practice of establishing greater control over possible threats through administrative structures. Supported by methods of network analysis, computational simulation, information infrastructure, and long-term policy goals, networked strategies offer an important alternative to hierarchical structures that prove vulnerable in uncertain environments.

INTRODUCTION

The last three years have seen a striking change in the ways in which citizens perceive and respond to sudden, urgent, destructive events and, more importantly, in citizen expectations of the government's capacity to anticipate and respond to such events. The sobering and painful events of September 11, 2001 initiated a critical review of government performance, both before and after the disaster, and triggered a plethora of new policies, procedures, and a reorganization of government functions to make the United States—and, presumably, the world—safer. The result has been a blurring of existing disaster management policies and practices that had been largely oriented toward mitigating and recovering from natural disasters and technical failures—earthquakes, floods, severe winds, fire, hazardous materials releases, and transportation accidents—with policies developed to prevent deliberate disasters initiated by human intent to do harm, such as terrorism, arson, and chemical/biological releases.

More than three years after 9/11, it is possible to gain some perspective on the measures that have been taken in response to deliberate threats and to weigh the

1094-2939/05/0615-0335$20.00

changes these measures have created in the capacity of local, state, and national governments to manage the risk of continuing threats from natural and deliberate hazards. In some instances, these measures were indeed constructive and necessary. In other instances, they proved to be clumsy efforts that primarily distracted already overburdened local response agencies from the daily management of risk. In still other instances, such as the passage of the U.S.A. Patriot Act, the measure appeared to threaten the very freedoms the law was designed to protect.

This review considers recent articles, reports, and books that address the question of security versus sustainable management of risk and disaster. In his 1988 book, *Searching for Safety*, Aaron Wildavsky frames this question as he seeks to identify the appropriate balance between anticipating risk and generating resilience in response to disaster. This review will also address new methodological approaches to anticipating risk, including network analysis and computational modeling as a means of generating credible scenarios for action under known constraints of resources and law. These methods provide a way to anticipate natural, technological, or deliberate threats that government agencies have not seriously considered before. In important ways, these methods of research are changing the perceptions, policies, and practice of managing risk and disasters over extended periods.

The dialogue between risk and security will continue. By developing new concepts, methods, and skills to reframe old questions of safety, security, and disaster management, academicians can contribute to the sustainable management of continuing risk.

COPING WITH UNCERTAINTY

The quintessential role of government is to protect its citizens from harm. This role, widely accepted and understood for over two centuries in the United States, has led to a series of public policies and government actions that were designed to anticipate risk, prepare citizens to manage risk, and assist them in recovering from damaging events (May 1985, May & Williams 1986). These policies and procedures, however, assume that the government itself remains intact and that citizens are the unintended victims of destructive events. The rationale underlying these policies is that the government's primary role is to pool resources from the wider society as a means of reducing the uncertainty and adverse impact from potentially extreme events. This formulation is based on the interpretation of extreme events as largely probabilistic occurrences that lay outside the control of individual citizens.

Since the mid-1980s, however, more careful documentation of losses from disaster events and more critical analyses of government practice in disaster operations have led to a different formulation of the problem of extreme events. Disaster was viewed as a problem that could be managed more effectively by informed action and appropriate investment of attention and resources in risk-prone communities

(McLoughlin 1985, Comfort 1988). At local, state and federal levels of jurisdiction, governments were regarded as the primary actors in mobilizing communities to engage in the mitigation of risk and preparedness for possible disaster. These activities, in turn, would increase the capacity of communities to respond effectively when extreme events did occur and to recover more quickly from the damage. This assessment reshaped the problem of harm from extreme events as a probabilistic occurrence beyond ordinary human control to one in which human actions and changing social, economic, physical, and political conditions contributed significantly to creating vulnerability to damaging events (Platt 1999, Mileti 1999). In this conception, extreme events were less random occurrences beyond human control than products of inadequate planning, negligence, or uninformed actions that led to cumulative failure of human and engineered systems exposed to recurring risk (Comfort et al. 1999, Comfort 1999). The challenge was to manage these recurring events, and government agencies were viewed as primarily responsible for designing appropriate policies and enabling citizens to take informed action to reduce risk.

The events of 9/11 significantly altered both the public perception of risk and government's role in reducing or managing this risk. Although terrorism was not a new form of attack on the U.S. government, the coordinated attacks on the World Trade Center and the Pentagon represented the most damaging attacks by foreign enemies on U.S. soil since the Japanese attack on Pearl Harbor in 1941. Even more devastating than the colossal damage inflicted on the civilian targets of the World Trade Center was the perception that the existing government policies to protect citizens from such an attack were inadequate or dysfunctional. The response to this sobering event was immediate, and the U.S. public was united in its commitment to prevent such attacks from occurring ever again.

The difficulty, however, lay in determining exactly how to prevent attacks that were conducted by an elusive network of like-minded individuals who were accountable to no nation-state and who were determined to discredit the efficacy of the U.S. government by attacking its citizens. The security of U.S. citizens as they engaged in routine activities on an ordinary day had been breached. The event itself indicated a failure of government policies to manage the risk of deliberate attack, but it was not at all clear in the immediate aftermath of the event what policies should be corrected or changed.

Designing Policy for Different States of Uncertainty

Clearly, different categories of harm can befall citizens, and different government actions can be taken to reduce these potential harms. But the basic issue in designing appropriate public policy and strategies for action lies in determining the source and degree of uncertainty that characterize potential harms. Risk, security, and disaster represent different states of uncertainty in reference to damaging events. Designing public policy for each state requires different allocations of attention, resources, organizational structure, methods, and measurement of performance.

Risk represents the possible occurrence of a harmful event that has some known likelihood of happening over time. Disaster represents the interdependent cascade of failure triggered by an extreme event that is exacerbated by inadequate planning and ill-informed individual or organizational actions. Security, however, includes government actions taken to prevent the potential for deliberate harm and, as such, it acknowledges the hostile intent of the perpetrator(s) against both citizens and government. Each type of uncertainty represents a type of low-probability, high-consequence event that challenges government performance and civic tolerance for failure. How policy makers should manage such events and make trade-offs in practice regarding the costs or benefits for government (in)action in deeply uncertain contexts is a continuing challenge.

In his thoughtful book, *Searching for Safety*, Wildavsky (1988) framed the issue as risk versus resilience. To Wildavsky, risk was ever present in a complex social world, and it would be impossible for any government to eliminate risk altogether. Rather, he acknowledged that society chooses the risks to be minimized and accepts the remainder, knowingly or not. Wildavsky viewed risk as the ability to anticipate a damaging event and to take proactive steps to reduce that risk, knowing that there was still some likelihood that the event could occur. This known likelihood, or probability of occurrence, was considered acceptable risk, or that amount of risk considered too infrequent to worry about or too costly to avoid. Although Wildavsky's formulation does not solve the problem of designing government policies for managing risk, it does frame the issue in dynamic terms. The degree of risk varies under different conditions, and governments can design policies to reduce risk and increase security for a price measured in economic or political terms. Conversely, governments can relax security and increase risk as conditions change. Wildavsky's lasting insight on this problem is that the degree of risk that a society accepts in an uncertain environment is a matter of choice. The likely error, in his judgment, lies in the validity of the information, or lack of same, on which the choice is based.

Increasing Vulnerability of Complex Systems to Extreme Events

The events of 9/11 and the anthrax attacks in the months that followed vividly illustrate the trends of the increasing vulnerability of civilian societies to hostile actors and to the harmful usurpation of interdependent services designed to facilitate global exchange in transportation, communications, commercial activity, and other regional services. This vulnerability is related to the increasing use of technology that makes possible the rapid exchange of goods, services, people, information, and knowledge at an ever-decreasing cost to a wider group of the world's population. Simultaneously, the global population lags in developing the shared values and goals to manage this technology responsibly, and it lacks mechanisms to minimize the risks engendered from human error, misjudgment, malfunction, and mal-intent. These risks lead to deliberate disaster, with sobering consequences for unprepared or ill-informed populations. Finding new methods of coping with deliberate disaster and discovering means to reduce security risks for civilian populations are primary challenges that cannot be ignored. This task represents a shared risk in which government agencies, private businesses, and nonprofit organizations must share the responsibility for taking informed action (Comfort 1999).

POLICY VS. PRACTICE IN MAINTAINING SECURITY

The intent of policy is to guide practice, but the reverse appears more consistently true. That is, good policy derives from practice. Yet this maxim is confounded in extreme events when there has been no previous incident that approximates the scale or scope of danger confronting public managers. This inability to imagine attacks on the security of U.S. cities on the scale of the 9/11 events limited government capacity to plan defensively for such threats. Government planning did occur, but it fell regrettably short of meeting the needs for coordinated action to protect the security of U.S. cities. To understand how this gap occurred and to design better strategies for improving government performance under security threats, it is useful to review the policies that were in place before 9/11, the policies that were put in place immediately after 9/11, and the reasoning underlying both strategies.

Policies Existing Before September 11, 2001

In the years immediately preceding 9/11, policy makers recognized the risk of terrorist attacks, as they had occurred sporadically throughout the 1990s. The first attack on the World Trade Center on February 26, 1993, the bombings of the U.S. embassies in Nairobi, Kenya and Dar es Salaam, Tanzania on August 7, 1998, and the attack on the U.S.S. Cole in Port Aden, Yemen on October 12, 2000 all signaled deliberate actions to harm U.S. personnel and property. These events alerted U.S. officials to the need to re-examine the government's capacity to manage risk from terrorist events. These events were primarily directed toward U.S. assets overseas, but federal agencies recognized that different actors with different responsibilities would need to re-organize their activities to reduce the threat and coordinate response in the event of a domestic attack.

In an effort to manage the risk of terrorist threats to U.S. personnel and institutions, federal agencies implemented the United States Government Interagency Domestic Terrorism Concept of Operations Plan in February 2001 (United States Government, 2001). Under this plan, known informally as the ConPlan, two types of response operations were to be initiated simultaneously in the event of a terrorist attack. The first was crisis management, or the effort to identify and pursue the perpetrators of the incident. The U.S. Department of Justice (DOJ) was designated as the lead agency for crisis management, and it coordinated its work with other agencies involved in pursuing individuals who may have engaged in illicit activity. These agencies included the Federal Bureau of Investigation (FBI); the Central Intelligence Agency (CIA), when international agents were involved; the Immigration and Naturalization Service (INS), which governed entry and exit of foreign nationals across U.S. borders; and the Bureau of Alcohol, Tobacco, and Firearms (ATF), which tracked the entry of illegal substances across U.S. borders. These agencies operated within the bounds of security required for a criminal investigation.

The second type of response to a terrorist attack was consequence management. This response included the immediate mobilization of search and rescue operations to save the lives of people harmed by the incident, the provision of disaster assistance to the people who suffered losses from the incident, and the recovery and reconstruction of the damaged communities. The Federal Emergency Management Agency (FEMA) had lead responsibility for consequence management, focusing first on lifesaving operations and second on assistance to the victims and recovery of the damaged community. Under the Federal Response Plan (FEMA 2000), eight federal agencies in addition to FEMA were designated to play lead roles in disaster operations, with 25 federal agencies assigned responsibilities under 12 specified emergency support functions (Comfort 2003). The lead agencies included the Department of Transportation (DOT), the National Communications Service (NCS), the Department of Defense (DOD), the U.S. Department of Agriculture (USDA), the Department of Health and Human Services (HHS), the Department of Housing and Urban Development (HUD), the Environmental Protection Agency (EPA), and the General Accounting Office (GAO). Two departments had dual emergency support functions: the USDA had the primary support function for firefighting, carried out by its sub-unit, the U.S. Forest Service (USFS), as well as responsibility for food; FEMA was responsible for information management as well as urban search-and-rescue operations. The American Red Cross (ARC), a nonprofit organization, was designated as the lead agency for mass care.

Under the ConPlan, the participating federal agencies retained their separate identities and distinct responsibilities for daily operations. The plan was intended to structure interagency coordination among federal agencies in the event of an extreme action directed against the nation. It did not specify responsibilities for coordination among state and local agencies that would respond to terrorist attacks, and it did not specify coordination of activities for the prevention of potential attacks. It was, however, the operations plan that was legally in effect on 9/11 (Comfort 2003).

Policies Implemented after September 11, 2001

The devastating consequences of the 9/11 terrorist attacks precipitated an almost immediate reaction to change government policy to increase security and reduce the danger of further terrorist attacks. Returning to Wildavsky's concept of the tension between risk and resilience in setting government policy, the balance in government action tipped in favor of reducing risk and against resilience as a means of countering threats. The tolerance for risk in U.S. society dropped to near zero, as reflected by two major policy changes: the passage of the U.S.A. Patriot Act and the establishment of a cabinet-level Department of Homeland Security. These policies, grafted onto existing policies for mitigating risk and managing emergencies, were performed, in large part, by agencies with distinct missions, histories, and organizational cultures. Despite significant efforts to integrate these functions organizationally, the intended level of security and reduction of risk has not been achieved. The questions of how and why these efforts have failed merit examination.

The U.S.A. Patriot Act

Aggrieved by the failure of U.S. intelligence agencies to identify the evolving threat that culminated in the 9/11 attacks, the U.S. Congress and the president sought new ways of monitoring potential threats and securing U.S. borders and institutions against potential threats. The "Uniting and Strengthening America by Providing Appropriate Tools Required to Intercept and Obstruct Terrorism (U.S.A. Patriot Act) Act of 2001" was passed by the 107th Congress and signed into law by President George W. Bush on October 26, 2001. Although the act includes a sunset provision that causes it to expire on December 31, 2005, the unusual powers granted to government agencies to conduct surveillance, intercept communications, extend searches, and hold information or persons who might be relevant to the search for terrorist activity without demonstrated evidence has raised significant questions regarding the power of the state to limit individual privacy in the name of increasing public security.

The U.S. Department of Homeland Security

Within weeks of 9/11, President George W. Bush established an Office of Homeland Security, and appointed Tom Ridge, then governor of Pennsylvania, to advise him on the development of a national strategy for homeland security. Governor Ridge accepted this position as Director of the White House Office on Homeland Security on October 6, 2001 and began an effort to organize a coordinated response among the federal agencies to increase their capacity for public security. In this position, he reported directly to the president but had no executive authority or budget. He could only advise, persuade, cajole, threaten, or negotiate agreements among the multiple federal agencies with differing responsibilities for border control, immigration, customs inspection, and intelligence gathering both within and outside the U.S. to share information and coordinate their activities. His first task was to identify which agencies performed what functions that were relevant to homeland security. The product of this analysis was a densely overlapping chart that identified 22 federal agencies with distinct responsibilities related to homeland security. The key issue, identified by Ridge as well as other informed analysts, was intergovernment coordination among not only these federal agencies, with their distinct cultures and competitive interests for budgets and personnel, but also with the state and local agencies that shared responsibility for implementing a comprehensive national security strategy (Posner 2002).

The proposal for a cabinet-level Department of Homeland Security generated substantive debate both for and against this massive structural reorganization. Those in favor believed that the reorganization would bring all relevant agencies together under one shared mission and grant a senior cabinet-level executive the authority and budget to coordinate performance among them. They argued that a cabinet-level appointment was needed to gain and keep the attention of the president on these issues and to defend the national mission of securing the homeland against separate efforts to protect the identity and budgets of single agencies. Those who opposed the strategy, including initially the White House, argued that the individual agencies had distinctive capabilities that would be minimized in a larger, more complex organization. Further, the difficulty of integrating these disparate agencies would delay and distract them from performing their separate functions at expected professional levels, and it would take years to build trust and mutual understanding among them. Nonetheless, on January 23, 2003, President Bush signed Executive Order 13,284, which established the U.S. Department of Homeland Security.

Contrasting Practice

The test of a policy's effectiveness lies in its ability to transform practice. By this measure, the record is mixed regarding the effectiveness of these two major policies designed to reduce risk, increase security, and manage disaster more effectively and efficiently. Instead of reassuring citizens that their basic freedoms were being better protected, the U.S.A. Patriot Act has generated substantial resistance among citizens who worry that the powers of surveillance granted to the state are being misused for questionable purposes (Nelson 2002). Strongly held values of privacy and individual freedom gave rise to serious questions regarding the capacity of citizens to hold government authorities accountable for their exercise of powers authorized by the U.S.A. Patriot Act, including surveillance, wiretapping, and information sharing based on dubious intelligence-gathering activities.

As the principal investment in developing a national strategy for increasing public security, the Department of Homeland Security has not demonstrated its ability to change significantly the practice of the 22 agencies now gathered under its overarching framework. Although the agencies share the same email address @dhs.gov, they are nonetheless carrying out their basic functions largely independently, in arrangements that were negotiated with a carefully crafted goal of minimizing conflict and securing at least verbal collaboration among principals. Admittedly, the reorganization effort is a difficult task, and some work is indeed moving forward. Budgets are being allocated, although spending priorities have not always been congruent with security needs or implemented in a timely manner. Accurate assessments of existing capacities for security at both local and state levels have been difficult to obtain, and agencies frequently resort to familiar methods of political distribution in order to satisfy allocation deadlines.

The apparent incongruence between policies and practice regarding the development of an effective strategy for increasing public security compels a reexamination of the policies adopted. To a large extent, the policies designed and implemented followed time-honored government strategies of seeking greater control over the uncertainty generated by terrorist threats. By extending government control over citizen activity as a means of identifying potential terrorist threats, did governmental agencies alienate the very groups of citizens and organizations who could contribute most to reducing such threats? The number of foreign students seeking visas to study in the United States, for example, has declined significantly. Many of these students not only bring knowledge of the languages and cultures of nations in parts of the world that have generated terrorist groups, but they also have stayed in the United States after graduation and contributed substantially to the knowledge base of science and technology that is essential to U.S. economic proficiency. Although there has been no major terrorist attack within U.S. borders since 9/11, it is not evident whether the United States has the capacity to prevent or interrupt such an attack, despite $43.7 billion dollars of expenditures.

Clearly, the operational environment for detecting potential threats to public security has changed significantly. This environment is increasingly complex, dynamic, and adaptive in using sophisticated techniques of planning, technology, and biotechnology. Continuing terrorist threats show little sign of abatement, as documented by recent incidents in Indonesia, Spain, Saudi Arabia, Egypt, and Italy. These attacks appear to be orchestrated by networks of highly committed actors, operating freely across national boundaries and within the protection of legal jurisdictions. The standard approach of administrative hierarchy, adopted by the U.S. policies, appears mismatched to counter the flexible, stateless networks of organized terrorists in practice. More sobering is the compelling evidence presented in the 9/11 Commission Report (2004) that documents startling gaps in performance of government agencies and in the communication and coordination among them. Although the report reviews only the performance of agencies leading up to the 9/11 attacks, there is little evidence that the principal policies adopted by the U.S. since 9/11 have altered its basic approach of administrative hierarchy. The primary problem, as documented in the report, appeared to be the asymmetry of information among relevant organizations with shared risks and responsibilities. Government agencies, based on incomplete or untimely information, did not recognize the risks presented by seemingly ordinary, but highly interconnected, actions by terrorists operating in different locations. Given the nature of the threat—secretive, lethal, and ruthlessly ideological—the multijurisdictional administrative structure developed for responding to natural and technological disasters is largely inappropriate for networked threats that cross jurisdictional boundaries and target civilian populations. Despite acknowledgment of the need for increased collaboration and cooperation among agencies, governmental policy has relied instead on the creation of large structures for administrative control through the Department of Homeland Security. There is an urgent need for fresh concepts and new measures of government action in uncertain environments that can counter effectively the rapidly evolving, dynamic strategies of networked threats.

THE LOGIC OF UNCERTAINTY

If standard administrative structures prove too rigid to perform effectively against the dynamic and flexible networks of terrorists, what forms and conceptual frameworks could serve as constructive models? Returning to the documented experience of practicing disaster managers, several approaches are useful that could be incorporated or combined to inform administrative practice. Four of these approaches will be outlined briefly below. None is entirely new. Each is intended to reduce risk, and all four are familiar concepts to practicing decision-makers working in environments of uncertainty. The four approaches differ from standard administrative practice: all acknowledge that dynamic environments require learning processes that enable flexible adaptation and collective action rather than attempts to exert control through an administrative hierarchy of rules and constraints. In designing such systems, managers recognize the centrality of information flow among participating agents that include technical systems as well as human actors.

After Action Reviews

After field operations are concluded in any major disaster, it is standard practice for the operations chiefs to call for an "after action review." These events, also called "hot washes" in the vernacular of emergency service personnel, constitute a rigorous review of the operations just concluded. They are intended as a candid, thorough examination of actual operations to determine what went right, what went wrong, and how to improve performance before the next event. Emergency personnel know how difficult it is to manage complex operations in the urgent context of disaster. They also know that mistakes cost both lives and property and that their credibility with the communities they serve depends upon performance. They recognize that plans and standard operating procedures defined at one time in one context may not be the most effective means of managing a different incident in a different setting. Any disaster represents a failure of existing policy, and the critical objective of these reviews is to identify mistakes in operations in order to avoid making the same mistakes again. Differences between the existing policy and the actual conduct of operations serve as the basis for organizational change and continued learning. After action reviews represent a method of organizational learning that is taken very seriously by the participating personnel. These events provide a way to compare the organization's existing model of performance against the actual requirements of field operations. On this basis of collective review, recommendations for change in design, strategy, and tactics are incorporated into the organization's performance model for the next event.

Recognition-Primed Decision Making

Researchers from several disciplines have studied the process of decision making under stress (Weick 1995, Weick & Roberts 1993, Rochlin 1993, Flin 1996). Noting that decision making capacity often drops under stress (Flin 1997), several researchers have observed that decision makers use models other than the standard rational model of assessing the problem, identifying alternatives, and reviewing these alternatives in the light of likely consequences. Gary Klein (1993) notes that managers under stress engage in "recognition-primed decision making." That is, they do not search through long lists of standard operating procedures to determine whether the organization is performing effectively in a given context. Rather, they scan the context in which the organization is operating and check the margins to determine whether observed performance is consistent with their mental model of effective performance. This means that expert personnel are so attuned to their organization and to their usual operating environment that they quickly detect the anomalies, or the points of dysfunction, and focus their scarce time and attention on correcting what is going wrong. In the urgent environment of disaster, time is critical, and identifying the potential threats before they occur is fundamental to avoiding failure and maintaining the operation of the system, even if it suffers some damage. This mode of decision making is consistent with Wildavsky's concept of anticipating risk and taking action to correct potential failures before they escalate to major collapse.

The Edge of Chaos

A third approach derives from the literature of complex adaptive systems. Biologist Stuart Kauffman (1993) regards all systems as operating on a continuum that ranges from order to chaos. Systems operating at the order end of the continuum move toward chaos. Conversely, systems operating at the chaotic end of the continuum move toward order. To Kauffman, there is a narrow band at the center of the continuum in which there is sufficient structure to hold and exchange information but sufficient flexibility to adapt to a changing environment. He terms this area the "edge of chaos," the most creative arena for organizational action. Decision makers who function in this range are likely to be highly innovative in managing scarce resources under urgent time constraints. This model has been observed in disaster field observations (Comfort 1999), most often enacted by a team of experienced disaster managers who not only respect and trust one another but who also complement and correct one another's actions in practice.

The Bowtie Model

A fourth approach builds on the previous models and offers a more systematic approach to managing uncertainty in operational environments. The key function in the previous models is the design of information processes to support learning, while simultaneously updating action strategies to adapt more effectively to a changing environment. Csete & Doyle (2004) combine feedback processes with simultaneity in transmitting information from heterogeneous sources to facilitate coordinated action in complex environments. Termed "bowtie" architecture, the design identifies key sources of data that "fan in" simultaneously to a central processing unit or "knot" where the data are integrated, analyzed, and interpreted from the perspective and performance of the whole system. This new information is then "fanned out" to the relevant actors or operating units that use the information to make adjustments in their specific operation informed by the global perspective. This design is similar to an Emergency Operations Center, where status reports from multiple agencies are transmitted to the service chiefs who review the data from the perspective of the whole community. The set of service chiefs collectively integrate, analyze, and interpret the data in reference to the performance of the whole response system and then transmit the relevant information to the respective agency personnel, who adjust the performance of their units informed by the operations perspective for the entire system.

This theoretical framework acknowledges the importance of both design and self-organizing action in guiding coordinated action in a complex, dynamic environment. It can be modeled as a set of networks that facilitate the exchange of incoming and outgoing information through a set of analytical activities that support coordinated decision making. The information flow is multi-way, but it gains efficiency through integrated analysis and coordinated action toward a clearly articulated goal for the whole system. It operates by identifying the key sources of information, the key processes of analysis and interpretation for the whole system, and the key routes of transmission. It maintains self-organizing functions in that personnel, with informed knowledge, adjust their own performance to achieve the best performance for the whole system. Design, self-organization, and feedback are central to effective performance of distinct organizational units within the global system.

This theoretical model, using the bowtie architecture, can best be implemented as a socio-technical system. That is, it uses the facilities of an advanced technical information infrastructure to inform the human decision makers who are responsible for maintaining the daily operations of the community. These facilities include the technical capacity to perform the processes of monitoring, integrating, analyzing, and transmitting information regarding community operations in a timely, accurate, and manageable fashion for the human decision makers. The model relies on the human capacity to learn, and it uses the design of a technical infrastructure to facilitate the learning process. Communication of information serves as the driving force for the model and transmits a continuous assessment of the status of the system's vital functions in real time. The performance of the system is measured by the shared commitment to informed action among the participants to achieve the stated goal. The elements of the model are illustrated in Figure 1 below.

Action Models

In each of the four models described above, the objective is to critique actual performance against a prior model of organizational structure in order to improve performance in a continuous process of collective learning. The decision makers use their experience to identify gaps in the organizational system model in order to

Figure 1   Bowtie model of an emergency operations center.

correct performance for the next event. The logic of these approaches is to identify what the organization does not know in changing environments or new situations and to devise better means of coping with unknown conditions. Acknowledgment of error is not a negative action but rather serves as the basis for learning and contributes to improved future performance. The major resource in each of these models is the capacity of individuals to learn and to transmit that knowledge to other participants in the system. Each approach acknowledges the need to design organizational structures and processes that facilitate individual and organizational learning as well as to identify and correct potential errors on a timely basis. The cumulative effect, seen most clearly in the bowtie model, is to reduce the asymmetry of information, a major cause of dysfunction in complex systems requiring coordination among multiple actors. Yet, the design of learning organizations that can maintain sustainable security but also function effectively in the rapidly changing, urgent environment of disaster requires methods and measurement of performance for dynamic contexts.

MANAGING UNCERTAINTY IN COMPLEX ENVIRONMENTS

The classic response to uncertainty is to recognize the limitations of the existing system and to broaden the scope of actors, agents, and knowledge that can be marshaled for action, as needed. In managing risk, whether from natural, technological, or deliberate disaster, this basic principle of widening the set of resources available to reduce risk applies. Security is a problem not only for government agencies but also for private and nonprofit organizations. Although mitigation and response to natural and technological disasters have historically engaged nonprofit and private organizations as well as public agencies, security has largely been perceived as a function of public agencies. The events of 9/11 demonstrated vividly that maintaining security for a given region requires the collaborative effort of public, private, and nonprofit systems operating along functional lines rather than within jurisdictional boundaries. This perspective is articulated most cogently by

Salamon (Salamon & Elliott 2002) in his discussion of the tools of governance. Salamon & Elliot present a set of financial and organizational instruments for organizing collective action to serve public purposes.

Three concepts are central to implementing a policy for managing uncertainty in complex environments. Each suggests new methods of monitoring and measuring dynamic processes, methods that can contribute to reducing uncertainty in complex environments.

Interoperability of Social and Technical Systems

Interoperability is a term that was initially used in reference to communication systems; it meant the capacity of radio systems operating on different channels to communicate with one another during emergencies (National Governors Association 2002). It also has been used to describe the integration of different formats for technical decision support systems (Walker 2002). The Office of Domestic Preparedness (ODP) defines interoperability as "the ability of two or more public safety agencies to exchange information, when and where it is needed, even when different communication/information systems are involved" (2003, p. 2-1). Although ODP extends the concept of interoperability beyond radios to include fixed facilities, mobile platforms, and portable (personal) devices, its focus is still primarily on communications equipment (Public Safety Wireless Network Program 2002). This focus on communications was broadened in findings from a research workshop sponsored by the U.S. National Science Foundation (Rao 2003). The interdisciplinary researchers and practicing managers who gathered at this workshop recognized the need for interoperability of the highly diverse, large-scale networks of communications and information exchange used by public, private, and nonprofit organizations to provide societal services. The findings acknowledged the centrality of communications to the capacity of different types of organizations to coordinate their actions to manage risk effectively. This same pattern of interactive communication is essential between the operators of technical systems and managers of the organizational systems that use them. Potential failure of interoperability among large technical systems becomes a security threat for the region. Security in large regions of the country, both metropolitan and rural, depends upon the interoperability of different types of technical systems and the organizational systems that manage them. Sustainable security requires functioning electrical power, transportation, communications, gas, water, and sewage distribution systems. These systems are often privately owned, yet serve critical public functions. Managing this technical infrastructure and maintaining its safe operation for public use becomes a key organizational function in developing sustainable security. This task is inherently interdisciplinary and interorganizational, and it explores the interaction between social and technical systems. For example, a report of a failure in a technical system is transmitted to managers of related organizational systems who seek to coordinate response actions and reallocate resources to maintain operations in the larger meta-system that incorporates both.

New models are currently being developed that characterize the operations of these interacting systems (Comfort et al. 2004). One measure represents the demands placed on a technical system, for example, transportation. A second measure represents the response to those demands as messages sent to emergency organizations reporting the technical failure and actions taken by these organizations to correct the failure and maintain the operation of the system. For example, traffic can be modeled on a complex roadway system using cameras and sensors. Should an accident occur and congestion form, information regarding alternate routing or other forms of transportation can be transmitted immediately to support decision-makers in taking constructive action to clear the congestion. Distribution patterns of communication among both technical and social organizations engaged in response operations can be modeled, showing the likely pattern of interaction among the two subsystems as conditions change. This dual dynamic reflects the reciprocal adjustment that each subsystem makes in response to the other, but it also reveals the threshold point of fragility, or the point at which performance in the regional transportation system fails. Such models capture the interaction between risk and resilience (Wildavsky 1988, Comfort 1994), similar to the dynamics in disaster operations.

In these models, information is the primary resource in both technical and organizational subsystems that enables adaptive performance. Consequently, information management, data quality, data currency, and accessibility are requisite for effective management of the larger socio-technical system. Maintaining effective performance requires public investment to create a technical infrastructure that enables scalability of information across the graduated levels of detail needed to support informed action in a complex environment. Scalable information is also essential to enable different audiences with different interests, capabilities, and experience to comprehend a massive event and mobilize common action.

Networks and Computational Simulation

If governance is accepted as a set of interacting networks, traditional methods of monitoring and measuring public performance are inadequate. A related line of research has been developed by sociologists studying the performance of organizations operating in dynamic conditions over time. Kathleen Carley (2000) and her colleagues initially studied how individuals performed under different conditions of resources, information, and time stress (Carley & Prietula 1994, Carley & Lee 1998). In later work, they have extended their analyses to develop computational models of organizational performance under changing conditions (Carley et al. 2001). This method of inquiry offers a systematic means to explore alternative scenarios for organizational action.

A similar approach has also been used to model fragility in disaster response systems (Comfort et al. 2003, 2004), using a theoretical framework of complex systems. Based on discrete dynamics, complexity theory reveals the power of self-organization embedded in complex systems. The interactions among agents who participate in response operations form a disaster response system that reveals a spontaneous order. Agent-based simulation is used to model those interactions (Carley 2000, 1999) and to study the dynamics of disaster response as a complex system. Although the initial definition of the system focuses on identifying the individual agents and their roles, the scope and order of the system emerges from the interactions among the participating agents. These interactions among the agents define the overall system properties. Both social (Wasserman & Faust 1994) and evolving network theories (Watts 2003, Barabasi 2002) are used to identify the structure of a disaster response network among organizations as well as the core information that is exchanged among the agents. These networks, identified as scale-free, differ from the random networks assumed in earlier social network analysis. That is, the networks are characterized by nodes of dense interaction, with links connecting actors to the nodes, rather than being distributed randomly across a grid of interaction. This pattern of interaction has been termed a small world network, in which it is possible to reach a large number of actors through a very small number of densely connected nodes (Watts 2003, Barabasi 2002). The scale-free networks prove robust under stressful conditions, but are vulnerable if key nodes are disabled. This vulnerability was illustrated by the collapse of telephone communications following the World Trade Center attacks in New York City when the Verizon Communications Center, located under Building 7, was destroyed.

The exploration of networks as an organizational form is particularly relevant to the context of security, which analyzes threats and counter-threats as interacting dynamics. Much of this work has been done by researchers examining threats in battlefield contexts (Alberts et al. 2001). This research uses network analysis and computational simulation as means to identify potential threats, mobilize counter actions, and estimate the potential fragility—or threshold point of failure—for each type of network. The focus is to assess and analyze the characteristics, organizational structures, and dynamics of security threats and counter-threats from the perspective of an interacting, complex system operating on multiple levels in many locations. This approach acknowledges the robustness and fragility of the interacting networks operating within societal and global systems. It focuses on identifying the information structures, mechanisms, evolving knowledge bases, and cultures that serve as resources to both terrorist and counter-terrorist actors/agents. The research investigates the flow of information among the different actors and between their levels of operation as a critical measure of both risk and resilience in an interactive, dynamic process. This approach also acknowledges the importance of learning at individual, organizational, network, and system scales of operation, and uses this process as a major resource in both identifying potential terrorist threats and developing resilient, robust strategies for counter-terrorism. It assumes that the dual dynamics of terrorism and counter-terrorism operate within a global sociotechnical system in which change at one level precipitates change—in vulnerability as well as strength—at other operating levels.

Network analysis and computational simulation offer useful means of exploring different strategies of organizational behavior under changing conditions over time.

These methods enable researchers to test alternative strategies of communication and coordination with other agencies, including potential adversaries. In a world in which threats to security are likely to continue, this approach becomes a necessary part of professional development.

Long-Term Policy Analysis and the Generation of Alternative Scenarios

The problem of uncertainty is particularly acute in efforts to forecast unusual or unstable future strategies. In situations of deep uncertainty, standard methods of analysis based on known data fail. There are too many unknowns to approximate any reliable trends, or to test any potential hypotheses. Addressing the problem of deep uncertainty in a novel way, Lempert et al. (2003) propose an approach to explore potential strategies of action for "the next one hundred years." Their approach is relatively simple. Using computational simulation, they generate a very large number of scenarios for the future, using a range of conditions and patterns of interaction among actors. They do not claim that any one of the scenarios actually predicts the future. Rather, they suggest that a plausible future scenario may be included in the set. They eliminate unlikely scenarios that do not fit the existing context or that practicing decision makers rule out as unworkable. Although no single scenario may be entirely accurate, they suggest that the set of scenarios refined through review and discussion represents a range of situations that could occur. By stretching the imaginations of participating policy makers and analysts, they suggest that this method of exploring the future contributes to the professional development of managers, enabling them to recognize and act on both positive and negative conditions as they emerge.

This method warrants careful consideration, as it is grounded in systematic, rigorous, and detailed analysis of the characteristics and interactions of the actors/agents involved in the selected system. It differs from traditional methods of forecasting in that it considers large ensembles of scenarios; seeks robust, rather than optimal strategies; employs adaptive strategies; and designs analysis for interactive exploration among relevant stakeholders. Its weakness is that it cannot predict which of the potential scenarios is most likely to happen.

In developing potential scenarios, researchers may use a range of research methods for data collection, analysis, modeling, and synthesis of findings. These methods include

- Systematic review and content analysis of documentary reports, case studies, experiments, datasets, and records of terrorist events to characterize the operating agents, structures, modes, and conditions of terrorist and counterterrorist networks.

- Characterization of existing conditions of the networks as baselines for measurement of change.

- Organizational analysis of the interdependencies within and between identified networks, using computational methods.

- Computational modeling of the dynamics of the sets of candidate networks and the interaction between them as well as the thresholds of fragility and resilience within each system.
- Evaluation of the plausibility of the models by practicing managers in public, private, and nonprofit organizations.
- Visual representation of findings to increase effective dissemination to relevant audiences and to increase dialogue, information exchange, and organizational learning among them.

The expected outcomes from this research should enable practicing managers to think about new ways of managing uncertainty and to recognize potential opportunities for constructive action as well as to avoid destructive situations before they occur. This approach seeks to enable practicing policy makers to develop long-term strategies for managing risk that will reduce potential harm to citizens before it occurs.

PUBLIC VALUES IN UNCERTAIN ENVIRONMENTS

In situations of deep uncertainty, rationality is limited. At this point, public values can play a critical role in linking known and unknown conditions within a community. Clearly articulated and cogently presented, public values can serve to bridge the interests and commitments of disparate groups and to support collective action toward a constructive future. The intent is to foster a dialogue that includes all participants in the community. In democratic societies, the function of a continuing dialogue is to identify potential error before it occurs and to make corrections in course as the system adapts to changing conditions. Iris Young (2002) argues that public dialogue is fundamental to democracy, because through dialogue, citizens can explore alternative futures and hold those who exercise public power accountable. Through dialogue, citizens develop the moral authority to act in uncertain conditions.

Recognizing the importance of dialogue to enabling collective action under uncertainty provides a critical lens through which to review the policy actions taken to reduce risk after 9/11. Countering a distinguished tradition of legal protection of privacy through U.S. courts, the U.S.A. Patriot Act enabled government agencies to engage in practices that abridged the norms of individual freedom without warrant or evidence. For example, persons seeking entry to the U.S. could be held in custody without evidence of wrongdoing and without resort to legal counsel (Sec. 213, U.S.A. Patriot Act 2001). Foreign students who were in the U.S. were subjected to new restrictions on travel or renewal of their visas (Sec. 416, U.S.A. Patriot Act 2001). Delays in submitting reports to Congress as a means of monitoring the appropriate execution of intelligence activities were authorized (Sec. 904, U.S.A. Patriot Act 2001). Authority to intercept wire, oral, and electronic communications presumably related to terrorism was broadly granted (Sec. 201, U.S.A. Patriot Act 2001).

Although the rationale for these actions was to increase public security and prevent threats to U.S. citizens, the effect of the U.S.A. Patriot Act often increased fear of privacy violations among citizens (Nelson 2002) and decreased the cooperation essential to sharing information among informed persons that is central to disrupting terrorist networks. Rather than reassuring citizens that enhanced government surveillance activities were being done only for their protection and in limited areas, the jarring experience of government controls placed on citizen activity without requisite evidence appeared to threaten the very freedoms the law was designed to protect.

The question is how to balance security, privacy, and responsible public access to information. Although it provides no certain answers, public dialogue does contribute to the development of intellectual capital within a society. That is, it stimulates among a broad group of citizens a blend of knowledge, professional judgment, trust, and leadership that is critical for innovative action. It supports the development of leaders who have the capacity to articulate a clear vision for the future and to formulate effective strategies for informed action.

FUTURE STRATEGIES

Given the continuing rate of change in a global society in which populations are growing, moving into hazardous areas, and engaging in novel and often questionable behaviors, the risk of natural, technological, and deliberate disasters is certain to increase. As these risks increase, the challenges of anticipating and managing them become more varied and more complex. Strategies of control quickly become outdated and obsolete. Rather, managing risk can best be understood as a continuing process of inquiry, adaptation, and learning.

Three approaches appear most constructive in supporting this task. The first is framing the problem as a continuous process of inquiry, recognizing the complexity and interdependence of risk factors. The theoretical framework of complex adaptive systems supports this formulation and provides an intellectual basis for analysis. The second is the skillful use of computational simulation to generate alternative scenarios for review and discussion of possible futures. Such exercises, based on rigorous characterization of existing conditions, stimulate imaginative exploration of alternative futures. As possible scenarios are reviewed, debated, and considered, they enable citizens to explore innovative strategies and adapt more appropriately to changing conditions. A third approach acknowledges the central role of technology in creating and maintaining sustainable communities and considers the processes of risk reduction, disaster management, and security management as integrated through a socio-technical system.

None of these methods alone can guarantee security, but cumulatively they offer a means of increasing the capacity of communities to manage their own risk. The critical function they perform is reducing the asymmetry of information among different actors and enabling public, private, and nonprofit organizations, as well as households and citizens, to take responsible action to reduce risk. In doing so, the problem of security is transformed from establishing hierarchical external controls over citizen behavior to enabling informed, timely action by multiple actors/agents in a coordinated effort to anticipate and reduce risk. This approach, building on well-designed information processes, appropriate technical information infrastructure, human capacity for learning, and timely feedback, offers the promise of sustainable management of risk and disaster through harnessing human innovation and adaptation in dynamic environments.

ACKNOWLEDGMENTS

I acknowledge Thomas W. Haase, Esq., for his thoughtful assistance in the preparation of this article, and his careful review of the provisions of the U.S.A. Patriot Act. I also thank Melissa Moran and Lin Huang for their research support.

The *Annual Review of Political Science* is online at http://polisci.annualreviews.org

LITERATURE CITED

9/11 Commission. 2004. *Final Report of the National Commission on Terrorist Attacks Upon the United States*, Official Gov. Ed. http://www.gpoaccess.gov/911/

Alberts DS, Garstka JJ, Hayes RE, Signori DA. 2001. *Understanding Information Age Warfare*. Washington, DC: Dep. Defense Command and Control Res. Program

Barabasi AL. 2002. *Linked: The New Science of Networks*. Cambridge: MA: Perseus. 304 pp.

Carley KM. 1999. On the evolution of social and organizational networks. In *Networks In and Around Organizations*, ed. SB Andrews, D Knoke, 16:3–30. Stamford, CT: JAI Press. 287 pp.

Carley KM. 2000. Organizational adaptation in volatile environments. In *Computational Modeling in Organizational Behavior: The Third Scientific Discipline*, ed. CL Hulin, DR Ilgen, pp. 241–268. Washington, DC: Am. Psychol. Assoc.

Carley KM, Lee JS. 1998. Dynamic organizations: organizational adaptation in a changing environment. In *Advances in Strategic Management*, ed. J Baum, pp. 269–97. Stamford, CT: JAI Press

Carley KM, Lee JS, Krackhardt D. 2001. Desta-bilizing networks. *Connections* 24(3):31–34

Carley KM, Prietula MJ, eds. 1994. *Computational Organizational Theory*. Hillsdale, NJ: Lawrence Erlbaum Assoc. 318 pp.

Comfort LK, ed. 1988. *Managing Disaster: Strategies and Policy Perspectives*. Durham, NC: Duke Univ. Press. 420 pp.

Comfort LK. 1994. Risk and resilience: inter-organizational learning following the Northridge Earthquake of January 17. *J. Contingencies and Crisis Manag.* 2(3):174–88

Comfort LK. 1999. *Shared Risk: Complex Systems in Seismic Policy*. Amsterdam and Oxford: Pergamon. 322 pp.

Comfort LK. 2003. Managing intergovernmental response to terrorism and other extreme events. *Publius* 32(4):29–49

Comfort LK, Hauskrecht M, Lin JS. 2004. *Dynamic networks: modeling changes in environments exposed to risk*. Presented at the Annu. Res. Conf., Assoc. Pub. Policy and Manag., Atlanta

Comfort LK, Ko K, Zagorecki A. 2003. *Modeling fragility in rapidly evolving disaster response systems*. Work. Pap., Inst. Gov. Stud., Univ. Calif., Berkeley

Comfort LK, Ko K, Zagorecki A. 2004. Coordination in rapidly evolving systems: the role of information. *Am. Behav. Sci.* 48(3): 295–313

Comfort LK, Wisner B, Cutter S, Pulwarty R, Hewitt K, et al. 1999. Reframing disaster policy: the global evolution of vulnerable communities. *Environ. Hazards* 1(1):39–44

Csete M, Doyle J. 2004. Bowties, metabolism, and disease. *Trends Biotech.* 22(9):446–50

Federal Emergency Management Agency. 2000. *Federal Response Plan.* Washington, DC: Fed. Emerg. Manag. Agency

Flin RH. 1996. *Sitting in the Hot Seat: Leaders and Teams for Critical Incident Management.* New York: John Wiley & Sons. 270 pp.

Flin RH, ed. 1997. *Decision Making Under Stress: Emerging Themes and Applications.* Aldershot, Hants, UK: Ashgate. 339 pp.

Kauffman SA. 1993. *The Origins of Order: Self-Organization and Selection in Evolution.* New York: Oxford Univ. Press. 734 pp.

Klein GA. 1993. A recognition primed decision making (RPD) model of rapid decision making. In *Decision Making in Action: Models and Methods*, ed. G Klein, J Orasanu, R Calderwood, CE Zsambok, pp 138–147. Norwood, NJ: Ablex

Lempert RJ, Popper SW, Bankes SC. 2003. *Shaping the Next One Hundred Years: New Methods for Quantitative, Long-Term Policy Analysis.* Santa Monica, CA: Rand. 170 pp.

May PJ. 1985. *Recovering from Catastrophes: Federal Disaster Relief Policy and Politics.* Westport, CT: Greenwood. 186 pp.

May PJ, Williams W. 1986. *Disaster Policy Implementation: Managing Programs Under Shared Governance.* New York: Plenum. 198 pp.

McLoughlin D. 1985. A framework for integrated emergency management. *Public Adm. Rev.* 45:165–72

Mileti D, ed. 1999. *Disasters by Design: A Reassessment of Natural Hazards in the United States.* Washington, DC: Joseph Henry Press. 351 pp.

Nelson L. 2002. Protecting the common good:

technology, objectivity, and privacy. *Public Adm. Rev.* 62(4):63–69

National Governors Association. 2002. *Homeland Security: A Governor's Guide to Emergency Management,* Vol. II. Washington, DC: Natl. Gov. Assoc. Center for Best Practices

Office of Domestic Preparedness. 2002. *Developing Multi-Agency Interoperability Communication Systems: User's Handbook.* Washington, DC: Dep. of Homeland Secur.

Platt R. 1999. *Disasters and Democracy.* Washington, DC: Island Press. 320 pp.

Posner PL. 2002. *Homeland Security: Effective Intergovernmental Coordination is Key to Success*, GAO-02-1013T. Washington, DC: Gen. Account. Off.

Public Safety Wireless Network Program. 2002. *Fire and EMS Communications Interoperability*, Information Brief. Washington, DC: Dep. Justice and Dep. Treas.

Rao R. 2003. *Cyberinfrastructure research for homeland security.* Natl. Sci. Found. Workshop Rep. University of California, San Diego

Rochlin GI. 1993. Defining high-reliability organizations in practice: a taxonomic prologue. In *New Challenges to Understanding Organizations*, ed. KH Roberts, 2:11–32. New York: Macmillan. 256 pp.

Salamon LA, Elliott OV, eds. 2002. *The Tools of Government: A Guide to the New Governance.* Oxford: Oxford Univ. Press. 669 pp.

United States Government. 2001. *United States Government Interagency Domestic Terrorism Concept of Operations Plan.* http://www.fbi.gov/publications/conplan/conplan.pdf.

U.S.A. Patriot Act. 2001. *Public Law 107–56.* http://frwebgate.access.gpo.gov/cgi-bin/getdoc.cgi?dbname=107_cong_public_laws&docid=f:publ056.107.pdf

Walker D. 2002. *Homeland Security: Critical Design and Implementation Issues.* Testimony before the Select Committee on Homeland Security, US House of Representatives, July 17, 2002, GAO-02-957T. Washington, DC: Gen. Account. Off.

Wasserman S, Faust K. 1994. *Social Network*

Analysis: Methods and Applications. Cambridge: Cambridge Univ. Press. 857 pp.

Watts DJ. 2003. *Six Degrees: The Science of a Connected Age.* New York: W.W. Norton. 368 pp.

Weick KE. 1995. *Sense Making in Organizations.* Thousand Oaks, CA: Sage. 235 pp.

Weick KE, Roberts K. 1993. Collective mind and organizational reliability: the case of flight operations on an aircraft carrier deck. *Admin. Sci. Q.* 38:357–81

Wildavsky AB. 1988. *Searching for Safety.* New Brunswick, NJ: Transaction Books. 253 pp.

Young IM. 2002. *Inclusion and Democracy.* Oxford: Oxford Univ. Press. 528 pp.

Annu. Rev. Polit. Sci. 2005. 8:357–98
doi: 10.1146/annurev.polisci.8.082103.104858
Copyright © 2005 by Annual Reviews. All rights reserved
First published online as a Review in Advance on Mar. 4, 2005

THEORIZING THE EUROPEAN UNION:
International Organization, Domestic Polity,
or Experiment in New Governance?

Mark A. Pollack

Department of Political Science, Temple University, Philadelphia, Pennsylvania
19122-6089; email: mark.pollack@temple.edu

Key Words European integration, rationalism, constructivism, institutionalism,
multi-level governance

■ **Abstract** The study of the European Union (EU) has been transformed during the
past decade, and three distinct theoretical approaches have emerged. The first approach,
which seeks to explain the process of European integration, has largely abandoned the
long-standing neofunctionalist-intergovernmentalist debate in favor of a rationalist-
constructivist debate reflecting broader developments in international relations theory.
A second approach, however, has rejected the application of international relations
theory in favor of comparative politics approaches which analyze the EU using off-
the-shelf models of legislative, executive, and judicial politics in domestic politics. A
third and final approach sees the EU as an emerging system of multi-level governance
in which national governments are losing influence in favor of supranational and subnational actors, raising important normative questions about the future of democracy
within the EU.

INTRODUCTION

More than five decades into its history, the European Union (EU) remains a compelling experiment in political organization beyond the nation-state as well as the
object of intense scholarly interest from a variety of theoretical perspectives. During its first four decades, from the 1950s through the 1990s, the study of the EU was
dominated by students of international relations, and the primary theories of European integration—neofunctionalism and intergovernmentalism—remained essentially static and essentially parasitical on other fields, with only periodic attempts
to generalize from the study of the EU to the study of politics more generally.

Over the course of the past decade, however, empirical and scholarly developments have fundamentally changed the shape of EU studies and their potential
contribution to political science. Three developments are particularly noteworthy.
First, within the field of international relations, students of the EU have largely
left behind the neofunctionalist/intergovernmentalist debate of previous decades in

favor of mainstream international relations theories, most notably rational choice institutionalism and constructivism, which has emerged as the primary intellectual divide in the field. In a second major development, however, students of comparative politics have moved in increasing numbers to study the EU, not as an instance of regional integration or regional cooperation, but as a political system featuring both a horizontal and a vertical separation of powers, analytically more similar to the U.S. political system than to other international organizations. Such work has raised and begun to answer fundamentally new questions about legislative, executive, and judicial behavior in the EU, seeking to approximate the model of "normal science" among mainstream comparativists. These contrasting images of the EU as an international organization or a political system comparable to other domestic systems have, however, been rejected by a governance school, which views the EU as neither an international organization nor a domestic political system, but rather a new and unique experiment in governance beyond the nation-state. Drawing in parts from both comparative politics and international relations, this third approach portrays an EU in which nation-state governments are losing ground to both subnational and supranational actors, raising important questions about the governance capacity and democratic legitimacy of the EU and exploring recent experiments in new governance such as the EU's Open Method of Coordination (OMC).

In this article, I explore each of these developments in turn, tracing the emergence of the rationalist/constructivist divide in international relations approaches, the development of a comparative politics school striving toward a "normal science" of political behavior in the EU, and the challenge from a governance school exploring the analytic as well as normative implications of governance beyond the nation-state. The article is organized in four parts. In the first, I provide a brief overview of the most influential theories of European integration, with particular attention to the emergence of a rationalist-constructivist divide and the prospects for reconciliation among these two theories. The second section examines the emergence of a comparative-politics agenda in EU studies and the concept of the EU as a political system characterized by a horizontal and a vertical separation of powers. In the third section, I examine the recent development of a governance approach to the EU. In the fourth section, I assess the overall state of the field, noting the tendency toward fragmentation but also the increasing dialogue among scholars from different theoretical traditions and the increasingly sophisticated empirical work being carried out by practitioners of all three approaches.

THEORIES OF EUROPEAN INTEGRATION

For many years, the academic study of the European Communities (EC)—as they were previously called—was virtually synonymous with the study of European integration. From its humble beginnings with the European Coal and Steel Community in 1951, the initially modest and largely technocratic achievements of the European Communities seemed less significant than the potential that they represented for the gradual integration of the countries of Western Europe into something else: a supranational polity. When the integration process was going well, as it was during the 1950s and early 1960s, neofunctionalists and other theorists sought to explain the process whereby European integration proceeded from modest sectoral beginnings to something broader and more ambitious. When the integration process was going badly, as it was from the 1960s through the early 1980s, intergovernmentalists and others sought to explain why it had not proceeded as smoothly as its founders had hoped. Regardless of the differences among these bodies of theory, the early literature on the European Communities sought to explain the process of European integration (rather than, say, policy-making), and in doing so, it drew largely (but not exclusively) on theories of international relations.

From the beginnings of the integration process through the early 1990s, the dominant theoretical traditions in EU studies were neofunctionalism, which saw European integration as a self-sustaining process driven by sectoral spillovers toward an ever-closer union, and intergovernmentalism, which emphasized the gatekeeping role of EU member governments and their resistance to any wholesale transfer of sovereignty from the member states to a new center in Brussels. By the 1990s, however, this debate had largely faded, replaced by a new divide between rationalist approaches, such as liberal intergovernmentalism and rational choice institutionalism, and constructivist approaches, which emphasized the potentially transformative potential of the EU.

Neofunctionalism

In 1958, on the eve of the establishment of the European Economic Community (EEC) and Euratom, Ernst Haas published his magisterial text, *The Uniting of Europe*, setting out a neofunctionalist theory of regional integration. As elaborated in subsequent work by Haas and other scholars (see Haas 1961, Lindberg & Scheingold 1970), neofunctionalism posited a process of functional spillover in which the initial decision by governments to place a certain sector, such as coal and steel, under the authority of central institutions inevitably creates pressures to extend the authority of the institutions into neighboring areas of policy such as currency exchange rates, taxation, and wages. Thus, Haas and other neofunctionalists predicted that sectoral integration would produce the unintended consequence of promoting further integration in additional issue areas.

Augmenting this process of functional spillover was a complementary process of political spillover, in which both supranational actors, such as the European Commission, and subnational actors, such as interest groups within the member states, create additional pressures for further integration. At the subnational level, Haas suggested that interest groups operating in an integrated sector would have to interact with the international organization charged with the management of their sector. Over time, these groups would come to appreciate the benefits from integration and would thereby transfer their demands, expectations, and even their loyalties from national governments to a new center, thus becoming an important force for further integration. As a result of such sectoral and political spillovers, according to the neofunctionalists, sectoral integration would become self-sustaining, leading to the creation of a new political entity with its center in Brussels.

By 1965, however, French President Charles de Gaulle had precipitated the so-called Luxembourg Crisis, insisting on the importance of state sovereignty and rejecting the transfer of additional authority to Brussels. The EEC, which had been scheduled to move to qualified majority voting in 1966, continued to take decisions de facto by unanimity, the Commission emerged weakened from its confrontation with de Gaulle, and the nation-state appeared to have reasserted itself. These tendencies were reinforced by developments in the 1970s, when economic recession led to the rise of new nontariff barriers to trade among EC member states and when the intergovernmental aspects of the Community were strengthened by the 1974 creation of the European Council, a regular summit meeting of EU heads of state and government. Even some of the major advances of this period, such as the creation of the European Monetary System in 1978, were taken outside the structure of the EEC Treaty, with no formal role for the Commission or other supranational EC institutions.

Intergovernmentalism and Liberal Intergovernmentalism

Reflecting these developments, a new intergovernmentalist school of integration theory emerged, beginning with Stanley Hoffmann's (1966) claim that the nation-state, far from being obsolete, had proven "obstinate." Most obviously with de Gaulle, but later with the accession of new member states like Britain, Ireland, and Denmark in 1973, member governments made clear that they would resist the gradual transfer of sovereignty to the Community, and that EC decision making would reflect the continuing primacy of the nation-state. Under these circumstances, Haas himself (1976) pronounced the "obsolescence of regional integration theory," and other scholars, including Paul Taylor (1983) and William Wallace (1983), argued that neofunctionalists had underestimated the resilience of the nation-state.

During the 1990s, intergovernmentalism was substantially reformulated by Andrew Moravcsik (1993, 1998), who put forward a modified liberal intergovernmentalist theory of European integration. By contrast with some authors who saw the relaunching of the integration process as a vindication of earlier neofunctionalist models (Tranholm-Mikkelson 1991, Sandholtz & Zysman 1989, Burley & Mattli 1993), Moravcsik argued that even these steps forward could be accounted for by an intergovernmental model emphasizing the power and preferences of EU member states. Put simply, Moravcsik's liberal intergovernmentalism is a three-step model combining a liberal theory of national preference formation with an intergovernmental model of EU-level bargaining and a model of institutional choice emphasizing the importance of credible commitments. In the first or liberal stage of the model, national chiefs of government (or COGs) aggregate the interests of their domestic constituencies, as well as their own interests, and articulate their respective national preferences toward the EU. Thus national preferences are complex, reflecting the distinctive economics, parties, and institutions of each member state, but they are determined domestically, not shaped by participation in the EU as some neofunctionalists had proposed.

In the second or intergovernmental stage of Moravcsik's model, national governments bring their preferences to the bargaining table in Brussels, where agreements reflect the relative power of each member state and where supranational organizations such as the Commission exert little or no influence over policy outcomes. By contrast with neofunctionalists, who emphasized the entrepreneurial and brokering roles of the Commission and the upgrading of the common interest among member states in the Council, Moravcsik and other intergovernmentalists emphasized the hardball bargaining among member states and the importance of bargaining power, package deals, and side payments as determinants of the most important EU decisions.

Finally, Moravcsik puts forward a rational choice theory of institutional choice, arguing that EU member states adopt particular EU institutions—pooling sovereignty through qualified majority voting or delegating sovereignty to supranational actors like the Commission and the European Court of Justice (ECJ) —in order to increase the credibility of their mutual commitments. In this view, sovereign states seeking to cooperate among themselves invariably face a strong temptation to cheat or defect from their agreements. Moravcsik argues that pooling and delegating sovereignty through international organizations allows states to commit themselves credibly to their mutual promises by monitoring state compliance with international agreements and filling in the blanks of broad international treaties such as those that have constituted the EC/EU.

In empirical terms, Moravcsik argues that the EU's historic intergovernmental agreements, such as the 1957 Treaties of Rome and the 1992 Treaty on European Union, were not driven primarily by supranational entrepreneurs, unintended spillovers from earlier integration, or transnational coalitions of interest groups, but rather by a gradual process of preference convergence among the most powerful member states, which then struck central bargains among themselves, offered side payments to smaller member states, and delegated strictly limited powers to supranational organizations that remained more-or-less obedient servants of the member states. In theoretical terms, all three elements of Moravcsik's argument were placed explicitly into a rationalist framework, which provided a common set of assumptions about the key actors in the process of European integration and the (domestic) sources of their preferences.

During the 1990s, Moravcsik's liberal intergovernmentalism emerged as the leading theory of European integration, yet its basic theoretical assumptions were questioned by international relations scholars coming from two different directions. A first group of scholars, collected under the rubrics of rational choice and historical institutionalism, accepted Moravcsik's rationalist assumptions but rejected his spare, institution-free model of intergovernmental bargaining as an accurate description of the integration process. By contrast, a second school of thought, drawing from sociological institutionalism and constructivism, raised more fundamental objections to Moravcsik's theory, rejecting the methodological institutionalism of rational choice theory in favor an approach in which national preferences and identities were shaped, at least in part, by EU norms and rules.

The "New Institutionalisms," Rational Choice and Historical

The rise of institutionalist analysis of the EU did not develop in isolation, but reflected a gradual and widespread reintroduction of institutions into a large body of theories (such as pluralism, Marxism, and neorealism) in which institutions either had been absent or were considered epiphenomenal. By contrast with these institution-free accounts of politics, which dominated much of political science between the 1950s and the 1970s, three primary institutionalisms—rational choice, historical, and sociological or constructivist—developed during the course of the 1980s and early 1990s, each with a distinct definition of institutions and a distinct account of how they matter in the study of politics (Hall & Taylor 1996).

The first of these approaches began with the effort by American political scientists to understand the origins and effects of U.S. Congressional institutions on legislative behavior and policy outcomes. Rational choice scholars noted that majoritarian models of Congressional decision making predicted that policy outcomes would be inherently unstable, because a simple majority of policy makers could always form a coalition to overturn existing legislation, yet substantive scholars of the U.S. Congress found considerable stability in Congressional policies. In this context, Kenneth Shepsle (1979, 1986) argued that Congressional institutions, and in particular the committee system, could produce structure-induced equilibrium by ruling some alternatives as permissible or impermissible and by structuring the voting power and the veto power of various actors in the decision-making process.

Shepsle and others have since examined the agenda-setting power of Congressional committees; devised principal-agent models of Congressional delegation to regulatory bureaucracies and to courts (Moe 1984, Kiewiet & McCubbins 1991); and, most recently, have pioneered a transaction-cost approach to the design of political institutions, arguing that legislators deliberately and systematically design political institutions to minimize the transaction costs associated with the making of public policy (Epstein & O'Halloran 1999, Huber & Shipan 2002). Although originally formulated and applied in the context of American political institutions, these rationalist institutionalist insights travel to other domestic and international contexts and were quickly taken up by students of the EU. Responding to the increasing importance of EU institutional rules such as the cooperation and codecision procedures, authors including Fritz Scharpf, George Tsebelis, and Geoffrey Garrett sought to model, in rational choice terms, the selection and workings of EU institutions, including the adoption, execution, and adjudication of EU public policies. Although beginning with the study of the EU as an international organization, many of these studies drew increasingly on relevant literatures from comparative politics, and are therefore reviewed in the next section of this review.

(For reviews of institutionalism in EU studies, see Jupille & Caporaso 1999, Dowding 2000, Aspinwall & Schneider 2001, and Pollack 2004.)

By contrast with the formal definition of institutions in rational choice terms, sociological institutionalism and constructivist approaches in international relations defined institutions much more broadly to include informal norms and conventions as well as formal rules, and they argued that such institutions could constitute actors, shaping their identities and hence their preferences in ways that rational choice approaches could not capture (these approaches are examined in the next section).

Historical institutionalists took up a position between these two camps, focusing on the effects of institutions *over time*, in particular the ways in which a given set of institutions, once established, can influence or constrain the behavior of the actors who established them. In its initial formulations (Hall 1986, Thelen & Steinmo 1992), historical institutionalism was seen as having dual effects, influencing both the constraints on individual actors and their preferences, and thereby encompassing the core insights of both the rationalist and constructivist camps. What makes historical institutionalism distinctive, however, is its emphasis on the effects of institutions on politics over time. In a sophisticated presentation of this strand of historical institutionalist thinking, Paul Pierson (2000) has argued that political institutions are characterized by increasing returns, insofar as those institutions and policies create incentives for actors to stick with existing institutions, adapting them only incrementally in response to changing circumstances. Insofar as political institutions are indeed subject to increasing returns, politics should be characterized by certain interrelated phenomena, including: inertia, or lock-ins, whereby existing institutions may remain in equilibrium for extended periods despite considerable political change; a critical role for timing and sequencing, in which relatively small and contingent events at critical junctures early in a sequence shape events that occur later; and path dependence, in which early decisions provide incentives for actors to perpetuate institutional and policy choices inherited from the past, even when the resulting outcomes are manifestly inefficient.

In recent years, these insights have been applied increasingly to the development of the EU, with various authors emphasizing the temporal dimension of European integration as a process occurring over time. At its best, this literature does not simply point to the stickiness or the path dependence of EU institutions, but develops and tests specific hypotheses about which types of institutions are subject to lock-ins, how those institutions shape historical trajectories over time, and under what conditions early choices either do—or do not—set the EU down a path from which it is increasingly costly to deviate. Pierson's (1996) study of path dependence in the EU, for example, seeks to understand European integration as a process that unfolds over time and the conditions under which path-dependent processes are most likely to occur. Working from essentially rationalist assumptions, Pierson argues that despite the initial primacy of member governments in the design of EU institutions and policies, gaps may occur in the ability of member governments to control the subsequent development of institutions and policies, for four reasons. First, member governments in democratic societies may, because of electoral concerns, apply a high discount rate to the future, agreeing to EU policies that lead to a long-term loss of national control in return for short-term electoral returns. Second, even when governments do not heavily discount the future, unintended consequences of institutional choices can create additional gaps, which member governments may or may not be able to close through subsequent action. Third, Pierson argues, the preferences of member governments are likely to change over time, most obviously because of electoral turnover, leaving new governments with new preferences to inherit an *acquis communautaire* negotiated by, and according to the preferences of, a previous government. Given the frequent requirement of unanimous voting (or qualified majority—still a high hurdle) to overturn past institutional and policy choices, individual member governments are likely to find themselves "immobilized by the weight of past initiatives" (Pierson 1996, p. 137). Finally, EU institutions and policies can become locked in not only as a result of change-resistant institutions from above, but also through the incremental growth of entrenched support for existing institutions from below, as societal actors adapt to and develop a vested interest in the continuation of specific EU policies.

At their best, historical institutionalist analyses offer not only the banal observation that institutions are sticky, but also a tool kit for predicting and explaining under what conditions we should expect institutional lock-ins and path-dependent behavior. More specifically, we should expect that, ceteris paribus, institutions and policies will be most resistant to change (*a*) where their alteration requires a unanimous agreement among member states, or the consent of supranational actors like the Commission or the European Parliament (EP); and (*b*) where existing EU policies mobilize cross-national bases of support that raise the cost of reversing or significantly revising them. Both of these factors vary across issue areas, and we should therefore expect variation in the stability and path-dependent character of EU institutions and policies.

In sum, for both rational choice and historical institutionalists, EU institutions matter, shaping both the policy process and policy outcomes in predictable ways, and indeed shaping the long-term process of European integration. In both cases, however, the effects of EU institutions are assumed to influence only the incentives confronting the various public and private actors—the actors themselves are assumed to remain unchanged in their fundamental preferences and identities. Indeed, despite their differences on substantive issues, liberal intergovernmentalism, rational choice institutionalism and most historical institutionalism arguably constitute a single rationalist research program: a community of scholars operating from similar basic assumptions and seeking to test hypotheses about the most important determinants of European integration. By contrast, constructivist and sociological institutionalist approaches argue that the most profound effects of EU institutions are precisely in the potential remaking of national preferences and identities in the crucible of EU institutions.

Constructivism and the Reshaping of European Identities and Preferences

Like rational choice theories, constructivist theory did not begin with the study of the EU. Indeed, as Thomas Risse (2004) points out in an excellent survey, constructivism came to EU studies relatively late, with the publication of a special issue of the *Journal of European Public Policy* in 1999 as a turning point. Yet constructivist theorists have been quick to apply their theoretical tools to the EU since then, promising to shed light on potentially profound effects of the EU on the peoples and governments of Europe.

Constructivism, like rational choice, is not a substantive theory of European integration per se, but a broader metatheoretical orientation with implications for the study of the EU. As Risse (2004, p. 161) explains:

> ... [It] is probably most useful to describe constructivism as based on a social ontology which insists that human agents do not exist independently from their social environment and its collectively shared systems of meanings ("culture" in a broad sense). This is in contrast to the methodological individualism of rational choice according to which "[t]he elementary unit of social life is the individual human action" (Elster 1989, p. 13). The fundamental insight of the agency-structure debate, which lies at the heart of many social constructivist works, is not only that structures and agents are mutually codetermined. The crucial point is that constructivists insist on the *constitutiveness* of (social) structures and agents (Adler 1997, pp. 324–5; Wendt 1999, Ch. 4). The social environment in which we find ourselves, "constitutes" who we are, our identities as social beings.

For constructivists, then, institutions are understood broadly to include not only formal rules but also informal norms, and these rules and norms are expected to constitute actors, that is, to shape their identities and their preferences. Actor preferences are not exogenously given and fixed, as in rationalist models, but endogenous to institutions, and individuals' identities shaped and reshaped by their social environment. Taking this argument to its logical conclusion, constructivists generally reject the rationalist conception of actors as utility-maximizers operating according to a "logic of consequentiality," in favor of March and Olsen's (1989, pp. 160–62) conception of a "logic of appropriateness."

In the field of EU studies, a growing number of scholars have argued that EU institutions shape not only the behavior but also the preferences and identities of individuals and member governments (Sandholtz 1996, Jørgensen 1997, Lewis 1998). This argument has been made most forcefully by Thomas Christiansen, Knud Erik Jørgensen, and Antje Wiener in their introduction to a 1999 special issue of the *Journal of European Public Policy* on "The Social Construction of Europe":

> A significant amount of evidence suggests that, as a process, European integration has a transformative impact on the European state system and its

constituent units. European integration itself has changed over the years, and it is reasonable to assume that in the process agents' identity and subsequently their interests have equally changed. While this aspect of change can be theorized within constructivist perspectives, it will remain largely invisible in approaches that neglect processes of identity formation and/or assume interests to be given endogenously (Christiansen et al., 1999, p. 529).

The authors begin with the claim that the EU is indeed reshaping national identities and preferences, and they reject rationalist approaches for their inability to predict and explain these phenomena. Not surprisingly, such claims have been forcefully rebutted by rationalist theorists, including most notably Andrew Moravcsik (Moravcsik 1999, Checkel & Moravcsik 2001).

Constructivist theorists, according to Moravcsik (1999) raise an interesting and important set of questions about the effects of European integration on individuals and states. Yet, he argues, constructivists have failed to make a significant contribution to our empirical understanding of European integration, for two reasons. First, constructivists typically fail to construct distinct falsifiable hypotheses, opting instead for broad interpretive frameworks that can make sense of almost any possible outcome and are therefore not subject to falsification through empirical analysis. Second, Moravcsik argues, even if constructivists posit hypotheses that are in principle falsifiable, they generally do not formulate and test those hypotheses in ways that distinguish clearly between constructivist predictions and their rationalist counterparts. Until constructivists test their hypotheses, and do so against prevailing and distinct rationalist models, he argues, constructivism will not come down "from the clouds" (Checkel & Moravcsik 2001).

Constructivists might, of course, respond that Moravcsik privileges rational choice explanations and sets a higher standard for constructivist hypotheses (since rational choice scholars typically do not attempt to test their own hypotheses against competing constructivist formulations). Many postpositivist scholars, moreover, dispute Moravcsik's image of EU studies as science, with its attendant claims of objectivity and of an objective, knowable world. For such scholars, Moravcsik's call for falsifiable hypothesis testing appears as a power-laden demand that "nonconformist" theories play according to the rules of a rationalist, and primarily American, social science (Jørgensen 1997). To the extent that constructivists do indeed reject positivism and the systematic testing of competing hypotheses, the rationalist/constructivist debate would seem to have reached a metatheoretical impasse in which constructivists and rationalists fail to agree on a common standard for judging what constitutes support for one or another approach.

In recent years, however, an increasing number of constructivist theorists have embraced positivism, and these scholars have produced a spate of constructivist work that attempts rigorously to test hypotheses about socialization, norm diffusion, and collective preference formation in the EU (Wendt 1999, Checkel 2003, Risse 2004). Some of these studies, including Liesbet Hooghe's (2002, 2005) extensive analysis of the attitudes of Commission officials and several studies of national officials participating in EU committees (Beyers & Dierickx 1998, Egeberg 1999), use quantitative methods to test hypotheses about the nature and determinants of officials' attitudes, including socialization in national as well as European institutions. Such studies, undertaken with methodological rigor and with a frank reporting of findings, seem to demonstrate that that EU-level socialization, although not excluded, plays a relatively small role by comparison with national-level socialization, or that EU socialization interacts with other factors in complex ways. Other studies, including Checkel's (1999, 2003) study of citizenship norms in the EU and the Council of Europe, and Lewis's (1998, 2003) analysis of decision making in the EU Committee of Permanent Representatives, utilize qualitative rather than quantitative methods, but are similarly designed to test falsifiable hypotheses about whether, and under what conditions, EU officials are socialized into new norms, preferences, and identities.

As a result of these and other studies, the metatheoretical gulf separating rationalists and constructivists appears to have narrowed considerably, and EU scholars have arguably led the way in confronting, and possibly reconciling, the two theoretical approaches. Perhaps most constructively, three EU scholars (Jupille et al. 2003) have recently put forward a framework for promoting integration of— or at least a fruitful dialogue between—rationalist and constructivist approaches to international relations. Rationalism and constructivism, the authors argue, are not hopelessly incommensurate, but can engage each other through "four distinct modes of theoretical conversation," namely:

1. competitive testing, in which competing theories are pitted against each other in explaining a single event or class of events;

2. a "domain of application" approach, in which each theory is considered to explain some subset of empirical reality, so that, for example, utility maximizing and strategic bargaining obtains in certain circumstances, whereas socialization and collective preference formation obtains in others;

3. a sequencing approach, in which one theory might explain a particular step in a sequence of actions (e.g., a constructivist explanation of national preferences) while another theory might best explain subsequent developments (e.g., a rationalist explanation of subsequent bargaining among the actors); and

4. "incorporation" or "subsumption," in which one theory claims to subsume the other so that, for example, rational choice becomes a subset of human behavior ultimately explicable in terms of the social construction of modern rationality.

Looking at the substantive empirical work in their special issue, Jupille, Caporaso, and Checkel find that most contributions to the rationalist-constructivist debate utilize competitive testing, whereas only a small number (e.g., Schimmelfennig 2003a) have adopted domain of application, sequencing, or subsumption approaches. Nevertheless, they see substantial progress in the debate, in which both sides generally accept a common standard of empirical testing as the criterion for useful theorizing about EU politics.

Integration Theory Today

In place of the traditional neofunctionalist/intergovernmentalist debate, the 1990s witnessed the emergence of a new dichotomy in EU studies, pitting rationalist scholars against constructivists. During the late 1990s, it appeared that this debate might well turn into a metatheoretical dialogue of the deaf, with rationalists dismissing constructivists as "soft" and constructivists denouncing rationalists for their obsessive commitment to parsimony and formal models. During the past several years, however, a more constructive dialogue between the two approaches has emerged, including a steady stream of empirical studies allowing us to adjudicate between the competing claims of the two approaches. Furthermore, whereas the neofunctionalist/intergovernmentalist debate was limited almost exclusively to the study of European integration, the contemporary rationalist/constructivist debate in EU mirrors larger debates among those same schools in international relations theory more broadly. Indeed, not only are EU studies relevant to the wider study of international relations, they are in many ways the vanguard of international relations theory, insofar as the EU serves as a laboratory for broader processes such as globalization, institutionalization, and socialization.

THE EU IN COMPARATIVE PERSPECTIVE

Thus far, we have examined the EU literature from the perspective of one concerned overwhelmingly with the causes and the direction of European integration as a process. Throughout its history, however, many scholars have approached the EU not solely or primarily through the lenses of international relations theory, but as a polity or political system akin to other domestic political systems. This tendency was most pronounced in the work of federalist writers, who explicitly compared the EU to federal and confederal systems in Germany, Switzerland, and the United States of America (Capelletti et al.1986, Scharpf 1988, Sbragia 1993), as well as in the work of systems theorists such as Lindberg & Scheingold (1970), who saw the EU as a political system characterized by political demands (inputs), governmental actors, and public policies (outputs). At the same time, an increasing number of EU scholars sought deliberately to bracket the question of integration and the EU's final destination, focusing instead on a better understanding of the EU policy process in all its complexity and diversity (Wallace & Wallace 1977).

By the mid-1990s, a growing number of scholars sought to understand the EU as a political system using the theoretical tools developed in the study of domestic polities. This perspective was championed most effectively by Simon Hix (1994, 1999), who issued a call to arms to comparativists in a series of publications. Previous studies of the EU, Hix argued, had drawn almost exclusively from theories of international integration, and they had problematized the EU as a process of integration; in doing so, however, they neglected the politics of the EU, as well as its characteristics as a political system. The EU, Hix argued, was clearly less than a Weberian state, lacking in particular a monopoly on the legitimate use of force; yet he echoed Lindberg and Scheingold by suggesting that the EU could be theorized as a political system, with a dense web of legislative, executive, and judicial institutions that adopted binding public policies and hence influenced the authoritative allocation of values in European society. Furthermore, by contrast with earlier studies that examined EU politics through the single dimension of integration (ranging from nationalism at one extreme to centralization at the other), Hix suggested that EU politics takes place in a two-dimensional space, with integration representing one dimension, alongside a second dimension spanning the traditional left-right divide over the extent and the nature of government intervention in the economy. As such, Hix concluded, the EU could and should be studied using "the tools, methods and cross-systemic theories from the general study of government, politics and policy-making. In this way, teaching and research on the EU can be part of the political science mainstream" (Hix 1999, p. 2).

Hix's call to arms among comparativists has not escaped criticism, with a number of authors arguing that Hix's dichotomous formulation of the division of labor between international and comparative politics—with the former using international relations theoretical tools to understand integration, and the latter using comparative tools to understand politics—represented an oversimplification of our object of study and a disciplinary step backward from integration to fragmentation of subfields within political science. Indeed, Jupille et al. (2003) suggested that "converging empirical and intellectual trends, especially in the area of political economy, increasingly undermine ... the distinction between comparative and international" (p. 10; see also Hurrell & Menon 1996). Empirically, the phenomenon of globalization has drawn scholars' attention to the links between international developments and domestic politics, not just in the EU but globally. In theoretical terms, an increasing number of theories—Peter Gourevitch's (1978) "second-image reversed," Robert Putnam's (1988) "two-level games" model, and various models of globalization (Keohane & Milner 1998, Caporaso 1997)—all theorized mechanisms linking domestic politics to developments at the international level, suggesting that purely comparative approaches might miss this domestic-international interaction. Furthermore, as we have just seen, rational choice theories of politics promised precisely to provide a single overarching theoretical framework linking together American, comparative, and international politics (Milner 1998). Under the circumstances, according to Jupille, "it would be perverse if the erosion of such disciplinary boundaries were to be resisted in EU Studies, the object of study of which seems precisely to fall in the interstices of the two subfields!" (Jupille 2005).

For all of these reasons, the comparative–international relations divide did not prove to be the important schism in EU studies that many had expected, and much useful work has integrated domestic and international politics within a single theoretical framework. Nevertheless, comparative political scientists have moved increasingly into EU studies, in part because the EU has intruded increasingly into what had previously been seen as exclusively domestic arenas, and in part because an increasing number of scholars accepted Hix's claim that the EU could be theorized as a political system and analyzed using off-the-shelf categories from the comparative study of domestic polities. This movement of comparativists into EU studies is reflected in quantitative data collected by Jupille (2005), who demonstrates the rise of EU studies from an almost entirely international relations–based initiative to one that features equally in the pages of international relations and comparative journals (see also Keeler 2004).

Although such comparative work on the EU is extraordinarily diverse, comprising numerous middle-range "islands of theory" (Dalton 1991) and empirical research, much of it can fairly be characterized as comparative, rationalist, and positivist in nature. First, as Hix (1998) argues, much of the work on EU politics proceeds from the assumption that the EU is not a *sui generis* system of governance, but is a variant on existing political systems and can therefore be understood with the aid of off-the-shelf models of politics in other (primarily national) contexts. In recent years, a growing number of these theories have drawn from the study of American politics, since the EU arguably resembles the US in possessing both a horizontal and a vertical separation of powers.

Second, in terms of the rationalist/constructivist divide sketched in the previous section, most of the work reviewed in this section is either implicitly or explicitly rationalist, taking the assumption that actors (be they states, individuals, or supranational organizations) have fixed, exogenously given preferences, and that they act systematically to maximize those preferences within the constraints of EU institutions. Within this rationalist literature, a growing subset not only employs the language of rational choice (i.e., "soft" rational choice) but also draws from and elaborates formal and game-theoretic models of EU decision making.

Finally, much of the work discussed here can be characterized as implicitly or explicitly positivist, seeking to test theory-driven hypotheses systematically, often (though by no means always) with the aid of quantitative as well as qualitative methods. Much of this work has appeared in mainstream American and European journals of political science, such as the *American Journal of Political Science*, the *American Political Science Review*, the *British Journal of Political Science*, and the *European Journal of Political Science*, but the spiritual home of this body of literature is undoubtedly the journal *European Union Politics*, which has published a steady stream of articles featuring formal models of decision making and innovative use of new and existing data sets to test hypotheses about political behavior in the EU. The editors of the journal, and many of its contributors, explicitly put forward a model of "normal science" in which scholars deduce theories of specific aspects of EU politics (e.g., legislative or executive or judicial politics) and seek to test them comparatively with the most precise available data (Gabel et al. 2002, p. 481). A thorough examination of this literature is beyond the scope of this review, and I therefore focus here on two dimensions, namely the horizontal or federal division of powers between the EU and member-state levels and the vertical or separation-of-powers division among the legislative, executive, and judicial branches of the EU.

The Horizontal Separation of Powers: The EU as a Federal System

The EU did not begin life as a federal union, nor, in the view of most analysts, does it constitute a fully developed federation today. In political terms, the word "federal" was regarded as taboo by the British and other delegations that negotiated the 1992 Maastricht Treaty on European Union (it was referred to obliquely as "the f-word"). In analytical terms, some scholars question whether the EU can or should be accurately described as a federal state:

> The contemporary EU is far narrower and weaker a federation than any extant national federation—so weak, indeed, that we might question whether it is a federation at all. The EU plays almost no role—at most a weak sort of international coordination—in most of the issue-areas about which European voters care most, such as taxation, social welfare provision, defense, high foreign policy, policing, education, cultural policy, human rights, and small business policy. European Union institutions are tightly constrained, moreover, by supermajoritarian voting rules, a tiny administration, radical openness, stringent provisions for subsidiarity, a distinct professional ethos, and the near-total absence of the power to tax and coerce. The EU was designed as, and remains primarily, a limited international institution to coordinate national regulation of trade in goods and services, and the resulting flows of economic factors. Its substantive scope and institutional prerogatives are limited accordingly. The EU constitutional order is not only barely a federal state; it is barely recognizable as a state at all (Moravcsik 2001, pp. 163–64).

Nevertheless, federalism was a powerful normative ideal motivating many of the founding fathers of the European movement and much of the early scholarship on the EU. By the 1980s, moreover, the institutions and policy processes of the European Communities had developed strong analytical similarities to those of existing federations, and theories of federalism therefore took on greater importance, not just as a normative ideal motivating European integration, but as a positive theoretical framework capable of explaining and predicting the workings of the EU as a political system.

The term federalism has been the subject of numerous overlapping definitions, but most of these formulations rely on the three elements emphasized by R. Daniel Kelemen, who has described federalism as "an institutional arrangement in which (*a*) public authority is divided between state governments and a central government, (*b*) each level of government has some issues on which it makes final decisions, and (*c*) a federal high court adjudicates disputes concerning federalism" (2003, p. 185). In most federal systems, the structure of representation is twofold, with popular or functional interests represented through a directly elected lower house, whereas territorial units are typically represented in an upper house whose members may be either directly elected (as in the U.S. Senate) or appointed by state governments (as in the German *Bundesrat*). In both of these senses, the EU already constitutes a federal system with a constitutionally guaranteed separation of powers between the EU and member-state levels, and a dual system of representation through the EP and the Council of Ministers—and hence the literature on comparative federalism provides a useful toolkit for theorizing the workings of the EU.

Perhaps the most difficult issue in the EU, as in other federal systems, is the question of the distribution of powers among the federal and state levels of government. Economic models of fiscal federalism have long suggested that the functions of macroeconomic stabilization and distribution are best exercised at the federal level, because these functions would be likely to go unprovided or underprovided if left to the individual states; and indeed, most mature federations feature a strong fiscal role for government, smoothing out asymmetric shocks across states and providing for redistribution of funds from wealthier to poorer states (Börzel & Hösli 2003, pp. 180–81). Helen Wallace (2000) has pointed out that the choice of a given level of government—federal/EU versus national/state—can be theorized through the metaphor of a pendulum, where the choice of policy arena varies depending on a number of contextual, functional, motivational, and institutional factors.

In this view, the history of the EU can be viewed as a series of centralizing initiatives (e.g., the founding years of the 1950s and the relaunching of the integration process in the 1980s) followed by periods of retrenchment or devolution (e.g., the Gaullist revolt of the 1960s and the post-Maastricht backlash of the 1990s) (Donahue & Pollack 2001). The struggle over European integration, in this view, is not a *sui generis* process but a constitutionally structured process of oscillation between states and central governments familiar from other federal systems.

Ironically, while emphasizing the similarity of the EU to other federal systems, students of comparative federalism have also pointed to an exceptional aspect of the EU, which is the absence or at least the weakness of fiscal federalism and the dominance of regulatory federalism at the EU level. By contrast with most federal systems, which engage in substantial fiscal transfers across state boundaries, the EU budget has been capped at a relatively small 1.27% of its GDP, the majority of which is devoted to agricultural and cohesion spending. The EU is therefore unable to engage in substantial redistribution or macroeconomic stabilization through fiscal policy, and it only indirectly influences the structure of European welfare states, which remain predominantly national. In the absence of a substantial budget, therefore, the EU has engaged primarily in regulatory activity, earning it the moniker of a "regulatory state" in the work of Giandomenico Majone (1996). The regulatory output of the EU, in Majone's view, has been driven by both demand and supply factors. On the demand side, the imperative of creating a single internal market has put pressure on EU member states to adopt common or harmonized EU-wide regulations, most notably on products, in order to remove nontariff barriers to trade and ensure the free movement of goods, services, labor and capital throughout the EU. On the supply side, an entrepreneurial Commission has seen regulation as a viable way to enhance its own policy competence despite the financial limits imposed by the EU's strict budgetary ceiling.

In empirical terms, the EU has engaged in a vast project of economic regulation, driven largely by the creation and maintenance of the internal market, and these EU regulations have been adopted according to a regulatory mode of governance within which the Commission plays a vital entrepreneurial role, the Council and EP a collective role as a bicameral legislature, and the ECJ and national courts a dual role in enforcing EU regulations and challenging national regulations that might impede the free movement of labor. As in other federal systems, the adoption of far-reaching central regulations has taken the EU into areas of regulation not originally envisaged by the framers of the treaties, generating significant controversy and increasing demands since the 1990s for adherence to the principle of subsidiarity, the notion that the EU should govern as close as possible to the citizen and therefore that the EU should engage in regulation only where necessary to ensure the completion of the internal market and/or other fundamental aims of the treaties. Even in the regulatory field, therefore, the horizontal separation of powers is not fixed but fluid, and the result resembles not so much a layer cake as a marble cake, in which EU and member-state authorities are concurrent, intermixed, and constantly in flux.

The Vertical Separation of Powers

Unlike the parliamentary states of Western Europe, but like the United States, the EU can also be characterized by a vertical separation of powers in which three distinct branches of government take the leading role in the legislative, executive, and judicial functions of government, respectively. This does not mean, of course, that any one institution enjoys sole control of any of these three functions; indeed, as Amie Kreppel points out, the Madisonian conception of separation of powers "requires to a certain extent a comingling of powers in all three arenas (executive, legislative, and judicial)" (2002, p. 5). In the case of the EU, for example, the legislative function is today shared by the Council of Ministers and the EP, with an agenda-setting role for the Commission; the executive function is shared by the Commission, the member states, and (in some areas) independent regulatory agencies; and the judicial function is shared by the ECJ, the Court of First Instance, and wide array of national courts bound directly to the ECJ through the preliminary reference procedure (Alter 2001).

Reflecting this separation of powers, comparative-politics scholars have during the past decade devoted extraordinary attention to theorizing, predicting, and explaining legislative, executive, and judicial behavior using off-the-shelf theories drawn from the rational choice study of American and comparative politics. A thorough discussion of these three arenas is clearly beyond the scope of this review; nevertheless, a brief overview of the literature will illustrate the application of comparative and rationalist theories to each of these three domains and the promise and limits of such applications.

LEGISLATIVE POLITICS: TOWARD BICAMERALISM   Without doubt, the largest and most systematic strand within the comparative/EU literature has been that on the EU legislative process. Drawing heavily on theories of legislative behavior and legislative organization, students of EU legislative politics have applied, tested, and adapted off-the-shelf theories of legislative politics to understand the process of legislative decision making inside the Council of Ministers and the EP, as well as the respective powers of these two legislative bodies as the EU has moved gradually from an essentially intergovernmental body to one increasingly resembling a classic bicameral legislature. Looking first at the Council of Ministers, a number of authors have attempted to model the relative voting power of member states in the Council of Ministers and the formation of voting coalitions among the member governments under different decision rules. Under unanimity voting, for example, EU legislative rules provide each member government with equal voting weight and with the opportunity to veto a decision that could leave them worse off than the status quo. Moving from unanimity to qualified majority voting, however, raises the possibility that states can form winning coalitions reflecting their respective interests and the voting weights within the EU's system of qualified majority voting. In this context, a number of scholars have used increasingly elaborate formal models of Council voting to establish the relative voting weights—and hence the bargaining power—of various member states. Nevertheless, as Garrett & Tsebelis (1996) have pointed out, voting weights are not the sole index of a member state's legislative influence, because not all coalitions of member states are equally likely to form in Council negotiations. Instead, a thorough understanding of member-states' legislative influence must also take into account the relative preferences of member governments: Those governments with preferences close to the center of the distribution on a given issue are thus most likely to be in a winning majority independent of their formal voting weight, whereas other governments may be preference outliers (in terms of either the integration or the left-right dimension) and therefore more likely to be isolated in EU decision making, again independent of their formal voting weights.

The EP, similarly, has been the subject of extensive theoretical modeling and empirical study over the past two decades, with a growing number of scholars studying the legislative organization of the EP and the voting behavior of its members (MEPs) through the lenses of comparative legislative studies. The early studies of the EP, in the 1980s and early 1990s, emphasized the striking fact that, in spite of the multinational nature of the EP, the best predictor of MEP voting behavior is not nationality but an MEP's "party group," with the center-left Party of European Socialists, the center-right European People's Party, and other, smaller party groups demonstrating extraordinarily high measures of cohesion in empirical studies of roll-call votes (e.g., Kreppel 2001). These MEPs were shown to contest elections and cast their votes in a two-dimensional issue space, including not only the familiar nationalism/supranationalism dimension but also and especially the more traditional, domestic dimension of left-right contestation (Hix 2001). In a similar vein, many students of the EP noted the tendency of the two major party groups to form oversized voting coalitions, ostensibly to ensure large majorities and increase the EP's influence relative to the Council; recent studies, however, have pointed to a tentative retreat from oversized coalitions toward more normal patterns of minimum-winning coalitions on the left or the right (Kreppel & Hix 2003). Still other studies have focused on the legislative organization of the EP, including not only the party groups but also the EP's powerful committees, whose members play an important agenda-setting role in preparing legislation for debate on the floor of Parliament (Kreppel 2001, McElroy 2004). These scholars have shown that the EP can increasingly be studied as a normal parliament whose members vote predictably and cohesively within a political space dominated by the familiar contestation between parties of the left and the right (Hix et al. 2002).

Through the 1980s and the 1990s, the legislative powers of the EP grew sequentially, from the relatively modest and nonbinding consultation procedure of the EEC Treaty through the creation of the cooperation procedure in the 1980s and the creation and reform of a codecision procedure in the 1990s. This expansion of EP legislative power, and the complex nature of the new legislative procedures, has fostered the development of a burgeoning literature and led to two vigorous debates in the legislative studies community about the nature and extent of the EP's and the Council's respective influence across the various procedures. The first of these debates concerned the introduction of the cooperation procedure, which gave the EP a second reading of EU legislation and allowed the EP to propose amendments that, if accepted by the Commission, could then be adopted by the Council by qualified majority, but rejected only by unanimity. In an influential article, George Tsebelis (1994) argued that this provision gave the EP conditional agenda-setting power, insofar as the EP would now enjoy the ability to make specific proposals that would be easier for the Council to adopt than to amend. Other scholars disputed Tsebelis's model, arguing that the EP's proposed amendments had no special status without the approval of the Commission, which therefore remained the principal agenda setter in the EU legislative process (Moser 1996). Subsequent empirical studies by Tsebelis and others appeared to confirm the basic predictions of Tsebelis's model, namely that the EP enjoyed much greater success in influencing the content of legislation under cooperation than under the older consultation procedure (Tsebelis 1996, Kreppel 1999, Corbett et al. 2000).

A second controversy emerged in the literature over the impact of EP under the codecision procedure introduced by the 1993 Maastricht Treaty (codecision I) and reformed by the 1997 Treaty of Amsterdam (codecision II). Under the Maastricht provisions, codecision would elevate the EP to a nearly equal status with the Council within the EU's bicameral legislature; specifically, legislation adopted under codecision could be negotiated between the two chambers in a conciliation committee, the results of which would have to be approved by the requisite majority in both chambers. In a major exception to the principle of strict bilateralism, however, the Maastricht version of codecision allowed the Council to reassert its initial position, which would become law unless rejected by an absolute majority in the EP. In a series of controversial articles, Tsebelis and Garrett argued that contrary to common perceptions of the codecision procedure as a step forward for the EP, Parliament had actually lost legislative power in the move from cooperation to codecision I, in favor of the Council, which gained the agenda-setting power to present the EP in its third reading with any possible alternative that the latter would prefer over the status quo (Tsebelis 1997; Tsebelis & Garrett 1997a,b). By contrast, other rational choice scholars disputed Garrett and Tsebelis's claims, noting that alternative specifications of the model predicted more modest agenda-setting power for the EP under cooperation and/or a stronger position for the EP in codecision (Scully 1997a–c; Crombez 1997; Moser 1997). Here again, quantitative and qualitative empirical analysis has provided at least tentative answers to the question of EP influence across the various legislative procedures, with the most extensive study suggesting that the EP has indeed enjoyed greater legislative influence under codecision I than under cooperation, largely at the expense of the Commission, which no longer plays the crucial intermediary role between the EP and the Council (Tsebelis et al. 2001). In any event, the Treaty of Amsterdam subsequently simplified the codecision procedure, removing the Council's third reading and creating a more symmetrical codecision II procedure in which "the Council and the Parliament are now coequal legislators and the EU's legislative regime is truly bicameral" (Tsebelis & Garrett 2000, p. 24).

EXECUTIVE POLITICS: DELEGATION AND DISCRETION   Rational choice institutionalists have devoted increasing attention during the past decade to the question of delegation to, and agency and agenda-setting by, supranational organizations such as the Commission. These studies generally address two specific sets of questions. First, they ask why and under what conditions a group of member-state principals might delegate powers to supranational agents, such as the Commission, the European Central Bank (ECB), or the ECJ. With regard to this first question, rationalists like Moravcsik (1998), Majone (1996), and Pollack (2003) have drawn from the theoretical literature on delegation in American, comparative, and international politics in order to devise and test hypotheses about the motives of EU member governments in delegating specific powers and functions to the Commission and other supranational actors.

Simplifying considerably, such transaction-cost accounts of delegation argue that as rational actors, member-state principals delegate powers to supranational organizations primarily to lower the transaction costs of policy making, in particular by allowing member governments to commit themselves credibly to international agreements and to benefit from the policy-relevant expertise provided by supranational actors. Despite differences in emphasis, the empirical work of these scholars has demonstrated that EU member governments delegate powers to the Commission, the ECB, and the ECJ largely to reduce the transaction costs of policy making, in particular through the monitoring of member-state compliance, the filling-in of framework treaties ("incomplete contracts"), and the speedy and efficient adoption of implementing regulations that would otherwise have to be adopted in a time-consuming legislative process by the member governments themselves. By the same token, however, the same studies generally concede that transaction-cost models do a poor job of predicting patterns of delegation to the EP, which appears to have been delegated powers primarily in response to concerns about democratic legitimacy rather than to reduce the transaction costs of policy making.

In addition to the question of delegation, rational choice institutionalists have devoted greater attention to a second question posed by principal-agent models: What if an agent such as the Commission, the ECJ, or the ECB behaves in ways that diverge from the preferences of the principals? The answer to this question in principal-agent analysis lies primarily in the administrative procedures that the principals may establish to define ex ante the scope of agency activities, as well as the procedures that allow for ex post oversight and sanctioning of errant agents. Applied to the EU, principal-agent analysis leads to the hypothesis that agency autonomy is likely to vary across issue areas and over time, as a function of the preferences of the member states, the distribution of information between principals and agents, and the decision rules governing the application of sanctions or the adoption of new legislation (Pollack 2003, Tallberg 2000).

Much of this literature on delegation and agency focuses on the rather arcane question of comitology, the committees of member-state representatives established to supervise the Commission in its implementation of EU law. For rational choice theorists, comitology committees act as control mechanisms designed by member-state principals to supervise their supranational agent (the Commission) in its executive duties. More specifically, rational choice analysts have analyzed the differences among the three primary types of comitology committees—advisory committees, management committees, and regulatory committees—noting that, in formal models of executive decision making, the Commission is least constrained under the advisory committee procedure and most constrained under the regulatory committee procedure, with the management committee procedure occupying a middle ground. Rationalists predict that under these circumstances, the influence of the Commission as an agent should vary with the type of committee governing a given issue area; empirical research suggests that member governments do indeed design and use comitology committees as instruments of control and that Commission autonomy and influence vary as a function of the administrative and oversight procedures adopted by the Council (Dogan 1997, Franchino 2001, Pollack 2003).

Finally, students of executive politics in the EU have turned increasingly to the study of a relatively new phenomenon: the proliferation of new executive bodies at the EU level, including the ECB and a diverse array of independent regulatory agencies. The ECB, created by the Maastricht Treaty and now serving as the collective central bank of the Euro-zone, is without doubt the most spectacular example of supranational delegation in the history of the EU. Indeed, both rational choice scholars and EU practitioners have referred to the ECB as the most independent central bank in the world, owing to the long and nonrenewable terms of office of its members and the insulation of the bank and its mandate, which can be altered only by a unanimous agreement of the member states. For rationalist scholars, the creation of the ECB is a classic case of delegation to increase the credibility of member-state commitments to a stable, noninflationary common currency (Moravcsik 1998). Arguing from a sociological institutionalist perspective, however, Kathleen McNamara has argued that the functional advantages of delegation to independent central banks are disputable, and that the creation of the ECB therefore represents a process of institutional isomorphism, in which organizational forms considered to be successful and legitimate in one setting diffuse and are copied in other settings "even if these rules are materially inappropriate to their needs" (2002). During the past decade, a growing number of European independent regulatory agencies have emerged, including the European Agency for the Evaluation of Medicinal Products (EMEA), the European Food Safety Authority (EFSA), and more than a dozen others. Although most of these agencies are in their infancy, early research has catalogued the diverse functions of these various agencies, as well as the wide range of control mechanisms designed by member governments to limit the discretion of these agencies in ways appropriate to their various tasks, suggesting again that EU member governments delegate functions to executive actors for the reasons specified in rationalist theories and tailor control mechanisms to the functions and expected preferences of the respective agencies (Everson et al. 2001).

JUDICIAL POLITICS AND THE ECJ   In addition to the lively debate about the nature of EU executive politics, rational choice institutionalists have also engaged in an increasingly sophisticated research program into the nature of EU judicial politics and the role of the ECJ in the integration process. Writing in the early 1990s, for example, Geoffrey Garrett first drew on principal-agent analysis to argue that the Court, as an agent of the EU's member governments, was bound to follow the wishes of the most powerful member states. These member states, Garrett argued, had established the ECJ as a means to solve problems of incomplete contracting and monitoring compliance with EU obligations, and they rationally accepted ECJ jurisprudence, even when rulings went against them, because of their longer-term interest in the enforcement of EU law (Garrett 1992). Garrett and Weingast (1993, p. 189) argued that in such a setting, the ECJ might identify "constructed focal points" among multiple equilibrium outcomes, but the Court was unlikely to rule against the preferences of powerful EU member states, as Burley & Mattli (1993) had suggested in a famous article drawing on neofunctionalist theory.

Responding to Garrett's work, other scholars have argued forcefully that Garrett's model overestimated the control mechanisms available to powerful member states and the ease of sanctioning an activist Court, which has been far more autonomous than Garrett suggests. Such accounts suggest that the Court has been able to pursue the process of legal integration far beyond the collective preferences of the member governments, in part because of the high costs to member states of overruling or failing to comply with ECJ decisions. The ECJ enjoys powerful allies, moreover, in the form of national courts and individual litigants, the ECJ's "other interlocutors," which refer hundreds of cases per year to the ECJ via the "preliminary reference" procedure of Article 234 (Weiler 1994; Mattli & Slaughter 1995, 1998; Stone Sweet & Caporaso 1998; Stone Sweet & Brunell 1998; Alter 2001). In this view, best summarized by Stone Sweet & Caporaso (1998, p. 129), "the move to supremacy and direct effect must be understood as audacious acts of agency" by the Court. Responding to these critiques, rational choice analyses of the ECJ have become more nuanced over time, acknowledging the limits of member-state control over the court and testing hypotheses about the conditions under which the ECJ enjoys the greatest autonomy from its national masters (Garrett 1995, Garrett et al. 1998, Kilroy 1999).

Finally, the literature on the ECJ and legal integration has increasingly moved from the traditional question of the ECJ's relationship with national governments toward the study of the ECJ's other interlocutors, including most notably the national courts that bring the majority of cases before the ECJ and the individual litigants who use EU law to achieve their aims within national legal systems. Such studies have problematized and sought to explain the complex and ambivalent relationship between the ECJ and national courts, which may be simultaneously challenged and empowered as a result of ECJ legal supremacy, as well as the varying litigation strategies of one-shot litigants and repeat players before the courts (Mattli & Slaughter 1998, Alter 2001, Conant 2002). These and other studies have demonstrated the complexities of ECJ legal integration; the interrelationships among supranational, national, and subnational political and legal actors; and the limits of EU law in national legal contexts.

Toward Normal Science?

An increasing number of scholars have approached the study of EU policy making, employing the theoretical tools of comparative politics, formal and informal models drawn from rational choice, and a positivist commitment to systematic empirical testing. The resulting literature, although sometimes highly abstract and inaccessible to the general reader, has substantially advanced our understanding of EU policy making; of the respective roles and influence of the Commission, Council, EP, and ECJ; and increasingly of the relationship between EU institutions and their national and subnational interlocutors. Furthermore, with the creation and dissemination of a range of new databases, the scope for systematic testing and falsification of theories will only increase in the years to come, making the EU an increasingly promising arena for the practice of "normal science."

THE GOVERNANCE APPROACH: THE EU AS A POLITY

On the basis of the previous section, the reader might easily conclude that the story of EU studies is a linear progression from international relations theories of European integration to rational choice theories derived from comparative politics and tested in a positivist manner using data on the political behavior of actors within the EU. Such a story, however, would be misleading. The comparative politics approach to the study of the EU has not replaced the international relations study of regional integration, but now exists alongside it, asking different questions and employing different theoretical and methodological tools to answer them. Just as important, the traditional international relations and comparative politics approaches to the EU now coexist with yet a third approach, typically labeled the governance approach, which draws from both international relations and comparative politics and which considers the EU not as a traditional international organization or as a domestic political system, but rather as a new and emerging system of "governance without government."

The governance approach is not a single theory of the EU or of European integration, but rather a cluster of related theories emphasizing common themes (Jachtenfuchs 2001, Jachtenfuchs & Kohler-Koch 2004). Nevertheless, Hix (1998) has usefully contrasted the governance school from its rationalist/comparativist/positivist alternative, arguing that the governance approach constitutes a distinctive research agenda across four dimensions. First, in contrast to the comparative approach, which theorizes the EU as a political system in which formal rules shape the behavior of governmental and nongovernmental actors, the governance approach theorizes EU governance as nonhierarchical, mobilizing networks of private and public actors who engage in deliberation and problem-solving efforts guided as much by informal norms as by formal institutions. Second, whereas comparativists see the EU as a variant of existing political systems, practitioners of the governance approach are suspicious of off-the-shelf models from comparative politics, advocating the need for a new vocabulary (Schmitter 1996, p. 133) to capture the distinctive features of EU governance. Third, in contrast to the methodological individualism of rationalist analyses, students of EU governance often emphasize the capacity of the EU to foster deliberation and persuasion, a model of policy making in which actors are open to changing their beliefs and their preferences and in which good arguments can matter as much or more than bargaining power. Fourth, governance theorists, like comparativists, frequently express a normative concern with the democratic deficit in the EU; but whereas comparativists emphasize majoritarian or parliamentary models of democracy in their assessments, governance theorists emphasize the promise of the EU as a deliberative democracy in which collective problem solving offers a normatively superior alternative to majoritarian rule in a multinational union. Finally, whereas Hix and other many comparative scholars are committed to a positivist model of hypothesis testing and generalization, governance scholars tend to eschew hypothesis testing in favor of "thick description" and normative critique of contemporary EU governance.

The EU literature on governance thus defined has exploded in the course of the past decade, and space precludes a full and fair discussion of all the intellectual currents and empirical claims in that literature (seminal statements include Jachtenfuchs 1995, Scharpf 1999, Jachtenfuchs 2001, Hooghe & Marks 2001, and Jachtenfuchs & Kohler-Koch 2004). This review will focus instead on a few key issues, including (*a*) the concept of governance as derived from both the comparative and international relations literatures; (*b*) early applications to the EU, in the literatures on multi-level governance and policy networks; (*c*) a substantial literature on the governance capacity of member states and of EU institutions and the problems of legitimacy faced by the latter; and (*d*) a novel set of claims about the EU as a process of deliberative supranationalism capable of resolving these normative dilemmas.

Governing without Government

In Hix's (1998) critique, the governance approach is presented as *sui generis*, treating the EU as fundamentally different from other polities. In practice, however, the governance approach has drawn from a broader literature on governance in both comparative politics and international relations; indeed, Rod Rhodes (1996) identifies at least six distinct uses of the term in the literature, including familiar concepts such as corporate governance, the new public management, and normative conceptions of good governance. At their most far-reaching, theorists of governance advance the radical claim that contemporary governments lack the knowledge and information required to solve complex economic and social problems and that governance should therefore be conceived more broadly as the negotiated interactions of public and private actors in a given policy arena. In this view, modern society is radically decentered, and government features as only one actor among many in the larger process of socioeconomic governance (Kooiman 1993).

Perhaps the most systematic definition of governance has been offered by Rhodes (1996, p. 660), who defines governance in terms of "self-organizing, interorganizational networks" of both public and private actors in the definition and delivery of public services. In this view, governance through public-private networks complements Williamson's (1985) traditional classification of markets and hierarchies as the two ideal-typical modes of "authoritatively allocating resources and exercising control and coordination." Governance in this sense is not new, in the sense that governments have always cooperated with various public and private actors in the provision of services, but the adoption of neoliberal policies in Europe and the United States has prompted a general move toward governance by such networks, as states shrink the size of the public sector and attempt to off-load responsibility for service provision to the private and voluntary sectors.

This shift from government to governance, moreover, raises new analytical and normative questions, including the interlinked issues of fragmentation, steering, and accountability. Fragmentation may result when centralized state bureaucracies outsource the provision of public services to a broad array of public, quasi-public, and private organizations, reducing central government control over policy outcomes. At best, Rhodes and others argue, governments may steer public policies in a given direction, but policy outcomes will depend in practice on the interactions of multiple actors over whom governments have only imperfect control.

Finally, the delegation of public functions by governments to independent agencies and private actors raises questions about democratic accountability to the electorate.

Within international relations theory, the analysis of governance typically begins with the systemic view of states coexisting in a condition of anarchy, and the primary question is whether, and under what conditions, states can cooperate to realize joint gains, despite the absence of a global government to enforce agreements among them. James Rosenau and others have argued that in this context, an international order can be maintained, even in the absence of world government, through processes of international governance. Governance, according to Rosenau,

> ... is not synonymous with government. Both refer to purposive behavior, to goal-oriented activities, to systems of rule; but government suggests activities rather are backed by formal authority, by police powers to ensure the implementation of duly constituted policies, whereas governance refers to activities backed by shared goals that may or may not derive from legal and formally prescribed responsibilities and that do not necessarily rely on police powers to overcome defiance and attain compliance. Governance, in other words, is a more encompassing phenomenon than government. It embraces governmental institutions, but it also subsumes informal, nongovernmental mechanisms whereby persons and organizations within its purview move ahead, satisfy their needs, and fulfill their wants (1992, p. 4).

Elaborating on this basic conception, other international relations theorists have examined the workings of various international regimes, defined as "social institutions that consist of agreed-upon principles, rules, norms, decision-making procedures and programs that govern the interactions of actors in specific issue-areas" (Young 1997, p. 4). Moreover, although traditional regime theories assumed that states were the primary or the only actors within international regime, an increasing number of international relations theorists have argued for the importance of different types of networks, including transgovernmental networks of lower-level government or judicial actors interacting across borders with their foreign counterparts (Slaughter 2004) and transnational networks of private actors forming a global civil society to lobby states and to influence individual behavior directly through joint actions such as international campaigns or boycotts (Wapner 1996).

Multi-Level Governance and EU Policy Networks

Drawing from both international relations and comparative politics, the governance approach in EU studies similarly emphasizes the core themes of nonhierarchical networks, public-private interactions, and "governance without government." By most accounts (Jachtenfuchs 2001; Bache & Flinders 2004, p. 3), the governance approach to the EU can be traced, at least in part, to Gary Marks' work on the making and implementation of the EU's Structural Funds. Writing in opposition to intergovernmentalists like Moravcsik, who claimed that the process of

European integration reflected the preferences of member governments and in fact strengthened those governments by providing them with privileged positions in EU policy making, Marks (1993) argued that the Structural Funds of the 1980s and 1990s provided evidence for a very different image of the EU, one in which central governments were losing control both to the Commission (which played a key part in designing and implementing the funds) and to local and regional governments inside each member state (which were granted a partnership role in planning and implementation by the 1988 reforms of the funds). In making this argument, Bache & Flinders point out:

> The multi-level governance concept . . . contained both vertical and horizontal dimensions. "Multi-level" referred to the increased interdependence of governments operating at different territorial levels, while "governance" signaled the growing interdependence between governments and nongovernmental actors at various territorial levels (Bache & Flinders 2004, p. 3).

Marks' analysis married the fundamental insights of the aforementioned policy networks literature with the view of an EU in which supranational and subnational actors were chipping away at the traditional dominance and control of national governments.

Later studies of the EU Structural Funds questioned Marks' far-reaching empirical claims, noting in particular that EU member governments played central roles in the successive reforms of the funds, and that these member states remained effective gatekeepers, containing the inroads of both the Commission and subnational governments into the traditional preserve of state sovereignty (Pollack 1995, Bache 1998). Following these challenges, proponents of the multi-level governance approach have retreated somewhat from the early and more far-reaching claims about the transformative effects of EU structural policy, while continuing to explore both the vertical dimension of territorial reform and the horizontal dimension of EU policy networks.

With regard to the vertical aspect of multi-level governance, Liesbet Hooghe, Gary Marks, and others returned to EU regional policies, seeking to delineate and explain the substantial variation in the empowerment of supra- and subnational actors in the various member states by the EU's Structural Funds. The most thorough examination of EU regional policies (Hooghe 1996) qualified the far-reaching claims of earlier studies, demonstrating that in some cases, new and existing regional authorities were able to draw upon EU resources and on their place in emerging policy networks to enhance regional autonomy, whereas in other states, such as the United Kingdom and Greece, central governments were able to retain a substantial gatekeeping role between the EU and subnational governments. Despite this cross-national variation in outcomes, Hooghe & Marks (2001) find and purport to explain what they call "an immense shift of authority" from national governments to the European arena and to subnational, regional governments in many states including France, Italy, Spain, Belgium, and the United Kingdom. Although it remains controversial whether such devolution was driven wholly or in part by European integration or by purely national considerations, it is clear that many regional governments have taken a proactive stance in European policy making, establishing permanent offices in Brussels and interacting directly with EU institutions (Marks et al. 1996). Like the literature on federalism, the literature on multi-level governance focuses in large part on the territorial aspects of governance in Europe; by contrast with the federalism literature, however, multi-level governance scholars are concerned not only with the distribution of authority between the nation-state and the EU, but also and more broadly with the shift of authority away from national governments and toward both supranational and subnational actors (Hooghe & Marks 2001, Bache & Flinders 2004).

At the same time, other scholars have focused on the horizontal or network aspects of European integration, drawing on the categories of network theory to describe and explain the workings of transnational and transgovernmental networks that can vary from the relatively closed policy communities of public and private actors in areas such as research and technological development to the more open and porous issue networks prevailing in areas such as environmental regulation. The openness and interdependence of these networks, it is argued, determine both the relative influence of various actors and the substantive content of EU policies (particularly in their early stages, when the Commission drafts policies in consultation with various public and private actors) (Peterson & Bomberg 1999, Peterson 2004). This network form of governance, moreover, has been accentuated further during the past decade by the creation of formal and informal networks of national regulators in areas such as competition (antitrust) policy, utilities regulation, and financial regulation. In contrast to most students of legislative politics who emphasize the importance of formal rules in shaping actors' behavior and polity outcomes, students of policy networks emphasize the informal politics of the EU, in which such networks of private and public actors substantially determine the broad contours of the policies that are eventually brought before the Council and the EP for their formal adoption.

A final offshoot from the multi-level governance tradition examines the phenomenon of "Europeanization," the process whereby EU institutions and policies influence national institutions and policies within the various member states. Such studies date to the 1970s, when a small number of scholars examined how EU membership had influenced national political institutions and public policies (see, e.g., Wallace 1973). During the 1990s, the study of Europeanization became a cottage industry, with a growing number of studies seeking to explain both the process of Europeanization and the significant variation in outcomes observed across both member states and issue areas. In one particularly influential formulation, Cowles et al. (2001) suggested that the extent of Europeanization should be the dual product of (a) adaptational pressures resulting from the varying "goodness of fit" between EU and national institutions and policies and (b) domestic intervening variables including the number of veto points and the organizational and political cultures embedded in existing national institutions. Subsequent scholars have elaborated further on this basic framework, sketching alternative rationalist and constructivist mechanisms whereby the EU might influence national politics, in the first instance by constraining national choices, in the second case by instilling new norms and reshaping national identities and preferences (Börzel & Risse 2000). More recently, Frank Schimmelfennig and Ulrich Sedelmeier (2003a,b; 2005) have led teams of researchers who have sought explicitly to test alternative rationalist and constructivist hypotheses about the effect of EU membership on the new member states in central and eastern Europe. Simplifying only slightly, they find some evidence of EU-led policy learning and socialization, as predicted by constructivist models, but the content and the timing of policy reforms in the new members suggests that the greatest impact of the EU has resulted from explicit EU conditionality, a classic rationalist mechanism.

Governance Capacity and Democratic Legitimacy

A second major branch of the governance approach to the EU has emerged from the European political economy literature of the 1980s and 1990s, associated with scholars such as a Wolfgang Streeck (1996) and Fritz Scharpf (1999), whose work analyzes and undertakes a normative critique of the EU. In this view, European integration has purportedly undermined the autonomy and domestic governance capacity of EU member states through negative integration, while failing to establish a substantial and democratically legitimate governance capacity at the supranational EU level.

This critique of the EU's governance capacity, and the resulting democratic deficit, is typically made in two stages. First, it is argued that EU internal market regulations and ECJ decisions have increasingly eroded, invalidated, or replaced national social regulations, thereby thwarting the social aims and the democratically expressed preferences of national electorates and their legislatures. Moreover, even where EU legislation and ECJ jurisprudence leave national laws, taxation systems, and welfare programs untouched, it is often argued that the free movement of capital mandated by the EU may set in motion a process of regulatory competition in which national governments face pressures to adjust national regulations in an effort to make them more attractive to mobile capital. The recent adoption of the euro, and the limitations on national budget deficits contained in the EU Stability and Growth Pact, may have constrained national autonomy still further, depriving states of fiscal policy tools that have proven effective in the past pursuit of economic and social goals. In the words of Claus Offe (2000), the *acquis communautaire* (the body of legislation mandated by the EU and devoted primarily to market liberalization) now threatens the *acquis nationale* of strong liberal democracy and well-developed welfare states. The full extent of this purported race to the bottom remains a matter of dispute, with Scharpf (1999) and others acknowledging that the extent of competitive deregulation appears to vary systematically across issue areas, but the prospect of undermining national regulations and welfare states poses important analytic and normative challenges to social democrats and to students of democratic theory.

This challenge to national governance raises a second question: whether the race to the bottom might be averted, and democracy regained, at the EU level. On this score, many contributors to the debate are pessimistic, pointing to the distant and opaque nature of EU decision making; the strong role of indirectly elected officials in the Council of Ministers and unelected officials in the Commission; the weakness of the EP and the second-order nature of its elections; and the bias in the treaties in favor of market liberalization over social regulation (Williams 1991, Scharpf 1999, Greven 2000). Joseph Weiler (1995) and others have suggested that even if these institutional flaws in the EU treaties were to be addressed, Europe lacks a *demos*, a group of people united by a sense of community or "we-feeling" that could provide the constituent basis for an EU-level democracy. Governance theorists argue that for all of these reasons, the EU faces a profound crisis of legitimacy, and much of the governance literature is given over to proposals for increasing the democratic accountability and the governance capacity of the EU. Whereas in the past EU institutions had relied primarily on output legitimacy (i.e., the efficiency or popularity of EU policy outputs), today there are increased calls for reforms that would increase the input legitimacy (i.e., the democratic accountability of EU institutions to the electorate).

Simplifying slightly, we can identify three distinct reform tracks proposed in the literature: parliamentarization, constitutionalization, and deliberation. The first of these, parliamentarization, would involve *inter alia* the strengthening of the EP's legislative and budgetary powers, a strengthening of EU party groups and the increased salience of EU (rather than national) issues in European elections, and the subordination of the Commission to the EP as in the national parliamentary systems of Europe. Recent treaty reforms have taken several steps in the direction of parliamentarization, but EU member states remain reluctant to make the EP a fully equal partner in some areas, and in any event, Weiler (1995) and others point out that majoritarian rule at the EU might exacerbate rather than ameliorate the EU's crisis of legitimacy by subjecting national communities, or *demoi*, to a long-term minority position in a union of 25 member states.

A second and more modest proposal is constitutionalization, the creation of overarching rules and procedural controls that would ensure minimum levels of transparency and public participation in EU policy making. To some extent, the Commission opened the debate on these questions in 2001 with its *White Paper on Governance* (CEC 2001), which called for various reforms including the online publication of policy information, a code of conduct for consultation with civil-society groups, strengthened rules on public access to EU documents, and the establishment of a systematic dialogue with local and regional governments in the member states. Even these reforms, however, would fail to bring the EU on a par with many national governments, which remain far more visible, transparent, and accountable to their citizens than EU institutions.

In light of these difficulties, an increasing number of authors have suggested a third model for the EU, namely a deliberative democracy in which citizens, or at least their representatives, would collectively deliberate in search of the best solution to common problems. This deliberative turn constitutes a major theme in the study of EU governance, and merits a more extended discussion.

Argument, Persuasion, and the "Deliberative Turn"

The recent emphasis on deliberation in the EU derives largely from the work of Jürgen Habermas (1985, 1998), whose theory of communicative action has been adapted to the study of international relations and to the study of EU governance. The core claim of the approach, as popularized by Risse (2000) in the field of international relations, is that there are three "logics of social action," namely (*a*) the logic of consequentiality (or utility maximization) emphasized by rational-choice theorists, (*b*) the logic of appropriateness (or rule-following behavior) associated with constructivist theory, and (*c*) a logic of arguing derived largely from Habermas's theory of communicative action.

In Habermasian communicative action, or what Risse (2000, p. 7) calls the logic of arguing, political actors do not simply bargain based on fixed preferences and relative power; they may also "argue," questioning their own beliefs and preferences and remaining open to persuasion and to the power of the better argument. In the view of many democratic theorists, moreover, such processes lead to the promise of a normatively desirable deliberative democracy, in which societal actors engage in a sincere collective search for truth and for the best available public policy, and in which even the losers in such debates accept the outcome by virtue of their participation in the deliberative process and their understanding of the principled arguments put forward by their fellow citizens (Elster 1998, Bohman 1998).

Habermas and his followers concede that genuine communicative action or argumentative rationality is likely only under a fairly restrictive set of three preconditions. First, the participants in a deliberation must demonstrate an ability to empathize, to see the world through others' eyes. Second, the participants must also share a "common lifeworld, . . . a supply of collective interpretations of the world and of themselves, as provided by language, a common history, or culture." Third, an ideal speech situation requires that the discourse be undertaken openly and that all actors have equal access to the discourse (Risse 2000, pp. 10–11). These are demanding preconditions, and all the more so at the international level, where a common lifeworld cannot be taken for granted and where relationships of power are ubiquitous. For this reason, Risse concedes, we should expect international deliberation or arguing only under certain conditions, including most notably:

- the existence of a common lifeworld provided by a high degree of international institutionalization in the respective issue-area;

- uncertainty of interests and/or lack of knowledge about the situation among the actors; and

- international institutions based on nonhierarchical relations enabling dense interactions in informal, network-like settings (2000, pp. 19–20).

These conditions are by no means satisfied everywhere in international politics; but where they are present, according to Habermasian and other constructivist scholars, international actors will engage in arguing rather than bargaining, presenting their arguments in a common language of law or science and proceeding to decisions on the basis of the better argument rather than the bargaining power of the respective actors. Empirical studies of deliberation face significant methodological hurdles in distinguishing between arguing and bargaining, or between genuine communicative action and cheap talk (Checkel 2001, Magnette 2004). Despite these challenges, a growing number of studies have pointed to at least suggestive evidence of deliberation in international institutions such as the UN Security Council (Johnstone 2003).

The promise of deliberation has received extraordinarily attention within the study of the EU, whose dense institutional environment and networked forms of governance are seen as a particularly promising place to look for evidence of international deliberation. This analytical claim, moreover, has been married to a normative case for what Christian Joerges (2001) has called deliberative supranationalism, which he claims offers a potentially compelling solution to the challenge of democratic legitimacy within the EU (see also Eriksen & Fossum 2000, 2003).

In empirical terms, EU scholars have identified the promise of deliberation in three EU-related forums: comitology committees, the Constitutional Convention of 2003–2004, and the new governance mechanisms of the EU's Open Method of Coordination (OMC). With regard to the first of these, Christian Joerges and Jürgen Neyer (1997a,b) draw on Habermasian accounts of deliberative democracy as well as constructivist analysis in political science to argue that EU comitology committees provide a forum in which national and supranational experts meet and deliberate in a search for the best or most efficient solutions to common policy problems. In this view, comitology is not an arena for hardball intergovernmental bargaining, as rationalists assume, but rather a technocratic version of deliberative democracy in which informal norms, deliberation, good arguments, and consensus matter more than formal voting rules, which are rarely invoked. In support of their view, Joerges and Neyer (1997a,b) present evidence from their study of EU foodstuffs regulation, where they find that the importance of scientific discourse limits the ability of delegates to discuss distributional issues, particularly in scientific advisory committees, which in turn focuses debate and deliberation onto scientific questions. In addition, the authors point out, delegates not only meet regularly in comitology committees but often meet as part of advisory committees and working groups involved in the adoption of the legislation in question, an ideal setting for long-term socialization into common European norms. In this way, comitology committees pass from being institutions for the strategic control of the Commission to being forums for deliberative interaction among experts for whom issues of control and distribution, as well as the carefully contrived institutional rules of their respective committees, recede into the background in favor of a collective search for the technically best solution to a given policy problem. Joerges and Neyer's claims remain controversial, however, with rational choice scholars arguing that EU member states design and utilize comitology committees systematically as instruments of control and that evidence of deliberation in such committees remains sketchy (Pollack 2003, pp. 114–145). Other critics, moreover, question the normative value of deliberative supranationalism in comitology committees, noting that such expert deliberation takes place largely out of the public eye (Zürn 2000).

A second EU arena often identified as a promising venue for deliberation was the Convention on the Future of Europe, which met to consider changes to the EU treaties and which concluded with a concrete proposal for a draft constitution for consideration by the EU's member governments. Composed of representatives of EU institutions, national governments, national parliaments, and representatives from candidate countries, the convention was explicitly conceived as a deliberative body, in contrast with the intergovernmental conference that had produced the contentious and inelegant Treaty of Nice in 2000 (Maurer 2003, Closa 2004). In a careful and theoretically informed study, Paul Magnette (2004) suggests that the actual meeting of the convention illustrated elements of both arguing and bargaining. On the one hand, Magnette argues, the public nature of the debates and the imperative of achieving consensus among the participants compelled participants to publicly justify their positions in terms of broad constitutional principles and the common good and to refrain from overt threats or horse trading. On the other hand, Magnette concedes, representatives of national governments did on occasion present fixed national positions in debate, and there is at best mixed evidence that participants in the debate were genuinely open to persuasion and to changing their preferences as in a Habermasian "ideal speech situation." Furthermore, "the *conventionnels* knew and acknowledged that their experience would be followed by a classic IGC, and tended to anticipate it. They deliberated, but under the shadow of the veto" (Magnette 2004, p. 220).

Finally, the promise of deliberation has also been emphasized by students of the OMC. Based on previous EU experience in areas such as economic policy coordination and employment policy, the OMC was codified and endorsed by the Lisbon European Council in March 2001, and it is characterized as an intergovernmental and legally nonbinding form of policy coordination based on the collective establishment of policy guidelines, targets, and benchmarks, coupled with a system of periodic peer review in which member governments present their respective national programs for consideration and comment by their EU counterparts. By and large, the OMC has been utilized not as a replacement for, but as a complement to, the traditional "Community method" in areas where member governments have been reluctant to adopt binding regulations, as in the areas of employment policy, social inclusion, and pensions reform. The OMC remains controversial both politically and in the academic community. For many commentators, the OMC offers a flexible means to address common policy issues without encroaching on sensitive areas of national sovereignty, representing a middle ground between communitarization and purely national governance. In addition, the basic elements of the OMC—institutionalized cooperation, iteration within nonhierarchical networks, and emphasis on exchange of information and learning—all suggested that OMC networks were potentially promising arenas, and potential test cases, for Habermasian deliberation (Hodson & Maher 2001, Scott & Trubek 2002).

Careful empirical work, however, has at least tempered the more far-reaching claims put forward by the supporters of the OMC. On the one hand, in-depth studies of the European Employment Strategy and other OMC processes suggests that the OMC has led to some sharing of experiences and the creation of a common language and common indicators for the analysis of public policy, and some scholars suggest that bargaining power in OMC committees depends at least in part on the strength of one's arguments and not solely on the size of one's country. "Strategic bargaining" according to one study, "is not the general mode of interaction in the committees" (Jacobsson & Vifell 2003, p. 21). On the other hand, however, a number of scholars have argued that when it comes time to negotiate politically sensitive provisions, detailed targets, or public recommendations to the member governments, national representatives revert to a presentation of fixed national positions, engaging clearly in bargaining rather than arguing behavior and demonstrating few signs of having been persuaded to change their basic approach to employment or other issues (see, e.g., Jacobsson & Vifell 2003, Jobelius 2003, Borrás & Jacobsson 2004, Zeitlin et al. 2005). In sum, although EU institutions and policy procedures such as comitology, the Convention on the Future of Europe, and the OMC might seem to be most likely arenas for Habermasian deliberation, evidence for such behavior remains at best partial, and the EU's status as a deliberative democracy open to question.

Legitimate Governance?

The governance approach to the EU is a distinctive one, drawing on both comparative politics and international relations theories and asking analytically and normatively important questions about the workings of EU policy networks, the transformation of territorial governance, and the prospects for deliberative democracy at the EU level. To be sure, the governance approach is not without its flaws or critics, and even its proponents concede that it remains a constellation of interrelated claims rather than a single, coherent theory (Jachtenfuchs 2001, Jachtenfuchs & Kohler-Koch 2004). In empirical terms, one can argue that the analytical and normative elaboration of the governance approach has frequently outpaced the empirical work needed to assess the plausibility of its claims. Nevertheless, students of EU governance have made significant progress in formulating a research program and in producing more empirical evidence and more nuanced claims about territorial change, Europeanization, and deliberation in an enlarged EU.

CONCLUSIONS

In a 1972 essay, Donald Puchala likened integration theorists and the EU to blind men touching an elephant, each one feeling a different part of the elephant and purporting to describe a very different animal. Today, theories of the EU are even more diverse than in Puchala's day, comprising three distinct approaches with lively debates both within and among all three. Puchala's metaphor was meant to suggest the relative immaturity and weakness of integration theory and the limits of its insights, yet there is a more optimistic reading of the dizzying array of theories purporting to provide insights into the workings of the EU and the telos of European integration.

In contrast to 1972, when Puchala was writing, the 1990s and early 2000s have witnessed a partial retreat from grand theorizing about the integration process in favor of a series of mid-range theories addressing a variety of topics including *inter alia* the workings of the EU's legislative, executive and judicial processes, the prospects of socialization or deliberation in EU institutions, the effects of European integration on national institutions and policies, and a wide range of other questions (see e.g. Pollack 2005 for an application of the three approaches examined above to the study of EU policy making). As with the study of other political systems, this diversity of mid-range questions has spawned a corresponding theoretical diversity, with various theories purporting to problematize and explain different aspects of the EU, in much the same way that distinctive bodies of theory have problematized different aspects of the American political experience. Furthermore, although one might be justified in fearing a cacophony of competing theories and a consequent dialogue of the deaf, there is in fact evidence that the opposite has occurred, with more dialogue across different theories and different theoretical approaches and with increasingly careful empirical work in all three traditions, allowing us to adjudicate among competing claims and to come to at least preliminary conclusions about the most important analytical and normative questions facing the EU at the start of the 21st century.

ACKNOWLEDGMENTS

The author is grateful to the College of Liberal Arts of Temple University for research support during the writing of this article, and to Orfeo Fioretos, Jerry Loewenberg, Helen Wallace, William Wallace, and Daniel Wincott for insightful comments on earlier drafts.

**The *Annual Review of Political Science* is online at
http://polisci.annualreviews.org**

LITERATURE CITED

Adler E. 1997. Seizing the middle ground: constructivism in world politics. *European Journal of International Relations* 3:319–63

Alter KJ. 2001. *Establishing the Supremacy of European Law: The Making of an International Rule of Law in Europe.* New York: Oxford Univ. Press

Aspinwall M, Schneider G, eds. 2001. *The Rules of Integration: Institutionalist Approaches to the Study of Europe.* New York: Manchester Univ. Press

Bache I. 1998. *The Politics of European Union Regional Policy: Multi-Level Governance or Flexible Gatekeeping?* Sheffield: Sheffield Acad.

Bache I, Flinders M. 2004. Themes and issues in multi-level governance. In *Multi-Level Governance*, ed. I Bache, M Flinders, pp. 1–11. New York: Oxford Univ. Press

Beyers J, Dierickx G. 1998. The working groups of the Council of Ministers: Supranational or intergovernmental negotiations? *J. Common Mark. Stud.* 36:289–317

Bohman J. 1998. Survey article: The coming of age of deliberative democracy. *J. Polit. Philos.* 6:400–25

Borrás S, Jacobsson K. 2004. The open method of coordination and new governance patterns in the EU. *J. Eur. Public Policy* 11:185–208

Börzel TA, Hösli M. 2003. Brussels between Bern and Berlin. Comparative federalism meets the European Union. *Governance* 16:179–202

Börzel TA, Risse T. 2000. *When Europe hits home: Europeanization and domestic change.* RSC Work. Pap. No. 2000/56, Robert Schuman Cent. Adv. Stud., Eur. Univ. Inst., Florence. http://www.iue.it/RSCAS/WP-Texts/00_56.pdf

Burley AM, Mattli W. 1993. Europe before the Court: A political theory of legal integration. *Int. Organ.* 47:41–76

Capelletti M, Seccombe M, Weiler JHH, eds. 1986. *Integration through Law: Europe and the American Federal Experience.* New York: de Gruyter

Caporaso JA. 1997. Across the great divide: Integrating comparative and international politics. *Int. Stud. Q.* 41:563–92

Checkel J. 1999. Norms, institutions, and national identity in contemporary Europe. *Int. Stud. Q.* 43:83–114

Checkel J. 2001. *Taking deliberation seriously.* ARENA Work. Pap. WP 01/14. http://www.arena.uio.no/publications/wp01_14.htm.

Checkel JT. 2003. 'Going native' in Europe? Theorizing social interaction in European institutions. *Comp. Polit. Stud.* 36:209–31

Checkel JT, Moravcsik A. 2001. A constructivist research program in EU studies? *Eur. Union Polit.* 2:219–49

Christiansen T, Jørgensen KE, Wiener A. 1999. The social construction of Europe. *J. Eur. Public Policy* 6:528–44

Closa C. 2004. The convention method and the transformation of EU constitutional politics. See Eriksen et al. 2004, pp. 183–206

Comm. Eur. Communities. 2001. *European Governance: A White Paper.* COM(2001) 428 final of 25 July

Conant L. 2002. *Justice Contained: Law and Politics in the European Union.* Ithaca: Cornell Univ. Press

Corbett M, Jacobs F, Shackleton M. 2000. *The European Parliament.* London: Catermill. 4th ed.

Cowles MG, Caporaso JA, Risse T, eds. 2001. *Transforming Europe: Europeanization and Domestic Change.* Ithaca: Cornell Univ. Press

Crombez C. 1997. The co-decision procedure in the European Union. *Legis. Stud. Q.* 22:97–119

Dalton R. 1991. Comparative politics in the industrial democracies: From the golden age to island hopping. In *Political Science*, ed. WJ Crotty, 2:15–43. Evanston: Univ. of Illinois Press

Dogan R. 1997. Comitology: Little procedures with big implications. *West Eur. Polit.* 20:31–60

Donahue JD, Pollack MA. 2001. Centralization and its discontents: The rhythms of Federalism in the United States and the European Union. See Nicolaidis & Howse 2001, pp. 73–117

Dowding K. 2000. Institutionalist research on the European Union: A critical review. *Eur. Union Polit.* 1:125–44

Egeberg M. 1999. Transcending intergovernmentalism? Identity and role perceptions of national officials in EU decision making. *J. Eur. Public Policy* 6:456–74

Elster J. 1989. *Nuts and Bolts for the Social Sciences.* New York: Cambridge Univ. Press

Elster J, ed. 1998. *Deliberative Democracy.* New York: Cambridge Univ. Press

Epstein D, O'Halloran S. 1999. *Delegating Powers: A Transaction Cost Politics Approach to Policy Making under Separate Powers.* New York: Cambridge Univ. Press

Eriksen EO, Fossum JE. 2000. Post-national integration. In *Democracy in the European Union,* ed. EO Eriksen, JE Fossum, pp. 1–28. London: Routledge

Eriksen EO, Fossum JE. 2003. *Closing the Legitimacy Gap?* www.arena.uio.no/ecsa/papers/ FossumEriksen.pdf

Eriksen EO, Fossum JE, Menéndez AJ, eds. 2004. *Developing a Constitution for Europe.* London: Routledge

Everson M, Majone G, Metcalfe L, Schout A. 2001. *The Role of Specialized Agencies in Decentralising EU Governance.* Presented to Comm. Work. Group Governance. http://www.europa.eu.int/comm/governance/ areas/group6/contribution_en.pdf

Franchino F. 2001. *Delegating powers in the European Union.* Presented at 7th Bienn. Int. Conf. Eur. Community Stud. Assoc., Madison, Wis., 31 May–2 June

Gabel M, Hix S, Schneider G. 2002. Who is afraid of cumulative research? The scarcity of EU decision-making data and what can be done about this. *Eur. Union Polit.* 3:481–500

Garrett G. 1992. International cooperation and institutional choice: The European Community's internal market. *Int. Organ.* 46:533–60

Garrett G. 1995. The politics of legal integration in the European Union. *Int. Organ.* 49:171–81

Garrett G, Keleman RD, Schulz H. 1998. The European Court of Justice, national governments, and legal integration in the European Union. *Int. Organ.* 52:149–76

Garrett G, Tsebelis G. 1996. An institutional critique of intergovernmentalism. *Int. Organ.* 50:269–99

Garrett G, Weingast B. 1993. Ideas, interests, and institutions: Constructing the European Community's internal market. In *Ideas and Foreign Policy,* ed. J Goldstein, RO Keohane, pp. 173–206. Ithaca: Cornell Univ. Press

Gourevitch P. 1978. The second image reversed. *Int. Organ.* 32:881–912

Greven MT. 2000. Can the European Union finally become a democracy? See Greven & Pauly 2000, pp. 35–61

Greven MT, Pauly LW, eds. 2000. *Democracy Beyond the State? The European Dilemma and the Emerging Global Order.* Lanham, MD: Rowman & Littlefield

Haas EB. 1958. *The Uniting of Europe.* Stanford: Stanford Univ. Press. Reprinted 2004 Notre Dame Univ. Press

Haas EB. 1961. European integration: The European and universal process. *Int. Organ.* 4:607–46

Haas EB. 1976. Turbulent fields and the theory of regional integration. *Int. Organ.* 30:173–212

Habermas J. 1985. *The Theory of Communicative Action,* Vols. 1, 2. Boston: Beacon

Habermas J. 1998. *Between Facts and Norms: Contributions to a Discourse Theory of Law and Democracy.* Cambridge: MIT Press

Hall PA. 1986. *Governing the Economy: The Politics of State Intervention in Britain and France.* New York: Oxford Univ. Press

Hall PA, Taylor RCR. 1996. Political science and the three new institutionalisms. *Polit. Stud.* 44:936–57

Hix S. 1994. The study of the European community: The challenge to comparative politics. *West Eur. Polit.* 17:1–30

Hix S. 1998. The study of the European Union II: The 'New Governance' agenda and its rival. *J. Eur. Public Policy* 5:38–65

Hix S. 1999. *The Political System of the European Union.* London: Palgrave

Hix S. 2001. Legislative behaviour and party competition in European Parliament: An application of nominate to the EU. *J. Common Mark. Stud.* 39:663–88

Hix S, Noury A, Roland G. 2002. *A 'normal' parliament? Party cohesion and competition in the European Parliament, 1979–2001.* EPRG Work. Pap., No. 9. http://www. lse.ac.uk/Depts/eprg/working-papers.htm.

Hodson D, Maher I. 2001. The open method of coordination as a new mode of governance: The case of soft economic policy co-ordination. *J. Common Mark. Stud.* 39:719–46

Hoffmann S. 1966. Obstinate or obsolete? The fate of the nation-state and the case of Western Europe. *Daedalus* 95:862–915

Hooghe L, ed. 1996. *Cohesion Policy and European Integration: Building Multi-Level Governance.* New York: Oxford Univ. Press

Hooghe L. 2002. *The European Commission and the Integration of Europe.* New York: Cambridge Univ. Press

Hooghe L. 2005. Several roads lead to international norms, but few via international socialization: A case study of the European Commission. *Int. Organ.* In press

Hooghe L, Marks G. 2001. *Multi-Level Governance and European Integration.* Lanham, MD: Rowman & Littlefield

Huber JD, Shipan CR. 2002. *Deliberate Discretion? The Institutional Foundations of Bureaucratic Autonomy.* New York: Cambridge Univ. Press

Hurrell A, Menon A. 1996. Politics like any other? Comparative politics, international relations and the study of the EU. *West Eur. Polit.* 19:386–402

Jachtenfuchs M. 1995. Theoretical perspectives on European governance. *Eur. Law J.* 1:115–33

Jachtenfuchs M. 2001. The governance approach to European integration. *J. Common Mark. Stud.* 39:245–64

Jachtenfuchs M, Kohler-Koch B. 2004. Governance and institutional development. See Wiener & Diez 2004, pp. 97–115

Jacobsson K, Vifell A. 2003. *Integration by deliberation? On the role of committees in the open method of coordination.* Pap. Workshop The Forging of Deliberative Supranationalism in the EU, Eur. Univ. Inst., Florence, 7–8 Feb.

Jobelius S. 2003. *Who formulates the European employment guidelines? The OMC between deliberation and power games.* Presented at Annu. Conf. EPSAnet, "Changing Societies—The Role for Social Policy," Copenhagen, 13–15 Nov.

Joerges C. 2001. *Deliberative Supranationalism: A Defence.* In *European Integration.* Online pap. (EIoP) Vol. 5 (2001)

No. 8. http://eiop.or.at/eiop/texte/2001-008a.htm.

Joerges C, Neyer J. 1997a. From intergovernmental bargaining to deliberative political process: The constitutionalization of comitology. *Eur. Law J.* 3:273–99

Joerges C, Neyer J. 1997b. Transforming strategic interaction into deliberative problem-solving: European comitology in the foodstuffs sector. *J. Eur. Public Policy* 4:609–25

Johnstone AI. 2003. Security council deliberations: The power of the better argument. *Eur. J. Int. Law* 14:437–87

Jørgensen KE. 1997. Introduction: Approaching European governance. In *Reflective Approaches to European governance,* ed. KE Jørgensen, pp. 1–12. New York: St. Martin's Press

Jupille J. 2005. Knowing Europe: Metatheory and methodology in EU studies. In *Palgrave Guide to European Union Studies,* ed. M Cini, A Bourne. London: Palgrave. In press

Jupille J, Caporaso JA. 1999. Institutionalism and the European union: Beyond international relations and comparative politics. *Annu. Rev. Polit. Sci.* 2:429–44

Jupille J, Caporaso JA, Checkel JT. 2003. Integrating institutions: Rationalism, constructivism, and the study of the European union. *Comp. Polit. Stud.* 36:7–40

Keeler JTS. 2004. *Mapping EU Studies: The Evolution from Boutique to Boom Field, 1960–2001.* Pap. Univ. Wis.-Madison, April 28, and Eur. Univ. Inst., Fiesole, Italy, May 5

Kelemen RD. 2003. The structure and dynamics of EU federalism. *Comp. Polit. Stud.* 36:184–208

Keohane RO, Milner HV. 1998. *Internationalization and Domestic Politics.* New York: Cambridge Univ. Press

Kiewiet RD, McCubbins M. 1991. *The Logic of Delegation: Congressional Parties and the Appropriations Process.* Chicago: Univ. Chicago Press

Kilroy B. 1999. *Integration through law: ECJ and governments in the EU.* PhD diss., Univ. Calif. Los Angeles

Kooiman J. 1993. Social-political governance: Introduction. In *Modern Governance*, ed. J Kooiman, pp. 1–6. London: Sage

Kreppel A. 1999. The European Parliament's influence over EU policy outcomes. *J. Common Mark. Stud.* 37:521–38

Kreppel A. 2001. *The European Parliament and Supranational Party System: A Study in Institutional Development.* New York: Cambridge Univ. Press

Kreppel A. 2002. *The Environmental Determinants of Legislative Structure: A Comparison of the US House of Representatives and the European Parliament.* Presented at Conf. Exporting Congress? The Influence of the U.S. Congress on World Legislatures, Jack D. Gordon Inst. Public Policy Citizenship Stud., Fla. Int. Univ., Miami, Dec. 6–7

Kreppel A, Hix S. 2003. From 'Grand Coalition' to left-right confrontation: explaining the shifting structure of party competition in the European Parliament. *Comp. Polit. Stud.* 36:75–96

Lewis J. 1998. Is the 'hard bargaining' image of the council misleading? The committee of permanent representatives and the local elections directive. *J. Common Mark. Stud.* 36:479–504

Lewis J. 2003. Institutional environments and everyday EU decision making: Rationalist or constructivist? *Comp. Polit. Stud.* 36:97–124

Lindberg LN, Scheingold SA. 1970. *Europe's Would-Be Polity.* Englewood Cliffs, NJ: Prentice-Hall

Magnette P. 2004. Deliberation or bargaining? Coping with constitutional conflicts in the convention on the future of Europe. See Eriksen et al. 2004, pp. 207–25

Majone G. 1996. *Regulating Europe.* New York: Routledge

March JG, Olsen JP. 1989. *Rediscovering Institutions.* Glencoe, IL: Free Press

Marks G. 1993. Structural policy and multi-level governance in the EC. In *The State of the European Community. Vol. 2. The Maastricht Debates and Beyond*, ed. A Cafruny, G Rosenthal. Boulder, CO: Reinner, pp. 391–410

Marks G, Hooghe L, Blank K. 1996. European integration from the 1980s: State–centric v. multi–level governance. *J. Common Mark. Stud.* 34:341–78

Marks G, Scharpf FW, Schmitter PC, W Streeck W, eds. 1996. *Governance in the European Union.* London: Sage

Mattli W, Slaughter AM. 1995. Law and politics in the European Union: A reply to Garrett. *Int. Organ.* 49:183–90

Mattli W, Slaughter AM. 1998. Revisiting the European Court of Justice. *Int. Organ.* 52:177–209

Maurer A. 2003. Less bargaining—more deliberation: The convention method for enhancing EU democracy. *Int. Polit. Ges.* 1:167–90

McElroy G. 2004. *Party leadership and representative committees in the European Parliament.* Presented at Annu. Meet. Am. Polit. Sci. Assoc., Chicago, 2–5 Sept.

McNamara KR. 2002. Rational fictions: Central Bank independence and the social logic of delegation. *West Eur. Poli.* 25:47–76

Milner HV. 1998. Rationalizing politics: The emerging synthesis of international, American, and comparative politics. *Int. Organ.* 52:759–86

Moe T. 1984. The new economics of organization. *Am. J. Polit. Sci.* 28:739–77

Moravcsik A. 1993. Preferences and power in the European Community: A liberal intergovernmentalist approach. *J. Common Mark. Stud.* 31:473–524

Moravcsik A. 1998. *The Choice for Europe: Social Purpose and State Power from Messina to Maastricht.* Ithaca: Cornell Univ. Press

Moravcsik A. 1999. Is something rotten in the State of Denmark? Constructivism and European integration. *J. Eur. Public Policy* 6:669–81

Moravcsik A. 2001. Federalism in the European Union: Rhetoric and reality. See Nicolaidis & Howse 2001, pp. 161–87

Moser P. 1996. The European Parliament as an agenda-setter: What are the conditions? A critique of Tsebelis. *Am. Polit. Sci. Rev.* 90:834–38

Moser P. 1997. The benefits of the conciliation procedure for the European Parliament: comment to George Tsebelis. *Aussenwirtschaft* 52:57–62

Nicolaidis K, Howse R. 2001. *The Federal Vision: Legitimacy and Levels of Governance in the United States in the European Union.* New York: Oxford Univ. Press

Offe C. 2000. The democratic welfare state in an integrating Europe. See Greven & Pauly 2000, pp. 63–89

Peterson J. 2004. Policy networks. See Wiener & Diez 2004, pp. 17–35

Peterson J, Bomberg E. 1999. *Decision-Making in the European Union.* London: Palgrave

Pierson P. 1996. The path to European integration: A historical institutionalist analysis. *Comp. Polit. Stud.* 29:123–63

Pierson P. 2000. Increasing returns, path dependence, and the study of politics. *Am. Polit. Sci. Rev.* 94:251–67

Pollack MA. 1995. Regional actors in an intergovernmental play: The making and implementation of EC structural policy. In *The State of the European Union*, ed. S Mazey, C Rhodes, III:361–90. Boston: Rienner

Pollack MA. 2003. *The Engines of Integration: Delegation, Agency and Agenda Setting in the European Union.* New York: Oxford Univ. Press

Pollack MA. 2004. The new institutionalisms and European integration. See Wiener & Diez 2004, pp. 137–56

Pollack MA. 2005. Theoretical and comparative insights into EU policy-making. In *Policy-Making in the European Union*, ed. H Wallace, W Wallace, MA Pollack. New York: Oxford Univ. Press. In press

Pollack MA, Shaffer GC. 2001. Who governs? In *Transatlantic Governance in the Global Economy*, ed. MA Pollack, GC Shaffer, pp. 287–305. Lanham, MD: Rowman & Littlefield

Puchala DJ. 1972. Of blind men, elephants, and international integration. *J. Common Mark. Stud.* 10:267–84

Putnam RD. 1988. Diplomacy and domestic politics: The logic of two-level games. *Int. Organ.* 42:427–60

Rhodes RAW. 1996. The new governance: Governing without government. *Polit. Stud.* 44:652–57

Risse T. 2000. Let's argue! Communicative action and world politics. *Int. Organ.* 54:1–39

Risse T. 2004. Social constructivism and European integration. See Wiener & Diez 2004, pp. 159–76

Rosenau JN. 1992. Governance, order and change in world politics. In *Governance Without Government: Order and Change in World Politics*, ed. JN Rosenau, EO Czempiel, pp. 1–29. New York: Cambridge Univ. Press

Sandholtz W. 1996. Membership matters: Limits of the functional approach to European institutions. *J. Common Mark. Stud.* 34:403–29

Sandholtz W, Zysman J. 1989. 1992: Recasting the European bargain. *World Polit.* 42:95–128

Sbragia A. 1993. The European Community: a balancing act. *Publius* 23:23–38

Scharpf FW. 1988. The joint-decision trap: Lessons from German federalism and European integration. *Public Adm.* 66:239–78

Scharpf FW. 1999. *Governing in Europe: Democratic and Effective?* New York: Oxford Univ. Press

Schimmelfennig F. 2003a. Strategic action in a community environment: The decision to enlarge the European Union to the East. *Comp. Polit. Stud.* 36:156–83

Schimmelfennig F, Sedelmeier U, eds. 2005. *The Europeanization of Central and Eastern Europe.* Ithaca: Cornell Univ. Press

Schmitter PC. 1996. Examining the present Euro-polity with the help of past theories. See Marks et al. 1996, pp. 1–14

Scott J, Trubek DM. 2002. Mind the gap: Law and new approaches to governance in Europe. *Eur. Law J.* 8:1–18

Scully RM. 1997a. The EP and the co-decision procedure: A reassessment. *J. Legis. Stud.* 3:57–73

Scully RM. 1997b. The EP and co-decision: A rejoinder to Tsebelis and Garrett. *J. Legis. Stud.* 3:93–103

Scully RM. 1997c. Positively my last words on co-decision. *J. Legis. Stud.* 3:144–46

Shepsle KA. 1979. Institutional arrangements and equilibrium in multidimensional voting models. *Am. J. Polit. Sci.* 23:27–60

Shepsle KA. 1986. Institutional equilibrium and equilibrium institutions. In *Political Science: The Science of Politics*, ed. H Weisberg. New York: Agathon

Slaughter AM. 2004. *A New World Order*. Princeton: Princeton Univ. Press

Stone Sweet A, Brunell TL. 1998. Constructing a supranational constitution: Dispute resolution and governance in the European community. *Am. Polit. Sci. Rev.* 92:63–81

Stone Sweet A, Caporaso JA. 1998. From free trade to supranational polity: The European Court and integration. In *European Integration and Supranational Governance*, ed. W Sandholtz, A Stone Sweet, pp. 92–133. New York: Oxford Univ. Press

Streeck W. 1996. Neo-voluntarism: A new social policy regime? See Marks et al. 1996, pp. 64–94

Tallberg J. 2000. The anatomy of autonomy: An institutional account of variation in supranational influence. *J. Common Mark. Stud.* 38:843–64

Taylor P. 1983. *The Limits of European Integration*. New York: Columbia Univ. Press

Thelen K, Steinmo S. 1992. Introduction. In *Structuring Politics: Historical Institutionalism in Comparative Politics*, ed. K Thelen, S Steinmo, pp. 1–32. New York: Cambridge Univ. Press

Tranholm-Mikkelson J. 1991. Neo-functionalism: Obstinate or obsolete? A reappraisal in light of the new dynamism of the EC. *Millennium* 20:1–21

Tsebelis G. 1994. The power of the European Parliament as a conditional agenda setter. *Am. Polit. Sci. Rev.* 88:129–42

Tsebelis G. 1996. More on the European Parliament as a conditional agenda-setter: Response to Moser. *Am. Polit. Sci. Rev.* 90:839–44

Tsebelis G. 1997. Maastricht and the democratic deficit. *Aussenwirtschaft* 52:29–56

Tsebelis G, Garrett G. 1997a. Agenda setting, vetoes, and the European Union's co-decision procedure. *J. Legis. Stud.* 3:74–92

Tsebelis G, Garrett G. 1997b. More on the co-decision endgame. *J. Legis. Stud.* 3:139–43

Tsebelis G, Garrett G. 2000. Legislative politics in the European Union. *Eur. Union Polit.* 1:9–36

Tsebelis G, Jensen C, Kalandrakis A, Kreppel A. 2001. Legislative procedures in the European Union: An empirical analysis. *Br. J. Polit. Sci.* 31:573–99

Wallace H. 1973. *National Governments and the European Communities*. London: Chatham House

Wallace H. 2000. The policy process: A moving pendulum. In *Policy-Making in the European Union*, ed. H Wallace, W Wallace, pp. 39–64. New York: Oxford Univ. Press

Wallace H, Wallace W, eds. 1977. *Policy-Making in the European Communities*. London: Wiley

Wallace W. 1983. Less than a federation, more than a regime: The Community as a political system. In *Policy-Making in the European Union*, ed. H Wallace, W Wallace, C Webb, pp. 403–36. London: Wiley

Wapner P. 1996. *Environmental Activism and World Civic Politics*. Albany: SUNY Press

Weiler JHH. 1994. A quiet revolution: The European Court of Justice and its interlocutors. *Comp. Polit. Stud.* 24:510–34

Weiler JHH. 1995. Does Europe need a constitution? Reflections on demos, telos, and the German Maastricht decision. *Eur. Law J.* 1:219–58

Wendt A. 1999. *Social Theory of International Politics*. New York: Cambridge Univ. Press

Wiener A, Diez T, eds. 2004. *European Integration Theory*. New York: Oxford Univ. Press

Williams S. 1991. Sovereignty and accountability in the European Community. In *The New European Community*, ed. RO Keohane, S

Hoffmann, pp. 155–76. Boulder, CO: Westview

Williamson O. 1985. *The Economic Institutions of Capitalism: Firms, Markets, Regional Contracting.* New York: Free Press

Young OR. 1997. *Global Governance: Drawing Insights from the Environmental Experience.* Cambridge: MIT Press

Zeitlin J, Pochet P, Magnusson L, eds. 2005. *The Open Method of Coordination in Action: The European Employment and Social Inclusion Strategies.* Brussels: PIE-Peter Lang.

Zürn M. 2000. Democratic governance beyond the nation-state. See Greven & Pauly 2000, pp. 90–105

Annu. Rev. Polit. Sci. 2005. 8:399–423
doi: 10.1146/annurev.polisci.6.121901.085727
Copyright © 2005 by Annual Reviews. All rights reserved
First published online as a Review in Advance on Mar. 4, 2005

THE GLOBALIZATION RORSCHACH TEST:
International Economic Integration, Inequality, and the Role of Government

Nancy Brune[1] and Geoffrey Garrett[2]

[1]*Department of Political Science, Yale University, New Haven, Connecticut 06520;
email: nbrune@isop.ucla.edu*
[2]*Ronald W. Burkle Center for International Relations and Department of Political
Science, University of California, Los Angeles, California 90095;
email: ggarrett@international.ucla.edu*

Key Words   globalization, inequality, economic growth, government spending, privatization

■ **Abstract**   In this review, we address three principal questions that have dominated the debate over the distributive effects of globalization. First, how has globalization affected inequality among countries? Second, how has globalization affected inequality within countries? Third, how has globalization affected the ability of national governments to redistribute wealth and risk within countries? We conclude that despite the proliferation of research on the consequences of globalization, there is no solid consensus in the relevant literature on any of these questions, largely because scholars disagree about how to measure globalization and about how to draw causal inferences about its effects. We also suggest possible foci for future research.

> *We've seen the result [of globalization]. The spread of sweatshops. The resurgence of child labor, prison and forced labor. Three hundred million more in extreme poverty than 10 years ago. Countries that have lost ground. A boom in busts in which a generation of progress is erased in a month of speculation. Workers everywhere trapped in a competitive race to the bottom.*
>
> AFL-CIO President John J. Sweeney at the
> International Confederation of Free Trade Unions Convention,
> April 4, 2000 (see http://www.aflcio.org/mediacenter/
> prsptm/sp04042000.cfm for text of this speech)

> *[T]hose who protest free trade are no friends of the poor. Those who protest free trade seek to deny them their best hope for escaping poverty.*
>
> President George W. Bush (*Los Angeles Times*, 2001)

1094-2939/05/0615-0399$20.00

399

INTRODUCTION

The polarized debate over the effects of economic globalization—the international integration of markets for goods, services, and capital—resembles a giant Rorschach test: Analysts have access to the same information, but they draw completely different conclusions. Supporters claim that globalization is good for international business; they consider it the best way to enrich and empower poor people and poor countries. But for critics, globalization only lines the pockets of a small global elite at the expense of labor, poor countries, and the environment—and there is little that eviscerated national governments can do about it.

Why is the debate so polarized? The age-old push and pull of distributive and partisan politics over the spoils of the market is at least partially responsible. But the scholarly community has not helped—and not because of lack of effort. Studying the effects of globalization on the economy and on politics is a growth industry across the social sciences. The problem is that no consensus has yet emerged from all this research, for two reasons. First, measuring globalization is notoriously difficult, and the measurement methods are contested. It is also very difficult to draw inferences about cause and effect between economic integration and other outcome variables, which tend to trend together.

In this essay, we try to make sense of the debate over globalization. We do not make definitive statements about the facts nor about causal relationships. Rather, we strive to focus the debate on three key questions that preoccupy political economists:

1. How has globalization affected inequalities in the distribution of incomes *between* richer and poorer countries?

2. How has globalization affected inequalities in the distribution of incomes *within* countries?

3. How has globalization affected the capacity of the state to redistribute wealth and economic risk?

From the standpoint of mainstream economic theory, the answers to these questions are clear. Since the publication of Adam Smith's *The Wealth of Nations* in 1776, it has been an article of faith that openness to the international economy is good for national economic growth.[1] The Ricardian notion of comparative advantage still provides the basic rationale: Openness to both trade and international capital allows countries to specialize in (and then to export) their comparative advantage while importing products in which they are disadvantaged. Other arguments, such as the importance of openness to realizing scale economies, have been added to the equation over time. But these only reinforce the mantra that openness is good.

---

[1]For a recent dissenting view by a Nobel-prize winning economist that has stirred up considerable controversy, if not consternation in the field, see Samuelson (2004).

Globalization should be particularly beneficial to developing countries. Poorer countries should always be catching up to richer ones because it is easier to borrow technology than to invent it and because labor tends to be more productive (lower costs per unit of production) in poorer countries. Openness should accelerate the catch-up process by exposing developing countries to the knowledge of the developed world (not only technology but also management skills and the like) as well as by ensuring that markets and investment are available to them.

Turning to the distribution of income within countries, the canonical Heckscher-Ohlin-Samuelson (HOS) model of trade, which can readily be adapted to international investment, implies that globalization should affect inequality very differently in developed versus developing countries. Openness should increase inequality in countries where capital and skilled labor are abundant, but it should have the opposite effect where less-skilled labor is relatively abundant. The intuition is simple: With fewer barriers to international flows of goods and investment, relative wages will rise in sectors in which a country has comparative advantage. Higher-income countries tend to be comparatively advantaged in capital and skilled labor, whereas lower income countries have a comparative advantage in less-skilled labor. Globalization should thus increase inequality in wealthier countries, but reduce it in poorer ones.

Finally, most economists and left-wing critics agree that openness to the international economy constrains governments from intervening in the domestic economy. Although economists tend to view smaller government as a virtue, the Left decries it for undermining the historical ability of government to alter market allocations of wealth and risk in favor of the less fortunate. But both sides share the view that international competition reduces government interventions in the economy (generous unemployment insurance or restrictions on the ability of firms to fire workers, for example). Moreover, capital mobility allows investors to vote with their feet, leaving countries whose policies are unfavorable to business. But are these standard suppositions about inequality and the scope of government borne out in reality? The answer depends on how economic integration is measured and on how one analyzes the linkages among globalization, the distribution of income among and within countries, and the size of government. As a result, arguments have been made that run directly counter to the conventional wisdom.

We organize the remainder of this review around these issues. The first section discusses the different ways globalization can be measured. The second section assesses the impact of globalization on differences in per capita incomes across nations. The third section examines the relationship between international economic integration and inequality within countries. The fourth section analyzes the impact of globalization on the government's ability to intervene in the economy to redistribute wealth and risk. The final section summarizes our conclusions about the state of the field and future directions for study.

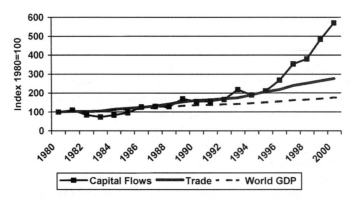

Figure 1   Global trade and private capital flows, 1980–2000. Capital flows are measured as the sum of absolute values of direct, portfolio, and other investment inflows, and outflows as a share of GDP. Trade is exports and imports as a share of GDP. Data from World Bank World Development Indicators CD-ROM 2004.

MEASURING GLOBALIZATION

International Economic Flows

Figure 1 presents basic facts about globalization in the 1980s and 1990s, normalized so that 1980 = 100. International trade (exports and imports) grew more than four times as quickly as global Gross Domestic Product (GDP), increasing about 280% during the two decades to reach more than $16 trillion (in 1995 dollars)—half of world GDP. Capital flows across national borders—inflows and outflows of both foreign direct investment (FDI) and portfolio investment[2]—grew by almost 600% to roughly $10 trillion per year, or 30% of global GDP.

The simplest way to examine the causal impact of globalization is to correlate global increases in economic flows with other outcomes of interest. For example, if the global distribution of income has become more unequal in recent decades, it is tempting to conclude that globalization is implicated as a causal agent (as in Milanovic 2003). But several important phenomena—the expansion of democracy as well as markets, the information technology revolution, etc.—trended together during the 1980s and 1990s. This covariation makes it very difficult to draw irrefutable conclusions about causality among these data series. This critique holds equally true even if one uses more sophisticated indicators of international economic integration. For example, following the seminal work of Feldstein & Horioka (1980), many economists believe that the correlation between national savings and investment across a group of countries is a far better indicator

---

[2]This category includes shorter term investments and bank lending, but excludes foreign exchange transactions that are estimated at almost two trillion dollars a day.

of capital mobility than is the magnitude of flows themselves. Whereas high flows might merely suggest instability in the investment environment, declining saving-investment correlations would indicate that domestic investment is less constrained by domestic savings—meaning capital would be more internationally mobile.

Moreover, these global aggregates belie considerable variations in the connections between specific national economies and international markets. Table 1 presents a list of the most and least internationally integrated countries based on economic flows in the late 1990s. The top ten biggest traders were very rich, very small, or both, whereas the smallest traders were very large, very poor, or both (consistent with gravity models of trade). A similar pattern was evident for capital flows, though here per capita income played the dominant role.

TABLE 1   Cross-national differences in trade and capital flows

Average (1996–2000)				Change Δ (1996–2000)–(1980–1984)			
Trade (% GDP)		Capital flows (% GDP)		Trade growth (%)		Capital flows growth (%)	
Top ten countries							
Singapore	319	Bahamas	396	Lao PDR	822	Bahamas	10,964
Hong Kong	274	Bahrain	207	Ghana	581	Lao PDR	2453
Eq. Guinea	213	Eq. Guinea	184	China	153	Malta	1327
Luxembourg	208	Ireland	168	Mexico	146	Hungary	1279
Guyana	207	Hong Kong	166	Nicaragua	116	India	1219
Malaysia	205	Malta	128	Philippines	108	Bahrain	1152
Malta	190	Belgium	82	Nigeria	105	Ireland	1144
Maldives	176	Switzerland	78	Maldives	103	Sweden	1026
Swaziland	165	U. K.	73	Thailand	103	Syria	919
Estonia	163	Panama	73	Turkey	103	Albania	864
Bottom ten countries							
Rwanda	31	Tanzania	4	Niger	−27	Costa Rica	−47
Fr. Polynesia	30	Sudan	4	Saudi Arabia	−27	Haiti	−47
India	27	Madagascar	4	Botswana	−29	St. Lucia	−47
Burundi	27	Iran	3	Japan	−29	Saudi Arabia	−47
Sudan	26	Belarus	3	Macao, China	−34	Guinea-Bissau	−61
U.S.	24	Bangladesh	3	Bahrain	−34	Botswana	−65
Argentina	22	Samoa	3	Egypt	−39	Rwanda	−71
Brazil	19	Nepal	2	C African Rep.	−40	Panama	−73
Japan	19	Haiti	2	Suriname	−72	Vanuatu	−74
Myanmar	2	Rwanda	1	Myanmar	−91	Antigua/ Barbuda	−76

The rankings were quite different, however, with respect to changes in international economic flows during the 1980s and 1990s. With respect to changes in trade, several countries in the top ten—China, Mexico, Thailand, and Turkey—are probably no surprise to close observers of the international economy. But very few would have guessed that Ghana, Laos, Nicaragua, or Nigeria would appear on the list, nor that the top ten would fail to include a single industrialized democracy. The bottom ten (featuring countries where trade as a portion of GDP declined by more than 25%) was more predictable, dominated by nations from the Middle East and Sub-Saharan Africa. But the list also includes Japan, where declining trade went hand-in-hand with economic stagnation. The list of countries in which international capital flows increased the most is eclectic; the bottom ten was more predictable. But the sheer magnitude in the decline in capital flows in these countries is worth emphasizing (more than 45% from 1980–1984 levels), given common perceptions that economic integration is ubiquitous. Should one measure the extent to which a country is globalized in terms of the level of international economic flows or changes in these flows? Sensible arguments have been made on both sides. Proponents of levels-based analyses argue that political economic dynamics are very different in Singapore than in the United States, even though trade has grown more quickly in recent years in the United States. But this argument can be reversed: Globalization is a process, not a steady-state phenomenon. From this perspective, open economies such as those of Belgium and the Netherlands, which have been dealing with the effects of international markets for decades, do not face the same types of new globalization pressures faced by large countries like China and India, where rates of recent growth in international transactions have been much steeper.

Other scholars believe that all flows-based measures—levels or changes—are flawed because they are driven by phenomena that are unrelated to real openness. For example, given how strongly trade is predicted by per capita income, market size, and geography, some argue that residuals in such gravity models indicate effective openness to international trade (Dowrick 1994). Similarly on the capital side, Frankel (1993) pioneered the analysis of covered interest rate differentials between countries, that is, the difference between interest rates in one country and those in an offshore benchmark (typically, the eurodollar), controlling for forward exchange rate expectations. Frankel suggests that high flows might indicate volatility in the investment climate rather than openness to cross-border movements, per se.

Foreign Economic Policy

But perhaps one should not concentrate on economic flows, or revealed indicators of openness, at all. Much of the debate about globalization holds governments at least partially accountable for the effects of changing tariffs and non-tariff barriers to trade and current and capital account policies. Figure 2 presents global averages

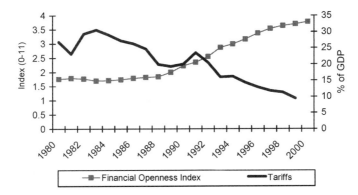

Figure 2   Global policy changes: tariffs and financial openness, 1980–2000. The financial openness index (FOI) is based on an index of 0–9. The tariffs measure is reported as a share of GDP. Tariffs data from World Bank (2004); financial openness index data from Brune (2004).

for tariffs and a new financial openness index (FOI) (Brune 2004). Higher tariffs represent less openness; higher FOI scores indicate more openness. These global trends in economic policy changes are very similar to trends in international economic flows, indicating that openness has increased dramatically in recent years.

Table 2 reports the top and bottom ten countries in terms of both levels and changes in tariffs and the FOI. Comparing the columns provides a very different picture of national economic policies depending on which measure is used. The list of most-open countries in terms of tariffs and financial openness policies includes several small economies, such as Hong Kong and Switzerland, where governments have actively pursued international economic integration. The list of countries with the highest tariffs was dominated by Southeast Asia and Sub-Saharan Africa. With respect to financial openness, more than 50 countries, many from North Africa, the Middle East, Southeast Asia, and Sub-Saharan Africa, retain completely closed capital and current accounts. In terms of changes in economic policies, the top ten lists with respect to both tariffs and financial openness featured several Latin American countries. Nations from North Africa and the Middle East were strongly represented in both bottom ten lists, and several actually increased tariffs as well as restrictions on the current and capital accounts during the 1990s.

Table 3 presents the correlations among levels and changes of economic flows and foreign economic policies at the national level. The most striking feature of the table is the weakness of most associations. Only three correlations in the table exceed 0.50, between: levels and changes in capital flows; levels and changes in the FOI; and levels of trade and capital flows in the late 1990s. For the remainder, there are not only marked differences in the integration of different countries into the international economy, but also dramatic variations in the extent of integration.

TABLE 2   Cross-national differences in average tariffs and financial openness

Average (1996–2000)			Change Δ (1996–2000)–(1980–1984)			
Tariffs (% GDP)		Financial openness (0 = closed, 9 = open)	Tariffs (%)		Financial openness (%)	
Top ten countries						
Hong Kong	0	Denmark	9	Switzerland	−100	Ireland	800
Switzerland	0	Switzerland	9	C. African Rep.	−78	New Zealand	800
Estonia	0	Vanuatu	9	Bangladesh	−74	Zambia	800
Singapore	0	Liberia	8.8	Benin	−71	El Salvador	780
U.A.E.	4	Panama	8.4	Dominica	−70	Denmark	733
Iceland	4	Hong Kong	8	Uruguay	−70	Nicaragua	700
Lithuania	4	Ireland	8	Brazil	−68	Peru	700
Norway	4	Netherlands	8	Peru	−68	Trinidad/ Tobago	700
New Zealand	5	New Zealand	8	Ecuador	−67	Uganda	660
Oman	5	Palau	8	Grenada	−64	Jamaica	640
Bottom ten countries						
Namibia	24	50 countries scored 0 including:		Papua N.Guinea	17	Yemen	−11
Bangladesh	25	Afghanistan		Madagascar	18	Lebanon	−14
Mauritius	26	Brazil		Poland	19	Bahrain	−18
Egypt	28	Chile		Czech Rep.	22	Saudi Arabia	−20
Tunisia	30	China		Yemen	23	Oman	−21
Burkina Faso	32	India		Guinea	53	U.S.	−27
Bahamas	32	Iran		Saudi Arabia	61	St. Lucia	−30
India	34	Iraq		Syria	63	Indonesia	−40
Cambodia	35	Sub-Saharan Africa		Oman	82	Seychelles	−44
Pakistan	44	Post-Communist countries		Zimbabwe	152	Zimbabwe	−50

Scholars have used different combinations of measures to answer similar questions about the effects of globalization. Milanovic (2003) assumed that globalization—however measured—has been increasing over time and has affected changes in the global inequality and growth he observed. Dollar & Kraay (2001b) and the related World Bank *World Development Report* (2003) based their work on growth and poverty on levels and (to a lesser extent) changes in trade. Rodrik (1998b) also used trade levels to measure globalization and its effect on the public economy, although he subsequently criticized Dollar & Kraay for doing the same (Rodrik 2000 & 2001). Garrett (2001) and Garrett & Mitchell (2001) used

TABLE 3   Correlations between globalization flows and policies. Correlations between levels and changes (Δ) in trade, tariffs, capital flows (Cap flows), and financial openness (FOI)

	Cap flows (96–00)	Tariffs (96–00)	FOI (96–00)	Δ Trade flows	Δ Cap	Δ FOI	Δ Tariffs
Trade (96–00)	.52	−.30	0.11	.05	0.05	−.07	0.05
Cap flows (96–00)		−.07	0.15	−.10	0.81	−.01	0.10
Tariffs (96–00)			−.53	0.06	0.27	−.25	.19
FOI (96–00)				−.10	−.11	0.51	−.20
Δ Trade					0.47	−.04	0.00
Δ Cap flows						−.03	.14
Δ FOI							−.26

changes in trade and capital mobility to reassess Rodrik's work on the public economy. Birdsall & Hamoudi (2002) argue that policy-based measures are better indicators of globalization, as Garrett (1998a), Quinn (1997), and Swank (2003) have done with respect to the effects of capital controls on government spending, taxation, and growth, and as Garrett (2004) did with respect to tariff reductions and growth. Clearly, studies on the consequences of globalization have been significantly influenced by how scholars have measured the phenomenon.

GLOBALIZATION AND DIFFERENCES IN PER CAPITA INCOMES BETWEEN COUNTRIES

The most frequently debated effect of globalization concerns inequality. But at least four important measurement issues have been raised in discussions of income distribution trends around the world:

1. Should inequality be measured among countries or within them?
2. Should inequality be measured globally or disaggregated into national experiences?
3. Should incomes be compared in terms of market exchange rates or adjusted for purchasing power parity?
4. Should the experiences of countries be counted equally or weighted by national population?

This section concentrates on the latter three questions with respect to differences in incomes between countries; the next section explores inequality within countries.

Global Gini Coefficients

Economists have long debated whether cross-country comparisons of per capita income should be computed using the rates at which currencies are actually exchanged (determined either by market forces or government fiat) or using rates that are adjusted according to purchasing power parity (PPP, determined by adjusting per capita incomes according to the prices of the same goods and services in different countries). Traded exchange rates, in theory, should converge over time on those adjusted by PPP. But in practice, market exchange rates have consistently undervalued the currencies (and hence incomes) of developing countries in recent years, often by a factor of two or more.

As a result, moving from market exchange rates to PPP-based comparisons substantially lessens the estimated amount of inter-country inequality in the world at any given point. But there is still considerable debate on the more important issue of whether global inequality has been increasing or decreasing in recent years. The United Nations' *Human Development Report 2002* used traded exchange rates to show that inequality between countries has risen, as did Schultz (1998) and Dowrick & Akmal (2003). However, using PPP-adjusted rates, Sala-i-Martin (2002) found little recent change in inequality between countries.

A bigger estimation issue concerns the appropriate weightings to use for countries of different sizes (see Firebaugh 1999 for a thorough consideration of the effects of country size on estimates of international inequality). Studies that treat countries as equal units of analysis tend to find evidence of increasing divergence in per capita incomes across countries in recent years (Sheehey 1996). In contrast, weighting countries according to their population results in estimates of decreasing international inequality (Boltho & Toniolo 1999, Firebaugh 1999, Schultz 1998).

Figure 3 demonstrates the impact of population-weighted versus "all-countries-equal" measures of inter-country inequality, using a single Gini coefficient (higher scores denote more inequality, on a scale from 0 to 1) for all countries in the world. The impact of China, with annual economic growth rates of nearly 10% for the last two decades and more than one sixth of the world's population, is clear. Moreover, economic growth in India, the world's second largest country, has approached Chinese rates in the past decade. If one weights the experiences of these two countries in terms of the proportion of the world's population (one-third) they represent, global inter-country inequality declined by about 8% during the 1980s and 1990s, from a Gini of approximately 0.54 in 1980 to one of 0.50 in 2000. However, if one were to count them only as two countries (i.e., the unweighted average in Figure 3), the inter-country Gini coefficient would have increased by about the same amount during the same twenty-year period.

Of course, even population-weighted inter-country Gini coefficients do not capture true global inequality because they do not take into account the distribution of income within a country. Measuring real global inequality is difficult. As Sala-i-Martin (2002) notes, one cannot simply combine intra- and inter-country Ginis because the former refer to individuals (or households), whereas the latter refer to

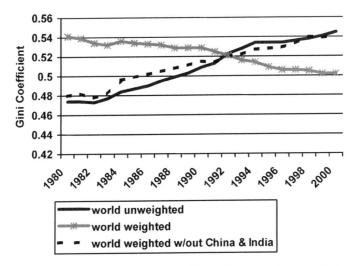

Figure 3   Between-country inequality: weighted and unweighted, 1980–2000. Data from Milanovic (2005).

countries. Nonetheless, several scholars have calculated global (i.e., comparing all people on earth) indices of inequality (Bourguignon & Morrision 1999, Dikhanov & Ward 2003, Dowrick & Akmal 2003, Milanovic 2003, Sala-i-Martin 2002). The strongest conclusion to emerge from these studies is that changes in the global distribution of income in recent decades have been largely the product of inter-country trends rather than changes in the income distributions within countries (Bourguignon & Morrison 2002, Goesling 2001, Kozeniewicz & Moran 1997, Li et al. 1998).

Differences in National Growth Rates

Even if one were confident that a single measure (such as a global Gini) could capture the amount of inter-country inequality in the world, problems of causal inference with respect to the impact of globalization on that inequality would still abound. The simplest analytic move would be to note first that the world has globalized in recent decades and then to assume that this has caused the observed changes in inter-country inequality, all the while disregarding the influences of democratization, privatization, and deregulation that have also swept around the world in the recent past. More important, the extent to which different countries are integrated into global markets varies considerably.

As a result of these considerations, many studies of the relationship between globalization and international inequality compare the experiences of different countries rather than global trends: Have globalized countries experienced faster rates of per capita economic growth than non-globalized countries? Have the benefits of globalizing been greater in developing countries than in developed ones? Economic theory suggests that the answer to both questions is yes, but proving this econometrically is difficult. The primary problem is that even if trade does increase economic growth rates, there is little doubt that growth stimulates trade (indeed, this is at the core of gravity models of trade). The ensuing issues of endogeneity, simultaneity, and reverse causation have led economists interested in the trade-growth relationship to search for instruments for trade that cannot be caused by growth, such as a country's size and geographic location (Frankel & Romer 1999).

Economists also believe that openness should speed what Robert Barro (1997) terms conditional convergence in cross-national incomes. The deadweight losses of protectionism are likely to be larger in less developed countries. FDI and trade transfer technology and know-how (i.e., management skills) to poorer countries. Financial integration offers an escape from the capital scarcities that constrain investment in poor countries and allows greater distribution of risk. Moreover, integration into international markets imposes external disciplines on developing countries that their political systems cannot produce domestically.

Have developing countries benefited from integration into the world economy? Two influential studies, based on trade integration, say that they have. Using a composite openness index, Sachs & Warner (1995) conclude that trade is an important driver of economic growth in developing countries. But numerous methodological questions have been raised about this index, notably by Rodriguez & Rodrik (1999), who caution that the index is almost tautologically connected with economic growth. Using very different measures and methods, Dollar & Kraay (2001b) draw the same conclusion about the benefits of trade as Sachs and Warner. But Rodrik (2000) again charges that many of the methodological choices made by Dollar & Kraay reflected a particular ideology ("trade is good") rather than sound scientific judgment. Rodrik contends that because Dollar & Kraay relied heavily on increases in trade flows to measure globalization, the alternative interpretation—that countries that have grown quickly, for whatever reason, have become magnets for trade—cannot be rejected.

Garrett (2004), using changes in tariffs rather than changes in trade flows, argues that whereas low-income developing countries (such as China and India) have benefited from lowering protectionist barriers, countries in the middle of the global income distribution (like Mexico and Poland) have, if anything, suffered. Others (Dikhanov & Ward 2003, Sala-i-Martin 2002, Sutcliffe 2003) argue that whereas a small group of industrialized countries at the top of the distribution have benefited from trade openness, middle-income (and poor) countries have been getting poorer. Dikhanov & Ward (2003) estimate that the share of OECD population falling into the wealthiest global decile increased from 42.5% to 55.3%. Only 8.6% of OECD's population was in the poorest decile. In 1999, Africa contributed 50% of the poorest global decile, whereas in 1970, its share was only 16%. Also, 39% of Africans were found in the lowest global decile in 1999, compared with 17% in 1990.

In contrast, Birdsall (2002) contends that globalizers among low-income countries have fared badly because they have not yet reached the minimum development threshold—in terms of human capital, physical infrastructure, political institutions, and the like—to benefit from international openness. Agenor (2003) claims that low-income countries have been hurt not because globalization goes too far, but because it does not go far enough.

Countries opening their borders to capital flows should also benefit from the efficient allocation of investment. But these gains must be balanced against the potential costs ensuing from volatility. There has been less empirical work on the capital mobility-growth relationship than on the causal impact of trade, but again the results are contradictory. Using a binary indicator of capital account openness for a sample of roughly 100 developing and developed countries, Rodrik (1998a) argued that there was no association between the level of capital account openness and growth. In contrast, Quinn (1997) used a more nuanced four-point scale for about 60 nations (and a greater proportion of developed countries), and concludes that countries that opened their capital accounts more quickly (i.e., a change measure) grew faster. Subsequently Edwards (2001) showed that using both Quinn and Rodrik's measures, capital account openness tended to be good for growth in developed countries, but not for developing nations. Edwards' findings are consistent with the post–Asia crisis consensus in the policy community—including the International Monetary Fund (IMF)—that the efficiency benefits of capital mobility are only likely to outweigh the costs in countries where domestic financial institutions are well enough developed to manage the risks associated with volatile inflows and outflows (Fischer 1998).

In sum, this section demonstrates the enormous amount of scholarly attention that has been paid in recent years across the social sciences to changes in the international distribution of income and the effects of globalization on them. Unfortunately, the work is sufficiently diverse in its methods, measures, and conclusions to have given pundits on all sides ample evidence to reinforce their prejudices.

In fact, only two conclusions can be drawn from the literature. First, two developing countries, China and India, have achieved spectacular growth rates in recent years. Because of their size, their experiences have a marked impact on how we view the effects of globalization. They have both opened to international trade (but much less to international capital), and they have achieved spectacular rates of growth. But whether, when, and how their experiences generalize to other countries is unclear.

Second, the wave of capital account liberalization in developing countries did not have the large benefits predicted by its proponents during the halcyon days of the "Washington consensus"—a group of influential Washington-based international financial institutions—in the late 1980s and early 1990s. Countries need strong domestic financial institutions to maximize the gains from global financial integration and to deal with its inherent volatility. For much of the developing world, this means that gradualism with respect to capital account liberalization is likely to be the best policy for years to come.

The jury is still out on the trade-growth nexus, particularly with respect to the impact of removing protectionist barriers to trade. Economic growth stimulates trade, creating enormous barriers to isolating the independent effects of trade growth on economic activity. Thus, scholars should focus on the vital policy questions of whether, when, and how countries should remove tariff and non-tariff barriers to trade.

GLOBALIZATION AND INEQUALITY WITHIN COUNTRIES

Two stylized facts are frequently bandied about with respect to the impact of globalization on inequality within countries. First, globalization is deemed to have undercut manufacturing employment in the industrialized countries in what 1992 presidential candidate Ross Perot called a "giant sucking sound" of jobs lost to the developing world. Second, the resulting new jobs in the developing world are in sweatshops that pay workers much less than would be paid for similar work done in developed countries. As a result of the parallel dynamics, so goes the popular wisdom, workers around the world are losing out from globalization—increasing inequality with countries all around the world.

The very influential HOS perspective supports the first stylized fact, predicting an increase in income inequality in the first world. But it contradicts the second by arguing that less skilled workers newly employed in manufacturing in developing countries should differentially benefit from globalization, lowering inequality within these nations.

Much of the policy debate, however, focuses not on the relative incomes but rather on the absolute plight of people at the bottom of the income distribution, i.e., poverty. But measuring poverty is more art than science. The official poverty line for an individual in the United States, according to the Department of Health and Human Services (2003), was $8980. By this definition, most of the world lives in poverty. But in the development community, the poverty threshold is defined as individuals living on less than "a dollar a day."[3] As Table 4 indicates, although roughly one sixth of the world's population (over a billion people) continues to live in poverty, the World Bank claims that the rate of poverty around the world declined appreciably during the 1990s. The World Bank's findings are reflected in other studies such as Sutcliffe (2003) and Dikhanov & Ward (2003) but disputed by Wade (2004), Reddy & Pogge (2003) and Ravallion (2003).

This headline statistic of poverty reduction, however, belies enormous regional variations. Excluding China from the calculation, for example, halves the estimated amount of poverty reduction. Moreover, as the case of China illustrates,

---

[3]The World Bank now reports the poverty data using $1.08 per day as the cut off (a dollar a day, measured in PPP terms, and adjusted for inflation in recent years). Data from World Bank (2000).

TABLE 4   Global poverty[a]

Region	1990	2000	Poverty reduction (1990–2000)
East Asia	29.4% 470.1 m	14.5% 261.4 m	50.7%
East Asia, excluding China	24.1% 109.5 m	10.6% 57.0 m	56.0%
China	31.5% 360.6 m	16.1% 204.4 m	48.9%
Eastern Europe & Central Asia	1.4% 6.3 m	4.2% 19.9 m	−200.0%
Latin America & the Caribbean	11.0% 48.4 m	10.8% 55.6 m	1.8%
Middle East & North Africa	2.1% 5.1 m	2.8% 8.2 m	−33.3%
South Asia	41.5% 466.5 m	31.9% 432.1 m	23.1%
Sub-Saharan Africa	47.4% 241.0 m	49.0% 322.9 m	−3.4%
Total	28.3% 1237.3 m	21.6% 1100.2 m	23.7%
Total, excluding China	27.2% 876.7 m	23.3% 895.8 m	14.3%

[a]Data presented in terms of percentage of population living below the poverty line and levels (in millions of individuals) by region.

Source: http://www.worldbank.org/research/povmonitor/

changes in poverty rates are affected by two distinct phenomena: how quickly a country (or region) is growing, and how the benefits of this economic growth are distributed among its citizens. We have already discussed differences in the growth trajectories among countries. With respect to inequality within countries, the basic phenomenon that researchers wish to measure is how widely a country's national income is shared. The standard measure, the Gini, captures the idea that complete equality would be manifest if every person earned the same income, whereas complete inequality would result if a single person held all national income. Although the hypothetical extremes on the Gini coefficient are 0 (complete equality) to 1.00 (complete inequality), the effective range for Ginis measuring national income distributions is between 0.30 and 0.50.

The most widely used data set on within-country inequality is the World Income Inequality Database (WIID 2000), a time series of national Gini coefficients that builds on the foundational work of Deninger & Squire (1996) at the World Bank. Using the WIID data, Figure 4 shows that within-country inequality for the world

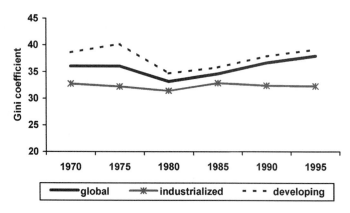

Figure 4   Within-country inequality, WIID, by level of development, 1970–1999. Figure 4 was constructed using WIID data (supplemented by World Bank data), averaged over five years.

(comprising unweighted national averages for all countries with available data) decreased in the 1970s but has subsequently increased, particularly in the developing world. Income inequality increased marginally in high-income countries in recent years, but not by the amount one might have expected from all the punditry on the subject. Thus, the WIID data report inequality trends that are precisely the opposite of what the HOS model implies about the effects of globalization.

The WIID data suffers, however, from two important limitations. First, it mixes apples and oranges in terms of what is actually measured. For example, some surveys used in WIID were based on incomes people received, others on expenditures people made; some surveys were for households, others for individuals; some report gross incomes, some net incomes (after taxes and government transfers). The second shortcoming is the WIID's limited coverage of the developing world, both in terms of countries and years of data. It is thus not surprising that others have tried to find better measures of inequality. The most recent data is from the University of Texas Inequality Project (UTIP). UTIP derives wage inequality measures from industrial surveys of wages in the manufacturing sector conducted by the United Nations Industrial Development Organization (UNIDO). The advantage of UTIP is that it comprises many more country-year observations, with much greater representation from the developing world, than does WIID. For example, for the period 1980–1998 for all countries, there are 429 country-year observations in the national WIID dataset and 1741 in the UTIP dataset. The bad news is that not everyone is employed in the manufacturing sector (with services dominant in developed countries and agriculture dominant in developing countries). UTIP deals with this problem by adjusting its scores in accordance with the observed relationship between UNIDO industrial pay data and WIID income inequality data, where both measures exist (see Galbraith & Kum (2002) for a lengthy discussion

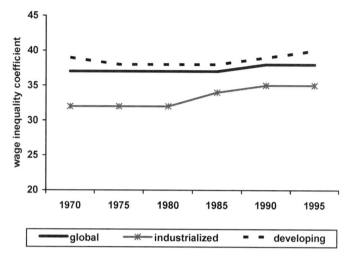

Figure 5   Within-country inequality, UTIP, by level of development, 1970–1998. Figure 5 was constructed using UTIP data (2004), averaged over five years.

of WIID, UNIDO and UTIP). Interestingly, however, as Figure 5 indicates, the patterns of within-country inequality in UTIP tend to trend in the same directions as the WIID data: a modest decline in global inequality in the 1970s, followed by rising inequality since. But the distribution of the increase in inequality in UTIP is closer to that predicted by HOS, with the increases concentrated in the developed world.

What about the globalization-inequality relationship at the national level? For rich countries, the evidence is mixed. Income inequality has clearly increased in the United States and the United Kingdom, and most analysts conclude that globalization is at least partially responsible. Galbraith & Kum (2002) using UTIP data, as well as Cornia & Kiiski (2001) and Sala-i-Martin (2002) using WIID data, argue that this finding can be generalized to other developed nations. But there are several other WIID-based studies arguing that openness is associated with less inequality in the industrial world (Barro 2000, Higgins & Williamson 1999, Lundberg & Squire 2003, and Spilimbergo et al. 1999). The same lack of consensus is evident with respect to globalization and within-country inequality in the developing world. Different studies conclude that market integration has increased inequality (Agenor 2003, Cornia & Court 2001, Kremer & Maskin 2002), reduced inequality (Barro 2000, Heston & Summers 1991, Higgins & Williamson 1999, Kapstein & Milanovic 2002, Schultz 1998), or has had no impact in less developed nations (Dollar & Kraay 2001a).

Despite these contradictory studies, three conclusions can be made about inequality within countries and the impact of globalization on it. First, changes in the distribution of income among countries have been far greater in recent years than changes in the distribution of income within countries, with big effects on poverty in the developing world. But even if globalization-induced higher growth rates are indeed lifting all boats, the adjustment costs of greater openness tend to be borne more by the poor in developing countries, as Wood (1994) first argued.

Second, Gini coefficients differ more across countries than they do over time. In wealthy countries, the strength of organized labor has played a major role in influencing cross-national differences in inequality (Lange & Scruggs 2002, Rueda & Pontusson 2000, Wallerstein 1999). In the developing world, initial distributions of land and education seem to have had a marked impact on national inequality trajectories (Birdsall & Londono 1997, 1998).

Third, in cases where inequality has increased in recent years, skill-biased technological change (i.e., computerization) has been a far more important cause of that increase than globalization. In the United States, estimates of the proportion of increased income inequality that can be attributed to trade growth vary between 10% and 33% (Feenstra & Hanson 1999, Katz & Autor 1999).

GLOBALIZATION AND GOVERNMENT SPENDING

We now turn to the impact of international economic integration on the ability of governments to use the policy tools of the state to redistribute wealth and risk within their countries. There are two very different positions in the literature, but they share the presumption (the veracity of which we explored in the previous section) that globalization adversely affects lower socioeconomic strata in society. The compensation argument suggests that government has expanded in order to cushion globalization's dislocations on those who have been harmed by it. Some go further to suggest that smart government interventions—for example, in education, in securing property rights, and in research and development—actually increase national competitiveness in global markets. The competition thesis, in contrast, contends that competitive pressures in international goods and services markets, as well as mobile capital in search of higher rates of return, have placed substantial downward pressure on the interventionist government policies that the markets view as inefficient.

Figure 6 presents data on the size of government for general government consumption expenditures and revenues from privatization (both as a share of GDP) in the 1980s and 1990s. Government consumption represents spending on the public provision of public services such as health, education, and public administration (essentially the wage bill of government). As Rodrik (1998b) notes, because transfer programs like public pensions and unemployment insurance are small in the developing world, general government consumption is a good bellwether for general trends in the public economy around the world. Total revenues from

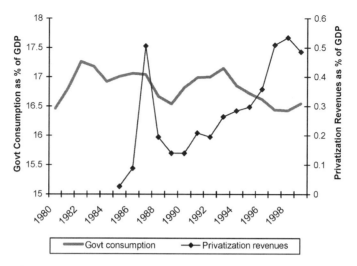

Figure 6   The size of government and privatization, 1990–1999.
Data on government consumption from World Bank (2004); data
on privatization revenues from Brune et al. 2004.

privatization, in contrast, speak to microeconomic reforms, highlighting the decline of state-owned firms, conventionally understood to prop up employment and
wages in enterprises that are not subject to market competition. In the past two
decades, very little nationalization has taken place, making privatization revenues
an easy quantitative indicator of market-oriented microeconomic reform.

The most striking fact about global government consumption spending is that
it has hovered in a very narrow band, between 16.5% and 17.5% of GDP, throughout the past two decades. Interestingly, the same pattern of slight declines in the
1980s followed by increases in the 1990s holds in both developed and developing
countries.

Although government consumption spending remained stable, privatization
swept around the world during the 1980s and 1990s. Global privatization revenues have been much smaller than government spending, however. More than
one trillion dollars in state-owned assets have been sold off around the world since
the mid-1980s (Brune et al. 2004). All tolled, this sums to only about 3% of today's
global GDP.

Turning to the cross-national evidence, the relationship between international
economic integration and the public economy has been studied for decades (see
Garrett 1998a for a review of the literature). Cameron (1978) first showed that trade
and the size of government were positively correlated in the OECD. Twenty years
later, Rodrik (1998b) and others (Dion 2004, Rudra & Haggard 2001) demonstrated
that this relationship held for developing countries, as well. These studies, however,
were based on levels of trade and spending. There is growing evidence that the

relationship is reversed when changes in trade and spending are considered, that is, faster trade growth has been associated with slower growth (or deeper cuts) in government spending both in the OECD (Garrett & Mitchell 2001, Kapstein 1999, Kapstein & Milanovic 2002) and in the developing world (Garrett 2001, Kaufman & Segura-Ubiergo 2001). Alternatively, this relationship may be reversed when other interactive effects are considered: Rudra (2002) finds that in low-income countries with weak labor power, globalization leads to less social welfare spending.

There is less research on relationship between financial openness and size of government. Rodrik (1997) hypothesized that the positive trade-spending nexus would be reversed for capital mobility—on the reasonable assumption that governments would be forced to cut taxes, and ultimately spending, to keep footloose capital from exiting—and presented some preliminary evidence to this effect for the OECD. Subsequent research, however, has failed to reveal any clear negative correlations, and indeed it has revealed some positive ones, between capital mobility and the size of the public sector among the industrial democracies (Garrett & Mitchell 2001, Quinn 1997, Swank 2002, Swank & Steinmo 2002). Marginal tax rates have declined; but investment allowances, depreciations, and other deductions have also been reduced. The result has been a broader base of capital taxation and stable tax revenues from corporate income. Data limitations have militated against similar work on taxation in the developing world, but Garrett (2001) found no evidence that increasing capital mobility reduced government spending for a sample of nearly one hundred developed and developing nations.

In light of the ambiguous relationship between openness and the size of government, recent studies have probed deeper by disaggregating government spending into categories such as transfers and expenditures on health and education. According to Kaufman & Segura-Ubiergo (2001), the negative effect of openness has operated primarily through social security transfers (mainly pensions) in developing countries, whereas health and education expenditures have proved far less vulnerable. This is consistent with Garrett's (1998a) work on the OECD. Dion (2004) goes further by arguing that trade openness has been associated with more investment in human capital (especially in authoritarian regimes).

There is much less research on the impact of globalization on privatization than there is on spending and taxing. The conventional wisdom, however, is that because state-owned enterprises are inherently inefficient, one should expect globalization (and hence more competition) to have fueled privatization. But in the most systematic study of privatization around the world, Brune et al. (2004) did not find any association between a country's trade and foreign direct investment patterns and the size of its privatization program. Instead, privatization revenues tended to be higher in countries under IMF programs, not because the IMF demanded larger scale privatization programs, but rather because the markets valued formerly state-owned assets more highly in countries subject to the general policy disciplines associated with the IMF.

After reviewing all the research on the impact of international economic integration on government policy, the evidence does not lend strong support to the conventional view that globalization will drive out inefficient government programs. The strongest support for this contention concerns changes at the margins in economic integration and in government spending and taxation, but the evidence is far from compelling.

There are two reasons for the resilience of government. As the recent difficulties the French and German governments have encountered in trying to reform their welfare states have demonstrated, political support for the public economy remains very high—all the more so when citizens feel that globalization is threatening their traditional quality of life. It is probably also true, however, that government is not as inefficient as is often presumed. Government spending on education, health care, and physical infrastructure may well produce economically important collective goods that are undersupplied by the market but also vitally important in the era of globalization. It is also not clear that public sector monopolies are any less efficient than the private sector ones that have emerged following state divestiture.

CONCLUSION

In this review, we have considered the voluminous literature on the effects of globalization on inequality among and within countries and on the size and scope of government. Neither the optimistic vision of the Washington consensus nor the inveterate pessimism of its critics have been vindicated. Rather, both sides can point to studies that support their positions. This lack of consensus is the product both of substantial measurement issues with respect to globalization and inequality and of the difficulties in drawing strong causal inferences among factors that tend strongly to covary.

It would be wrong, however, to suggest that we have not made any progress toward better understanding globalization and its impact. With respect to measuring globalization, studies that focus more on changes than levels of international economic activity, and on policy constraints rather than on flows themselves, seem better designed to generate insight into the causal relationships, particularly with respect to the roles that governments have played in accentuating or curtailing market trends. With respect to international inequality, scholars now understand the enormous impact of the individual experiences of China and India on global distributional outcomes. With respect to inequality within countries, we know that the large differences between national levels of inequality have been remarkably resilient to change in recent decades, and where they have changed appreciably, technological innovation seems to have been at least as important as globalization.

There is clearly a long way to go, however, before we will really understand the effects of globalization. Perhaps the best way forward is to acknowledge the limitations of the kind of cross-national quantitative research that dominates the literature. Small differences in methods and measurement often have very large effects on overall results. Scholars might be better off using simpler measures of statistical association, making sure they are robust to different measures, and then thinking harder about the underlying microfoundations of the proposed causal arguments. Well-designed comparative case studies may often be gainfully employed to buttress and illuminate large-N studies. But the bottom line is that more work should be done; the underlying issues at stake are far too important to do otherwise.

ACKNOWLEDGMENTS

The authors thank Alexandra Guisinger, David Nickerson, and Jason Sorens for their assistance with data collection. Many of the thoughts discussed here have also been influenced by conversations with Sebastian Edwards, Stephan Haggard, Edward Leamer, Robert Kaufman, Ronald Rogowski, Kenneth Scheve, Mathew Slaughter, and George Tsebelis.

The *Annual Review of Political Science* is online at
http://polisci.annualreviews.org

LITERATURE CITED

Agenor P. 2003. *Does globalization hurt the poor?* Policy Res. Work. Pap. Ser. 3067, World Bank

Barro R. 1997. *Determinants of Economic Growth: A Cross-Country Empirical Study.* Cambridge, MA: MIT Press

Barro R. 2000. Inequality and growth in a panel of countries. *J. Econ. Growth* 5(1):87–120

Birdsall N. 2002. *Asymmetric globalization: global markets require good global politics.* Work. Pap. No. 12, Cent. Glob. Dev., Washington, DC

Birdsall N, Hamoudi A. 2002. *Commodity dependence, trade and growth: when 'openness is not enough.'* Work. Pap. 7, Cent. Glob. Dev.

Birdsall N, Londono J. 1997. Asset inequality matter: an assessment of the World Bank's approach to poverty reduction. *Am. Econ. Rev.* 87:32–37

Birdsall N, Londono J. 1998. No trade-off: efficient growth via more equal human capital accumulation. In *Beyond Trade-offs: Market Reforms and Equitable Growth in Latin America,* ed. N Birdsall, C Graham, R Sabot,

pp. 111–146. Washington, DC: Brookings Inst.

Boltho A, Toniolo G. 1999. The assessment: the twentieth century—achievements, failures, lessons. *Oxford Rev. Econ. Policy* 15(4):1–17

Bourguignon F, Morrison C. 2002. Inequality among world citizens: 1820–1992. *Am. Econ. Rev.* 92(4):727–44

Brune N. 2004. *Explaining financial liberalization around the world.* PhD thesis. Yale Univ.

Brune N, Garrett G, Kogut B. 2004. The IMF and the global spread of privatization. *IMF Staff Pap.* 51(2):195–219

Cameron D. 1978. The expansion of the public economy. *Am. Polit. Sci. Rev.* 72:1243–61

Cornia G, Court J. 2001. *Inequality, growth and poverty in the area of liberalization and globalization.* WIDER Policy Brief, UN Univ. World Inst. Dev. Econ. Res.

Cornia G, Kiiski S. 2001. *Trends in income distribution in the post-World War II period: evidence and interpretation.* WIDER Discuss. Pap. 89, UN Univ. World Inst. Dev. Econ. Res.

Deninger K, Squire L. 1996. A new dataset measuring income inequality. *World Bank Econ. Rev.* 10:565–91

Department of Health and Human Services (2003). *The 2003 DHHS Poverty Guidelines.* http://aspe.hhs.gov/poverty/03poverty.htm.

Dikhanov Y, Ward M. 2003. *Evolution of the global distribution of income.* Work. Pap. Centre for the Study of Globalisation and Regionalisation (CSGR). University of Warwick

Dion. 2004. *Globalization, political institutions, and social spending change in middle income countries, 1980–1999.* Presented at 2004 Annu. Meet. Am. Polit. Sci. Assoc., Chicago

Dollar D, Kraay A. 2001a. *Growth is good for the poor.* Work. Pap. 2587, World Bank

Dollar D, Kraay A. 2001b. *Trade, growth and poverty.* Work. Pap. 2615, World Bank

Dowrick S. 1994. *Openness and Growth: RBA Annual Conference Volume 1994–02.* Sydney: Reserve Bank Aust.

Dowrick S, Akmal M. 2003. *Contradictory trends in global income inequality: a tale of two biases.* Work. Pap. School of Economics. Australian National University

Edwards S. 2001. *Capital mobility and economic performance: Are emerging economies different?* Work. Pap. 8076, Nat. Bur. Econ. Res.

Feenstra R, Hanson G. 1999. The impact of outsourcing and high-technology capital on wages: estimates for the United States, 1979–1990. *Q. J. Econ.* 114:907–40

Feldstein M, Horioka C. 1980. Domestic savings and international capital flows. *Econ. J.* 90:314–29

Firebaugh G. 1999. Empirics of world income inequality. *Am. J. Sociol.* 104:1597–630

Fischer S. 1998. Capital account liberalization and the role of the IMF. In *Should the IMF Pursue Capital Account Convertibility? Essays in International Finance 207*, ed. S. Fischer, pp. 1–10. Princeton, NJ: Dep. Econ., Princeton Univ.

Frankel JA. 1993. *On Exchange Rates.* Cambridge, MA: MIT Press

Frankel JA, Romer D. 1999. Does trade cause growth? *Am. Econ. Rev.* 89:379–99

Galbraith JK, Kum H. 2002. *Inequality and economic growth.* Work. Pap. 21, Univ. Texas Inequal. Proj.

Garrett G. 1998a. Global markets and national politics. *Int. Organ.* 52:787–824

Garrett G. 1998b. *Partisan Politics in the Global Economy.* New York: Cambridge Univ. Press

Garrett G. 2001. Globalization and government spending around the world. *Stud. Comp. Int. Dev.* 35(4):3–29

Garrett G. 2004. Globalization's missing middle. *Foreign Affairs* 83(6):72–83

Garrett G, Mitchell D. 2001. Globalization, government spending and taxation in the OECD. *Eur. J. Polit. Res.* 39:145–77

Goesling B. 2001. Changing income inequalities within and between nations: new evidence. *Am. Sociol. Rev.* 66:745–61

Heston A, Summers R. 1991. The Penn World Tables (Mark 5): an expanded set of international comparisons, 1950–1988. *Q. J. Econ.* 106:327–68

Higgins M, Williamson J. 1999. *Explaining inequality the world round.* Work. Pap. 7224, Nat. Bur. Econ. Res.

Kapstein E. 1999. *Sharing the Wealth.* New York: Norton

Kapstein E, Milanovic B. 2002. *Income and Influence: Social Policy in Emerging Market Economies.* Kalamazoo, MI: Upjohn Inst. Employ. Res.

Katz L, Autor D. 1999. Changes in the wage structure and earnings inequality. In *Handbook of Labor Economics*, ed. O Ashtenfelter, D Card, ch. 3A. 1463–1555. Amsterdam: North-Holland

Kaufman R, Segura-Ubiergo A. 2001. Globalization, domestic politics and social spending in Latin America. *World Polit.* 53(4):553–67

Kozeniewicz R, Moran T. 1997. World-economic trends in the distribution of income, 1965–1992. *Am. J. Sociol.* 102:1000–39

Kremer M, Maskin E. 2002. *Globalization and inequality.* Work. Pap., Brookings Inst. Group Glob. Inequal.

Lange P, Scruggs L. 2002. Where have all the members gone? *J. Polit.* 64(1):126–53

Li H, Squire L, Zou H. 1998. Explaining international and intertemporal variations in income inequality. *Econ. J.* 108:26–43

Los Angeles Times, July 18, 2001

Lundberg M, Squire L. 2003. The simultaneous evolution of growth and inequality. *Econ. J.* 113(487):326–44

Milanovic B. 2003. *Can we discern the effect of globalization on income distribution?* Policy Res. Work. Pap. Ser. No. 2876, World Bank

Milanovic B. 2003. The two faces of globalization. *World Dev.* 31(4):667–83

Milanovic B. 2005. *Worlds Apart: Measuring Global and International Inequality.* Princeton, NJ: Princeton Univ. Press. In press

Quinn D. 1997. The correlates of change in international financial regulation. *Am. Polit. Sci. Rev.* 91:531–51

Ravallion M. 2003. *How NOT to count the poor: a reply to Reddy and Pogge.* Work. Pap., Columbia Univ.

Reddy S, Pogge T. 2003. *How NOT to count the poor.* Work. Pap., Columbia Univ.

Rodriguez F, Rodrik D. 1999. *Trade policy and economic growth: a skeptic's guide to the cross-national evidence.* Work. Pap. 7081, Nat. Bur. Econ. Res.

Rodrik D. 1997. *Has Globalization Gone Too Far?* Washington, DC: Inst. Int. Econ.

Rodrik D. 1998a. Who needs capital-account convertibility? In *Should the IMF Pursue Capital Account Convertibility? Essays in International Finance No. 207*, ed. S. Fischer, pp. 55–65. Princeton, NJ: Dep. Econ., Princeton Univ.

Rodrik D. 1998b. Why do more open economies have bigger government? *J. Polit. Econ.* 106:997–1032

Rodrik D. 2000. Comments on "Trade, Growth, and Poverty," by D. Dollar and A. Kraay, Work. Pap., Harvard University, Kennedy School of Government

Rodrik D. 2001. Trading in illusions. *Foreign Policy* 123:54–62

Rudra N. 2002. Globalization and the decline of the welfare state in less-developed countries. *Int. Organ.* 56(2):411–445

Rudra N, Haggard S. 2001. *Globalization, domestic politics, and welfare.* Presented at Annu. Conf. Am. Polit. Sci. Assoc., 2001, San Francisco

Rueda D, Pontusson J. 2000. Wage inequality and varieties of capitalism. *World Polit.* 52:350–83

Sachs J, Warner A. 1995. Economic reform and the process of global integration. *Brookings Pap. Econ. Act.* 1:1–118

Sala-i-Martin X. 2002. *The disturbing "rise" of global income inequality.* Work. Pap. 8904, Nat. Bur. Econ. Res.

Samuelson P. 2004. Where Ricardo and Mill rebut and confirm arguments of mainstream economists supporting globalization. *J. Econ. Perspect.* 18(3):135–46

Schultz TP. 1998. Inequality in the distribution of personal income in the world. *J. Popul. Econ.* 11:307–44

Sheehey E. 1996. The growing gap between rich and poor countries. *World Dev.* 24:1379–84

Spilimbergo A, Londono J, Szekely M. 1999. Income distribution, factor endowments and trade openness. *J. Dev. Econ.* 59(1):77–101

Sutcliffe B. 2003. *A more or less unequal world? World income distribution in the 20th century.* Work. Pap. 54, Polit. Econ. Res. Inst., Univ. Mass.,

Swank D. 2002. *Global Capital, Political Institutions and Policy Change in Developed Welfare States.* New York: Cambridge Univ. Press

Swank D. 2003. Withering welfare? Globalization, political economic institutions, and the foundations of contemporary welfare states. In *States and Global Markets: Bringing Domestic Institutions Back In*, ed. L Weiss, pp. 58–82. Cambridge, UK: Cambridge Univ. Press

Swank D, Steinmo S. 2002. The new political economy of taxation in advanced capitalist democracies. *Am. J. Polit. Sci.* 46(3):477–89

UN Dev. Programme. 2002. *Human Development Report*. New York: Oxford Univ. Press

UN Univ. 2000. World Income Inequality Database Beta 3 (WIID). Helsinski: World Inst. Dev. Econ. Res.

Wade R. 2004. Is globalization reducing poverty and inequality? *World Dev.* 32(4): 567–89

Wallerstein M. 1999. Wage-setting institutions and pay inequality in advanced industrial societies. *Am. J. Polit. Sci.* 43:649–80

Wood A. 1994. *North-South Trade, Employment and Inequality*. Oxford: Clarendon

World Bank. 2000. *World Development Report: Attacking Poverty*. Washington, DC: World Bank

World Bank. 2003. *Sustainable Development in a Dynamic World: Transforming Institutions, Growth, and Quality of Life*. World Dev. Rep. Washington, DC: World Bank

World Bank World Development Indicators (book and CD-ROM). 2004. Washington, DC: World Bank

Annu. Rev. Polit. Sci. 2005. 8:425–51
doi: 10.1146/annurev.polisci.8.082103.104905
Copyright © 2005 by Annual Reviews. All rights reserved
First published online as a Review in Advance on Mar. 4, 2005

CONSTRUCTING JUDICIAL REVIEW

Mark A. Graber

*Department of Government and Politics, University of Maryland, College Park,
Maryland 20742 and University of Maryland School of Law, Baltimore,
Maryland 21201; email: mgraber@gvpt.umd.edu*

Key Words   Constitution, courts, democracy, law

■ **Abstract**   New works by five young political scientists are establishing a new
paradigm for studying judicial review. In different ways, Terri Peretti, Ran Hirschl,
George Lovell, Kevin McMahon, and Thomas Keck point out that judicial review is
established and maintained by elected officials. Adjudication is one of many means that
politicians and political movements employ when seeking to make their constitutional
visions the law of the land. Elected officials provide vital political foundations for
judicial power by creating constitutional courts, vesting those courts with jurisdiction
over constitutional questions, staffing those courts with judges prone to exercising
judicial power, assisting or initiating litigation aimed at having those courts declare
laws unconstitutional, and passing legislation that encourages justices to make public
policy in the guise of statutory or constitutional interpretation. Judicial review does not
serve to thwart or legitimate popular majorities; rather, it is a practice that alters the
balance of power between the numerous political movements that struggle for power
in a pluralist democracy.

INTRODUCTION

During his 1858 debates with Stephen Douglas, Abraham Lincoln correctly linked
the Supreme Court's ruling prohibiting bans on slavery in all American territories
to the reigning Democratic coalition. "[T]he *Dred Scott* decision," he observed,
"would never have been made in its present form if that party that made it had
not been sustained previously by the election" (1953b [1858], p. 232). Jacksonian
presidents and politicians for a decade had foisted responsibility for slavery onto
the federal judiciary. President-elect James Buchanan's inaugural address in 1857
declared that the status of slavery in the territories was "a judicial question, which
legitimately belongs to the Supreme Court of the United States" (1897 [1857],
p. 431). Jacksonians from all regions of the United States approved the actual
decision the justices made. "If the case had been disposed on narrow grounds,"
Douglas asserted three months after the judicial decision had been handed down,
"who can doubt... the character of the denunciations which would have been hurled
upon the elevated heads of those illustrious judges, with much more plausibility

and show of fairness than they are now acknowledged for having decided the case . . . upon its merits" (Schwartz 1993, p. 124).

Contemporary constitutional commentators commonly posit greater tensions between elected officials and justices. "[W]hen the Supreme Court declares unconstitutional a legislative act or the action of an elected executive," Alexander Bickel (1962, pp. 160–17) famously wrote, "it thwarts the will of representatives of the actual people of the here and now." Theories justifying judicial review must overcome the countermajoritarian difficulty by explaining why judicial decisions challenging majoritarian beliefs are nevertheless consistent with American democracy. Many leading law professors are abandoning that effort. Mark Tushnet (1999) would "tak[e] the Constitution away from the courts." Larry Kramer (2004a, 2004b) champions "popular constitutionalism" when calling for far greater judicial deference to Congress than recently exhibited by the Rehnquist Court. Lincoln is the patron saint of this movement. Ignoring the Illinois Republican's comments during his debates with Douglas, contemporary commentators opposed to judicial supremacy commonly cite the passage in Lincoln's first inaugural that declares,

> the candid citizen must confess that if the policy of the Government upon vital questions affecting the whole people is to be irrevocably fixed by decisions of the Supreme Court, the instant they are made in ordinary litigation between parties in personal actions the people will have ceased to be their own rulers, having to that extent practically resigned their Government into the hands of that eminent tribunal (Lincoln 1953a [1861], p. 268).

Contemporary political scientists who study constitutional courts prefer the Lincoln of 1858 to the Lincoln of 1861. They think studies of judicial review ought to place more emphasis on the cooperative relationships between Jacksonian elected officials and justices that help explain *Dred Scott* v. *Sandford* (1856) than on the potential for conflict between Republican elected officials and Jacksonian justices that, with the exception of one ruling on circuit (*Ex parte Merryman* 1861), remained latent during the Civil War. Public law students of courts believe justices rarely impose their will on popular majorities. With rare exception, Robert Dahl's (2001, p. 580) seminal article maintains, "the Supreme Court is inevitably part of the dominant national alliance." Judicial decisions declaring laws unconstitutional help "the representatives of the actual people of the here and now" secure various political concerns. As one study (Graber 1993, p. 37) concludes, "Elected officials in the United States encourage or tacitly support judicial policymaking both as a means of avoiding political responsibility for making tough decisions and as a means of pursuing controversial policy goals that they cannot publicly advance through open legislative and electoral politics." Howard Gillman (2002, 512) details how judicial decisions during the late nineteenth century sharply limiting antitrust prosecutions (*United States v. E.C. Knight Co.* 1895), striking down the federal income tax (*Pollock v. Farmers' Loan and Trust Co.* 1895), issuing injunctions against labor unions (*In re Debs* 1894), and banning state regulation of interstate railroads (*Wabash, St. Louis & Pacific Railway Co. v. Illinois* 1886), "are best viewed as 'politically inspired,' " as "part of the Republican party's effort to restructure national institutions better to facilitate national economic development." Keith Whittington (2001a) documents the tendency for judicial supremacy, the view that justices have the final authority to determine what the constitution means, to be championed by leaders of decaying political coalitions who must rely on the federal judiciary to buttress policies that no longer command powerful electoral support.

Five important books by young political scientists have recently been published on the political construction of judicial review. Terri Peretti (1999) looks at the empirical foundations of the countermajoritarian problem and finds them wanting. Her work suggests that rather than obsessing about a political court, constitutional commentators should recognize that the more political the court, the more democratic the outcome. Ran Hirschl (2004) examines the causes and consequences of the global explosion of judicial power and constitutionalism. He concludes that in Israel, Canada, New Zealand, and South Africa, judicial review was established by politicians with neoliberal policy goals, and has helped advance those political commitments. George Lovell (2003) and Kevin McMahon (2004) describe how particular episodes of judicial policy making in American history were politically constructed. Lovell details the ways legislators during the first third of the twentieth century empowered the federal judiciary to limit strikes by inserting ambiguous language in legislation ostensibly intended to promote the interests of workers. McMahon explores how the Roosevelt administration created a more hospitable environment for progressive politics in the South by appointing committed racial liberals to the federal bench and assisting litigation aimed at eradicating Jim Crow practices. Thomas Keck (2004) exposes the judicial activism of the Rehnquist Court. His analysis explains why both judicial policy making and liberal judicial policy making have survived conservative calls for judicial restraint. The public expects the courts to protect rights, he concludes, and the Rehnquist Court frequently champions policies favored by crucial members of the dominant Republican coalition.

Individually, all are fine studies. All make important contributions to constitutional theory and development. All should be required reading for graduate students doing dissertations on constitutional courts and academic lawyers writing on the role of federal judiciaries. All contain various flaws associated with dissertations that are turned into first books, most notably extensive literature reviews that distract readers from the main argument.

Collectively, these studies announce a new paradigm. Judicial review is established and maintained by elected officials. Adjudication is one of many means politicians and political movements employ when seeking to make their constitutional visions the law of the land. Elected officials provide vital political foundations for judicial power by creating constitutional courts, vesting those courts with jurisdiction over constitutional questions, staffing those courts with judges prone to exercising judicial power, assisting or initiating litigation aimed at having those courts declare laws unconstitutional, and passing legislation that encourages justices to make public policy in the guise of statutory or constitutional interpretation. Judicial review does not serve to thwart or legitimate popular majorities; rather that practice alters the balance of power between the numerous political movements that struggle for power in a pluralist democracy.

The political science emphasis on judicial review as politically constructed has some affinity with the emphasis on popular constitutionalism in contemporary academic law. Both highlight constitutional deliberation outside the courtroom. Law professors, however, maintain the sharp distinction between elected officials and unelected justices characteristic of the countermajoritarian problem. Waldron (1999), Tushnet (1999), and Kramer (2004a, 2004b) invoke constitutional interpretation by nonjudicial officials when questioning judicial supremacy. Barry Friedman (1993), Louis Fisher (1988), and Neal Devins (1996) claim that official constitutional meanings are determined by dialogues between elected officials and justices. The new paradigm in political science rejects this view that constitutional politics is best understood as a struggle or conversation between courts and elected institutions. Constitutional politics involves alliances between some elected officials and some justices who share common constitutional visions against other elected officials and justices with rival constitutional agendas. Judicial supremacy is frequently promoted by elected officials who have various reasons for preferring judicial to legislative resolution of certain constitutional issues (Whittington 2001a) and is rarely an effort by imperial justices to forestall constitutional deliberation in other branches of government.

This review details this new paradigm of judicial review that has developed in political science during the past decade. The first part presents the work Peretti and Hirschl have done on justices as coalition partners, assisting some office holders to retain, consolidate, or expand their authority. The second part examines how Lovell and McMahon employ this coalitional framework to explain judicial activism on behalf of the politically strong and weak. The third part uses Keck's study of the Rehnquist Court to explain why judicial practices and precedents associated with the liberal Warren Court have now been embraced by conservatives on and off the federal bench. The final part suggests how normative debate over judicial review might be reframed by scholars who recognize that judicial power rests on political foundations. Rather than worry about whether courts are behaving in a countermajoritarian fashion, scholars should explore the ways in which judicial review promotes and weakens the political accountability of elected officials. Rather than oppose judicial review to democracy, scholars should compare the groups, interests, and values privileged by judicial review to the groups, interests, and values privileged by other democratic arrangements.

JUSTICES AS COALITION MEMBERS

The persons responsible for the Constitution erroneously assumed that governing officials would primarily identify with their governing institution. In *The Federalist Papers* 51, Madison declared, "the great security against a gradual concentration of the several powers in the same department, consists in giving to those who administer each department the necessary constitutional means and personal motives to resist encroachments of the others . . . . The interest of the man must be connected with the constitutional rights of the place" (1987 [1788]). This expectation was abandoned with the rise of political parties. For the next two hundred years, representatives, senators, and presidents formed coalitions with persons in other branches of government. Elected officials retain some distinctive interests in the particular prerogatives of their office. Nevertheless, interbranch cooperation on most issues is the norm. Presidents and members of congress routinely work together to secure shared interests and constitutional visions.

In her book *In Defense of a Political Court* (1999), Terri Peretti contends that interbranch cooperation between justices and elected officials is also constitutionally appropriate. "[P]olitical motivation on the part of the justices," Peretti maintains, is "critical to insuring that the Court exercises its power of judicial review in a responsible, legitimate, and democratic manner" (p. 3). The legal hope for neutrality is a phantasm. Judicial decisions require contested value choices that cannot be logically deduced from purely legal standards. Peretti (1999, p. 50) notes, "Given the indeterminate nature of the constitutional text, particular interpretations can be chosen and defended only by recourse to the decisionmakers' personal values." The standard parade of horribles associated with political judging proves illusory. Political checks on the courts assure that justices make decisions well within politically acceptable standards. Institutional legitimacy is predicated on desirable results, not on jurisprudential methods mastered only by a few elite law professors. Among these desirable results is the tendency for judicial decisions to promote consensus democracy. Peretti insists that judicial review increases "the chance that government policy will in the end prove more satisfactory to the diverse interests in our nation" (1999, p. 6).

Peretti does a particularly effective job devastating fears of a political court. She points out that justices are unlikely to promote idiosyncratic values with no resonance in the rest of the political system. "[W]hen a justice decides in accordance with her personal values," Peretti (1999, p. 5) asserts, "she is vindicating those values deliberately 'planted' on the Court by a recently elected president." When judicial preferences diverge too sharply from those of the elected branches of government, elected officials have tools that reign in wayward courts, and "[p]olitical checks on the Court are effective" (Peretti 1999, p. 5). Justices respond to political threats, frequently pulling their legal punches before hostile legislative proposals become law. Political decision making does not weaken and may enhance judicial legitimacy. Peretti observes, "the Supreme Court lacks salience for most Americans," "there is not overwhelming public support for the belief that the Court makes its decisions in a neutral or nonpolitical manner," and "attitudes toward public policy [are] the best predictors of support for the Court" (Peretti 1999, pp. 167, 170, 174). Such poorly reasoned decisions as *United States v. Nixon* (1974) enjoy substantial public support because most Americans believed President Richard Nixon was wrong to withhold the Watergate tapes from the special prosecutor (Page 1990, pp. 1026–27). No better summary of political science wisdom on the nature of judicial policy making exists. Law professors writing on the judicial function should not be allowed to publish unless they submit affidavits swearing that they have read the middle chapters of *In Defense of a Political Court.*

Peretti concludes that judicial review is democratically desirable. The judicial power to declare laws unconstitutional, in her view, promotes representation and pluralism. The United States is a pluralist democracy committed to "expanding the opportunities for groups to advance and protect their interests" (Peretti 1999, p. 212). That justices use the same criteria as other governing officials when making decisions does not make judicial review unnecessary. Peretti (1999, p. 219) believes, "having the Court serve as an institutional recourse for legislative or administrative losers is regarded as a desirable redundancy in the process of developing policies that command widespread agreement." Remarkably, a work that challenges so much conventional wisdom offers the very conventional justification of judicial review as enhancing the voice of the politically powerless. Peretti (1999, p. 238) contends that the "relative freedom from direct and immediate political reprisals may be used to defend groups or values that do not receive adequate representation in the other branches."

Claims that judicial review promotes pluralism and participation require some measure of adequate representation. States are represented in the House of Representatives and the executive branch. Whether the Senate is necessary to provide states with an appropriate degree of political power depends on the degree to which states ought to be represented in the national government. Peretti, unfortunately, tends to invoke pluralism to avoid considering these difficult problems concerning how much representation democracies should provide various interests. If, as she consistently suggests, "there is no determinate, ascertainable consensus on either contemporary values or higher moral principles" (Peretti 1999, p. 44), then what grounds exist for determining whether a group or value is receiving adequate representation?

The interests that appear before the Supreme Court are almost always represented in the elected branches of government. Whether the constitution prohibits abortion is as vigorously debated in state legislatures as in the federal judiciary. Both prochoice and prolife values have champions in virtually every political forum that exists in the United States. What varies across institutions is balance of power between them. At present, proponents of legal abortion are better represented on the Supreme Court than in the Bush administration. They also have more power in the Senate than in the House of Representatives. Allowing the Supreme Court to declare laws unconstitutional alters the balance of power between prolife and prochoice forces, just as the filibuster rule in the Senate enables prochoice forces to defeat antiabortion bills passed by the House of Representatives. Whether these rules are desirable has nothing to do with pluralism per se. The crucial issue is whether judicial review (or filibustering in the Senate) provides prochoice concerns with their democratically appropriate degree of power.

Peretti's emphasis on participation, pluralism, and outsider groups seems divorced from her claims that elected officials cooperate with justices to advance common constitutional visions. Presidents have no incentive to appoint justices who favor groups or values that do not receive adequate representation in the other branches. Presidents want justices who favor groups or values that the president believes do not receive adequate representation in other governing institutions. These presidential incentives suggest that judicial review in practice may have no inherent tendency to promote participation, pluralism, or outsider groups. The more natural inference from Peretti's analysis is that the judicial power to declare laws unconstitutional augments the power of groups and institutions that have the power to appoint and influence justices at the expense of those groups and institutions that do not.

Ran Hirschl's *Towards Juristocracy* (2004) takes a more nuanced look at how constitutionalism and judicial review influence the balance of power in society. Hirschl's "hegemonic preservation thesis" observes how the rise of judicial review in Israel, South Africa, Canada, New Zealand, and many other countries resulted from actions taken by elected officials and interest groups fearful of losing political power. In the literature's most sophisticated study of comparative constitutionalism, he details how constitutional reform has served as a vehicle for transferring "an unprecedented amount of power from representative institutions to judiciaries" (Hirschl 2004, p. 1). As Peretti observed in the United States, judicial review abroad involves cooperation between justices and other governing officials; it is not the means by which an apolitical judiciary checks the rest of the political system. "When their policy preferences have been, or are likely to be, increasingly challenged in majoritarian decision-making arenas," Hirschl (2004, p. 12) observes, "elites that possess disproportionate access to, and influence over, the legal arena may initiate a constitutional entrenchment of rights and judicial review in order to transfer power to supreme courts." Fulfilling this constitutional mission, courts throughout the world are more likely to protect liberties exercised by the politically powerful than protect powerless minorities. The right to make unlimited campaign contributions is presently gaining more judicial solicitude globally than rights to basic necessities. Hirschl's study of comparative constitutional law in action "contrast[s] the limited impact of constitutionalization on enhancing the life conditions of the have-nots with its significant contribution to the removal of so-called market rigidities and the promotion of economic liberties" (2004, p. 14).

Hirschl's magisterial study reinforces Peretti's view of justices as coalition actors. "The most plausible explanation for voluntary, self-imposed judicial empowerment," he claims, is "that political, economic, and legal power-holders who either initiate or refrain from blocking such reforms estimate that it serves their interests to abide by the limits imposed by increased judicial intervention in the political sphere" (Hirschl 2004, p. 11). Three groups in particular play major roles in the political alliances responsible for transferring power from legislatures to national judiciaries: "threatened political elites, who seek to preserve or enhance their political hegemony . . . ; economic elites, who view the constitutionalization of rights . . . as a means of placing boundaries on government action and promoting a free-market business friendly agenda; and judicial elites" (Hirschl 2004, p. 12). In contrast to Bickel's (1962) assertion that judicial review "thwarts the will of representatives of the actual people," Hirschl concludes that judicial decisions declaring laws unconstitutional promote policies preferred by the people's most entrenched representatives.

These judicial decisions striking down national legislation hardly promote participation and pluralism. Justices are typically allied with secular elites who champion neo-liberal agendas. Courts protect more marginalized citizens only when doing so is "congruent with the prevalent conceptualization of rights as safeguards against state interference with the private sphere" (Hirschl 2004, p. 218). Suspicious of state power and the infusion of religious values in the public sphere, justices throughout the world have struck down laws that discriminate on the basis of sexual orientation, adopted liberal views of women's rights, and provided some protections for the rights of criminal suspects. Rarely do marginalized persons needing state assistance gain judicial solicitude. In most cases, justices in Israel, South Africa, Canada, and New Zealand have rejected positive rights claims, promoted negative economic liberties, and preferred management to labor. "The difference in absolute numbers between cases involving successful negative rights claims and cases involving successful positive rights claims," Hirschl (2004, p. 108) observes, "is tremendous."

The hegemonic preservation thesis may help explain early American constitutionalism. Gordon Wood (1991) details how the constitution of 1787 was in significant part an effort by established republic elites to ward off a more populist politics. The Marshall Court was allied first with the remnants of the Federalist party and then with the more nationalistic wing of the dominant Republican party (Graber 1998). Judicial review assisted those who would use national government power to promote commerce. Rather than promoting pluralism and participation, the Marshall Court augmented the power of the more nationalistic and modernizing forces in American politics. Such Marshall Court decisions as *Fletcher v. Peck* (1810), *McCulloch v. Maryland* (1819), and *Gibbons v. Odgen* (1824) protected vested property rights and national economic interests against more local forces. The Taney Court was allied with proslavery interests and those northerners who wanted slavery off the national legislative agenda. *Dred Scott* is not Exhibit A for pluralism in America.

If Hirschl provides a corrective to Peretti's pluralism, Peretti has something to teach Hirschl as well. After detailing the political foundations of judicial review in numerous countries, *Towards Juristocracy* complains that judicial review is undemocratic. According to Hirschl (2004, p. 217), "self-interested political and economic elites" are "attempt(ing) to insulate policy-making from the vagaries of democratic politics." Yet, this insulation seems a democratic choice. The crucial decisions authorizing constitutionalism and constitutional review were publicly debated and voted on. The constitutional orders that Hirschl studies all contain mechanisms that enable national legislative overrides of judicial decisions. That these provisions are rarely invoked (Hirschl 2004, p. 18) suggests that juristocracy

is a form of, rather than an alternative to, democracy. Whether juristocracy is a desirable form of democracy depends, in part, on whether secular, neoliberal values are desirable democratic values.

PROTECTING THE POWERFUL AND/OR POWERLESS

Neoliberal courts protect the strong and the weak. Constitutional courts in Israel, for example, have supported banks and suspected terrorists (Hirschl 2004, pp. 22–23, 111–12). The Supreme Court of the United States has similarly protected the most and least powerful Americans. *Dred Scott* asserted that slaveholders had the right to bring their human property into the territories. *Gideon v. Wainwright* (1963) ruled that the most impecunious criminal defendant has a right to an attorney supplied by the government. Traditional accounts treat cases in which the justices protect the strong as instances when a judicial elite ignored the voice of the people's elected representatives. Cases in which the justices protect the weak are thought to demonstrate a distinctive judicial capacity to "listen for voices from the margin" (Fiss 1989, p. 255). Recent scholarship on the political construction of judicial power provides different explanations. Lovell (2003) details how judicial decisions favoring business enterprises during the progressive era were responses to legislative invitations to make labor policy. McMahon (2004) maintains that judicial protection for disenfranchised persons of color was rooted in the electoral strategies adopted by the Roosevelt Administration.

Lovell's *Legislative Deferrals* might be read as an American case study of hegemonic preservation. During the nineteenth century, management ruled supreme. Workers had few legal rights. Some state courts considered unions to be common law conspiracies. Legislative support for labor rights increased during the progressive era. Many states and the national government began considering measures providing some legal protections for strikes. Unable to fully stem this popular tide in electoral politics, conservatives empowered courts to make crucial labor polices. Courts responded by declaring prolabor measures unconstitutional and (mis)interpreting statutes to maintain the antilabor status quo. Most egregiously, the Supreme Court in *Duplex Printing Press Company v. Deering* (1921) interpreted what was thought to be the prolabor Clayton Act as granting labor no immunity from antitrust laws.

Lovell (2003, p. 43) tells this important tale in ways that debunk conventional analyses of progressive-era labor decisions as instances when "bad courts" undid the handiwork of "good legislators." Courts made antilabor policy only when legislators gave justices legal maneuvering room. According to Lovell, "Hostile judicial rulings occurred in part because legislators deliberately . . . empowered judges to make important substantive decisions in labor policy" by strategic use of ambiguous language (2003, p. 45). His examination of federal labor legislation from 1900 to 1936 concludes, "the collective decision made in Congress was that the meaning of legislation should emerge only in the broader context of judicial rulings" (Lovell, 2003, p. 155). Many elected officials openly proclaimed their

intention to empower courts. Representative William Sulzer declared with respect to the Erdman Act, "We can not tell now just how the courts will construe some of the provisions of the bill, and until that is done no one can tell whether this bill be in the interest of the workers" (Lovell 2003, p. 68). When prolabor representatives introduced clearer provisions, their proposals were defeated. Faced with the choice between ambiguous statutes likely to be interpreted by courts as preserving an antilabor status quo and passing no legislation, many representatives declared those measures a boon for unions and then blamed courts for depriving workers of their hard earned legislative triumphs.

Justices and legislators cooperated when making labor policy during the first third of the twentieth century. When Congress passed laws unambiguously announcing prolabor policy, the vast majority of justices handed down prolabor decisions. Only a few conservative diehards on the federal bench sought to interpret away the plain ban on labor injunctions set out in the Norris-LaGuardia Act of 1932 (Lovell 2003, pp. 164–65). Justices most often indulged their antiunion sentiments when Congress self-consciously delegated policy choices to the judiciary. The Clayton Act contained numerous legislative deferrals. Congress repeatedly considered and rejected language that would have more clearly mandated that no labor activities were subject to the Sherman Anti-Trust Act and that no court could enjoin secondary boycotts. Lovell (2003, p. 188) describes how "legislators deliberately refrained from establishing a specific policy position and instead deliberately created ambiguity that gave judges discretion to make substantive policy choices." Rejecting proposed statutory language declaring union activities legal, Congress chose to declare unions legal and forbid interference with "lawful" union activities. What constituted lawful activities was for judges to determine (Lovell 2003, pp. 107–25). During the legislative debates, representatives recognized that Congress had decided not to decide. The precise rights of labor unions, Andrew Volstead of Minnesota declared during the debates over the Clayton Act, would "of necessity go into the courts after [the bill] becomes a law before anyone will know definitively just what it means" (Lovell 2003, p. 118).

Representatives aligned with management and labor had incentives to endorse these statutory bargains. Conservatives accepted statutory ambiguities confident that courts would give such provisions an antilabor interpretation (Lovell 2003, p. 130). Union activists inside and outside of Congress acquiesced partly because such language was the best they could secure and partly because the appearance of legislative victories was necessary to stave off more radical challenges to their leadership. "By declaring victory," Lovell (2003, p. 48) writes, "labor leaders could justify and maintain internal support for their conventional political strategy of working within the existing two-party system."

Lovell's close analysis of ostensibly prolabor legislation exposes problems with claims that labor abandoned electoral politics when courts consistently denied unions the fruits of their legislative victories (see Hattam 1993; Forbath 1991). "Earlier scholars," Lovell documents, "have overestimated labor's political success in the legislative branch, and . . . as a result . . . have overestimated the importance

of judicial power" (2003, p. xix). Labor leaders consistently oversold legislation. The Clayton Act was not labor's Magna Carta, as Samuel Gompers maintained (Lovell 2003, p. 1); rather, to obtain any legislation, labor consistently had to accept language that empowered courts to maintain the status quo if justices so wished. Statutes that labor publicized as legislative victories were "a confusing hodgepodge of provisions that passed despite widespread disagreement among legislators about what the provisions meant" (Lovell 2003, p. 146). "The reason judges were able to produce an outcome that differed from the AFL's stated expectations," Lovell concludes, "was not that the judges did not have to stand for election against an AFL juggernaut that had produced a prolabor Congress . . . . The problem was that the AFL could not find a majority in the divided Congress that would enact stronger legislation that better secured the AFL's policy goals" (2003, p. 156).

Legislative Deferrals makes a particularly important contribution to public law scholarship by identifying and criticizing what Lovell (2003, p. 5) calls the legislative baseline theory. According to this theory, legislation always "establish(es) a particular policy position for Congress." Theories of statutory interpretation concern how courts should identify that policy choice. Theories of the judicial function in constitutional cases concern whether courts should honor that policy choice. Much legislation, however, is best understood as a legislative refusal to make the appropriate policy choices. Congress commonly rejects clear statutory language in favor of language that forces courts to make policy choices in the guise of interpretation. Countermajoritarian problems do not occur when Congress passes such measures; there is no concrete wish of the people to which courts may defer. "[T]he conventional divide between 'democratic' and 'counter-majoritarian' branches is too simplistic," Lovell (2003, p. xviii) states, when "legislators . . . deliberately include ambiguous language in statutes that allows judges to make policy choices as they resolve interpretive controversies."

This wonderful analysis of legislative politics might have been pushed one step further. Conservatives did more than provide language courts might have interpreted as restricting union activities. The Taft, Harding, and Coolidge administrations fought to staff the federal judiciary with political actors prone to construe ambiguous Constitutional and statutory language against labor. When he was president and chief justice, Taft was particularly committed to securing a promanagement court (Murphy 1961). Labor's very limited ability to influence the staffing of federal courts further demonstrates that unions were not as politically powerful as some literature suggests. A labor movement not strong enough to obtain unambiguously prolabor legislation was also not strong enough to prevent the appointment of unambiguously antilabor federal judges. The politically powerful were well represented on the federal bench because they were (nearly) as well represented in the elected branches of government.

Kevin McMahon's *Reconsidering Roosevelt on Race* (2004) conversely demonstrates that the justices who declared Jim Crow practices unconstitutional inherited their capacities to "listen for voices from the margin" from their political sponsors in the executive branch who had previously heard the cries of oppressed African

Americans. McMahon successfully employs a presidency-centered focus to link elected officials and judicial activism on behalf of the powerless. McMahon maintains that *Brown v. Board of Education* (1954) was as rooted in decisions made by the Roosevelt Administration as in the litigation campaign against segregated schools. Civil rights began occupying a substantial place on the federal judicial agenda only after executive branch officials converted the Supreme Court from a bastion of laissez-faire to a bulwark of racial liberalism. New Dealers supported adjudication on behalf of the powerless as a means for expanding their political coalition, implementing Roosevelt's "immediate policy preferences," and "realizing the president's 'constitutional vision'" (McMahon 2004, p. 179). When making civil rights decisions, the Supreme Court was responding as much to Roosevelt as to the NAACP. According to McMahon (2004, p. 214), "The justices behaved in a fashion consistent with an institutional mission substantially influenced by FDR's policy toward the judiciary."

Judicial protection for powerless African Americans promoted policies and Constitutional visions favored by politically powerful elites in the executive branch of the national government. For both partisan and principled reasons, American presidents during the 1940s and 1950s sought to promote racial liberalism. Roosevelt was convinced that newly enfranchised black voters would support the New Deal. Were the justices to declare the poll tax unconstitutional, "a vast pool of potentially progressive voters would be tapped, southern representation in Washington dramatically altered, and [Roosevelt's] institutional program implemented" (McMahon 2004, p. 102). Truman and Eisenhower competed for black votes when they campaigned. In 1948, Truman highlighted "the Justice Department's litigation campaign as a means to convince black American voters to . . . support his bid for the presidency" (McMahon 2004, p. 191). Mary Dudziak (2000), as well as Philip Klinkner and Rogers Smith (1999), details how executive branch officials regarded Jim Crow as a foreign policy embarrassment during the Cold War. More laudable motives were also at work. As elections moved the base of the Democratic party northward, party leadership became increasingly controlled by persons who abhorred Jim Crow (McMahon 2004, p. 100). Unable to break the southern Democratic stranglehold on Congress, the presidential wing of the Democratic party turned to courts to achieve a measure of racial justice.

McMahon details important connections between the partisan and constitutional politics of the New Deal. Roosevelt's struggles with the Court that led to the failed Court-packing plan of 1937, his struggles with southern Democrats that led to the failed purge of 1938, and increased judicial protection for civil rights and civil liberties after 1937 are all well known. McMahon demonstrates how these events, too often treated as distinctive, were part of a unified whole. Roosevelt intended that the Court-packing plan be a vehicle for ending judicial protection of property rights and increasing judicial protection for racial minorities. His "judicial policy sought to disrupt southern politics" (McMahon 2004, p. 17). Southern Democrats opposed the Court-packing plan, fearful that Roosevelt judicial appointees were likely to be racial liberals. "The Court-packing plan," McMahon (2004, p. 81)

points out, "was the last straw for many congressional southerners already unnerved by . . . the president's increasingly progressive policies and the addition of black American voters to the Roosevelt coalition." When the justices struck down racial discriminations, such pillars of Jim Crow as Senator Richard Russell of Georgia complained that the Supreme Court had become "the political arm of the Executive Branch" (McMahon 2004, p. 6).

McMahon's chapters discussing how Roosevelt sought to imbue the judiciary with his constitutional vision echo prominent themes in Peretti's work. Judicial nominees were screened to ensure they were sound on rights questions. The Justice Department promoted Wiley Rutledge for a vacancy after an internal review concluded he was a "liberal who would stand up for human rights" (McMahon 2004, p. 138). Executive branch officials with presidential encouragement initiated or supported litigation to secure more egalitarian racial policies. Influenced by Justice Department activity, a Supreme Court packed with racial liberals declared white-only primaries unconstitutional (*Smith v. Allwright* 1944) and revived Reconstruction statutes protecting persons of color from lynching and political brutality (*Screws v. United States* 1945) (McMahon 2004, pp. 150–75). Executive encouragement mattered. McMahon (2004, p. 20) points out, "given New Deal jurisprudence's penchant toward deference, it is highly unlikely that the Court would have trod a progressive civil rights trail without the support of the executive branch."

These Supreme Court decisions protecting African Americans belie conventional distinctions between judicial restraint and judicial activism. Conventionally, deferential justices accept the judgment of elected officials that existing legislation is constitutional. The justices after 1937 deferred to elected officials in this sense when they declared New Deal economic measures constitutional. The justices also deferred to the executive branch in *Smith v. Allwright*, but in this instance they accepted the judgment of national elected officials that existing legislation was unconstitutional. By sponsoring or assisting litigation on behalf of racial minorities, executive branch officials enabled the Stone Court to reconcile its hands-off approach to economic regulation with activist interventions in southern politics. "By asking the 'Roosevelt Justices' to entertain the race issue," McMahon (2004, p. 7) declares, "the Roosevelt Justice Department helped them resolve the apparent contradiction between their actions and the 'mistaken' activism of the 'old' anti-New Deal Court."

McMahon wisely avoids claiming that the Supreme Court was a puppet in the hands of the Roosevelt administration. He recognizes that Supreme Court justices are not "mere clones of the president when issuing their rulings from the high bench" (McMahon 2004, p. 8). Not all New Deal justices aggressively supported increased protection for persons of color. Many, most notably Felix Frankfurter, were skeptical about increased judicial solicitude for civil liberties. The most that can be said is that Roosevelt appointees shared a common distaste for southern racial practices. How that distaste would be manifested was not set in stone at the moment of appointment. *Reconsidering Roosevelt on Race* explains "why the

Roosevelt justices came to be greater advocates of racial equality" (McMahon 2004, p. 9).

McMahon does not explain why these same Roosevelt justices were not as aggressive when championing the rights of labor. The New Deal Court did sustain some legislation granting rights to labor unions (i.e., *NLRB v. Jones and Laughlin Steel Company* 1937). In *NLRB v. Mackey Co.* (1938), however, the justices permitted permanent replacements for striking workers, and in *NLRB v. Sands Mfg. Co.* (1939), they prohibited strikes during the life of a collective bargaining agreement. These decisions were partly consequences of the same legislative deferrals that took place before the New Deal. In *Legislative Deferrals*, Lovell convincingly demonstrates that "the Wagner Act was never an unqualified victory for labor organizations" (2003, p. 219). "Legislators rejected proposals to address these issues more decisively in the statutory language" (Lovell 2003, p. 234), leaving crucial decisions to be made by courts. Yet neither Lovell nor McMahon explain why New Deal justices made these antilabor decisions. When New Dealers spoke of civil rights and liberties, they were speaking as much of the rights of labor as the rights of persons of color. Roosevelt judicial appointees were screened to ensure they supported the President's labor policy (McMahon 2004, pp. 86–95). Nevertheless, while the New Deal Court sustained federal labor laws and provided some First Amendment protection for union activities, that tribunal never became a bastion of labor rights. New Deal justices apparently accepted their mission to protect potential members of the Democratic coalition while giving far less support to the group at the heart of the New Deal order.

Hirschl's comparative perspective may shed some light why New Deal justices did not always support labor. In *Towards Juristocracy*, Hirschl observes that the justices at the turn of the twenty-first century typically favored management over workers (2004, pp. 139–46). This tendency has not been absolute. Economic elites at times have championed unions and collective bargaining as means for stabilizing the work force. During the New Deal, prominent industrialists affiliated with the Democratic party concluded that American participation in an international political economy required the protections for labor set out in the Norris-LaGuardia and the Wagner Acts (Ferguson 1989). New Deal judicial elites sustained those measures, but had no desire to further the cause of labor beyond what was embodied in New Deal measures. When statutory ambiguities were litigated, the neoliberal elites on the Roosevelt Court reverted to form and favored management. Anticipating the contemporary judicial practice Hirschl discusses, New Deal justices supported labor only when statutory language clearly warranted that result.

ENTRENCHING JUDICIAL REVIEW

First-generation judicial review is rarely countermajoritarian. The Roosevelt Court did not thwart the will of the Roosevelt Administration. The justices in Israel, Canada, South Africa, and New Zealand who are declaring constitutional

limitations on government power are members of the coalition responsible for the constitutionalization of rights. Judicial power in these regimes is exercised consistently with majority intentions and expectations. Problems of democratic accountability typically occur only with second-generation judicial review. Inherited judicial practices may become legally entrenched. Constrained by past precedent, justices might not be able to change course after coalitions opposed to the constitutionalization of particular rights establish control over the elected branches of government.

Thomas Keck's *The Most Activist Supreme Court in History* (2004) details how both rights-based judicial activism and rights-based liberal judicial activism are presently hard-wired into the American constitutional order. Presidents Richard Nixon, Ronald Reagan, George Bush, Sr., and George Bush, Jr., all praised judicial restraint and condemned liberal judicial activism. The Rehnquist Court, however, aggressively exercises judicial power. Keck points out "Justice Felix Frankfurter's doctrine of judicial deference has no surviving heirs" (2004, p. 200). Although "the standard conservative view of the Supreme Court has amounted to a critique of liberal 'judicial activism' and a call for 'judicial restraint,' " *Keck* notes that "in a wide variety of doctrinal contexts, the justices of the Rehnquist Court have proven willing both to declare constitutional limitations on government and to become involved in heated political questions" (2004, pp. 1–2). Most remarkably, what Keck (2004, p. 284) reasonably labels the "O'Connor Court" engages in both liberal and conservative activism. The justices on that tribunal protect abortion rights and the rights of cigarette advertisers. This Janus-faced policy making, Keck maintains, is rooted in public expectations and inherited legal practices. *The Most Activist Supreme Court in History* claims that the more moderate conservatives on the Rehnquist Court have not reversed past liberal rulings because past precedents entrenched both such decisions as *Roe v. Wade* and conceptions of the judicial role underlying those precedents. Republican judicial appointees frequently engage in conservative judicial activism because inherited legal logics are better employed constructing conservative constitutional limitations on government than tearing down liberal constitutional limitations.

Keck devastates claims that contemporary conservatives on the federal bench have no judicial agenda other than to return control over basic polity questions to elected officials. During the past decade, the Rehnquist Court has declared twice as many federal laws unconstitutional each year as the next most activist tribunal (Keck 2004, p. 40). States and localities that discriminate against women (*United States v. Virginia* 1996), ban abortion (*Planned Parenthood v. Casey* 1992), regulate consensual sexual behavior (*Lawrence v. Texas* 2003), pass campaign finance reforms (*Colorado Republican Federal Campaign Committee v. FEC* 1996), attempt to regulate commercial advertising (*44 Liquormark, Inc. v. Rhode Island* 1996), restrict land use (*Lucas v. South Carolina Coastal Council* 1992), implement affirmative action programs (*Richmond v. J.A. Croson Co.* 1989), and use race when redistricting congressional districts (*Shaw v. Reno* 1993) have felt the wrath of the Rehnquist Court. Judicial opinions make clear that the federal judiciary is

responsible for interpreting the constitution and need not defer to constitutional judgments statutorily expressed by the elected branches of government. Congress, Justice Kennedy declared in *Boerne v. Flores* (1997, p. 519), "has been given the power 'to enforce,' not the power to determine what constitutes a constitutional violation." The plurality opinion in *Planned Parenthood v. Casey* (1992, 867) asserted, "the Court's interpretation of the Constitution calls the contended sides of a national controversy to end their national division." The most conservative justices on the present bench, Chief Justice William Rehnquist, Justice Antonin Scalia, and Justice Clarence Thomas, vote to declare laws unconstitutional as often as their more moderate peers and far more often than their liberal peers (Keck 2004, p. 251). Their jurisprudence, Keck (2004, p. 5) details, cannot be explained by any commitment to restraint or originalism. The common thread is a "broad New Right critique of liberalism as the source of cultural decay, economic stagnation, and American decline."

Keck (2004, p. 7) clearly documents "the survival of liberal activism, on the one hand, and the emergence of conservative activism, on the other." Thanks to Justices O'Connor and Kennedy, the main pillars of Warren Court jurisprudence are still standing. Some have been strengthened. Legal abortion remains the law of the land. The right to privacy has been expanded to cover all voluntary sexual activity between consenting adults. Affirmative action lives, although race-based preferences must satisfy a weak version of strict scrutiny (*Grutter v. Bollinger* 2003). Even *Miranda v. Arizona* (1966) has been reaffirmed (*Dickerson v. United States* 2000). Rather than overturn these landmarks of liberal jurisprudence, the Rehnquist Court prefers staking out new areas for conservative judicial activism. Commerce clause limitations on the federal government have been revived (*United States v. Lopez* 1995), as well as state sovereignty restrictions rooted in an exceptionally broad reading of the Tenth and Eleventh Amendments (*Printz v. United States* 1997, *Seminole Tribe of Florida v. Florida* 1996). Warren Court precedents protecting the rights of political dissenters have been expanded to protect the rights of cigarette advertisers (*Lorillard Tobacco Co. v. Reilly* 2001). Justices Thomas and Scalia, the two most vehement opponents of liberal activism, are aggressive proponents of conservative activism. Both would use the judicial power to end affirmative action (*Grutter v. Bollinger*), place sharp limits on campaign finance reform (*McConnell v. FEC* 2003), and challenge understandings of federal power to regulate the national economy dating from at least the New Deal (*United States v. Morrison* 2000).

Surprising connections exist between past liberal and present conservative activism. Much contemporary conservative activism owes a debt to Justice Hugo Black's efforts during the 1940s and 1950s to nationalize the Bill of Rights and combat McCarthyism. Black consistently employed textual and originalist logics in his opinions. While Frankfurterian liberals insisted that courts defer to legislatures, Black and his judicial allies claimed that the persons responsible for the Constitution intended to place certain fundamental liberties beyond the reach of popular majorities. As Black became more conservative during the 1960s, he

employed the same legal logics when opposing Warren Court decisions on privacy and voting rights. These dissents, Keck (2004, p. 68) observes, "supplemented Frankfurter's deference with more explicit appeals to constitutional text, to their own reasoned judgments, and to an emerging critique of liberal egalitarianism." That changing attack on judicial liberalism "would influence conservative critiques of the Court for years to come." When conservatives began coming to judicial power during the 1970s, critiques of Warren Court decision making could be employed to promote conservative activism. Justice Rehnquist could employ history to attack judicial solicitude for abortion rights and promote judicial solicitude for state rights. Other conservatives could employ antiegalitarian logics when condemning judicial decisions protecting obscenity and championing judicial decisions opposing affirmative action.

Keck maintains that Rehnquist Court activism has two other foundations. The first is a respect for precedent and reasoned elaboration that O'Connor and Kennedy inherited from Justice John Marshall Harlan. Committed to this centrist vision, the moderate conservatives are reluctant to strike down liberal precedents such as *Roe v. Wade* (1973) and *Regents of Univ. of California v. Bakke* (1978). Their commitment to lived traditions justifies occasional activism, such as their recent decision to strike down bans on homosexual sodomy in *Lawrence v. Texas*. The second foundation is hostility to Great Society values that Rehnquist, Scalia, and Thomas inherited from New Right political activists. Keck notes that Rehnquist Court justices who sometimes speak the language of originalism abandon history when past practice supports liberal outcomes (2004, pp. 2–3). *The Most Activist Supreme Court in History* details how "the conservatives' effort to tie their specific modern constitutional doctrines to the 1787 Constitution has been both inconsistent and unsuccessful." Justices Thomas (*Grutter* 2003, pp. 349–50, 378) cites Frederick Douglass and the Declaration of Independence when opposing affirmative action, but he ignores the substantial evidence that the persons responsible for the equal protection clause approved benign racial classifications (see Schnapper 1985). The notion that justices should not enforce their notions of morality are forgotten when justices consider whether environmental regulations take property in violation of the Fifth Amendment.

Keck insists that Rehnquist Court activism is best explained by past legal decisions that entrenched both a judicial commitment to protect rights and a judicial commitment to protect certain legal rights. The Rehnquist Court turned to judicial activism because a more Frankfurterian commitment to judicial restraint had been decisively abandoned by the late Warren and Burger Court. "The very mission of an independent Supreme Court," Keck claims, "had come to be identified . . . with the enforcement of rights-based limits on political action" (2004, p. 7). Few precedential or political foundations presently exist for judicial restraint. Contemporary law is activist and, as the failed Bork nomination demonstrates, the general public supports that activism (Keck 2004, pp. 163–64). Contemporary justices wishing to act in a countermajoritarian fashion would be well advised to consider abjuring the judicial power to declare laws unconstitutional.

The judicial decisions of the 1960s are better understood as creating a public committed to judicial activism than as entrenching constitutional rules that might frustrate future majorities. The broad public demand for judicial decisions protecting fundamental rights, Keck observes, left only activist paths open to judicial conservatives. Justices O'Connor and Kennedy chose largely to accept liberal activism where previously established and develop additional areas of conservative activism. The other justices chose to endorse new conservative rights while abandoning liberal precedents (Keck 2004, p. 7). No member of the Rehnquist Court has made any serious effort to reduce the judicial presence in American life. All pursue constitutional visions supported by prominent figures in the elected branches of government.

Conservative constitutional practice casts some doubt on the constraining force of past liberal precedent. The more centrist justices on the Rehnquist Court have expanded weak lines of liberal precedent, while stronger lines have been nearly abandoned. When Richard Nixon took office, rights to basic necessities had greater precedential support than rights to procreative choice (Graber 1997). Nevertheless, as Keck (2004, p. 119) notes, "one of the first areas in which the Burger Court successfully halted its predecessor's line of liberal activism was that of economic equality." The death penalty seemed moribund when conservatives come to judicial power. The Supreme Court in 1972 declared unconstitutionally arbitrary all state laws imposing capital punishment (*Furman v. Georgia* 1972). The Burger and Rehnquist Courts then sustained most rewritten state statutes, despite evidence that substantial arbitrariness remains in the death sentencing process. *McCleskey v. Kemp* (1987) found no constitutional problem with capital punishment in Georgia, even though persons who murdered whites were more than four times as likely to receive the death penalty than those who murdered persons of color.

The different status of past liberal precedent suggests the need for greater emphasis on political and social entrenchments. The sexual revolution is here to stay. As the plurality opinion in *Planned Parenthood v. Casey* (1992, p. 856) asserted, Americans "for two decades . . . have organized intimate relationships and made choices that define their views of themselves and their places in society, in reliance on the availability of abortion in the event that contraception should fail." Young Republicans are as sexually active as young Democrats. Many gravitate toward libertarianism and see nothing objectionable in any form of intimacy between consenting adults. Affirmative action is now mainstream. Both corporate America and the military, staunch Republican allies, filed amicus briefs in *Grutter v. Bollinger*, urging the justices not to declare all race classifications unconstitutional. Justice O'Connor's majority opinion (*Grutter* 2003, p. 331) quoted the military brief's contention that a "highly qualified, racially diverse officer corps . . . is essential to the military's ability to fulfill its principle mission to provide national security." By comparison, no conservative constituency has the same stake in abolishing capital punishment or constitutionalizing a right to basic necessities.

Casey, *Lawrence*, and *Grutter* are not instances of liberal judicial policy making (see Levinson 2003). Formerly liberal precedents survived the political death of

liberalism by gaining conservative constituencies. Perhaps, following Hirschl's analysis, the Rehnquist Court ought to be understood as behaving consistently with the global tendency of justices to engage in neoliberal policy making. The justices have tended to support liberal results that limit state action or favor a secular elite, but they have abandoned lines of liberal activism that called for more state intervention on behalf of the powerless.

Entrenchment is a legal, political, and social phenomenon. A good case can be made that Rehnquist Court justices would not have declared abortion a constitutional right or sustained affirmative action had such decisions not been supported by past precedents. Nevertheless, *stare decisis* was not the only foundation of *Casey* and *Grutter*. Politics mattered. *Roe* (1973) and *Bakke* (1978) created future majorities. Those judicial decisions facilitated lifestyle and business choices that, over time, created bipartisan support for abortion rights and affirmative action. *Roe* and *Bakke* are legally entrenched partly because the practices they legalized are politically and socially entrenched. Had the Supreme Court banned affirmative action during the 1970s, American businesses might not have relied on that practice so extensively thirty years later. Similarly, had the Supreme Court handed down a different decision in *Bush v. Gore* (2000), the present majority coalition might have substantially different policy preferences.

Keck reorients the debate over the Rehnquist Court. He is right to note that "we need a new and better conversation about what the contemporary Supreme Court is doing" (2004, p. 14). The present debate is over judicial activism. All participants purport to oppose aggressive judicial policy making. President George Bush publicly deplores judicial activists (Kirkpatrick 2004, p. A24). Justice Antonin Scalia gives speech after speech condemning justices for making moral choices that he believes are constitutionally entrusted to the elected branches of government (Sherman 2004, p. 26). Liberals echo these complaints about activist justices. Law review articles accuse the Rehnquist Court of "dissing Congress" (Colker & Brudney 2001). "Instead of a Court interested in collaborating with Congress and encouraging popular participation in the formation of constitutional values," Dean Kramer (2004b, p. 984) complains, "we now have Justices telling us that a presumption of constitutionality is 'unwarranted' because Congress cannot be trusted to be faithful to the Constitution." Something is obviously amiss. Conservatives are not acknowledging their activism. Liberals try to shoehorn Warren Court activism into more narrow channels or indicate less enthusiasm for that activism than was expressed during the 1960s. This constant bickering about judicial activism, Keck observes, has "preempted a more productive conversation about constitutional meaning, distracting our attention from the actual locus of constitutional conflict" (2004, p. 288). As judicial policy making has become a relatively enduring element of American constitutionalism, Americans should focus as much on how judicial review is appropriately exercised as on whether judicial power should be exercised.

Constitutional theorists in the United States would be better off acknowledging that politicians in office seek to use courts to advance their agendas and debating the merits of those agendas. The debate over whether the Rehnquist Court is right to declare Tenth Amendment limitations on Congressional power should be part of the larger debate over whether the Republican party is right to promote a more robust constitutional federalism. Several political scientists (Whittington 2001b, Pickerill & Clayton 2004) point out that state sovereignty is enjoying a resurgence inside and outside of courts. When declaring national laws unconstitutional, the justices are largely advancing constitutional values articulated in successful Republican campaigns. Rather than direct criticisms at the Rehnquist Court for substituting their values for those of elected officials, political scientists should discuss whether the dominant Republican coalition is correctly construing the Constitution.

Scholarship that makes explicit connections between Republican constitutional visions and Republican judicial activism may find particularly troubling the federal laws recently declared unconstitutional. Dahl (2001, pp. 571–72) notes that when justices declare federal laws unconstitutional, they typically strike down policies enacted by a deposed coalition. The Great Society liberals on the Warren Court routinely sustained measures championed by Great Society liberals in the legislative and executive branches of the national government. Judicial activism was directed at the South and rural America (Powe 2000, p. 494). The Rehnquist Court typically strikes down laws supported by Reagan Republicans. Twenty of the federal statutes declared unconstitutional by that tribunal were enacted after 1980 (Keck 2004, pp. 204–07). All but one were signed by a Republican president or passed by a Congress in which either the House, the Senate, or both were controlled by Republicans. Republican legislative support for federal measures declared unconstitutional by Republican justices has often been close to unanimous. These practices raise important questions about whether the Rehnquist Court is pursuing or concealing a Republican constitutional vision.

Lovell's discussion of political accountability during the progressive era provides useful guidelines for thinking about Republican/Rehnquist judicial activism. In *Legislative Deferrals*, Lovell notes that political actors have different reasons for invoking judicial power. Some openly champion judicial policy making. Many elected officials have publicly proclaimed that crucial provisions in their legislative handiwork were vague and that such language was intended to promote judicial policy making. Some acknowledged that they promoted judicial power as the best available means for securing conservative labor policies. Other politicians empowered courts in order to conceal their political choices, proclaiming clear legislative victories that they knew had not been won. Problems of democratic accountability occurred during the first third of the twentieth century, Lovell declares, because those "[l]egislators were never forced to say 'no' to the demands of labor organizations." Ostensibly prolabor elected officials "could instead create deceptive responses that were attractive to legislators precisely because they made legislators and the legislative process appear responsive" to union demands that were being ignored (2003, p. 260).

Lovell attacks judicial review as enabling elected officials to "deflect conflicting political pressures without having to take full responsibility for making divisive choices" (2003, p. 255). This criticism provides both the appropriate focus for questions of political accountability and a reasonable standard for evaluating political coalitions that seek to augment judicial power. Examining the political foundations of judicial power, Lovell (2003, p. 263) points out, "shifts attention away from decisions made by judges to decisions made in the other branches." Whether judicial review is being democratically exercised depends as much on why elected officials empower courts as on how justices exercise that power. Elected officials thwart democracy only when they employ courts to disguise policy choices. They behave within democratic parameters when forming public alliances with courts to pursue a common constitutional vision. The Roosevelt and Truman administrations satisfied this standard for democratic accountability by openly employing a combination of judicial appointments and litigation strategies to improve the status of persons of color in the South. Interested voters could easily discern the position of Democratic presidents on race issues and cast their ballots accordingly.

The fundamental constitutional commitments of contemporary Republican party elites are far more difficult to discern. During the 2004 presidential debates, George Bush refused to provide any clue about the policies his judicial appointees would make other than that they would sustain the use of "under God" in the Pledge of Allegiance and would not protect slavery. Republicans convey sympathy for religious minorities when they vote for such measures as the Religious Freedom Restoration Act, which mandates that states provide exemptions to religious believers from neutral laws. Republicans express the opposite sentiments when they appoint and praise federal justices who insist that states have no obligations to provide such exemptions to religious believers (*Employment Division v. Smith* 1990). Voters concerned with the flag are likely to be confused when Republican presidents first call for bans on flag-burning and then celebrate those justices who declare those prohibitions unconstitutional (*United States v. Eichman* 1990). Accountability is nearly impossible as long as conservatives deny that they are as committed to judicial activism as Great Society liberals. "[T]he continued use of judicial restraint rhetoric by conservatives," Keck (2004, p. 291) points out, "renders it difficult for the American public to express its views on the Rehnquist Court's distinctive constitutional jurisprudence."

The Republican refusal to take responsibility for Republican judicial policy making creates the fundamental democratic problem with Rehnquist Court activism. Holding elected officials responsible for the present course of judicial decision making is not easy when the conservative political sponsors of contemporary judicial conservatives obfuscate their responsibility for rulings protecting gay rights or limiting federal power to prohibit crimes of violence against women. Americans in 1964 were given a relatively clear choice between the party that supported liberal judicial activism and the party that did not (Powe 2000, p. 238). Warren Court activism was at least temporarily vindicated by the landslide Johnson victory. Americans at the turn of the twenty-first century are largely offered misleading cliches about fidelity to the constitution. At no point during recent campaigns have prominent Republican elected officials been asked to reconcile their votes for such measures as the Americans with Disabilities Act with their support for justices who insist crucial provisions of that law are unconstitutional (*Board of Trustees of the University of Alabama v. Garrett 2001*). As a result, Rehnquist Court activism has never been democratically validated. "If no Republican politicians are willing to support the O'Connor [Rehnquist or Scalia] Court's decisions on the campaign trail," Keck (2004, p. 291) concludes, "then the public is denied the opportunity" to influence whether that constitutional vision should be the law of the land and whether that vision ought to be implemented partly by the Supreme Court.

THE NEW PARADIGM

The new paradigm for thinking about judicial power is now fully formed. Its mantra, "judicial review is politically constructed," is replacing previous chants that "judicial review is a deviant institution in American democracy" (Bickel 1962, p. 18). Judicial review is democratically as well as politically constructed. Lovell (2003, p. 31) notes, "judges who act as independent rivals of Congress are almost all the creation of Congress itself, and . . . the powers they exercise have been granted by Congress and remain subject to Congressional revocation." Judicial activism is sponsored by elected officials. Lucas Powe's acclaimed study concludes that the Warren Court "was a functioning part of the Kennedy-Johnson liberalism of the mid and late 1960s" (2000, p. 490). Some constitutional commentators recognize these alliances between justices and elected officials when offering normative accounts of judicial policy making. Jack Balkin & Sanford Levinson (2001, p. 1102) advance a "theory of partisan entrenchment," under which "each party has the political 'right' to entrench its vision of the Constitution in the judiciary if it wins a sufficient number of elections."

Juristocracy is a democratic choice. Legislative majorities in Israel, Canada, New Zealand, and South Africa choose to constitutionalize rights and empower courts to protect those rights. During his victorious 1948 presidential campaign, Truman pledged himself to promote judicial activism on behalf of persons of color. In no instance considered by the five books surveyed above was judicial review foisted upon an unwilling populace. Americans will better grasp the foundations of judicial power in the United States by remembering that the judicial authority to declare laws unconstitutional was first explicitly established by Section 25 of the Judiciary Act of 1789, not by the last paragraphs of *Marbury v. Madison* (1803) (Graber 2003). A presidential candidate who promised to appoint to the federal bench only justices committed to never declaring a law unconstitutional would be electorally slaughtered.

The understanding that judicial review is democratically constructed does not immunize judicial review from democratic challenge. Persons commonly debate the merits of majoritarian and consensus regimes while recognizing that both are democratic (Lijphart 1999). Juridical democracy or juristocracy is likely superior to some forms of democracy and inferior to others. The crucial democratic point is judicial review rarely pits the people against the courts. Political struggles over judicial power are between people who want courts to make certain policy decisions and people who prefer those decisions to be made by other institutions. *The People Themselves* (Kramer 2004a) champions a more limited role for judicial policy making. *The People Rising* (Pertschuk & Schaetzel 1989) celebrates the defeat of a Supreme Court nominee, Judge Robert Bork, who championed a more limited role for judicial policy making. The merits of judicial review lie in the extent to which that practice serves values internal to democracy, rather than in the choice between democratic and some other values. All democratic institutions privilege some people at the expense of others. Whether judicial review is desirable depends on the interests democracies should privilege and whether judicial review privileges those interests in a democratically appropriate manner.

Democratically constructed judicial review may weaken political accountability. Lovell points out that prominent national legislators during the progressive era obscured their responsibility for antilabor policies by blaming justices for adverse decisions. Keck details how contemporary conservatives use a rhetoric of judicial restraint to mask their responsibility for staffing the federal judiciary with justices who have declared more federal laws unconstitutional than any other judicial cohort in American history. Unlike traditional approaches to judicial review, attention to political foundations places legislators at the center of debates over political accountability. Democratically constructed courts are politically accountable. Justices almost always make policy within parameters acceptable to most elected officials and respond to clear changes in political sentiment. Accountability problems result when politicians use courts to confuse voters. Prolabor voters in the progressive era may have supported representatives who condemned courts for antilabor decisions, not fully aware that those representatives made the statutory choices that empowered courts to make promanagement rulings.

Whether alternative institutional arrangements will cure this problem is doubtful. Voters will always have difficulty determining accountability when government is divided and power fragmented. Legislators who cannot use ambiguous language to foist political responsibility on to judges may use ambiguous language to foist political responsibility on to administrative agencies. When elected officials cannot foist political responsibility elsewhere, they often refrain from taking any action. Before the Supreme Court decided *Roe v. Wade* (1973), proponents of legal abortion could not induce state legislators to repeal statutory bans, and opponents of legal abortion could not induce state executives to enforce those prohibitions (Graber 1996). Having courts make policy choices when legislatures refuse to act may be the best institutional means that imperfect democracies have for improving political accountability. If elected officials will not take responsibility for making policy, they can at least be called to account for the policies made by their judicial appointees.

The more serious problem with democratically constructed judicial review is that the wrong groups, interests, and values may be privileged. Courts, like other political institutions, are not neutral between power holders. Peretti and McMahon provide evidence that judicial review augments the power of the president (and national government) at the expense of Congress (and states). Hirschl provides evidence that judicial review privileges the secular elite at the expense of the peasantry. His analysis suggests that both liberals and conservatives thinking about judicial review confront tragic choices. Courts tend to provide more protection for criminal suspects, and less for labor unions, than legislatures do. Judicial review tends to prevent elected officials from making certain invidious discriminations and from redistributing property. The groups whose values and interests are most often promoted by judicial power include the upper-middle class, libertarians, and, to no one's surprise, lawyers.

Alternative political arrangements will not solve this problem of bias. "All forms of political organization," E.E. Schattschneider (1960, p. 69) observes, involve "the mobilization of bias. Some issues are organized into politics while others are organized out." Different democratic institutions privilege different forms of participation, different interests, different values, and, most likely, different elites. Institutional alterations that disempower elite lawyers may do more to empower elite investors than the general populace. Reduced judicial oversight of administrative agencies may do more to increase the power of regulated industries than the public.

The democratic merits of alternative institutional arrangements cannot be assessed on purely procedural grounds. Determining what constitutes adequate representation or diversity requires some assessment of the substantive values that democracies should protect. Whether democratic institutions should privilege neoliberal outcomes depends in part on the merits of neoliberalism as a public philosophy. Professors Peretti, Hirschl, Lovell, McMahon, and Keck have done yeomen work detailing the actual democratic issues at stake when elected officials vest courts with the power to declare laws unconstitutional. Let the real normative debates begin.

APPENDIX: CASES CITED

Board of Trustees of the University of Alabama v. Garrett, 531 U.S. 356 (2001)

Boerne v. Flores, 521 U.S. 507 (1997)

Brown v. Board of Education, 347 U.S. 483 (1954)

Bush v. Gore, 531 U.S. 98 (2000)

Colorado Republican Federal Campaign Committee v. FEC, 518 U.S. 604 (1996)

Dickerson v. United States, 530 U.S. 428 (2000)

Dred Scott v. Sandford, 60 U.S. 393 (1856)

Duplex Printing Press Company v. Deering, 254 U.S. 443 (1921)

Employment Division v. Smith, 494 U.S. 872 (1990)

Ex parte Merryman, 17 F. Cas. 144 (C.C.D. Md. 1861)

Fletcher v. Peck, 10 U.S. 87 (1810)

44 Liquormark, Inc. v. Rhode Island, 517 U.S. 484 (1996)

Furman v. Georgia, 408 U.S. 238 (1972)

Gibbons v. Ogden, 22 U.S. 1 (1824).

Gideon v. Wainwright, 372 U.S. 335 (1963)

Grutter v. Bollinger, 539 U.S. 306 (2003).

In re Debs, 158 U.S. 564 (1894)

Lawrence v. Texas, 539 U.S. 558 (2003)

Lorillard Tobacco Co. v. Reilly, 533 U.S. 525 (2001)

Lucas v. South Carolina Coastal Council, 505 U.S. 1003 (1992)

Marbury v. Madison, 5 U.S. 137 (1803)

McCleskey v. Kemp, 481 U.S. 279 (1987)

McConnell v. FEC, 540 U.S. 93 (2003)

McCulloch v. Maryland, 17 U.S. 316 (1819)

Miranda v. Arizona, 384 U.S. 436 (1966)

NLRB v. Jones and Laughlin Steel Company, 301 U.S. 1 (1937)

NLRB v. Mackey Co., 304 U.S. 333, 345 (1938)

NLRB v. Sands Mfg. Co., 306 U.S. 332 (1939)

Planned Parenthood v. Casey, 505 U.S. 833 (1992)

Pollock v. Farmers' Loan and Trust Co. 158 U.S. 601 (1895)

Printz v. United States, 521 U.S. 898 (1997)

Regents of Univ. of California v. Bakke, 438 U.S. 265 (1978)

Richmond v. J.A. Croson Co., 488 U.S. 469 (1989)

Roe v. Wade, 410 U.S. 113 (1973)

Screws v. United States, 325 U.S. 91 (1945)

Seminole Tribe of Florida v. Florida, 517 U.S. 44 (1996)

Shaw v. Reno, 509 U.S. 630 (1993)

Smith v. Allwright, 321 U.S. 649 (1944)

United States v. E.C. Knight Co., 156 U.S. 1 (1895)

United States v. Eichman, 496 U.S. 310 (1990)

United States v. Lopez, 514 U.S. 549 (1995)

United States v. Morrison, 529 U.S. 598 (2000)

United States v. Nixon, 418 U.S. 683 (1974)

United States v. Virginia, 518 U.S. 515 (1996)

Wabash, St. Louis & Pacific Railway Co. v. Illinois, 118 U.S. 557 (1886)

**The *Annual Review of Political Science* is online at
http://polisci.annualreviews.org**

LITERATURE CITED

Balkin JM, Levinson S. 2001. Understanding the Constitutional Revolution. *Va. Law Rev.* 87:1045–109

Bickel AM. 1962. *The Least Dangerous Branch: The Supreme Court at the Bar of Politics*. Indianapolis: Bobbs-Merrill

Buchanan J. 1897(1857). Third Annual Message. In *A Compilation of the Messages and Papers of the Presidents, Vol. 5*, ed. JD Richardson. Washington, DC: GPO

Colker R, Brudney JJ. 2001. Dissing Congress. *Mich. Law Rev.* 100:80–144

Dahl RA. 2001. Decision-making in a Democracy: The Supreme Court as a National Policymaker. *Emory Law J.* 50:563–82

Devins NE. 1996. *Shaping Constitutional Values: Elected Government, the Supreme Court, and the Abortion Debate*. Baltimore: Johns Hopkins Univ. Press. 193 pp.

Dudziak ML. 2000. *Cold War Civil Rights: Race and the Image of American Democracy*. Princeton: Princeton Univ. Press. 342 pp.

Ferguson T. 1989. Industrial conflict and the coming of the New Deal: The triumph of multinational liberalism in America. In *The Rise and Fall of the New Deal Order, 1930–1980*, ed. S Fraser, G Gestle, pp. 3–31. Princeton: Princeton Univ. Press

Fisher L. 1988. *Constitutional Dialogues: Interpretation as Political Process*. Princeton: Princeton Univ. Press. 320 pp.

Fiss OM. 1989. The law regained. *Cornell Law Rev.* 74:245–55

Forbath W. 1991. *Law and the Shaping of the American Labor Movement*. Cambridge: Harvard Univ. Press

Friedman B. 1993. Dialogue and judicial review. *Mich. Law Rev.* 91:577–682

Gillman H. 2002. How political parties can use the Courts to advance their agendas: Federal Courts in the United States, 1875–1891. *Am. Polit. Sci. Rev.* 96:511–24

Graber MA. 1993. The non-majoritarian difficulty: Legislative deference to the judiciary. *Stud. Am. Polit. Dev.* 7:35–73

Graber MA. 1996. *Rethinking Abortion: Equal Choice, the Constitution and Reproductive Politics*. Princeton: Princeton Univ. Press

Graber MA. 1997. The Clintonification of American Law: Abortion, welfare, and liberal constitutional theory. *Ohio State Law J.* 58:731–818

Graber MA. 1998. Federalist or Friends of Adams: The Marshall Court and Party Politics. *Stud. Am. Polit. Dev.* 12:229–66

Graber MA. 2003. Establishing Judicial Review: Marbury versus The Judiciary Act of 1789. *38 Tulsa Law Rev.* 38:609–50

Hattam V. 1993. *Labor Visions and State Power*. Princeton: Princeton Univ. Press

Hirschl R. 2004. *Toward Juristocracy: The Origins and Consequences of the New Constitutionalism*. Cambridge: Harvard Univ. Press

Keck TM. 2004. *The Most Activist Supreme Court in History: The Road to Modern Judicial Conservatism*. Chicago: Univ. Chicago Press

Kirkpatrick DD. 2004. Conservative Groups Differ on Bush Words on Marriage. *The New York Times*, Jan. 22:A24

Klinkner PA, Smith RM. 1999. *The Unsteady March: The Rise and Decline of Racial Equality in America*. Chicago: Univ. Chicago Press. 424 pp.

Kramer LD. 2004a. *The People Themselves: Popular Constitutionalism and Judicial Review*. New York: Oxford

Kramer LD. 2004b. "Popular Constitutionalism, circa 2004. *Calif. Law Rev.* 92:959–1011

Levinson SV. 2003. Redefining the Center: Liberal Decisions from a Conservative Court. *The Village Voice*, July 2–8, p. 38

Lijphart A. 1999. *Patterns of Democracy: Government Forms and Performance in Thirty-Six Countries.* New Haven: Yale Univ. Press

Lincoln A. 1953a [1861]. First Inaugural Address. In *The Collected Works of Abraham Lincoln*, ed. RP Basler, 4:262–71. New Brunswick: Rutgers

Lincoln A. 1953b[1858]. Mr. Lincoln's Reply, Fifth Debate with Stephen A. Douglas, at Galesburg, Illinois. In *The Collected Works of Abraham Lincoln*, ed. RP Basler, 3:219–37. New Brunswick: Rutgers

Lovell GI. 2003. *Legislative Deferrals: Statutory Ambiguity, Judicial Power, and American Democracy.* New York: Cambridge

Madison J, Hamilton A, Jay J. 1987 [1787-88]. *The Federalist Papers*, ed. I Kramnick. New York: Penguin

McMahon KJ. 2004. *Reconsidering Roosevelt on Race: How the Presidency Paved the Road to Brown.* Chicago: Univ. Chicago Press

Murphy WF. 1961. In His Own Image: Mr. Chief Justice Taft and Supreme Court Appointments. In *1961: The Supreme Court Review*, ed. PB Kurland, pp. 159–93. Chicago: Univ. Chicago Press

Page BI. 1990. The rejection of Bork preserved the Court's limited popular constituencies. *Northwest. Univ. Law Rev.* 84:1024–30

Peretti TJ. 1999. *In Defense of a Political Court.* Princeton: Princeton Univ. Press

Pertschuk M, Schaetzel W. 1989. *The People Rising: The Campaign Against the Bork Nomination.* New York: Thunder's Mouth Press

Pickerill JM, Clayton CW. 2004. The Rehnquist Court and the Political Dynamics of Federalism. *Perspect. Polit.* 2:233–48

Powe LA Jr. 2000. *The Warren Court and American Politics.* Cambridge: Harvard Univ. Press

Schattschneider EE. 1960. *The Semisovereign People: A Realist's View of Democracy in America.* Hinsdale, IL: Dryden

Schnapper E. 1985. Affirmative action and the legislative history of the Fourteenth Amendment. *Va. Law Rev.* 71:753–98

Schwartz B. 1993. *A History of the Supreme Court.* New York: Oxford Univ. Press

Sherman EA. 2004. Justice's Anti-Social Stand Dubious. *The Boston Herald*, Oct. 3:26

Tushnet M. 1999. *Taking the Constitution Away from the Courts.* Princeton: Princeton Univ. Press

Waldron J. 1999. *Law and Disagreement.* New York: Oxford Univ. Press. 332 pp.

Whittington KE. 2001a. The Political Foundations of Judicial Supremacy. In *Constitutional Politics: Essays on Constitution Making, Maintenance, and Change*, ed. SA Barber, RP George, pp. 261–97. Princeton: Princeton Univ. Press

Whittington KE. 2001b. Taking what they give us: Explaining the Court's Federalism Offensive. *Duke Law J.* 51:477–521

Wood GI. 1991. *The Radicalism of the American Revolution.* New York: Knopf

SUBJECT INDEX

A

Abortion politics, 137, 430
Academic journals
  considering relevance in
  evaluating submissions,
  42
Academic promotions
  considering real-world
  relevance in, 42
Academic surveys in public
  opinion research,
  300–14
  country coverage in
  cross-national research
  programs, 303–9
  features of cross-national
  survey programs, 312–13
Acquiescence bias, 323
Action models
  and the logic of
  uncertainty, 346–47
"Adjustment and anchoring"
  heuristic, 7
Adversary in the September
  11 attacks
  failure to understand the
  nature of, 150–51
  nature of causing U.S.
  policy makers to miss
  opportunities to counter
  the known threat, 165–66
Afghanistan, 5, 15, 152, 155,
  157, 162, 166
African National Congress,
  139
Afrobarometer, 310, 330
  Sampling Protocol for, 316
After action reviews
  and the logic of
  uncertainty, 344
Agenda-setting

role for the European
  Commission, 373
Agent impact
  in the canonical
  principal-agent model,
  205
Agent-based simulation, 350
"Aggressive uncuriosity," 18
Airpower
  coercive, 33
Al Qaeda threat, 129–30, 145
  warnings prior to the
  September 11 attacks,
  151–52
Albright, Madeleine, 164
Algeria, 15, 139–40
Allende, Salvador, 5
Allgemeinen
  Bevölkerungsumfrage
  der
  Sozialwissenschaften
  (ALLBUS), 301–2
Allocation deadlines, 342
Alsace loss, 11
Alternative scenarios
  long-term policy analysis
  and the generation of,
  351–52
America, 15
  access to as a scarce global
  resource, 112
  associational life in, 228
  development of interest
  group politics in, 251–67
  looking foolish and brutal,
  164
  "traditional"
  migrant-receiving by, 110
American Bill of Rights, 89
American Constitution, 77
  architects of, 264

American Enterprise
  Institute, 41
*American Journal of Political
  Science*, 370
American National Election
  Studies (ANES), 122,
  301
American Patriot Movement,
  130
American policy makers
  missing opportunities to
  counter known threats
  prior to September 11,
  153–66
  bureaucratic pathologies,
  156–62
  cognitive failures, 153–56
  limits on policy makers,
  162–64
  nature of the adversary,
  165–66
American Political Science
  Association, 39
*American Political Science
  Review*, 2, 43, 370
American Red Cross (ARC),
  340
The American Voter, 301
Americans for Democratic
  Action, 210
AmeriCorps, 229, 237
Analogies
  in assessing domain, 9
Anchoring
  See "Adjustment and
  anchoring" heuristic
ANES
  See American National
  Election Studies
Anglican Church of Kenya,
  134–35

Anglo-French Entente, 5
Annan, Kofi, 288n
Anthrax attacks, 338
Anti-Americanism, 166
Antiapartheid movement, 182
Anti-immigrant political
    campaigns, 185, 187
Apartheid, 137, 139
Apocalyptic literature, 130
Application issues
    See Theoretical
    applications of theory to
    policy
Appointments Commission,
    92
Apprenticeships
    in successful deliberation,
    64
"Appropriateness"
    logic of, 365
ARC
    See American Red Cross
Architecture
    of the mind, 58
Arguing
    logic of, 387
Aspirations
    in assessing domain, 5–7
Associational life
    in America, 228
Asymmetry in the canonical
    principal-agent model
    in information, 205
    in preferences, 205–6
ATF
    See Bureau of Alcohol,
    Tobacco, and Firearms
At-home civil society actors
    in cross-border migrant
    political power
    relationships, 190–91
Attitudes
    See Nonattitudes;
    Perception; Public
    attitudes
"Attitudes to Europe" survey,
    300

Attlee, Clement, 78
Attrition of interest groups
    new leverage on, 261–64
Australia, 93
    "traditional"
    migrant-receiving by, 110
Austria
    Freedom Party in, 104

B

"Back translation," 320–21
Backward induction based on
    common knowledge
    in the canonical
    principal-agent model,
    206
Bank of England, 74
Bankers and credible
    commitment
    moral hazards for
    principals, 220–22
Baptist Bible Fellowship, 135
Bargaining
    See "Strategic bargaining";
    Ultimatum bargaining
Base-closing commission
    a moral hazard for the
    principals, 222–23
Behavioral economics, 2
Behavioral theory of choice,
    3, 17
Berger, Sandy, 154, 164
Berlin Wall
    fall of, 280
Berryhill, Michael, 239
BES
    See British Election
    Studies
Between-country inequality
    in per capita incomes, 409
Beyond the Nation State, 272,
    279, 281, 284, 286,
    288–89
Bias, 319
    acquiescence, 323
    of interest groups, new
    leverage on, 261–64

"mobilization of," 448
    social acceptability, 324
    See also "Heuristic and
    biases" research
Bicameral democracies, 93
    and legislative politics,
    374–76
Bickel, Alexander, 425–26
Bilateral bargaining, 216–17
bin Laden, Osama, 130, 148n,
    152, 155
Bismarck, Otto von, 37
Blair, Tony, 91
Bonding activities, 232
Bork, Robert, 447
Bosnia and Kosovo, 28, 34
Bowling Alone, 121
Bowtie models, 345–46
    of emergency operations
    center, 347
    and the logic of
    uncertainty, 345–46
"Bracero" temporary worker
    program, 110
"Brain drain" problem, 106
Brazil/Japan migration
    system, 102
Bridging activities, 232
Bringing Rights Home, 88
Britain, 15
    Constitutional reform in,
    73–95
    puzzle of the Constitution,
    94–95
British Election Studies
    (BES), 301
*British Journal of National
    Front Studies*, 122
*British Journal of Political
    Science*, 370
British Social Attitudes
    survey, 301
Brookings Institution, 41
Brown v. Board of Education,
    436
Brzezinski, Zbigniew, 9
Bundesrat, 372

reforming, 93
Bureau of Alcohol, Tobacco, and Firearms (AFT), 340
Bureaucratic pathologies after the September 11 attacks, 156–62
  continued CIA weakness, 156–58
  FBI shortcomings, 158–60
  inadequate institutional management, 161–62
  lack of domestic response, 161
  military resistance to action, 160–61
Bureaucratic pathologies before the September 11 attacks, 148–49
Burger Court, 442
Bush, George H.W., 9
Bush, George W., 5–7, 13, 145, 148n, 153–55, 191n, 341–42, 399, 430, 443, 445

C

California's anti-immigrant initiative, 108, 187
Canada, 93, 106
  "traditional" migrant-receiving by, 110
Candidate Countries Eurobarometer (CC-EB), 300, 317
CAPI/CATI
  See Computer assisted personal/telephone interviewing
Capital account liberalization, 411
Capital flows
  cross-national differences in, 403
  private, and global trade, 402
  See also Private capital flows

Carter, Jimmy, 4, 9
Catholic Church, 183, 241
Catholicism
  feminist, 183
Catholics for the Right to Choose, 183
Cato Institute, 41
Causality, 32–33
CC-EB
  See Candidate Countries Eurobarometer
Center for American Women and Politics
  National Education for Women leadership program, 236
Center for the Study of Developing Societies, 310
Central America, 29
Change and continuity in interest group politics, 254–58
  "doing history" and employing multidimensional methods, 257–58
  emergence of interest groups in national politics, 257
  underestimating group mobilization in the Progressive Era, 255–56
  See also International change
Changed Voting Changed Politics, 86
Chaos
  the edge of, and the logic of uncertainty, 345
Chief executives
  power of, 207
Child labor
  result of globalization, 399
Chile, 5, 12, 137
China, 31, 106, 136, 322, 419
Choices

behavioral theory of, 3, 17
  framing, 11
  processes of making, 56
Chomsky, Noam, 163n
Christian Identity movement, 128, 130
Christian Reconstructionism movement, 130
Christian Right Studies, 122
Churchill, Winston, 78
CIA weakness, 145, 340
  before the September 11 attacks, continual, 156–58
CIS Index
  See *U.S. Congressional Committee Hearings Index (CIS Index)*
Citizen input, 50
  deliberative democracy encouraging greater, 50–54
Citizen values
  enhancement of, 232–35
Citizens' Councils, 241
Citizens in transnational civil society, 177–83
  ideological affinity versus counterpart-based coalitions, 182–83
  importance of a transnational civil society for transnational citizenship, 178–79
  most cross-border networks and coalitions not constituting transnational movements, 179–80
  past internationalisms illuminating the meaning of transnational citizenship, 181–82
  shared targets not necessarily generating shared political community, 180–81
Citizenship
  cross-border, 173

"flexible," 190
good, 227
low-intensity, 193
"world," 176
Citizenship and civic
    engagement, 227–45
    civic engagement and the
        good citizen, 242–45
    civic participation as a
        cure-all, 229–32
    civic participation not a
        panacea, 232–42
    and the enhancement of
        citizen values, 232–35
    See also "Transnational
        citizenship"
Citizenship and Immigration
    Services
    See U.S. Immigration and
        Naturalization Service
Civic divide
    versus political divide,
        235–39
Civic participation as a
    cure-all, 229–32
    impact on civic values and
        attitudes, 230–31
    impact on democracy and
        society, 231–32
    impact on political
        behavior, 231
Civic participation not a
    panacea, 232–42
    the civic versus political
        divide, 235–39
    diversity and the
        enhancement of citizen
        values, 232–25
    the importance of group
        goals, 239–42
Civic values and attitudes,
    230–31
Civil liberties
    failure of intelligence
        agencies to respect, 149,
        160
    organizations

promoting, 107
Civil Rights Act of 1964, 133
Civil society
    "transmission belt" model
        of, 242
Civil society actors
    at-home, in cross-border
        migrant political power
        relationships, 190–91
Clarke, Richard, 152, 154,
    162
"Clash of civilizations," 31,
    121
Clayton Act, 433–35
Clinton, Bill, 145, 148n, 155,
    161, 163, 229
"Closed" questions
    standardized, 298, 324
Coalitions
    counterpart-based, versus
        ideological affinity,
        182–83
    justices as members of,
        428–33
Coase Theorem, 17
Codecision
    power of, 81
Coercive airpower, 33
Cognitive failures
    causing U.S. policy makers
        to miss opportunities to
        counter the known al
        Qaeda threat, 153–56
Cognitive heuristics, 51, 55,
    57
Cognitive problems
    for analysts and policy
        makers before the
        September 11 attacks,
        147–48
Cold War, 29–31, 109
    end of, 280
"Collective action" problems,
    51
Colombia, 106
Comitology committees, 388,
    390

Commercial polls, 298–99
Committee of Permanent
    Representatives, 367
Committee on Standards in
    Public Life, 94
Common knowledge
    backward induction based
        on, 206
Communicative action
    theory of, 387
Communism, 31
Communist Party, 299
Comparative Study of
    Electoral Systems
    (CSES), 301, 325
Competitive testing, 367
Competitive voluntarism, 240
Completeness
    of a good theory, 27
Complex adaptive systems,
    345
Complex systems
    increasing vulnerability to
        extreme events, 338–39
Complexity theory, 349
Computational simulations,
    353
    networks and, 349–51
Computer assisted
    personal/telephone
    interviewing
    (CAPI/CATI), 314
Conduct of foreign policy
    characteristics of a good
        theory, 26–28
    contribution of theory to,
        25–34
    theoretical applications of
        theory to policy, 28–34
    types of knowledge needed
        by policy makers, 25–26
Conflict avoidance, 234
Congressional Information
    Service, 256
ConPlan
    See United States
        Government Interagency

Domestic Terrorism
Concept of Operations
Plan
Conseil Constitutionnel, 77
Consequences
of immigration, 102–6
Consequentiality
logic of, 387
Consistency
logical, of a good theory,
26–27
Constitution Unit, 78–79, 86
Constitutional Convention,
388
*Constitutional Futures: A
History of the Next Ten
Years*, 78
Constitutional Reform Act,
75
Constitutional reform in
Britain, 73–95
the British Constitution as
a puzzle, 94–95
the Constitution and
limited government,
80–81
devolution and
quasi-federalism, 81–85
electoral reform and
proportional
representation, 85–87
end of the historic
Constitution, 73–78
the Human Rights Act and
parliamentary
sovereignty, 87–91
the referendum, 78–80
reform of the House of
Lords, 91–94
"Constitutional Treaty," 280
Constitutional Update, 77
Constitutionalization, 386
Constraints
in periodizing interest
groups in American
politics, 261
Construction

of judicial review, 425–50
Constructivism, 358, 366
pragmatic, 285
and the reshaping of
European identities and
preferences, 365–68
Contentious politics
literature, 124n
Contextualization, 321
Continuity
See Change and continuity
in interest group politics
Contract laborers
importing, 104
Convention on the Future of
Europe, 389–90
Cooperation
in principal-agency theory,
217–18
Correlations
between globalization
flows and policies, 407
Côte d'Ivoire
civil war in, 129
Council of Europe, 87, 367
Council of Ministers, 372,
374, 386
Council on Foreign Relations,
39n
Counterpart-based coalitions
versus ideological affinity,
182–83
Counterterrorism, 145, 158,
160–62, 166
Counterterrorism Support
Group, 162
Counterterrorist Center
(CTC), 157
Countries of origin
immigration's effects on,
105–6
Country coverage
in cross-national research
programs, 303–9
Court of First Instance, 373
Court of Justice of the EU, 87
Court-packing plan, 436

Coverage
in cross-national public
opinion research, 315–16
Covert action, 162
Credible commitment, 224
of investors and bankers,
220–22
Cross-border citizenship, 173
Cross-border migrant politics,
183–91
direct transnational
political enfranchisement,
183–85
flexible forms of
transnational citizenship,
189–90
indirect transnational
political enfranchisement,
185
power relationships
between organized
migrants and at-home
civil society actors,
190–91
three main forms of
transnational citizenship,
188–89
transnational citizenship
versus "long-distance
nationalism," 186–87
transnational versus
translocal membership,
187–88
Cross-border networks and
coalitions
defining, 172
not constituting
transnational movements,
179–80
Cross-border voting rights,
184
Cross-national research,
314–24
country coverage in, 303–9
differences in average
tariffs and financial
openness, 406

differences in trade and capital flows, 403
equivalence of meaning, 320–24
features of surveys, 312–13
intellectual assumptions of, 325–26
political efficacy vignettes, 323
quality issues, 314–20
"Crowe Commission," 150
CSES
See Comparative Study of Electoral Systems
CTC
See Counterterrorist Center
Cuban missile crisis, 4, 219
Cultural software, 58
Culture
functions of, 126
as a motive for political engagement, 132
motives for religion in political life, 125–31
"Cumulative causation" theory of, 102

D

Decision making, 15
"recognition-primed," 344–45
Declaration of Independence, 441
Defense of the Realm Act, 299
de Gaulle, Charles, 279, 360
Delegation
in executive politics, 376–78
Deliberation, 386
characteristics of, 54–60
difficulties of, 62
institutionalizing, 50
Deliberation Day, 242–43
Deliberative democracy in practice, 49–65, 380, 386

encouraging greater citizen input, 50–54
mechanisms of successful deliberation, 63–64
product of deliberative talk, 60–62
Deliberative supranationalism, 381
Democracies
expanding, 402
impact of civic participation on, 231–32
institutions of, 34
liberal, 51
organizational, 241
See also Deliberative democracy in practice
Democratic Unionist Party, 82
Department for Constitutional Affairs, 89
Department of Defense (DOD), 340
Department of Health and Human Services (HHS), 340, 412
Department of Housing and Urban Development (HUD), 340
Department of Transportation (DOT), 340
"Desert One" hostage rescue mission, 160
Determinants of international migration, 100–2
Determinism, 58
Deterrence
theory of, 29
Deutsch, Karl, 291
Development of interest group politics
in America, 251–67
Devolution
in Britain, 81–85
challenging integrity of the United Kingdom, 83
Diagnosis

in applying theory to policy, 29–31
Diasporic nationalisms, 186n
Diffuse reciprocity, 291
Direct transnational political enfranchisement, 183–85
in cross-border migrant politics, 183–85
cross-border voting rights, 184
elected transnational authorities, 185
legislative representation of expatriates, 185
migrants voting where they are not citizens, 184–85
Director of Central Intelligence, 151
Disaster
defining, 338
Disaster management, 335–54
coping with uncertainty, 336–39
future strategies, 353–54
the logic of uncertainty, 344–47
managing uncertainty in complex environments, 347–52
policy vs. practice in maintaining security, 339–43
public values in uncertain environments, 352–53
risk and security in, 335–54
Disconnect between IR theory and policy, 34–41
bridging by division of labor, 40–41
different agendas of scholars and policy makers, 37–38
generality and abstraction of IR theory, 34–35
limited explanatory power

of available theories,
35–37
professionalism in the
profession, 38–39
Discretion
in executive politics,
376–78
"Disinformation," 151
*The Dismal Fate of New
Nations*, 290
Dispositional systems, 56
Distrust
mutual, 240
Diversity
and the enhancement of
citizen values, 232–35
Division of labor, 40–41
gulf growing wider, 40–41
trickle-down model, 40
DOD
See Department of Defense
DOJ
See U.S. Department of
Justice
Domain assessment, 3–11
analogies, 9
aspirations, 5–7
emotion, 10–11
heuristics, 7–9
status quo as reference
point, 4–5
"Domain of application"
approach, 367
Domains
of gain or loss, 3
of transnational rights and
membership, 192
Domestic interest groups
in immigration policy
making, 106–7
Domestic response
lack of before the
September 11 attacks, 161
Dominican Republic, 106
"Domino" theory, 15, 29
DOT
See Department of

Transportation
Douglas, Stephen, 425–26
Douglass, Frederick, 441
Dred Scott decision, 77,
425–26, 433
Durkheim, Émile, 125, 131
Dynamism in interest groups,
259–61
nationalism and
professionalism, 260
number, 259–60
opportunities and
constraints, 261
variety, 260

E

East Asia Barometer, 310
EC
See European Community
ECB
See European Central Bank
ECJ
See European Court of
Justice
Economic flows
international, 402–4
Economic globalization,
400
Economic integration
global, 101, 401
Economics
behavioral, 2
psychological, 2
The Economists' Voice, 43
Eden, Anthony, 4
EEC
See European Economic
Community
EEC Treaty, 360, 375
Efficiency tradeoffs
in the canonical
principal-agent model,
206
EFSA
See European Food Safety
Agency
Einstein, Albert, 27

Eisenhower, Dwight D.,
14–15
Elected transnational
authorities, 185
Electoral Commission, 75, 79
Electoral reform in Britain
and proportional
representation, 85–87
Electoral Reform Society, 79
El Salvador, 106
EMEA
See European Agency for
the Evaluation of
Medicinal Products
Emergency operations centers
bowtie model of, 346–47
Emotional factors
in assessing domain, 10–11
Empirical law, 25
Encyclopedia of Associations,
254–56, 260
Endowment effect, 17
The English Constitution, 77
Enhancement of citizen
values
diversity and, 232–35
Entebbe raid, 9
Entrenchment
of judicial review, 438–46
EP
See European Parliament
EPA
See U.S. Environmental
Protection Agency
"Epistemic communities"
of professionals, 285
Equilibrium prediction
subgame-perfect, 216
Equivalence of meaning
in cross-national research,
320–24
ESS
See European Social
Survey
Euratom, 359
Euro
Britain's adherence to, 78

Eurobarometer, 105, 300, 317, 320
European Agency for the Evaluation of Medicinal Products (EMEA), 378
European Central Bank (ECB), 281, 376
European Coal and Steel Community, 278, 293, 358
European Commission, 300, 364, 366
    agenda-setting role for, 373
European Communities Act, 81, 94
European Community (EC), 5, 78, 94, 358–59
European Convention on Human Rights, 75, 87–88, 90
European Court of Human Rights, 108
European Court of Justice (ECJ), 361, 373, 376, 379
European Economic Community (EEC), 277–79, 300, 359
European Employment Strategy, 390
European Food Safety Agency (EFSA), 378
European integration, 358–68
    constructivism and the reshaping of European identities and preferences, 365–68
    integration theory today, 368
    intergovernmentalism and liberal intergovernmentalism, 360–62
    neofunctionalism, 359–60
    "new institutionalisms," rational choice and historical, 362–64

in world politics, 277–81
European Journal of Political Science, 370
European Monetary System, 360
European Parliament (EP), 80–81, 92, 364
European Parliamentary Elections Act, 74
European Social Survey (ESS), 310, 315, 317, 319–20, 327–28
European Union (EU), 175, 195, 281
    challenging integrity of the United Kingdom, 83
    citizenship norms in, 367
    Committee of Permanent Representatives, 367
    common refugee and asylum policies within, 111
    Court of Justice, 87
    Open Method of Coordination, 358, 388–90
    promise of, 380
    Stability and Growth Pact, 385
    Structural Funds, 382–83
    as "supranational," 177
European Union (EU) as a polity
    governance approach to, 379–91
European Union (EU) policy making in comparative perspective, 368–79
    the horizontal separation of powers with the EU as a federal system, 371–73
    the vertical separation of powers, 373–79
European Union Politics, 370
"Europeanization," 384
Euro-zone, 377
Evaluation

in applying theory to policy, 33–34
Evidence-based medicine, 327
Executive Order #13, 284, 341
Executive politics
    delegation and discretion, 376–78
Exodus metaphor, 141
Expatriates
    legislative representation of, 185
Expected utility theory, 3
Explanatory power
    of available theories, limitations in, 35–37
    of a good theory, 27
Extreme events
    increasing vulnerability of complex systems to, 338–39

F
Face-to-face surveys, 298
Falwell, Jerry, 123, 128–29, 133
FBI shortcomings, 145, 340
    before the September 11 attacks, 158–60
FDA
    See U.S. Food and Drug Administration
FDI
    See Foreign direct investment
Federal Emergency Management Agency (FEMA), 340
Federal Reserve Board, 221
Federal systems
    EU as, 371–73
Federal Trade Commission (FTC), 208, 210
Federalism
    "executive," 84
    resisted by the United

Kingdom, 83, 93
See also Quasi-federalism
The Federalist Papers, 264,
428
FEMA
See Federal Emergency
Management Agency
Feminist Catholicism, 183
Financial openness
cross-national differences
in, 406
global policy changes in,
405
Financial openness index
(FOI), 404–5
FIOB
See Oaxacan Indigenous
Binational Front (FIOB)
First International, 181
Fiscal burden
imposed by immigrants
where they settle, 103–4
"Flexible" citizenship, 190
FOI
See Financial openness
index
"Force of the better
argument," 54
Forced labor
result of globalization, 399
Foreign Affairs, 39, 42, 277
Foreign direct investment
(FDI), 402
Foreign economic policy,
404–7
Foreign policy
contribution of theory to
the conduct of, 25–34
Foreign Policy, 39
Foreign Policy Studies group,
41
France, 11, 15, 93, 148, 190,
299, 320
National Front in, 104
Franco-Prussian War, 37
Frankfurter, Felix, 437,
439–40

Free trade
protesting, 399
Smith/Ricardo theory of,
27, 29
Freedom of Information Act,
75
Freedom Party
in Austria, 104
Freedoms
U.S.A. Patriot Act
threatening, 336, 352–53
Freeh, Louis, 151, 160
Friendly fire, 147
Friends of the Earth, 179
FTC
See Federal Trade
Commission (FTC)
Full Gospel Church, 126–27,
133–34
Functional concerns
holding the United
Kingdom together, 83
"Functional-equivalence"
procedure for
measurement, 322
Functionalism
linking with integration
studies, 272
Future strategies
regarding risk, security,
and disaster management,
353–54
Futurology, 78

G

Gallipoli campaign, 149
Gallup, George, 298
Gallup polls, 299
Game theory, 16, 36, 216–18,
369
GAO
See General Accounting
Office (GAO)
Garvey, Marcus, 181
Gaullist revolt, 372
General Accounting Office
(GAO), 340

General Agreement on Tariffs
and Trade, 293
General Social Survey (GSS),
301, 314, 319, 330
General theories, 35
Generality
sacrificing, 36
Generality and abstraction
of IR theory, 34–35
Generalized reciprocity, 230
Germany, 5, 7, 14, 28, 93,
146, 292
Nazi, 240, 290
See also Turkey/Germany
migration system
Gideon v. Wainwright, 433
Gilbert and Sullivan, 94
Gini coefficients
global, 408–9
Global Attitudes Surveys, 311
Global Barometers, 302–310
Global civil society, 177
Global Compact, 286
Global economic integration,
101
"Global ethnography," 189
Global Gini coefficients
and per capita incomes,
408–9
Global justice movement, 183
Global metropoles
creation of, 108
Global poverty
and inequality within
countries, 413
Global privatization revenues,
417
Global trade
and private capital flows,
402
Globalization, 319, 368–69
backlash against, 99
challenging integrity of the
United Kingdom, 83
and differences in per
capita incomes between
countries, 407–12

economic, 400
"from above," 173
"from below," 171
increasing al Qaeda's
potency, 165
and inequality within
countries, 412–16, 419
measuring, 402–7
results of, 399
of survey research, 298
Globalization and
government spending,
416–19
the size of government and
privatization, 417
Globalization of public
opinion research,
297–331
brief history, 298–314
categories of evidence
about treatment, 328
intellectual assumptions of
cross-national surveys,
325–26
methodological issues in
cross-national research,
314–24
proposed weighting of
sample surveys, 328
survey-related web sites,
330–31
Glorious Revolution of 1688,
76
Goals
See Group goals
Good citizenship, 227
Good theories
characteristics of, 26–28
clarity of, 28
completeness of, 27
dealing with a major
problem, 27
explanatory power of, 27
logical consistency of,
26–27
prescriptive richness of,
27–28

Governance
legitimate, 390
multi-level, and EU policy
networks, 382–85
Governance approach to the
EU as a polity, 379–91
argument, persuasion, and
the "deliberative turn,"
387–90
governing without
government, 381–82
Governance capacity
and democratic legitimacy,
385–87
The Governance of England,
74
Government
governing without, 381–82
limited, in Britain, 80–81
role in international
economic integration,
399–420
Government of Wales Act, 74
Government spending
and globalization, 416–19
the size of government and
privatization, 417
Government-sponsored polls,
299–300
Great Depression, 261
Great Society, 441, 444–45
Greater London Authority
(Referendum) Act, 74
Greenpeace, 179
Group diversity, 235
Group goals
the importance of, 239–42
Group mobilization in the
Progressive Era
underestimating, 255–56
"Groupthink," 147
Group-threat theories, 105
GSS
See General Social Survey
Guatemala, 106
Guestworker migration, 101
Guevara, Che, 181

H
Haas, Ernst B., 271–94, 359
on European integration,
277–81
intellectual orientation of,
273–77
on international change,
281–88
on nationalism, 288–93
Haas, Peter, 275, 277, 285,
288
Habermas, Jürgen, 387–89
Hamas, 130
Heckscher-Ohlin model of
international trade, 104
Heckscher-Ohlin-Samuelson
(HOS) model, 401, 412,
414
Heritage Foundation, 41
Heterogeneous groups, 234
"Heuristic and biases"
research, 7–8
Heuristics
in assessing domain, 7–9
HHS
See Department of Health
and Human Services
Historic Constitution
end of in Britain, 73–78
History of global public
opinion research,
298–314
academic surveys, 300–14
commercial polls, 298–99
government-sponsored
polls, 299–300
Hobbes, Thomas, 273, 287
Holmes, Sherlock, 139
Home Rule, 82
Homeland defense, 164
Homogeneous groups, 234
HOS
See Heckscher-Ohlin-
Samuelson
model
Host-state economies
immigration affecting, 103

"Hot washes," 344
House of Commons, 92
House of Lords
  reforming, 80, 91–94
House of Lords Act, 75
HUD
  See Department of Housing
    and Urban Development
Human capital
  loss of, 106
*Human Development Report
  2002*, 408
Human Rights Act, 75, 88,
    90, 94
  in Britain, and
    parliamentary
    sovereignty, 87–91
Humanitarian considerations,
    102, 109
Huntington, Samuel, 31–32,
    121
Hussein, Saddam, 5, 30

I

Identification of loss aversion,
    12–16
  loss-aversion effects cf.
    artifacts, 13
  loss-aversion effects cf.
    rational decisions, 14–16
  measuring loss aversion in
    the field, 13–14
Identities and equivalencies
  method of, 329
Identity
  motives for religion in
    political life, 125–31
"Identity-equivalence"
  procedure for
  measurement, 321
Ideological affinity
  versus counterpart-based
    coalitions, 182–83
ILO
  See International Labor
    Organization
Imagination

"failure of," 153–54
IMF
  See International Monetary
    Fund
Immigration consequences,
    102–6
  affecting the host-state
    economies, 103
  altering the size and
    structure of
    receiving-state
    populations, 103
  effects on countries of
    origin, 105–6
  imposing a net fiscal
    burden where they settle,
    103–4
  perceived negative
    consequences, 104–5
  posing security threats, 104
Immigration controls, 99
Immigration and
    Naturalization Service
    (INS), 340
Immigration policy making,
    106–10
  domestic interest groups,
    106–7
  international factors,
    108–10
  political institutions, 107–8
  significance of, 110–12
Imperatives
  "moral-cognitive," 292
*In Defense of a Political
  Court*, 429, 430
In the Shadow of Power, 38
Incentives in congressional
  oversight
  congressional control
    through, 209–10
  congressional control
    without, 214–16
  limited impact of, 212–14
  modeling "multiple
    principals," 213–14
  resistance at the

EPA, 212–13
  structure and the limits of
    incentives, 213
  tradeoffs in, 204–5
Independent Commission on
  the Voting System, 85
India, 106, 419
Indirect transnational political
  enfranchisement
  in cross-border migrant
    politics, 185
Indochina, 29
Induction based on common
  knowledge
  backward, in the canonical
    principal-agent model,
    206
Inequality between countries
  in per capita incomes, 409
Inequality within countries
  and global poverty, 413
  and globalization, 412–16
  within-country inequalities
    by level of development,
    414–15
Inevitability of intelligence
  failures
  before the September 11
    attacks, 146–51
Information asymmetry
  in the canonical
    principal-agent model,
    205
Information shortcuts, 51
Initiative
  resting with a unified
    principal in the canonical
    principal-agent model,
    206
"Inman Report," 150
Inquiry
  continuous process of, 353
INS
  See Immigration and
    Naturalization Service
Institute for Concrete Social
  Research, 299

Institutional management
  before the September 11
  attacks, inadequate,
  161–62
"Institutionalisms"
  rational choice and
  historical, 362–64
Institutionalization, 368
  of deliberation, 50
"Integrated" transnational
  participation, 189
Integration studies
  linking with functionalism,
  272
Integration theory, 368
Intellectual contributions of
  Ernst B. Haas, 271–94
  European integration,
  277–81
  intellectual orientation,
  273–77
  international change,
  281–88
  on nationalism, 288–93
Intelligence failures before
  the September 11
  attacks, 149, 152
  bureaucratic pathologies,
  148–49
  cognitive problems for
  analysts and policy
  makers, 147–48
  inevitability of, 146–51
  nature of the adversary,
  150–51
  political limits on effective
  policy, 149–50
Intensities
  of transnational rights and
  membership, 192
Interest group attrition, 263
Interest group politics
  development of in
  America, 251–67
  parties and interest groups
  as interwoven systems of
  representation, 264–66

periodizing interest groups
  in American politics,
  259–64
recognizing patterns and
  transformations, 266–67
reviving interest group
  research, 252–54
studying change and
  continuity, 254–58
Interest group research,
  251–54
  reviving, 252–54
Interest groups in America,
  259–61
  nationalism and
  professionalism in, 260
  number of, 259–60
  opportunities and
  constraints in, 261
  variety of, 260
Intergovernmentalism
  and liberal
  intergovernmentalism,
  360–62
"Intermestic" phenomena,
  108
International Affairs
  Fellowships, 39n
International change, 283–87
  alternatives to realism and
  idealism, 286–87
  how voluntary cooperation
  occurs, 283–84
  kinds of institutional
  arrangements that foster
  cooperation, 284
  organizational learning
  promoted by scientific
  knowledge and by the
  involvement of experts,
  285
  the role of actor cognition,
  284–85
  in world politics, 281–88
International Criminal Court,
  175
International economic

flows, 402–4
  cross-national differences
  in trade and capital flows,
  403
  global trade and private
  capital flows, 402
International economic
  integration, inequality
  globalization and
  differences in per capita
  incomes between
  countries, 407–12
  globalization and
  government spending,
  416–19
  globalization and
  inequality within
  countries, 412–16
  measuring globalization,
  402–7
  and the role of government,
  399–420
International factors
  in immigration policy
  making, 108–10
International Labor
  Organization (ILO), 276,
  282
International migration
  determinants of, 100–2
International Monetary Fund
  (IMF), 293, 411–18
International Organization
  special issue, 285
International politics
  neo-realist theory of, 35
International relations (IR),
  272
  altering the prevailing
  norms of the academic IR
  discipline, 41–43
  contribution of theory to
  the conduct of foreign
  policy, 25–34
  disconnect between theory
  and policy, 34–41
  mainstream theories

of, 358, 368
relationship between
  theory and policy in,
  23–43
International Social Survey
  Program (ISSP), 302,
  317, 320
International solidarity
  ideological affinity versus
  counterpart-based
  coalitions, 182–83
International trade
  effective openness to, 404
  Heckscher-Ohlin model of,
  104
Interoperability
  of social and technical
  systems, 348–49
Inter-University Consortium
  for Political and Social
  Research, 300
Investors and credible
  commitment
  moral hazards for
  principals, 220–22
IR
  See International relations
Iran, 123
  hostage crisis in, 4, 9
Iranian Revolution, 132
Iraq War, 5–6, 13, 15, 28, 34,
  150, 208
IRCA
  See U.S. Immigration
  Reform and Control Act
Ireland, 93
"Iron triangles," 263
"Is there a Hole in the
  Whole," 285–86, 288
Islamic revivalists, 130
Islamic Revolution, 123
Islamic terrorists, 28
  See also individual persons
  and groups
Israel, 9, 94, 147–48, 184
  U.S. support for atrocities
  of, 163n

ISSP
  See International Social
  Survey Program
Italy, 93, 101
"Ivory tower," 40–41

J

Jackson, Jesse, 132n
James, William, 123
James II, King of England, 76
Japan, 12, 101, 292
  migrant-receiving by, 110
  See also Brazil/Japan
  migration system
Jesus Christ
  imminent return of, 137
Jihad, 141
  al Qaeda's manual for, 165
Johnson, Lyndon, 222
*Journal of Economic
  Perspectives*, 42
*Journal of European Public
  Policy*, 365
Judicial politics
  and the ECJ, 378–79
Judicial review
  cases of, 448–50
  constructing, 425–50
  entrenching, 438–46
  justices as coalition
  members, 428–33
  the new paradigm for,
  446–48
  protecting the powerful
  and/or powerless, 433–38
Juristocracy, 446

K

Kaiser Family Foundation, 61
Kandinsky, Wassily, 81
Kean, Thomas, 153
Kennan, George, 274n
Kennedy, John, 4, 219
Khobar Towers attack, 150
Khomeini, Ayatollah, 123,
  132
Khruschev, Nikita, 299

Kim Il Sung, 5
Kim Jong Il, 5–6
King, Martin Luther, Jr., 132
Knowledge needed by policy
  makers
  types of, 25–26
Korean War, 4, 8, 15
Kosovo, 28, 34

L

Labor unions, 106
Latin America
  democracies in, 12
  labor exportation by, 106
Latinobarómetro, 310
Latino studies, 178
Leadership
  in successful deliberation,
  63
Legal Studies, 75
Legislative Deferrals, 433,
  435, 438, 444
Legislative politics
  toward bicameralism,
  374–76
Legislative representation of
  expatriates, 185
Legitimate governance, 52,
  62, 390
Liberal democracies, 51
Liberal
  intergovernmentalism,
  360–62
Liberal progressive
  nationalism, 291
Liberal theory, 33
Libertarian paranoia, 240
Limited government in
  Britain
  and the Constitution, 80–81
Lincoln, Abraham, 425–26
Lisbon European Council,
  389
Lobbying
  aggressive, 107
Lobbying community,
  254–55, 258, 263

Local Government Act, 74
Locke, John, 78
"Logic of appropriateness,"
    365
Logic of arguing, 387
Logic of consequentiality,
    387
Logic of uncertainty, 344–47
    action models, 346–47
    after action reviews, 344
    the bowtie model, 345–46
    the edge of chaos, 345
    recognition-primed
        decision making, 344–45
Logical consistency
    of a good theory, 26–27
"Logics of social action,"
    387
London Assembly, 82, 85
"Long-distance nationalism"
    versus transnational
    citizenship, in
    cross-border migrant
    politics, 186–87
Longitudinal data, 267
Long-term policy analysis
    and the generation of
    alternative scenarios,
    351–52
Lord Chancellor's office, 75
Loss aversion
    cf. artifacts, 13
    cf. rational decisions,
        14–16
    empirical applications of,
        11–17
    identifying, 12–16
    policy implications of,
        16–17
Low-intensity citizenship,
    193
Luxembourg Crisis, 360

M

Maastricht Treaty, 280, 371,
    375, 377
    backlash against, 372

Madison, James, 251, 264,
    373, 428
Major, John, 94
Major problems
    a good theory dealing with,
        27
Mapping transnational rights
    and membership,
    191–94
    domains and intensities of
        transnational rights and
        membership, 192
Marbury v. Madison, 77, 446
"Marginality," 105
Market and Opinion Research
    International, 79
Marshall Court, 432
Marshall Plan, 278
Marxist perspectives, 29, 101,
    105, 362
Mass movements
    portrayals of, 124
Mass-mediated cues, 55
Mayor of London, 82
Meaning
    equivalence of in
        cross-national research,
        320–24
Means
    for religion in political life,
        131–36
Measurement, 54
    in cross-national public
        opinion research, 318–19
    "functional-equivalence"
        procedure for, 322
    "identity-equivalence"
        procedure for, 321
    of loss aversion in the field,
        13–14
Measurement of
    globalization, 402–7
    correlations between
        globalization flows and
        policies, 407
    cross-national differences
        in average tariffs and

financial openness, 406
    foreign economic policy,
        404–7
    global policy changes in
        tariffs and financial
        openness, 405
    international economic
        flows, 402–4
Mechanisms of successful
    deliberation, 63–64
    apprenticeship, 64
    leadership, 63
    rules, 63
    stakes, 63–64
    stories, 63
"Metacode," 58
Methodological issues in
    cross-national research,
    314–24
    equivalence of meaning,
        320–24
    political efficacy vignettes,
        323
    quality issues, 314–20
Mexican revolution, 181
Mexico, 106, 322
    See also U.S.-Mexico
        border
Michigan model of election
    studies, 325
Microeconomics, 36
Middle East, 33
Middle-range theory, 36
Migrants voting where they
    are not citizens, 184–85
Migration-related deaths
    See U.S. Immigration
        Reform and Control Act
Migratory pressures
    continuing to increase, 113
Military resistance to action
    before the September 11
    attacks, 160–61
Mill, John Stuart, 77
Mobilization
    of bias, 448
    of interest groups, new

leverage on, 261–64
Modeling "multiple
    principals," 213–14
Modernization, 290
Mohammad, Khalid Shaykh,
    157
Monnet, Jean, 278
Montreal Protocol, 5
Moore, Barrington, 174
"Moral-cognitive
    imperatives," 292
Moral hazard, 224
    of the principal, 220–23
Moral Majority organization,
    128–29, 134
Moroccan crisis, 5
*The Most Activist Supreme
    Court in History*, 439,
    441
Mueller, John, 155n
Multidimensional methods
    "doing history" and,
    257–58
Multidimensional research
    strategies, 258
Multiethnic societies, 34
Multilateral
    cosmopolitanism, 291
Multilateral Investment
    Agreement, 180
Multi-level governance
    and EU policy networks,
    382–85
Multinational corporations,
    108
Multiple citizenship, 172
"Multiple modernities,"
    291–92
Multiple principals, 211–12
    modeling, 213–14
"Multi-sited ethnography,"
    189
Munich crisis, 10

N
Napoleonic wars, 94
Nasser, Gamal

Abdel, 9, 14–15
National Assembly of Wales,
    78, 81–82
National Communications
    Service (NCS), 340
National Council of
    Churches, 132, 136
National Education for
    Women leadership
    program, 236
National Election Study, 105
National Election Survey, 316
National Front
    in France, 104
National growth rates in per
    capita incomes
    differences in, 409–12
National Health Service, 82
National Issues Conference,
    53
National Issues Forums
    (NIFs), 60
National Labor Relations
    Board (NLRB), 211–12
National politics
    emergence of interest
    groups in, 257
National Science Foundation
    (NSF), 301, 310, 348
National security
    relation to population
    movements, 108–10
National Security Council,
    24, 158–59
*Nationalism, Liberalism and
    Progress*, 289
Nationalisms, 186
    liberal progressive, 291
    periodizing interest groups
    in American politics, 260
    virulent and intolerant, 288
    in world politics, 288–93
NATO, 274n, 293
    decision to expand, 32
Natural-science-based truth
    tests
    in positivism, 276

Nazi Germany, 240, 290
NCS
    See National
    Communications Service
Neofunctionalism, 278–79,
    359–60
    expectations of, 284
Neo-realist theory of
    international politics, 35,
    362
Networks
    and computational
    simulation, 349–51
    exploration of, 350
    "principled issue," 178
New Christian Right, 123
New Deal, 137, 261, 438
New Europe Barometer, 302
"New institutionalisms"
    rational choice and
    historical, 362–64
The New Republic, 239
New Zealand, 94
Nicaragua, 123n, 136
NIFs
    See National Issues Forums
9/11 Commission, 152–53,
    157, 161, 164, 343
Nitze, Paul, 24
Nixon, Richard, 429, 442
NLRB
    See National Labor
    Relations Board
Nobel Prize awards, 2, 13, 43,
    288n
Nonattitudes
    problem of, 325
Noncomparability, 327
Nonresponse
    in cross-national public
    opinion research,
    316–17
Normandy landings, 151
Normative theory, 49
Norms of the academic IR
    discipline
    academic journals

evaluating submissions, 42
academic promotions, 42
altering the prevailing, 41–43
junior faculty and real-world participation, 42
Norris-LaGuardia Act of 1932, 434, 438
North American Free Trade Agreement, 180
North Korea, 5–6
Northern Ireland Act, 74
Northern Ireland Assembly, 81–82, 84
NSF
  See National Science Foundation
Nuclear terror, 273

O

"Oaxacalifornia," 190
Oaxacan Indigenous Binational Front (FIOB), 188–89
"Observational equivalence," 222
ODP
  See Office of Domestic Preparedness
OECD, 417–18
Office of Domestic Preparedness (ODP), 348
Open Method of Coordination (OMC), 358, 388–90
Organization for European Economic Cooperation, 278
Organizational democracy, 241
Organizations
  vertical, 241
Organized migrants
  in cross-border migrant political power

relationships, 190–91
Outcome-based incentives in the canonical principal-agent model, 206

P

Paisley, Ian, 82
Pakistan, 153, 162–63
Pan-Africanist movement, 181
Paradigm for judicial review changing, 446–48
Paranoia
  libertarian, 240
Pareto-suboptimal game, 217
Parliament Act of 1949, 80
Parliamentarization, 386
Parliamentary sovereignty in Britain
  and the Human Rights Act, 87–91
Parsimony
  sacrificing, 36
Party caucuses and party leaders
  as moral hazards for principals, 222
Party-label legislation, 222
PAT
  See Principal-agency theory
Patterns
  recognizing in interest groups, 266–67
Pavitt, James, 158
Pax Americana, 31
Pearl Harbor, 4, 146n, 147, 337
The People Rising, 447
The People Themselves, 447
Per capita incomes
  between-country inequality, 409
  differences in national growth rates, 409–12

global Gini coefficients, 408–9
globalization and differences between countries, 407–12
Perceived negative consequences of immigration, 104–5
Perception
  vs. reality, 102
Periodizing interest groups in American politics, 259–64
  new leverage on the mobilization, bias, policy networks, and attrition of interest groups, 261–64
  sources of dynamism, 259–61
Perot, Ross, 412
Personhood
  emerging norms of, 108
Perspectives on Politics, 43
Pew Charitable Trusts, 61, 311
Pew Global Attitudes Project, 310, 316
Philippines, 324
Pierce, William, 130
Planned Parenthood v. Casey, 440, 442
Pledge of Allegiance, 445
Pluralism, 362
Poland, 123n
Policies
  achieving particular results in, 32–33
  anticipating how and why they might fail, 33
  correlations with globalization flows, 407
  designing for different states of uncertainty, 337–38
  evaluating desirability and feasibility of, 32
  global changes in tariffs

and financial openness,
405
relevance of, 25
theoretical applications of
theory to, 28–34
Policies for maintaining
security
existing before September
11, 2001, 339–40
implemented after
September 11, 2001,
340–41
Policy analysis
long-term, and the
generation of alternative
scenarios, 351–52
Policy analysts
prior to the September 11
attacks, cognitive
problems for, 147–48
Policy instruments
particular, determining
likely working of, 33
Policy makers, 2, 24, 27, 33,
37
limits on, causing U.S.
policy makers to miss
opportunities to counter
the known al Qaeda
threat, 162–64
types of knowledge needed
by, 25–26
Policy mistakes
prior to the September 11
attacks, 152–53
Policy networks
in the EU, 382–85
of interest groups, new
leverage on, 261–64
Policy subgovernments, 263
Political Action surveys, 311
Political behavior
impact of civic
participation on, 231
Political Change in Britain,
301
Political community

shared, not necessarily
generated by shared
targets, 180–81
Political distribution, 342
Political divides
versus civic divides,
235–39
Political efficacy vignettes
in cross-national research,
323
Political enfranchisement
cross-border voting rights,
184
direct transnational,
183–85
elected transnational
authorities, 185
indirect transnational, 185
legislative representation of
expatriates, 185
migrants voting where they
are not citizens, 184–85
Political engagement
culture as a motive for, 132
Political evolution of
principal-agent models,
203–24
contributions of political
science to
principal-agency theory,
223–24
principal-agency theory
extended and challenged
in congressional
oversight, 208–16
principal-agency theory as
received from economics,
204–8
Political institutions
in immigration policy
making, 107–8
Political life
making sense of religion
in, 121–41
Political limits on effective
policy
before the September 11

attacks, 149–50
Political Parties, Elections
and Referendums Act,
75
Political pluralism
"modernized theory" of,
252
Political Science Quarterly,
39
Politics and immigration,
99–113
consequences of
immigration, 102–6
determinants of
international migration,
100–2
immigration policy
making, 106–10
significance of immigration
policy, 110–12
Policy makers
prior to the September 11
attacks, cognitive
problems for, 147–48
Polls
commercial, 298–99
government-sponsored,
299–300
Population movements
national security's relation
to, 108–10
Portfolio investment, 402
Portugal, 93
Positivism, 370, 380
natural-science-based truth
tests of, 276
Postpositivist scholars, 366
Poverty
global, and inequality
within countries, 413
Power, 30
of chief executives, 207
See also Separation of
powers
Power relationships between
organized migrants and
at-home civil society

actors
in cross-border migrant
politics, 190–91
Powerful and/or powerless
people
protecting through judicial
review, 433–38
PPP
See Purchasing power
parity
Practice
in maintaining security,
342–43
"Pragmatic constructivism,"
285
Prediction
in applying theory to
policy, 31–32
Preferences, 10
asymmetry in the canonical
principal-agent model,
205–6
Prescription
in applying theory to
policy, 32–33
Prescriptive richness
of a good theory, 27–28
President's Council of
Economic Advisors, 24
Principal-agency theory
(PAT), 203–5, 216–18
contributions of political
science to, 223–24
and cooperation, 217–18
and credible commitment
problems, 218–23
the principal's moral
hazard, 220–23
from ultimatum bargaining
to bilateral bargaining,
216–17
Principal-agency theory
(PAT) as received from
economics, 204–8
a canonical application to
political science, 207–8
the canonical

principal-agent model,
205–6
the trade-off in risk and in
incentives, 204–5
Principal-agency theory
(PAT) extended and
challenged in
congressional oversight,
208–16
congressional control
through incentives,
209–10
congressional control
without incentives,
214–16
limited impact of
incentives, 212–14
with multiple principals,
211–12
Principal-agent model, 205–6
agent impact, 205
asymmetry in preferences,
205–6
backward induction based
on common knowledge,
206
efficiency tradeoffs, 206
information asymmetry,
205
initiative lying with a
unified principal, 206
outcome-based incentives,
206
ultimatum bargaining, 206
Principal's moral hazards,
220–23
base-closing commission,
222–23
investors, bankers, and
credible commitment,
220–22
party caucuses and party
leaders, 222
"Principled issue" networks,
178
Prison labor
result of globalization, 399

Prisoner's dilemma game, 16,
218
Privacy
tradition of protecting
countered, 352
Private capital flows
global trade and, 402
Privatization
global revenues from, 417
and the size of government,
417
Procedural-control
hypothesis, 215
Professionals
"epistemic communities"
of, 285
hard to control, 211
in the IR profession,
38–39
periodizing interest groups
in American politics, 260
Progressive Era
underestimating group
mobilization in, 255–56
Progressive taxation, 103
Proportional representation
and electoral reform in
Britain, 85–87
Proposition 187, 108, 187
Prospect theory in political
science, 1–18
assessing domain, 3–11
empirical applications of
loss aversion, 11–17
identifying loss aversion,
12–16
policy implications of loss
aversion, 16–17
Psychological economics, 2
Public attitudes
about immigration, 103
Public opinion research
brief history, 298–314
categories of evidence
about treatment, 328
globalization of, 297–331
intellectual assumptions of

cross-national surveys,
325–26
methodological issues in
cross-national research,
314–24
proposed weighting of
sample surveys, 328
survey-related web sites,
330–31
Public policy
issue of immigration for,
105
Public services
consumed by immigrants,
103
Public values
in uncertain environments,
352–53
Purchasing power parity
(PPP), 408

Q

Quality issues in public
opinion research,
314–20
coverage, 315–16
measurement, 318–19
nonresponse, 316–17
sampling, 317–18
Quasi-federalism
in Britain, 81–85

R

Race to the bottom, 399
Racism
white, 105
Rahman, Omar Abdel, 130
RAND Corporation, 40–41
Random selection, 52–53
The Rape of the Constitution,
75
Rational choice, 16
Rational choice
institutionalism, 358
Reagan, Ronald, 213
Reality
vs. perception, 102

Real-world participation
encouraging junior faculty
in, 42
Real-world relevance
considering in academic
promotions, 42
Receiving-state populations
immigration's effect
altering the size and
structure of, 103
Reciprocity
diffuse, 291
generalized, 230
Recognition-primed decision
making
and the logic of
uncertainty, 344–45
*Reconsidering Roosevelt on
Race*, 435, 437
Reference points
status quo, 4–5
Referendums, 74
in Britain, 78–80
Reform
of the Bundesrat in
Germany, 93
of the House of Lords in
Britain, 91–94
Reform Act of 1832, 77
Refugee crises, 109
"Regime decay," 284
Regime transformation, 259
Rehnquist Court, 425–26,
428, 439, 441–44
Rehnquist, William, 440
Relativity
theory of, 27
Religion in political life
background, 122–25
making sense of, 121–41
means and resources,
131–36
motives from culture and
identity, 125–31
opportunity, 136–40
Religious organizations
capacity for accumulating

wealth, 134
Remittances
from emigrants, 106
Reparations, 133
Representation
proportional, and electoral
reform in Britain, 85–87
systems of, 264–66
"Representativeness"
heuristic, 7
Resistance
at the EPA, 212–13
Resistance to action
in the military before the
September 11 attacks,
160–61
Resource allocation, 156
Resource mobilization
theories of, 125, 131n
Resources
for religion in political life,
131–36
Revolution, quiet
of Constitutional reform in
Britain, 73–95
Rhodesia
religious conflict in, 128
Ridge, Tom, 341
Rights Brought Home, 88
Risk
defining, 338
Risk acceptance, 1, 3, 5
Risk aversion, 2–3, 5
Risk management, 335–54
coping with uncertainty,
336–39
future strategies, 353–54
the logic of uncertainty,
344–47
managing uncertainty in
complex environments,
347–52
policy vs. practice in
maintaining security,
339–43
public values in uncer_ₐn
environments, 352 ₅3

tradeoffs in, 204–5
Risk reduction, 353
"Risk theory," 28
Risky behavior, 10
Roe v. Wade, 439, 447
Roosevelt, Franklin D., 10,
    435–36, 445
Ruby Ridge, 159
Rule-following behavior, 387
Rules
    in successful deliberation,
    63
Rumsfeld, Donald, 5
Russell Sage Foundation, 301
Russia, 15
    See also Soviet Union

S
"Safety valve," 105
Sampling methodologies, 53
    in cross-national public
    opinion research, 317–18
Sandinista uprising, 123n
Saudi Arabia, 148n, 153,
    162–63
Scalia, Antonin, 440, 443
Schengen agreement, 110
Scholars
    different agendas than
    policy makers, 37–38
Scotland Act, 74
Scottish Parliament, 78, 81,
    84
Searching for Safety, 336,
    338
*Second Treatise on
    Government*, 78
Second Vatican Council, 137
Securities and Exchange
    Commission, 208, 210
Security
    defining, 338
    managing, 353
Security issues
    contrasting practice,
    342–43
    policies existing before

September 11, 2001,
    339–40
    policies implemented after
    September 11, 2001,
    340–41
    policy vs. practice in
    maintaining, 339–43
    threats posed by
    immigration, 104
    the U.S. Department of
    Homeland Security,
    341–42
    the U.S.A. Patriot Act, 341
Self-organization
    power of embedded in
    complex systems, 349
Separation of powers, 373
    horizontal, 371–73
    vertical, 373–79
September 11 terrorist
    attacks, 7, 335, 338–39
    missed opportunities for
    intelligence, 152
    nature of the September 11
    failure, 151–53
    policy mistakes, 152–53
    reasons U.S. policy makers
    missed opportunities to
    counter the known threat,
    153–66
    responding to the next
    failure, 166
    strategic surprise and,
    145–67
    warnings of an al Qaeda
    threat, 151–52
Sequencing approach, 367
Shared political community
    shared targets not
    necessarily generating,
    180–81
Shelton, Henry, 160
Sherman Anti-Trust Act, 434
"Signal to noise ratio," 147
Simulation
    computational, and
    networks, 349–51

Sinn Fein, 82
Smith, Adam, 400
Smith/Ricardo theory of free
    trade, 27, 29
Smoot-Hawley Tariff, 9
Snowball method, 51
Social acceptability bias, 324
Social democracy
    traditional ideals of, 76
Social Democratic and
    Labour Party, 82
Social identity theory, 233
Social movement
    organizations, 179
Social movement theory
    (SMT), 122, 124–26,
    131–32
Social movements
    with a religious base, 136
Social networks
    transborder, 101
Social science theory, 36
Social systems
    interoperable technical
    systems, 348–49
*Social Theory of International
    Politics*, 35, 38
Socialization, 368
Society
    impact of civic
    participation on, 231–32
Sociological Journal, 299
Solidarity movement, 123n
South African Council of
    Churches, 139
South Korea
    migrant-receiving by, 110
Soviet Union, 146n
    collapse of, 5, 29–30
    Third World policies of,
    29
Spain, 93, 101
SRC
    See Survey Research
    Center
Stability and Growth Pact,
    385

Stakes
  in successful deliberation,
    63–64
"State of Democracy in South
    Asia" survey, 310, 330
Status hierarchy, 40
Status quo
  as reference point in
    assessing domain, 4–5
St. Elizabeth's Church,
    126–27
Storytelling
  bringing order to human
    experience, 58–59
  in successful deliberation,
    63
"Strategic bargaining," 390
Strategic questions of
    international change,
    283–87
  alternatives to realism and
    idealism, 286–87
  how voluntary cooperation
    occurs, 283–84
  kinds of institutional
    arrangements that foster
    cooperation, 284
  organizational learning
    promoted by scientific
    knowledge and by the
    involvement of experts,
    285
  the role of actor cognition,
    284–85
Strategic surprise and the
    September 11 attacks,
    145–67
  nature of the September 11
    failure, 151–53
  reasons U.S. policy makers
    missed opportunities to
    counter the known threat,
    153–66
  responding to the next
    failure, 166
Structural Funds,
    382–83

Structure
  and the limits of incentives,
    213
Subgame-perfect equilibrium
    prediction, 216
Subjective expected utility
    theory, 1
"Subsumption," 367
Suez crisis, 4, 9, 14–15, 146
Surveillance systems, 56
Survey research, 257
  face-to-face, 298
  globalization of, 298
Survey Research Center
    (SRC), 300–1
Sweatshops
  result of globalization, 399
Sweden, 235
Systems of representation
  interwoven, parties and
    interest groups as, 264–66

T
Taliban, 155, 158, 165
Taney Court, 432
Tariffs
  cross-national differences
    in average, 406
  global policy changes in,
    405
Taxation
  progressive, 103
Technical systems
  interoperable social
    systems, 348–49
Temporary guestworker
    migration, 101
Tenet, George, 151–52, 154–56
Terror
  nuclear, 273
Terrorists, 146, 165–66
  Islamic, 28
  vetting of candidates by,
    157n
Theoretical applications of
    theory to policy, 28–34
  diagnosis, 29–31

evaluation, 33–34
  prediction, 31–32
  prescription, 32–33
Theories
  contribution to the conduct
    of foreign policy, 25–34
  See also Good theories
Theories of European
    integration, 358–68
  constructivism and the
    reshaping of European
    identities and preferences,
    365–68
  integration theory today,
    368
  intergovernmentalism and
    liberal
    intergovernmentalism,
    360–62
  neofunctionalism, 359–60
  "new institutionalisms,"
    rational choice and
    historical, 362–64
Theorizing the European
    Union
  EU policy making in
    comparative perspective,
    368–79
  the governance approach,
    with the EU as a polity,
    379–91
  international organization,
    domestic polity, or
    experiment in new
    governance, 357–91
  theories of European
    integration, 358–68
  toward normal science,
    370, 379
*Theory of International
    Politics*, 38
Theory-practice gap, 40
Thomas, Clarence, 440
Thomas Road Baptist
    Church, 133
*Thorburn v. Sunderland City
    Council*, 90

Tocqueville, Alexis de, 94, 236, 251
Towards Juristocracy, 431–32, 438
Town meetings, 59
Trade
  cross-national differences in, 403
Trade-growth nexus, 412
Tradeoffs
  in risk and in incentives, 204–5
  See also Efficiency tradeoffs
Transborder social networks, 101
Transformation
  regime, 259
Transformations in interest groups
  recognizing, 266–67
Transformations in world politics
  European integration, 277–81
  the intellectual contributions of Ernst B. Haas, 271–94
  intellectual orientation, 273–77
  international change, 281–88
  on nationalism, 288–93
Translation problems, 320–31
Translocal membership
  versus transnational, in cross-border migrant politics, 187–88
"Transmission belt"
  model of civil society, 242
  from theory to policy, 42
"Transnational citizenship," 171–95
  citizens in transnational civil society, 177–83
  claiming rights versus gaining citizenship, 176

cross-border migrant politics, 183–91
  defining, 172, 174–76
  flexible forms of, 189–90
  importance of a transnational civil society for, 178–79
  versus "long-distance nationalism," in cross-border migrant politics, 186–87
  mapping transnational rights and membership, 191–94
  past internationalisms illuminating the meaning of, 181–82
  three main forms of, 188–89
Transnational movements
  most cross-border networks and coalitions not constituting, 179–80
Transnational participation "integrated," 189
Transnational political enfranchisement
  indirect, 185
Treaties of Rome, 361
Treaty of Amsterdam, 375
Treaty on European Union, 361
Treaty of Nice, 389
Trickle-down model
  of division of labor, 40
Trigger strategy, 218
Truman, Harry, 4, 8–9, 445
Turkey/Germany migration system, 102
The Turner Diaries, 130
Tutu, Desmond, 135
"Two-level games" model, 369

U

Ulster Unionist Party, 82
Ultimatum bargaining, 216–17

in the canonical principal-agent model, 206
Uncertainty
  coping with, 336–39
  designing policy for different states of, 337–38
  and the increasing vulnerability of complex systems to extreme events, 338–39
Uncertainty management in complex environments, 347–52
  interoperability of social and technical systems, 348–49
  long-term policy analysis and the generation of alternative scenarios, 351–52
  networks and computational simulation, 349–51
Unemployment rate, 1
Unified principals
  initiative lying with, 206
Unitary states, 82
United Kingdom
  challenges to the integrity of, 83
  federalism resisted by, 83
  held together by functional concerns, 83
United Nations (UN), 175–76, 293, 408
  evolution of peacekeeping by, 284
  Global Compact, 286
  Security Council, 388
United Nations Industrial Development Organization (UNIDO), 414–15
United States Government Interagency Domestic Terrorism Concept of

Operations Plan (ConPlan), 339
The Uniting of Europe, 275–78, 281–84, 286, 359
University of Texas Inequality Project (UTIP), 414–15
U.S. Agency for International Development, 310
U.S. Congress, 221–22
control through incentives, 209–10
control without incentives, 214–16
roll call votes in, 107
U.S. Congressional Committee Hearings Index (CIS Index), 256–58
U.S. Department of Agriculture (USDA), 340
U.S. Department of Homeland Security and maintaining security, 341–42
U.S. Department of Justice (DOJ), 339
U.S. Environmental Protection Agency (EPA), 340
resistance at, 212–13
U.S. Food and Drug Administration (FDA), 213–14
U.S. Forest Service (USFS), 340
U.S. Immigration and Naturalization Service, 111–12
U.S. Immigration Reform and Control Act (IRCA), 111
U.S. Supreme Court, 89–90, 108, 425–26, 436–37
US v. Carolene Products Co., 90

U.S. War Department, 299
U.S.A. Patriot Act
and maintaining security, 341–42
threatening freedoms, 336, 352–53
USDA
See U.S. Department of Agriculture
USFS
See U.S. Forest Service
U.S.-Mexico border, 100, 102, 183
U.S.S. Cole
attack on, 339
Utility maximization, 387
UTIP
See University of Texas Inequality Project

V

Values
See Citizen values; Civic values and attitudes; Public values
Vance, Cyrus, 9
Vermont town meetings, 59
Vertical organizations, 241
Vertical separation of powers, 373–79
executive politics, delegation and discretion in, 376–78
judicial politics and the ECJ, 378–79
legislative politics, toward bicameralism, 374–76
Vietnam War, 15
Vignettes
problems using, 322–23, 329
See also Political efficacy vignettes
Voice and Equality, 121
Voluntarism
competitive, 240
Voluntary association

members, 233
The Voter Decides, 301
Voting
by migrants where they are not citizens, 184–85
Voting rights
cross-border, 184
Vulnerability
of complex systems to extreme events, on the rise, 338–39

W

Waco assault, 159
Wagner Act, 438
Waltz, Kenneth, 293
WAPOR
See World Association for Public Opinion Research
Warning fatigue, 154
Warnings
of an al Qaeda threat prior to the September 11 attacks, 151–52
Warren Court, 440, 443, 446
Washington Information Directory, 254–56
Washington lobbying community, 254–55, 258, 263
Washington Representatives, 254–55
The Wealth of Nations, 400
Weapons of mass destruction, 150
Web sites
survey-related, 330–31
Weber, Max, 125, 131, 203, 223, 292, 369
Weighting
of sample surveys, 328
Westminster Parliament, 84, 89
Westphalian sovereignty, 110
When Knowledge is Power, 285–87

White Paper on Governance, 386
White racism, 105
WIID
  See World Income
    Inequality Database
William of Orange, 76
Wilson, Woodrow, 39n
Within-country inequalities, 412–16
  and global poverty, 413
  by level of development (UTIP), 415
  by level of development (WIID), 414
World Association for Public Opinion Research (WAPOR), 327
World Bank, 193, 293, 406, 412–13

"World" citizenship, 176
World Council of Churches, 136
World Development Report, 406
World Income Inequality Database (WIID), 413, 415
World politics
  intellectual orientation in, 273–77
  transformation in, 271–94
World Trade Center attacks, 154, 337, 350
World Trade Center bombing (1993), 339
World Trade Organization, 180
World Values Survey (WVS), 302, 315, 326, 330

World War I, 28, 104, 261
World War II, 9, 104, 293
  British intelligence during, 150
  brutal reality of, 273
WVS
  See World Values Survey

Y
Yom Kippur War, 146

Z
Zacatecan federations, 190
Zapatista rebellion, 182
Zero-sum models, 265
ZUMA (Zentrum für Umfragen, Methoden und Analysen) Center for Survey Research and Methodology, 300

CUMULATIVE INDEXES

CONTRIBUTING AUTHORS, VOLUMES 1–8

A

Achen CH, 5:423–50
Adcock R, 2:537–65
Amadae SM, 2:269–95
Andeweg RB, 3:509–36
Annan NA, 2:363–67
Austen–Smith D, 1:259–87

B

Bailey M, 6:99–118
Baker PJ, 5:87–110
Baldwin D, 3:167–82
Balsiger J, 7:149–75
Banks JS, 1:259–87
Baum L, 6:161–80
Beck N, 4:271–93
Beckwith K, 4:371–90
Behnegar N, 1:95–116
Bendor J, 4:235–69;
   6:433–71
Bennett WL, 7:125–48
Berger S, 3:43–62
Berman L, 6:181–204
Bogdanor V, 8:73–98
Bowles N, 2:1–23
Brass P, 3:305–30
Braybrooke D, 6:99–118
Broz JL, 4:317–43
Brune N, 8:399–423
Bueno de Mesquita B,
   2:269–95
Bunce V, 4:43–65
Butler D, 1:451–64
Byman D, 8:145–70

C

Cain BE, 2:163–87
Callan E, 7:71–90
Cameron C, 7:409–35

Caporaso JA, 2:429–44
Chambers S, 6:307–26
Cheibub JA, 5:151–79
Clarke HD, 1:357–78
Collier D, 2:537–65
Comfort LK, 8:335–56
Converse PE, 3:331–53
Cook FL, 7:315–44
Cornelius WA, 8:99–119
Cox G, 2:145–61

D

de la Garza RO, 7:91–123
Delli Carpini MX, 7:315–44
Dietz MG, 6:399–431
Downs G, 3:25–42
Druckman JN, 3:1–24

E

Eulau H, 2:75–89
Evans G, 3:401–17

F

Fabbrini S, 2:465–91;
   6:119–37
Fearon JD, 1:289–313
Feaver P, 2:211–41
Feder SA, 5:111–25
Finnemore M, 4:391–416
Fisher S, 8:297–333
Fox J, 8:171–201
Franzese RJ Jr, 5:369–421
Fridy KS, 8:121–43
Frieden JA, 4:317–43

G

Galston WA, 4:217–34
Garrett G, 8:399–423
Geddes B, 2:115–44

Gerber A, 2:189–210
Gibson CC, 5:201–21
Gill A, 4:117–38
Gillman H, 7:363–82
Glaser CL, 3:251–76
Glazer A, 4:235–69
Goldgeier JM, 4:67–92
Goldstein K, 7:205–26
Goldstone JA, 4:139–87
Goodin RE, 6:55–76
Gould AC, 5:87–110
Graber D, 6:139–60
Graber MA, 8:425–51
Green DP, 2:189–210;
   6:509–31
Grofman B, 7:25–46

H

Hammond T, 4:235–69
Hankin J, 3:419–47
Harris RA, 8:251–70
Hart DM, 7:47–69
Hart J, 1:379–99
Hasen RL, 7:297–313
Haslam J, 6:77–98
Hazell R, 3:379–400
Heath A, 8:297–333
Hechter M, 4:189–215
Hibbing JR, 8:227–49
Hutchings VL, 7:383–408
Huth PK, 2:25–48

J

Jackman RW, 1:47–73
Jackman S, 7:483–505
Jacobs LR, 7:315–44
Jacobson H, 3:149–66
Jewell ME, 7:177–203
Johnson J, 5:223–48

Jones BD, 2:297–321
Jones CO, 6:1–22
Jupille J, 2:429–44

K

Kalyvas SN, 2:323–43
Kateb G, 6:275–305
Katzenstein PJ, 8:271–96
Keefer P, 7:247–72
Keohane RO, 8:271–96
Kinder DR, 1:167–98
Knight J, 1:425–49

L

Laitin DD, 3:117–48
Laver M, 1:1–25; 6:23–40
Lehoucq F, 6:233–56
Leskiw CS, 4:295–316
Levi L, 3:475–507
Levin MA, 2:163–87
Levy JS, 1:139–66
Lewis–Beck MS, 3:183–219
Lichbach MI, 1:401–23
Limongi F, 5:151–79
Lovenduski J, 1:333–56
Lupia A, 3:1–24; 7:463–82

M

Mair P, 1:211–29
Marcus GE, 3:221–50
Masters RD, 4:345–69
Matsusaka JG, 7:463–82
Mayhew DR, 3:449–74
McCarty N, 7:409–35
McCormick GH, 6:473–507
McDermott R, 5:31–61
Mercer J, 8:1–21
Miller GJ, 8:203–25
Miller RA, 1:47–73
Milner HV, 2:91–114
Minogue K, 7:227–46
Mitra SK, 2:405–28
Molina O, 5:305–31
Monroe KR, 1:315–31;
    3:419–47

Moon J, 6:257–74
Morehouse SM, 7:177–203
Morrow JD, 3:63–83
Mudde C, 1:211–29
Munck GL, 7:437–62
Murphy RD, 5:63–85

O

Okamoto D, 4:189–215
O'Neill K, 7:149–75
Ostrom E, 2:493–535

P

Patterson D, 4:93–115
Patterson M, 1:315–31
Pollack MA, 8:357–98
Polsby NW, 1:199–210;
    5:331–67
Powell GB Jr, 7:273–96
Powell R, 5:1–30

R

Rae DW, 4:417–38
Ray JL, 1:27–46
Rhodes M, 5:305–31
Riccucci, NM 1:231–57
Richardson B, 4:93–115
Ridout TN, 7:205–26
Rosecrance R, 6:377–98
Rosenblum MR, 8:99–119
Routh SR, 6:181–204
Ruggie JG, 8:271–96
Ruin O, 6:41–54
Ryan A, 2:345–62
Ryfe DM, 8:49–71

S

Sapiro V, 7:1–23
Schickler E, 5:331–67
Schmitter PC, 8:271–96
Schofield N, 3:277–303
Schudson M, 5:249–69
Seher RL, 6:509–31
Shafer BE, 2:445–63
Sikkink K, 4:391–416

Silverman AL, 8:121–43
Simmons BA, 1:75–93
Sinclair D, 3:379–400
Smith S, 8:297–333
Snyder J, 7:345–62
Spruyt H, 5:127–49
Stegmaier M, 3:183–219
Stewart MC, 1.357–78
Stinchcombe A, 2:49–73
Stoker L, 3:475–507
Stokes SC, 2:243–67

T

Tarrow S, 4:1–20
Tetlock PE, 4:67–92
Theiss–Morse E, 8:227–49
Thelen K, 2:369–404
Thomas RG, 6:205–32
Thompson FR, 1:231–57
Thompson P, 6:377–98
Tichenor DJ, 8:251–70
Tilly C, 4:21–41
Tucker JA, 5:271–304

V

Valentino NA, 7:383–408
VanDeveer SD, 7:149–75
Van Vechten RB, 3:419–47
Vasquez J, 4:295–316
Vinjamuri L, 7:345–62
Von der Muhll GE,
    6:345–76

W

Wade R, 3:85–115
Wald KD, 8:121–43
Wallerstein M, 3:355–77
Walt SM, 8:23–48
Watts RL, 1:117–37
Western B, 3:355–77
Whitefield S, 5:181–200
Wilkerson JD, 6:327–43

Z

Zlomke S, 2:75–89

CHAPTER TITLES, VOLUMES 1–8

Volume 1 (1998)

Models of Government Formation	M Laver	1:1–25
Does Democracy Cause Peace?	JL Ray	1:27–46
Social Capital and Politics	RW Jackman, RA Miller	1:47–73
Compliance with International Agreements	BA Simmons	1:75–93
The Intellectual Legacy of Leo Strauss (1899–1973)	N Behnegar	1:95–116
Federalism, Federal Political Systems, and Federations	RL Watts	1:117–37
The Causes of War and the Conditions of Peace	JS Levy	1:139–66
Communication and Opinion	DR Kinder	1:167–98
Social Science and Scientific Change: A Note on Thomas S. Kuhn's Contribution	NW Polsby	1:199–210
The Party Family and Its Study	P Mair, C Mudde	1:211–29
Reinventing Government	FR Thompson, NM Riccucci	1:231–57
Social Choice Theory, Game Theory, and Positive Political Theory	D Austen-Smith, JS Banks	1:259–87
Domestic Politics, Foreign Policy, and Theories of International Relations	JD Fearon	1:289–313
Narrative in Political Science	M Patterson, KR Monroe	1:315–31
Gendering Research in Political Science	J Lovenduski	1:333–56
The Decline of Parties in the Minds of Citizens	HD Clarke, MC Stewart	1:357–78
Neglected Aspects of the Study of the Presidency	J Hart	1:379–99
Contending Theories of Contentious Politics and the Structure-Action Problem of Social Order	MI Lichbach	1:401–23
Justice and Fairness	J Knight	1:425–49
Reflections on British Elections and Their Study	D Butler	1:451–64

Volume 2 (1999)

Studying the Presidency	N Bowles	2:1–23
Deterrence and International Conflict: Empirical Findings and Theoretical Debates	PK Huth	2:25–48

Ending Revolutions and Building New Governments	A Stinchcombe	2:49–73
Harold D. Lasswell's Legacy to Mainstream Political Science: A Neglected Agenda	H Eulau, S Zlomke	2:75–89
The Political Economy of International Trade	HV Milner	2:91–114
What Do We Know About Democratization After Twenty Years?	B Geddes	2:115–44
Electoral Rules and Electoral Coordination	G Cox	2:145–61
Term Limits	BE Cain, MA Levin	2:163–87
Misperceptions About Perceptual Bias	A Gerber, DP Green	2:189–210
Civil-Military Relations	P Feaver	2:211–41
Political Parties and Democracy	SC Stokes	2:243–67
The Rochester School: The Origins of Positive Political Theory	SM Amadae, B Bueno de Mesquita	2:269–95
Bounded Rationality	BD Jones	2:297–321
The Decay and Breakdown of Communist One-Party Systems	SN Kalyvas	2:323–43
Isaiah Berlin: Political Theory and Liberal Culture	A Ryan	2:345–62
Isaiah Berlin (1909–1997)	NA Annan	2:363–67
Historical Institutionalism in Comparative Politics	K Thelen	2:369–404
Effects of Institutional Arrangements on Political Stability in South Asia	SK Mitra	2:405–28
Institutionalism and the European Union: Beyond International Relations and Comparative Politics	J Jupille, JA Caporaso	2:429–44
American Exceptionalism	BE Shafer	2:445–63
American Democracy from a European Perspective	S Fabbrini	2:465–91
Coping with Tragedies of the Commons	E Ostrom	2:493–535
Democracy and Dichotomies: A Pragmatic Approach to Choices about Concepts	D Collier, R Adcock	2:537–65

Volume 3 (2000)

Preference Formation	JN Druckman, A Lupia	3:1–24
Constructing Effective Environmental Regimes	G Downs	3:25–42
Globalization and Politics	S Berger	3:43–62
Alliances: Why Write Them Down?	JD Morrow	3:63–83

Wheels Within Wheels: Rethinking the
   Asian Crisis and the Asian Model   R Wade   3:85–115
Post-Soviet Politics   DD Laitin   3:117–48
International Institutions and System
   Transformation   H Jacobson   3:149–66
Success and Failure in Foreign Policy   D Baldwin   3:167–82
Economic Determinants of Electoral
   Outcomes   M Stegmaier,   3:183–219
                                              MS Lewis-Beck
Emotions in Politics   GE Marcus   3:221–50
The Causes and Consequences of Arms
   Races   CL Glaser   3:251–76
Constitutional Political Economy: On the
   Possibility of Combining Rational
   Choice Theory and Comparative Politics N Schofield   3:277–303
Foucault Steals Political Science   P Brass   3:305–30
Assessing the Capacity of Mass Electorates PE Converse   3:331–53
Unions in Decline? What Has Changed
   and Why   B Western,   3:355–77
                                              M Wallerstein
The British Constitution: Labour's
   Constitutional Revolution   R Hazell, D Sinclair 3:379–400
The Continued Significance of Class
   Voting   G Evans   3:401–17
The Psychological Foundations of Identity
   Politics   KR Monroe,   3:419–47
                                              RB Van Vechten,
                                              J Hankin
Electoral Realignments   DR Mayhew   3:449–74
Political Trust and Trustworthiness   M Levi, L Stoker   3:475–507
Consociational Democracy   RB Andeweg   3:509–36

Volume 4 (2001)

Transnational Politics: Contention and
   Institutions in International Politics   S Tarrow   4:1–20
Mechanisms in Political Processes   C Tilly   4:21–41
Democratization and Economic Reform   V Bunce   4:43–65
Psychology and International Relations
   Theory   JM Goldgeier,   4:67–92
                                              PE Tetlock
Political Traditions and Political Change:
   The Significance of Postwar Japanese
   Politics for Political Science   B Richardson,   4:93–115
                                              D Patterson
Religion and Comparative Politics   A Gill   4:117–38
Toward a Fourth Generation of
   Revolutionary Theory   JA Goldstone   4:139–87

Political Consequences of Minority Group Formation	M Hechter, D Okamoto	4:189–215
Political Knowledge, Political Engagement, and Civic Education	WA Galston	4:217–34
Theories of Delegation	J Bendor, A Glazer, T Hammond	4:235–69
Time-Series–Cross-Section Data: What Have We Learned in the Past Few Years?	N Beck	4:271–93
The Origins and War Proneness of Interstate Rivalries	J Vasquez, CS Leskiw	4:295–316
The Political Economy of International Monetary Relations	JL Broz, JA Frieden	4:317–43
Biology and Politics: Linking Nature and Nurture	RD Masters	4:345–69
Women's Movements at Century's End: Excavation and Advances in Political Science	K Beckwith	4:371–90
Taking Stock: The Constructivist Research Program in International Relations and Comparative Politics	M Finnemore, K Sikkink	4:391–416
Viacratic America: *Plessy* on Foot *v. Brown* on Wheels	DW Rae	4:417–38

Volume 5 (2002)

Bargaining Theory and International Conflict	R Powell	5:1–30
Experimental Methods in Political Science	R McDermott	5:31–61
Politics, Political Science, and Urban Governance: A Literature and A Legacy	RD Murphy	5:63–85
Democracy and Taxation	AC Gould, PJ Baker	5:87–110
Forecasting for Policy Making in the Post–Cold War Period	SA Feder	5:111–25
The Origins, Development, and Possible Decline of the Modern State	H Spruyt	5:127–49
Democratic Institutions and Regime Survival: Parliamentary and Presidential Democracies Reconsidered	J Cheibub, F Limongi	5:151–79
Political Cleavages and Post-Communist Politics	S Whitefield	5:181–200
Of Waves and Ripples: Democracy and Political Change in Africa in the 1990s	CC Gibson	5:201–21
How Conceptual Problems Migrate: Rational Choice, Interpretation, and the Hazards of Pluralism	J Johnson	5:223–48
The News Media as Political Institutions	M Schudson	5:249–69

The First Decade of Post-Communist Elections and Voting: What Have We Studied, and How Have We Studied It?   JA Tucker   5:271–304

Corporatism: The Past, Present, and Future of a Concept   O Molina, M Rhodes   5:305–31

Landmarks in the Study of Congress since 1945   NW Polsby, E Schickler   5:331–67

Electoral and Partisan Cycles in Economic Policies and Outcomes   RJ Franzese Jr.   5:369–421

Toward a New Political Methodology: Microfoundations and ART   CH Achen   5:423–50

Volume 6 (2003)

Richard E. Neustadt: Public Servant as Scholar   CO Jones   6:1–22

Government Termination   M Laver   6:23–40

Political Science on the Periphery: Sweden   O Ruin   6:41–54

Folie Républicaine   RE Goodin   6:55–76

The Cold War as History   J Haslam   6:77–98

Robert A. Dahl's Philosophy of Democracy, Exhibited in His Essays   M Bailey, D Braybrooke   6:99–118

Bringing Robert A. Dahl's Theory of Democracy to Europe   S Fabbrini   6:119–37

The Media and Democracy: Beyond Myths and Stereotypes   D Graber   6:139–60

The Supreme Court in American Politics   L Baum   6:161–80

Why the United States Fought in Vietnam   L Berman, SR Routh   6:181–204

What Is Third World Security?   RGC Thomas   6:205–32

Electoral Fraud: Causes, Types, and Consequences   F Lehoucq   6:233–56

Rawls and Habermas on Public Reason: Human Rights and Global Justice   JD Moon   6:257–75

Democratic Individualism and Its Critics   G Kateb   6:275–305

Deliberative Democratic Theory   S Chambers   6:307–26

The Political Economy of Health in the United States   JD Wilkerson   6:327–43

Ancient Empires, Modern States, and the Study of Government   GE Von der Muhll   6:345–76

Trade, Foreign Investment, and Security   R Rosecrance, P Thompson   6:377–98

Current Controversies in Feminist Theory   MG Dietz   6:399–431

Herbert A. Simon: Political Scientist   J Bendor   6:433–71

Terrorist Decision Making   GH McCormick   6:473–507

What Role Does Prejudice Play in Ethnic Conflict?   DP Green, RL Seher   6:509–31

Volume 7 (2004)

Not Your Parents' Political Socialization: Introduction for a New Generation	V Sapiro	7:1–23
Downs and Two-Party Convergence	B Grofman	7:25–46
"Business" Is Not an Interest Group: On the Study of Companies in American National Politics	DM Hart	7:47–69
Citizenship and Education	E Callan	7:71–90
Latino Politics	RO de la Garza	7:91–123
Global Media and Politics: Transnational Communication Regimes and Civic Cultures	WL Bennett	7:125–48
Actors, Norms, and Impact: Recent International Cooperation Theory and the Influence of the Agent-Structure Debate	K O'Neill, J Balsiger, SD VanDeveer	7:149–75
States as Laboratories: A Reprise	SM Morehouse, ME Jewell	7:177–203
Measuring the Effects of Televised Political Advertising in the United States	K Goldstein, TN Ridout	7:205–26
Oakeshott and Political Science	K Minogue	7:227–46
What Does Political Economy Tell Us About Economic Development—and Vice Versa?	P Keefer	7:247–72
Political Representation in Comparative Politics	GB Powell Jr.	7:273–96
A Critical Guide to *Bush v. Gore* Scholarship	RL Hasen	7:297–313
Public Deliberation, Discursive Participation, and Citizen Engagement: A Review of the Empirical Literature	MX Delli Carpini, FL Cook, LR Jacobs	7:315–44
Advocacy and Scholarship in the Study of International War Crime Tribunals and Transitional Justice	L Vinjamuri, J Snyder	7:345–62
Martin Shapiro and the Movement from "Old" to "New" Institutionalist Studies in Public Law Scholarship	H Gillman	7:363–82
The Centrality of Race in American Politics	VL Hutchings, NA Valentino	7:383–408
Models of Vetoes and Veto Bargaining	C Cameron, N McCarty	7:409–35
Democratic Politics in Latin America: New Debates and Research Frontiers	GL Munck	7:437–62

Direct Democracy: New Approaches to
   Old Questions | A Lupia, | 7:463–82

JG Matsusaka

Bayesian Analysis for Political Research | S Jackman | 7:483–505

Volume 8 (2005)

Prospect Theory and Political Science	J Mercer	8:1–21
The Relationship Between Theory and Policy in International Relations	SM Walt	8:23–48
Does Deliberative Democracy Work?	DM Ryfe	8:49–71
Constitutional Reform in Britain: The Quiet Revolution	V Bogdanor	8:73–98
Immigration and Politics	WA Cornelius, MR Rosenblum	8:99–119
Making Sense of Religion in Political Life	KD Wald, AL Silverman, KS Fridy	8:121–43
Strategic Surprise and the September 11 Attacks	D Byman	8:145–70
Unpacking "Transnational Citizenship"	J Fox	8:171–201
The Political Evolution of Principal-Agent Models	GJ Miller	8:203–25
Citizenship and Civic Engagement	E Theiss-Morse, JR Hibbing	8:227–49
The Development of Interest Group Politics in America: Beyond the Conceits of Modern Times	DJ Tichenor, RA Harris	8:251–70
Transformations in World Politics: The Intellectual Contributions of Ernst B. Haas	JG Ruggie, PJ Katzenstein, RO Keohane, PC Schmitter	8:271–96
The Globalization of Public Opinion Research	A Heath, S Fisher, S Smith	8:297–333
Risk, Security, and Disaster Management	LK Comfort	8:335–56
Theorizing the European Union: International Organization, Domestic Policy, or Experiment in New Governance?	MA Pollack	8:357–98
The Globalization Rorschach Test: International Economic Integration, Inequality, and the Role of Government	N Brune, G Garrett	8:399–423
Constructing Judicial Review	MA Graber	8:425–51

ANNUAL REVIEWS
Intelligent Synthesis of the Scientific Literature

Annual Reviews – Your Starting Point for Research Online
http://arjournals.annualreviews.org

- Over 900 Annual Reviews volumes—more than 25,000 critical, authoritative review articles in 31 disciplines spanning the Biomedical, Physical, and Social sciences—available online, including all Annual Reviews back volumes, dating to 1932

- Current individual subscriptions include seamless online access to full-text articles, PDFs, Reviews in Advance (as much as 6 months ahead of print publication), bibliographies, and other supplementary material in the current volume and the prior 4 years' volumes

- All articles are fully supplemented, searchable, and downloadable—see http://polisci.annualreviews.org

- Access links to the reviewed references (when available online)

- Site features include customized alerting services, citation tracking, and saved searches

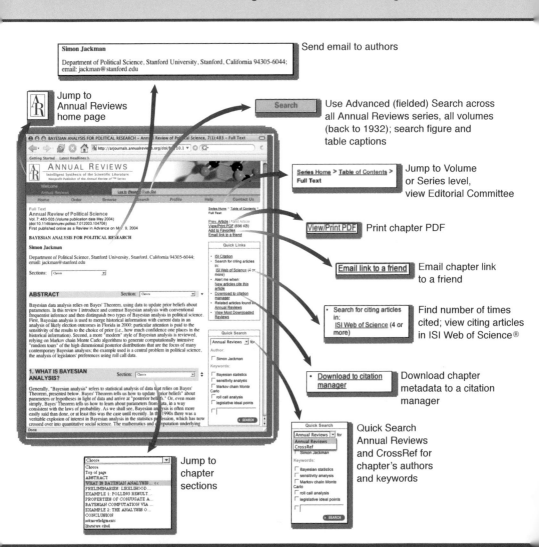

Send email to authors

Jump to Annual Reviews home page

Use Advanced (fielded) Search across all Annual Reviews series, all volumes (back to 1932); search figure and table captions

Jump to Volume or Series level, view Editorial Committee

View/Print PDF — Print chapter PDF

Email link to a friend — Email chapter link to a friend

Search for citing articles in: ISI Web of Science (4 or more) — Find number of times cited; view citing articles in ISI Web of Science®

Download to citation manager — Download chapter metadata to a citation manager

Quick Search Annual Reviews and CrossRef for chapter's authors and keywords

Jump to chapter sections